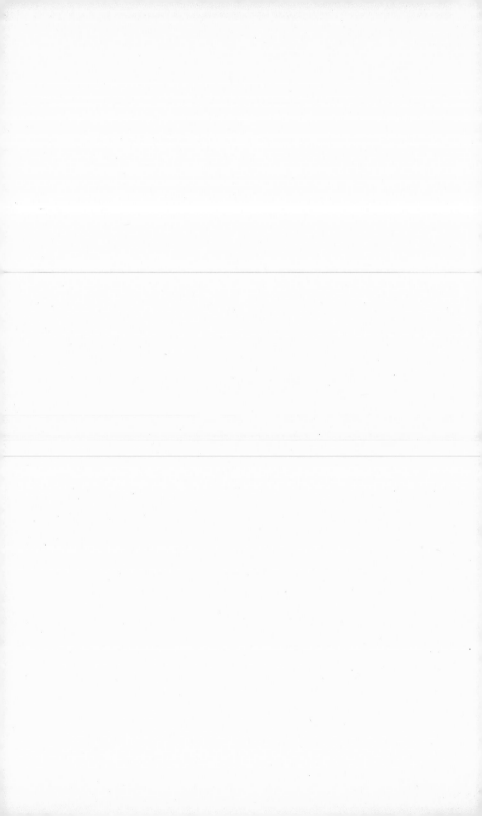

Longman Annotated English Poets

GENERAL EDITOR: JOHN BARNARD

FOUNDING EDITOR: F. W. BATESON

Frontispiece. An anonymous portrait of Dryden, dated 1657 but probably *c*. 1662, in the Bodleian Library, Oxford. Reproduced by permission of the Librarian.

THE POEMS OF

JOHN DRYDEN

– Volume I –
1649–1681

EDITED BY
PAUL HAMMOND

LONGMAN
London and New York

Longman Group Limited,
Longman House, Burnt Mill,
Harlow, Essex CM20 2JE, England
and Associated Companies throughout the world.

*Published in the United States of America
by Longman Publishing, New York*

First published 1995

ISBN 0 582 49213 0

British Library Cataloguing in Publication Data
A catalogue record for this book is
available from the British Library

Library of Congress Cataloging-in-Publication Data
(Revised for vol. 2)

Dryden, John, 1631–1700.
  The poems of John Dryden.

  (Longman annotated English poets)
  Includes bibliographical references and index.
  Contents: v. 1. 1649–1681 — v. 2. 1682–1685.
  I. Hammond, Paul, 1953–   . II. Title.
  III. Series.
PR3412.H35 1994   821'.4   94–14270
ISBN 0–582–19213–0 (v. 1)
ISBN 0–582–23944–3 (v. 2)

Set by 3 in Linotron 202 Bembo Roman 10/11

Printed and Bound by Bookcraft (Bath) Ltd

Contents

Note by the General Editor

Longman Annotated English Poets was launched in 1965 with the publication of Kenneth Allott's edition of *The Poems of Matthew Arnold*. F. W. Bateson wrote that the 'new series is the first designed to provide university students and teachers, and the general reader with complete and fully annotated editions of the major English poets'. That remains the aim of the series, and Bateson's original vision of its policy remains essentially the same. Its 'concern is primarily with the *meaning* of the extant texts in their various contexts'. The two other main principles of the series were that the text should be modernized and the poems printed 'as far as possible in the order in which they were composed'.

These broad principles still govern the series. Its primary purpose is to provide an annotated text giving the reader any necessary contextual information. However, flexibility in the detailed application has proved necessary in the light of experience and the needs of a particular case (and each poet is by definition, a particular case).

First, proper glossing of a poet's vocabulary has proved essential and not something which can be taken for granted. Second, modernization has presented difficulties, which have been resolved pragmatically, trying to reach a balance between sensitivity to the text in question and attention to the needs of a modern reader. Thus, to modernize Browning's text has a double redundancy: Victorian conventions are very close to modern conventions, and Browning had firm ideas on punctuation. Equally, to impose modern pointing on the ambiguities of Herbert or Marvell would create a misleading clarity. Third, in the very early days of the series Bateson hoped that editors would be able in many cases to annotate a *textus receptus*. That has not always been possible, and where no accepted text exists or where the text is controversial, editors have been obliged to go back to the originals and create their own text. The series has taken, and will continue to take, the opportunity not only of providing thorough annotations not available elsewhere, but also of making important scholarly textual contributions where necessary. A case in point is the edition of *The Poems of Tennyson* by Christopher Ricks, the Second Edition of which (1987) takes into account a full collation of the Trinity College Manuscripts, not previously available for an edition of this kind. Yet the series' primary purpose remains annotation and the editions do not attempt a comprehensive recording of textual variants.

The requirements of a particular author take precedence over 'principle'. It would make little sense to print Herbert's *Temple* in the order of composition even if it could be established. Where Ricks rightly decided that Tennyson's reader needs to be given the circumstances of composition, the attitude to Tennyson and his circle, allusions, and important variants, a necessary consequence was the exclusion of twentieth-century critical responses. Milton, however, is a very different case. John Carey and Alastair Fowler, looking to the needs of their readers, undertook synopses of the main lines of the critical debate over Milton's poetry. Finally, chronological ordering by date of composition will almost always have a greater or lesser degree of speculation or arbitrariness. The evidence is usually partial, and is confused further by the fact that poets do not always write one poem at a time and frequently revise at a later period than that of composition. In the case of Dryden, a public poet, the dates of composition and publication in one form or another are very close, and his work is ordered by the latter dating.

JOHN BARNARD
University of Leeds
January 1994

Introduction

The present volume is the first part of a four-volume edition of Dryden's poems. Volumes I and II, which include the poems up to 1685 (the end of the reign of Charles II), have been edited by Paul Hammond and are being published simultaneously; volumes III (1686 to 1696) and IV (1697 to the posthumously published poems) will be edited jointly by Paul Hammond and David Hopkins. The edition will be complete except for the translation of Virgil (1697), which has been excluded from the present scheme because of its bulk, though it is hoped that it may eventually prove possible to add this as a fifth volume. The aim of the edition is to present a complete rethinking of the text, canon and dating of Dryden's poetry, together with a substantial body of annotation which draws upon previous editions, on subsequent scholarship, and on extensive new research.

Canon

Dryden did not collect his poems into volumes which constituted an authorially sanctioned canon. The poems were originally published in the form which was appropriate to their initial purpose: *Absalom and Achitophel*, intervening in a national crisis, appeared as a printed pamphlet for a wide readership, while *Mac Flecknoe*, prompted by a particular literary dispute, circulated in manuscript for the *cognoscenti*; occasional prologues were spoken in the theatre, and printed as separate sheets only when their content was politically significant; poems which promoted the work of Dryden's friends, such as 'To the Earl of Roscommon' or 'To the Memory of Mr Oldham', were published as part of the works of those writers. Translations appeared in miscellanies or in the composite translations of Ovid, Juvenal and other classical writers which the publisher Jacob Tonson organized. Although Dryden's poems were usually reprinted after their first appearance, there was no systematic attempt to keep his works in print, or to assemble a clearly defined *œuvre* under his own name. Tonson did reprint some of Dryden's major poems in a common format between 1688 and 1693, so that they could be bound together into a collection, but this project was limited in its scope. Some important poems remained unavailable for long periods: *Astraea Redux* was not reprinted for nearly thirty years; *Religio Laici* was not reprinted after Dryden's conversion to Rome.

The shorter occasional pieces generally remained attached to the works for which they were commissioned, so that readers could have found 'To the Memory of Mr Oldham' (one of Dryden's finest poems) only if they sought out copies of *Remains of Mr John Oldham in Verse and Prose*. Many of Dryden's prologues and epilogues (though not all) were reprinted in *Miscellany Poems* (1684), but this collection is the work of various hands, and is not the equivalent of an individual writer's 'Collected Poems'. One must also stress that some famous poems—*Absalom and Achitophel*, *The Medal* and *Mac Flecknoe*—were published anonymously, and continued to be published without Dryden's name throughout his lifetime, even though their authorship quickly became known. Whatever the rhetorical strategies behind such anonymity, it is part of a reluctance to build a canon over his own name which is a striking (though rarely noted) feature of Dryden's career. (I have discussed the publication of Dryden's poetry in more detail in 'The Circulation of Dryden's Poetry', *PBSA* lxxxvi (1992) 379–409, and the issue of anonymity in 'Anonymity in Restoration Poetry', *SC* viii (1993) 123–142.) Consequently, in assembling a canon for him, modern editors do something which Dryden himself never attempted, and it is important that readers of this edition should be aware that the canon presented here is something which no seventeenth-century reader would have recognized.

The boundaries of the Dryden canon are, however, relatively uncontroversial, particularly when compared with that of some of his contemporaries, such as the Earl of Rochester. A number of poems were attributed to Dryden in Restoration sources which have not been accepted by modern editors, and a few later attributions have also been contested; a list of these rejected attributions will be provided in an appendix to volume IV. The canon accepted for the present edition differs only occasionally from that defined in James Kinsley's Oxford edition of 1958. The 'Prologue to *Julius Caesar*' is omitted, following the arguments of Paul Hammond in *ES* lxv (1984) 409–19; 'The Fair Stranger' is omitted in the light of work by Peter Beal (see Beal 395); and 'To Mr L. Maidwell', which was discovered in 1984, and 'Carmen Lapidarium', discovered in 1993, are collected here for the first time. Where there remains some doubt about a poem's authorship, this is indicated in the headnote. Although the 1697 Virgil is omitted, this edition does include the translations from Virgil which were written and published separately in the 1680s.

Chronology

For the first time in any edition of Dryden, the poems are printed chronologically in the order of their first appearance in the public domain, as far as this can now be ascertained. G. R. Noyes and the California editors use an arrangement which is partly generic and partly chronological; Kinsley orders the poems according to their first appearance in print. Both of these methods are illuminating in their different ways, but since Dryden's work was often highly topical there is also a case for attempting a strictly chronological organization by date of publication. For the Restoration period 'publication' is not synonymous with 'appearance in print': a prologue was published by being spoken on the stage, an epitaph by being inscribed on a monument; a satire may have been made public through manuscript circulation. In some cases there was an interval of several years between the publication of a poem in this form and its appearance in print: *Mac Flecknoe* is a good example, for it was published in manuscript in 1676 but not printed until the pirated edition of 1682. References to the poem indicate that it had some currency before 1682, and so to include it under the latter date would be to obscure its original occasion and early history. Some editors attempt to arrange their author's works according to the chronology of composition. Whatever one thinks of the assumptions which guide such a choice, with its stress on the private act of composition and the primacy of the biographical framework, it would not be an appropriate principle for the editor of Dryden. For most of Dryden's poems there is little or no independent evidence about the date of composition, and in most cases his poetry seems to have been published fairly soon after it was written. Where information is available about a poem's composition, it is recorded in the headnote.

Copy-texts

The decision to print the poems in the order of their publication is related to the decision about which text to follow. In theory there are good arguments for adhering to the text as it first appeared; there are also good arguments for preferring that text which received the author's final revision and approval; many editors adopt the first printed text but incorporate the author's later revisions. The practice adopted in the present edition is to print the text as it was when it was first made available to readers or audiences, and to record revisions in the notes. Many of Dryden's poems are occasional pieces, designed, at least in the first instance, to speak to a particular moment, though they also have a wider reach and a more lasting interest. That is one important reason for ordering the poems chronologically. To appreciate each poem's relation to its original occasion, one ought to have the text as it was at the time of first publication, not the text which was revised later. In fact, Dryden (unlike Pope, who revised compulsively) did not make a habit of revising his poems, and such changes as he did make after publication are generally small.

However, any revisions pose problems for an editor, and there seems to be no ideal way of handling them. Some second thoughts were included as press corrections, or in the errata lists, or in Dryden's prefaces: one could hardly refuse to incorporate these. The inclusion of such changes creates an 'ideal text' of the first publication; but at what point does 'first publication' stop? Some poems went through a complex and hasty process of reprinting which involved partial resetting of the type, and intermittent revision to the text. *Annus Mirabilis, The Medal, Religio Laici, The Art of Poetry* and *Threnodia Augustalis* all exemplify this kind of revision during the period of the poem's 'first publication'. In such cases it is not always possible to be clear about what constitutes a poem's first edition, or to maintain the bibliographer's traditional distinction between separate 'editions' of a work and separate 'states' or 'issues' of the same edition. Some editorial judgement has to determine the point at which 'first publication' was completed. This edition includes in the text all those revisions which were made during the poem's first publication; but changes which were made when a significant period of time had elapsed after the poem's original occasion are instead included in the notes.

Some cases are clear. Dryden made significant revisions to his early poem 'To the Lady Castlemaine' some twenty years after its first publication, but in circumstances so different from those which prompted the poem originally that it would be inappropriate to print the readings finalized by Dryden in the 1690s in preference to those from the 1670s, and then to present the result under the poem's original date. Dryden also refined the phrasing of 'To the Memory of Anne Killigrew' (first published in 1686) when he reprinted it in 1693; in this case the editor reluctantly sets aside Dryden's maturer poetic decisions in order to print the poem as it first appeared, and as it was known to readers for seven years. In both these cases Dryden is taking pieces which began life as occasional poems, and preparing them for inclusion in Tonson's miscellany *Examen Poeticum* (1693); in so doing he could be said to be producing a 'final' text, and an editor who preferred 'final thoughts' would be justified in adopting these readings. But unless the editor believed that there could be a platonically ideal text, a timeless and definitive form of a poem, the adoption of revised readings would logically entail printing the poem under the date '1693', or with a split date such as '1686/1693'. The present edition does not claim to have devised the correct way of editing Dryden, but rather to have provided a treatment of the text which emphasizes the circumstances in which the poems were first produced. In instances such as 'To the Memory of Anne Killigrew', readers of this edition can easily reconstruct Dryden's revised text from the variant readings provided at the foot of the page.

Even this apparently clear policy faces dilemmas, however. Dryden made important revisions to his translation of Virgil after its first publication in 1697, and if the Longman edition is ultimately able to include the Virgil, it would seem bizarre to reject the alterations in the second edition of 1698, which are part of a continuing process of correction and revision which Dryden made to his Virgil, starting with the proof corrections and errata to *1697*. In this case it would be sensible to regard these stages of revision as Dryden's continuous attempt to achieve a single correct text, and so one would include the revised readings.

It may be clear that the kinds of revision undertaken on 'To the Lady Castlemaine' and the translation of Virgil are sufficiently different to warrant different treatment within this overall policy. But *Absalom and Achitophel* poses a difficult test case. It was first printed as a folio late in 1681: Luttrell's copy (a gift from its publisher Tonson) is dated 17 November. There are four states of this edition. Besides two Dublin editions, there was a further folio edition published by Tonson in 1681, before he published a quarto edition, still bearing the date 1681. This quarto includes twelve lines on Shaftesbury and four on Monmouth which are not present in the folio. The date of the quarto is unknown, but it can hardly be much more than a month after the first folio edition. Various hypotheses have been put forward about these additional lines. Were they originally in Dryden's manuscript, but cut before the publication of the folio, and then restored in the quarto? Or were they composed after the appearance of the folio and added in the quarto to alter the representation of Shaftesbury and Monmouth? In terms of the textual policy of this edition, however, the question to be settled is clear, though difficult: does one follow the folio text because it is what Dryden and Tonson presented to the public in mid-November 1681 as the appropriate text for that occasion; or does one include the lines from the quarto because they were the product of Dryden's almost immediate second thoughts, published quite soon after the initial occasion, and still addressed to the same general crisis? (The additional arguments that the quarto text was reissued by Dryden and Tonson in the 1684 *Miscellany Poems*, and that it became the text which all readers have subsequently known, would concern an editor who followed final intentions, but are irrelevant in terms of the textual policy of this edition.) The argument seems finely balanced. In the end, the Longman edition includes the lines from the quarto text, but inside square brackets, so as to indicate clearly that contemporary readers in late 1681 would have had two versions of the poem available to them.

The decision to follow the first published text normally entails adhering to the first printed edition, but in some cases it is necessary to use manuscript evidence to reconstruct the text as it first appeared. The manuscript tradition sometimes enables us to move behind the printed texts of prologues and epilogues to recover the words which were originally spoken from the stage (examples are the 'Prologue to *Marriage A-la-Mode*' and the 'Prologue Spoken at *Mithridates*'). In the case of 'To the Lady Castlemaine' and *Mac Flecknoe* the present edition uses manuscript evidence to reconstruct the text as it was when it began to circulate in manuscript. In these cases this edition offers a text which has never before been printed, though it was the text which the poems' first readers and audiences would have known. In general, this edition aims to provide a tidy version of the poem as it first appeared: misprints are corrected, press corrections and authorial revisions made around the time of the first publication are incorporated into the text, while later revisions are reported in the notes.

The headnotes to each poem give details of the copy-text, and a summary of the poem's publication history, including all the printed editions which appeared in Dryden's lifetime. Detailed information about printed editions may be found in Macdonald's bibliography, while Day's edition of the songs provides further details for those pieces. In cases where a poem had a significant manuscript circulation, this is noted; a full list of manuscript copies of Dryden's poems is supplied by Peter Beal. An analysis of the circulation of Dryden's poetry in both printed books and manuscripts is provided by my article in *PBSA* lxxxvi (1992) 379–409.

The notes to each poem record all the departures which this edition makes from the wording of the copy-text (i.e. 'substantive' variants), except that obvious misprints are silently corrected, and press corrections and errata are also incorporated silently, unless they seem likely to be authorial revisions, in which case the emendations are recorded in the notes. The notes also record substantive variants in subsequent texts published in Dryden's lifetime, but only if these seem to derive from authorial revision. Variant readings in later texts which appear merely to be misprints or compositorial changes are ignored. There is, of course, an element of editorial discretion involved in this distinction, but fuller collations are available in the Oxford and California editions for readers who wish to consult them. In some cases variants which seem to be the result of revision by someone other than Dryden are recorded if they are of special interest, for example where contemporary changes are made to prologues and epilogues spoken in the playhouse.

Spelling and punctuation
The present edition modernizes spelling, punctuation, capitals and italics, the 'accidentals' of the text. There is always a place for an edition which preserves the accidentals of the original printed texts, which is the policy adopted by both Kinsley and the California edition. But that is not the only defensible or desirable way of editing Dryden. It is important to recognize that the accidentals of seventeenth-century texts derive principally from the compositors in the printing houses, not from the authors. Joseph Moxon's contemporary account of printing is quite clear on this point:

> the carelesness of some good Authors, and the ignorance of other Authors, has forc'd *Printers* to introduce a Custom, which among them is look'd upon as a task and duty incumbent on the *Compositer*, viz. to discern and amend the bad *Spelling* and *Pointing* of his *Copy* . . . it is necessary that a *Compositer* . . . know the present traditional *Spelling* of all English Words, and that he have so much Sence and Reason, as to *Point* his Sentences properly: when to begin a Word with a *Capital Letter*, when (to render the Sence of the Author more intelligent to the Reader) to *Set* some Words or Sentences in *Italick*.
> (Joseph Moxon, *Mechanick Exercises on the Whole Art of Printing (1683–4)*, edited by Herbert Davis and Harry Carter, second edition (Oxford, 1962) 192–3)

This account has been substantiated and illustrated by modern investigations of seventeenth-century printing. If the autograph manuscript of Dryden's *Heroic Stanzas* (BL MS Lansdowne 1045;

reproduced in Appendix A) is compared with the printed editions of 1659 and 1692 it becomes apparent that there is little correlation between the schemes of spelling, punctuation, italics and capitals used by Dryden and those used by his compositors (see Paul Hammond, *PBSA* lxxvi (1982) 457–70). Compositors sometimes worked not from the author's manuscript, but from a fair copy made by a professional scribe, who would introduce his own style: we know that a scribal copy was made in the case of Dryden's Virgil (*Letters* 84–5). Different printing houses had different styles, as did individual compositors within the same shop: this can result in different pages within the same book having markedly different schemes of accidentals (for examples from Oldham's works see Harold F. Brooks, *SB* xxvii (1974) 188–226). Fashions also changed in the course of this period: in 1700 punctuation is heavier and capitalization more lavish than in 1660, but forty years later the fashion had changed back again. Authors sometimes read proofs, but not always, particularly if they were away from London, as Dryden often was; and no author (or editor), however fortunate, can be certain that his printer and publisher will follow his wishes. Indeed, we know that Dryden was sometimes dissatisfied with the printing of his work. He drew attention to the poor punctuation in *Annus Mirabilis* (see headnote) and *Sylvae* (see 'Preface to *Sylvae*', ll. 426–7), and 'bestowd nine entire days' on correcting the first edition of his Virgil, complaining to Tonson that 'the Printer is a beast, and understands nothing I can say to him of correcting the press' (*Letters* 97). In the errata to his Virgil, Dryden says that he has had to leave many errors to be corrected by the reader: 'There are other Errata both in false pointing, and omissions of words, both in the Preface and the Poem, which the Reader will correct without any trouble. I omit them, because they only lame my *English*, not destroy my meaning' (*Works* v 65). In the almost total absence of authorial manuscripts we cannot have a text directly based on Dryden's spelling and punctuation: some of his preferences survive into the printed texts, but many do not. His own spelling tended to be more archaic than that of his compositors, so the process of modernization had already begun by the time his poems first reached print. Moreover, those poems which were published by being spoken or sung can have no accidentals which derive from their first publication, and those which were circulated in manuscript acquired whatever accidentals their transcribers chose. Some readers may still prefer to have Dryden's poems in the dress supplied by Restoration compositors and scribes, and some nuances of meaning, rhythm and rhyme are undoubtedly lost through modernization; on the other hand, seventeenth-century accidentals can puzzle and mislead even quite experienced modern readers, and the accidentals supplied by a modern editor may well be found more helpful.

In modernizing spelling for their edition of Milton in this series, John Carey and Alastair Fowler explained their procedure thus:

> [Spelling] is not a grammatical symbol but a vocabulary symbol. That is to say, all that can generally be expected of orthographic signals is that they should enable the reader to make the right vocabulary selection. Now modern spelling is perfectly well able to do this for a seventeenth-century text. It is usually easy to find exact modern equivalents for old spellings, because orthographic signals are essentially simple binary signals. True, spelling also conveys some information about how words sound. But in English the relation between orthography and the phonetic reality it renders is remote. Certainly with our knowledge of the pronunciation of the seventeenth century in its present state there can be few instances where the old spelling indicates the sound to a modern reader better than the new.
>
> (p. xi)

This is also the position adopted in this edition. Occasionally the original spelling suggests a pronunciation so distinct from the modern one that it needs to be preserved in the text: 'murther' for 'murder' and 'sate' for 'sat' are examples. Otherwise the principal instances where the sound of the word in the seventeenth century was different from that which a modern reader would expect are recorded in the notes: these generally affect stress and rhyme. The modernization of spelling may alter how a rhyme appears to the eye rather than the ear: in a case where 'rest' rhymes with 'blest', the modernized spelling 'blessed' will suggest a less exact rhyme to the eye, but will not alter the sound of the line. Sometimes the spelling of the seventeenth-century text does indicate how the rhythm of the line is envisaged (though this may be how the compositor or scribe envisaged it, rather than the poet). It was a frequent habit to print -'*d* for -*ed* to indicate an unstressed syllable; in the present edition the reverse convention is adopted, and words are marked only where a stress is required which a modern reader would regard as unusual. Thus for a monosyllabic pronunciation we print 'blessed' (not 'bless'd') and for a disyllabic pronunciation 'blessèd'. Contractions are, however, more problematic. The manuscript of the *Heroic Stanzas* shows that Dryden took care to indicate with apostrophes that certain words were to be slurred in pronunciation in order to avoid a hypermetrical line:

> Him at that age her favo'urites ranck'd among
>
> (l. 31)
>
> T'is true, his Count'nance did imprint an awe,
> And natu'rally all Soules to his did bowe;
>
> (ll. 73–4)
>
> When past all offe'rings to Feretrian Jove
>
> (l. 77)

The fact that in this manuscript Dryden often spells a word in full, with the apostrophe looking like a slur over (rather than between) the letters, suggests that in some cases he wanted syllables to be run together rather than dropped completely. The printed texts of this poem, however, do not follow Dryden's contractions at all systematically. Similarly, when Dryden asked Tonson to correct an error in 'To the Earl of Roscommon', he wrote the correct line thus:

> That heer his Conque'ring Ancestors were nursd:
>
> (*Letters* 23)

Again, Dryden marks a contraction without omitting any letters. While the verbal correction ('was' to 'were') was made in the next printing, the contraction was ignored (along with Dryden's archaic spelling 'heer'). There is no entirely satisfactory way of dealing with this question. The present edition tends to prefer to print words in full, thus allowing readers to find the rhythm of the line for themselves, for excessive use of apostrophes can squeeze the line into a metrical strait-jacket and obscure the varieties of rhythm which Dryden uses. This edition does, however, follow the seventeenth-century practice of using the apostrophe more freely between words when vowels come together, thus preferring to print 'th' event' rather than 'the event'. Even in these cases, however, the elided sound is probably to be slurred rather than allowed to disappear completely.

The punctuation of Dryden's verse is difficult to render satisfactorily for a modern reader, whether one preserves or alters the seventeenth-century pointing. Here the Longman Dryden departs from the practice adopted by John Carey and Alastair Fowler in the Longman Milton, where they adhered scrupulously to the original punctuation of their copy-texts. Comparison of the manuscript of the *Heroic Stanzas* with the printed texts does not inspire confidence in the consistency or sensitivity of compositorial pointing. Dryden's contemporaries were moving from a generally rhetorical to a more grammatical punctuation. (For a discussion of seventeenth-century theories of punctuation see Vivian Salmon, *Anglia* cvi (1988) 285–314.) In the manuscript of the *Heroic Stanzas* Dryden prefers a light, rhetorical punctuation, while the compositors make the pointing heavier and more grammatical. (Though there are difficulties in using a manuscript from 1658 of a poem in quatrains in order to extrapolate principles which could apply to the pointing of couplet verses over the next forty years of Dryden's career, the evidence is nevertheless instructive.) In later poems such as *Absalom and Achitophel* or *Religio Laici*, long passages of argument in couplets are punctuated with repeated colons and semi-colons in a way which gives them an appropriate mixture of strength and impetus. To move over entirely to a modern system of grammatical punctuation would be detrimental to such poetry. The method adopted in this edition is a compromise: it takes the punctuation of the copy-text as its basis, lightens it a little, removes conventions which would puzzle modern readers (such as the use of a question mark for an exclamation mark, or a semi-colon for what would now be a dash), and aims at giving it clarity and consistency. The result is generally a more rhetorical pointing than one finds in modern practice, and a more grammatical pointing than in seventeenth-century usage.

Italics have been removed consistently, since the schemes of emphasis which they represent appear to be generally compositorial rather than authorial, and they frequently distract a modern reader.

Capitals are more problematic. The capitalization in early printed editions is often taken by modern readers to indicate personification, but this is not a safe inference. For example, in the case of the words 'fate' and 'fortune' in the *Heroic Stanzas*, the printed texts sometimes use capitals where Dryden's manuscript does not, and vice versa. A reader who did not know the origin of the accidentals in the printed texts might reasonably infer that their capitals implied a degree of personification and that the lower-case letters did not. The present edition therefore adopts modern conventions, capitalizing only proper names and those words which seem quite clearly to be personifications. This does not, however, solve the problem of personification, which is not a simple and rigid matter. Major ideas in the period, such as Art, Nature, Reason or Sense, are often given capitals in the early texts to indicate their almost talismanic force, which is not the same as personification. But in the period from 1660 to 1700 such a critical and philosophical vocabulary did not achieve the quasi-institutionalized status which it was to have in the writings of Pope and his contemporaries; more lavish use of capitals for such words might be needed in an edition of Pope than would be appropriate in an edition of Dryden. All in all, it is for the reader to work out the significance of such terms, and a sparing use of capitalization is probably the most helpful policy.

Annotation

The provision of substantial, though concise, annotation is one of the major aims of this edition. Dryden has been well served by generations of editors and commentators, and much of their work has been incorporated into the present edition. It is hoped that due acknowledgement has been given to the originators of notes adopted here, though material from eighteenth-, nineteenth- and early twentieth-century editions which has become common currency in Dryden studies is not always attributed. It should, therefore, be said at the outset that Sir Walter Scott, George R. Noyes and W. D. Christie made important contributions to the study of Dryden from which all his readers have benefited, whether directly or indirectly. More recently, James Kinsley and the various editors of the California edition have brought the techniques of modern scholarship—editorial, historical and critical—to bear on Dryden's work with valuable results. However, it is now more than thirty-five years since the publication of Kinsley's edition and the first volumes of the California series, and the new Longman edition has been able to profit from many books and articles which have appeared during this time. In addition, new research on the canon, dating, text, language, sources and cultural contexts of Dryden's work is published for the first time in this edition.

The headnote aims to introduce each poem fully but succinctly. It begins by recording under 'Date and publication' the date and form of the poem's publication, and the history of its subsequent republication up to Dryden's death. Textual problems are also noted at this point. The section headed 'Context' provides details of the cultural contexts within which the poem was composed, to which it contributed, and through which it would have been interpreted by its early readers. The kind of information offered in this section varies considerably from poem to poem. A section headed 'Authorship' is included in the headnote if the poem was originally published anonymously, has been attributed to Dryden since his death, or is of doubtful authenticity. Under 'Sources' the headnote summarizes the major sources for the poem, while 'Reception' records the most important responses of readers up to 1700. Unlike some other volumes in the Longman series, this edition does not attempt to summarize modern critical debate. The marked increase in the rate at which critical books and articles are published, together with a growing diversity of critical theory and practice, means that any attempt to summarize critical opinion is now a much larger and more controversial task than it was when this series was launched in the 1960s, and one which is better tackled separately.

The annotation aims primarily at providing modern readers with the kinds of information which would have been available to well-informed Restoration readers, though without assuming that this can enable us to read as if we were actually Dryden's contemporaries. Many of the notes are lexical, elucidating Dryden's vocabulary more fully than has previously been attempted. There are many cases where words which now seem unproblematic carried meanings (or a range of meanings) which are no longer current; some words (such as 'patriot' or 'liberty') acquired strongly politicized meanings in this period; and Dryden himself used a number of words which carried special connotations for him personally, sometimes because of their use by other poets. Many glosses are drawn from the *Oxford English Dictionary* (*OED*), and references to the different numbered senses identified there are included if there is any doubt about the sense in which Dryden is using a word. Some of the lexical notes add to or correct the information in the *OED*, or supply examples which antedate the *OED*'s first recorded usages. Other annotations explain references, outline the historical context for Dryden's poems, and identify sources, echoes and allusions. When parallel phrasing in other poems is noted, this is usually introduced by the formula 'cp.', thus inviting the reader to consider whether this is a direct borrowing by Dryden of a phrase in another writer, or an example of a shared contemporary rhetoric. Particular attention has been given to Dryden's use of contemporary pamphlet material in his topical poems, so that *Annus Mirabilis, Absalom and Achitophel* and *The Medal* are shown to be more deeply informed by the polemics of the period than has previously been realized. Similarly the notes to *Religio Laici* draw substantially upon contemporary theological debate to elucidate the poem's arguments for the modern reader. The notes to *Mac Flecknoe* and 'To the Memory of Mr Oldham' record how these poems draw heavily and pertinently upon the writings of Flecknoe, Shadwell and Oldham themselves. Prologues and Epilogues are located within their appropriate theatrical and topical milieux. But Dryden's poems were never written merely for the moment: they are not journalism in verse. The poems are alive with Dryden's imaginative, literary and philosophical interests, and accordingly the notes give attention to those self-borrowings and recurrent echoes within Dryden's own work which point to his deepest concerns: for example his ideas about fortune, liberty and reason, and his abiding fascination with man's place in the natural world. The level of annotation varies. Generally, more attention has been given to the more significant and difficult poems, so that *Absalom and Achitophel* is more heavily annotated than *To My Lord Chancellor*. But in its sense of priorities this edition does take issue implicitly with some of the conventional valuations of Dryden's work. There are strong critical and historical reasons for thinking that Dryden's translations are far more important, and potentially more attractive to modern readers, than the prevailing consensus would suggest—a consensus which is reflected in the relative lack of attention which was given to Dryden's translations in most previous editions. Accordingly a special effort has been made in volumes I and II to annotate the translations, particularly those in *Sylvae*, in greater detail than readers might expect, and this policy will be continued in the subsequent volumes, notably for the masterpieces included in Dryden's *Fables Ancient and Modern* of 1700.

However, the annotation of Dryden's translations presents special difficulties, both for the editor and for the reader. In the 'Preface to Ovid's Epistles' (1680) Dryden made his famous distinction between three types of translation: metaphrase, 'or turning an author word by word, and line by line, from one language into another'; paraphrase, 'or translation with latitude, where the author is kept in view by the translator, so as never to be lost, but his words are not so strictly followed as his sense, and that too is admitted to be amplified, but not altered'; and imitation, 'where the translator (if now he has not lost the name) assumes the liberty not only to vary from the words and sense, but to forsake them both as he sees occasion: and taking only some general hints from the original, to run division on the ground-work, as he pleases' (ll. 234–48). Dryden's practice as a translator generally falls into the second of these categories, though he varies his method somewhat according to the poems which he is rendering, and in each of his translations uses all three methods to some degree.

Dryden was, of course, translating from seventeenth-century texts of the Greek, Latin and medieval classics, and these often varied from twentieth-century texts. Therefore what appear at first glance to be mistakes or departures from the original may actually be direct renderings of the text or glosses in one of the standard seventeenth-century editions, as J. McG. Bottkol showed in a pioneering article (*MPh* xl (1943) 241–54). As well as translating the originals, Dryden saw it as his duty to clarify them by explaining references and allusions which might puzzle his contemporary English readers. He thus incorporated into his versions material from the footnotes and the *interpretatio* (the running paraphrase in Latin prose) which are provided in most seventeenth-century editions of the classics. He also made use of ideas from other poets who had handled the same theme, often prompted to include comparable material from other classical poets by the quotations in the footnotes of his editions, but also recalling other English poets who had written on that particular topic: thus a translation from Horace may draw not only upon the Horatian text but also on the editorial glosses and on analogous material in, say, Virgil and Cowley. Moreover, Dryden seems to have wanted his versions to be, amongst other things, a distillation of the best elements from the work of previous English translators. He consequently included vocabulary, phrases, rhymes, end-words to which he supplied his own rhymes, and, on occasion, whole lines, from the English poets who had translated his originals before him. Some of these predecessors were obscure and undistinguished, but it was part of Dryden's practice to consult as many translations and editions as he could find. Consequently, Dryden's translations are works of scholarship and imagination interacting the one with the other.

The editor of Dryden's translations has to decide how to plot the ever-changing relationship of Dryden's versions to their originals, and how much to record of the scholarly activity which went into the making of these poems. The annotations offered here attempt in the first instance to explicate these works as autonomous English poems, glossing their vocabulary and noting their allusions. They also attempt to guide readers who are interested in exploring the relationship between these translations and their originals, and in understanding the methods and materials which went into their composition. However, the treatment of this area has of necessity to be selective if the reader is not to be overwhelmed by myriad details of doubtful interest. The notes therefore record only substantial or significant departures from the original, and those borrowings from editors, translators and other poets which most illuminate the aims, emphases and artistry of Dryden's poem. No attempt has been made to record minor similarities of vocabulary, phrasing or rhyme-words, since readers who wish to study Dryden's translations at that level of detail will need to examine the sources for themselves. The note 'D.'s addition' is a shorthand phrase indicating words or lines which have no direct equivalent in the original; sometimes these are outright departures from Dryden's source, but on other occasions they make explicit meanings which might seem to be latent or implicit in the original. The annotations to the translations are, therefore, illustrative, and invitations to further study, not exhaustive.

Conclusion

This does not claim to be a 'definitive' edition. Indeed, though that term is often used by editors and reviewers, it is difficult to see how any edition could properly make such a claim, or even aim at such a status. There are—as this introduction has argued—various ways of editing texts, and each is grounded upon particular assumptions about authors, texts and readers, assumptions which are not only bibliographical but aesthetic, political and philosophical as well. The aim of this edition is to arrange Dryden's poems in the order in which they appeared before the public; to provide a text which holds the minimum of difficulties and distractions for the modern reader; and to equip those readers with historical and linguistic materials which may enable and enhance their responses to Dryden's work. In effect, the texts and notes in this edition are a translation—both of Dryden's texts and of the fabric of his culture—into a form which modern readers can use for their own transactions with the past. 'Authenticity'—the unmediated recovery of some supposed original—is in any case impossible.

Much of Dryden's work discusses—and is itself a form of—translation: he is fascinated by the handing on (*translatio*) of culture from one society or one generation to another, and by the rewriting of the past which is the necessary task of each new age; moreover, his own poetry frequently takes the form of translation, whether by rendering classical poetry in English for modern readers, or by redeploying the tropes of contemporary political debate to his own purposes. Shadwell seemed to see no problem in reusing the ideas of Ben Jonson as the currency of Restoration theatre; but for Dryden this was a cultural transformation which was fraught with difficulty, for he had pondered long over the alterations of language and *mores* which seemed to fix an almost unbridgeable gulf between himself and those masters of the past whose insights were vital to the present—vital to his society and to his own soul. This loss provoked his creativity: the literature of the past could not be mimicked, but it could be translated, made new. It may therefore be appropriate to think of this edition as aiming to provide, in its own way, an appropriate 'translation' of Dryden for new generations.

Acknowledgements

Dryden's publisher Jacob Tonson once sent him two melons by way of friendly encouragement; the encouragement which I have received over a long period from successive publishers at Longman has taken different forms, but has been no less welcome.

The following acknowledgements apply to both volumes I and II of this edition.

Several institutions have given practical support to this work, for which I am very grateful. Trinity College, Cambridge, Dryden's own college, elected me to a Prize Fellowship, which enabled me to begin this edition. I have received generous research grants from Trinity, the British Academy, and the University of Leeds. The School of English at Leeds has provided research expenses and regular study leave, and made the final stages of the work easier by allowing Ms Elizabeth Paget to retype substantial portions of the commentary, which she has done with great accuracy.

Much of the work for this edition was carried out in Leeds University Library, particularly in the Brotherton Collection of rare books and manuscripts, from which most of the copy-texts are drawn: I am grateful to Mr Christopher Sheppard and his colleagues in the Collection for their help, expertise and patience. For permission to cite manuscript material I am indebted to Mr Nicholas Fisher; the Bodleian Library; the British Library; Cambridge University Library; the William Andrews Clark Memorial Library, Los Angeles; Leeds University Library; Chetham's Library Manchester; and the Keeper of Manuscripts at Nottingham University Library.

I am grateful for permission to quote portions of Dryden's works from *The Works of John Dryden*, edited by H. T. Swedenberg and others, in progress; copyright © 1956–1989 by the Regents of the University of California.

Dryden's poetry frequently attests to the importance of literary and scholarly friendships, and he would have expected these to be given due prominence and acknowledgement here. The teachers who introduced me as an undergraduate to Dryden's work, and first showed me some of its fascination and its wisdom, were Dr Carl Baron and the late Mr Harold Mason; subsequently Dr Richard Luckett guided my research on Oldham and Restoration translation. Over the years I have gained much from exchanging information and ideas with Professor James Winn, and he has made valuable comments on portions of this edition in draft. Mrs Elsie Duncan-Jones kindly shared with me her unpublished researches on Dryden, Marvell and Flecknoe. Mr Hilton Kelliher generously supplied me with proofs of the article in which he announced his discovery of Dryden's 'Carmen Lapidarium', and allowed me to make use of his translation. Mr J. W. Binns has also advised me on this poem. Mr Simon Bentley has contributed information on astrology, and Mrs Jennifer Stead has supplied me from her store-cupboard of knowledge about seventeenth-century food. Dr Stuart Gillespie, Dr John Mason, Dr Susan Owen and Dr Richard Perkins have allowed me to use material from their unpublished doctoral theses; Dr Gillespie has also contributed suggestions for improving the annotation to *Sylvae*. Dr Richard Sharpe has been generous with his hospitality during my visits to Oxford, and has often tracked down material for me in the Bodleian Library. Dr David Hopkins, who will be co-editor for volumes III and IV, has read volumes I and II scrupulously in typescript, and made innumerable suggestions for their improvement; his enthusiasm for Dryden has been a constant encouragement. Professor John Barnard has been an exemplary general editor, meticulous and patient, and as a colleague and a friend has quietly smoothed my path.

My parents, Maureen and Ron, have been an unfailing source of loving support throughout the fifteen years in which I have worked on this project.

Dryden's dedications are generally grand, prominent statements which associate his writing with the powerful patrons of his age. Rather than place a formal dedication of my own in front of his works, I will simply record that the editorial portion of these two volumes is dedicated to Nick, with love.

January 1993 Paul Hammond

List of Illustrations

Frontispiece. An anonymous portrait of Dryden, dated 1657 but probably c. 1662, in the Bodleian Library, Oxford (Poole portrait no. 177). Reproduced by permission of the Bodleian Library.

Plate 1. Thomas Baker's transcript of Dryden's 'Carmen Lapidarium', in Cambridge University Library MS Mm 1.36 page 406. Reproduced by permission of the Syndics of Cambridge University Library.

Plate 2. The first page of the autograph manuscript of Dryden's *Heroic Stanzas*, from British Library MS Lansdowne 1045 f. 101^r. Reproduced by permission of the British Library Board.

Plate 3. Title page of the first edition of *Annus Mirabilis* (1667), from a copy in the Brotherton Collection, Leeds University Library. Reproduced by permission of the Librarian.

Plate 4. The monument to the Marquis of Winchester in Englefield Church, showing the epitaph composed by Dryden. Photograph by Mr Ian Maclean.

Plates 5–7. Title page and pages 6–7 from the first issue of the first edition of *Absalom and Achitophel* (1681), from a copy in the Brotherton Collection, Leeds University Library. Reproduced by permission of the Librarian. Page 6 shows the original readings 'Kold', 'Kody' and 'Patron's' corrected by hand to 'Bold', 'Body' and 'Patriott's'. Pages 6 and 7 together show the passage on Shaftesbury as it was before the addition of the present lines 180–91.

Plate 8. First page of *Mac Flecknoe* from Leeds University Library Brotherton Collection MS Lt 54 page 1. Reproduced by permission of the Librarian. The manuscript is a scribal miscellany compiled c. 1680, and illustrates the circulation of the poem before its first appearance in print in 1682.

Chronological Table of Dryden's Life and Publications

For documentation and further details see Winn, Macdonald and *Letters*.

1631   (*9 August*) D. born at Aldwincle, Northamptonshire, the son of Erasmus Dryden and Mary Pickering; brought up in the nearby village of Titchmarsh; probably educated initially at the village school.

1644   Possible date of D.'s entry to Westminster School, London (scholars' conjectures range from 1642 to 1646).

1649   Publication of *Lachrymae Musarum*, a collection of elegies on the death of Lord Hastings, to which D. contributed.

1650   Admitted to Trinity College, Cambridge, as a Westminster scholar; his tutor was John Templer.
        Contributes commendatory verses to John Hoddesdon's *Sion and Parnassus*.

1652   (*19 July*) D. punished by the Master and Seniors for his (unspecified) disobedience to the Vice-Master.
        (*August*) D. writes 'Carmen Lapidarium' on the death of John Smith.

1654   (*February*) D. graduates BA and subsequently leaves Cambridge.
        (*June*) Death of D.'s father, Erasmus (buried *14 June*). He leaves D. a farm, but insufficient income to make him financially independent.

1657   (*19 October*) D. signs a receipt for £50 from John Thurloe, Cromwell's Secretary of State; how long he had been employed by the government is not known, but he was probably introduced by his cousin Sir Gilbert Pickering, Cromwell's Lord Chamberlain.

1657–60 D. has some form of employment with the bookseller Henry Herringman during these years, and may have written occasional prefaces and advertisements for books published by him.

1658   (*3 September*) Death of Cromwell.
        (*23 November*) D. walks in Cromwell's funeral procession along with Milton and Marvell as the Secretaries of the French and Latin Tongues.

1659   (*January*) *Heroic Stanzas* printed in *Three Poems Upon the Death of his late Highness Oliver*.

1660   D. contributes a commendatory poem to Sir Robert Howard's *Poems*; he is lodging with Howard in London at around this time.

(*May*) Restoration of the monarchy and return of Charles Stuart as King Charles II.

(*June*) Publication of *Astraea Redux*.

1661   (*April*) Publication of *To His Sacred Majesty* on the coronation.

1662   (*January*) Publication of *To My Lord Chancellor*.

(*September*) Publication of commendatory verses in Walter Charleton's *Chorea Gigantum* (dated 1663).

(*19 November*) D. elected a Fellow of the Royal Society (proposed by Charleton).

1663   (*5 February*) First performance of D.'s first play, *The Wild Gallant*, at the Theatre Royal, Vere Street; subsequently performed at court *23 February*, probably due to the influence of Lady Castlemaine; D.'s verses 'To the Lady Castlemaine' (circulated in MS) may date from this occasion, or from the play's printing in 1669.

(*1 December*) D. marries Elizabeth Howard, daughter of the Earl of Berkshire, and sister of Sir Robert Howard.

Late in 1663 or early in 1664 *The Rival Ladies* performed at the Theatre Royal, Bridges Street.

1664   (*January*) *The Indian Queen* performed at the Theatre Royal; first recorded performance on *25 January* in the presence of the King.

(*c. November*) *The Rival Ladies* published.

1665   (*February/March*) *The Indian Emperor* performed at the Theatre Royal.

(*March*) *The Indian Queen* published in Sir Robert Howard's *Four New Plays*.

(*5 June*) London theatres close because of the plague. Around this time D. leaves with his wife for her father's country estate at Charlton, Wiltshire. During his year at Charlton D. works on *Secret Love*, *Of Dramatic Poesy* and *Annus Mirabilis*.

1666   (*27 August*) D.'s first son, Charles, born.

(*2–5 September*) Fire of London.

(*November*) London theatres reopen.

(*November/December*) Likely date for the performance of

the revised version of *The Wild Gallant*, with a new Prologue and Epilogue.

1667   (*January*) *Annus Mirabilis* published.

(*March*) *Secret Love* performed at the Theatre Royal.

(*15 August*) *Sir Martin Mar-All* performed at Lincoln's Inn Fields.

(*Autumn*) *Of Dramatic Poesy* and *The Indian Emperor* published.

(*7 November*) *The Tempest* performed at Lincoln's Inn Fields.

1668   D.'s second son, John, born.

(*January*) *Secret Love* published.

(*February*) 'Prologue to *Albumazar*' spoken.

(*13 April*) D. appointed Poet Laureate.

(*Spring*) D. signs contract with the King's Company to write three plays a year in return for a share of the profits.

(*12 June*) *An Evening's Love* performed at the Theatre Royal.

(*Autumn*) *Sir Martin Mar-All* published. Shadwell's *The Sullen Lovers* published with a preface attacking D.'s remarks on Jonson. Sir Robert Howard's *The Duke of Lerma* published with a preface attacking D.'s views on the use of rhyme in plays. D. replies in 'A Defence of An Essay of Dramatic Poesy' prefixed to the second edition of *The Indian Emperor* (*early September*).

1669   (*Spring*) *The Wild Gallant* published.

(*2 May*) D.'s third son, Erasmus-Henry, born.

(*June*) *Tyrannic Love* performed at the Theatre Royal.

1670   (*c. February*) *The Tempest* published.

(*18 August*) D. appointed Historiographer Royal.

(*Autumn*) *Tyrannic Love* published.

(*December*) *The First Part of The Conquest of Granada* performed at the Theatre Royal.

1671   (*January*) *The Second Part of The Conquest of Granada* performed at the Theatre Royal.

(*c. February*) *An Evening's Love* published.

(*November*) *Marriage A-la-Mode* performed at the Theatre Royal.

(*7 December*) First performance of Buckingham's *The Rehearsal*, in which D. is satirized as Mr Bayes.

1672   The song 'Farewell, fair Armida' appears in various printed miscellanies.

(*25 January*) Theatre Royal destroyed by fire.

(*February*) *The Conquest of Granada* published.

(*26 February*) 'Prologue to *Wit without Money*' spoken.

(*Summer: after 4 July*) 'Prologue and Epilogue to *Secret Love*, Spoken by the Women'.

(*Summer or Autumn*) *The Assignation* performed at Lincoln's Inn Fields.

1673   (*Spring*) 'Prologue to *Arviragus* revived' spoken. Probable date of first performance of *Amboyna*. D.'s poems and plays extensively attacked in *The Censure of the Rota* and *The Friendly Vindication*; he is defended in *Mr Dreyden Vindicated* and *A Description of the Academy of the Athenian Virtuosi*.

(*June*) *Marriage A-la-Mode* and *The Assignation* published.

(*July*) 'Prologue and Epilogue at Oxford' spoken.

(*Autumn*) *Amboyna* published.

1674   *Notes and Observations on the Empress of Morocco* published (written jointly by D., Crowne and Shadwell).

(*26 March*) 'Prologue and Epilogue Spoken at the Opening of the New House'.

(*Spring*) *The State of Innocence* written, but not staged, because of the expense.

(*July*) 'Prologue and Epilogue at Oxford' spoken.

1675   (*February*) Epilogue written for a performance of *Calisto* at court.

(*17 November*) *Aureng-Zebe* performed at Drury Lane.

(*Winter*) Rochester's *An Allusion to Horace* (which includes an attack on D.) circulates in MS.

1676   (*February*) *Aureng-Zebe* published.

(*11 March*) 'Epilogue to *The Man of Mode*' spoken.

(*June*) Death of D.'s mother (buried *14 June*).

(*July*) 'Prologue at Oxford' spoken. Publication of Shadwell's *The Virtuoso*; its Dedication has an implicit attack on D.

(*July/August*) *Mac Flecknoe* composed, and put into circulation in MS.

1677   (*February*) *The State of Innocence* published.

(*12 May*) 'Prologue to *Circe*' spoken.

(*Autumn*) 'To Mr Lee, on his *Alexander*' published in Lee's *The Rival Queens*. D. writes 'Heads of an Answer to Rymer' on the endpapers of Thomas Rymer's *The Tragedies of the Last Age* (1677).

| | (*December*) *All for Love* performed at the Theatre Royal. |
| 1678 | (*c. February*) 'Epilogue to *Mithridates*' spoken. |

(*11 March*) *The Kind Keeper* performed at Dorset Garden.

(*March*) 'Prologue to *A True Widow*' spoken. *All for Love* published.

(*Autumn*) *Oedipus* (by D. and Lee) performed at Dorset Garden.

1679 (*March*) *Oedipus* published.

(*c. April*) *Troilus and Cressida* performed at Dorset Garden.

(*July*) 'Prologue at Oxford' spoken.

(*Summer*) 'Prologue to *Caesar Borgia*' spoken.

(*Autumn*) *Troilus and Cressida* published by Tonson, marking the beginning of his association with D. *The Kind Keeper* published dated 1680.

(*c. December*) 'Prologue to *The Loyal General*' spoken.

(*18 December*) D. attacked and badly injured in Rose Alley, probably because he was thought to have written *An Essay upon Satire* (by Mulgrave).

1680 (*February*) *Ovid's Epistles* published, with Preface and three translations by D.

(*July*) 'Prologue at Oxford' spoken.

(*November*) *The Spanish Friar* performed at Dorset Garden.

1681 (*c. February*) 'Epilogue to *Tamerlane the Great*' spoken.

(*March*) *The Spanish Friar* published.

(*19 March*) 'Epilogue Spoken to the King' at the Oxford Parliament.

(*Spring*) 'Prologue and Epilogue to *The Unhappy Favourite*' spoken.

(*June*) *His Majesties Declaration Defended* published.

(*July*) 'Prologue at Oxford' spoken.

(*October*) 'Prologue and Epilogue spoken at *Mithridates*'.

(*November*) *Absalom and Achitophel* published, followed by many rejoinders.

1682 (*February*) 'Prologue and Epilogue to *The Loyal Brother*' spoken.

(*15/16 March*) *The Medal* published, followed by rejoinders.

(*21 April*) 'Prologue to His Royal Highness' spoken.

(*May*) Publication of *The Medal of John Bayes*, an outspoken attack on D., probably by Shadwell.

(*31 May*) 'Prologue to the Duchess' spoken.

(*July*) *The Duke of Guise* ready for performance, but banned by the Lord Chamberlain.

(*October*) *Mac Flecknoe* printed in a pirated edition.

(*November*) *The Second Part of Absalom and Achitophel* published. *Religio Laici* published. 'Prologue and Epilogue to the King and Queen' spoken.

(*28 November*) *The Duke of Guise* performed at the Theatre Royal.

(*c. December*) 'Prologue and Epilogue to *The Princess of Cleves*' spoken.

1683   Song 'High state and honours' printed in *Choice Ayres and Songs*.

(*February*) *The Duke of Guise* published, followed by pamphlets attacking it.

(*Spring*) *The Vindication of The Duke of Guise* published.

(*May*) Vol. I of *Plutarch's Lives* published, containing D.'s 'Life of Plutarch'.

(*Autumn*) Soame's *The Art of Poetry* published, with revisions by D.

(*November*) 'Epilogue to *Constantine the Great*' spoken.

1684   'To the Earl of Roscommon' published in Roscommon's *Essay on Translated Verse*. 'To Mr L. Maidwell' written and left in MS. First version of *King Arthur* composed.

(*February*) *Miscellany Poems* published, with contributions by D.

(*March*) Probable date of D.'s letter to Laurence Hyde, asking for help in securing payment of his salary.

(*April*) 'Prologue to *The Disappointment*' spoken.

(*July*) *The History of the League* published.

(*Autumn*) 'To the Memory of Mr Oldham' published in Oldham's *Remains*. *Albion and Albanius* staged before the King.

1685   (*January*) *Sylvae* published, with contributions by D.

(*6 February*) Death of Charles II; accession of James II.

(*March*) *Threnodia Augustalis* published.

(*3 June*) Revised version of *Albion and Albanius* performed at Dorset Garden.

(*11 June*) Duke of Monmouth lands at Lyme Regis; defeated at the Battle of Sedgemoor (*6 July*), and executed (*15 July*).

(*Summer*) Publication of commendatory verses in Northleigh's *The Triumph of our Monarchy*.

1686   D.'s conversion to the Church of Rome is not precisely
          datable, but probably occurred in 1685; on *19 January
          1686* Evelyn recorded: '*Dryden* the famous play-poet &
          his two sonns, & Mrs. *Nelle* (Misse to the late . . .) were
          said to go to Masse; & such purchases were no greate
          losse to the Church.'
          D. contributes to *A Defence of the Papers*, a work defend-
          ing papers on catholicism attributed to Charles II and
          Anne Hyde.
          (*November*) Publication of 'To the Pious Memory of Mrs
          Anne Killigrew' in her *Poems*.

1687   (*May*) *The Hind and the Panther* published. D. says in the
          address 'To the Reader' that it had been written 'during
          the last Winter and the beginning of this Spring; though
          with long interruptions of ill health, and other hin-
          drances'.
          (*Summer*) Publication of commendatory verses in Hig-
          den's *A Modern Essay on the Tenth Satyr of Juvenal*.
          (*July*) Publication of Montague and Prior's satirical *The
          Hind and the Panther Transvers'd*.
          (*22 November*) St Cecilia's Day celebration, at which D.'s
          'A Song for St Cecilia's Day' was performed; the printed
          text appeared around this time, and was probably distrib-
          uted at the performance.
          (*December*) Composition of 'On the Marriage of Anastasia
          Stafford'.

1688   Lines on Milton printed in Tonson's new edition of *Para-
          dise Lost*.
          Publication of Tom Brown's attack on D., *The Reasons of
          Mr Bays Changing his Religion*.
          (*June*) Publication of *Britannia Rediviva*, celebrating the
          birth of a son to James II and Queen Mary (on *10 June*).
          (*July*) Publication of D.'s translation of Bouhours' *The
          Life of St Francis Xavier*.
          (*5 November*) Prince William of Orange lands at Torbay.
          (*11 December*) James II flees London, but is captured and
          returned; finally escapes to France.

1689   (*January*) Convention Parliament offers the crown to
          William and Mary. As a result of the revolution D. loses
          his offices as Poet Laureate and Historiographer Royal
          (replaced by Shadwell); he returns to the theatre to make a
          living.

(*November*) Contributes Prologue for performance of Behn's *The Widow Ranter*.

(*4 December*) *Don Sebastian* performed at the Theatre Royal.

1690 Tom Brown publishes another attack on D., *The Late Converts Expos'd*.

(*January*) *Don Sebastian* published.

(*May*) Politically controversial Prologue for Beaumont and Fletcher's *The Prophetess* spoken and immediately suppressed.

(*October*) *Amphitryon* performed at the Theatre Royal; printed at the end of the month.

(*December*) Prologue for Harris's *The Mistakes* spoken.

1691 D. contributes Preface to Walsh's *A Dialogue concerning Women*.

(*February/March*) Publication of Purcell's music for *The Prophetess*, with a dedication to the Duke of Somerset drafted for Purcell by D.

(*May/June*) *King Arthur* performed at Dorset Garden (originally written in 1684); published *early June*.

1692 (*c. February*) Publication of commendatory verses in Southerne's *The Wives' Excuse*.

(*March*) Publication of *Eleonora*, mourning the Countess of Abingdon.

(*April*) *Cleomenes* performed at the Theatre Royal; it is published in *May*. D. contributes a 'Character of Saint-Evremond' to a translation of his *Miscellaneous Essays*.

(*September*) Contributes Prologue to the anonymous *Henry the Second*.

(*October*) Publication of *The Satires of Juvenal and Persius* (dated 1693).

1693 D. contributes 'A Character of Polybius' to *The History of Polybius*.

(*July*) Publication of *Examen Poeticum*, with contributions by D.

(*December*) 'To My Dear Friend Mr Congreve' published in Congreve's *The Double Dealer* (dated 1694).

1694 (*January*) *Love Triumphant* performed at the Theatre Royal.

(*March*) *Love Triumphant* published.

(*15 June*) D. signs contract with Tonson for a complete translation of Virgil, which occupies most of the next three years.

	(*July*) *Annual Miscellany for the Year 1694* published with contributions by D.
1695	(*June*) D.'s translation of Du Fresnoy's *De Arte Graphica* published.
1696	(*February*) Contributes Epilogue to *The Husband his own Cuckold* by his son John, and adds a Preface when it is printed in *July*.
	(*Spring: before June*) *An Ode on the Death of Mr Henry Purcell* published (Purcell died *21 November 1695*).
1697	(*July*) Publication of *The Works of Virgil*.
	(*22 November*) *Alexander's Feast* performed at the St Cecilia's Day celebration; the printed text appeared about this time, and was probably distributed at the performance.
1698	(*February*) Commendatory verses published in Granville's *Heroick Love*.
	(*March*) Publication of Jeremy Collier's *A Short View of the Immorality and Profaneness of the English Stage* including criticism of D.'s plays.
	(*June*) Commendatory verses published in Motteux's *Beauty in Distress*. D.'s translation of Annals Book I published in *The Annals and History of Cornelius Tacitus*.
1699	(*20 March*) Contract for *Fables* drawn up with Tonson.
	(*October*) D. plans to translate Homer and seeks patronage for the project.
1700	(*March*) *Fables Ancient and Modern* published.
	(*April*) *The Pilgrim* performed (adapted from a play by Fletcher).
	(*1 May*) Death of D.; buried on *2 May* in St Anne's Church, Soho; reburied in Chaucer's grave in Westminster Abbey, *13 May*.
	(*June*) *The Pilgrim* published.
	Various poems published in memory of D., including *Luctus Britannici* (*June*) and *The Nine Muses*, by women admirers (*September*).
1704	*Poetical Miscellanies: The Fifth Part* includes material by D.
1709	*Ovid's Art of Love* includes Book I translated by D. (written in 1693).
1711	D.'s 'The Life of Lucian' (written *c*. 1696) published in *The Works of Lucian*.
1717	D.'s 'Aesacus transformed into a Cormorant' (written *c*. 1692) published in *Ovid's Metamorphoses*.

Abbreviations

The Works of Dryden
AA   *Absalom and Achitophel*
2AA   *The Second Part of Absalom and Achitophel*
AM   *Annus Mirabilis*
EDP   *Of Dramatic Poesy, An Essay*
EP   *Examen Poeticum* (1693)
HP   *The Hind and the Panther*
MF   *Mac Flecknoe*
MP   *Miscellany Poems* (1684)
RL   *Religio Laici*

Journals
BJRL   *Bulletin of the John Rylands University Library of Manchester*
BNYPL *Bulletin of the New York Public Library*
CQ   *Cambridge Quarterly*
DUJ   *Durham University Journal*
EA   *Études Anglaises*
ECS   *Eighteenth-Century Studies*
EIC   *Essays in Criticism*
ELH   *English Literary History* (now known as 'ELH')
ELN   *English Language Notes*
EMS   *English Manuscript Studies*
ES   *English Studies*
HJ   *Historical Journal*
HLB   *Harvard Library Bulletin*
HLQ   *Huntington Library Quarterly*
JEGP   *Journal of English and Germanic Philology*
JHI   *Journal of the History of Ideas*
JWCI   *Journal of the Warburg and Courtauld Institutes*
MLN   *Modern Language Notes*
MLQ   *Modern Language Quarterly*
MLR   *Modern Language Review*
MPh   *Modern Philology*
N & Q   *Notes and Queries*
PBSA   *Papers of the Bibliographical Society of America*
PLL   *Papers on Language and Literature*
PLPLS *Proceedings of the Leeds Philosophical and Literary Society (Literary and Historical Section)*

PMLA	*Publications of the Modern Language Association of America* (now known as 'PMLA')
PP	*Past and Present*
PQ	*Philological Quarterly*
PTRS	*Philosophical Transactions of the Royal Society*
RECTR	*Restoration and Eighteenth-Century Theatre Research*
RES	*Review of English Studies*
RS	*Renaissance Studies*
SB	*Studies in Bibliography*
SC	*Seventeenth Century*
SECC	*Studies in Eighteenth-Century Culture*
SEL	*Studies in English Literature 1500–1900*
SP	*Studies in Philology*
SRev	*Southern Review*
TCBS	*Transactions of the Cambridge Bibliographical Society*
TN	*Theatre Notebook*
TRHS	*Transactions of the Royal Historical Society*
YES	*Yearbook of English Studies*

Other abbreviations

Aen.	Virgil, *Aeneid*
BL	British Library, London
BodL	Bodleian Library, Oxford
Carm.	Horace, *Carmina* ('Odes')
CSPD	*Calendar of State Papers Domestic*
Ecl.	Virgil, *Eclogues*
Ed.	The present editor
Eds	The general consensus among previous editors
FQ	Spenser, *The Faerie Queene*
Geo.	Virgil, *Georgics*
HMC	Historical Manuscripts Commission
LS	*The London Stage* (see Bibliography for details)
Met.	Ovid, *Metamorphoses*
NT	New Testament
OT	Old Testament
PL	Milton, *Paradise Lost*
POAS	*Poems on Affairs of State* (see Bibliography for details)
PR	Milton, *Paradise Regained*
s.d.	stage direction
Serm.	Horace, *Sermones* ('Satires')
SR	*The Stationers' Register*
TC	*The Term Catalogues*

tr.   translated by
UL   University Library

Note on the use of abbreviated titles for Dryden's poems
Each poem has been given a standardized short title which is used throughout, except that the full original title is given at the beginning of each poem.

Bibliography

This bibliography lists only the editions used for principal references and quotations, and those works of scholarship and criticism which are cited by author or short title. In this bibliography the place of publication is London unless otherwise stated, but in the rest of this edition the place of publication is not given. Throughout the edition the date given for plays is the date of their appearance in print, unless first performance is specified.

The Works of Dryden

Christie *The Poetical Works of John Dryden*, edited by W. D. Christie (1870)

Day *The Songs of John Dryden*, edited by Cyrus Lawrence Day (New York, 1932)

Ker *Essays of John Dryden*, edited by W. P. Ker, 2 vols (Oxford, 1900)

Kinsley *The Poems of John Dryden*, edited by James Kinsley, 4 vols (Oxford, 1958)

Letters *The Letters of John Dryden*, edited by Charles E. Ward (Durham, NC, 1942)

Malone *The Critical and Miscellaneous Prose Works of John Dryden*, edited by Edmond Malone, 3 vols (1800)

Noyes *The Poetical Works of Dryden*, edited by George R. Noyes (Boston, Mass., 1909; second edition 1950)

Scott *The Works of John Dryden*, edited by Walter Scott, 18 vols (1808)

Watson John Dryden, *Of Dramatic Poesy and other critical essays*, edited by George Watson, 2 vols (1962)

Works *The Works of John Dryden*, edited by H. T. Swedenberg et al., 20 vols (Berkeley, Calif., 1956–   )

Dryden's writings are generally cited from *Works*, while pieces which have not yet appeared in *Works* are cited from Kinsley or from the first printed editions. References to *Works* are given by line numbers for the poetry (e.g. ll. 12–34), by act, scene and line numbers for the plays (e.g. I ii 34–56), and by volume and page number for the prose and for the editorial commentary (e.g. i 2–3). When a note in the present edition draws upon or discusses material in the equivalent note in *Works*, this is signalled by a simple citation (*Works*) without further references. The same applies to the citation of other editors.

Classical works
Classical writers are quoted from the Loeb Library, unless there is a particular reason for citing the editions which Dryden is known to have used (for these see Bottkol's article, and the headnotes to Dryden's translations). Translations are generally based on the Loeb versions, but are adapted where necessary.

Seventeenth-century works

Boileau   *Oeuvres complètes de Boileau*, edited by Charles-H. Boudhors, 7 vols (Paris, 1934–43)

Buckingham   George Villiers, Duke of Buckingham, *The Rehearsal*, edited by D. E. L. Crane (Durham, 1976)

Burnet   *Burnet's History of my Own Time, Part I: The Reign of Charles the Second*, edited by Osmund Airy, 2 vols (Oxford, 1897–1900)

Burton   Robert Burton, *The Anatomy of Melancholy*, Everyman's Library (1932)

Carew   *The Poems of Thomas Carew*, edited by Rhodes Dunlap (Oxford, 1949)

Cowley   Abraham Cowley, *Poems*, edited by A. R. Waller (Cambridge, 1905)
                 Abraham Cowley, *Essays, Plays and Sundry Verses*, edited by A. R. Waller (Cambridge, 1906)

Danchin   *The Prologues and Epilogues of the Restoration 1660–1700*, edited by Pierre Danchin, *Part One: 1660–1676*, 2 vols (Nancy, 1981) *Part Two: 1677–1690*, 2 vols (Nancy, 1984)

Denham   *The Poetical Works of Sir John Denham*, edited by Theodore Howard Banks, second edition (n.p., 1969)

Downes   John Downes, *Roscius Anglicanus* [first published 1708], edited by Judith Milhous and Robert D. Hume (1987)

Etherege   *The Dramatic Works of Sir George Etherege*, edited by H. F. B. Brett-Smith, 2 vols (Oxford, 1927)

Evelyn   *The Diary of John Evelyn*, edited by E. S. de Beer, 6 vols (Oxford, 1955)

Godwyn   Thomas Godwyn, *Romanae Historiae Anthologia*, revised edition (Oxford, 1631)

Grey   *Debates of the House of Commons, From the Year 1667 to the Year 1694*, edited by Anchitell Grey, 10 vols (1763)

Jonson	*Ben Jonson*, edited by C. H. Herford, Percy and Evelyn Simpson, 11 vols (Oxford, 1925–52)
Langbaine	Gerard Langbaine, *An Account of the English Dramatick Poets* (1691)
Luttrell	Narcissus Luttrell, *A Brief Historical Relation of State Affairs 1678–1714*, 6 vols (1857)
Marvell	*The Poems and Letters of Andrew Marvell*, edited by H. M. Margoliouth; third edition revised by Pierre Legouis and E. E. Duncan-Jones, 2 vols (Oxford, 1971)
Milton	*The Poems of John Milton*, edited by John Carey and Alastair Fowler (1968)
	The Complete Prose Works of John Milton, edited by Don M. Wolfe et al., 8 vols (New Haven, Conn., 1953–82)
Montaigne	Montaigne, *Œuvres complètes*, edited by Maurice Rat (Paris, 1962)
Oldham	*The Poems of John Oldham*, edited by Harold F. Brooks with Raman Selden (Oxford, 1987)
Otway	*The Works of Thomas Otway*, edited by J. C. Ghosh, 2 vols (Oxford, 1932)
Pepys	*The Diary of Samuel Pepys*, edited by Robert Latham and William Matthews, 11 vols (1970–83)
POAS	*Poems on Affairs of State*, edited by George De F. Lord et al., 7 vols (New Haven, Conn., 1963–75)
Rochester	*The Complete Poems of John Wilmot, Earl of Rochester*, edited by David M. Vieth (New Haven, Conn., 1968)
Ross	Alexander Ross, *Mystagogus Poeticus, or The Muses Interpreter* (1647)
Rymer	*The Critical Works of Thomas Rymer*, edited by Curt A. Zimansky (New Haven, Conn., 1956)
Shadwell	*The Complete Works of Thomas Shadwell*, edited by Montague Summers, 5 vols (1927)
Shakespeare	*The Arden Edition of the Works of William Shakespeare*, 39 vols (1949–)
	William Shakespeare, *The Sonnets and A Lover's Complaint*, edited by John Kerrigan (Harmondsworth, 1986)
Southerne	*The Works of Thomas Southerne*, edited by Robert Jordan and Harold Love, 2 vols (Oxford, 1988)
Spence	Joseph Spence, *Observations, Anecdotes, and Characters*

	of Books and Men, edited by James M. Osborn, 2 vols (Oxford, 1966)
Spenser	*Spenser's Faerie Queene*, edited by J. C. Smith, 2 vols (Oxford, 1909)
	Spenser's Minor Poems, edited by Ernest de Selincourt (Oxford, 1910)
Spingarn	*Critical Essays of the Seventeenth Century*, edited by J. E. Spingarn, 3 vols (Oxford, 1908–9)
Sprat	Thomas Sprat, *The History of the Royal-Society of London* (1667)
Waller	*The Poems of Edmund Waller*, edited by G. Thorn Drury, 2 vols (1901)
Wycherley	*The Plays of William Wycherley*, edited by Arthur Friedman (Oxford, 1979)

Modern scholarship and criticism

This list is not intended to be even a basic bibliography of Dryden studies; it simply provides the details of those works which it has been convenient to cite in this edition by author or short title. Readers wishing to find listings of Dryden scholarship and criticism might consult *John Dryden: A Survey and Bibliography of Critical Studies, 1895–1974*, edited by David J. Latt and Samuel Holt Monk (Minneapolis, Minn., 1976); more recent work is listed in regular bibliographies in the periodicals *Restoration*, *The Scriblerian* and *The Year's Work in English Studies*. A selective bibliography is included in Paul Hammond, *John Dryden: A Literary Life* (Basingstoke, 1991).

Ashcraft	Richard Ashcraft, *Revolutionary Politics and Locke's 'Two Treatises of Government'* (Princeton, NJ, 1986)
Beal	Peter Beal, *Index of English Literary Manuscripts*, vol. 2, part 1 (1987)
Bottkol	J. McG. Bottkol, 'Dryden's Latin Scholarship', *MPh* xl (1943) 241–54
Garrison	James D. Garrison, *Dryden and the Tradition of Panegyric* (Berkeley, Calif., 1975)
Gillespie	Stuart Gillespie, 'Dryden's *Sylvae*: A study of Dryden's translations from the Latin in the second Tonson miscellany, 1685' (unpublished PhD thesis, Cambridge 1987)
	Stuart Gillespie, 'A Checklist of Restoration English Translations and Adaptations of

Classical Greek and Latin Poetry, 1660–1700',
Translation and Literature i (1991) 52–67

Haley   K. H. D. Haley, *The First Earl of Shaftesbury*
(Oxford, 1968)

Harth   Phillip Harth, *Contexts of Dryden's Thought*
(Chicago, Ill., 1968)

Hawkins   Edward Hawkins, *Medallic Illustrations of the
History of Great Britain to the Death of George II*,
2 vols (1885)

Highfill   Philip H. Highfill, Jr, Kalman A. Burnim and
Edward A. Langhans, *A Biographical Diction-
ary of Actors, Actresses, Musicians, Dancers,
Managers and other stage personnel in London,
1660–1800* (Carbondale, Ill., 1973–   )

Hoffman   Arthur W. Hoffman, *John Dryden's Imagery*
(Gainesville, Fla., 1962)

Hotson   Leslie Hotson, *The Commonwealth and Restoration Stage* (Cambridge, Mass., 1928)

Hume   Robert D. Hume, *The Development of English
Drama in the Late Seventeenth Century* (Oxford,
1976)

Hutton   Ronald Hutton, *The Restoration: A Political and
Religious History of England and Wales 1658–
1667* (Oxford, 1985)
Ronald Hutton, *Charles the Second: King of
England, Scotland, and Ireland* (Oxford, 1989)

LS   *The London Stage 1660–1800*, Part I: 1660–
1700, edited by William van Lennep (Carbon-
dale, Ill., 1965)

Macdonald   Hugh Macdonald, *John Dryden: A Bibliography
of Early Editions and of Drydeniana* (Oxford,
1939). (For corrections and additions to Macdonald's bibliography see James M. Osborn,
MPh xxxix (1941) 69–98, 197–212.)

McFadden   George McFadden, *Dryden the Public Writer
1660–1685* (Princeton, NJ, 1978)

Mason   J. R. Mason, 'To Milton through Dryden and
Pope' (unpublished PhD thesis, Cambridge
1987)

Milhous and Hume Judith Milhous and Robert D. Hume, 'Dating
Play Premieres from Publication Data, 1660–
1700', *HLB* xxii (1974) 374–405

Miner	Earl Miner, *Dryden's Poetry* (Bloomington, Ind., 1971)
Ogg	David Ogg, *England in the Reign of Charles II*, second edition (Oxford, 1956)
Osborn	James M. Osborn, *John Dryden: Some Biographical Facts and Problems*, revised edition (Gainesville, Fla., 1965)
Owen	Susan Owen, 'Drama and Politics in the Exclusion Crisis: 1678–83' (unpublished PhD thesis, Leeds 1992)
Price	Curtis A. Price, *Music in the Restoration Theatre: With a Catalogue of Instrumental Music in the Plays 1665–1713* (Ann Arbor, Mich., 1979)
	Curtis Alexander Price, *Henry Purcell and the London Stage* (Cambridge, 1984)
Spurr	John Spurr, *The Restoration Church of England, 1646–1689* (New Haven, Conn., 1991)
Tilley	M. P. Tilley, *A Dictionary of the Proverbs in England in the Sixteenth and Seventeenth Centuries* (Ann Arbor, Mich., 1950)
Verrall	A. W. Verrall, *Lectures on Dryden* (Cambridge, 1914)
Winn	James Anderson Winn, *John Dryden and his World* (New Haven, Conn., 1987) (cited as 'Winn')
	James Anderson Winn, *'When Beauty Fires the Blood': Love and the Arts in the Age of Dryden* (Ann Arbor, Mich., 1992) (cited with short title)
Zwicker	Steven N. Zwicker, *Dryden's Political Poetry: The Typology of King and Nation* (Providence, R.I., 1972)

THE POEMS

1 Upon the Death of the Lord Hastings

Date and publication. Printed in *Lachrymae Musarum; The Tears of the Muses . . . Upon the death of the most hopefull, Henry Lord Hastings* (1649); reissued 1650. D.'s poem is signed 'Johannes Dryden, Scholae Westm. Alumnus.' Contributors included Herrick, Denham, Cotton and Marvell. The poems by D. and Marvell are among eight in gatherings F and G which were sent in after the rest of the volume was printed; five of these extra poems are by alumni of Westminster School.

Context. Henry Lord Hastings was born on 16 January 1630 and died of smallpox on 24 June 1649, the eve of the day arranged for his marriage with Elizabeth de Mayerne, the daughter of the King's physician, Sir Theodore Turquet de Mayerne. He was the eldest and last surviving son of Ferdinando, sixth Earl of Huntingdon. The circumstances are described by Michael Gearin-Tosh (*Essays and Studies* xxxiv (1981) 105–22) who suggests that *Lachrymae* was in part an opportunity for royalists covertly to mourn Charles I. For a later echo of *Lachrymae* by D. see *AA* 1. 227*n*.

Sources. In addition to specific verbal echoes of earlier elegies, the poem draws generally on the tradition of elegy (see Ruth Wallerstein, *Studies in Seventeenth-Century Poetic* (1950) 115–42) and on Royalist poetry (see James A. Winn, *MLR* lxxix (1984) 21–31).

Upon the Death of the Lord Hastings

    Must noble Hastings immaturely die,
    The honour of his ancient family?
    Beauty and learning thus together meet,
    To bring a winding for a wedding sheet?
5 Must virtue prove death's harbinger? Must she,
    With him expiring, feel mortality?
    Is death, sin's wages, grace's now? Shall art
    Make us more learnèd, only to depart?
    If merit be disease, if virtue death;
10 To be good, not to be; who'd then bequeath

¶1. 7. *death, sin's wages*] from Romans vi 23.
9–12. Perhaps an echo of the speech 'To be, or not to be . . .' (*Hamlet* III i 56–76 (J. M. Aden, *N & Q* cc (1955) 22–3).
10. bequeath] devote [oneself] to (*OED* 7).

Himself to discipline? Who'd not esteem
Labour a crime, study self-murther deem?
Our noble youth now have pretence to be
Dunces securely, ign'rant healthfully.
15 Rare linguist! whose worth speaks itself, whose praise,
Though not his own, all tongues besides do raise;
Than whom great Alexander may seem less,
Who conquered men, but not their languages.
In his mouth nations speak; his tongue might be
20 Interpreter to Greece, France, Italy.
His native soil was the four parts o' th' earth,
All Europe was too narrow for his birth.
A young apostle, and (with rev'rence may
I speak 't) inspired with gift of tongues as they.
25 Nature gave him, a child, what men in vain
Oft strive, by art though furthered, to obtain.
His body was an orb, his sublime soul
Did move on virtue's and on learning's pole,
Whose reg'lar motions better to our view
30 Than Archimedes' sphere the heavens did show.
Graces and virtues, languages and arts,

15–20. Several elegists praised his linguistic skill, e.g. Sir Aston Cokaine: 'his sweet tongue could fall / Into the ancient Dialects; dispence / Sacred *Judaea*'s amplest Eloquence, / The Latine Idiome elegantly true, / And Greek as rich as *Athens* ever knew: / The *Italian* and the *French* do both confess / Him perfect in their Modern Languages' (*Lachrymae* 4).

16. raise] extol (*OED* 18b).

21. four parts] The river which flowed out of the garden of Eden divided into four (Genesis ii 10).

24. The apostles were inspired with the gift of tongues at Pentecost (Acts ii).

27–30. Richard Busby, headmaster of Westminster School, taught astronomy and had a collection of astronomical texts (Winn, *MLR* lxxix (1984) 23).

27. orb] Used of the concentric hollow spheres inside which the earth was supposed to turn. The circle or sphere was a common seventeenth-century image of perfection: cp. Jonson, *Epigrammes* xcviii 3 (drawing on Horace, *Serm.* II vii 86–8) and cxxviii 8; and D.'s *Heroic Stanzas* ll. 18–20; *AA* ll. 838–9; *Eleonora* ll. 272–3.   *sublime*] awkwardly accented here on the first syllable.

30. Archimedes' sphere] Archimedes made a sphere which represented the motions of the sun, moon and five planets (see Cicero, *De Re Publica* i 21–2; Claudian, *In sphaeram Archimedis*; John Wilkins, *Mathematicall Magick* (1648) 164–5; R. N. Ringler, *ELN* i (1963–4) 256–61).   *show*] The spelling *shew* in *1649* provides an acceptable rhyme with *view*.

Beauty and learning, filled up all the parts.
Heaven's gifts, which do like falling stars appear
Scattered in others, all, as in their sphere,
35 Were fixed and conglobate in 's soul, and thence
Shone through his body with sweet influence,
Letting their glories so on each limb fall,
The whole frame rendered was celestial.
Come, learnèd Ptolemy, and trial make
40 If thou this hero's altitude canst take;
But that transcends thy skill; thrice happy all,
Could we but prove thus astronomical.
Lived Tycho now, struck with this ray (which shone
More bright i' th' morn than others' beam at noon),
45 He'd take his astrolabe, and seek out here
What new star 'twas did gild our hemisphere.
Replenished then with such rare gifts as these,
Where was room left for such a foul disease?
The nation's sin hath drawn that veil which shrouds
50 Our dayspring in so sad benighting clouds.
Heaven would no longer trust its pledge, but thus

33–5. Echoes Carew: 'Aske me no more where those starres light, / That downewards fall in dead of night: / For in your eyes they sit, and there, / Fixed become as in their sphere' ('A Song' printed in his *Poems* (1640); *Poems* edited by Dunlap 103).

35. conglobate] gathered into a globe (from the Latin *conglobo*; the first example of the adjective in the *OED*, though Sir Thomas Browne used the verb in *Pseudodoxia Epidemica* (1646) iii 7).

36. influence] astrologically, the effect of the planets and stars on human life.

38. celestial] in contrast to sublunary bodies, which are corruptible.

39–40. The Alexandrian astronomer Ptolemy (c. AD 100–178) had measured the ecliptic of the sun.

41–2. Cp. *Eleonora* ll. 263–9.

42. i.e. if we could attain such immeasurable virtue.

43. Tycho Brahé (1546–1601), the Danish astronomer, discovered a new star in the constellation of Cassiopeia in 1572.

49. the nation's sin] The execution of Charles I on 30 January 1649. Other elegists are more outspoken, e.g. Denham: 'as the Leader of the Herd fell first, / A Sacrifice to quench the raging thirst / Of inflam'd Vengeance for past Crimes: so none / But this white fatted Youngling could atone, / By his untimely Fate, that impious Smoke / That sullied Earth, and did Heaven's pity choke' (*Lachrymae* 41).

50. dayspring] from Luke i 78–9, used of Christ.

Recalled it, rapt its Ganymede from us.
Was there no milder way but the small pox,
The very filth'ness of Pandora's box?
55 So many spots, like naeves, our Venus soil?
One jewel set off with so many a foil?
Blisters with pride swelled, which through 's flesh did
    sprout
Like rose-buds, stuck i' th' lily skin about.
Each little pimple had a tear in it,
60 To wail the fault its rising did commit,
Who, rebel-like, with their own lord at strife,
Thus made an insurrection 'gainst his life.
Or were these gems sent to adorn his skin,
The cab'net of a richer soul within?
65 No comet need foretell his change drew on,
Whose corpse might seem a constellation.
O had he died of old, how great a strife

52. Ganymede] The boy with whom Zeus fell in love, and took to heaven to
be his cupbearer. It can be a name for 'one that delights in divine counsell or
wisdome; and wisdome is the true beauty of the minde wherein God takes
pleasure' (Ross 96).
54. Pandora's box] Zeus, enraged at Prometheus's theft of fire from heaven,
sent Pandora to earth with a box which disgorged all kinds of evils; but hope
was found at the bottom.
55. naeves] spots, blemishes (from Latin, *naevus*). This is one of only three
uses cited by the *OED*, the first being in 1619.   *Venus*] Referring to
Hastings's beauty; possibly also referring to the Platonic celestial Venus
which represents the love of heavenly things (Ross 261). Cp. Nathaniel
Whiting, *Albino and Bellama* (1637): 'The purest-boulted floure that is, has
bran. / *Venus* her Naeue, *Helen* her stain' (sig. A4ʳ; Winn, *MLR* lxxix (1984)
25).
56. Cp. Thomas Pestell: 'The Case so bright, what radiance threw / The
Jewel that it did indue!' (*Lachrymae* 17).
59–60. Cp. Edward Montagu: *utque tumebat / Pustula, sic tumeat Lachryma,
mille oculis* ('and as the pimple swelled, so may a tear swell in a thousand
eyes': *Lachrymae* frontispiece).
63–6. Cp. Carew: 'Shee was a Cabinet / Where all the choysest stones of
price were set; / . . . Whose rare and hidden vertues, did expresse, / Her
inward beauties, and minds fairer dresse' ('Epitaph on the Lady S.' (1640);
Poems, edited by Dunlap 55); and William Cartwright: 'let us say / They were
small Stars fixt in a *Milky-way*, / Or faithfull Turquoises' ('On His Majesties
recovery from the small Pox 1633' in *Comedies* (1651) 192) (*Works*).
66. constellation] i.e. from which one could foretell its own fate.
67–8. An allusion to the ancient belief that by drawing in the last breath of a

Had been, who from his death should draw their life!
Who should, by one rich draught, become whate'er
70   Seneca, Cato, Numa, Caesar were—
Learned, virtuous, pious, great, and have by this
An universal metempsychosis.
Must all these aged sires in one funeral
Expire? All die in one so young, so small?
75   Who, had he lived his life out, his great fame
Had swoll'n 'bove any Greek or Roman name.
But hasty winter with one blast hath brought
The hopes of autumn, summer, spring to nought.
Thus fades the oak i' th' sprig, i' th' blade the corn,
80   Thus without young this phoenix dies new born.
Must then old three-legged grey-beards with their
         gout,
Catarrhs, rheums, achès live three ages out?
Time's offal, only fit for th' hospital,
Or t' hang an antiquary's room withal;
85   Must drunkards, lechers, spent with sinning, live
With such helps as broths, possets, physic give?
None live, but such as should die? Shall we meet
With none but ghostly fathers in the street?

---

dying man one could acquire his spirit: 'The *Romans* . . . had such a custome,
that the next of the kinne should receiue the last gaspe of breath from the
sicke bodie into his mouth' (Godwyn 76).

70–1. The Stoic philosopher Lucius Annaeus Seneca (*c*.4 BC to AD 41) was
the author of many treatises, letters and plays. Marcus Porcius Cato (234–149
BC) brought a stern traditional morality to Roman public life. Numa Pompi-
lius, by tradition the second King of Rome (715–673 BC) was credited with
establishing Roman religion. Gaius Julius Caesar (100–44 BC) was an out-
standing general and ruler.

72. metempsychosis] Transmigration of souls. The spelling in *1649* is *metempsu-
chosis*, which suggests a Greek pronunciation ('u' rather than 'y'); the accent is
on the third syllable.

73. aged] monosyllabic.

81–4. Cp. Juvenal, *Satire* x 190–5; ll. 305–12 in D.'s translation.

81. three-legged] As in the riddle of the sphinx: a staff is the third leg.

82. achès] disyllabic; pronounced as 'aitches'.

84. Cp. Earle's character of the antiquary: 'His chamber is hung commonly
with strange Beasts skins, and is a kind of Charnel-house of bones extraordinary' (*Microcosmographie* (1628), edited by Edward Arber (1868) 29).

86. possets] drinks of hot milk, curdled with liquor, to remedy colds.

Grief makes me rail; sorrow will force its way,
90 And showers of tears tempestuous sighs best lay.
The tongue may fail, but overflowing eyes
Will weep out lasting streams of elegies.
But thou, O virgin-widow, left alone
Now thy beloved, heaven-ravished spouse is gone
95 (Whose skilful sire in vain strove to apply
Med'cines, when thy balm was no remedy),
With greater than Platonic love, O wed
His soul, though not his body, to thy bed;
Let that make thee a mother, bring thou forth
100 Th' ideas of his virtue, knowledge, worth;
Transcribe th' orig'nal in new copies, give
Hastings o' th' better part: so shall he live
In 's nobler half, and the great grandsire be
Of an heroic divine progeny:
105 An issue which t' eternity shall last,
Yet but th' irradiations which he cast.
Erect no mausoleums: for his best
Monument is his spouse's marble breast.

---

90. Perhaps conventional; cp. Davenant (1651): 'Her sighs as show'rs lay
windes, are calm'd with tears' (*Gondibert* III ii 37).   *lay*] allay, calm (*OED*
3).

97–100. Kinsley cites Plato's *Symposium* (209) where Diotima says that lovers
whose procreation is spiritual rather than fleshly 'conceive and bear the things
of the spirit . . . wisdom and all her sister virtues'; and their union is 'even
more complete than that which comes of bringing children up, because they
have created something lovelier and less mortal than human seed'.

100. ideas] in the Platonic sense of eternal archetypes.

106. irradiations] Kinsley cites Browne's use of the term in discussing
generation: 'impregnation may succeed from seminal spirits, and vaporous
irradiations containing the active principle, without material and gross
immissions'; 'the generation of bodies is not meerly effected as some conceive, of souls, that is, by Irradiation' (*Pseudodoxia Epidemica* VII xvi, III ix).

107–8. For the formula cp. Cartwright: 'To whom the gratefull wife hath
sadly drest / One Monument here, Another in her Brest' ('An Epitaph on
Mr. *Poultney*' in *Comedies* (1651) 298).

2 To John Hoddesdon

Date and publication. Published in 1650 as commendatory verses to John Hoddesdon's *Sion and Parnassus, or Epigrams on severall texts of the Old and New Testament* (imprimatur 7 June 1650). The verses are signed 'J. Dryden of Trin. C.' (D. was admitted as a pensioner of Trinity College, Cambridge, on 18 May 1650 and matriculated on 6 July).

Context. The engraved portrait of Hoddesdon shows him aged 18. In 1652 he published a life of Thomas More and in 1654 *The Holy Lives of God's Prophets*. No more is known of him. Other commendatory verses in this volume were signed by Henricus Bromley, R. Marsh and W. James. Marsh and James were almost certainly Westminster boys (see Macdonald 3), and it is likely that Hoddesdon was also.

To his Friend the Author, on his Divine Epigrams

Thou hast inspired me with thy soul, and I
Who ne'er before could ken of poetry
Am grown so good proficient, I can lend
A line in commendation of my friend.
5 Yet 'tis but of the second hand: if aught
There be in this, 'tis from thy fancy brought;
Good thief who dar'st Prometheus-like aspire,
And fill thy poems with celestial fire;
Enlivened by these sparks divine, their rays
10 Add a bright lustre to thy crown of bays.
Young eaglet, who thy nest thus soon forsook,
So lofty and divine a course hast took

¶**2**. *3. good*] highly (*OED* 19b, 23b).
5–8. Prometheus's theft of fire from heaven was a common metaphor for artistic inspiration; cp. Thomas Randolph: 'Have I a sparke of that coelestiall flame / Within me, I confesse I stole the same / *Prometheus* like, from thee' ('A Gratulatory to Mr Ben. Iohnson' in his *Poems* (1638) 23); Winn (privately) cites Waller: 'for this theft thou hast climbed higher / Than did Prometheus for his fire' ('To Vandyck' ll. 49–50).
11–17. Cp. W. James's poem: 'Go on, go on; if thy first enterprise / Doth mount so high, we must get eagles eyes / To see thy next' (*Sion and Parnassus* sig. ¶ 3ᵛ). The young eagle was supposed to be trained by its mother to look directly at the sun (Pliny, *Naturalis Historia* x 3).

As all admire, before the down begin
To peep, as yet, upon thy smoother chin,
15 And, making heaven thy aim, hast had the grace
To look the sun of righteousness i' th' face.
What may we hope, if thou goest on thus fast,
Scriptures at first, enthusiasms at last!
Thou hast commenced betimes a saint: go on,
20 Mingling diviner streams with Helicon,
That they who view what epigrams here be
May learn to make like, in just praise of thee.
Reader, I've done, nor longer will withhold
Thy greedy eyes; looking on this pure gold
25 Thou'lt know adult'rate copper, which, like this,
Will only serve to be a foil to his.

16. Cp. Hoddesdon: 'Though Sols refulgent rayes dazle our sight, / . . . I'll
look to th' sunne, and looking may I be / Exhal'd a meteor to heav'ns axle-
tree' (*Sion and Parnassus* 51–2). The image of the *sun of righteousness* (from
Malachi iv 2) is also used several times by Hoddesdon (e.g. 126).
18. i.e. Hoddesdon will graduate from meditating on the written word of
God to being directly possessed by the divine spirit.   *enthusiasms*] possession by a god, supernatural inspiration (*OED* 1). At this date D. is using
the word in a complimentary, though perhaps teasing, way, but it became
increasingly pejorative (fancied inspiration, misguided religious fervour:
OED 2, from 1660). The delusions of those who fancied themselves to be
inspired were attacked by Henry More in *Enthusiasmus Triumphatus* (1656).
Winn (privately) notes that religious enthusiasm would have been discour-
aged at Westminster School. For D.'s later view see *AA* l. 530*n*; 'Prologue to
Oedipus' ll. 29–31*n*.
19. commenced] graduated. For the academic image cp. Hoddesdon: 'So often
to commence, yet never past / Master o' th' art *at last*' (*Sion and Parnassus*
100).
20. Helicon] The mountain sacred to the Muses; the name was often applied to
the fountains which rose there (*OED*).

3 Carmen Lapidarium

Date and publication. Written after the death of John Smith on 7 August 1652, this piece survives uniquely in Cambridge UL MS Mm.1.36 p. 406, in a transcript made *c.* 1720 by the antiquarian Thomas Baker (see Plate 1). It was first published by Hilton Kelliher, with an introduction and translation, in *TCBS* x (1993) 340–58.

Context. John Smith (1618–52) was one of the Cambridge Platonists, Fellow of Queens' College and University Lecturer in Mathematics. His religious writings were collected after his death as *Select Discourses* (1660). He came from Achurch, Northamptonshire, a village only two miles from D.'s home at Aldwincle, and was educated at Emmanuel College, Cambridge, as were D.'s father, and Thomas Hill, Rector of the Dryden family's other home village of Titchmarsh, Northamptonshire, and Master of Trinity since 1645. There were therefore local connections between D. and Smith. D. was an undergraduate at Trinity from 1650 to 1654. The form of the *carmen lapidarium*, which is a non-metrical prose poem, was used for inscriptions on tombs and in volumes of memorial verses (see Kelliher). This is D.'s only extant Latin work.

Authorship. The poem is attributed in the MS to 'Jo: Dryden e Coll: Trin.'; there is no reason to doubt the attribution, which is confirmed by the Northamptonshire connections.

In obitum viri pientissimi literatissimi magistri Johannis Smith Collegii Reginalis socii.
Carmen Lapidarium

Adsis viator, sed eruditus,
Adsis lector, sed academicus,
Uterque vel per sympathiam illacrymabilis
Cineribus doctis et academicis.
5 Forma ossea, corpus incorporeum, naturale cemiterium,
Hic jacet Johannes Smithius
Una recubat socius Collegii Reginalis
Una Academiae Praelector Mathematicus:
Misera mortalitas
10 Assidue cadavera confitetur

Rarius skeleton.
Diu versatus in geometria
Tandem (proh dolor) incohavit geodaesiam
Archimedes alter.

15   Encyclopaediae peripheriam aeque calluit
Ac probitatis quadraturam.
Tam bene in uranometria exercitatus
Ut vel inde colligeres
Cognationem aliquam dudum habuisse
20   Cum supernis sedibus.
Hoc unico deficiens
Quod cum orbis ambitum figura ac spatio concluderet,
Suae doctrinae cancellos ac dimensiones nesciret
Quippe infinitos.
25   Talem simul pietatem et indolem
Lenta, sed nimium propera Pthysis abstulit.
Quis melius potuit de Fabro ominarier,
Quum morbus in pulmonum folles incideret.
Tantum (scilicet) profecerat in theologia,
30   Ut carnem domaret consumendo,
Et priusquam exueret, subjugaret.
Praelusit etiam ad occasum novissimum
Quotidiana apoplexia.
Abi viator, et Praelectorem Mathematicum
35   Guttis lugeas arithmetice diffluentibus
Sed innumeris,
Et dicas nepotibus
Cantabrigiam, abrupta hac vitae linea
Amisisse figuram academiae.

¶3. *15–16.* Simon Patrick in his funeral sermon for Smith commented: 'If one should have asked him . . . "What is thy art and profession, thy business and employment?" he would not have answered, To be a great philosopher, mathematician, historian, or Hebraist, (all which he was in great eminency,) . . . but he would have answered, . . . "My art is to be good"' (John Smith, *Select Discourses*, edited by H. G. Williams (1859) 513).
21–4. Smith's vast learning and sharp insight are praised by Patrick 506–8.
29–31. Cp. Patrick: 'He was always very urgent upon us, that . . . we would endeavour to purge out the corruption of our natures, and to "crucify the flesh with all the affections and lusts thereof"' (510).
35. arithmetice] perhaps 'in due proportion'.

Lapidary Verses on the Death of that Most Pious and Learned Man, Mr John Smith, Fellow of Queens' College

Come hither, traveller, if you be learned, come hither, reader, if you be an academic, even if for very fellow-feeling you are unable to weep for learned and academic ashes. A bony frame, a body without substance, his own cemetery, [5] John Smith lies here, reposing at once Fellow of Queens' College and University Lecturer in Mathematics. Wretched mortality frequently manifests itself as a corpse, [10] more rarely as a skeleton. After long involvement in geometry, at length (O grief) he embarked upon geodesy, a second Archimedes. He was as skilled in the circle of learning [15] as in the square of goodness. So well practised was he in astronomy that from this alone you would infer he had long had an acquaintance with the heavenly abodes: [20] wanting only in this, that although the globe defines its circle by form and space, he would admit no bounds or dimensions to his learning, because they were infinite. Such piety and genius together [25] a long drawn out yet all too quick consumption bore away. Who could have foreseen a fitter end for a Smith, seeing that disease attacked the bellows of his lungs? Such (to be sure) was his skill in theology that he subdued the flesh by wearing it away, [30] and before he sloughed it off had conquered it. He foreshadowed his final dissolution by a daily apoplexy. Traveller depart, and mourn this mathematics lecturer with tears that flow numerously [35] though numberless; and tell future generations how Cambridge, when this line of life was severed, lost the appearance of a university.

(from the translation by Hilton Kelliher)

4 To Honor Dryden

Date and publication. The letter (now in the William Andrews Clark Library, University of California at Los Angeles) is the earliest extant by D.; it was written from Cambridge and dated 'May the 23^d / 16'; the last two figures of the year are no longer visible. Using a microscope Edmond Malone found the last figure 'manifestly a 5', and inferred from Honor's age that the third figure was also a 5. D. was no longer regularly in residence at Trinity on 23 April 1655, but he might have returned temporarily in May. Alternatively, what Malone read as a 5 might have been a 3. The letter was first printed in *The Gentleman's Magazine* lv (1785) i 337.

Context. Honor (*c.* 1637–*c.* 1714) was the daughter of D.'s uncle Sir John Dryden of Canons Ashby. D. addressed a verse epistle to her brother John in his *Fables* (1700).

To Honor Dryden

Madam,

If you have received the lines I sent by the reverend
Levite, I doubt not but they have exceedingly wrought
upon you; for being so long in a clergyman's pocket,
assuredly they have acquired more sanctity than their
5 author meant them. Alas, Madam, for aught I know they
may become a sermon ere they could arrive at you; and
believe it, having you for the text it could scarcely prove
bad, if it light upon one that could handle it indifferently.
But I am so miserable a preacher that though I have so
10 sweet and copious a subject, I still fall short in my expressions. And instead of an use of thanksgiving I am
always making one of comfort, that I may one day again
have the happiness to kiss your fair hand. But that is a
message I would not so willingly do by letter as by word
15 of mouth. This is a point I must confess I could willingly
dwell longer on, and in this case whatever I say you may

¶**4**. *Title.* Ed.
Letter.
2. *Levite*] clergyman.

confidently take for gospel. But I must hasten. And
indeed, Madam (beloved I had almost said), he had need
hasten who treats of you; for to speak fully to every part
20 of your excellencies requires a longer hour than most
parsons have allotted them. But in a word yourself hath
been the best expositor upon the text of your own
worth, in that admirable comment you wrote upon it, I
mean your incomparable letter. By all that's good (and
25 you, Madam, are a great part of my oath) it hath put me
so far besides myself that I have scarce patience to write
prose, and my pen is stealing into verse every time I kiss
your letter. I am sure the poor paper smarts for my
idolatry, which by wearing it continually near my breast
30 will at last be burnt and martyred in those flames of
adoration it hath kindled in me. But I forget, Madam,
what rarities your letter came fraught with besides
words: you are such a deity that commands worship by
providing the sacrifice; you are pleased, Madam, to force
35 me to write by sending me materials, and compel me to
my greatest happiness. Yet though I highly value your
magnificent presents, pardon me if I must tell the world
they are but imperfect emblems of your beauty; for the
white and red of wax and paper are but shadows of that
40 vermillion and snow in your lips and forehead. And the
silver of the inkhorn, if it presume to vie whiteness with
your purer skin, must confess itself blacker than the
liquor it contains. What then do I more than retrieve
your own gifts, and present you that paper adulterated
45 with blots which you gave spotless?

For since 'twas mine the white hath lost its hue,
To show 'twas ne'er itself but whilst in you;
The virgin wax hath blushed itself to red
Since it with me hath lost its maidenhead.

Verses.
3–8. Cp. *FQ* III viii 6, where Spenser describes how the witch made a false
Florimel from snow 'And virgin wex, that never yet was seald, / And
mingled them with perfect vermily, / That like a lively sanguine it seem'd to
the eye' (*Works*).

5   You, fairest nymph, are wax; O may you be
    As well in softness so as purity;
    Till fate and your own happy choice reveal
    Whom you so far shall bless to make your seal.

                    Fairest valentine the unfeigned
                      wish of your humble votary.

                                Jo: Dryden.

Cambridge
May the 23^d
16[ ]

        To the fair hands
        of Madam Honor Dryden
        these crave
        admittance.

5 Heroic Stanzas

Date and publication. Cromwell died on 3 September 1658. Because of ineffectual embalming, the body had to be buried privately at an unknown date before the state funeral on 23 November, at which an effigy was used. On 20 January 1659 Henry Herringman entered in *SR* 'a booke called *Three poems to the happy memory of the most renowned Oliver, late Lord Protector of this Commonwealth*, by Mr. Marvell, Mr. Driden, Mr. Sprat.' But Herringman did not proceed with publication, possibly because of changing political circumstances. It was William Wilson who at an unknown date in 1659 published *Three Poems Upon the Death of his late Highnesse Oliver Lord Protector of England, Scotland, and Ireland*, with Waller's 'Upon the Late Storm, and of the Death of his Highness ensuing the same', already printed, replacing Marvell's poem. D.'s poem was reprinted in 1681 with the title *An Elegy on the Usurper O.C. by the Author of Absalom and Achitophel, published to shew the Loyalty and Integrity of the Poet*, which was evidently a Whig attempt to embarrass D.; there were two similar unauthorized reprints in 1682, and another in 1687, which described D. as 'the Author of *The H—d and the P—r*'. An authorized reprint was issued by Tonson in 1691 or 1692 as part of a uniform set of D.'s earlier poems.

An autograph MS of this poem survives in BL MS Lansdowne 1045 (hereafter '*MS*'; see Plate 2), the only autograph MS of a poem by D. now known (apart from the verses in his letter to Honor Dryden). This was identified as being in D.'s hand by Anna Maria Crinò in *English Miscellany* xvii (1966) 311–20. Beal 403–4 lists fourteen other MSS of this poem, so it was evidently given some limited MS circulation through the Restoration period. A critical text based on *MS* was printed by Vinton A. Dearing et al. in *PBSA* lxix (1975) 502–26, and the texts of *MS*, *1659* and *1692* were compared (particularly in their use of accidentals) by Paul Hammond in *PBSA* lxxvi (1982) 457–70.

The relationship of *MS* to *1659* is not entirely clear: *MS* is probably a fair copy (perhaps intended for presentation) made before the poem was revised for its publication in *1659*. It is likely that the substantive variants in ll. 10, 67, 89, 90 and 145 are authorial revisions to the poem made for *1659*; it is possible that the same is true of the variants in ll. 57 and 138 (though Dearing regards them as errors made by *1659*). If the text in *MS* could be shown to have had any public circulation, the textual policy of this edition would point to the choice of *MS* as copy-text; however, since the poem seems to have reached its first public in *1659*, the present edition follows *1659*, emending only at l. 63 (apart from the usual silent emendation of indubitable misprints). Substantive variants between *MS* and *1659* are recorded in the notes, and a reprint of *MS* is provided in Appendix A.

Context. D. probably joined the service of the Protectoral government through his cousin Sir Gilbert Pickering, who was Cromwell's Lord

Chamberlain. (Later, Shadwell wrote that D. had been 'Clerk to *Nolls* Lord Chamberlain': *The Medal of John Bayes* (1682) 8.) On 19 October 1657 D. received £50 from John Thurloe, Cromwell's Secretary of State, for unspecified services. In 1659 he was allocated 9s. for mourning and walked in Cromwell's funeral procession as one of the secretaries of Latin and French tongues, who also included Milton and Marvell (see Paul Hammond, *TCBS* viii (1981) 130–6; Winn 557–8).

Sources. The stanza form had been used by Davenant in *Gondibert* (1651). Several similarities with Sprat's and Waller's poems on the death of Cromwell suggest that D. saw them before writing his own. Garrison 149–55 describes how the poem draws upon the arrangement of material favoured in classical orations.

Heroic Stanzas

Consecrated to the Glorious Memory Of his most Serene and Renowned Highness Oliver, Late Lord Protector of this Commonwealth, etc. Written after the Celebration of his Funeral

I

And now 'tis time; for their officious haste
Who would before have borne him to the sky,
Like eager Romans, ere all rites were past
Did let too soon the sacred eagle fly.

2

5   Though our best notes are treason to his fame,
Joined with the loud applause of public voice,
Since heaven what praise we offer to his name
Hath rendered too authentic by its choice;

¶5. *Title. glorious*] glorious [& happy *deleted*] *MS.*   *funeral*] Funeralls *MS.*
1–4. A reference to panegyrics written before the funeral.
3–4. At the deification of a Roman emperor an eagle was released from the top of his funeral pile to carry his soul to heaven (Herodian IV ii).
8. authentic] duly authorized.

3

Though in his praise no arts can liberal be,
10 Since they whose Muses have the highest flown
Add not to his immortal memory,
But do an act of friendship to their own:

4

Yet 'tis our duty and our interest too
Such monuments as we can build to raise,
15 Lest all the world prevent what we should do,
And claim a title in him by their praise.

5

How shall I then begin, or where conclude,
To draw a fame so truly circular?
For in a round what order can be shewed,
20 Where all the parts so equal perfect are?

6

His grandeur he derived from heaven alone,
For he was great ere Fortune made him so;
And wars, like mists that rise against the sun,
Made him but greater seem, not greater grow.

7

25 No borrowed bays his temples did adorn,
But to our crown he did fresh jewels bring;

10–12. Cp. Sprat: 'thy mighty name / Wants not Addition of another's Beam; / . . . The Muses are made great by Thee, not thou by Them' (*Three Poems* 13; *Works*).
10. Since] And MS.
13. Cp. Sprat: 'but yet our Duty calls our Songs' (13; *Works*).
15. prevent] anticipate.
16. title] legal right.
17. Cp. Sprat: 'What shall I say, or where begin?' (14; *Works*).
18–20. Cp. 'Upon the Death of the Lord Hastings' l. 27*n.*
19. round] sphere (*OED* 1); circle (*OED* 6).   *shewed*] The now obsolete form of *showed*; a perfect rhyme with *conclude*.
22–4. Cp. Sprat: 'whilst yet / Thou only to thy self wert great; / . . . As bodyes, in the Dark and Night, / Have the same Colours, the same Red and White, / As in the open day and Light; / The Sun doth only show / That they are bright, not make them so' (15–16; *Works*).
25. bays] laurels, forming the conqueror's crown.
25–8. Cromwell rejected the offer of the crown in 1657. Cp. Sprat: 'thou

Nor was his virtue poisoned soon as born
With the too early thoughts of being king.

8

Fortune (that easy mistress of the young,
30   But to her ancient servants coy and hard)
Him at that age her favourites ranked among
When she her best-loved Pompey did discard.

9

He private marked the faults of others' sway,
And set as sea-marks for himself to shun;
35   Not like rash monarchs who their youth betray
By acts their age too late would wish undone.

10

And yet dominion was not his design:
We owe that blessing not to him but heaven,

---

wast not born unto a Crown, / Thy Scepter's not thy Fathers, but thy own'
(16).

29–30. Echoes Machiavelli: 'Fortune is a mistresse; and it is necessary, to
keep her in obedience to ruffle and force her: and we see, that she suffers her
self rather to be mastered by those, than by others that proceed coldly. And
therefore, as a mistresse, shee is a friend to young men, because they are lesse
respective, more rough, and command her with more boldnesse' (*The Prince*,
tr. Edward Dacres (1640), Tudor Translations xxxix (1905) 352). Some contemporaries accused Cromwell of Machiavellian deviousness: see *Oliver
Cromwell and the English Revolution*, edited by John Morrill (1990) 263–4. For
links between Marvell's 'An Horatian Ode' and Machiavelli see Blair Worden
in *Politics of Discourse*, edited by Kevin Sharpe and Steven N. Zwicker (1987)
162–8. For the importance of Fortune in D.'s thought see 'Horace: *Odes* III
xxix' ll. 73–87*n*. Sprat says of Cromwell that 'Fortune did hang on thy
Sword' (23).

31–2. Cromwell was 45 when he won the Battle of Marston Moor in 1644,
and 59 when he died. Pompey was 45 when he returned to Rome from the
East at the height of his fortunes, which declined until his death in 48 BC, in
his fifty-ninth year. Lucan says: *sed poenas longi Fortuna fauoris / exigit a misero*
('but Fortune who had long favoured him [Pompey], now demands from her
victim the penalty of that favour': *Pharsalia* viii 21–2).

34. sea-marks] conspicuous objects distinguishable at sea, serving to guide or
warn sailors.

38. Cromwell habitually ascribed his victories to divine providence (see Blair

Which to fair acts unsought rewards did join,
40   Rewards that less to him than us were given.

11

Our former chiefs, like sticklers of the war,
First sought t' inflame the parties, then to poise;
The quarrel loved, but did the cause abhor,
And did not strike to hurt, but make a noise.

12

45   War, our consumption, was their gainful trade;
We inward bled whilst they prolonged our pain:
He fought to end our fighting, and essayed
To stanch the blood by breathing of the vein.

Worden, *PP* cix (1985) 55–99; essays by J. C. Davis and Anthony Fletcher in *Oliver Cromwell*, edited by Morrill). Sprat says: 'when the Heavens smil'd on thee in Fight, / When thy propitious God had lent / Successe and Victory to thy Tent; / To Heaven again the Victory was sent' (23–4).

41–8. Some parliamentary leaders, such as the Earl of Manchester, were reluctant to press home the victory at Marston Moor and hoped to reach a settlement with the King in favour of parliamentary rights and presbyterian religion. On 25 November 1644 Cromwell accused Manchester of 'unwillingness . . . to have this war prosecuted unto a full victory, and a design or desire to have it ended by accommodation on some such terms to which it might be disadvantageous to bring the King too low', and on 9 December he told the Commons: 'The important occasion now is no less than to save a Nation out of a bleeding, nay almost dying, condition . . . casting off all lingering proceedings like soldiers of fortune beyond sea, to spin out a war' (*The Writings and Speeches of Oliver Cromwell*, edited by W. C. Abbott, 4 vols (1937–47) i 302, 314).

41. sticklers] umpires at tournaments, wrestling or fencing matches, who part the combatants when they have fought enough (*OED*).

48. The opening ('breathing' *OED* 8) of a vein in order to let blood was standard medical practice for many complaints. This line, which completes the image begun at l. 45, was later read by D.'s enemies as a reference to the execution of Charles I. *1681* prints the line in italics, and marks it with an initial dagger. Shadwell says D. 'prais'd his opening the Basilick Vein' (*The Medal of John Bayes* (1682) 8), and Robert Gould says that had Charles II been murdered, 'thou hadst prais'd the Fact; his Father Slain, / Thou call'dst but gently breathing of a Vein' (*The Laureat* [1687]). *Works* notes that Sprat has similar images to D.'s: 'Thy Country wounded 'twas, and sick before, / Thy Wars and Armes did her restore: / . . . like the Cure of Sympathy, / Thy

13
Swift and resistless through the land he passed,
50   Like that bold Greek who did the east subdue;
And made to battles such heroic haste
As if on wings of victory he flew.

14
He fought secure of fortune as of fame,
Till by new maps the island might be shown
55   Of conquests, which he strewed where'er he came,
Thick as the galaxy with stars is sown.

15
His palms, though under weights they did not stand,
Still thrived; no winter could his laurels fade:
Heaven in his portrait showed a workman's hand,
60   And drew it perfect, yet without a shade.

---

strong and certain Remedy / Unto the Weapon didst apply' (18); and 'Thy hand . . . / Not only Lanc'd, but heal'd the Wound' (28).

50. *that bold Greek*] Alexander the Great.

52. The Greek goddess of victory, Nike, was represented as winged.

54–5. i.e. the island might be represented by new maps in which the sites of Cromwell's victories replace the features previously marked. A map in John Speed's *Theatre of the Empire of Great Britaine* (1631) marks 'The Invasions of England and Ireland With all their Civill Wars Since the Conquest', while Wenceslaus Hollar's *Comparison of the English and Bohemian Civil Wars* (print *c.* 1642) marks the battles of the Civil War on a map of England.

55–6. Cp. Sprat: 'Others' great Actions are / But thinly scatter'd here and there; / At best, all but one single Starr: / But thine the Milkie way' (14; *Works*).

57. *weights*] weight *MS*. It was commonly supposed that the palm tree thrives when weighted down; hence it became an emblem of virtue, truth or constancy overcoming hardships. The frontispiece to Ἐικὼν Βασιλική (1649) showed Charles I at prayer, two palms (one heavily weighted) and the motto *Crescit sub Pondere Virtus* ('Virtue rises under weight'). Another example, used to opposite political effect, is in Matthew Mew's poem in *Musarum Oxoniensium* Ἐλαιοφορία (1654) 34: *Sed pressa, palmae par virenti, / Ponderibus melius resurgit* ('Weighed down like a flourishing palm, [England] rises again better under weights').

59–60. This is the first of D.'s many references to painting, which he often saw as a parallel art to poetry (e.g. in *To Sir Godfrey Kneller*, and 'A Parallel, of Poetry and Painting' prefixed to his translation of Du Fresnoy's *De Arte Graphica* (1695)). Cp. ll. 94–6; *Astraea Redux* ll. 125–8*n*; *Threnodia Augustalis*

16

Peace was the prize of all his toils and care
Which war had banished, and did now restore;
Bologna's walls thus mounted in the air
To seat themselves more surely than before.

17

65 Her safety rescued Ireland to him owes,
And treacherous Scotland, to no interest true,
Yet blessed that Fate which did his arms dispose
Her land to civilize as to subdue.

18

Nor was he like those stars which only shine
70 When to pale mariners they storms portend;

---

l. 248n. For a discussion of D. and painting see Winn, *When Beauty, passim.*
61–4. Cp. Sprat: Cromwell made war 'That peace might land again upon the
shoare / Richer and better than before' (19; *Works*). The motto of the Protectorate was *Pax Quaeritur Bello* ('Peace is sought through war').
63–4. Guicciardini recounts that during the siege of Bologna by the Spanish
in 1512 a mine blew up part of the city wall on which was built a chapel
dedicated to the Virgin Mary. The chapel was lifted into the air by the
explosion, but then fell so exactly into its original place that the breach was
completely filled (*The Historie,* tr. Geffray Fenton (1579) 569).
63. walls] MS, *1692;* wall *1659.*
65–8. The native Irish had risen against the settlers in 1641; Cromwell said
that his Irish campaign of 1649–50 was undertaken by divine guidance in
defence of liberty and property (*Writings and Speeches* ii 36–9). Both sides in
the English Civil War would have regarded l. 66 as an apt summary of their
experience with the Scots, whose duplicity culminated in their sale of Charles
I to Parliament in 1647. Marvell in 'An Horatian Ode' had referred to the
Pict's 'party-colour'd Mind' (l. 106). Cromwell's conquest of Scotland was
accomplished chiefly by the Battle of Dunbar on 3 September 1650. Cp.
Waller: 'The Caledonians, armed with want and cold, / Have, by a fate
indulgent to your fame, / Been from all ages kept for you to tame. / . . . So
kind dictators made, when they came home, / Their vanquished foes free
citizens of Rome. / Like favour find the Irish' ('A Panegyric to My Lord
Protector' ll. 82–97; *Works*).
67. Yet blessed] May blesse *MS.*
68. The idea that Scotland needed to be civilized also appears in Waller's
earlier poem 'To My Lord of Falkland': 'To civilize, and to instruct the north'
(*Poems* i 75).
69–70. The rising and setting of Arcturus and the Hyades were associated

He had his calmer influence, and his mine
Did love and majesty together blend.

19

'Tis true, his count'nance did imprint an awe,
And naturally all souls to his did bow;
75   As wands of divination downward draw
And point to beds where sovereign gold doth grow.

20

When past all offerings to Feretrian Jove
He Mars deposed, and arms to gowns made yield,
Successful counsels did him soon approve
80   As fit for close intrigues as open field.

21

To suppliant Holland he vouchsafed a peace,
Our once bold rival in the British main,

---

with stormy weather (Horace, *Carm.* I iii 14; Virgil, *Aen.* iii 513–19).

71. *mine*] variant spelling of 'mien'.

75. 'A *Divining Wand* is a two-forked branch of an *Hazel-tree*, which is used for the finding out either of *Veins*, or hidden *Treasures* of *Gold* or *Silver*; and being carryed about, bends downwards (or rather is said to do so) when it comes to the place where they lye' (Cowley's note to his poem 'To Mr. Hobs': *Poems* 191; *Works*).

76. *grow*] See *AM* l. 553–6n.

77. *Feretrian Jove*] Romulus inaugurated the custom whereby arms taken personally by a Roman general from an enemy commander were offered to Jupiter Feretrius; his achievement was matched only twice (Livy I x; Propertius IV x).

78. Cicero applied the dictum *cedant arma togae* ('let arms yield to the toga') to his own consulship, in which sedition was defeated (*De Officiis* I xxii 77). *gowns*] togas, the dress of peace (*OED* 3). The antithesis is in Sprat: 'Or in thy Armes, or in thy Gown' (14).

79. *approve*] demonstrate (*OED* 1).

81–4. The First Dutch War (1652–4) was provoked by commercial rivalry. The English Navigation Act (1651) prohibited imports which were not carried in ships belonging to England or to the exporting country, thus impeding Dutch trade. Dutch ships were also required to strike their flags and topsails to English ships in the Channel. The treaty of 1654 enforced these provisions, and exacted compensation from the Dutch for the massacre of English traders at Amboyna and damage to English merchantmen.

Now tamely glad her unjust claim to cease,
And buy our friendship with her idol gain.

22

85   Fame of th' asserted sea through Europe blown
Made France and Spain ambitious of his love:
Each knew that side must conquer he would own,
And for him fiercely as for empire strove.

23

No sooner was the Frenchman's cause embraced
90   Than the light Monsieur the grave Don outweighed:
His fortune turned the scale where it was cast,
Though Indian mines were in the other laid.

24

When absent, yet we conquered in his right,
For though some meaner artist's skill were shown
95   In mingling colours, or in placing light,
Yet still the fair designment was his own.

83–4. Cp. Waller: 'Holland, to gain your friendship, is content / To be our outguard on the continent' ('A Panegyric' ll. 101–2; *Works*).

85–8. 'His greatness at home was but a shadow of the glory he had abroad. It was hard to discover which feared him most, France, Spain, or the Low Countries, where his friendship was current at the value he put on it' (Clarendon, *The History of the Rebellion*, edited by W. D. Macray, 6 vols (1888) vi 94).

85. asserted sea] British claims to the sovereignty of the surrounding seas, including the whole of the Channel and North Sea, had been stated by John Selden in *Mare Clausum* (1635), a reply to *Mare Liberum* (1609) by the Dutchman Hugo Grotius.   *assert*] lay claim to (*OED* 3, 4).

89–92. In 1656 England and France agreed to a joint campaign against Spain in Flanders, which led to the capture of Dunkirk in June 1658.

89. No] Nor *MS.*

90. the light] th' ayery *MS.*

91. European strategy was frequently viewed in terms of an imbalance of power brought about by shifting alliances between England, France and Spain, as in Waller's lines: 'Heaven . . . has placed this island to give law, / To balance Europe, and her states to awe' ('A Panegyric' ll. 21–2).

92. Spain's supplies of gold from the Americas had been disrupted by Admiral Blake's destruction of the plate fleet at Santa Cruz in 1657, which hampered her campaign in Flanders.

96. designment] original design (*OED* 4).

25

For from all tempers he could service draw:
The worth of each with its allay he knew,
And as the confidant of Nature saw
100   How she complexions did divide and brew.

26

Or he their single virtues did survey
By intuition in his own large breast,
Where all the rich ideas of them lay
That were the rule and measure to the rest.

27

105   When such heroic virtue heaven sets out,
The stars like commons sullenly obey;
Because it drains them when it comes about,
And therefore is a tax they seldom pay.

28

From this high spring our foreign conquests flow
110   Which yet more glorious triumphs do portend,
Since their commencement to his arms they owe,
If springs as high as fountains may ascend.

97–100. For the alchemical implications of this imagery see Jack M.
Armistead, *SEL* xxvii (1987) 383.

98. allay] mixture of elements which detracts from the object's purity and
value (*OED* 4).

100. complexions] the four humours which determined the temperament of
the body (*OED* 1b).

101–4. Cp. Sprat on the young Cromwell: 'Then the same vertues did appear
/ Though in a lesse, and more Contracted Sphear' (16). Cp. George
Lawrence's sermon on 13 October 1658: 'Those lines of Honour which by
refractions ran dispersedly in others, in him were knit up as their natural
centre: and what made others happy in division, was in him a Colledge of
vertues solemnly met and seated' (*Peplum Olivarii* (1658) 29). Lawrence cites
Claudian: *sparguntur in omnes, / in te mixta fluunt; et quae divisa beatos / efficiunt,*
collecta tenes ('To all other men blessings come scattered, to you they flow
commingled, and gifts that separately make one happy are all together
yours': *De Consulatu Stilichonis* i 33–5).

103. ideas] in the Platonic sense of eternal archetypes (*OED* 1); conception of
something in its highest perfection (*OED* 2). Cp. *AM* ll. 661–4.

29

He made us freemen of the continent,
Whom Nature did like captives treat before;
115 To nobler preys the English lion sent,
And taught him first in Belgian walks to roar.

30

That old, unquestioned pirate of the land,
Proud Rome, with dread the fate of Dunkirk h'ard,
And trembling wished behind more Alps to stand,
120 Although an Alexander were her guard.

31

By his command we boldly crossed the line,
And bravely fought where southern stars arise;
We traced the far-fetched gold unto the mine,
And that which bribed our fathers made our prize.

32

125 Such was our Prince; yet owned a soul above
The highest acts it could produce to show;

113–20. The capture of Dunkirk seemed to make Cromwell the arbiter of
Europe: Thurloe said he 'carried the keys of the continent at his girdle, and
was able to make invasions thereupon, and let in armies and forces upon it at
his pleasure'. In particular, Cromwell renewed support for Protestants in
Flanders, France and Piedmont, and pursued negotiations for a Protestant
league against Catholic Austria (C. H. Firth, *Last Years of the Protectorate* 2
vols (1909) ii 218–23). Cp. Marvell: 'Who once more joyn'd us to the Continent; / Who planted *England* on the *Flandrick shoar*' ('A Poem upon the Death
of O.C.' ll. 172–3).
115–16. Sprat says that after years when 'The Brittish Lyon hung his Main
and droopt / . . . whose least voice before / . . . shook the World at every
Roare / ', Cromwell made him 'again afright the neighbouring Floods' (24–
5).
118. h'ard] The spellings *h'ard* in MS and *har'd* in 1659 clearly indicate the
required pronunciation.
120. Alexander] Alexander VII, Pope from 1655 to 1667; implicitly not as
strong a defence as Alexander the Great.
121–3. An expedition commanded by Penn and Venables set out for the West
Indies in 1654 to disrupt Spanish supplies of gold. Their attack on San
Domingo in 1655 was an ignominious failure, but they did take Jamaica.
124. Spanish gold was thought to have corrupted the councillors of James I.
In 1656 Captain Stayner captured part of the Spanish bullion fleet near Cadiz.

Thus poor mechanic arts in public move,
Whilst the deep secrets beyond practice go.

33

Nor died he when his ebbing fame went less,
130   But when fresh laurels courted him to live;
He seemed but to prevent some new success,
As if above what triumphs earth could give.

34

His latest victories still thickest came,
As near the centre motion does increase;
135   Till he pressed down by his own weighty name
Did like the vestal under spoils decease.

35

But first the ocean as a tribute sent
That giant prince of all her watery herd;

127. mechanic arts] practical applications of theory (*OED* mechanical 2b).
128. practice] calculation (*OED* 8).
129–31. Just before Cromwell's death a Spanish attempt to retake Jamaica failed; after it, the campaign in Flanders continued with the capture of Ypres on 27 September. Cp. Waller: 'Our dying hero from the continent / Ravished whole towns; and forts from Spaniards reft, / As his last legacy to Britain left' ('Upon the Late Storm' ll. 14–16).
131. prevent] anticipate.
134. 'Nature at the approaches of Death usually puts forth the utmost of her activity. A Stone in its descent increaseth in the celerity of its Motion, as it comes nearer the Center' (John Templer [D.'s tutor], *Reason of Episcopall Inspection* (1676) 26).
135. Cp. Spenser's image of Rome: 'With her own weight down pressed now she lies' ('The Ruines of Time' l. 76).
136. The vestal virgin Tarpeia betrayed Rome to the Sabines, and in recompense asked for what they had on their left arms, meaning their gold bracelets; instead they heaped their bucklers upon her and killed her (Livy I xi).
137–8. On 3 June 1658 a large whale appeared in the Thames; 'after a long Conflict it was killed with the harping yrons, & struck in the head . . . & after a horrid grone it ran quite on shore & died' (Evelyn, *Diary*). It was later interpreted as a portent: 'Flaming Comets *Divination* hold, / But *Whales*, extinct, *Divinity* unfold: / *Jonah*'s Pulpit, (dead) turn'd Prophet, shew'd Thee / Thy Death, *swallow'd up into victorie*' (Samuel Slater, *A Rhetorical Rapture* (1658)).
138. her] the MS.

And th' isle, when her protecting genius went,
140 Upon his obsequies loud sighs conferred.

36

No civil broils have since his death arose,
But faction now by habit does obey;
And wars have that respect for his repose
As winds for halcyons when they breed at sea.

37

145 His ashes in a peaceful urn shall rest,
His name a great example stands, to show
How strangely high endeavours may be blessed,
Where piety and valour jointly go.

139–40. On 30 August, while Cromwell was on his death-bed, a great storm swept over England, which Waller made the theme of his memorial poem. James Heath later saw the whale and the storm as a 'prognostick that the great *Leviathan* of men, that Tempest and overthrow of Government, was now going to his own place' (*Flagellum* (1663) 205; C. H. Firth).
139. genius] guardian spirit.
144. halcyons] Ovid records that for the seven days in winter when halcyons breed in a nest floating on the sea the winds are still (*Met.* xi 745–8). This image was frequently used in mid-seventeenth-century poetry for a period of peace against a background of war. It was chiefly applied to Stuart rule, but also to Cromwell's achievements by Marvell in 'The Character of Holland' ll. 127–30 and 'A Poem upon the Death of O.C.' ll. 79–82. See D. Palomo, *HLQ* xliv (1980–1) 205–21.
145. In peacefull Urne his sacred Ashes rest *MS*.
148. Cp. Waller: 'so much power, and piety, in one' (*A Panegyric* l. 124; quarto text).

6 To Sir Robert Howard

Date and publication. Printed in 1660 as prefatory verses to Sir Robert Howard's *Poems, viz. 1. A Panegyrick to the King. 2. Songs and Sonnets. 3. The Blind Lady, a Comedy. 4. The Fourth Book of Virgil. 5. Statius his Achilleis, with Annotations. 6. A Panegyrick to Generall Monck*, which was published by Henry Herringman (*SR* 16 April; advertised in *Mercurius Publicus* 21–8 June); reissued 1696 by Francis Saunders. D.'s verses were reprinted in Saunders' *Collection of Poems by Several Hands* (1693), reissued as *The Temple of Death* (1695).

Context. Sir Robert Howard (1626–98) was the sixth son of the Earl of Berkshire. If D. was employed by Herringman, who published Howard's *Poems*, he may have met Howard in this way (Osborn 168–83). Howard may be referring to D. when he says that he 'prevail'd with a worthy Friend to take so much view of my blotted Copies, as to free me from grosse Errors' (sig. A5ʳ). D. may have lodged with Howard in London in the early 1660s until he married Howard's sister Elizabeth on 1 December 1663 (Winn 95–103, 119–28). Shadwell in *The Medal of John Bayes* (1682) 9 says that D. received financial help from Howard 'who kept him generously at his own House'. The two men collaborated on *The Indian Queen* (1664) but differed on the issue of rhymed plays. Their dispute began with D.'s Preface to *The Rival Ladies* (1664) and continued in Howard's Preface to *Four New Plays* (1665), D.'s *EDP* (1668), Howard's Preface to *The Great Favourite* (1668) and D.'s *Defence of An Essay* (1668). See also the 'Account of the Ensuing Poem' prefixed to *AM*, esp. l. 5*n*, and 'Prologue to *Albumazar*'. Ending their debate on drama, D. said: 'For his person and parts, I honour them as much as any man living, and have had so many particular Obligations to him, that I should be very ungrateful, if I did not acknowledge them to the World' (*Works* ix 22). Evelyn described Howard as 'a Gent: pretending to all manner of Arts & Sciences for which he had ben the subject of Comedy, under the name of Sir Positive; not ill-natur'd, but unsufferably boosting' (*Diary* 16 February 1685; Kinsley). Shadwell ridiculed him as Sir Positive At-all in *The Sullen Lovers* (1668) (see Pepys 8 May 1668; Kinsley). For the relations between D. and Howard, and Howard's career in the government, see Winn; H. J. Oliver, *Sir Robert Howard* (1963); McFadden 59–87.

To my Honoured Friend Sir Robert Howard,
on his Excellent Poems

As there is music uninformed by art
In those wild notes, which with a merry heart
The birds in unfrequented shades express,
Who better taught at home yet please us less:
5   So in your verse a native sweetness dwells,
Which shames composure, and its art excels.
Singing no more can your soft numbers grace
Than paint adds charms unto a beauteous face.
Yet as when mighty rivers gently creep,
10 Their even calmness does suppose them deep,
Such is your Muse: no metaphor swelled high
With dangerous boldness lifts her to the sky;
Those mounting fancies when they fall again
Show sand and dirt at bottom do remain.
15 So firm a strength, and yet withal so sweet,
Did never but in Samson's riddle meet.
'Tis strange each line so great a weight should bear,
And yet no sign of toil, no sweat appear.
Either your art hides art, as Stoics feign
20 Then least to feel, when most they suffer pain;
And we, dull souls, admire, but cannot see

¶6. *1–3*. Cp. Milton: 'Or sweetest Shakespeare fancy's child, / Warble his native wood-notes wild' (*L'Allegro* ll. 133–4; *Works*).
6. *composure*] composition, arrangement (*OED* 1); literary style (*OED* 8).
7. *numbers*] verses.
9–10. Echoes Denham's lines on the Thames: 'O could I flow like thee, and make thy stream / My great example, as it is my theme! / Though deep, yet clear, though gentle, yet not dull, / Strong without rage, without ore-flowing full' (*Cooper's Hill* (1655) ll. 189–92).
10. suppose] imply.
16. Samson's riddle] Samson's riddle was: 'out of the strong came forth sweetness'; the answer was the carcase of a lion in which he had found bees and honey (Judges xiv 5–18).
19. your art hides art] a version of the anonymous tag *ars est celare artem* ('the art lies in concealing the art').   *Stoics*] In the 'Dedication of the *Aeneis*' (1697) D. says that Howard 'is better conversant than any Man that I know, in the Doctrine of the Stoicks' (*Works* iv 294).

What hidden springs within the engine be:
Or 'tis some happiness that still pursues
Each act and motion of your graceful Muse.
25　Or is it Fortune's work, that in your head
The curious net that is for fancies spread
Lets through its meshes every meaner thought,
While rich ideas there are only caught?
Sure that's not all; this is a piece too fair
30　To be the child of chance, and not of care.
No atoms casually together hurled
Could e'er produce so beautiful a world.
Nor dare I such a doctrine here admit,
As would destroy the providence of wit.
35　'Tis your strong genius then which does not feel
Those weights would make a weaker spirit reel:
To carry weight and run so lightly too
Is what alone your Pegasus can do.
Great Hercules himself could ne'er do more
40　Than not to feel those heavens and gods he bore.
Your easier odes, which for delight were penned,
Yet our instruction make their second end:

22. For D.'s interest in unseen mechanisms of change cp. *Astraea Redux* ll.
125–30, 153–6, 163–8.　　*engine*] machine.

25. For Fortune see 'Horace: *Odes* III xxix' ll. 73–87*n.*

26. curious net] Rete Mirabile (D.'s note). A network of blood vessels at the
base of the brain in some animals, which Galen wrongly thought also existed
in man. Here the vital spirits from the heart were supposedly changed into
animal spirits to be distributed through the body by the nerves. Galen's
theory was first challenged in the sixteenth century, but not completely
overthrown by D.'s day.

27. meaner] less noble.

29–32. This argument against the Epicurean philosophy is used by Walter
Charleton in *The Darknes of Atheism Dispelled* (1652) 61–7. For D.'s interest in
Epicurus and Lucretius see headnote to 'Lucretius: The Beginning of the First
Book'.

34. providence of wit] the guiding role of intelligence in poetic creation, like the
role of divine providence in creating the world.

38. Pegasus] the winged horse of Greek mythology, often taken to symbolize
the flights of poetic inspiration.

40. Hercules relieved Atlas of his burden of supporting the heavens during his
eleventh labour.

41. easier odes] Howard's lyrics (*Poems* 10–27), chiefly love poems.

41–2. D. follows the Horatian dictum that poets should mix instruction with

We're both enriched and pleased, like them that woo
At once a beauty and a fortune too.
45 Of moral knowledge Poesy was queen,
And still she might, had wanton wits not been,
Who like ill guardians lived themselves at large,
And not content with that, debauched their charge.
Like some brave captain, your successful pen
50 Restores the exiled to her crown again,
And gives us hope that having seen the days
When nothing flourished but fanatic bays,
All will at length in this opinion rest:
'A sober Prince's government is best'.
55 This is not all; your art the way has found
To make improvement of the richest ground,
That soil which those immortal laurels bore,
That once the sacred Maro's temples wore.
Elisa's griefs are so expressed by you,
60 They are too eloquent to have been true:
Had she so spoke, Aeneas had obeyed
What Dido rather than what Jove had said.
If funeral rites can give a ghost repose,
Your Muse so justly has dischargèd those,
65 Elisa's shade may now its wandering cease,
And claim a title to the fields of peace.
But if Aeneas be obliged, no less
Your kindness great Achilles doth confess,
Who dressed by Statius in too bold a look
70 Did ill become those virgin's robes he took.

---

delight (*Ars Poetica* ll. 333–44).
45. Cp. 'For Moral Truth is the Mistress of the Poet as much as of the
Philosopher: Poesie must resemble Natural Truth, but it must *be* Ethical'
(*Defence of An Essay* (1668); *Works* ix 12).
46, 52. *wanton wits . . . fanatic bays*] a critique of both lascivious cavalier poets
and puritan didactic versifiers of the previous twenty years.
47. *at large*] without restraint, prodigally.
56–66. Referring to Howard's translation of *Aen.* iv.
58. *Maro*] Virgil (Publius Virgilius Maro).
59. *Elisa*] Virgil's alternative name for Dido.
68–70. In his *Achilleis*, translated by Howard, Statius (*c.* AD 45–96) describes
how Thetis disguised her son Achilles as a girl in order to avoid his being sent

To understand how much we owe to you,
We must your numbers with your author's view;
Then we shall see his work was lamely rough,
Each figure stiff as if designed in buff;
75 His colours laid so thick on every place,
As only showed the paint, but hid the face:
But as in perspective we beauties see
Which in the glass, not in the picture be,
So here our sight obligingly mistakes
80 That wealth which his your bounty only makes.
Thus vulgar dishes are by cooks disguised,
More for their dressing than their substance prized.
Your curious notes so search into that age
When all was fable but the sacred page,
85 That since in that dark night we needs must stray,
We are at least misled in pleasant way.
But what we most admire, your verse no less
The prophet than the poet doth confess:
Ere our weak eyes discerned the doubtful streak
90 Of light, you saw great Charles his morning break;
So skilful seamen ken the land from far,
Which shows like mists to the dull passenger.
To Charles your Muse first pays her duteous love,

---

to the Trojan War. D. later remarked that 'Statius never thought an expression could be bold enough; and if a bolder could be found he rejected the first' ('A Parallel, of Poetry and Painting' (1695); Works xx 76; cp. 73–4, and the Epistle Dedicatory to The Spanish Friar (1681) sig. A2ᵛ).

74. buff] stout leather.

77. perspective] An arrangement of mirrors which makes a designedly distorted picture intelligible to the eye (OED 2, 4b). The word was accented on the first and third syllables in the seventeenth century.

80. i.e. that wealth which appears to belong to Statius only through Howard's bounty.

81. vulgar] common, ordinary.

83. curious notes] Annotations on Statius (D.'s note). These extensive annotations explain classical mythology and customs, and quote and translate parallel passages in other Latin poems.   curious] careful, studious (OED 1).

88. confess] give evidence of (OED 5).

88–9. Howard's preface records that he composed the poem to Charles three years earlier, when a prisoner in Windsor Castle (sig. A3ᵛ).

90. Charles his] Charles's; a common seventeenth-century usage.

As still the ancients did begin from Jove.
95 With Monck you end, whose name preserved shall be,
As Rome recorded Rufus' memory,
Who thought it greater honour to obey
His country's interest than the world to sway.
But to write worthy things of worthy men
100 Is the peculiar talent of your pen:
Yet let me take your mantle up, and I
Will venture in your right to prophesy:

'This work by merit first of fame secure
Is likewise happy in its geniture:
105 For since 'tis born when Charles ascends the throne,
It shares at once his fortune and its own.'

95. *Monck*] For General Monck's role in the restoration of the monarchy see
Astraea Redux, headnote.
96. *Rufus*] *Hic situs est Rufus qui pulso Vindice quondam, / Imperium asseruit non
sibi sed patriae* (D.'s note: 'Here lies Rufus, who, having once defeated
Vindex, set free the sovereignty not for himself but for his country'). Vergi-
nius Rufus, an officer of the Roman army in Gaul, suppressed the revolt of
Vindex in AD 68, and resisted his soldiers' attempts to make him emperor.
He is said to have composed this epitaph for himself (Pliny, *Ep.* VI x).
104. *geniture*] birth (*OED* 1); horoscope (*OED* 2).

7 Astraea Redux

Date and publication. Astraea Redux. A Poem On the Happy Restoration & Return Of His Sacred Majesty Charles the Second was published by Herringman in 1660 (advertised in *Mercurius Publicus* 21–8 June); George Thomason's copy in the BL is dated 19 June. There are two states of *1660*, the second incorporating press corrections, including one substantive change which is probably authorial (see l. 208*n*), and another which could have been made by the printing house (see l. 195*n*). The poem was reprinted in the 1688 edition of *AM*. The present edition follows *1660* with the two press corrections included.

Context. General George Monck (1608–70), commander of the army in Scotland, led his forces into England on 1 January 1660, and occupied London on 3 February. He recalled those members of the Long Parliament who had been excluded by Colonel Pride; an election was held, and on 25 April the new 'Convention Parliament' met. Charles Stuart's Declaration of Breda, which proposed the basis of a political settlement, was accepted, and he was proclaimed King on 8 May. On 25 May he landed at Dover, and entered London on the 29th, his thirtieth birthday. Monck was created Duke of Albemarle. For the political changes see Ogg 1–34; Hutton, *The Restoration* 3–123. For the rhetoric of sermons welcoming Charles see Caroline Edie, *BJRL* lxii (1979–80) 61–86.

Sources. Charles was greeted by scores of similar panegyrics; samples from these are quoted by H. T. Swedenberg in his account of the political context of D.'s poem (*SP* l (1953) 30–44), and by Nicholas Jose in *Ideas of the Restoration in English Literature, 1660–71* (1984) 1–66. D. definitely knew Martin Lluelyn, *To the King's most excellent Majesty* (Thomason's copy in BL dated 24 May); Thomas Higgons, *A Panegyrick to the King* (10 June); Cowley, *Ode upon the blessed Restoration and Returne* (31 May); and Waller, *To the King* (9 June). But many of D.'s images are the common stock of other panegyrics, notably in the two university collections, Oxford's *Britannia Rediviva* (7 July) and *Academiae Cantabrigiensis ΣΩΣΤΡΑ* (10 July). Winn 561 suggests some parallels with poems by Malherbe. For the poem's relation to the wider tradition of panegyric, see Garrison 155–64.

Astraea Redux

A Poem on the Happy Restoration and Return of His Sacred Majesty Charles the Second

Iam redit et virgo, redeunt Saturnia regna.

Virgil

Now with a general peace the world was blessed,
While ours, a world divided from the rest,

¶**7**. *Title. Astraea Redux* means 'Justice brought back'. Ovid in *Met.* i 89–150 (ll. 113–92 in D.'s translation, 'The First Book of Ovid's *Metamorphoses*' (1693)) recounts that the golden age of Saturn was succeeded by the increasingly degenerate ages of silver, brass and iron; in the latter Astraea (Justice) left the earth. Virgil in *Ecl.* iv prophesies that the golden age is about to begin anew: *Iam redit et virgo, redeunt Saturnia regna* (l. 6: 'now the virgin [Astraea] returns, the kingdom of Saturn returns'). This prophecy was associated with Augustus (cp. ll. 320–3*n* below), and was later read as a prophecy of the birth of Christ. In the Renaissance, Astraea was associated with the monarch, particularly with Elizabeth I (see Frances Yates, *Astraea* (1975)), though James I was also greeted as Astraea in his coronation entry into London, when the motto from *Ecl.* iv appeared on the Temple Bar arch. For the Augustan imagery see Swedenberg, and Howard Erskine-Hill, *The Augustan Idea in English Literature* (1983) 213–22. D.'s handling (here and elsewhere) of the myth of the Golden Age is discussed by Thomas H. Fujimura in *PLL* xi (1975) 149–67. The example of Astraea is also used by Samuel Willes, *To the King's Most Sacred Majesty* (1660) 5, and in *Academiae Cantabrigiensis ΣΩΣΤΡΑ* sig. *3ᵛ.

1. This hyperbole is understandable. The war between France and Spain had been ended by the Treaty of the Pyrenees (7 November 1659) and this peace was sealed by the spectacular wedding of Louis XIV and Maria Theresa in June 1660; and the War of the North involving Sweden, Denmark and Brandenburg was concluded by the Treaties of Oliva and Copenhagen (May and June 1660).

1–2. D. echoes, and reverses, Sir Richard Fanshawe's 'An Ode Upon occasion of His Majesties Proclamation in the yeare 1630', which opens: 'Now warre is all the world about', and presents Britain as a haven of peace, 'A world without the world' (*Shorter Poems and Translations*, edited by N. W. Bawcutt (1964) 5–6; Michael Cordner, *N & Q* ccxxix (1984) 341–2). Cowley begins his poem by praising the stars which 'calm the stormy *World*, and still the rage of *Warrs*' (*Poems* 420).

2. From Virgil, *Ecl.* i 66: *penitus toto divisos orbe Britannos* ('the Britons,

A dreadful quiet felt, and worser far
Than arms, a sullen interval of war:
5   Thus when black clouds draw down the labouring
skies,
Ere yet abroad the wingèd thunder flies,
An horrid stillness first invades the ear,
And in that silence we the tempest fear.
Th' ambitious Swede like restless billows tossed,
10 On this hand gaining what on that he lost,
Though in his life he blood and ruin breathed,
To his now guideless kingdom peace bequeathed;
And heaven that seemed regardless of our fate,
For France and Spain did miracles create,
15 Such mortal quarrels to compose in peace
As nature bred and interest did increase.

---

completely cut off from the whole world'). This motto was used on the
Fenchurch arch in James I's coronation entry, and in Jonson's *The Masque of
Blacknesse* (1605) l. 248.

3. dreadful quiet] Echoes Tacitus: *ducemque terruit dira quies* ('a fearful quiet
terrified the general': *Annales* i 45; Christie).   *worser*] a common seventeenth-century variant of *worse*.

5. labouring] moving strenuously (*OED* labour 12); troubled (*OED* labour
15).

7. This line was ridiculed by several of D.'s critics: in *A Letter from a Gentleman to the Honourable Ed. Howard Esq* (1668) 6; in *The Censure of the Rota*
(1673) 9; *The Friendly Vindication of Mr. Dryden* (1673) 16; and Martin Clifford, *Notes upon Mr. Dryden's Poems* (1687) 13. *Works* cites a comparable line
from Cowley: 'A dreadful *Silence* fill'd the hollow place' (*Davideis* i; *Poems*
245).

9–12. Charles X of Sweden invaded Poland in 1655, but failed to secure it. In
1657–8 he twice invaded Denmark. He gained Scania, the island of Bornholm, and other territories which gave Sweden control of the Sound, but was
forced to give up his claim to Prussia. At his death in February 1660 his son
Charles XI was a minor, and his regents concluded peace in May–June 1660,
returning Bornholm to Denmark. Contemporary English interest in his
death is evidenced by *The Most Heavenly and Christian Speech of the Magnanimous and Victorious King of Sweden . . . on his Death-Bed* (1660) and the satirical
The Last Will and Testament of Carolus Gustavus (1660).

9–10. Cp. Sir Robert Howard: 'So when the Trojan Prince was almost lost /
In Storms, among ungentle billows tost' ('A Panegyrick to Generall Monck',
Poems (1660) 283).

13–18. See l. 1*n*. The lily was the emblem of the French monarchy.

We sighed to hear the fair Iberian bride
Must grow a lily to the lily's side,
While our cross stars denied us Charles his bed
20 Whom our first flames and virgin love did wed.
For his long absence church and state did groan,
Madness the pulpit, faction seized the throne;
Experienced age in deep despair was lost
To see the rebel thrive, the loyal crossed;
25 Youth that with joys had unacquainted been
Envied grey hairs that once good days had seen:
We thought our sires, not with their own content,
Had ere we came to age our portion spent.
Nor could our nobles hope their bold attempt
30 Who ruined crowns would coronets exempt:
For when by their designing leaders taught
To strike at power which for themselves they sought,
The vulgar, gulled into rebellion, armed;
Their blood to action by the prize was warmed.
35 The sacred purple then and scarlet gown
Like sanguine dye to elephants was shown.
Thus when the bold Typhoeus scaled the sky,
And forced great Jove from his own heaven to fly,
(What king, what crown from treason's reach is free,

17. Iberian bride] Maria Theresa, daughter of Philip IV of Spain.

27–8. D. applies the same image to pre-war dramatists in *EDP*: 'We acknowledge them our Fathers in wit, but they have ruin'd their Estates themselves before they came to their childrens hands' (*Works* xvii 73).

33. The vulgar] the common people.

35. The purple of bishops and scarlet of peers.

36. From Maccabees vi 34: 'And to the end they might provoke the elephants to fight, they showed them the blood of grapes and mulberries' (Winn, privately).

37–44. Typhoeus or Typhon was the monstrous offspring of Earth and Hell, who had a hundred heads which spoke with changeable voices. When he assaulted Olympus the gods fled to Egypt; Zeus eventually buried him under Mount Etna, where he generated winds which wreak havoc at sea (Hesiod, *Theogony* ll. 820–80; Apollodorus I vi 3). The image is used similarly in *Academiae Cantabrigiensis ΣΩΣΤΡΑ* sigs *4ʳ; B4ᵛ and D1ʳ. *Mercurius Publicus* (24–31 May) describing Charles's entry into London recalled that '*Jupiter* himself was not quiet in Heaven till after a long war with the Giants' (351). The myth of Typhon had been variously applied by seventeenth-century writers. Francis Bacon interpreted it as an allegory of rebellion in his *De Sapientia Veterum* (1609) ch. 2.

40   If Jove and heaven can violated be?)
     The lesser gods that shared his prosperous state
     All suffered in the exiled Thunderer's fate.
     The rabble now such freedom did enjoy
     As winds at sea that use it to destroy:
45   Blind as the Cyclops, and as wild as he,
     They owned a lawless salvage liberty,
     Like that our painted ancestors so prized
     Ere empire's arts their breasts had civilized.
     How great were then our Charles his woes, who thus
50   Was forced to suffer for himself and us!
     He, tossed by Fate, and hurried up and down,
     Heir to his father's sorrows with his crown,
     Could taste no sweets of youth's desirèd age,
     But found his life too true a pilgrimage.
55   Unconquered yet in that forlorn estate,
     His manly courage overcame his fate.
     His wounds he took like Romans on his breast,
     Which by his virtue were with laurels dressed.

45. Cyclops] Polyphemus, who was blinded by Odysseus (*Odyssey* ix 375–97). The commonwealth without a king is compared to Polyphemus without an eye by Ross 73; John Gauden, Κακοῦργοι (1660; sermon preached 28 February, printed text dated 28 March by Thomason on his copy in BL) 63; and Waller, ll. 19–21. D. uses the image again in *The Medal* ll. 226–7.

46–8. For this picture of man in the state of nature cp. Virgil's account of society before the reign of Saturn: *Aen.* viii 314–18 (translated in D.'s 'The Eighth Book of the *Aeneis*' ll. 417–24). In *AA* ll. 53–6 D. again associates the Commonwealth with the lawless state of nature. In *1 Conquest of Granada* D. has Almanzor imagine the state of nature as a time of innocence, anticipating Rousseau: 'I am as free as Nature first made man / 'Ere the base Laws of Servitude began / When wild in woods the noble Savage ran.' (I i 207–9). See also 'To Dr Charleton' l. 13*n*.

46. salvage] variant form of *savage* (the spelling recalls the word's Latin origin from *silva*, 'wood').

49. Charles his] Charles's (again at l. 111).

51. Cp. Higgons: 'Thus great Æneas when his Troy was lost, / And nought but ruine left of all that State, / Wander'd at Land, and on the Floods was tost, / And hurried up and down the World by Fate' (*A Panegyrick* 10). See also Cowley (st. xiii) and Robert Howard (*Poems* (1660) 283).

52. Apparently echoed by J. Ailmer in the anthology *Britannia Rediviva*: 'Heir to thy Fathers Sufferings, and his Crown' (sig. Bb3ʳ).

55. estate] condition.

57. Roman soldiers considered it a dishonour to receive wounds behind.

As souls reach heaven while yet in bodies pent,
60 So did he live above his banishment.
That sun which we beheld with cozened eyes
Within the water, moved along the skies.
How easy 'tis when Destiny proves kind
With full-spread sails to run before the wind;
65 But those that 'gainst stiff gales laveering go
Must be at once resolved and skilful too.
He would not like soft Otho hope prevent
But stayed and suffered Fortune to repent:
These virtues Galba in a stranger sought,
70 And Piso to adopted empire brought.
How shall I then my doubtful thoughts express
That must his sufferings both regret and bless!
For when his early valour heaven had crossed,
And all at Worcester but the honour lost,
75 Forced into exile from his rightful throne
He made all countries where he came his own;

59. Referring either to the soul's capacity for mystical contact with God while still on earth, or to the bodily translation of some prophets to heaven (e.g. Enoch and Elijah).

61–2. i.e. we could see Charles's movements only indirectly, like people who see the sun's movements reflected in water.

61. *cozened*] deceived.

65. *laveering*] tacking.

67–70. Galba, Emperor of Rome AD 68–9, adopted Piso as his heir instead of the effeminate Otho. Otho revolted, had Galba and Piso murdered, and briefly gained power. But he was attacked by Vitellius, and after being defeated at Brixellum killed himself in despair (Suetonius).

67. *prevent*] anticipate.

68. *suffered*] allowed.

74. Recalls the statement of François I of France to his mother after his defeat at Pavia (1525): 'all is lost except our honour'. Cp. Higgons: 'And won Renown, although you lost the field' (*A Panegyrick* 8). Charles was defeated by Cromwell at the Battle of Worcester in 1651 and subsequently escaped to France.

76–86. This passage resembles (and perhaps contributed to) T. Topping's verses in the anthology *Britannia Rediviva*: 'the Universe must be his School: / Thus Fate prov'd kind even against her will, / And whiles she did neglect him, taught him skill. / Thrice happy we! that our great Monarch thus / Must learn to Govern *Europe* first, then us. / While other Kings only their Crowns inherit, / The Crown is his by Birth-right and by Merit' (sig. Cc3ᵛ).

76–7. Cp. Waller: 'For, having viewed the persons and the things, / The

And viewing monarchs' secret arts of sway
A royal factor for their kingdoms lay.
Thus banished David spent abroad his time,
80   When to be God's anointed was his crime,
And when restored made his proud neighbours rue
Those choice remarks he from his travels drew.
Nor is he only by afflictions shown
To conquer others' realms, but rule his own:
85   Recov'ring hardly what he lost before,
His right endears it much, his purchase more.
Inured to suffer ere he came to reign,
No rash procedure will his actions stain;
To business ripened by digestive thought,
90   His future rule is into method brought:
As they who first proportion understand
With easy practice reach a master's hand.

---

councils, state, and strength of Europe's kings, / You know your work' (ll.
41–3); and cp. Jonson, 'To William Roe': 'th'art now, to goe / Countries, and
climes, manners, and men to know, / T'extract, and choose the best of all
these knowne, / And those to turne to bloud, and make thine owne' (ll. 1–4;
Epigrammes cxxviii). D. commented again on the results of Charles's exile in
his 'Defence of the Epilogue': 'His own misfortunes and the Nations,
afforded him an opportunity, which is rarely allow'd to Sovereign Princes, I
mean of travelling, and being conversant in the most polish'd Courts of
Europe; and, thereby, of cultivating a Spirit, which was form'd by Nature, to
receive the impression of a gallant and generous education. At his return, he
found a Nation lost as much in Barbarism as in Rebellion: and as the excellency of his Nature forgave the one, so the excellency of his manners
reform'd the other' (*Works* xi 216; Kinsley).

78. factor] deputy: i.e. by being a kind of understudy, Charles learned the art
of government.

79. See 2 Samuel xv–xxi. For the comparison of David and Charles see the
headnote to *AA*.

80. Cp. Lluelyn: 'But to be born our Prince, was all Thy Crimes' (*To the
King's . . . Majesty* 3).

82. remarks] observations.

85. hardly] with difficulty (*OED* 6).

86. purchase] acquisition of property by one's own action, as distinct from
inheritance (*OED* 5).

89. digestive] tending to methodize and reduce to order (*OED* 6; sole
example).

91–2. An image from drawing.

Well might the ancient poets then confer
On night the honoured name of counsellor,
95   Since struck with rays of prosperous fortune blind,
We light alone in dark afflictions find.
In such adversities to sceptres trained,
The name of Great his famous grandsire gained;
Who yet a king alone in name and right,
100 With hunger, cold and angry Jove did fight;
Shocked by a covenanting league's vast powers,
As holy and as catholic as ours,
Till Fortune's fruitless spite had made it known
Her blows not shook but riveted his throne.
105   Some lazy ages, lost in sleep and ease,
No action leave to busy chronicles;
Such whose supine felicity but makes
In story chasms, in epoches mistakes;
O'er whom Time gently shakes his wings of down
110 Till with his silent sickle they are mown:
Such is not Charles his too, too active age,
Which governed by the wild distempered rage
Of some black star infecting all the skies,
Made him at his own cost like Adam wise.

93–4. Proverbial. In his comments on the adage *In nocte consilium* in his
Adagiorum Chiliades Erasmus cites Sophocles, Plato and Plutarch. Cp. also
Spenser, *FQ* I i 33.

98–104. Charles's maternal grandfather Henri IV of France (1553–1610)
became nominal King in 1589. A Protestant, he was opposed by many of his
subjects through the Catholic League, until he became a Catholic in 1593.
Henri extended the powers of the crown and restored prosperity to the
country. D.'s perception of a parallel with the English Solemn League and
Covenant (1643) was anticipated by the royalist pamphlet *Mercurius Rusticus*
(1646): 'the *holy League* in *France*, the *Prototype* of the present *Rebellion* in
England' (sig. N1ʳ). D. said that he sketched a play about the Catholic League
in 1660, which was completed in 1682 as *The Duke of Guise*. D. returns to the
parallel in the Postscript to his translation of Maimbourg's *History of the
League* (1684; *Works* xviii 393–415).

105–6. *ease . . . chronicles*] Christie notes that D. similarly rhymes *ease* and
articles in 'To Sir George Etherege' ll. 36–7; for a comparable pronunciation
of *miracles* see *Threnodia Augustalis* l. 414n.

107. *supine*] accented on the second syllable. See *Threnodia Augustalis* l. 14n.

108. *epoches*] dates of historical events (*OED* 3); probably trisyllabic, as in the
Greek 'ἐποχή.

112. *distempered*] immoderate, intemperate (*OED* 5).

115   Tremble ye nations who, secure before,
        Laughed at those arms that 'gainst ourselves we bore;
        Roused by the lash of his own stubborn tail
        Our lion now will foreign foes assail.
        With alga who the sacred altar strows?
120   To all the sea-gods Charles an offering owes:
        A bull to thee, Portunus, shall be slain,
        A lamb to you, the tempests of the main:
        For those loud storms that did against him roar
        Have cast his shipwracked vessel on the shore.
125   Yet as wise artists mix their colours so
        That by degrees they from each other go,
        Black steals unheeded from the neighbouring white
        Without offending the well-cozened sight:
        So on us stole our blessèd change, while we
130   Th' effect did feel, but scarce the manner see.
        Frosts that constrain the ground, and birth deny
        To flowers, that in its womb expecting lie,
        Do seldom their usurping power withdraw,
        But raging floods pursue their hasty thaw:
135   Our thaw was mild, the cold not chased away,

115–18. Cp. Waller, 'To My Lord of Falkland': 'our proud neighbours . . . ere long shall mourn / (Though now they joy in our expected harms) / . . . A lion so with self-provoking smart, / (His rebel tail scourging his noble part) / Calls up his courage; then begins to roar / And charge his foes, who thought him mad before' (ll. 34–40). With D.'s political viewpoint here contrast *Heroic Stanzas* ll. 113–16.

119. alga] seaweed.   *strows*] strews.

121. Portunus] the god of harbours (see *Aen.* v 241–3; Ovid, *Fasti* vi 545–8).

122. A lamb is sacrificed to the Tempests in *Aen.* v 772.

125–30. Sir Robert Howard also saw the Restoration as happening by degrees: 'Yet by degrees you mov'd, as after Night / The Sun begins to shew the World its light. / At whose approach, darknesse its place resignes, / And though it seems to move not, yet it shines. / So softly you began to spread your beams, / Through all our factions, dark in all extreams' ('A Panegyrick to Generall Monck', *Poems* (1660) 285).

125–8. This technique is advocated by William Sanderson: 'the sight must be sweetly deceived, by degrees, in breaking the Colours, by insensible passage, from higher Colours, to more dimme'; 'deceiving the Eye with a stealth of change' they 'lightly and smoothly coosin the Eye' (*Graphice* (1658) 23, 48).

130. Cp. Cowley: 'The manner *How* lies hid, th' *effect* we see' (*Davideis* ii; *Poems* 284).

131–6. Cp. *AM* ll. 1133–8.

But lost in kindly heat of lengthened day.
Heaven would no bargain for its blessings drive,
But what we could not pay for, freely give.
The Prince of Peace would, like himself, confer
140 A gift unhoped without the price of war:
Yet as he knew his blessing's worth, took care
That we should know it by repeated prayer,
Which stormed the skies and ravished Charles from
    thence,
As heaven itself is took by violence.
145 Booth's forward valour only served to show
He durst that duty pay we all did owe:
Th' attempt was fair, but heaven's prefixèd hour
Not come; so like the watchful traveller
That by the moon's mistaken light did rise,
150 Lay down again, and closed his weary eyes.
'Twas Monck whom Providence designed to loose
Those real bonds false freedom did impose.
The blessèd saints that watched this turning scene
Did from their stars with joyful wonder lean
155 To see small clues draw vastest weights along,
Not in their bulk but in their order strong.

136 kindly] nurturing.
137–40. The idea of God's free gift comes from Romans v 15–18.
139. Prince of Peace] a title for the Messiah from Isaiah ix 6.
144. The phrasing is from Matthew xi 12 ('the kingdom of heaven suffereth violence'); the idea of prayer as importunate is from Luke xi 5–10.
145. Booth] In August 1659 Sir George Booth led a rising for Charles in Cheshire, but was defeated by the Republic's forces under John Lambert. *forward*] ready, prompt (*OED* 6).
147–8. hour / Not come] echoing John viii 20.
151. Monck] See headnote.
155. clues] threads. The image is of a pulley; D. could have found such machines described and illustrated in John Wilkins, *Mathematicall Magick* (1648) 86–102. This apparent paradox was the subject of University Act verses at Cambridge: see *Minima vis potest movere maximum pondus* [*c.* 1585–90], which has a large woodcut of cogwheels. Bacon said that historians must attend to the hidden causes of public events, for God 'doth hang the greatest weight upon the smallest wires' (*The Advancement of Learning* (1605) II ii 5). Cp. Cowley: 'Strange *Play* of *Fate*! when might'iest humane things / Hang on such small, *Imperceptible Strings!*' (*Davideis* iv; *Poems* 374).
156. order] arrangement.

Thus pencils can by one slight touch restore
Smiles to that changèd face that wept before.
With ease such fond chimeras we pursue
160   As fancy frames for fancy to subdue,
But when ourselves to action we betake
It shuns the mint like gold that chymists make.
How hard was then his task, at once to be
What in the body natural we see
165   Man's architect distinctly did ordain
The charge of muscles, nerves and of the brain;
Through viewless conduits spirits to dispense,
The springs of motion from the seat of sense.
'Twas not the hasty product of a day,
170   But the well-ripened fruit of wise delay.
He like a patient angler, ere he strook
Would let them play a while upon the hook.
Our healthful food the stomach labours thus,
At first embracing what it straight doth crush.
175   Wise leeches will not vain receipts obtrude,
While growing pains pronounce the humours crude;
Deaf to complaints, they wait upon the ill
Till some safe crisis authorize their skill.

157. pencils] paint brushes (*OED* 1).
160. fancy] the imagination.
162. It] The antecedent is probably *fancy* (but possibly *chimera* or *action*).
mint] place of assay; test.   *chymists*] alchemists.
163–8. i.e. 'How hard for Monck to perform [in the body politic] the three
functions which we see that God, in designing the natural body, has ordained
to be the separate responsibility of muscles, nerves and brain: to send through
invisible channels of communication impulses from the brain which will
stimulate action'. The image comes from contemporary physiology: 'The
animal spirits . . . resemble a very subtle wind, or rather a flame which is very
pure and very vivid, and which, continually rising up in great abundance
from the heart to the brain, thence proceeds through the nerves to the
muscles, thereby giving the power of motion to all the members' (Descartes,
Discours de la Méthode (1637) V; *Philosophical Works* tr. Elizabeth S. Haldane
and G. R. T. Ross, 2 vols (1911) i 115).
167. viewless] invisible.
175–6. The medical metaphor is the theme of John Gauden's sermon
Κακοῦργοι (see l. 45*n*).
175. leeches] doctors.   *receipts*] recipes.
176. humours] bodily fluids which were thought to determine health.
crude] undigested (*OED* 3).

Nor could his acts too close a vizard wear
180   To scape their eyes whom guilt had taught to fear,
And guard with caution that polluted nest
Whence Legion twice before was dispossessed;
Once sacred house which when they entered in
They thought the place could sanctify a sin,
185   Like those that vainly hoped kind heaven would wink
While to excess on martyrs' tombs they drink:
And as devouter Turks first warn their souls
To part, before they taste forbidden bowls,
So these when their black crimes they went about
190   First timely charmed their useless conscience out.
Religion's name against itself was made;
The shadow served the substance to invade:
Like zealous missions they did care pretend
Of souls in show, but made the gold their end.
195   Th' incensèd powers beheld with scorn from high
An heaven so far distant from the sky,
Which durst with horses' hoofs that beat the ground
And martial brass belie the thunder's sound.
'Twas hence at length just Vengeance thought it fit

181–2. Parliament was dissolved by Cromwell in 1653 and by Lambert in
1659. *Legion* is the devil in Luke viii 26–36.
185. wink] close its eyes.
186. Probably a reference to the desecration of churches during the Civil War:
soldiers quartered in Westminster Abbey 'set Formes about the Communion
Table, there they eat, and there they drink Ale' (*Mercurius Rusticus* (1646)
216). Henry King's elegy for Charles I catalogues similar outrages (*Poems*
(1664) 25–7). St Augustine knew of some early Christians who held sacrilegious banquets on tombs (*Patrologia Latina* xxxii 1342).
187–8. 'One [Turk] drinking wine . . . made great clamors; being asked the
cause, he said he did it to warne his soule to flee into some corner of the
bodie, or else be quite gone, lest it should be polluted with that sinne' (*Purchas
his Pilgrimage* (1614) 294); cp. Burton, *Anatomy of Melancholy* (1621) III iv 1. 3.
189–90. Commanders of the Parliamentary armies held prayer meetings
before major actions.
190. timely] quickly (*OED* 1).
191. made] pressed into military service, enlisted (*OED* 15a).
195–8. Salmoneus tried to imitate the thunder and lightning of Jove by
waving torches and driving his chariot over brass arches, in order to be
worshipped as a god by his subjects. Jove struck him with a thunderbolt
(Virgil, *Aen.* vi 585–94).
195. beheld] *1660 second state*; behold *1660 first state*.

200   To speed their ruin by their impious wit.
      Thus Sforza, cursed with a too fertile brain,
      Lost by his wiles the power his wit did gain.
      Henceforth their fogue must spend at lesser rate
      Than in its flames to wrap a nation's fate.
205   Suffered to live, they are like helots set
      A virtuous shame within us to beget:
      For by example most we sinned before,
      And glass-like, clearness mixed with frailty bore.
      But since reformed by what we did amiss,
210   We by our sufferings learn to prize our bliss:
      Like early lovers whose unpractised hearts
      Were long the May-game of malicious arts,
      When once they find their jealousies were vain
      With double heat renew their fires again.
215   'Twas this produced the joy that hurried o'er
      Such swarms of English to the neighbouring shore,
      To fetch that prize by which Batavia made
      So rich amends for our impoverished trade.

200. wit] intelligence.
201–2. Lodovico Sforza, *il Moro* (1451–1508) poisoned his nephew Giovanni and succeeded him as Duke of Milan. He was betrayed by his own mercenaries to Louis XII of France in 1500, and died a prisoner. 'He carried a mind vaine, and full of thoughts busie and ambitious, and nourishing alwayes intentions dissembled, he kept no reckoning of his promises and faith. . . . This was a grosse error in his policie, to breed the storme, . . . fire suffered to runne, burnes without limite, even to the consuming of such as first kindled it' (Guicciardini, *Historie*, tr. G. Fenton, third edition (1618) 183, 30–1).
203. fogue] fury, passion (*OED*'s first example); a borrowing from French.
205–6. The Spartans would sometimes make their slaves (Helots) drunk and exhibit them to their young men to show them the evil of drunkenness (Plutarch, *Lycurgus* 28).
208. And glass-like] *1660 second state*; Like glass we *1660 first state*.
216. Clarendon recalled that 'Breda swarmed with English, a multitude repairing thither . . . with presents, and protestations how much they had longed and prayed for this blessed change, and magnifying their sufferings under the late tyrannical government, when many of them had been zealous ministers and promoters of it' (*History* xvi 234). One such was D.'s cousin John Pickering (Pepys, 16, 22 May 1660).
217. Batavia] Holland.
218. In 1660 English trade was depressed, partly because of competition from Holland for the conveyance of goods (Ogg 219–23).

O had you seen from Scheveline's barren shore
220 (Crowded with troops, and barren now no more)
Afflicted Holland to his farewell bring
True sorrow, Holland to regret a king;
While waiting him his royal fleet did ride,
And willing winds to their low'red sails denied,
225 The wavering streamers, flags and standard out,
The merry seamen's rude but cheerful shout,
And last the cannons' voice that shook the skies ⎫
And, as it fares in sudden ecstasies, ⎬
At once bereft us both of ears and eyes. ⎭
230 The *Naseby* now no longer England's shame,
But better to be lost in Charles his name
(Like some unequal bride in nobler sheets)
Receives her lord: the joyful *London* meets
The princely York, himself alone a freight;
235 The *Swiftsure* groans beneath great Gloucester's
weight.
Secure as when the halcyon breeds, with these
He that was born to drown might cross the seas.
Heaven could not own a providence and take

219–20. Charles embarked from Sheveling (now Scheveningen) near The Hague on 23 May. Pepys noted on 22 May that 'the shore was so full of people . . . as that it was as black (which otherwise is white sand) as everyone would stand by another'.

222. The United Provinces of the Netherlands was a republic. (Holland was one of the chief constituent states, though its name was loosely applied in English to the whole federation.)

226. rude] rough.

227–9. 'My Lord fired all his guns round twice, and all the fleet after him; which in the end fell into disorder, which seemed very handsome. . . . Nothing in the world but going of guns almost all this day' (Pepys, 22 May).

228. fares] happens. *ecstasies*] trances.

230–1. 'After dinner, the King and Duke . . . altered the name of some of the Shipps, *viz.* the *Nazeby* into *Charles* . . .' (Pepys, 23 May).

232. unequal] of lower social status.

233–5. 'The Duke of Yorke went on board the *London*, and the Duke of Glocester the *Swiftsure*' (Pepys, 23 May).

235. From *Aen.* vi 412–13: *accipit alveo / ingentem Aenean. gemuit sub pondere cumba* ('[Charon] received great Aeneas in his boat. The boat groaned under the weight').

236. For halcyons see *Heroic Stanzas* l. 144n.

238. own a providence] say that the world is governed by divine providence.

The wealth three nations ventured at a stake.
240 The same indulgence Charles his voyage blessed
Which in his right had miracles confessed.
The winds that never moderation knew,
Afraid to blow too much, too faintly blew;
Or out of breath with joy could not enlarge
245 Their straitened lungs, or conscious of their charge.
The British Amphitryte smooth and clear
In richer azure never did appear;
Proud her returning Prince to entertain
With the submitted fasces of the main.

250 And welcome now, great monarch, to your own;
Behold th' approaching cliffs of Albion;
It is no longer motion cheats your view,
As you meet it, the land approacheth you.
The land returns, and in the white it wears
255 The marks of penitence and sorrow bears.
But you, whose goodness your descent doth show,
Your heavenly parentage, and earthly too;
By that same mildness which your father's crown
Before did ravish, shall secure your own.

---

243. Thomas Fuller writes that the wind 'fearing that his *Breath* might be too rough, / Prov'd *over-civil*, and was scarce enough' (*A Panegyrick to his Majesty* 8).

244–5. Or . . . or] Either . . . or.

246. Amphitryte] wife of Neptune and goddess of the sea.

249. submitted fasces] When the consul Publius Valerius appeared before the people to answer allegations of ambition he ordered the lictors to walk with lowered fasces (*submissis fascibus*) as a sign of the people's superior authority (Livy ii 7). Many panegyrists write of Neptune surrendering his trident (e.g. Robert Wild, *Iter Boreale* 19; *Britannia Rediviva* sigs B3ʳ, F4ʳ). For D.'s later uses of the image see 'Verses to her Highness the Duchess' (prefixed to *AM*) ll. 15–16; *AM* ll. 197–200; *Threnodia Augustalis* ll. 516–17; and his addition of the line 'And *Neptune* shall resign the Fasces of the Sea' to Virgil's praise of Augustus in 'The First Book of the *Georgics*' l. 42.

253. Hoffman 12 sees this as an accurate image for the Restoration, which was not a surrender, but a rapprochement on agreed terms.

254. white] The cliffs of Dover; to stand publicly in a white sheet was a form of penance for fornication or adultery.

258–65. For mercy as a characteristic of Charles cp. *AA* l. 939 and *Threnodia Augustalis* l. 86*n*.

260 Not tied to rules of policy, you find
Revenge less sweet than a forgiving mind.
Thus when th' Almighty would to Moses give
A sight of all he could behold and live,
A voice before his entry did proclaim
265 Long-suffering, goodness, mercy in his name.
Your power to justice doth submit your cause,
Your goodness only is above the laws,
Whose rigid letter while pronounced by you
Is softer made. So winds that tempests brew
270 When through Arabian groves they take their flight,
Made wanton with rich odours, lose their spite.
And as those lees that trouble it, refine
The agitated soul of generous wine,
So tears of joy for your returning spilt,
275 Work out and expiate our former guilt.
Methinks I see those crowds on Dover's strand,
Who in their haste to welcome you to land
Choked up the beach with their still growing store,
And made a wilder torrent on the shore;
280 While spurred with eager thoughts of past delight,
Those who had seen you court a second sight,
Preventing still your steps, and making haste
To meet you often wheresoe'er you passed.
How shall I speak of that triumphant day
285 When you renewed th' expiring pomp of May?

260. rules of policy] As in Machiavelli, who wrote that an incoming ruler should decide what cruelty was necessary and inflict it immediately (*Prince* ch. 8). For Machiavelli, cp. *Heroic Stanzas* ll. 29–30*n*.
261, 266–9. In the Declaration of Breda (14 April) Charles offered pardon to all except those whom Parliament decided to exclude; this was effected in the Act of Indemnity of 29 August.
262–5. See Exodus xxxiii 19 to xxxiv 10; and cp. *AA* ll. 1007–9*n*.
267. The idea may recall Cowley: 'To do much *Good* his *sole Prerogative*' (*Davideis* iv; *Poems* 377).
272–3. *Trouble* and *agitate* are technical terms from fermentation (W. Hughes, *Compleat Vineyard* (1670) 53).   *generous*] rich, strong; a common epithet for wine.
276–8. Pepys (25 May) noted: 'Infinite the Croud of people and the gallantry of the Horsmen, Citizens, and Noblemen of all sorts.' The scene is described by John Price in *A Letter written from Dover* (1660).
282. Preventing] going ahead of.

(A month that owns an interest in your name:
You and the flowers are its peculiar claim.)
That star that at your birth shone out so bright
It stained the duller sun's meridian light,
290 Did once again its potent fires renew,
Guiding our eyes to find and worship you.
    And now time's whiter series is begun,
Which in soft centuries shall smoothly run;
Those clouds that overcast your morn shall fly
295 Dispelled to farthest corners of the sky.
Our nation with united interest blessed,
Not now content to poise, shall sway the rest:

286–7. This idea is also used by Whichcote: *Mensis erat* Maius *quem Tu*
nascendo *beasse / Diceris, & roseis condecorasse genis* ('It was the month of May
which you are said to have blessed with your birth, and to have ornamented
it with roses': *Academiae Cantabrigiensis ΣΩΣΤΡΑ* sig. A3ʳ).
287. peculiar] special.
288–9. On the day of Charles's birth in 1630 a bright star was seen in the
midday sky. This is a commonplace of panegyrics on the Restoration, but D.
particularly echoes Cowley: the star 'At *Charls* his *Birth*, did, in despight / Of
the proud *Sun*'s Meridian Light, / His future *Glories*, and this *Year* foreshow /
. . . Auspicious *Star* again arise' (*Poems* 421). Roettier's medal commemorating Charles's landing at Dover shows a star over the King's ship
(Hawkins i 457–8).
289. stained] obscured the lustre of (*OED* 1b, c).
291. Evocations of the birth of Christ were likewise common; cp. 'I've seen
your Star, and worship' (William Fairebrother, *An Essay of a Loyal Brest* (1660)
2; cp. *Britannia Rediviva* sigs a3ᵛ, Bb2ʳ). At his birth Herrick had written: 'At
Noone of Day, was seene a silver Star, / Bright as the Wise-mens Torch,
which guided them / To Gods sweet Babe, when borne at *Bethlehem*' ('A
Pastorall upon the Birth of Prince *Charles*' ll. 20–2, in *Hesperides*; Kinsley).
Cp. also the implications of D.'s epigraph (see note on title).
292–3. The renewal of time is a feature of the return of the golden age in
Virgil's *Ecl.* iv 4–7. Cp. Cowley: 'Such are the *years* (great *Charles*) which
now we see / Begin their *glorious March* with Thee' (*Poems* 427); John
Tatham, *London's Glory* (1660) 1; and *AM* ll. 69–72; *AA* ll. 1028–9 (Kinsley).
292. whiter] more innocent (*OED* 7); more fortunate (*OED* 8); senses of the
Latin *alba.*   *series]* perhaps also a Latinism: cp. *innumerabilis annorum series
et fuga temporum* ('innumerable series of years and flight of time'; Horace,
Carm. III xxx 5–6).
293. soft] The Latin *mollis* when applied to time can have the sense of 'propitious' (e.g. Virgil, *Aen.* iv 293).
297. See *Heroic Stanzas* l. 91n.

Abroad your empire shall no limits know,
But like the sea in boundless circles flow.
300 Your much-loved fleet shall with a wide command
Besiege the petty monarchs of the land:
And as old Time his offspring swallowed down,
Our ocean in its depths all seas shall drown.
Their wealthy trade from pirates' rapine free,
305 Our merchants shall no more adventurers be:
Nor in the farthest east those dangers fear
Which humble Holland must dissemble here.
Spain to your gift alone her Indies owes,
For what the powerful takes not, he bestows;
310 And France that did an exile's presence fear
May justly apprehend you still too near.
At home the hateful names of parties cease
And factious souls are wearied into peace.
The discontented now are only they
315 Whose crimes before did your just cause betray:
Of those your edicts some reclaim from sins,
But most your life and blessed example wins.
O happy prince, whom heaven hath taught the way
By paying vows, to have more vows to pay!

302. Chronos (Time) swallowed his children because it was prophesied that one of his sons would dethrone him (Hesiod, *Theogony* ll. 453–67).
305. *adventurers*] Merchants will still be sharers in commercial enterprises (*OED* 4), but they will no longer be waging war at their own risk (*OED* 3).
306–7. The Dutch had a virtual monopoly of the spice trade with the Far East; now they will humbly have to pretend not to notice (*dissemble*, *OED* 3) the threats to their economic survival posed by English naval dominance in the Channel.
308–9. Jamaica had been captured from Spain in 1655, and attempts were made to colonize Guiana; but the only threat to the wealthy and extensive Spanish possessions on the American mainland was to come from pirates.
310. Mazarin offered financial inducements to Charles to leave France for Germany in 1654 as he was negotiating an alliance with Cromwell. Under this treaty, signed on 24 October 1655, France excluded Charles, James and seventeen royalists from her territories.
316. Sir Charles Firth saw that this refers to Charles's 'Proclamation against vicious, debauched, and prophane persons' of 30 May 1660.
319. 'By keeping (*OED* pay 7a) your kingly vows of faithfulness to your people and church you have attracted more vows of obedience from them, which you must in turn honour' (and perhaps 'reward': *OED* pay 4).

320   O happy age! O times like those alone
       By Fate reserved for great Augustus' throne!
       When the joint growth of arms and arts foreshow
       The world a monarch, and that monarch *you*.

320–3. In Virgil, *Aen.* vi 791–4 Anchises prophesies the return of the golden
age with Augustus: *hic vir, hic est, tibi quem promitti saepius audis,* / *Augustus
Caesar, divi genus, aurea condet* / *saecula qui rursus Latio regnata per arva* / *Saturno
quondam* ('*Augustus*, promis'd oft, and long foretold, / Sent to the Realm that
Saturn rul'd of old; / Born to restore a better Age of Gold': tr. by D., ll. 1079–
81). Higgons also saw a parallel: 'When Rome was ruin'd with intestine hate,
/ Augustus took the rudder of the State' (*A Panegyrick* 5).
322. foreshow] The spelling *foreshew* in *1660* provides a perfect rhyme with
you.
323. Cp. Lluelyn: 'We still request a King, and that King, Thee' (*To the King's
. . . Majesty* 5; *Works*).

8 To His Sacred Majesty

Date and publication. *To His Sacred Maiesty, A Panegyrick On His Coronation* was published by Herringman in 1661 around 23 April, the date of the coronation. *1661* was issued in two states, the second having a variant reading (presumably an authorial revision) in line 32. The poem was reprinted, with a French translation, in *Complementum Fortunatarum Insularum* (1662), and in the 1688 edition of *AM*.

Context. Charles II was crowned in Westminster Abbey on 23 April 1661, after a procession the previous day from the Tower to Whitehall. The occasion is described by Pepys (22–3 April), Evelyn (22–3 April), and John Ogilby in *The Relation of His Majestie's Entertainment* (1661), expanded as *The Entertainment of His Most Excellent Majesty Charles II* (1662).

Sources. D.'s use of biblical typology is discussed by Zwicker 71–7. The poem is related to the tradition of panegyric by Garrison 165–75.

To His Sacred Majesty
A Panegyric on his Coronation

In that wild deluge where the world was drowned,
When life and sin one common tomb had found,
The first small prospect of a rising hill
With various notes of joy the ark did fill:
5   Yet when that flood in its own depths was drowned,
It left behind it false and slippery ground;
And the more solemn pomp was still deferred
Till new-born nature in fresh looks appeared.
Thus (royal sir) to see you landed here

¶8. *1–8.* See Genesis viii and Ovid, *Met.* i 343–9 (D.'s 'The First Book of Ovid's *Metamorphoses*' ll. 462–73). D. uses the image of the ark again in 'Epilogue Spoken to the King' ll. 17–18, 'Prologue to *The Unhappy Favourite*' ll. 1–6, and 'To the Duchess of Ormonde' ll. 70–9. Winn notes that D. is reversing an image common in the Civil War, e.g. in *England's Miraculous Preservation Emblematically Described* (1646), which shows the Long Parliament in the ark, while Charles I, Laud and their supporters drown in the waves (Winn 339–41, including illustration). But the image had already been used as a compliment to Charles in the anonymous poem *To the King, upon His Majesties Happy Return* (1660) 3: 'Twice has the World been trusted in a Barque; / The New, the *Charles* contain'd, the Old, the Ark'.

10   Was cause enough of triumph for a year:
     Nor would your care those glorious joys repeat
     Till they at once might be secure and great;
     Till your kind beams by their continued stay
     Had warmed the ground, and called the damps away:
15   Such vapours while your powerful influence dries
     Then soonest vanish when they highest rise.
     Had greater haste these sacred rites prepared,
     Some guilty months had in your triumphs shared:
     But this untainted year is all your own,
20   Your glories may without our crimes be shown.
     We had not yet exhausted all our store
     When you refreshed our joys by adding more:
     As heaven of old dispensed celestial dew,
     You give us manna and still give us new.
25   Now our sad ruins are removed from sight,
     The season too comes fraught with new delight;
     Time seems not now beneath his years to stoop,
     Nor do his wings with sickly feathers droop;
     Soft western winds waft o'er the gaudy spring,
30   And opened scenes of flowers and blossoms bring
     To grace this happy day, while you appear
     Not King of us alone, but of the year.
     All eyes you draw, and with the eyes the heart,
     Of your own pomp yourself the greatest part:
35   Loud shouts the nation's happiness proclaim,
     And heaven this day is feasted with your name.
     Your cavalcade the fair spectators view

17–20. Had Charles been crowned before 25 March, the first day of 1661 in the old calendar, two months of his exile (25 March to 25 May 1660) would have been included in his coronation year.
21–2. Cp. 'Lucretius: Against the Fear of Death' ll. 138–9.
23–4. See Exodus xvi 11–15.
26–32. Jonson used similar imagery in James I's coronation entry (*Part of the Kings Entertainment* ll. 626–8) and to Charles I in *The King's Entertainment at Welbeck* (ll. 5–36) (*Ben Jonson* vii 103, 791–2).
29. gaudy] bright.
32. Not King of us alone] *1661 second state;* Not only King of us *1661 first state.*
37–40. On 22 April Charles rode from the Tower to Whitehall with a 'magnificent Traine on horseback . . . thro the streetes, strew'd with flowers, houses hung with rich *Tapissry,* Windos & *Balconies* full of Ladies' (Evelyn, *Diary*).

From their high standings, yet look up to you;
From your brave train each singles out a prey,
40   And longs to date a conquest from your day.
Now charged with blessings while you seek repose,
Officious slumbers haste your eyes to close;
And glorious dreams stand ready to restore
The pleasing shapes of all you saw before.
45   Next·to the sacred temple you are led,
Where waits a crown for your more sacred head:
How justly from the church that crown is due,
Preserved from ruin and restored by you!
The grateful choir their harmony employ
50   Not to make greater but more solemn joy.
Wrapped soft and warm your name is sent on high,
As flames do on the wings of incense fly;
Music herself is lost, in vain she brings
Her choicest notes to praise the best of kings:
55   Her melting strains in you a tomb have found,
And lie like bees in their own sweetness drowned.
He that brought peace, and discord could atone,
His name is music of itself alone.

42. Officious] ready to do kind offices (*OED* 1).
48. The Long Parliament had abolished episcopacy and set up a presbyterian form of church government; the Book of Common Prayer was dropped, and many church lands were sold. The re-establishment of the Church of England at the Restoration was controversial, and incomplete at the time of this poem. The Convention Parliament of 1660 had postponed decisions on an ecclesiastical settlement, and on 25 October 1660 Charles declared that these questions would be referred to a national synod. The Savoy Conference met from 5 April to 23 July 1661, but without reconciling differences between puritans and anglicans. A new Prayer Book was accepted by Parliament in April 1662, and the Act of Uniformity in May 1662 imposed a liturgy, theology and organization to which many puritans refused to conform. See further Hutton, *The Restoration* 125–80; Robert S. Bosher, *The Making of the Restoration Settlement* (1951); Ian Green, *The Re-Establishment of the Church of England 1660–1663* (1978). The re-establishment of the Church of England was a major theme in several panegyrics, e.g. Robert Whitehall, *The Coronation* and Carew Reynell, *The Fortunate Change*.
49. grateful] pleasing (*OED* 1).
56. A proverbial idea (Pliny, *Naturalis Historia* xi 67; Tilley B 204), used again in *EDP* in a discussion of rhyme (*Works* xvii 77; Winn, *When Beauty* 74).
57. atone] reduce to harmony.
58. Punning on the Latin name for Charles, *Carolus* (Winn, *When Beauty* 75).

Now while the sacred oil anoints your head,
60 And fragrant scents, begun from you, are spread
Through the large dome, the people's joyful sound
Sent back, is still preserved in hallowed ground;
Which in one blessing mixed descends on you,
As heightened spirits fall in richer dew.
65 Not that our wishes do increase your store:
Full of yourself you can admit no more;
We add not to your glory, but employ
Our time like angels in expressing joy.
Nor is it duty or our hopes alone
70 Create that joy, but full fruition;
We know those blessings which we must possess,
And judge of future by past happiness.
No promise can oblige a prince so much
Still to be good, as long to have been such.
75 A noble emulation heats your breast,
And your own fame now robs you of your rest:
Good actions still must be maintained with good,
As bodies nourished with resembling food.
You have already quenched sedition's brand,
80 And zeal (which burnt it) only warms the land.
The jealous sects that dare not trust their cause
So far from their own will as to the laws,

61. *dome*] church (from Latin *domus Dei*, 'house of God'; *pace OED* 2 not specifically a cathedral: Thomas Otway calls St George's Chapel, Windsor a *dome* in *Windsor Castle* (1685) 11); cp. D.'s 'Dido to Aeneas' l. 109.
64. An image from distilling; cp. *AM* ll. 51–2.
78. 'Nature doth nourish and amplify all parts of an Animal with the same matter, or humour . . . out of which she constituted or framed them at the first. Because, whatsoever is superadded to the parts, during their growth, ought to be of the same substance, with what was praeexistent' (Walter Charleton, *Natural History of Nutrition* (1659) 2–3; *Works*).
79. In January 1661 Thomas Venner led a rising in London by a small group of Fifth Monarchy Men. The rebels were quickly captured and executed, but the rising prompted extensive searches and arrests of dissenters, until the government realized that Venner's move was not part of a nation-wide conspiracy.
81–4. During the Civil War and Commonwealth the more radical Protestant sects had opposed attempts by Parliament to establish a presbyterian church. In the Declaration of Breda Charles had promised 'a liberty to tender consciences, and that no man shall be disquieted or called in question for differ-

You for their umpire and their synod take,
And their appeal alone to Caesar make.
85 Kind heaven so rare a temper did provide
That guilt repenting might in it confide.
Among our crimes oblivion may be set,
But 'tis our King's perfection to forget.
Virtues unknown to these rough northern climes
90 From milder heavens you bring, without their crimes:
Your calmness does no after-storms provide,
Nor seeming patience mortal anger hide.
When empire first from families did spring,
Then every father governed as a king;
95 But you that are a sovereign prince allay
Imperial power with your paternal sway.
From those great cares when ease your soul unbends,
Your pleasures are designed to noble ends:
Born to command the mistress of the seas,
100 Your thoughts themselves in that blue empire please.
Hither in summer evenings you repair
To take the fraischeur of the purer air:
Undaunted here you ride when winter raves,

ences of opinion in matter of religion which do not disturb the peace of the
kingdom'. His subsequent Declaration of 25 October 1660 referred ecclesiastical differences to a national synod. Meanwhile, dissenters petitioned the
King for permission to follow their own practices. See further l. 48*n*.
84. Echoing Acts xxv 11.
87–8. Alluding to the Act of Oblivion (1660), pardoning past offences, which
was passed with Charles's active encouragement. D. implies that the people
had forgotten their obligations to their King.
89–90. Cp. 'from each clime / You brought their virtues with you, not their
crime' (Anon, *A Poem upon his Maiesties Coronation* (1661) 8; exact date
unknown).
93–4. A commonplace long before Filmer's *Patriarcha* (1680); e.g. in Hooker:
'as the chiefest person in every houshold was always as it were a king, so
when numbers of housholds joined themselves in civill societie together,
kings were the first kind of governors amongst them' (*Of the Lawes of
Ecclesiasticall Politie* (1593) I x 4; citing Aristotle, *Politics* i 2); cp. also James I:
the King is the people's 'naturall father and kindly maister' (*Basilicon Doron*
(1599); edited by James Craigie, 2 vols (1944–50) i 54).
102. fraischeur] freshness (French; *OED*'s first example is from 1599); for D.'s
liking for French borrowings cp. *Astraea Redux* l. 203*n*.

With Caesar's heart that rose above the waves.
105   More I could sing, but fear my numbers stays;
No loyal subject dares that courage praise.
In stately frigates most delight you find,
Where well-drawn battles fire your martial mind.
What to your cares we owe is learnt from hence,
110   When ev'n your pleasures serve for our defence.
Beyond your court flows in th' admitted tide,
Where in new depths the wondering fishes glide:
Here in a royal bed the waters sleep,
When tired at sea within this bay they creep.
115   Here the mistrustful fowl no harm suspects,
So safe are all things which our King protects.
From your loved Thames a blessing yet is due,
Second alone to that it brought in you;

104. When Caesar was in a ship on the rough river Aoüs the pilot was about
to turn back when Caesar revealed his identity and said, 'Go boldly on, and
fear nothing; you carry Caesar and his fortune in your boat' (Plutarch, *Caesar*
38; cp. Lucan, *Pharsalia* v 568–93).

105. stays] holds back.

107–10. Cp. John Sheffield's *Character of Charles II*: 'The great and almost
only pleasure of mind he appeared addicted to, was shipping and sea-affairs;
which seemed to be so much his talent both for knowledge, as well as
inclination, that a war of that kind was rather an entertainment, than any
disturbance to his thoughts' (*Works* (1723) ii 59–60). For Charles's interest in
the navy see also *AM* ll. 53–60; Robert Latham in Pepys, *Diary* x 56–8;
Hutton, *Charles the Second passim.* The anonymous *A Poem upon his Maiesties
Coronation* said: 'The Seamans Art, and his great end, Commerce / Through
all the corners of the Universe, / Are not alone the subject of Your care, / But
Your delight' (9).

111–16. The alterations made to St James's Park, London, by the King
included a canal to the Thames and a decoy stocked with wild fowl. See
Waller's poem *On St. James's Park, as lately improved by His Majesty* (1661);
Pepys, 16 September, 11 October 1660; Evelyn, 9 February 1665.

113–14. Cp. Cowley, 'Where their vast *Court* the *Mother-waters* keep, / And
undisturb'd by *Moons* in silence sleep' (*Davideis* i, *Poems* 244; cp. *MF* ll. 72–
3*n*).

117–28. At the time of the coronation there were two possibilities for the
royal marriage: a Spanish princess, who would bring wealth from the
Spanish West Indies (the *ore* of l. 125), or Catherine of Braganza, from
Portugal, whose dowry would include Tangier, Bombay and trading rights
with the Portuguese East Indies (the *incense* of l. 126). Charles's choice of
bride and alliance would affect the outcome of the Portuguese war for inde-

A queen, from whose chaste womb, ordained by Fate,
120 The souls of kings unborn for bodies wait.
It was your love before made discord cease:
Your love is destined to your country's peace.
Both Indies (rivals in your bed) provide
With gold or jewels to adorn your bride.
125 This to a mighty king presents rich ore,
While that with incense does a god implore.
Two kingdoms wait your doom, and as you choose,
This must receive a crown, or that must lose.
Thus from your royal oak, like Jove's of old,
130 Are answers sought, and destinies foretold:
Propitious oracles are begged with vows,
And crowns that grow upon the sacred boughs.
Your subjects, while you weigh the nations' fate,
Suspend to both their doubtful love or hate:
135 Choose only, sir, that so they may possess
With their own peace their children's happiness.

---

pendence from Spain. Pepys recorded discussion of the question on 14 and 28 February 1661. On 8 May Charles told Parliament that he would marry Catherine of Braganza, 'with full consideration of the good of my subjects in general, as of myself' (Kinsley).

122. Your] Eds; Your your *1661*.

127. doom] decision.

129–32. One of the coronation arches depicted 'the ROYAL OAK bearing Crowns, and Scepters, instead of Acorns; amongst the Leaves, in a Label, MIRATURQUE NOVAS FRONDES ET NON SUA POMA—"Leaves unknown / Admiring, and strange Apples not her own." As designing its Reward for the Shelter afforded His Majesty after the Fight at *Worcester*' (John Ogilby, *The Relation of His Majestie's Entertainment* (1661) 6).

129. like Jove's] At Dodona (*Odyssey* xiv 327–8). Cp. Whitehall: 'Great *Joves* concerne, and *chiefest* care, who took, / Your *Sacred Self* into his *Sacred Oak*' (5).

9 To My Lord Chancellor

Date and publication. To My Lord Chancellor, Presented on New-years-day was published by Herringman in 1662, and reprinted in the 1688 edition of *AM*.

Context. Edward Hyde (1609–74) was one of Charles I's chief counsellors during the Civil War, and was particularly entrusted with the care of the Prince of Wales. From 1646 to 1660 he was in exile, and suffered financial hardship. For most of this period he was Charles II's close adviser, though not without opposition from Queen Henrietta Maria and other courtiers. In 1658 he was appointed Charles's Lord Chancellor, a post which he continued to hold after the Restoration, when he was effectively head of the government. He was created Earl of Clarendon at the coronation. The initially secret marriage of his daughter Anne to the Duke of York on 3 September 1660 was one of several factors which contributed to his unpopularity. 'Clarendon's decline may be dated from the summer of 1661, when the implications of the Restoration Settlement had become revealed; for by Catholic and Non-conformist alike he was held responsible for the denial of toleration; by the Courtiers, he was thought to be the agent whereby parliament had made insufficient financial provision for the crown; by the Cavaliers, he was blamed for the land settlement, and for the insufficient reward to loyalists' (Ogg 205). He survived an attempt to impeach him in July 1663, but on 30 August 1667 he was dismissed and on 29 November went into exile. He spent his last years on his literary masterpiece, published as *History of the Rebellion* (1702–4) and *Life . . . Written by Himself* (1759). He rightly said of himself: 'His Integrity was ever without Blemish; and believed to be above Temptation. He was firm and unshaken in his Friendships' (*Life* 35).

Nothing is known of any connection between D. and Clarendon prior to this poem, but in January 1662 Clarendon reminded the King to pay money promised to the Earl of Berkshire, and on 27 February warrants were issued promising to pay the Earl £8,000 and his daughter Elizabeth £3,000. Winn 127 suggests that the payment to Elizabeth was intended as a dowry, and thus facilitated her marriage to D. on 1 December 1663. Evidence of later connections between D. and Clarendon is equally fragmentary. In February 1663 the Earl of Orrery thanked Clarendon's son Henry, Viscount Cornbury, for his favour to D. (BodL MS Clarendon 79 f. 84). In a letter *c*. March 1684 thought to be addressed to Hyde's son Laurence, D. says that 'on some occasions, perhaps not known to you, [I] have not been unserviceable to the memory & reputation of My Lord your father' (*Letters* 21). No more is known about the connection.

In the Renaissance it was customary for writers to present a poem in Latin or English to their patron at Christmas or on New Year's Day (J. W. Binns, *Intellectual Culture in Elizabethan and Jacobean England* (1990) 75). For New Year's gifts in the Restoration see Pepys (Index: xi 196). Expensive gifts were exchanged between the King and government office-holders (Pepys ii *5n*).

To My Lord Chancellor
Presented on New Year's Day

My Lord,
While flattering crowds officiously appear
To give themselves, not you, an happy year;
And by the greatness of their presents prove
How much they hope, but not how well they love;
5   The Muses (who your early courtship boast,
Though now your flames are with their beauty lost)
Yet watch their time, that if you have forgot
They were your mistresses, the world may not:
Decayed by time and wars, they only prove
10 Their former beauty by your former love;
And now present, as ancient ladies do
That courted long at length are forced to woo:
For still they look on you with such kind eyes
As those that see the church's sovereign rise
15 From their own order chose, in whose high state
They think themselves the second choice of Fate.
When our great monarch into exile went,
Wit and religion suffered banishment:

¶9. 5. 'Whilst He was only a Student of the Law, and stood at Gaze, and irresolute what Course of Life to take, his chief Acquaintance were *Ben. Johnson, John Selden, Charles Cotton, John Vaughan, Sir Kenelm Digby, Thomas May*, and *Thomas Carew*' (*Life* 16). Later his friends included Lucius Cary, Viscount Falkland, and the theologians and men of letters who were associated with Falkland's house at Great Tew: Sidney Godolphin, Edmund Waller, Gilbert Sheldon, George Morley, John Earle, John Hales, William Chillingworth and Thomas Hobbes. Hyde shared rooms with William Davenant in the Middle Temple and wrote a prefatory poem for his *Albovine* (1629); he may also have composed verses for Donne's *Death's Duell* (1632).
11. *present*] i.e. present themselves (*OED* 2b).
14. *those*] cardinals at a papal election.
17–18. Cp. Denham: 'The *Laurel* and the *Crown* together went, / Had the same *Foes*, and the same *Banishment*' ('Prologue to His Majesty' (1660) ll. 7–8). D. returns to the idea in *EDP* (*Works* xvii 34, 63). For royalists' appropriation of the arts to their political ends in the 1650s see Derek Hirst, *SC* v (1990) 133–55.

Thus once when Troy was wrapped in fire and smoke,
20   The helpless gods their burning shrines forsook;
They with the vanquished prince and party go,
And leave their temples empty to the foe:
At length the Muses stand restored again
To that great charge which Nature did ordain;
25   And their loved Druids seem revived by Fate,
While you dispense the laws and guide the state.
The nation's soul (our monarch) does dispense
Through you to us his vital influence;
You are the channel where those spirits flow,
30   And work them higher as to us they go.
    In open prospect nothing bounds our eye
Until the earth seems joined unto the sky:
So in this hemisphere our utmost view
Is only bounded by our King and you:
35   Our sight is limited where you are joined,
And beyond that no farther heaven can find.
So well your virtues do with his agree,
That though your orbs of different greatness be,
Yet both are for each other's use disposed,
40   His to enclose, and yours to be enclosed:

19–20. See *Aen.* ii 351–2.

25. Druids] writers and artists, the Muses' 'priests'.

27–30. i.e. The King, the nation's soul, dispenses his vital influence through Clarendon, who is like the system of arteries by which these spirits are transmitted throughout the body politic, and in which these spirits are refined into higher form to constitute the Rational Soul, the seat of the nation's understanding and will (*Works*).

37. virtues] the powers of a heavenly body which influence human life (*OED* 1, 9).

38–40. See 'Upon the Death of the Lord Hastings' l. 27*n.*

38. orbs] [celestial] spheres.

39–42. Cp. Marvell: 'And with such to inclose / Is more than to oppose. / . . . Nature that hateth emptiness, / Allows of penetration less:' ('An Horatian Ode' ll. 19–20, 41–2; E. E. Duncan-Jones, privately). Since D. worked with Marvell in the same office in Cromwell's government he could easily have seen a MS of the poem, which was first printed in Marvell's *Miscellaneous Poems* (1681), and even then excised from most copies. For D.'s later echoes of this poem see ll. 105–6*n*, *AM* ll. 849–60*n*, *AA* ll. 353–4*n*, 387–8*n*, 805–8*n*, 887*n*, *Threnodia Augustalis* ll. 230–5*n*.

Nor could another in your room have been,
Except an emptiness had come between.
Well may he then to you his cares impart,
And share his burden where he shares his heart.
45 In you his sleep still wakes; his pleasures find
Their share of business in your labouring mind:
So when the weary sun his place resigns,
He leaves his light and by reflection shines.
      Justice that sits and frowns where public laws
50 Exclude soft mercy from a private cause,
In your tribunal most herself does please,
There only smiles because she lives at ease;
And like young David finds her strength the more
When disencumbered from those arms she wore.
55 Heaven would your royal master should exceed
Most in that virtue which we most did need,
And his mild father (who too late did find
All mercy vain but what with power was joined)
His fatal goodness left to fitter times,
60 Not to increase but to absolve our crimes:
But when the heir of this vast treasure knew
How large a legacy was left to you,
(Too great for any subject to retain)
He wisely tied it to the crown again:
65 Yet passing through your hands it gathers more,
As streams through mines bear tincture of their ore.
While emp'ric politicians use deceit,
Hide what they give, and cure but by a cheat,
You boldly show that skill which they pretend,
70 And work by means as noble as your end;
Which, should you veil, we might unwind the clue
As men do nature, till we came to you:

41–2. i.e. if a lesser man than Hyde occupied this office there would be a gap,
a vacuum, between his orb and the King's.
53–4. See 1 Samuel xvii 38–9: David took off his armour to fight Goliath
more easily.
55–60. For Charles's mercy cp. *Threnodia Augustalis* l. 86n.
67. *emp'ric*] quack, charlatanical.
71. *clue*] thread.
72. i.e. the study of nature leads man to discover evidence of her maker, God,
at work.

And as the Indies were not found before
Those rich perfumes which from the happy shore
75 The winds upon their balmy wings conveyed,
Whose guilty sweetness first their world betrayed;
So by your counsels we are brought to view
A rich and undiscovered world in you.
By you our monarch does that fame assure
80 Which kings must have or cannot live secure:
For prosperous princes gain the subjects' heart
Who love that praise in which themselves have part:
By you he fits those subjects to obey,
As heaven's eternal monarch does convey
85 His power unseen, and man to his designs
By his bright ministers the stars inclines.
    Our setting sun from his declining seat
Shot beams of kindness on you, not of heat;
And when his love was bounded in a few
90 That were unhappy that they might be true,
Made you the favourite of his last sad times,
That is, a sufferer in his subjects' crimes:
Thus those first favours you received were sent,
Like heaven's rewards, in earthly punishment.
95 Yet Fortune, conscious of your destiny,
Ev'n then took care to lay you softly by,
And wrapped your fate among her precious things,
Kept fresh to be unfolded with your King's.
Shown all at once, you dazzled so our eyes,
100 As new-born Pallas did the gods surprise,
When springing forth from Jove's new-closing wound

73–6. As they approached Virginia in 1584 Amadas and Barlowe 'smelt so
sweet, and so strong a smel, as if we had bene in the midst of some delicate
garden abounding with all kinde of odoriferous flowers, by which we were
assured, that the land could not be farre distant' (Hakluyt, *Voyages* (1903–5)
viii 298). Cp. Diodorus Siculus III xlvi 4.
79. *assure*] secure to himself, make sure of (*OED* 1b).
87. *Our setting sun*] Charles I.
88. *kindness*] nurturing power.
100. Pallas Athene, goddess of war and of learning; for her birth fully grown
from the head of Zeus (Jove) see Hesiod, *Theogony* 924–6. Lines 102–4 recall
Ovid, *Met.* vi 80–1.

She struck the warlike spear into the ground,
Which sprouting leaves did suddenly enclose,
And peaceful olives shaded as they rose.
105   How strangely active are the arts of peace,
Whose restless motions less than war's do cease!
Peace is not freed from labour but from noise,
And war more force but not more pains employs;
Such is the mighty swiftness of your mind
110 That (like the earth's) it leaves our sense behind,
While you so smoothly turn and roll our sphere,
That rapid motion does but rest appear.
For as in nature's swiftness, with the throng
Of flying orbs while ours is borne along,
115 All seems at rest to the deluded eye
(Moved by the soul of the same harmony):
So carried on by your unwearied care
We rest in peace and yet in motion share.
Let envy then those crimes within you see
120 From which the happy never must be free
(Envy that does with misery reside,
The joy and the revenge of ruined pride);
Think it not hard if at so cheap a rate
You can secure the constancy of Fate,
125 Whose kindness sent, what does their malice seem,
By lesser ills the greater to redeem.
Nor can we this weak shower a tempest call,
But drops of heat that in the sunshine fall.

105–6. Cp. Marvell: 'So restless *Cromwel* could not cease / In the inglorious
Arts of Peace' ('An Horatian Ode' ll. 9–10; E. E. Duncan-Jones, privately).
111–18. i.e. 'You direct the course of England among the nations, as God
turns the earth on its axis and rolls it in its orbit among the other planets, so
smoothly that it seems to be at rest.' Copernicus discussed the illusion that
the earth is at rest in *De Revolutionibus Orbis* (1543) i 8 (Kinsley).
119–26. 'He foresaw, and told many of his Friends, "that the Credit He was
thought to have with the King, and which He knew was much less than it
was thought to be . . . would in a short Time raise such a Storm of Envy and
Malice against him, that He should not be able to stand the Shock."' (*Life*
27). Pepys was told on 27 July 1661 that 'my Lord Chancellor is much envyed
and that many great men, such as the Duke of Buckingham and my Lord of
Bristoll, do endeavour to undermine him.'

You have already wearied Fortune so
130　She cannot farther be your friend or foe,
But sits all breathless, and admires to feel
A fate so weighty that it stops her wheel.
In all things else above our humble fate,
Your equal mind yet swells not into state,
135　But like some mountain in those happy isles
Where in perpetual spring young nature smiles,
Your greatness shows: no horror to affright,
But trees for shade, and flowers to court the sight;
Sometimes the hill submits itself a while
140　In small descents which do its height beguile;
And sometimes mounts, but so as billows play
Whose rise not hinders but makes short our way.
Your brow which does no fear of thunder know
Sees rolling tempests vainly beat below;
145　And (like Olympus' top) th' impression wears
Of love and friendship writ in former years.
Yet unimpaired with labours or with time,
Your age but seems to a new youth to climb.
Thus heavenly bodies do our time beget,
150　And measure change, but share no part of it.
And still it shall without a weight increase,
Like this new year whose motions never cease;

131. admires] wonders.
134–42. Cp. Denham, *Cooper's Hill*: Windsor 'above the Valley swells / Into
my eye, and doth it self present / With such an easie and unforc't ascent, /
That no stupendious precipice denies / Access, no horror turns away our
eyes: / But such a Rise, as doth at once invite / A pleasure, and a reverence
from the sight' (ll. 40–6).
134. equal] fair, just (*OED* 5); calm, tranquil (*OED* 9, first example 1680), a
sense of the Latin *aequus*, as in Horace, *Carm.* III xxi 33.　　*state*] primarily
'pomp', 'magnificent place'; but perhaps also 'the climax of a disease' (*OED*
7).
137. horror] ruggedness (*OED* 1).
139. submits] becomes lower (*OED* 8c).
140. beguile] give a misleading impression of.
143–6. For the serenity of Olympus see *Odyssey* vi 42–6.
151. Cp. *Heroic Stanzas* ll. 57–8n.
152–6. As the cycle of the returning new year follows the course of the sun,
so Hyde's course follows Charles's; it will therefore prove *weightless* (free

For since the glorious course you have begun
Is led by Charles, as that is by the sun,
155   It must both weightless and immortal prove,
Because the centre of it is above.

---

from earthly cares) because the lighter elements of fire and air move upwards,
and *immortal* because it has its centre in the King (and, beyond the King, in
God).

10 To Dr Charleton

Date and publication. This is the prefatory poem to Walter Charleton's *Chorea Gigantum, or, The most Famous Antiquity of Great-Britain, Vulgarly called Stoneheng . . . Restored to the Danes* (1663: dedication to the King dated 27 April 1662, imprimatur 11 September; *SR* 18 September 1662). Published by Herringman. It exists in two states with revisions to D.'s poem in the second state (followed here).

Context. Walter Charleton (1620–1707) was educated under John Wilkins at Oxford and quickly acquired a medical reputation, being appointed physician in ordinary to Charles I. Besides his medical writings he published a series of books which followed Gassendi in expounding a version of Epicureanism which was purged from atheism: *The Darknes of Atheism Dispelled by the Light of Nature* (1652); *Physiologia Epicuro-Gassendo-Charletoniana* (1654); *Epicurus' Morals* (1656); and *The Immortality of the Human Soul* (1657). Osborn 174–5 suggests that the advertisement to the latter, and that in Charleton's *Natural History of Nutrition* (1659), might have been written by D. for Herringman. For Charleton's life to 1659 see L. Sharp, *Annals of Science* xxx (1973) 311–40. On 12 November 1662 he proposed D. for membership of the Royal Society; D. was elected on 19 November and admitted on 26 November. But this does not imply that D. had a strong interest in the Society: he was inactive, did not pay his dues, and was expelled in 1666 (see Michael Hunter, *Notes & Records of the Royal Society* xxxi (1976–7) 9–114). Charleton contributed to the translation of Plutarch which D. supervised in 1683–6. For D., Charleton and contemporary medicine see Hugh Ormsby-Lennon, *SECC* vii (1978) 389–411.

Chorea Gigantum, which has an effusive dedication to Charles II, argues that Stonehenge was built by the Danes as a place where their kings were inaugurated; this was in reply to Inigo Jones's theory in *The Most Notable Antiquity of Great Britain* (1655) that it had been a Roman temple dedicated to the god Coelus. The copy of *Chorea* which Charleton gave to D. is now in the Folger Shakespeare Library, inscribed: 'For my Learned & obliging Friend, Mr. John Driden'. Sir Robert Howard wrote the other prefatory poem.

Sources. D.'s ideas and phrasing (including his images of political freedom) probably owe something to pp. 1–5 of Charleton's *Physiologia*, where philosophers are divided into four groups: (i) slavish followers of Aristotle who 'believe all, examine nothing; and, as if the Lamp of their own Reason were lent them by their Creator for no use at all, resign up their judgments' (cp. ll. 1–4); (ii) 'assertors of philosophical liberty' (cp. l. 21) who 'admit of no Monarchy in Philosophy, besides that of Truth'; they 'vindicate the native privilege of our Intellectuals, from the base villenage of Praescription' (cp. 'free-born', l. 3); these include Harvey; (iii) the 'renovators' of the ancient philosophers, such as Ficino who revived Plato, as Gassendi did Epicurus; (iv) the 'electors' who 'cull and select out of all others, what they most approve'. Charleton claims for himself 'the lowest room' in group (iv): cp. ll. 33–42.

To my Honoured Friend Dr Charleton, on his learned and useful works;

and more particularly this of Stonehenge, by him restored to the true founders

The longest tyranny that ever swayed
Was that wherein our ancestors betrayed
Their free-born reason to the Stagirite,
And made his torch their universal light.
5 So truth, while only one supplied the state,
Grew scarce and dear, and yet sophisticate,
Until 'twas bought, like emp'ric wares or charms,
Hard words sealed up with Aristotle's arms.
Columbus was the first that shook his throne,
10 And found a temperate in a torrid zone:
The feverish air fanned by a cooling breeze,
The fruitful vales set round with shady trees,

¶10. *1–4*. Cp. Cowley, 'To Mr. Hobs': 'Long did the mighty *Stagirite* retain / The *universal Intellectual* reign' (*Poems* 188).
3. Stagirite] Aristotle (born at Stagirus).
6. sophisticate] corrupt, adulterated (*OED* 1).
7. emp'ric wares] quack medical remedies.
8. For the wording cp. the advertisement on the last page of Sir Kenelm Digby, *A Late Discourse* (1660), for Buckworth's lozenges, which were available 'sealed up with their Coat of Armes' from Herringman's shop (Hugh Ormsby-Lennon, *SECC* vii (1978) 407).
9–10. Aristotle believed that the heat was so intense in the torrid zone between the tropics of Cancer and Capricorn that no one could live there. Columbus and later voyagers discovered the delights of the West Indies.
10. Echoes Marvell: 'War turn'd the temperate, to the Torrid Zone' ('On the Victory obtained by Blake over the Spaniards' (1657) l. 124).

And guiltless men who danced away their time,
Fresh as their groves, and happy as their clime.
15 Had we still paid that homage to a name
Which only God and nature justly claim,
The western seas had been our utmost bound,
Where poets still might dream the sun was drowned;
And all the stars that shine in southern skies
20 Had been admired by none but salvage eyes.
    Among th' assertors of free reason's claim,
Th' English are not the least in worth or fame.
The world to Bacon does not only owe
Its present knowledge, but its future too.
25 Gilbert shall live till loadstones cease to draw,
Or British fleets the boundless ocean awe;
And noble Boyle, not less in nature seen
Than his great brother read in states and men.
The circling streams, once thought but pools of blood
30 (Whether life's fuel, or the body's food)

13. The *locus classicus* for the Renaissance view of the innate goodness of uncivilized man is Montaigne's essay *Des Cannibales*, which includes the detail, 'Toute la journée se passe à dancer' (Montaigne 205). D. appears to have coined the phrase 'the noble savage' (*I Conquest of Granada* I i 209), and he dramatized the meeting of Indian and European cultures in *The Indian Emperor* (1667). See also *Astraea Redux* ll. 46–8*n*, and the 'Prologue to *The Indian Queen*'.   *who*] *1663 second state; that 1663 first state.*

20. salvage] savage; cp. *Astraea Redux* l. 46*n*.

22. Th' English are not the] *1663 second state; The English are not 1663 first state.*

23. Bacon] Francis Bacon (1561–1626) was frequently credited in the 1660s with laying the foundations of empirical philosophy: see Michael Hunter, *Science and Society in Restoration England* (1981) 14 and *passim.*

25. Gilbert] William Gilbert (1540–1603), physician to Elizabeth I and author of *De Magnete* (1600), which described the properties of magnets and the implications for navigation. Charleton discusses the loadstone in *Physiologia* 383–413.

27–8. Robert Boyle (1627–91), natural philosopher, chemist and theologian; and his brother Roger (1621–79), Earl of Orrery, politician, poet and dedicatee of D.'s *The Rival Ladies* (1664).

29–31. William Harvey (1578–1657) published his discovery of the circulation of the blood in *Exercitatio Anatomica De Motu Cordis Et Sanguinis In Animalibus* (1628).

30. This question is discussed by Charleton in his *Natural History of Nutrition,* where he argues for the former explanation (see A. H. de Quehen, *N & Q* ccxxii (1977) 544–5).

From dark oblivion Harvey's name shall save,
While Ent keeps all the honour that he gave.
Nor are you, learnèd friend, the least renowned,
Whose fame, not circumscribed with English ground,
35 Flies like the nimble journeys of the light,
And is, like that, unspent too in its flight.
Whatever truths have been, by art or chance,
Redeemed from error or from ignorance,
Thin in their authors, like rich veins of ore,
40 Your works unite, and still discover more.
Such is the healing virtue of your pen,
To perfect cures on books, as well as men.
Nor is this work the least: you well may give
To men new vigour, who make stones to live.
45 Through you the Danes, their short dominion lost,
A longer conquest than the Saxons boast.
Stonehenge, once thought a temple, you have found
A throne, where kings, our earthly gods, were
     crowned;
Where by their wondering subjects they were seen,
50 Joyed with their stature and their princely mien.
Our sovereign here above the rest might stand,
And here be chose again to rule the land.

32. *Ent*] Charleton's friend Sir George Ent (1604–89), an original FRS, defended Harvey in his *Apologia Pro Circuitione Sanguinis* (1641).

35–6. Charleton had written that the motion of light is not instantaneous (*Physiologia* 206); D.'s *unspent* echoes a notion found in Aristotle and repeated by Charleton, that light perpetuates itself in flight (*Works*).

39. *of*] *1663* second state; in *1663* first state.

41. *virtue*] power.

42. *perfect*] stressed on the first syllable, though a verb.

43–4. Howard praises Charleton's care, 'Which unto *Men* not only life can give, / But makes their *Monuments* themselves to live.'   *stones*] There may be a secondary reference to Charleton's treatise on the formation of stones in the body, *Spiritus Gorgonicus* (1650) (S. A. Golden, *Explicator* xxiv (1966) no. 53).

47–8. Cp. Howard: 'That great *Respects* not onely have been found / Where *Gods* were *Worship'd*, but where *Kings* were *Crown'd*.'

50. *Joyed with*] *1663* second state; Chose by *1663* first state.

52. In 1660 the Danes changed their elective monarchy into an hereditary one (E. R. Wasserman, *JEGP* lv (1956) 201–12).   *rule*] *1663* second state; sway *1663* first state.

These ruins sheltered once his sacred head,
Then, when from Worcester's fatal field he fled;
55   Watched by the genius of this royal place,
And mighty visions of the Danish race.
His refuge then was for a temple shown:
But, he restored, 'tis now become a throne.

53–4. Charleton recalls in his preface that Charles found shelter at Stonehenge after the Battle of Worcester in 1651.
55. *watched*] guarded (*OED* 10).   *royal*] *1663 second state*; Kingly *1663 first
state*.
56. *visions*] persons appearing in a dream (*OED* 1d).
57–8. Cp. Howard: 'once a *Temple* thought, now prov'd a *Throne*.'

11 Prologue and Epilogue to *The Wild Gallant*

Date and publication. *The Wild Gallant*, D.'s first play, was given its initial performance on 5 February 1663 at the Theatre Royal, Vere Street. Herringman published *The Wild Gallant: A Comedy* in 1669 (*TC* 19 May); reprinted 1669, 1684 and 1694.

Context. The play was not successful. Pepys saw it at court on 23 February: 'it was ill acted and the play so poor a thing as I never saw in my life almost, and so little answering the name, that from beginning to end I could not, nor can at this time, tell certainly which was the wild gallant. The King did not seem pleased at all, all the whole play, nor anybody else. . . . My Lady Castlemayne was all worth seeing tonight.' D. himself admits in his preface: 'I made the Town my Judges; and the greater part condemn'd it. . . . Yet it was receiv'd at Court; and was more than once the Divertisement of His Majesty, by His own Command' (*Works* viii 3). Perhaps this performance at court was the favour which D. owed to the Countess of Castlemaine (see 'To the Lady Castlemaine'). The play was revived later, perhaps in 1667, when it was entered in *SR* on 7 August: see 'Prologue and Epilogue to *The Wild Gallant* revived'.

Prologue to *The Wild Gallant,* as it was first acted

> Is it not strange to hear a poet say
> He comes to ask you how you like the play?
> You have not seen it yet! alas, 'tis true,
> But now your love and hatred judge, not you;
> 5 And cruel factions, bribed by interest, come

¶**11**. *Prologue.*
1–6. Though this courtship of the audience is natural in a first play, it foreshadows D.'s determination to please his customers throughout his dramatic career: it was an attitude which was criticized by Shadwell in his prefaces, Buckingham in *The Rehearsal* (1672) and Rochester in *An Allusion to Horace* (in MS, 1675–6): 'Canst thou be such a vain, mistaken thing / To wish thy works might make a playhouse ring / With the unthinking laughter and poor praise / Of fops and ladies, factious for thy plays?' (ll. 104–7).

> Not to weigh merit, but to give their doom.
> Our poet therefore, jealous of th' event,
> And, though much boldness takes, not confident,
> Has sent me whither you, fair ladies, too
> 10 Sometimes upon as small occasions go,
> And from this scheme, drawn for the hour and day,
> Bid me inquire the fortune of his play.

The curtain drawn discovers two astrologers; the Prologue is pre-sented to them.

> *First Astrologer reads.* A figure of the heavenly bodies in
> their several apartments, Feb. the 5th half an hour after
> 15 three after noon, from whence you are to judge the
> success of a new play called *The Wild Gallant.*
> *2 Ast.* Who must judge of it, we or these gentlemen?
> We'll not meddle with it, so tell your poet. Here are in
> this house the ablest mathematicians in Europe for his
> 20 purpose.
> They will resolve the question ere they part.
> *1. Ast.* Yet let us judge it by the rules of art.
> First Jupiter, the ascendant's lord disgraced,
> In the twelfth house, and near grim Saturn placed,

---

6. *doom*] verdict.

7. *jealous of th' event*] apprehensive about the outcome.

8. *takes*] pleases.

11. *scheme*] Like *figure* (l. 13) this is a horoscope showing the disposition of the planets and signs of the zodiac in the twelve houses of the heavens at the moment for which the horoscope is drawn. D. had a lifelong interest in astrology; cp. his letter to his sons in Rome in 1697: 'Towards the latter end of this Moneth, September, Charles will begin to recover his perfect health, according to his nativity, wch casting it my self, I am sure is true, & all things hetherto have happend accordingly to the very time that I predicted them' (*Letters* 93–4). On the numerous astrological references in D.'s work, see W. B. Gardner, *SP* xlvii (1950) 506–21; on their use here see F. C. Osenburg, *ELN* vii (1969) 35–9; on D.'s own horoscope see Simon Bentley and Paul Hammond, *Restoration* ix (1985) 56–60.

14–15. *half an hour after three*] Performances usually began in the middle of the afternoon; cp. 'But, when a Play's revived, you stay and dine, / And drink till three, and then come dropping in' (*Covent Garden Drolery* (1672) 83).

19. *mathematicians*] astrologers.

23–9. The lord of the ascendant is the planet which rules the ascending sign. Jupiter is a beneficent planet which is particularly associated with justice. It rules Sagittarius by day (l. 26) and Pisces by night; and is now disgraced because it is in the unfavourable twelfth house of the heavens, and near the

25   Denote short life unto the play: ——
        2. Ast.   —— Jove yet,
      In his apartment Sagittary, set
      Under his own roof, cannot take much wrong;
        1. Ast. Why then the life's not very short, nor long;
        2. Ast. The luck not very good, nor very ill,
30   *Pro.* That is to say, 'tis as 'tis taken still.
        1. Ast. But brother, Ptolemy the learnèd says
      'Tis the fifth house from whence we judge of plays.
      Venus the lady of that house I find
      Is peregrine; your play is ill designed:
35   It should have been but one continued song,
      Or at the least a dance of three hours long.
        2. Ast. But yet the greatest mischief does remain,
      The twelfth apartment bears the lord of Spain;
      Whence I conclude it is your author's lot
40   To be endangered by a Spanish plot.
        Pro. Our poet yet protection hopes from you,

---

maleficent planet Saturn. This combination of favourable and unfavourable influences foreshows indifferent success. This chart is actually impossible for 3.30 p.m. on 5 February 1663. The ascendant would have been Leo, which is not ruled by Jupiter. The chart could, however, apply to the early morning, e.g. to 3.30 a.m. D. may have made a mistake, or altered the nativity to provide more apt material (Simon Bentley, privately).

31. Ptolemy] the Alexandrian geographer and astronomer (*c.* AD 100–178) whose *Tetrabiblos* was the basic text of classical astrology.

32. fifth house] 'By this house we judge of . . . Playes . . . it's Consignificators are Leo and Venus, who doth joy in this house, in regard it's the house of Pleasure, Delight and Meriment' (William Lilly, *Christian Astrology* (1647) 53).

34. peregrine] situated in an indifferent sign, which neither prejudices nor increases her influence.

35–6. A glance at the vogue for more music and spectacle on the stage, as in Davenant's *The Siege of Rhodes*, revived by the Duke's Company in 1661.

38–40. Jupiter, the lord of Spain (Ptolemy II iii 62), is in the twelfth house, that of secret enemies and afflictions.

40. Spanish plot] Alludes to Sir Samuel Tuke's *The Adventures of Five Hours*, an adaptation of Antonio Coello's *Los Empeños de Seis Horas*, first produced by the Duke's Company at Lincoln's Inn Fields on 8 January 1663. It was very successful, having thirteen performances. For the wording of ll. 39–40 cp. Tuke's Prologue: 'You'l wonder much, if it should prove his Lot, / To take all *England* with a *Spanish* Plot'.

But bribes you not with anything that's new.
Nature is old which poets imitate,
And for wit, those that boast their own estate
45 Forget Fletcher and Ben before them went,
Their elder brothers, and that vastly spent:
So much 'twill hardly be repaired again,
Not though supplied with all the wealth of Spain.
This play is English, and the growth your own;
50 As such it yields to English plays alone.
He could have wished it better for your sakes,
But that in plays he finds you love mistakes:
Besides, he thought it was in vain to mend
What you are bound in honour to defend,
55 That English wit, howe'er despised by some,
Like English valour still may overcome.

Epilogue to *The Wild Gallant*, as it was first acted

The wild gallant has quite played out his game;
He's married now, and that will make him tame:
Or if you think marriage will not reclaim him,
The critics swear they'll damn him, but they'll tame
    him.
5 Yet though our poet's threatened most by these,
They are the only people he can please:
For he to humour them has shown today
That which they only like, a wretched play.
But though his play be ill, here have been shown
10 The greatest wits and beauties of the town:

44–7. Cp. *EDP* (1668): 'We acknowledge them our Fathers in wit, but they
have ruin'd their Estates themselves before they came to their childrens
hands' (*Works* xvii 73).
46. *elder brothers*] A punning reference to Beaumont and Fletcher's *The Elder
Brother* (1637), revived in 1660–1 by the King's Company.
52. *mistakes*] The plot of Tuke's play turns on misunderstandings.

And his occasion having brought you here,
You are too grateful to become severe.
There is not any person here so mean
But he may freely judge each act and scene;
15   But if you bid him choose his judges, then
He boldly names true English gentlemen;
For he ne'er thought a handsome garb or dress
So great a crime to make their judgement less:
And with these gallants he these ladies joins,
20   To judge that language their converse refines.
But if their censures should condemn his play,
Far from disputing, he does only pray
He may Leander's destiny obtain:
Now spare him, drown him when he comes again.

Epilogue.
23–4. Leander used to swim the Hellespont to see Hero; one night he was
drowned in a storm.

12 To the Lady Castlemaine

Date and publication. The poem was probably written and presented to Lady Castlemaine in 1663, when D.'s first play *The Wild Gallant* was performed at court, perhaps through her influence (see 'Prologue and Epilogue to *The Wild Gallant*' and *nn*). The MSS which say that the poem was occasioned by her help in getting the play printed (see note on the title) must be wrong, because the play was not printed until 1669, and these verses were known in London literary circles in 1664, when they are mentioned in *The Session of the Poets* (see *POAS* i 331; but that edition's dating of the *Session* to 1668 has been challenged by Gillian Brown in *RECTR* xiii (1974) 19–26, who argues convincingly for a date of 1664). The text in *EP* describes the occasion as 'Her incouraging his first Play'. The poem was first printed in John Bulteel's *A New Collection of Poems and Songs* (1674), and was circulating in MS in the early 1670s: it survives in BodL MSS Eng. Poet. e 4 (transcribed 1672; siglum: '*E*') and Top. Oxon. e 202 ('*T*'); BL MS Burney 390 ('*B*'); Nottingham UL MS Portland PwV 30 ('*P*'); and Society of Antiquaries MS 330 ('*A*'). It was subsequently printed in *EP* (1693) in a revised text. The two printed texts and the first four of the five MSS are collated and discussed by Paul Hammond in *PBSA* lxxviii (1984) 81–90. He argues that *1674* and the MSS preserve the text of the poem as it was first written, and that this original text can be reconstructed by following those readings where (i) *1674* and MSS agree against *1693*, or (ii) at least one witness from among *1674* and MSS agrees with *1693*. The best witness to the original text turns out to be *P* (*A*, not collated by Hammond, is close to *E*). Since the poem is an occasional piece which was originally made public in manuscript, this edition reconstructs the text which belongs to that occasion by following *P*, emending it at ll. 26, 32, 39, 43, 47, 48, 50 and 51, where other witnesses seem closer to the original text. The revisions which D. made for *1693* are recorded in the notes to ll. 6, 10, 35, 37–8, 40, 51, 52 and 55–8. There is an element of doubt about the original readings at ll. 47 and 51. D.'s revisions, made some thirty years after the poem was first written, generally smooth out awkward phrasing and remove some embarrassing hyperbole. The textual notes given here record only this edition's departures from *P*, and D.'s revisions in *1693* to the original text.

Context. Barbara Villiers (*c.* 1641–1709) was the daughter of the second Viscount Grandison, who died in 1643 of wounds received fighting for Charles I at the siege of Bristol. In 1659 she married Roger Palmer, who was created Earl of Castlemaine in 1661 in recognition of his wife's services to Charles II. She was the King's chief mistress from 1659 to 1670, and bore him five children. In 1670 she was created Duchess of Cleveland. She and D. were related by marriage: her uncle and aunt both married first cousins of Lady Elizabeth Howard, D.'s wife. Her power over the King was at its height in 1662–3, when she made him appoint her a Lady of the Queen's Bedchamber. She was the subject of numerous satirical verses.

Reception. The poem is alluded to in *The Session of the Poets* (in MS, 1664; printed in *POAS* i 331), and echoed by Oldham in 'A Letter from the Country' ((1678), *Poems* 430).

To the Lady Castlemaine

 As seamen shipwracked on some happy shore
 Discover wealth in lands unknown before,
 And what their art had laboured long in vain,
 By their misfortunes happily obtain;
5 So my much-envied Muse, by storms long tossed,
 Is cast upon your hospitable coast,
 And finds more favour by her ill success,
 Than she could hope for by her happiness.
 Once Cato's virtue did the gods oppose,
10 When they the victor, he the vanquished chose;
 But you have done what Cato could not do,
 To choose the vanquished, and restore him too.
 Let others still triumph, and gain their cause
 By their deserts, or by the world's applause;
15 Let merit crowns, and justice laurels give,
 But let me happy by your pity live.
 True poets empty fame and praise despise,
 Fame is the trumpet, but your smile the prize:
 You sit above and see vain men below
20 Contend for what you only can bestow;
 But those great actions others do by chance,
 Are, like your beauty, your inheritance:
 So great a soul, such sweetness joined in one,
 Could only spring from noble Grandison.
25 You, like the stars, not by reflection bright,

¶**12.** *Title. Ed.*; who got his play printed *added in P* (*and similar wording in A, B, E, T*); Upon Her incouraging his first Play *added in 1693.*
6. cast] thrown *1693* (D.'s revision, probably to avoid the awkward assonance with *coast*).
9–10. From Lucan: *victrix causa deis placuit, sed victa Catoni* ('the victorious cause pleased the gods, but the defeated one pleased Cato': *Pharsalia* i 128).
10. When] While *1693* (D.'s revision).
13. triumph] stressed on the second syllable.
19–20. Cp. 'Lucretius: The Beginning of the Second Book' ll. 7–15.

Are born to your own heaven, and your own light;
Like them are good, but from a nobler cause,
From your own knowledge, not from nature's laws.
Your power you never use, but for defence,
30   To guard your own, or others' innocence;
Your foes are such as they, not you, have made,
And virtue may repel, though not invade.
Such courage did the ancient heroes show,
Who, when they might prevent, would wait the blow,
35   With that assurance as they meant to say,
We will o'ercome, but scorn the safest way.
Well may I rest secure in your great fate,
And dare my stars to be unfortunate.
What further fear of danger can there be?
40   Beauty, that captives all things, sets me free.
Posterity will judge by my success
I had the Grecian poet's happiness,
Who, waiving plots, found out a better way:
Some god descended and preserved the play.
45   When first the triumphs of your sex were sung
By those old poets, beauty was but young,
And few admired her native red and white,
Till poets dressed them up to charm the sight;
So beauty took on trust, and did engage
50   For sums of praises till she came to age.

---

26. *and*] *1674, 1693; omitted in A, B, E, P, T.*
31. She had political enemies (she worked to undermine Clarendon), as well
as critics such as Pepys and Evelyn, who objected to her very public sexual
relationship with the King.
32. *though*] *1674, 1693; but A, B, E, P, T.*
34. *prevent*] anticipate.
35. *that*] such *1693* (D.'s revision).
37–8. Omitted in *1693* (D.'s revision).
39. *further*] *1674, 1693, B, E, T*; farther *A, P.*
40. *that*] which *1693* (D.'s revision).
42–4. The device of the *deus ex machina* was used particularly by Euripides.
42. *happiness*] fortunate skill (*OED* 3).
43. *Who*] *1674, 1693*; Which *A, E, P, T*; With *B.*
47. *her*] *1674*; their *A, B, E, P, T*; the *1693.*
48. *them*] *1693, A, B, E*; her *1674, P, T.*
49. *took*] charmed.   *engage*] pledge its credit.
50. *to*] *1693, A, B, E*; of *1674, T*; on *P.*

But this vast growing debt to poetry
You, Madam, justly have discharged to me,
When your applause and favour did infuse
New life to my condemned and dying Muse:
55 Which, that the world as well as you may see,
Let these rude verses your acquittance be:
Received in full this present day and year,
One sovereign smile from beauty's general heir.

51. *this vast growing*] *1674*; this vast *P, T*; your vast wondrous *A, B, E*; this long growing *1693* (D.'s revision).
52. *Madam, justly*] justly (Madam) *1693* (D.'s revision).
55–8. Omitted in *1693* (D.'s revision).
56. *rude*] rough.   *acquittance*] receipt for payment of a debt.

13 Prologue to *The Rival Ladies*

Date and publication. The date of the first performance is unknown, but it was probably late in 1663 or early in 1664, as the play appears to have been written in response to the success of Sir Samuel Tuke's *The Adventures of Five Hours.* For this dating, inferred from the normal interval between première and publication, see Milhous and Hume 380. *The Rival Ladies: A Tragi-Comedy* was published by Herringman in 1664 (*SR* 27 June; advertised in *The Newes* 3 November); reprinted 1669, 1675, 1693. The play was dedicated to Roger Boyle, Earl of Orrery. The printed play has no epilogue, but the copy of the Prologue in BodL MS Ashmole 36, 37 adds the following Epilogue (ff. 267^v–268^r):

Epilogue by the Doctor
'Tis true, what as a iest our Poet meant,
His little witt was in ye Prologue spent:
None left t' excuse my part, unles you would
Forbeare to damme it till t' were understood.
T'would go ill wth us, should you give o^r play
Halfe y^{ose} hard words y^{at} I gave you to day.
 The Dcōrs man comes in & brings in an Urinall
 wth black water in it, & whispers ye Dcōr in his Eare.
Whilst wee in vaine excuses wast our breath
The Poet & his Muse are sick to death;
Hees past my cure: as his condicon stands,
I leave him to y^{ese} abler Doctors hands.

This may have been used in performance but dropped for publication; see R. G. Ham, *RES* xiii (1937) 76–80. Its authorship is uncertain.

Context. The play was staged by the King's Company at the Theatre Royal, Bridges Street, and was seen by Pepys on 4 August 1664, 'a very innocent and most pretty witty play'.

Prologue to *The Rival Ladies*

'Tis much desired you judges of the town
Would pass a vote to put all prologues down;
For who can show me, since they first were writ,
They e'er converted one hard-hearted wit?
5 Yet the world's mended well; in former days
Good prologues were as scarce as now good plays:
For the reforming poets of our age
In this first charge spend their poetic rage;

Expect no more when once the prologue's done—
10 The wit is ended ere the play's begun.
You now have habits, dances, scenes and rhymes,
High language often, ay, and sense sometimes;
As for a clear contrivance, doubt it not—
They blow out candles to give light to the plot;
15 And for surprise, two bloody-minded men
Fight till they die, then rise and dance again.
Such deep intrigues you're welcome to this day,
But blame yourselves, not him who writ the play:
Though his plot's dull as can be well desired,
20 Wit stiff as any you have e'er admired,
He's bound to please, not to write well; and knows
There is a mode in plays as well as clothes.

¶**13**. *11. habits*] The use of elaborate costumes is documented chiefly for the Duke's Company: they used the coronation robes of the King and Duke of York in *Love and Honour* (1661) and *Henry V* (1664). Their *Henry VIII* (1663) likewise used spectacular costumes.   *dances*] These soon became an important element in the entertainment; Pepys records his enjoyment of the dances in *A Midsummer Night's Dream* (29 September 1662), *The Villain* (18 October 1662) and *The Humorous Lieutenant* (8 May 1663).   *scenes*] Davenant made great use of movable scenery and machines in his theatre in Lincoln's Inn Fields. Killigrew's rival King's Company followed suit when they moved into the Theatre Royal in Drury Lane in 1663; their lavish productions included *The Indian Queen*.   *rhymes*] D. defends rhyme as superior to blank verse in the Dedication of *The Rival Ladies* (*Works* viii 98–101). Its use in drama was one of the points debated between D. and Sir Robert Howard (see 'To Sir Robert Howard', headnote).

12. High language] Contemporary dramatic language was often inflated, and was regularly derided by critics, e.g. in Buckingham's *The Rehearsal* (1672); in the controversy over Settle's *The Empress of Morocco* (1673–4); and in Rochester's *Timon* (written 1674) ll. 113–50.

14. The device of reducing stage illumination to denote darkness in scenes of mistake and intrigue was common (e.g. in D.'s *An Evening's Love* (1671) Act V), and is ridiculed by Shadwell in the inset play in *A True Widow* (1679) Act IV.

15–16. In *The Rehearsal* two groups of soldiers kill one another, and Bayes (a caricature of D.) says: 'Now here's an odd surprize: all these dead men you shall see rise up presently, at a certain Note that I have made, in *Effaut flat*, and fall a Dancing' (II v 7–9).

Therefore kind judges——
A second Prologue enters.
2.   ——Hold; would you admit
For judges all you see within the pit?
25   1. Whom would he then except, or on what score?
2. All who, like him, have writ ill plays before,
For they, like thieves condemned, are hangmen made
To execute the members of their trade;
All that are writing now he would disown,
30   But then he must except ev'n all the town;
All choleric, losing gamesters, who in spite
Will damn today because they lost last night;
All servants whom their mistress' scorn upbraids,
All maudlin lovers, and all slighted maids;
35   All who are out of humour, or severe;
All that want wit, or hope to find it here.

23–36. This is the first of D.'s recurrent expressions of contempt for the taste and judgement of his audiences.

23. In the Epilogue to Tuke's *Adventures* there is an interruption by a second speaker, followed by a discussion as to which members of the audience are competent critics.

24. pit] The Restoration theatre was commonly divided socially: the upper gallery for servants; the boxes for 'quality'; the middle gallery for citizens' wives and daughters; and the pit, 'where sit the *Judges, Wits* and *Censurers*, or rather the *Censurers without either Wit or Judgment.* These are the *Bully-Judges,* that *damn and sink the Play at a venture* . . . in common with these sit the *Squires, Sharpers, Beaus, Bullies* and *Whores*, and here and there an extràvagant *Male* and *Female Cit*' ([Edmund Stacy], *The Country Gentleman's Vade Mecum* (1699) 39; see further Harold Love, *YES* x (1980) 21–44); cp. 'Prologue to *Marriage A-la-Mode*' l. 36n; 'Prologue for the Women' ll. 11–17.

34. slighted maids] Alluding to Sir Robert Stapylton's comedy *The Slighted Maid*, performed by the Duke's Company in February–May 1663. In the Preface to *Troilus and Cressida* (1679) D. says of this play that 'there is no Scene in the first Act, which might not by as good reason be in the fifth' (*Works* xiii 230).

36. want] lack.

14 Prologue, Epilogue and Songs from *The Indian Queen*

Date and publication. The play's first recorded performance was at court on 25 January 1664, given by the King's Company; in late January and early February there were successful public performances at the Theatre Royal, Bridges Street. *The Indian-Queen, A Tragedy* was first printed in Sir Robert Howard's *Four New Plays*, published by Herringman in 1665 (*SR* 4 February 1664; imprimatur 7 March 1665); reprinted in his *Five New Plays* (1692). An operatic version, with music by Henry and Daniel Purcell, was produced in 1695 (see Price, *Henry Purcell* 125–43); this had additional songs, of uncertain authorship, which were printed in *The Songs in the Indian Queen* (1695) (see *Works* viii 325–30). Song I was printed with Purcell's music in *Deliciae Musicae* (1696) and *Orpheus Britannicus* (1698).

Authorship. The play was probably a collaboration between D. and Howard (for whom see 'To Sir Robert Howard'). Though it was printed as Howard's, D. says in a prefatory note to *The Indian Emperor* that part of the previous play was written by him (*Works* ix 27). J. H. Smith in *SP* li (1954) 54–74 and *Works* viii 283 suppose extensive collaboration between D. and Howard; H. J. Oliver in *Sir Robert Howard* (1963) 63–7 assigns the play wholly to Howard, while McFadden 49 awards it wholly to D. Winn 147–9 assumes a close collaboration between the two, but assigns the songs to D. (*When Beauty* 178). Actual evidence is lacking.

Prologue

As the music plays a soft air, the curtain rises softly, and discovers an Indian boy and girl sleeping under two plantain trees; and when the curtain is almost up, the music turns into a tune expressing an alarm, at which the boy wakes and speaks.

> *Boy.* Wake, wake, Quevira; our soft rest must cease,
> And fly together with our country's peace;
> No more must we sleep under plantain shade,
> Which neither heat could pierce, nor cold invade;
> 5   Where bounteous nature never feels decay,

¶**14**. *Prologue.*
s.d. It was unusual for a prologue to be presented from the main stage, rather than in front of the curtain. For the use of a 'curtain tune' see Price, *Music in the Restoration Theatre* 55–6.

And opening buds drive falling fruits away.
Que. Why should men quarrel here, where all possess
As much as they can hope for by success?
None can have most, where nature is so kind
10   As to exceed man's use, though not his mind.
Boy. By ancient prophecies we have been told
Our world shall be subdued by one more old;
And see, that world already's hither come.
Que. If these be they, we welcome then our doom:
15   Their looks are such, that mercy flows from thence,
More gentle than our native innocence.
Boy. Why should we then fear these are enemies,
That rather seem to us like deities?
Que. By their protection let us beg to live;
20   They came not here to conquer, but forgive.
If so, your goodness may your power express,
And we shall judge both best by our success.

---

6. The simultaneous presence of different stages of growth was a standard
feature of the earthly paradise; cp. Tasso: 'ere their fruit drop off, the blos-
some comes, / This springs, that fals, that ripeneth, and this blomes' (*Gerusalemme Liberata*, tr. Fairfax (1600) xvi 10); and cp. Spenser, *FQ* III vi 42.

7–10. Cp. Montaigne, *Des Cannibales*: 'Ils ne sont pas en debat de la conqueste
de nouvelles terres, car ils jouyssent encore de cette uberté naturelle qui les
fournit sans travail et sans peine de toutes choses necessaires, en telle abon-
dance qu' ils n'ont que faire d' agrandir leurs limites. Ils sont encore en cet
heureux point, de ne desirer qu' autant que leurs necessitez naturelles leur
ordonnent; tout ce qui est au delà est superflu pour eux' (208).

11. ancient prophecies] Davenant's *The Cruelty of the Spaniards in Peru* (1658)
mentions the prophecy that 'Bearded People should come from the Sea to
destroy them' (7–8).

16. native innocence] Cp. 'To Dr Charleton' l. 13*n*.

17–18. The Indians initially thought the Spaniards to be gods; cp. Davenant:
'wonder doth engender fear: / And from our fear does adoration rise: / Else
why do we encline / To think them Pow'rs divine' (17–18).

Epilogue to *The Indian Queen*

Spoken by Montezuma

You see what shifts we are enforced to try
To help out wit with some variety;
Shows may be found that never yet were seen,
'Tis hard to find such wit as ne'er has been:
5   You have seen all that this old world could do,
We therefore try the fortune of the new,
And hope it is below your aim to hit
At untaught nature with your practised wit:
Our naked Indians then, when wits appear,
10   Would as soon choose to have the Spaniards here.
'Tis true, y' have marks enough, the plot, the show,
The poet's scenes, nay more, the painter's too;
If all this fail, considering the cost,
'Tis a true voyage to the Indies lost:
15   But if you smile on all, then these designs,
Like the imperfect treasure of our minds,
'Twill pass for current wheresoe'er they go,
When to your bounteous hands their stamps they owe.

Epilogue.
1. shifts] desperate stratagems.
11. marks] targets.
12–14. The play was 'so beautified with rich Scenes as the like had never ben seene here as happly (except rarely any where else) on a mercenarie *Theater*' (Evelyn, *Diary*, 5 February 1664). Pepys heard that 'for show, they say, [it] exceeds *Henry the 8th*' (27 January). For the fashion for 'shows' cp. *The Rehearsal*, where Bayes says: 'NOW, Gentlemen, I will be bold to say, I'l shew you the greatest Scene that ever *England* saw: I mean not for words, for those I do not value; but for state, shew, and magnificence. In fine I'll justifie it to be as grand to the eye every whit, I gad, as that great Scene in Harry the Eight, and grander too' (V i 1–6).
17. current] legal tender, acceptable currency.
18. stamps] designs impressed on coins.

Songs

I

You twice ten hundred deities,
To whom we daily sacrifice;
You powers that dwell with Fate below,
And see what men are doomed to do,
5   Where elements in discord dwell;
Thou god of sleep arise, and tell
Great Zempoalla what strange fate
Must on her dismal vision wait.

By the croaking of the toad,
10   In their caves that make abode,
Earthy dun that pants for breath,
With her swelled sides full of death;
By the crested adders' pride
That along the cliffs do glide;
15   By thy visage fierce and black,
By the death's-head on thy back;
By the twisted serpents placed
For a girdle round thy waist;
By the hearts of gold that deck
20   Thy breast, thy shoulders and thy neck;
From thy sleepy mansion rise,
And open thy unwilling eyes,
While bubbling springs their music keep,
That use to lull thee in thy sleep.
God of dreams rises.

Song I. From Act III Scene ii: Ismeron invokes the God of Dreams to discover the significance of the Empress Zempoalla's dream.
1. 'The Gods of *Mexico* were two thousand in number' (*Purchas his Pilgrimes* (1625) iii 1134).
11. dun] toad.
16–20. 'The Images had for a girdle great Snakes of gold, and for Collars and Chaines about their necks, ten hearts of men made of gold . . . and in their necks death painted' (*Purchas* iii 1134).

II

Supposed sung by aerial spirits

Poor mortals that are clogged with earth below
    Sink under love and care,
    While we that dwell in air
Such heavy passions never know.
5   Why then should mortals be
    Unwilling to be free
    From blood, that sullen cloud
    Which shining souls does shroud?
    Then they'll show bright,
10   And like us light,
When leaving bodies with their care,
    They slide to us and air.

III

You to whom victory we owe,
    Whose glories rise
    By sacrifice,
And from our Fates below;
5   Never did yet your altars shine
Feasted with blood so near divine;
    Princes to whom we bow,
    As they to you,
These you can ravish from a throne,
10 And by their loss of power declare your own.

Song II. In the same scene.
7. *cloud*] Perhaps both (i) the modern sense; and (ii) a variant form of *clod*, an earthy mass, often used of the human body as the vehicle of the soul (*OED* clod 1, 2, 4; cloud 2).
Song III. From Act V Scene i: sung by the priest as he prepares to sacrifice the Inca, his daughter Orazia, and his general Montezuma, who have been defeated in war.

15 Prologue, Epilogue and Songs from *The Indian Emperor*

Date and publication. The play was probably first performed in February or March 1665 (Milhous and Hume 381, against *LS* and *Works* ix 293, which suggest April); see 'Epilogue' l. 20*n*. *The Indian Emperour, or, The Conquest of Mexico by the Spaniards* was entered by Herringman in *SR* on 26 May 1665, but publication was delayed, no doubt by the plague and the Fire of London. It was eventually published in 1667: the Dedication to the Duchess of Monmouth is dated 12 October 1667, and Pepys bought it 'newly printed' on 28 October. The second edition (1668) was revised by D.; three more editions followed in 1670, and the play was reprinted in 1681, 1686, 1692, 1694 and 1696 (three times). For the complex textual history of these editions see the work by Fredson Bowers and others summarized in *Works* ix 381–2. Purcell's setting for the first song was printed in *The Banquet of Musick* (1692), *A Collection of Songs . . . by Mr Henry Purcell* (1696) and *Orpheus Britannicus* (1698); see Curtis Price, *Henry Purcell* 40–4. Pelham Humphrey's setting for Song II was printed in *Choice Ayres, Songs, & Dialogues* (1675, reprinted 1676; facsimile in Day 7–8). The words of the song were printed in R.V., *New Court-Songs, and Poems* (1672; siglum: '*NCS*'), *Methinks the Poor Town has been troubled too long* (1673, reprinted 1673; '*MPT*') and *The Wits Academy* (1677; '*WA*'); they are also found in BodL MS Rawl. Poet. 65. These three miscellanies and the MS contain variant readings which probably derive from changes made in the playhouse; variants in the text set by Humphrey were probably introduced by the composer to suit his musical ideas. The more significant variants are recorded in the notes.

Context. The play was staged by the King's Company at the Theatre Royal, Bridges Street. It is not known how popular it was before the theatres were closed on 5 June 1665 because of the plague, but it reopened in January 1667 and became one of D.'s most successful plays. Purcell composed music for a revival in 1691. It is a sequel to *The Indian Queen*.

Prologue

Almighty critics! whom our Indians here
Worship, just as they do the devil, for fear;
In reverence to your power I come this day
To give you timely warning of our play.

5 The scenes are old, the habits are the same
   We wore last year, before the Spaniards came.
   Our prologue th' old cast too——
   For to observe the new, it should at least
   Be spoke by some ingenious bird or beast.
10 Now if you stay, the blood that shall be shed
   From this poor play be all upon your head.
   We neither promise you one dance, or show;
   Then plot and language, they are wanting too.
   But you, kind wits, will those light faults excuse:
15 Those are the common frailties of the Muse,
   Which who observes, he buys his place too dear,
   For 'tis your business to be cozened here.
   These wretched spies of wit must then confess
   They take more pains to please themselves the less.
20 Grant us such judges, Phoebus, we request,
   As still mistake themselves into a jest;
   Such easy judges, that our poet may
   Himself admire the fortune of his play,
   And arrogantly, as his fellows do,
25 Think he writes well because he pleases you.
   This he conceives not hard to bring about
   If all of you would join to help him out:
   Would each man take but what he understands,
   And leave the rest upon the poet's hands.

¶15. *Prologue.*

5–6. *The Indian Emperor* reused some of the lavish settings and costumes from
The Indian Queen, which was set in the period before the Spanish conquest.

7–9. *1667; omitted in 1668–96* (probably D.'s revision). These lines appear to
refer to animal prologues, though the recorded vogue for them is rather later:
the most notable example was the Epilogue to Thomas Scott's *The Unhappy
Kindness* (1697) spoken by Joseph Haines 'in the Habit of a Horse Officer,
mounted on an Ass' (*LS* 463).

16. *place*] i.e. seat in the theatre.

17. *cozened*] cheated.

20. In the Restoration there were various versions current of the *Session of the
Poets*, in which contemporary writers appear before Apollo to claim the bays
(for one *c.* 1664 see *POAS* i 327–37).

Epilogue

By a Mercury

To all and singular in this full meeting,
Ladies and gallants, Phoebus sends me greeting.
To all his sons by whate'er title known,
Whether of court, of coffee house or town;
5   From his most mighty sons, whose confidence
Is placed in lofty sound and humble sense,
Ev'n to his little infants of the time
That write new songs, and trust in tune and rhyme.
Be 't known that Phoebus (being daily grieved
10   To see good plays condemned, and bad received)
Ordains your judgement upon every cause
Henceforth be limited by wholesome laws.
He first thinks fit no sonneteer advance
His censure farther than the song or dance.
15   Your wit burlesque may one step higher climb,
And in his sphere may judge all doggerel rhyme;

Epilogue.
6. Cp. 'Prologue to *The Rival Ladies*' l. 12*n*.
8. *That*] 1667; *Who* 1668–96 (probably D.'s revision).
12. *wholesome*] beneficial, salutary.
13. *sonneteer*] This is the *OED*'s first example. 'Sonnet' was applied at this time to any short verses and songs, not just the fourteen-line poem.
15. *burlesque*] D.'s first use of the word, which seems to have established itself slowly in England; it was used loosely at first, and then acquired a more precise meaning. In Randle Cotgrave's *A Dictionarie of the French and English Tongues* (1611) it is defined as 'jeasting . . . mocking, flouting', and in Thomas Blount's *Glossographia* (1656) as 'drolish, merry, pleasant'. Burlesque poetry, which mocked heroic poetry, was popular in Italy and France, a notable example being Paul Scarron's *Le Virgile Travesty en Vers Burlesques* (1648–53), imitated in English by Charles Cotton as *Scarronides* (1664). The Prologue to *The Knight of the Burning Pestle* explains the word carefully: 'our *Fletchers* wit, / Has here burlesqu'd all he himself had writ. / Burlesqu'd, that is has turn'd to ridicule, / As one would say, has wisely play'd the fool' (*Covent Garden Drolery* (1672) 78). Some succeeding lines suggest that the word was also applied to personal abuse: 'Not only every wit, Lampoons his brother, / But men are all burlosque [*sic*] to one another'. For further definitions and discussions see D.'s 'An Account of the Ensuing Poem' (prefixed to *AM*) ll. 272–8; *A Description of the Academy of the Athenian Virtuosi* (1673)

All proves, and moves, and loves, and honours too,
All that appears high sense, and scarce is low.
As for the coffee-wits he says not much,
20 Their proper business is to damn the Dutch:
For the great dons of wit——
Phoebus gives them full privilege alone
To damn all others, and cry up their own.
Last, for the ladies, 'tis Apollo's will
25 They should have power to save, but not to kill:
For Love and he long since have thought it fit
Wit live by beauty, beauty reign by wit.

Songs

I

Kalib ascends all in white in the shape of a woman and sings:

I looked and saw within the book of Fate,
    Where many days did lour,
    When lo one happy hour
Leaped up, and smiled to save thy sinking state;
5   A day shall come when in thy power
      Thy cruel foes shall be;
      Then shall thy land be free,
      And thou in peace shall reign:
    But take, O take that opportunity,
10 Which once refused will never come again.

34; Davenant's *The Play-house to be Lett* in *The Works of Sr William D'avenant* (1673) 75–6; and *The Critical Works of Thomas Rymer*, edited by Curt A. Zimansky (1956) 4, 89.

17. proves] seventeenth-century spelling of *proofs*: results, issues (*OED* 7).

20. The Second Dutch War began on 22 February 1665.

Song I. From Act II Scene i. Montezuma seeks to know the outcome of the war; the high priest summons up the spirit Kalib, who sings this song.

8. shall] *1667*; shalt *1668* (possibly D.'s revision).

II

A pleasant grotto discovered: in it a fountain spouting; round about it
Vasquez, Pizarro and other Spaniards lying carelessly unarmed,
and by them many Indian women, one of which sings the following
song.

    Ah fading joy, how quickly art thou past!
       Yet we thy ruin haste;
    As if the cares of human life were few
       We seek out new;
5 And follow Fate that does too fast pursue.

    See how on every bough the birds express
      In their sweet notes their happiness:
      They all enjoy and nothing spare,
    But on their mother nature lay their care.
10 Why then should man, the lord of all below,
      Such troubles choose to know
    As none of all his subjects undergo?

    Hark, hark, the waters fall, fall, fall;
      And with a murmuring sound
15   Dash, dash upon the ground,
      To gentle slumbers call.

Song II. From Act IV Scene iii.
2. And what too soon would die / Help to destroy. *added after this line in NCS,*
MPT, WA and MS (probably a playhouse variant; used in Humphrey's
setting).
5. In vain doth Natures bounteous hand supply / What peevish mortals to
themselves deny. *added after this line in NCS, MPT, WA and after l. 12 in MS*
(probably a playhouse variant; used in Humphrey's setting).   *follow Fate*]
draw fate on *MS* (probably a playhouse variant).   *that does*] *1667* (*also*
NCS, MPT, WA, substantially); which would *1668* (probably D.'s revision).
This line was criticized by R.F. in *A Letter from a Gentleman to the Honourable*
Ed. Howard Esq. (1668); D. replied in the Preface to the second edition of
Tyrannic Love (1672; *Works* x 113) saying that the image was borrowed from
Virgil, *Aen.* xi 695: *eludit gyro interior sequiturque sequentem* ('[Camilla] wheels
into an inner ring and pursues the pursuer'). Nevertheless, the textual variants suggest that both D. and others may have tinkered with this line in order
to avert criticism.
8. Not anxious how to get, or spare *NCS, MPT, WA* (probably a playhouse
variant; used in Humphrey's setting).
13–16. The verbal repetitions may imitate those in the song 'Slow, slow,
fresh fount' from Jonson's *Cynthia's Revels* I ii 65–75 (David Hopkins, privately).

16 Prologue and Epilogue to *The Wild Gallant* revived

Date and publication. There is no record of the revival, but the topical references in the Epilogue (ll. 39–40n, 44n, 47n) point to a date in December 1666. (Danchin suggests April 1667 and Winn 183 suggests May, after the success of *Secret Love*.) After the Fire of London public theatrical performances were resumed on 29 November 1666 (*LS*). The entry of the play in *SR* on 7 August 1667 also suggests that the play may have been staged in its revised form some months earlier. The present Prologue and Epilogue were first printed with the play: for details of its publication see the headnote to 'Prologue and Epilogue to *The Wild Gallant*'.

Prologue to *The Wild Gallant* revived

As some raw squire, by tender mother bred,
Till one and twenty keeps his maidenhead
(Pleased with some sport which he alone does find,
And thinks a secret to all human kind),
5   Till mightily in love, yet half afraid,
He first attempts the gentle dairymaid;
Succeeding there, and led by the renown
Of Whetstones Park, he comes at length to town,
Where entered by some school-fellow or friend
10 He grows to break glass-windows in the end;
His valour too, which with the watch began,
Proceeds to duel, and he kills his man.

¶**16.** *Prologue.* For the use of sexual imagery cp. 'Prologue to *An Evening's Love*' and n.
8. Whetstones Park] A lane between Holborn and Lincoln's Inn Fields which was a well-known resort of prostitutes (see Wycherley, *Love in a Wood* (1672) I ii 213; Pepys 16 November 1668; D.'s 'Ovid's Elegies, Book II: Elegy the Nineteenth' l. 31).
10–12. Such exploits were commonly attributed to the rakes; cp. Rochester: 'I'll tell of whores attacked, their lords at home; / Bawds' quarters beaten up, and fortress won; / Windows demolished, watches overcome;' (*The Disabled Debauchee* (*c.* 1675) ll. 33–5).

By such degrees, while knowledge he did want,
Our unfledged author writ a *Wild Gallant*.
15 He thought him monstrous lewd, I'll lay my life,
Because suspected with his landlord's wife;
But since his knowledge of the town began,
He thinks him now a very civil man.
And, much ashamed of what he was before,
20 Has fairly played him at three wenches more.
'Tis some amends his frailties to confess;
Pray pardon him his want of wickedness:
He's towardly, and will come on apace;
His frank confession shows he has some grace.
25 You balked him when he was a young beginner,
And almost spoiled a very hopeful sinner:
But if once more you slight his weak endeavour,
For aught I know, he may turn tail for ever.

Epilogue to *The Wild Gallant* revived

Of all dramatic writing, comic wit,
As 'tis the best, so 'tis most hard to hit.
For it lies all in level to the eye,
Where all may judge, and each defect may spy.
5 Humour is that which every day we meet,
And therefore known as every public street,
In which, if e'er the poet go astray
You all can point, 'twas there he lost his way.
But what's so common to make pleasant too
10 Is more than any wit can always do:

13. want] lack.
15–18. For Pepys's opinion of the original play see headnote to 'Prologue and
Epilogue to *The Wild Gallant*'.
20. This indicates that the scene in Act IV between Loveby (the 'wild gallant'), Lady Du Lake and two prostitutes was added by D. in his revision.
23. towardly] promising, apt to learn.

Epilogue.
5. humour] characteristics of human behaviour.

For 'tis, like Turks, with hen and rice to treat,
To make regalios out of common meat.
But in your diet you grow savages:
Nothing but human flesh your taste can please;
15 And as their feasts with slaughtered slaves began,
So you at each new play must have a man.
Hither you come, as to see prizes fought:
If no blood's drawn, you cry the prize is nought.
But fools grow wary now, and when they see
20 A poet eyeing round the company,
Straight each man for himself begins to doubt;
They shrink like seamen when a press comes out.
Few of 'em will be found for public use,
Except you charge an oaf upon each house,
25 Like the trained bands, and every man engage
For a sufficient fool to serve the stage;
And when with much ado you get him there,
Where he in all his glory should appear,
Your poets make him such rare things to say,
30 That he's more wit than any man i' th' play;
But of so ill a mingle with the rest,
As when a parrot's taught to break a jest.
Thus aiming to be fine, they make a show
As tawdry squires in country churches do.

11. 'The general *Food* of the *Turks*, both in City and Camp, is *Rice* and *Water*, Their most dainty addition being but a *Hen*, or some small lump of *Flesh*' (Francis Osborne, *Politicall Reflections upon the Government of the Turks* (1656) 62).

12. regalios] presents of choice food or drink.

17. prizes fought] prize fighting, which was sometimes staged in theatres on days when no plays were performed (Winn 184).

19–21. D. was censured for bringing real characters onto the stage in *The Friendly Vindication of Mr. Dryden* (1673), but it is not clear that he ever did so. Cp. 'Prologue to *Sir Martin Mar-all*'.

21. doubt] be apprehensive.

22. press] press gang.

24–6. i.e. exact a levy requiring each house to provide one fool for ridicule, either a man of the house, or an acceptable substitute.

25. trained bands] trained companies of citizen soldiers.

29. rare] remarkably fine (*OED* 6).

32. break a jest] crack a joke.

35 Things well considered, 'tis so hard to make
    A comedy which should the knowing take,
    That our dull poet, in despair to please,
    Does humbly beg by me his writ of ease.
    'Tis a land tax which he's too poor to pay:
40 You, therefore, must some other impost lay.
    Would you but change for serious plot and verse
    This motley garniture of fool and farce,
    Nor scorn a mode because 'tis taught at home,
    Which does, like vests, our gravity become;
45 Our poet yields you should this play refuse,
    As tradesmen, by the change of fashions, lose
    With some content their fripperies of France,
    In hope it may their staple trade advance.

36. take] please.

38. writ of ease] certificate of discharge from employment. Cp. 'Epilogue to *All for Love*' l. 19. Samuel Tuke in his Prologue to *The Adventures of Five Hours* (1663) says that if his plot fail, 'You'll give your Modern Poet his Writ of Ease' (l. 26).

39–40. In order to pay for the war against the Dutch, the House of Commons agreed on 12 October 1666 to raise £1,800,000. A debate lasted until 8 November on whether to raise the money by a sale of the chimney tax, by excise (the *impost* of l. 40) or by a land tax. The last two were the chief possibilities, with the court party favouring excise and the presbyterians land tax (*The Diary of John Milward*, edited by Caroline Robbins (1938) 16 and 31 October); see also Marvell, *Last Instructions to a Painter* ll. 329–32; *POAS* i 116. It was agreed on 8 November to raise the money through a poll tax and land tax; debate on the former lasted until 14 January 1667, and the latter was agreed on 19 January.

42. garniture] ornament.

44. vests] In October 1666 the King set a new fashion by abandoning the French style of dress in favour of the vest. Pepys describes it as 'a long Cassocke close to the body, of black cloth and pinked with white silk under it, and a coat over it, and the legs ruffled with black riband like a pigeon's leg—and upon the whole, I wish the King may keep it, for it is a very fine and handsome garment' (15 October; cp. Evelyn, *Diary* 18 October; E. S. de Beer, *JWCI* ii (1939) 105–15). The French fashion was resumed around 1670.

47. The King's proclamation of 10 November 1666 prohibited all imports of French goods with effect from 1 December 1666.

17 Prologue and Song from *Secret Love*

Date and publication. The play was probably first performed in late January 1667 (Arthur H. Scouten, *Restoration* ix (1985) 9–11). It was composed in D.'s period of residence at the house of his father-in-law at Charlton, Wiltshire, during the plague and Fire of London (mid-1665 to late 1666). In the letter to Sir Robert Howard dated 10 November 1666 prefacing *AM*, D. mentions that he has recently asked Howard to read a play of his, which is probably *Secret Love*. It was first performed by the King's Company at the Theatre Royal, Bridges Street. Pepys saw it on 2 March: 'a new play of Dryden's mightily commended for the regularity of it and the strain and wit; and the truth is, there is a comical part done by Nell, which is Florimell, that I never can hope ever to see the like done again by man or woman. The King and Duke of York was at the play; but so great performance of a comical part was never, I believe, in the world before as Nell does this, both as a mad girle and then, most and best of all, when she comes in like a young gallant; and hath the motions and carriage of a spark the most that ever I saw any man have. It makes me, I confess, admire her.' Herringman entered the play in *SR* on 7 August 1667, and published *Secret-Love, or the Maiden-Queen* in 1668; Pepys bought it 'newly printed' on 18 January. It was reprinted in 1669 (twice), 1679, 1691 and 1698. The song was printed in *The New Academy of Complements* (1671). The epilogue was by an anonymous 'person of honour'. For a prologue and epilogue from a later revival see 'Prologue and Epilogue to *Secret Love*, Spoken by the Women'.

Prologue

I

He who writ this, not without pains and thought,
From French and English theatres has brought
Th' exactest rules by which a play is wrought:

¶**17**. *Prologue.*
1–6. The other known products of D.'s Charlton period are *AM* and *EDP*. *Secret Love* is evidently the outcome of D.'s thinking about drama which takes theoretical form in *EDP*, where he discusses the comparative qualities of the English and French stages, the unities of time, place and action, and the work of his English precursors, Shakespeare, Jonson and Fletcher. In the Preface to *Secret Love* D. repeats his claim to regularity: 'it is regular, according to the strictest of Dramatick Laws, but that . . . is a commendation which many of our Poets now despise, and a beauty which our common Audiences

II

The unities of action, place and time,
5   The scenes unbroken, and a mingled chime
Of Jonson's humour, with Corneille's rhyme.

III

But while dead colours he with care did lay,
He fears his wit or plot he did not weigh,
Which are the living beauties of a play.

IV

10   Plays are like towns, which howe'er fortified
By engineers, have still some weaker side
By the o'erseen defendant unespied:

V

And with that art you make approaches now;
Such skilful fury in assaults you show,
15   That every poet without shame may bow.

do not easily discern' (*Works* ix 115). See also 'Epilogue to *An Evening's Love*'
ll. 17–22. Buckingham mocked D.'s 'rules' in *The Rehearsal* (1672) I i 94–141.
The author of *The Censure of the Rota* (1673) accused D. of boasting in this
Prologue, but D. was defended by Charles Blount in *Mr. Dreyden Vindicated*
(1673).

5. *scenes unbroken*] There is continuity of place and characters from one scene
to the next, following the French principle of *la liaison des scènes*. Crites
discusses this in *EDP* (*Works* xvii 18–19).

6. *Corneille's*] Apparently trisyllabic; the pronunciation was problematic for
Restoration Englishmen: cp. the trisyllabic Latinization in 'And there was
wrought in great *Corneliu's* Loom' (*Covent Garden Drolery* (1672) 80). Pierre
Corneille (1606–84) was an important influence on *EDP* (see *Works* xvii 337–
9).

7–9. In his Preface to *Secret Love* D. says: 'with all that symmetry of parts, it
may want an air and spirit (which consists in the writing) to set it off' (*Works*
ix 115).

7. *dead colours*] a technical term for preparatory layers of colour in a painting
(*OED*).

10–15. This image comes from Mme de Scudéry's Preface to *Ibrahim, ou
L'Illustre Bassa* (1641): 'mais quelque deffence que i'aye employée, ie sçay
qu'il est des ouurages de cette nature, comme d'une Place de guerre: où
quelque soin qu'ait apporté l'Ingenieur à la fortifier, il se trouue tousiours
quelque endroit foible, où il n'a point songé, & par où on l'attaque' (sig. o
iij'). Langbaine 169 noted this borrowing as an example of D.'s habit of

VI

Ours therefore humbly would attend your doom,
If soldier-like he may have terms to come
With flying colours, and with beat of drum.
The Prologue goes out, and stays while a tune is played, after which
he returns again.

Second Prologue

     I had forgot one half, I do protest,
20   And now am sent again to speak the rest.
     He bows to every great and noble wit, ⎫
     But to the little hectors of the pit   ⎬
     Our poet's sturdy, and will not submit. ⎭
     He'll be beforehand with 'em, and not stay
25   To see each peevish critic stab his play:
     Each puny censor, who his skill to boast,
     Is cheaply witty on the poet's cost.
     No critic's verdict should, of right, stand good,
     They are excepted all as men of blood:
30   And the same law should shield him from their fury

'transversing', which Bayes expounds in *The Rehearsal* (1672): 'Sir, my first
Rule is the Rule of Transversion . . . I take a book in my hand, either at home
or elsewhere, for that's all one, if there be any Wit in't, as there is no book but
has some, I Transverse it; that is, if it be Prose put it into Verse' (I i 96–104).
12. o'erseen] mistaken, betrayed into a blunder (*OED*).
16. doom] verdict.
18. s.d. Normally on the Restoration stage the prologue was followed by the
overture which preceded the raising of the curtain; the audience is therefore
surprised by the return of the Prologue (Price, *Music in the Restoration Theatre*
55–6).
22. hectors] swaggering braggarts; Thomas Blount defines *hector* as 'a roaring
boy that frequents Taverns, and lives chiefly by the reputation of his sword'
(*Glossographia*, first included in the 1661 edition).   *pit*] See 'Prologue to
The Rival Ladies' l. 24*n.*
24. be beforehand with] anticipate.
26. puny] subordinate (*OED* 1); raw, inexperienced (*OED* 3); feeble (*OED* 4).
29–31. D. is probably referring to the legal rule that people who were
convicted of crimes of violence against the person were excluded from serving on juries (Michael Macnair, privately). See also *POAS* ii 285.
29. excepted] objected to, ruled out.

Which has excluded butchers from a jury.
You'd all be wits——
But writing's tedious, and that way may fail;
The most compendious method is to rail:
35 Which you so like, you think yourselves ill used
When in smart prologues you are not abused.
A civil prologue is approved by no man—
You hate it as you do a civil woman:
Your fancy's palled, and liberally you pay
40 To have it quickened ere you see a play:
Just as old sinners, worn from their delight,
Give money to be whipped to appetite.
But what a pox keep I so much ado
To save our poet? He is one of you,
45 A brother judgement, and as I hear say,
A cursèd critic as e'er damned a play.
Good savage gentlemen, your own kind spare,
He is, like you, a very wolf or bear;
Yet think not he'll your ancient rights invade,
50 Or stop the course of your free damning trade:
For he (he vows) at no friend's play can sit
But he must needs find fault to show his wit.
Then, for his sake, ne'er stint your own delight,
Throw boldly, for he sets to all that write;
55 With such he ventures on an even lay,
For they bring ready money into play.
Those who write not, and yet all writers nick,
Are bankrupt gamesters, for they damn on tick.

34. compendious] saving time (OED 2).
38. civil] grave, sober (OED 10).
45. judgement] critic, judge (OED 8c).
54–8. Extended metaphor from gaming: *sets to*] challenges by laying down a stake; *nick*] beat with a winning throw.

Song

I feed a flame within which so torments me
That it both pains my heart, and yet contents me:
'Tis such a pleasing smart, and I so love it,
That I had rather die than once remove it.

5   Yet he for whom I grieve shall never know it,
My tongue does not betray, nor my eyes show it:
Not a sigh nor a tear my pain discloses,
But they fall silently like dew on roses.

Thus to prevent my love from being cruel,
10   My heart's the sacrifice as 'tis the fuel:
And while I suffer this to give him quiet,
My faith rewards my love, though he deny it.

On his eyes will I gaze, and there delight me;
While I conceal my love no frown can fright me:
15   To be more happy I dare not aspire;
Nor can I fall more low, mounting no higher.

Song. In Act IV Scene ii Asteria (played by Mrs Knep) sings to the Queen 'the Song you made of *Philocles*, / And call'd it *Secret-Love*'.
1. This line is used by Crazy in Shadwell's *The Humorists* (1671) and identified as 'stole out of a Play' by Drybob, Shadwell's caricature of D. (Winn 223).
8. Cp. Herrick: 'And give me such reposes, / That I, poore I, / May think, thereby, / I live and die / 'Mongst Roses. / / Fall on me like a silent dew' ('To Musique, to becalme his Fever' ll. 18–23; from *Hesperides* (1648); Kinsley).

18 Annus Mirabilis

Date and publication. In 1665 D. left London to avoid the plague, perhaps soon after the theatres closed on 5 June; the vivid description of the sounds of the Battle of Lowestoft (3 June) at the opening of *EDP* suggests that he was still in London then (see also the 'Verses to her Highness the Duchess' ll. 13–20, 30–2). He retired to Charlton, Wiltshire, the seat of his father-in-law Thomas Howard, Earl of Berkshire. He stayed there until the end of 1666, composing *Secret Love*, *AM* and *EDP*. The poem depicts events from March 1665 to September 1666, and was probably composed in the summer and autumn of 1666; the address to Sir Robert Howard is dated 10 November 1666. On grounds of style and tone *Works* (i 257) suggests that the verses on the fire were an afterthought, but this is mere speculation. *Annus Mirabilis: The Year of Wonders, 1666* was licensed by L'Estrange on 22 November 1666 and published by Herringman early in 1667 (*SR* 21 January). New light on the exact date and circumstances of the publication is shed by a letter from Sir Allen Brodrick to the Duke of Ormonde dated 29 December 1666: 'There is a Poem of the last Sumers Sea Fights by Mr Dreyden in the Press, which I had hoped to inclose for your Graces divertisement, the next shall certaynely bring it, for I suppose it deteyned only for the Ceremony of a New Years guift to the Prince and Generall.' On 1 January 1667 he wrote that 'I sent your Grace Mr Drydens by the last Post' (BodL MS Carte 35 ff. 191^r and 232^r; information from Nicholas von Maltzahn, privately). Pepys bought a copy on 2 February. Two alterations were made after the initial printing: in the second issue C6 was cancelled and replaced with a leaf giving a revised version of stanza 105; in the third issue C1 was also cancelled and a revised version of l. 267 substituted (this C1 cancellans exists in two settings): for the variants see the notes below. Since D. was in Wiltshire when *1667* was printed he asked Sir Robert Howard to see it through the press. Howard failed to spot a number of errors, and *1667* has a note 'To the Readers' (sig. a4^r) in which D. says: 'Notwithstanding the diligence which has been used in my absence, some faults have escap'd the Press: and I have so many of my own to answer for, that I am not willing to be charg'd with those of the Printer. I have onely noted the grossest of them, not such as by false stops have confounded the sense, but such as by mistaken words have corrupted it.' An errata list follows. The present text is from *1667*, third issue, with readings from the errata list silently incorporated. *AM* was reprinted in 1668 (probably pirated) and 1688, but there is no evidence that D. oversaw these editions. *1688* makes some necessary corrections (followed here) but also adds many errors; some changes of wording could be attributable to D. (see l. 649*n*), but they could easily have been made in the printing house.

Context. The euphoria of the Restoration soon gave way to dissension, and (in 1665–7) to a series of disasters (see Hutton, *The Restoration* 185–267). The year 1666 was widely expected to be a year of disaster, since 666 is the number of the beast in Revelation xiii 18 (see D. Brady, *BJRL* lxi (1978–9) 314–36). As Malone noted (ii 249) D.'s title echoes the titles of three pamphlets which reported recent prodigies and held that these were divine judgements on England for the ungodly behaviour of King and court: *Mirabilis Annus, the Year of Prodigies* (1661) and *Mirabilis Annus Secundus; or, the Second Year of Prodigies*, in two parts (1662). E. N. Hooker (*HLQ* x (1946) 49–67) argued that D. was responding to the apocalyptic prophecies of such opposition writers by portraying the war and the fire not as judgements but as trials which a virtuous country and city should bear patiently, submissive to the King and providence. Nevertheless, apprehension about 1666 was not confined to dissidents: Sandwich told Pepys that he dreaded the issue of that year (25 February 1666), and Pepys himself bought a copy of Francis Potter's *An Interpretation of the Number 666* (1642), which, he said, 'whether it be right or wrong, is mighty ingenious' (18 February; 4, 10 November 1666). Moreover, D. was not reacting solely to dissident prophecy. Michael McKeon (in his *Politics and Poetry in Restoration England* (1975), a major study of *AM* and its context) points out that dissidents did not have a monopoly of prophecy, and some royalist writers expected good things from 1666. Almanacs anticipated a 'Year of Wonders', and the appendix to Vincent Wing's almanac has the running title 'Annus Mirabilis'. To McKeon's examples we may add that 'Anno Mirabili 1666' appears in the title of *A Short and Serious Narrative of Londons Fatal Fire* (1667; exact date of publication unknown). The two major events which made 1666 a year of wonders were the Dutch War and the Fire of London.

Dutch War. The Second Dutch War was provoked by commercial rivalry; Pepys reported Capt. Cocke as saying that 'the trade of the world is too little for us two, therefore one must down' (2 February 1664). The main engagements were the Battle of Lowestoft (3 June 1665), an English victory which was not followed through; the Four Days Battle (1–4 June 1666), a defeat, but inconclusive; and the St James's Day Fight (25 July 1666), a decisive English victory. D. describes these, together with the disastrous raid on Bergen and the successful raid on the Vly. (*AM* was published before the humiliating Dutch appearance in the Medway in 1667.) James Kinsley in *RES* vii (1956) 30–7 shows how D. presents the naval war in a favourable light, suppressing examples of cowardice and incompetence, and ignoring the criticisms of the conduct of the war which contemporaries such as Pepys heard and made (e.g. Pepys 10, 24 June 1666; 4 April 1667). Contemporary accounts are reprinted in *The Rupert and Monck Letter Book 1666*, edited by J. R. Powell and E. K. Timmings (1969), hereafter cited as *Letter Book*. See also Pepys, *passim*. For modern accounts see Hutton, *The Restoration* 214–25, 237–45, Richard Ollard in Pepys x 110–20, and W. L. Clowes, *The Royal Navy*, 7 vols (1897–1903) ii 252–85. The diplomatic context is explained by Keith Feiling, *British Foreign Policy 1660–1672* (1930). The Battle of Lowestoft and the Four Days Battle were drawn by Willem van de Velde (*Van De Velde Drawings*, edited by M. Robinson (1958) 352–3; 309); his drawing of the raid on the Vly, and Hollar's engraving of the St James's Day Fight are reproduced in Richard Ollard, *Man of War* (1969).

Fire of London. The best contemporary reports of the fire are by Pepys and Evelyn (2–7 September). For modern accounts see W. G. Bell, *The Great Fire of London in 1666* (1920; 1951) and Robert Latham in Pepys x 138–40. The extent of the disaster is shown in Hollar's engraving of London before and after the fire (reproduced in *Wenceslaus Hollar: Prints and Drawings*, edited by Antony Griffiths and Gabriela Kesnerová (1983) 70–1). The fire prompted many moral reflections: Samuel Rolle in *The Burning of London* (1667) and Thomas Vincent in *Gods Terrible Voice in the City* (1667) saw it as a punishment for the people's sins; the same view was taken in the official Anglican sermons on the Fast Day by Edward Stillingfleet (*A Sermon . . . Octob. 10* (1666)) and William Sancroft (*Lex Ignea* (1666)). For poems on the fire and rebuilding of London see *London in Flames, London in Glory*, edited by Robert Aubin (1943).

Royal Society. Although D.'s praise of the Royal Society is brief (ll. 656–64) and his own association with it inconsiderable (see headnote to 'To Dr Charleton'), *AM* does share the Society's interest in ores, tides, eclipses, longitude and shipping. It is also notable that Sprat in his *The History of the Royal-Society of London* (published 1667, though pages 1–319 were set up and printed in 1665, so possibly available to D.) claims that experimental philosophy will reduce men's dependence upon prophecy: he says that Englishmen are swayed too much by omens and prodigies, 'especially this last year, this gloomy, and ill-boding humor has prevail'd. So that it is now the fittest season for *Experiments* to arise, to teach us a Wisdome, which springs from the depths of *Knowledge*, to shake off the shadows, and to scatter the mists, which fill the minds of men with a vain consternation' (362). Sprat and D. also share a concern for language: D.'s interest in the terms proper to each art ('Account' ll. 91–112), though primarily related to literary discussions of decorum and poetic vocabulary, may also be compared with the Society's adoption of 'a close, naked, natural way of speaking; positive expressions; clear senses; a native easiness: bringing all things as near the Mathematical plainness, as they can: and preferring the language of Artizans, Countrymen, and Merchants, before that, of Wits, or Scholars' (113); and D.'s use of similes drawn from scientific discoveries is in line with Sprat's view that 'the *Works of Nature* . . . are one of the best and most fruitful Soils for the growth of *Wit*' (415). See also Helen M. Burke, *ELH* lvii (1990) 307–34 for a discussion of the ideology of science as represented in *AM*.

Sources. Since D. composed *AM* in Wiltshire, he would have relied upon documentary sources for his account of the war and the fire. The war was reported in the *London Gazette*, *Current Intelligence* and various pamphlets (see *Letter Book*). His account of the Four Days Battle is closest to that in the official pamphlet *A True Narrative of the Engagement between His Majesties*

Fleet, and that of Holland (1666). The other engagements were described in *The Victory over the Fleet of the States General, obtained by His Majesties Navy Royal in the late Engagement, begun the 25 of July instant* (1666) and *A True and Perfect Narrative of the Great and Signal Success of a Part of His Majesties Fleet . . . Burning One hundred and Sixty Dutch Ships within the Ulie* (1666). For the fire he probably used the *London Gazette* lxxxv (3–10 September). The events of 1665–6 prompted a number of poems. Waller's *Instructions to a Painter* (1665) celebrated the Battle of Lowestoft, and drew a series of anonymous rejoinders: *Second Advice to a Painter* (Pepys saw a MS copy 14 December 1666; printed 1667); *Third Advice* (dated 1 October 1666; Pepys saw a MS copy 20 January 1667; printed 1667); *Fourth* and *Fifth Advice* and *Last Instructions* (the latter by Marvell), these last three covering the period from September 1666 to late 1667. For all these see *POAS* i 20–156. There is evidence only for D.'s knowing Waller's poem (see l. 64*n*), but *AM* clearly responds defensively to the critical climate in which the others were written (even Pepys contemplated writing a satire on the Four Days Fight: see the entry for 15 July 1666). Waller's analogues from natural history (parodied in the *Second Advice*) may have suggested to D. his own use of Georgic elements in *AM*. D. also used Waller's *Of a War with Spain* (1658). He also seems to have recalled William Smith's poems on the Battle of Lowestoft (see l. 228*n*) and the *Loyal London* (see ll. 17–20*n*). Simon Ford's thanksgiving sermon for Lowestoft, preached in Northampton, has some similarities with *AM*: it discusses the restriction of trade (9, 26; cp. *AM* ll. 5–6*n*), the ordering of tides (10), and the origins and development of shipping and navigation (14–15) (Θαυμάσια Κύριον ἐν Βυθῷ (1665)). D.'s stanza form, previously used in *Heroic Stanzas*, comes from Davenant's *Gondibert* (1651), as do some of the ideas in the 'Account'.

As the 'Account' shows, D. used several classical writers to help him define the appropriate mode for an historical poem. He tried to avoid the difficulties (exemplified for him in Lucan's *Pharsalia*) of taking too diverse a subject, and he used two Latin poets as his models. From Virgil's *Aeneid* he took a stress upon *pietas*, that submission to providence and dedication to one's country represented by Aeneas and by the protagonists of *AM* (see James D. Garrison, *Pietas from Vergil to Dryden* (1992) for this concept). D.'s poem thus suggests England's Augustan destiny, and sees the war with Holland in terms of Rome's struggle with Carthage. From the *Georgics* D. drew inspiration for his poem's delight in the ordinary, everyday world (both in nature, and in the details of human occupations), and its sense of the place of labour in a divinely ordered world. But while D. draws many images from Virgil, his wit is more akin to that of Ovid, whose ability to treat serious subjects wittily always influenced him. As his own notes show, D. draws upon other Latin authors for images or philosophical reflections. He also activates the Latinate roots of English, using many words of Latin origin in their primary meanings.

Reception. Pepys thought it 'a very good poem', but did not keep his copy (2

February 1667). Abraham Markland's 'Upon the Anniversary of His Majesties Birth and Restauration, May 29. (1667.)' uses the same stanza form as *AM*; other resemblances with *AM* include the King weeping at the fire, and the description of the wind which fanned the flames as 'a *Dutch* East-wind' (cp. *AM* l. 917) (*Poems on His Majestie's Birth and Restauration* (1667) 1–23). Many passages of *AM* were echoed in J[oseph] G[uillim]'s poem on the fire, Ἀκάματον Πῦρ (1667), and there are echoes in [James Wright], *Ecclesia Restaurata* (1677), but other contemporaries were scathing about D.'s wit (see ll. 521–8n, 697n, 1121–4n).

Annus Mirabilis:

The Year of Wonders, 1666.

An Historical Poem:

Containing the progress and various successes of our naval war with Holland, under the conduct of His Highness Prince Rupert, and His Grace the Duke of Albemarle. And describing the Fire of London.

Multum interest res poscat, an homines latius imperare velint.
Trajan Imperator ad Plin.

Urbs antiqua ruit, multos dominata per annos.
Virg.

¶18. *Title.* See headnote, '*Context*'.
Epigraphs. Multum . . . velint.] '[The validity of a course of action] depends very much upon whether the occasion demands it, or men are [just] eager to extend their power more widely' (Pliny, *Epistulae* x 22).   Urbs . . . annos] 'The ancient city falls, having dominated for many years' (Virgil, *Aen.* ii 363).

To the Metropolis of Great Britain, the most renowned and late flourishing City of London, in its representatives the Lord Mayor and Court of Aldermen, the Sheriffs and Common Council of it.

As perhaps I am the first who ever presented a work of this nature to the metropolis of any nation, so is it likewise consonant to justice that he who was to give the first example of such a dedication should begin it
5   with that city which has set a pattern to all others of true loyalty, invincible courage and unshaken constancy. Other cities have been praised for the same virtues, but I am much deceived if any have so dearly purchased their reputation; their fame has been won them by cheaper
10 trials than an expensive, though necesssary, war, a consuming pestilence, and a more consuming fire. To submit yourselves with that humility to the judgements of heaven, and at the same time to raise yourselves with that vigour above all human enemies; to be combated at
15 once from above and from below, to be struck down and to triumph; I know not whether such trials have been ever paralleled in any nation: the resolution and successes of them never can be. Never had prince or people more mutual reason to love each other, if suffer-
20 ing for each other can endear affection. You have come together a pair of matchless lovers, through many diffi-

Dedication. Relations between the court and London had been difficult for many years. During the Civil War London had provided a secure base of support for Parliament, and after the Restoration it continued to nourish Protestant and, later, Whiggish sentiments. During the plague many courtiers and clergy left London for safer places, and pamphlets voiced the resentment of Londoners at their abandonment. Relations became particularly awkward for Charles II during the Popish Plot (1678–9) and Exclusion Crisis (1680–1), and he moved Parliament to Oxford to avoid Whig pressure from Londoners: this tension is registered by D. in *AA*, and in *The Duke of Guise* (1683) which ridicules city sheriffs. Royal control over the city was effected through a new charter in 1683, a victory which D. celebrated in *Albion and Albanius* (1685).

culties; he, through a long exile, various traverses of
Fortune, and the interposition of many rivals, who violently ravished and withheld you from him; and cer-
25   tainly you have had your share in sufferings. But
Providence has cast upon you want of trade, that you
might appear bountiful to your country's necessities; and
the rest of your afflictions are not more the effects of
God's displeasure (frequent examples of them having
30   been in the reign of the most excellent princes) than
occasions for the manifesting of your Christian and civil
virtues. To you therefore this *Year of Wonders* is justly
dedicated, because you have made it so: you who are to
stand a wonder to all years and ages, and who have built
35   yourselves an immortal monument on your own ruins.
You are now a phoenix in her ashes, and, as far as
humanity can approach, a great emblem of the suffering
deity. But heaven never made so much piety and virtue to
leave it miserable. I have heard indeed of some virtuous
40   persons who have ended unfortunately, but never of
any virtuous nation: Providence is engaged too deeply,
when the cause becomes so general. And I cannot
imagine it has resolved the ruin of that people at home,
which it has blessed abroad with such successes. I am
45   therefore to conclude that your sufferings are at an end,
and that one part of my poem has not been more an
history of your destruction than the other a prophecy of
your restoration. The accomplishment of which happiness, as it is the wish of all true Englishmen, so is by
50   none more passionately desired than by

The greatest of your admirers, and most humble of
your servants,

JOHN DRYDEN.

22. *traverses*] obstructions, adversities (*OED* 7).
36–7. *phoenix . . . suffering deity*] The phoenix rising from the ashes of its
parent was an obvious symbol for the city, and was included in the original
design for the monument to the fire. It was also a traditional emblem of the
passion and resurrection of Christ.

An Account of the Ensuing Poem, in a letter to the Honourable Sir Robert Howard

Sir,

I am so many ways obliged to you, and so little able to return your favours, that, like those who owe too much, I can only live by getting farther into your debt.
5 You have not only been careful of my fortune, which was the effect of your nobleness, but you have been solicitous of my reputation, which is that of your kindness. It is not long since I gave you the trouble of perusing a play for me, and now, instead of an acknow-
10 ledgement, I have given you a greater, in the correction of a poem. But since you are to bear this persecution, I will at least give you the encouragement of a martyr: you could never suffer in a nobler cause. For I have chosen the most heroic subject which any poet could
15 desire: I have taken upon me to describe the motives, the beginning, progress and successes of a most just and necessary war; in it, the care, management and prudence of our King; the conduct and valour of a royal admiral, and of two incomparable generals; the invinc-
20 ible courage of our captains and seamen; and three glorious victories, the result of all. After this I have, in the fire, the most deplorable, but withal the greatest argument that can be imagined: the destruction being so swift, so

An Account of the Ensuing Poem. D.'s first critical essay was his Preface to *The Rival Ladies* (1664); the present essay is (with the closely preceding *EDP*) D.'s first extended piece of literary criticism. He is concerned chiefly with decorum—with the literary form which is appropriate for particular events, and with the language which is appropriate to that form.

Howard] See headnote ('*Date and publication*') and 'To Sir Robert Howard' above.

5. *careful of my fortune*] Howard seems to have helped D. and his wife Elizabeth in their negotiations with the Treasury to obtain the £3,000 dowry due to them out of a grant from the King to the Earl of Berkshire (Winn 168–9).

9. *a play*] *Secret Love*, written during D.'s period at Charlton.

19. *admiral*] James, Duke of York.   *generals*] Prince Rupert and George Monck, Duke of Albemarle.

22. *deplorable*] lamentable.   *argument*] topic.

sudden, so vast and miserable, as nothing can parallel in
25 story. The former part of this poem, relating to the
war, is but a due expiation for my not serving my King
and country in it. All gentlemen are almost obliged to
it: and I know no reason we should give that advantage
to the commonalty of England to be foremost in brave
30 actions, which the noblesse of France would never
suffer in their peasants. I should not have written this
but to a person who has been ever forward to appear in
all employments whither his honour and generosity
have called him. The latter part of my poem, which
35 describes the fire, I owe first to the piety and fatherly
affection of our monarch to his suffering subjects; and,
in the second place, to the courage, loyalty and magnanimity of the city: both which were so conspicuous that
I have wanted words to celebrate them as they deserve.
40 I have called my poem historical, not epic, though both
the actions and actors are as much heroic as any poem
can contain. But since the action is not properly one,

27. *gentlemen*] Charles and James preferred gentlemen commanders to professional seamen, but they were not always reliable under pressure (Ogg 273–
4; Pepys 10 January 1666 and *n*).
29. *commonalty*] common people (*OED* 3).   *foremost*] formost *1688*; for
most *1667*, *1668*.
30. *noblesse*] nobility (a long-standing English word).   *France*] The majority of the French nobility served in the army, other pursuits being considered dishonourable.
33. *employments*] At the outbreak of the Civil War the young Howard joined
the royalist army, and in 1646 was knighted for his bravery. In October 1660
Howard was appointed a commissioner for investigating the dispersal of
royal property during the Commonwealth; in November made colonel in the
Hampshire militia; in 1661 elected Member of Parliament for Stockbridge,
Hampshire; in 1662 appointed a commissioner for reforming the streets and
buildings of London. He was also a partner in the building and ownership of
the Theatre Royal, Bridges Street, from 1661. Howard's prominence as a
parliamentarian began in 1666 with his opposition to court interests, though
he soon changed sides (H. J. Oliver, *Sir Robert Howard* (1963) 42–4, 131–2).
generosity] nobility (*OED* 1).
35. *piety*] partly in the Latin sense (from *pietas*) of 'dutiful care for one's
country'; see headnote ('*Sources*') and cp. *AM* l. 255*n*.
37–8. *magnanimity*] fortitude (*OED* 2).
42. *action is not properly one*] It is a basic classical principle that the subject of a

nor that accomplished in the last successes, I have
judged it too bold a title for a few stanzas which are
45 little more in number than a single *Iliad*, or the longest
of the *Aeneids*. For this reason (I mean not of length, but
broken action, tied too severely to the laws of history) I
am apt to agree with those who rank Lucan rather
among historians in verse than epic poets: in whose
50 room, if I am not deceived, Silius Italicus, though a
worse writer, may more justly be admitted. I have
chosen to write my poem in quatrains, or stanzas of
four in alternate rhyme, because I have ever judged
them more noble, and of greater dignity, both for the

---

poem should have a unity (Aristotle, *Poetics* 1450b–51b; Horace, *Ars Poetica*
ll. 1–23).

43. last] latest.

45. little more in number] *AM* has 1216 lines; Virgil, *Aen.* xii has 952; Homer,
Iliad v has 909.

48. Lucan] AD 39–65, author of *Bellum Civile* (or *Pharsalia*), a poem on the
civil war between Caesar and Pompey. D.'s critical estimate of him derives
from Quintilian, who thought him *magis oratoribus quam poetis imitandus* (X i
90; 'more worthy of imitation by orators than poets'). Petronius concurred,
saying that historical events are better dealt with by historians than poets
(*Satyricon* 118), quoted by Fanshawe, translating Camoens's *The Lusiad*
(1655) sig. b2ᵛ, and by D. in *Of Heroique Playes* (1672; *Works* xi 11–12). J. C.
Scaliger censured Lucan for a lack of poetic unity caused by following too
closely the events of history, and contrasted him in this respect with Silius
Italicus (*Poetices Libri Septem* (1561) 325, 327). Davenant, in his Preface to
Gondibert (1651) 4, wrote: '*Lucan*, who chose to write the greatest actions that
ever were allowed to be true . . . did not observe that such an enterprise
rather beseem'd an Historian, then a Poet: for wise Poets think it more
worthy to seek out truth in the Passions, then to record the truth of Actions'.
In 1672 D. said that Lucan 'follow'd too much the truth of history, crowded
sentences [i.e. philosophical aphorisms] together, was too full of points, and
too often offer'd at somewhat which had more of the sting of an Epigram,
than of the dignity and state of an Heroick Poem' (*Works* xi 11).

50. Silius Italicus] AD 26–101, writer of *Punica*, the longest Latin poem,
12,200 verses on the Second Punic War. A translation by Thomas Ross was
published in 1661; an epigram on the frontispiece portrait of Charles II says
that the King surpasses Scipio and Hannibal.

52. quatrains] the form of D.'s *Heroic Stanzas*, of Davenant's *Gondibert* and of
Sir John Davies's *Nosce Teipsum* (1599).

54. for] *1688*; fro *1667*; from *1668*.

55   sound and number, than any other verse in use amongst
us; in which I am sure I have your approbation. The
learnèd languages have, certainly, a great advantage of
us, in not being tied to the slavery of any rhyme, and
were less constrained in the quantity of every syllable,
60   which they might vary with spondees or dactyls,
besides so many other helps of grammatical figures for
the lengthening or abbreviation of them, than the
modern are in the close of that one syllable which often
confines and more often corrupts the sense of all the
65   rest. But in this necessity of our rhymes I have always
found the couplet verse most easy (though not so
proper for this occasion), for there the work is sooner at
an end, every two lines concluding the labour of the
poet: but in quatrains he is to carry it farther on, and not
70   only so, but to bear along in his head the troublesome
sense of four lines together. For those who write correctly in this kind must needs acknowledge that the last
line of the stanza is to be considered in the composition
of the first. Neither can we give ourselves the liberty of
75   making any part of a verse for the sake of rhyme, or
concluding with a word which is not current English,
or using the variety of female rhymes, all which our
fathers practised; and for the female rhymes, they are
still in use amongst other nations: with the Italian in
80   every line, with the Spaniard promiscuously, with the
French alternately, as those who have read the *Alaric*,
the *Pucelle*, or any of their latter poems will agree with
me. And besides this, they write in alexandrines, or

55. *number*] metre or rhythm.

58. *slavery of any rhyme*] Milton's note on 'The Verse' added to the fourth
issue of *PL* (1668) also remarks on 'the troublesome and modern bondage of
rhyming'. D. had just defended the use of rhyme in drama in *EDP*. Latin
hexameter verse is scanned by quantity rather than stress, and permits spondees and dactyls. The inflexions of Latin allow considerable liberty in word-
order.

77. *female rhymes*] In the Preface to *Albion and Albanius* (1685) D. says:
'Female, or double Rhyme . . . is not natural to our Tongue, because it
consists too much of Monosyllables, and those too, most commonly clogg'd
with Consonants' (*Works* xv 10).

81. Alaric] *Alaric, ou Rome vaincüe* (1654) by Georges de Scudéry.

82. Pucelle] *La Pucelle, ou la France délivrée* (1656) by Jean Chapelain.

verses of six feet, such as amongst us is the old trans-
85 lation of Homer by Chapman; all which, by lengthening of their chain, makes the sphere of their activity the
larger. I have dwelt too long upon the choice of my
stanza, which you may remember is much better
defended in the Preface to *Gondibert*, and therefore I will
90 hasten to acquaint you with my endeavours in the
writing. In general I will only say, I have never yet seen
the description of any naval fight in the proper terms
which are used at sea; and if there be any such in another
language, as that of Lucan in the third of his *Pharsalia*,
95 yet I could not prevail myself of it in the English, the
terms of arts in every tongue bearing more of the idiom
of it than any other words. We hear, indeed, among our
poets of the thundering of guns, the smoke, the disorder and the slaughter; but all these are common
100 notions. And certainly, as those who in a logical dispute
keep in general terms would hide a fallacy, so those
who do it in any poetical description would veil their
ignorance.

84–5. translation of Homer by Chapman] His *Iliad* (1598–1611) is actually in
lines of seven feet, and his *Odyssey* (1614–15) in lines of five.
88–9. better defended in the Preface to Gondibert] 'I beleev'd it would be more
pleasant to the Reader, in a Work of length, to give this respite or pause,
between every *Stanza* (having endeavour'd that each should contain a period)
then to run him out of breath with continu'd *Couplets*. Nor doth alternate
Rime by any lowliness of cadence make the sound less Heroick' (*Gondibert*
(1651) 25).
92. proper terms] As W. P. Ker noted, Ronsard advocated the use of 'les noms
propres des mestiers' in his *Abrégé de l'Art Poëtique François* (1565). D.'s
interest here may be compared with the Royal Society's concern for style (see
headnote, '*Royal Society*'). D. returns to the subject of the poet being master
of the appropriate languages in his 'Discourse Concerning Satire' (*Works* iv
21), his note to 'The Second Book of the *Georgics*' (*Works* vi 814) and his
'Dedication of the *Aeneis*' (*Works* v 337), where he now says that he has
followed Virgil in not using the proper terms of navigation and other professions.
95. prevail] avail (*OED* 4c); cp. *AA* l. 461.
101. Kinsley cites the tag *Fraus latet in generalibus*; cp. *HP* ii 79.

descriptas servare vices operumque colores
105   *cur ego, si nequeo ignoroque, poeta salutor?*

For my own part, if I had little knowledge of the sea,
yet I have thought it no shame to learn; and if I have
made some few mistakes, 'tis only, as you can bear me
witness, because I have wanted opportunity to correct
110   them, the whole poem being first written and now sent
you from a place where I have not so much as the
converse of any seaman. Yet, though the trouble I had
in writing it was great, it was more than recompensed
by the pleasure; I found myself so warm in celebrating
115   the praises of military men, two such especially as the
Prince and General, that it is no wonder if they inspired
me with thoughts above my ordinary level. And I am
well satisfied that as they are incomparably the best
subject I have ever had, excepting only the royal family,
120   so also that this I have written of them is much better
than what I have performed on any other. I have been
forced to help out other arguments, but this has been
bountiful to me; they have been low and barren of
praise, and I have exalted them, and made them fruitful:
125   but here——*Omnia sponte sua reddit justissima tellus.* I
have had a large, a fair and a pleasant field, so fertile that
without my cultivating it has given me two harvests in
a summer, and in both oppressed the reaper. All other
greatness in subjects is only counterfeit, it will not endure
130   the test of danger; the greatness of arms is only real:
other greatness burdens a nation with its weight, this
supports it with its strength. And as it is the happiness
of the age, so is it the peculiar goodness of the best of
kings, that we may praise his subjects without offend-

104–5. 'If I am ignorant of and fail to adhere to the established varieties and
styles of works, why should I be hailed as a poet?' (Horace, *Ars Poetica* ll. 86–
7).
109. wanted] lacked.
125. Omnia . . . tellus] 'The most righteous earth returns everything of its
own free will': D.'s own hexameter, probably based on Virgil's *fundit humo*
facilem uictum iustissima tellus (*Geo.* ii 460), *omnis feret omnia tellus* (*Ecl.* iv 39),
and Ovid's *tellus animalia formis / sponte sua peperit* (*Met.* i 416–17; cp. *Fasti* iv
370).
127–8. two harvests in a summer] probably the praises of Prince Rupert and
General Monck.

135   ing him: doubtless it proceeds from a just confidence of
       his own virtue, which the lustre of no other can be so
       great as to darken in him, for the good or the valiant are
       never safely praised under a bad or a degenerate prince.
       But to return from this digression to a farther account
140   of my poem, I must crave leave to tell you, that as I
       have endeavoured to adorn it with noble thoughts, so
       much more to express those thoughts with elocution.
       The composition of all poems is or ought to be of wit,
       and wit in the poet, or wit writing (if you will give me
145   leave to use a school distinction) is no other than the
       faculty of imagination in the writer, which like a nimble
       spaniel beats over and ranges through the field of
       memory, till it springs the quarry it hunted after; or,
       without metaphor, which searches over all the memory

142. elocution] See 'Account' l. 169.

143–53. Cp. Davenant: '*Wit* is the laborious, and the lucky resultances of
thought, having towards its excellence (as we say of the strokes of Painting)
as well a happiness, as care. . . . *Wit* is not only the luck and labour, but also
the dexterity of thought, rounding the world, like the Sun, with unimagin-
able motion; and bringing swiftly home to the memory universall surveys'
(Preface to *Gondibert* (1651) 26–7; D. seems to have borrowed Davenant's
terms 'laborious' and 'lucky' to describe Shakespeare in *EDP* (*Works* xvii
55)). D. is developing his earlier account of poetic creation: in the Dedication
to *The Rival Ladies* (1664) he said that the play was once 'a confus'd Mass of
Thoughts, tumbling over one another in the Dark: When the Fancy was yet
in its first Work, moving the Sleeping Images of things towards the Light,
there to be Distinguish'd, and then either chosen or rejected by the Judgment'
(*Works* viii 95); cp. also 'To Sir Robert Howard' ll. 1–34. The threefold
analysis of the act of creation is derived from classical rhetoric (see 'Account'
ll. 166–70*nn*); D. has a similar division in his 'A Parallel of Poetry and
Painting' (*Works* xx 61–71).

144–51. wit writing . . . Wit written] 'The school distinction which D. has in
his mind is that of *Natura naturans* and *Natura naturata*. So in the case of Wit he
distinguishes between Wit the faculty and Wit the product' (Ker).

145. school distinction] a distinction from scholastic philosophy.

147. spaniel] Cp. Hobbes: 'Sometimes a man knows a place determinate,
within the compasse whereof he is to seek; and then his thoughts run over all
the parts thereof, in the same manner . . . as a Spaniel ranges the field, till he
find a sent' (*Leviathan* (1651) 10). D. had used the image in the Dedication to
The Rival Ladies: 'Imagination in a Poet is a faculty so Wild and Lawless, that,
like an High-ranging Spaniel it must have Cloggs tied to it, least it out-run
the Judgment' (*Works* viii 101). For Shadwell's parody of this image in *The
Humorists* see Winn 223.

150   for the species or ideas of those things which it designs to
represent. Wit written is that which is well defined, the
happy result of thought or product of that imagination.
But to proceed from wit in the general notion of it to the
proper wit of an heroic or historical poem, I judge it
155   chiefly to consist in the delightful imaging of persons,
actions, passions or things. 'Tis not the jerk or sting of
an epigram, nor the seeming contradiction of a poor
antithesis (the delight of an ill-judging audience in a
play of rhyme), nor the jingle of a more poor parono-
160   masia: neither is it so much the morality of a grave
sentence, affected by Lucan, but more sparingly used by
Virgil; but it is some lively and apt description, dressed
in such colours of speech that it sets before your eyes the
absent object as perfectly and more delightfully than
165   nature. So then, the first happiness of the poet's imagination is properly invention, or finding of the thought;
the second is fancy, or the variation, driving or mould-
ing of that thought as the judgement represents it
proper to the subject; the third is elocution, or the art of
170   clothing and adorning that thought so found and varied

---

150. species] mental impressions; ideas (*OED* 5c).   *ideas*] abstract or ideal
forms (ultimately from Plato).

152. happy] fortunate and skilful.

156–7. Cp. D.'s comment on Lucan, quoted in l. 48*n*.

159–160. paronomasia] play on words; pun.

160–1. grave sentence] Quintilian says that Lucan is *sententiis clarissimus* (X i 90;
'most famous for his sentences' [i.e. moral aphorisms]).

166. invention] The finding out or selection of topics to be treated (*OED* 1d); a
standard rhetorical term, *inventio* in classical rhetoric. For this and the following terms cp. the list of five elements of rhetoric (*inventio, dispositio, elocutio,
memoria, pronuntiatio*) in Cicero, *De Inventione* i 7 and *Ad Herennium* i 2.

167. variation] corresponds to *dispositio*.   *driving*] 1667, 1668, Watson; deriving 1688, Ker, Kinsley, Works. 'Deriving' would be inappropriate, as it
belongs to the first stage of composition; *driving* refers to the pursuit of the
idea once found: it is either an elaboration of the hunting image from l. 148 or
an image from painting or metalwork (spreading a colour or beating a metal
thinly (*OED* 12)). Cp. 'drive' in 'Preface to *Ovid's Epistles*' l. 165.

169. elocution] oratorical or literary expression of thought (*OED* 1); from
elocutio.

170. clothing] That thoughts were 'clothed' in words was a contemporary
commonplace (*OED* clothe 8b).

in apt, significant and sounding words: the quickness of
the imagination is seen in the invention, the fertility in
the fancy, and the accuracy in the expression. For the
two first of these Ovid is famous amongst the poets, for
175 the latter Virgil. Ovid images more often the movements and affections of the mind, either combating
between two contrary passions, or extremely discom-
posed by one: his words therefore are the least part of
his care, for he pictures nature in disorder, with which
180 the study and choice of words is inconsistent. This is the
proper wit of dialogue or discourse, and consequently
of the drama, where all that is said is to be supposed the
effect of sudden thought; which, though it excludes not
the quickness of wit in repartees, yet admits not a too
185 curious election of words, too frequent allusions or use
of tropes, or, in fine, anything that shows remoteness of
thought, or labour in the writer. On the other side,
Virgil speaks not so often to us in the person of another,
like Ovid, but in his own; he relates almost all things as
190 from himself, and thereby gains more liberty than the
other to express his thoughts with all the graces of
elocution, to write more figuratively, and to confess as
well the labour as the force of his imagination. Though
he describes his Dido well and naturally in the violence

171. sounding] high-sounding, imposing (*OED* 2).

175–201. D.'s praise of Ovid's invention and fancy is probably derived from
the classical critics' stress on his *ingenium* (Seneca, *Quaestiones Naturales* III
xxvii 14; Quintilian X i 88, 98). David Hopkins points out (privately) that
D.'s l. 176 seems to echo Daniel Heinsius's remark on Ovid's *imitatio affec-
tuum in quibus semper regnat* ('imitation of the affections, in which he always
excels') in the Preface to his edition of 1629 (sig. ★4ᵛ). Heinsius also places
Ovid second to Virgil (sig. ★3ʳ). Otherwise, D.'s comparison of Ovid and
Virgil seems to be original. In *EDP* he again says that Ovid shows dramatic
abilities in depicting 'the various movements of a Soul combating betwixt
two different Passions', and commends his stories of Myrrha and Byblis
(*Works* xvii 30–1). For D.'s later comments on Ovid see the Prefaces to *Ovid's
Epistles* (below), *Sylvae* (ll. 142–57) and *Fables* (edited by Kinsley ll. 216–
305), and 'Dedication of the *Aeneis*' (*Works* v 322, 339).

185. curious] exact.

186. tropes] See l. 230.

187–201. This comparative judgement was condemned as a 'soloecism of
commendation' in *The Friendly Vindication of Mr. Dryden* (1673) 13–14.

192. confess] reveal.

195 of her passions, yet he must yield in that to the Myrrha,
the Byblis, the Althaea of Ovid; for, as great an admirer
of him as I am, I must acknowledge that if I see not
more of their souls than I see of Dido's, at least I have a
greater concernment for them, and that convinces me
200 that Ovid has touched those tender strokes more delicately than Virgil could. But when action or persons are
to be described, when any such image is to be set before
us, how bold, how masterly are the strokes of Virgil!
We see the objects he represents us with in their native
205 figures, in their proper motions; but we so see them as
our own eyes could never have beheld them so beautiful
in themselves. We see the soul of the poet, like that
universal one of which he speaks, informing and moving through all his pictures, *Totamque infusa per artus*
210 *mens agitat molem, et magno se corpore miscet*; we behold
him embellishing his images, as he makes Venus
breathing beauty upon her son Aeneas:

> ——*lumenque juventae*
> *purpureum, et laetos oculis afflarat honores:*
215 > *quale manus addunt ebori decus, aut ubi flavo*
> *argentum, Pariusve lapis circundatur auro.*

See his tempest, his funeral sports, his combat of Turnus
and Aeneas, and in his *Georgics*, which I esteem the

---

195. *Myrrha*] She fell in love with her father: Ovid, *Met.* x 314–518, tr. D. in
Fables.
196. *Byblis*] She fell in love with her brother: *Met.* ix 454–665, tr. John
Oldham in his *Satyrs upon the Jesuits* (1681), and again by John Dennis (1692)
and Stephen Harvey (1694).   *Althaea*] She took vengeance on her son for
killing her brothers: *Met.* viii 445–514, tr. D. in *Fables*.
202. *be set*] *1668, 1688*; beset *1667*.
209–10. Totamque . . . miscet] 'and mind, pervading the frame, moves the
whole mass, and mingles with the mighty body' (Virgil, *Aen.* vi 726–7).
210. *molem*] *1688*; motem *1667, 1668*.
213–16. lumenque . . . auro] '[Venus] had breathed on him the bright light of
youth and joyful glory on his eyes: such grace as hands give to ivory, or when
silver or Parian marble is encircled by yellow gold' (Virgil, *Aen.* i 590–3).
217. *tempest*] *Aen.* i 84–156.   *funeral sports*] *Aen.* v 42–603.   *combat*]
Aen. xi.
218. *Georgics*] For this opinion cp. 'Preface to *Sylvae*' ll. 272–4 and D.'s note
to Virgil, *Geo.* i (*Works* vi 813–14).

divinest part of all his writings, the plague, the country,
220   the battle of bulls, the labour of the bees, and those
many other excellent images of nature, most of which
are neither great in themselves, nor have any natural
ornament to bear them up; but the words wherewith he
describes them are so excellent that it might be well
225   applied to him which was said by Ovid, *materiam supera-*
bat opus; the very sound of his words has often somewhat that is connatural to the subject, and while we read
him we sit, as in a play, beholding the scenes of what he
represents. To perform this he made frequent use of
230   tropes, which you know change the nature of a known
word by applying it to some other signification, and
this is it which Horace means in his *Epistle to the Pisos*:

> *dixeris egregie notum si callida verbum*
> *reddiderit junctura novum*——

235   But I am sensible I have presumed too far, to entertain
you with a rude discourse of that art which you both
know so well, and put into practice with so much happiness. Yet before I leave Virgil, I must own the vanity
to tell you, and by you the world, that he has been my
240   master in this poem: I have followed him everywhere, I
know not with what success, but I am sure with diligence enough: my images are many of them copied
from him, and the rest are imitations of him. My expressions also are as near as the idioms of the two lan-
245   guages would admit of in translation. And this, sir, I
have done with that boldness for which I will stand
accomptable to any of our little critics, who perhaps are
not better acquainted with him than I am. Upon your

---

219. plague] *Geo.* iii 478–566.   *country*] probably the praise of country life
in *Geo.* ii 458–542.
220. battle of bulls] *Geo.* iii 209–41.   *bees*] *Geo.* iv.
225–6. materiam superabat opus] 'The workmanship surpassed the material'
(Ovid, *Met.* ii 5).
233–4. dixeris . . . novum] 'You will have spoken well if a skilful method of
connecting makes a well-known word new' (Horace, *Ars Poetica* ll. 47–8).
236. rude] rough, unsophisticated.
238–40. Virgil . . . has been my master] See headnote ('*Sources*').
247. accomptable] accountable.

250 first perusal of this poem you have taken notice of some
words which I have innovated (if it be too bold for me
to say refined) upon his Latin; which, as I offer not to
introduce into English prose, so I hope they are neither
improper nor altogether unelegant in verse; and in this
Horace will again defend me:

255 *et nova, fictaque nuper habebunt verba fidem, si*
Graeco fonte cadant, parce detorta——

The inference is exceeding plain: for if a Roman poet
might have liberty to coin a word, supposing only that
it was derived from the Greek, was put into a Latin
260 termination, and that he used this liberty but seldom,
and with modesty; how much more justly may I challenge that privilege to do it with the same prerequisites,
from the best and most judicious of Latin writers? In
some places where either the fancy or the words were
265 his, or any other's, I have noted it in the margin, that I
might not seem a plagiary; in others I have neglected it,
to avoid as well the tediousness as the affectation of
doing it too often. Such descriptions or images, well
wrought, which I promise not for mine, are, as I have
270 said, the adequate delight of heroic poesy, for they
beget admiration, which is its proper object; as the
images of the burlesque, which is contrary to this, by
the same reason beget laughter: for the one shows
nature beautified, as in the picture of a fair woman,
275 which we all admire; the other shows her deformed, as

250. *innovated*] D. makes Latinate innovations in both phrasing and vocabulary; see ll. 251–2n, 1022n, 1028n, 1069n. Cp. 'Dedication of the *Aeneis*'
(*Works* v 333–5), and D.'s note to 'The Ninth Book of the *Aeneis*' l. 1095
(*Works* vi 828–9).
255–6. et . . . detorta] 'New words, and words recently made, will win
acceptance if they spring from a Greek source, and are drawn sparingly' (*Ars
Poetica* ll. 52–3).   cadant] Modern texts of Horace read *cadent*, but *cadant* is
preferred by some seventeenth-century editors, e.g. Lubinus, Bond, Marolles and Schrevelius.
270. *adequate*] appropriate, fitting (*OED* 2).
271. *admiration*] wonder, astonishment (*OED* 1).
272. *burlesque*] See 'Epilogue to *The Indian Emperor*' l. 15n.

in that of a lazar, or of a fool with distorted face and antic gestures, at which we cannot forbear to laugh because it is a deviation from nature. But though the same images serve equally for the epic poesy and for the
280 historic and panegyric, which are branches of it, yet a several sort of sculpture is to be used in them: if some of them are to be like those of Juvenal, *stantes in curribus Aemiliani*, heroes drawn in their triumphal chariots, and in their full proportion, others are to be like that of
285 Virgil, *spirantia mollius aera*: there is somewhat more of softness and tenderness to be shown in them. You will soon find I write not this without concern. Some who have seen a paper of verses which I wrote last year to her Highness the Duchess, have accused them of that
290 only thing I could defend in them: they have said I did *humi serpere*, that I wanted not only height of fancy, but dignity of words to set it off; I might well answer with that of Horace, *nunc non erat hic locus*, I knew I addressed them to a lady, and accordingly I affected the softness of
295 expression and the smoothness of measure, rather than the height of thought; and in what I did endeavour, it is no vanity to say I have succeeded. I detest arrogance, but there is some difference betwixt that and a just defence. But I will not farther bribe your candour or the
300 reader's. I leave them to speak for me, and, if they can, to make out that character, not pretending to a greater, which I have given them.

276. lazar] poor and diseased person, esp. leper. D. returns to the image in *Defence of An Essay* (1668), discussing *Bartholomew Fair*: Jonson 'hath made an excellent lazar of it; the copy is of price, though the original be vile' (*Works* ix 7). The analogy of painting and poetry is a classical commonplace (e.g. Horace, *Ars Poetica* l. 361) and recurs through D.'s criticism. Cp. *Heroic Stanzas* ll. 59–60n.

281. several] different.

282–3. stantes . . . Aemiliani] 'Aemiliani standing in their chariots' (*Satire* viii 3; actually 'Aemilianos': D. changes the case to suit his syntax).

285. spirantia mollius aera] '[Others will shape] more smoothly [statues of] breathing bronze' (*Aen*. vi 847).

287. concern] self-interest.

291. humi serpere] 'creep on the earth' (*Ars Poetica* l. 28).

293. nunc . . . locus] 'This was not now the place' (*Ars Poetica* l. 19; D. alters *his* ('for them') to *hic* ('this')).

299. candour] impartiality, justice (*OED* 3).

Verses to her Highness the Duchess, on the memorable victory gained by the Duke against the Hollanders, June the 3. 1665, and on her journey afterwards into the north

Madam,
When for our sakes your hero you resigned
To swelling seas, and every faithless wind;
When you released his courage, and set free
A valour fatal to the enemy,
5   You lodged your country's cares within your breast
(The mansion where soft love should only rest);
And ere our foes abroad were overcome,
The noblest conquest you had gained at home.
Ah, what concerns did both your souls divide!
10   Your honour gave us what your love denied;
And 'twas for him much easier to subdue
Those foes he fought with, than to part from you.
That glorious day which two such navies saw
As each unmatched might to the world give law,
15   Neptune, yet doubtful whom he should obey,
Held to them both the trident of the sea:

Verses. This poem was first printed as part of the prefatory material to *AM*; from ll. 287–90 above, it appears that the verses circulated in MS, but no separate MS copy is known. The Duchess of York (Anne Hyde: 1637–71) had visited the fleet at Harwich in May 1665 (the *Second Advice* has a scathing account, ll. 55–74). After James's narrow escape from death in the Battle of Lowestoft he was kept on shore to avoid further risks to his life. On 5 August 1665 the Duke and Duchess left plague-ridden London and made a triumphal progress to York, where rebellions had been reported. Waller also has complimentary lines to the Duchess in his *Instructions* ll. 81–90. D.'s lines are favourably alluded to in Christopher Wase's *Divination* (1666; a rejoinder to the *Second Advice*); Wase rejects several possible authors for the *Second Advice* including D.: 'Or else if love and honour crown each page, / You well had read the champion of the stage: / Here the kind Duchess is forbid to mourn / When her Lord parts, or joy at his return' (ll. 33–6; *POAS* i 56). For D.'s defence of the Duchess's posthumously published religious papers in 1686 see *Works* xvii 291–323.
15–16. *obey* / . . . *sea*] Scott noted that *sea* is often pronounced in D. to rhyme with *obey, way* etc. (cp. ll. 42–3). For the image cp. *Astraea Redux* l. 249n.

The winds were hushed, the waves in ranks were cast,
As awfully as when God's people passed;
Those yet uncertain on whose sails to blow,
20 These where the wealth of nations ought to flow.
Then with the Duke your Highness ruled the day, ⎫
While all the brave did his command obey, ⎬
The fair and pious under you did pray. ⎭
How powerful are chaste vows! The wind and tide
25 You bribed to combat on the English side.
Thus to your much-loved lord you did convey
An unknown succour, sent the nearest way.
New vigour to his wearied arms you brought
(So Moses was upheld while Israel fought).
30 While from afar we heard the cannon play
Like distant thunder on a shiny day,
For absent friends we were ashamed to fear
When we considered what you ventured there.
Ships, men and arms our country might restore,
35 But such a leader could supply no more.
With generous thoughts of conquest he did burn,
Yet fought not more to vanquish than return.
Fortune and victory he did pursue
To bring them as his slaves to wait on you.
40 Thus beauty ravished the rewards of fame,
And the fair triumphed when the brave o'ercame.
Then, as you meant to spread another way
By land your conquests far as his by sea,
Leaving our southern clime you marched along
45 The stubborn north, ten thousand Cupids strong.
Like commons the nobility resort

17. *cast*] thrown up, banked up (*OED* 30).
18. Exodus xiv 21–2.
29. When Joshua fought with Amalek, he was victorious so long as Moses kept his arms raised; when Moses grew weary his arms were supported (Exodus xvii 11–13).
30–1. Cp. the account of the naval battle at the opening of *EDP* (*Works* xvii 8–9).
36. *generous*] noble.
44. *along*] through (*OED* 1).
45. *stubborn north*] Opposition to Charles's rule was strong in the north of England, as seen in the Yorkshire rebellion of 1663 (Hutton, *The Restoration* 204–9).

In crowding heaps to fill your moving court;
To welcome your approach the vulgar run
Like some new envoy from the distant sun,
50 And country beauties by their lovers go,
Blessing themselves and wondering at the show.
So when the new-born phoenix first is seen,
Her feathered subjects all adore their queen,
And while she makes her progress through the east
55 From every grove her numerous train's increased;
Each poet of the air her glory sings,
And round him the pleased audience clap their wings.

And now, sir, 'tis time I should relieve you from the
tedious length of this account. You have better and more
305 profitable employment for your hours, and I wrong the
public to detain you longer. In conclusion, I must leave
my poem to you with all its faults, which I hope to find
fewer in the printing by your emendations. I know you
are not of the number of those of whom the younger
310 Pliny speaks, *Nec sunt parum multi qui carpere amicos suos
judicium vocant*; I am rather too secure of you on that
side. Your candour in pardoning my errors may make
you more remiss in correcting them, if you will not
withal consider that they come into the world with
315 your approbation, and through your hands. I beg from

50. *go*] walk.
52–7. The progress of the new-born phoenix, attended by other birds, was
first recounted in the late Latin poem *Phoenix*, sometimes attributed to Lactantius (ll. 151–8), and then in Claudian's *Phoenix* ll. 76–80. The former is
closer to D.'s passage. Claudian also makes a political application of the
phoenix simile in *De Consulatu Stilichonis* ii 414–20. The progress is described
at length in Du Bartas (tr. Sylvester, I v 645–712), which D. knew well as a
boy. The phoenix is normally masculine, but is feminine in 'Lactantius';
Sylvester changes the sex to feminine in his translation of Du Bartas, probably as a compliment to Elizabeth I (for the phoenix as an emblem of Elizabeth see Frances Yates, *Astraea* (1975) 58, 65–6). Cp. *Threnodia Augustalis* ll.
364–71*n*; 'To the Memory of Anne Killigrew' l. 134; 'Of the Pythagorean
Philosophy' ll. 600–11.

310–11. Nec . . . vocant] 'There are not a few who call it discernment to
disparage their friends' (*Epistulae* vii 28).

you the greatest favour you can confer upon an absent
person, since I repose upon your management what is
dearest to me, my fame and reputation; and therefore I
hope it will stir you up to make my poem fairer by
320   many of your blots: if not, you know the story of the
gamester who married the rich man's daughter, and
when her father denied the portion, christened all the
children by his surname, that if, in conclusion, they
must beg, they should do so by one name as well as by
325   the other. But since the reproach of my faults will light
on you, 'tis but reason I should do you that justice to the
readers, to let them know that if there be anything
tolerable in this poem, they owe the argument to your
choice, the writing to your encouragement, the correct-
330   ion to your judgement, and the care of it to your friendship, to which he must ever acknowledge himself to
owe all things, who is,

SIR,
The most obedient and most
faithful of your servants,
JOHN DRYDEN.

From Charlton in
Wiltshire, Novem.
10. 1666.

Annus Mirabilis:
The Year of Wonders,
MDCLXVI

1–24. Samuel Johnson noted that the opening of *AM* resembles the opening
of Waller's *Of a War with Spain, and Fight at Sea* (1658): 'Now, for some ages,
had the pride of Spain / Made the sun shine on half the world in vain; / While
she bid war to all that durst supply / The place of those her cruelty made die.
/ Of nature's bounty men forbore to taste, / And the best portion of the earth
lay waste, / From the new world her silver and her gold / Came, like a
tempest, to confound the old; / . . . When Britain, looking with a just disdain
/ Upon this gilded majesty of Spain, / And knowing well that empire must
decline, / Whose chief support and sinews are of coin, / Our nation's solid
virtue did oppose / To the rich troublers of the world's repose' (ll. 1–8, 13–
18).

I

In thriving arts long time had Holland grown,
　　Crouching at home, and cruel when abroad;
　　Scarce leaving us the means to claim our own;
　　　Our King they courted, and our merchants awed.

2

5　Trade, which like blood should circularly flow,
　　Stopped in their channels, found its freedom lost;
　　Thither the wealth of all the world did go,
　　　And seemed but shipwrecked on so base a coast.

---

1. Holland] England was at war with the United Provinces of the Netherlands, a republic made up of seven independent provinces; Holland was a
powerful maritime province, and its name was often used loosely for the
whole republic; 'Belgium' was another loose seventeenth-century term for
the same country (cp. l. 16 etc.).

2. Crouching] cringing, fawning (*OED* 2).　　　*cruel*] The cruelty of the Dutch
against English traders had recently been recorded by Thomas Mun in *England's Treasure by Forraign Trade* (1664) 206 and in *His Majesties Propriety, and
Dominion on the British Seas Asserted* (1665) (*Works*). The massacre of English
sailors by the Dutch at Amboyna in 1619 was still bitterly remembered, as in
D.'s play *Amboyna* (1673).

4. After the Restoration Holland desired peace and a trade agreement with
England; inconclusive negotiations took place in 1660–2.

5–6. Simon Ford (Θαυμάσια Κύριον ἐν Βυθῷ (1665)) says that the Dutch
'think the *Trade* of the *whole World* ought to run in no other *channell* but that
which unloads it selfe into their *private purses*' (9), and compares restriction of
trade to illness in the body, where 'the *blood* and *spirits* being any way *infected*
or *obstructed* (though in *remoter* parts) quickly by *circulation* communicate their
distempers to the *heart* it selfe' (26). The Speaker of the House of Commons
said: 'we found our Body Politick entring into a Consumption, our Treasures, that are the sinews of War, and the bond of Peace, are much exhausted;
the great aydes which are given to your Majesty for the maintenance of the
War, are but like the blood in its circulation, which will return again, and
nourish all the parts' (*The Speech of S^r. Edw. Turnor, K^t . . . Delivered on Friday
the Eighteenth day of January 1666* [i.e. 1666/7] (1666) 2).

5. Perhaps echoed by Denham in 'Our knowledge, like our blood, must
circulate' ('The Progress of Learning' l. 216, in his *Poems and Translations*
(1668)).

8. shipwrecked] 1667's spelling *shipwracked* indicates seventeenth-century pronunciation.　　　*base*] punning on the meaning 'low-lying' (*OED* 3); cp. the
French name for the Netherlands, Les Pays-Bas.

3
For them alone the heavens had kindly heat,
10   ^aIn eastern quarries ripening precious dew;
For them the Idumaean balm did sweat,
And in hot Ceylon spicy forests grew.

(a) In eastern quarries, etc: *Precious stones at first are dew, condensed and hardened by the warmth of the sun, or subterranean fires.*

4
The sun but seemed the labourer of their year;
^bEach waxing moon supplied her watery store
15   To swell those tides which from the line did bear
Their brim-full vessels to the Belgian shore.

(b) Each waxing, etc: *According to their opinion, who think that great heap of waters under the line is depressed into tides by the moon towards the poles.*

5
Thus mighty in her ships stood Carthage long,
And swept the riches of the world from far;

9. *kindly*] favourable to growth (*OED* 5b).

10. The origin of metals and stones was a subject of contemporary debate. At a meeting of the Royal Society on 27 May 1663 some members argued 'that minerals were produced by certain subterraneous juices, which passing through the veins of the earth, and having mingled therewith, do afterwards precipitate and crystallize into stones, ores and metals of various kinds and figures, according to the various kinds of salts contained in the juices and the earth' (Thomas Birch, *History of the Royal Society*, 4 vols (1756–7) i 247) (*Works*).

11. From Virgil: *odorato . . . sudantia ligno / balsama* ('balsam sweating from the odorous wood'; *Geo.* ii 118–19). Idumaea is a region in southern Palestine occupied by the Edomites.

12. The Royal Society had enquired about the cinnamon trees in Ceylon (Sprat 169) (*Works*).   *Ceylon*] stressed on the first syllable.

14–15. Descartes proposed in his *Principia* (1644) that tides result from lunar pressure, rather than lunar attraction; G. P. de Roberval further argued that the pressure of the moon being greatest at the equator, the waters are depressed there and pushed outwards towards the poles (reprinted by Marin Mersenne, *Novarum Observationum Physico-Mathematicarum tomus III* (1647) 31–2; C. W. Adams, *Isis* xliv (1953) 100–1).

15. line] equator.

17–20. The Second Punic War (218–201 BC) decisively established Rome as

Yet stooped to Rome, less wealthy but more strong:
20   And this may prove our second Punic War.

6

What peace can be where both to one pretend?
   (But they more diligent, and we more strong)
Or if a peace, it soon must have an end,
   For they would grow too powerful were it long.

7

25   Behold two nations then, engaged so far
   That each seven years the fit must shake each land;
Where France will side to weaken us by war,
   Who only can his vast designs withstand.

8

See how he feeds th' ^cIberian with delays,
30   To render us his timely friendship vain;
And while his secret soul on Flanders preys,
   He rocks the cradle of the babe of Spain.

(c) Th' Iberian: *the Spaniard.*

9

Such deep designs of empire does he lay
   O'er them whose cause he seems to take in hand;
35   And prudently would make them lords at sea
   To whom with ease he can give laws by land.

---

the dominant power in the Mediterranean; the Second Dutch War by no
means achieved a comparable result for England. The First Dutch War had
been fought successfully under Cromwell in 1653–4. The same comparison is
used by William Smith: 'With equall folly, and with equal fate / Mistaken
Carthage urg'd the *Romane* State' (*A Poem on the famous ship called the Loyal
London* (1666; licensed 15 June) 4). For further echoes of Smith's poem see ll.
601–16n, 1049–52n, 1205n. For comparisons of Holland and Carthage during
the First Dutch War see Marvell, 'The Character of Holland' ll. 141–2, and
L.S., *The Perfect Politician* (1660) 254–60 (a biography of Cromwell). For D.'s
later use of the comparison see 'Epilogue to *Amboyna*' l. 19n.
21. *pretend*] claim.
27–36. Louis XIV was bound by the treaty of 1662 to aid the Dutch against
aggression. His marriage with the Spanish princess Maria Theresa in 1660

10

This saw our King; and long within his breast
    His pensive counsels balanced to and fro;
He grieved the land he freed should be oppressed,
40   And he less for it than usurpers do.

11

His generous mind the fair ideas drew
    Of fame and honour which in dangers lay;
Where wealth, like fruit on precipices, grew,
    Not to be gathered but by birds of prey.

12

45 The loss and gain each fatally were great,
    And still his subjects called aloud for war;
But peaceful kings o'er martial people set
    Each other's poise and counterbalance are.

13

He first surveyed the charge with careful eyes,
50   Which none but mighty monarchs could maintain;

---

seemed to promise peace and dynastic union between France and Spain. In June 1664 Clarendon sent Sir Richard Fanshawe as ambassador to Madrid in an effort to repair England's bad relations with Spain, but through Fanshawe's incompetence and Louis's influence this came to nothing. It was in Louis's interest for England and Holland to weaken each other, and Dutch domination of the sea in the event of their victory would be counterbalanced by the proximity to Holland of Louis's powerful army. When Philip IV of Spain died in September 1665, leaving the throne to his infant son, Louis invaded the Spanish Netherlands (Flanders) and claimed them for his wife.

38. Cp. the Latin idiom *consilia eventis ponderare* (Cicero, *Pro Rabirio Postumo* 1).

40. On the military achievements of Britain under Cromwell see *Heroic Stanzas* ll. 81, 96, 113–24.

41. generous] noble.

45–8. On 2 June 1664 Charles wrote to his sister Henriette-Anne: 'I never saw so great an appetite to a war as is, in both this town and country, especially in the Parliament men, who, I am confident, would pawn their estates to maintain a war. But all this shall not govern me, for I will look merely [to] what is just and best for the honour and good of England, and will be very steady in what I resolve, and if I be forced to a war, I shall be ready with as good ships and men as ever was seen, and leave the success to God' (*Letters of Charles II*, edited by Arthur Bryant (1935) 159).

Yet judged, like vapours that from limbecks rise,
  It would in richer showers descend again.

14

At length resolved t' assert the watery ball,
  He in himself did whole armadoes bring;
55 Him agèd seamen might their master call,
  And choose for general were he not their King.

15

It seems as every ship their sovereign knows,
  His awful summons they so soon obey;
So hear the scaly herd when ^dProteus blows,
60   And so to pasture follow through the sea.

(d) When Proteus blows, *or* Caeruleus Proteus immania ponti
armenta, et magnas pascit sub gurgite phocas. *Virg.*

16

To see this fleet upon the ocean move,
  Angels drew wide the curtains of the skies;

51. limbecks] alembics, apparatuses used in distilling; for the alchemical implications see l. 1169*n*.
52. Cp. Virgil: *tum pater omnipotens fecundis imbribus Aether / coniugis in gre-
mium laetae descendit* (*Geo.* ii 325–6: 'Then the almighty father, the Sky,
descends in fruitful showers upon the lap of his joyful consort'). Cp. 'The
Sun exhales the vapours from the earth, and then sends them down again in
showres of plenty: So we to our great joy, do find that our obedience and
affection to your Majesty are returned upon our heads in plenty, peace and
protection' (*The Several Speeches of Sr. Edward Turner Kt.* (1661) 9). Cp. ll.
181–4.
53. assert] lay claim to (*OED* 3, 4); see *Heroic Stanzas* l. 85*n*.
54. See *To His Sacred Majesty* ll. 107–10*n*. Cp. Virgil: *magnum / agmen agens
Clausus magnique ipse agminis instar* (*Aen.* vii 706–7: 'Clausus bringing a large
army, and himself worth a large army').
59n. A version of *Geo.* iv 388, 394–5: *caeruleus Proteus . . . immania cuius / armenta
et turpis pascit sub gurgite phocas* ('sea-green Proteus drives his huge flock and ugly
seals to pasture under the sea'). The comparison of Charles with Proteus may
draw upon the use of Proteus as an emblem of the qualities of the wise ruler (see
Ross 371 and D.'s *Albion and Albanius* III i (*Works* xv 47–8)).
59. hear] Eds; here *1667, 1668, 1688.*
62–3. Cp. Du Bartas, tr. Sylvester: God 'Spred Heav'ns blew Curtains and
those Lamps . . . burnisht' (I i 463); and Sidney: '*Phoebus* drew wide the
curtaines of the skies' (*Astrophil and Stella* xiii 12).

And heaven, as if there wanted lights above,
For tapers made two glaring comets rise.

17

65   Whether they unctuous exhalations are,
        Fired by the sun, or seeming so alone,
     Or each some more remote and slippery star
        Which loses footing when to mortals shown:

18

     Or one that bright companion of the sun,
70   Whose glorious aspect sealed our new-born King;
     And now a round of greater years begun,
        New influence from his walks of light did bring.

63. there] 1668, 1688; their 1667.   wanted] lacked.
64. The first comet was discovered in Spain in November 1664, and was last seen in March 1665; the second was discovered at Aix in March 1665 and disappeared in April (see Pepys 15, 17 December 1664, 1 March 1665). There had been a comet in 1652 when the English defeated the Dutch at sea (John Gadbury, *De Cometis* (1665) 43). Gadbury says: 'It is a thing so *rare* and *unusual*, for to have *three Comets* in a *year*; nay, sometimes in an *Age*: that we may properly term *this*, wherein we live, not only, ANNUS (*sed* AETAS) MIRABILIS! not only, a WONDERFUL YEAR, but AGE' (62); but he also thought that the first comet portended 'shipwracks and sea-fights; Wars . . . destruction of Governments, Laws, Customs and Constitutions'; and the second 'Famine, the Plague, Exile', and he carefully leaves in Latin the implication that the King may die (45–8). D. omits these dire implications, as did Waller: 'Make Heaven concerned, and an unusual star / Declare the importance of the approaching war' (*Instructions* ll. 7–8).
65–72. D. offers four explanations for comets: (i) they are produced by vapours drawn up by the sun: this is the traditional theory, originating with Aristotle, and held by Gadbury ('not so much *enflamed*, as *illustrated* of the Sun' (6)); (ii) they are illusions, as suggested by Galileo in 1623, and recorded by Gadbury (5); (iii) they are falling stars: cp. Song I in *Tyrannic Love* l. 13n; Shakespeare, *The Rape of Lucrece* l. 1525 and *A Midsummer Night's Dream* II i 153; (iv) one of the comets is that which greeted the birth of Charles II and has now returned (cp. *Astraea Redux* ll. 288–9n).
67. slippery] Probably from Latin usage; *labor* ('slide') is often used of stars (e.g. *Geo.* i 366).
71. Cp. *Astraea Redux* ll. 292–3n.
72. walks] region where something moves (*OED* 8b); probably rendering *solisque vias* ('walks of the sun') in *Aen.* vi 796.

19

Victorious York did first, with famed success,
  To his known valour make the Dutch give place:
75 Thus heaven our monarch's fortune did confess,
  Beginning conquest from his royal race.

20

But since it was decreed, auspicious King,
  In Britain's right that thou shouldst wed the main,
Heaven as a gage would cast some precious thing,
80   And therefore doomed that Lawson should be
    slain.

21

Lawson amongst the foremost met his fate,
  Whom sea-green Syrens from the rocks lament;
Thus as an offering for the Grecian state
He first was killed who first to battle went.

73–4. The Duke of York took command of the fleet on 25 March 1665, and
put to sea in May with ninety-eight warships. The Dutch fleet was engaged
off Lowestoft on 2–3 June, and although both sides incurred heavy losses, the
Dutch suffered worst and withdrew. The news was received with delight in
London: see Pepys 8 June, and the opening of *EDP.*

75. confess] reveal by circumstances (*OED* 5).

77. auspicious] favoured by heaven (*OED* 3); cp. *AA* l. 230, *Threnodia Augustalis* l. 373.

78. wed the main] As in the annual ceremony on Ascension Day when the
Doge of Venice married the sea and cast a ring into it. The *Second Advice*
sarcastically says that this ceremony was eclipsed by the splendour of the
Duchess of York's visit to the fleet at Harwich (ll. 73–4; *POAS* i 40).

79. gage] pledge.

80–1. Lawson] Vice-Admiral Sir John Lawson commanded ships in the service of Parliament from 1642 to 1656, and in 1659–60 was Vice-Admiral of
the fleet which brought Charles from Holland. He served against the corsairs
in the Mediterranean 1661–4. At Lowestoft he was wounded in the knee;
gangrene set in and he died on 29 June.

80. Cp. 'They therefore doom that *Dargonet* must fall' (Davenant, *Gondibert* I
iv 18).

83–4. Protesilaus was the first Greek to land at Troy, and the first to be killed
(*Iliad* ii 695–702). Lawson's ship was in the van of the fleet.

22

85   *Their chief blown up, in air not waves expired,
          To which his pride presumed to give the law;
      The Dutch confessed heaven present, and retired,
          And all was Britain the wide ocean saw.

*The Admiral of Holland.

23

      To nearest ports their shattered ships repair,
90   Where by our dreadful cannon they lay awed:
      So reverently men quit the open air
          When thunder speaks the angry gods abroad.

24

                                    The attempt at Bergen.
      And now approached their fleet from India, fraught
          With all the riches of the rising sun;
95   And precious sand from ᵉsouthern climates brought
          (The fatal regions where the war begun).

(e) Southern climates: *Guinea.*

85. The Dutch commander Opdam's flagship, *De Eendracht*, blew up during an engagement with the Duke of York's ship *Royal Charles*. This was the turning-point in the battle. D. omits to mention that the Dutch were allowed to retire unharried into the Texel because James's secretary Henry Brounker, weary of the pursuit, fabricated an order from James to slacken sail while the Duke was asleep.

91–2. Cp. D.'s contemporaneous *Secret Love*: 'as, when it thunders / Men reverently quit the open Air / Because the angry Gods are then abroad' (III i 13–15) (*Works*).

93–124. In July 1665 the English fleet, commanded by the Earl of Sandwich, was cruising about the Dogger Bank waiting to intercept the rich fleet from the Indies under the Dutch admiral De Ruyter. An arrangement was negotiated with the King of Denmark to allow the English to attack the fleet in the neutral port of Bergen, in return for half the spoils. Sandwich dispatched Teddiman with fifteen ships, but the governor of Bergen urged delay pending firm orders from his king. Impatient, Teddiman entered the harbour on 2 August, was bombarded by the shore forts, and withdrew with the loss of 118 men.

95–6. southern climates] The valuable gold-bearing reefs on the coast of West Africa had been fought over by Dutch and English factors for fifty years. The immediate trigger of the Second Dutch War was the dispatch in August 1664 of a Dutch fleet under De Ruyter to retake the Gold Coast which had been captured earlier that year by Sir Robert Holmes.

25

Like hunted castors, conscious of their store,
    Their waylayed wealth to Norway's coasts they
        bring;
There first the north's cold bosom spices bore,
100   And winter brooded on the eastern spring.

26

By the rich scent we found our perfumed prey,
    Which flanked with rocks did close in covert lie;
And round about their murdering cannon lay,
    At once to threaten and invite the eye.

27

105 Fiercer than cannon, and than rocks more hard,
    The English undertake th' unequal war:
Seven ships alone, by which the port is barred,
    Besiege the Indies and all Denmark dare.

28

These fight like husbands, but like lovers those:
110   These fain would keep, and those more fain enjoy;
And to such height their frantic passion grows
    That what both love, both hazard to destroy.

29

Amidst whole heaps of spices lights a ball,
    And now their odours armed against them fly:

---

97. *castors*] beavers, who were hunted for the substance in their sacs which was used in making perfumes and medicines.

107. *Seven ships*] 'I got 8 sail in a line, and brought our broadsides on the ships in the harbour, which spread from one side to the other, the other 7 I placed against the Castle' (Teddiman's report to Sandwich, in *Journal of Edward Montagu* (1929) 262).

109. *lovers*] Cp. Waller: 'These dying lovers' (*Of a War with Spain* l. 89).

110–12. *enjoy . . . destroy*] Cp. Waller: 'glad to see the fire destroy / Wealth that prevailing foes were to enjoy' (ll. 77–8).

113–16. Cp. Waller: 'Spices and gums about them melting fry, / And, phoenix-like, in that rich nest they die' (ll. 83–4).

115 Some preciously by shattered porcelain fall,
     And some by aromatic splinters die.

30

     And though by tempests of the prize bereft,
         In heaven's inclemency some ease we find:
     Our foes we vanquished by our valour left,
120   And only yielded to the seas and wind.

31

     Nor wholly lost we so deserved a prey,
         For storms, repenting, part of it restored,
     Which, as a tribute from the Baltic Sea,
         The British Ocean sent her mighty lord.

32

125 Go, mortals, now, and vex yourselves in vain
     For wealth which so uncertainly must come,
     When what was brought so far, and with such pain,
         Was only kept to lose it nearer home.

33

     The son who, twice three months on th' ocean
         tossed,
130   Prepared to tell what he had passed before,

120. The wind was blowing from the south, out of the port, so Teddiman could not send in his fireships (*Journal* 262).

121–4. The Dutch ships were scattered by a storm on their way home from Bergen, and Sandwich captured seven warships, two East Indiamen and other merchantmen (*Journal* 277–81).

125–40. D.'s note to l. 137 cites Petronius, *Satyricon* 115 ('If you consider it rightly, shipwreck is everywhere'). In this note *1667* reads *naufragiunt est* in the text, which is corrected to *fit naufragium* in the errata; it is a peculiar correction, since the proper reading in Petronius is *naufragium est,* and the correction of *nt* to *m* is all that was needed. Christie noted that D.'s ll. 125–36 also draw upon the same passage: *Hunc, forsitan, proclamo, in aliqua parte terrarum secura expectat uxor, forsitan ignarus tempestatis filius, aut patrem utique reliquit aliquem, cui proficiscens osculum dedit. Haec sunt consilia mortalium, haec vota magnarum cogitationum. . . . Ite nunc, mortales, et magnis cogitationibus pectora implete. Ite cauti, et opes fraudibus captas per mille annos disponite. Nempe hic proxima luce patrimonii sui rationes inspexit, nempe diem etiam, quo venturus esset in patriam, animo suo fixit. Dii deaeque, quam longe a destinatione sua iacet.* ('Perhaps somewhere, I say, a carefree wife waits for him; perhaps a son, not

Now sees in English ships the Holland coast,
  And parents' arms in vain stretched from the shore.

                              34
  This careful husband had been long away,
    Whom his chaste wife and little children mourn,
135 Who on their fingers learned to tell the day
    On which their father promised to return.

                              35
  fSuch are the proud designs of human kind,
    And so we suffer shipwreck everywhere!
  Alas, what port can such a pilot find,
140   Who in the night of fate must blindly steer!

(f) Such are etc: *From Petronius*: Si bene calculum ponas ubique fit
naufragium.

                              36
  The undistinguished seeds of good and ill
    Heaven in his bosom from our knowledge hides,
  And draws them in contempt of human skill,
    Which oft for friends mistaken foes provides.

                              37
145 Let Münster's prelate ever be accursed,
    In whom we seek the gGerman faith in vain:

knowing about the storm; or he left a father, or someone whom he kissed as
he set out. Such are the plans of mortals, such are our great designs. . . . Go
now, mortals, and fill your hearts with great schemes. Go and carefully
invest your ill-gotten gains for a thousand years. Yesterday he must have
looked at the accounts of his investments, he must have imagined the day he
would reach his home town. O heavens, how far away he lies from his
destination!'). Thomas Flatman paraphrases the same passage in his *Poems and
Songs* (1674) 36–7. Cp. Waller, *Of a War with Spain* ll. 51–60.
134. Cp. also Lucretius iii 894–6 (tr. D. in 'Lucretius: Against the Fear of
Death' ll. 76–80) and *Geo.* ii 523–4, esp. Virgil's *casta* ('chaste').
141. 'Good and evill we know in the field of this World grow up together
almost inseparably; . . . those confused seeds which were impos'd on *Psyche*
as an incessant labour to cull out, and sort asunder, were not more intermixt'
(Milton, *Areopagitica* (1644); *Complete Prose Works* ii 514).
145. In June 1665 a treaty was made with Bernhard von Galen, Bishop of

> Alas, that he should teach the English first
>   That fraud and avarice in the church could reign!

(g) The German faith: *Tacitus saith of them*, Nullos mortalium fide aut armis ante Germanos esse.

38

> Happy who never trust a stranger's will,
150   Whose friendship's in his interest understood,
> Since money giv'n but tempts him to be ill
>   When power is too remote to make him good.

39

War declared by France.

> Till now, alone the mighty nations strove:
>   The rest at gaze without the lists did stand;
155 And threatening France, placed like a painted Jove,
>   Kept idle thunder in his lifted hand:

40

> That eunuch guardian of rich Holland's trade,
>   Who envies us what he wants power t' enjoy;
> Whose noiseful valour does no foe invade,
160   And weak assistance will his friends destroy.

41

> Offended that we fought without his leave,
>   He takes this time his secret hate to show;

Münster, whereby he would invade Holland in return for subsidies from England. No peace was to be made without agreement. He did invade, but was soon under pressure from French armies and from his German enemies. English subsidies dried up, and he was forced to make peace unilaterally in April 1666.

146n. 'No men exceed the Germans in loyalty or arms', *Annales* xiii 54. (The usual text is *armis aut fide.*)

154. at gaze] gazing in wonder or fascination (*OED* 3b).

155–63. For the early part of 1665 Louis's attitude was uncertain. He sent an embassy to try to reconcile England and Holland, but as the year wore on it became apparent that Louis would honour his treaty obligations to Holland, and he declared war on 6 January 1666. Louis was beginning to assert his claim to the Spanish Netherlands, and at this point wanted the friendship of the Dutch; neither did he want to see England strengthened.

Which Charles does with a mind so calm receive
As one that neither seeks nor shuns his foe.

42
165   With France to aid the Dutch the Danes unite,
        France as their tyrant, Denmark as their slave;
        But when with one three nations join to fight,
        They silently confess that one more brave.

43
        Louis had chased the English from his shore,
170   But Charles the French as subjects does invite.
        Would heaven for each some Solomon restore,
        Who by their mercy may decide their right.

44
        Were subjects so but only by their choice,
        And not from birth did forced dominion take,
·175   Our Prince alone would have the public voice,
        And all his neighbours' realms would deserts make.

45
        He without fear a dangerous war pursues,
        Which without rashness he began before:
        As honour made him first the danger choose,
180   So still he makes it good on virtue's score.

46
        The doubled charge his subjects' love supplies,
        Who in that bounty to themselves are kind:

165–6. After the fiasco at Bergen, England tried to cement an alliance with
Denmark by threats and promises; but in February 1666 Denmark joined the
other side, the decision being eased by a French subsidy.

169–76. Louis had given English residents in France three months to leave;
Charles promised protection to any French or Dutch nationals who wished to
leave their countries, particularly oppressed Protestants, in *His Majesties Declaration against the French* (9 February 1666); cp. Pepys 11 February.

171–2. See 1 Kings iii 16–28 for the judgement of Solomon.

176. deserts] *1667*'s spelling *desarts* indicates seventeenth-century pronunciation.

181–4. Cp. l. 52n.

181. *doubled charge*] On 9 February 1665 the House of Commons, in bellicose

So glad Egyptians see their Nilus rise,
    And in his plenty their abundance find.

47
Prince Rupert and Duke Albemarle sent to sea.

185 With equal power he does two chiefs create,
    Two such, as each seemed worthiest when alone;
Each able to sustain a nation's fate,
    Since both had found a greater in their own.

48
Both great in courage, conduct and in fame,
190   Yet neither envious of the other's praise;
Their duty, faith and interest too the same,
    Like mighty partners equally they raise.

49
The Prince long time had courted Fortune's love,
    But once possessed did absolutely reign;
195 Thus with their Amazons the heroes strove,
    And conquered first those beauties they would
        gain.

---

mood, voted £2,500,000 for the war, which was to be raised by a three-year assessment. In October 1665 the House voted a further £1,250,000.

185–6. Rupert and Albemarle were placed in joint command of a fleet of eighty ships (Pepys 23 April 1666).

188. i.e. their own lives had already demonstrated their capacity to triumph over adversity (see ll. 193–4*n*, 197–8*n*).

190. But see the quotation in ll. 197–8*n* below.

192. raise] rise (*OED* 35).

193–4. Prince Rupert (1619–82) was the son of the Queen of Bohemia and the Elector Palatine, and shared their exile in Holland and England during 1620–37. After he and his father lost the Battle of Vlotho (1638) he was imprisoned until 1641. During the Civil War he served his uncle Charles I as a successful but rash and brutal general, though he lost the Battle of Marston Moor. From 1649 to 1653 he harassed the Commonwealth's fleet.

193. For the image cp. *Heroic Stanzas* ll. 29–30*n*.

194. i.e. dominated Fortune like an autocratic (*absolute*) ruler.

195–6. For Theseus's campaign against the Amazons and his marriage to their Queen Antiope, see Plutarch, *Theseus* 26–7.

196–7. D. also links stanzas by repeating a rhyme at ll. 296–7, 524–5, 576–7, 1024–5, 1116–17.

50

The Duke beheld, like Scipio, with disdain
　　That Carthage which he ruined rise once more;
And shook aloft the fasces of the main
200　　To fright those slaves with what they felt before.

51

Together to the watery camp they haste,
　　Whom matrons passing to their children show:
Infants' first vows for them to heaven are cast,
　　And ʰfuture people bless them as they go.

(h) Future people: Examina infantium futurusque populus. *Plin. Jun.
in pan. ad Traj.*

52

205　With them no riotous pomp nor Asian train
　　T' infect a navy with their gaudy fears,
To make slow fights, and victories but vain—
　　But war, severely, like itself appears.

53

Diffusive of themselves where'er they pass,
210　　They make that warmth in others they expect:

197–8. Monck (for whom see *Astraea Redux*, headnote) had been a successful
commander of the fleet in the First Dutch War. Scipio Africanus defeated the
Carthaginians in Spain, and ended the Second Punic War by defeating Hannibal at Zama (202 BC). One contemporary viewed Monck's fortune more
critically: 'It was reported, before the General went from Whitehall, that he
had said he would undertake with forty sail of ships, to beat the Dutch out of
the sea. Fortune had so long attended him at sea and land, that perhaps he
took her for his slave, and she would now let him know to his cost, she was
his commandress . . . it is not unlikely, that he was greedy to engross all the
glory of besting the Dutch to himself' (MS account in *Letter Book* 212).
199. fasces of the main] Cp. *Astraea Redux* l. 249n.
200. The Scythians suppressed a slave rising by brandishing horse-whips
instead of spears; the slaves were awed, and fled (Herodotus iv 3–4).
201. watery camp] The Latin *campus* means 'plain'; cp. Virgil's *campos liquentis*
('liquid plains', *Aen.* vi 724).
204n. From Pliny, *Panegyricus* 26: 'swarms of children, the future populace'.
205. Asian] proverbially luxurious.

Their valour works like bodies on a glass,
  And does its image on their men project.

54

  Duke of Albemarle's battle, first day.
Our fleet divides, and straight the Dutch appear,
  In number and a famed commander bold;
215 The narrow seas can scarce their navy bear,
  Or crowded vessels can their soldiers hold.

55

The Duke, less numerous, but in courage more,
  On wings of all the winds to combat flies;
His murdering guns a loud defiance roar,
220 And bloody crosses on his flagstaffs rise.

56

Both furl their sails, and strip them for the fight,
  Their folded sheets dismiss the useless air:
ⁱTh' Elean plains could boast no nobler sight,
  When struggling champions did their bodies bare.

(i) Th' Elean etc: *Where the Olympic games were celebrated.*

211–12. For the image of the optic glass cp. 'Epilogue Spoken to the King' ll. 1–4.
213–16. On 29 May Rupert, with twenty ships, sailed to intercept the French fleet which was wrongly reported to be entering the Channel. Albemarle was left in the Downs with about sixty ships, and this division of the fleet was much criticized after the event. At the same time, the Dutch fleet of eighty-four warships under De Ruyter was leaving harbour. Orders for the recall of Rupert were delayed, but Albemarle moved to a new anchorage off the North Foreland. On 1 June Albemarle decided (against the advice of some of his officers) to engage the Dutch, who were sighted at anchor off Ostend. Thus began the Four Days Battle.
220. Each ship flew the Union Jack at the jack staff; an ensign of the squadronal colour (red, white or blue) with the red St George's cross in the canton at the ensign staff; and all except the admiral's ships flew long pennants with the St George's cross in the hoist at the main mast (Timothy Wilson, *Flags at Sea* (1986) 21–2).
221–2. In preparation for action 'they use to strip themselves into their short sailes, or fighting sailes, which is onely the fore sail, the maine and fore top sailes, because the rest should not be fired nor spoiled' (John Smith, *The Sea-Mans Grammar* (1653) 60) (*Works*).

57

225   Borne each by other in a distant line
            The sea-built forts in dreadful order move;
        So vast the noise, as if not fleets did join
            ^kBut lands unfixed and floating nations strove.

(k) Lands unfixed: *From Virgil*: Credas innare revulsas Cyclades.

58

        Now passed, on either side they nimbly tack,
230   Both strive to intercept and guide the wind,
        And in its eye more closely they come back
            To finish all the deaths they left behind.

59

        On high-raised decks the haughty Belgians ride,
            Beneath whose shade our humble frigates go:
235   Such port the elephant bears, and so defied
            By the rhinoceros her unequal foe.

60

        And as the built, so different is the fight:

225–44. Ogg 267 explains that the usual practice was 'for each fleet to file past
the other, firing into the enemy hulls and rigging; the ships in the van, having
fired their volleys, then bore round to take up position behind the rearmost
ships so as to repeat the attack. This was continued until the order of battle
was broken, when there was likely to be a general mêlée in which the
disabled ships might be boarded or burnt by fire-ships.' On this occasion, the
English ships passed twice through the Dutch fleet, 'the *Dutch* being on the
Leewards, their Guns mounted so high, that they onely shot our Rigging,
but did little execution on the Men or Hulls . . . they had much holed and
torn the Admirals Rigging' (*London Gazette* lviii).
228n. Virgil, *Aen.* viii 691–3: 'you would think that the Cyclades, torn from
their roots, were floating on the sea, or that high mountains were clashing
with mountains, so huge are the towered ships on which the heroes stand'.
revulsas] *1688*; revultas *1667*, *1668*. The comparison with the Cyclades is used
in William Smith's poem on the Battle of Lowestoft, *Ingratitude Reveng'd*
(*1665*), which includes the line 'Or two unfixed *Towns*, or floating *Woods*' (3);
the poem ends with an address to the City of London.
230. guide] manage (*OED* 4b).
235–6. A traditional idea: see Pliny, *Naturalis Historia* viii 29; Du Bartas tr.
Sylvester I vi 41–50.
235. port] bearing, demeanour.
237. built] style of construction, esp. of a ship (*OED*).

Their mounting shot is on our sails designed;
 Deep in their hulls our deadly bullets light,
240 And through the yielding planks a passage find.

61
Our dreaded admiral from far they threat,
 Whose battered rigging their whole war receives:
All bare, like some old oak which tempests beat,
 He stands, and sees below his scattered leaves.

62
245 Heroes of old, when wounded, shelter sought,
 But he, who meets all danger with disdain,
Ev'n in their face his ship to anchor brought,
 And steeple-high stood propped upon the main.

63
At this excess of courage, all amazed
250 The foremost of his foes a while withdraw:
With such respect in entered Rome they gazed,
 Who on high chairs the godlike fathers saw.

239–40. Cp. Waller: 'Through yielding planks the angry bullets fly' (*Of a War with Spain* l. 47).

241–8. 'Several other of our ships, had their Rigging and Sails very much shattered, and especially the Admiral (his Courage carrying him foremost to all Dangers) to such a degree, as she was forced in the sight of the Enemy to chop to an Anchor, till she had brought new Sayls to the Yards, the old being rendred useless' (*True Narrative* 4).

243–4. Delicately recalling that 'The Duke had all his Tackle taken off by Chain-shot, and his Breeches to his Skin were shot off' (*London Gazette* lix). The incident is less sympathetically recorded in *Third Advice* ll. 123–30 (*POAS* i 73). D. is also adapting Virgil: *ac velut annoso validam cum robore quercum / Alpini Boreae nunc hinc nunc flatibus illinc / eruere inter se certant; it stridor, et altae / consternunt terram concusso stipite frondes* ('And as when Alpine North winds strive with each other to uproot a mighty oak of aged strength, with blasts now on this side, now on that, a creaking ensues, and the lofty leaves strew the ground, as the trunk is shaken'; *Aen.* iv 441–4). John Ogilby's translation here includes the words 'Tempests . . . some old Oake . . . scatter'd Leavs' (1654) 278; differently worded in his 1649 and 1665 texts.

251–2. When the Gauls sacked Rome in 387 BC they were awed by the sight of the elders sitting in their chairs of state 'like gods' (*simillimos diis*; Livy v 41). *entered Rome*] a Latinate participial construction. *fathers*] rendering *patres*, the Roman honorific for senators.

64

And now, as where Patroclus' body lay,
　　Here Trojan chiefs advanced, and there the Greek:
255　Ours o'er the Duke their pious wings display,
　　And theirs the noblest spoils of Britain seek.

65

Meantime his busy mariners he hastes,
　　His shattered sails with rigging to restore;
And willing pines ascend his broken masts,
260　Whose lofty heads rise higher than before.

66

Straight to the Dutch he turns his dreadful prow,
　　More fierce th' important quarrel to decide:
Like swans in long array his vessels show,
　　Whose crests advancing do the waves divide.

67

265　They charge, re-charge, and all along the sea
　　They drive and squander the huge Belgian fleet;
Berkeley alone who nearest danger lay
　　Did a like fate with lost Creüsa meet.

253–4. The battle over the body of Patroclus is related in *Iliad* xvii.
255. *pious*] faithful in the duties owed to a friend or superior (*OED* 2); cp.
Latin *pius*, frequently applied by Virgil to Aeneas.　　*display*] spread out
(*OED* 1).
259. *willing*] perhaps a Latinate usage: cp. *volentia rura* ('willing Ground' in
D.'s translation) in *Geo.* ii 500.
265. 'We tackt and stood through the Body of their Fleet, . . . then tackt to
the Westward again' (*True Narrative* 4).　　*all along*] throughout (*OED* 1).
266. *squander*] scatter (*OED* 2).
267–8. *who nearest danger lay*] *1667 third issue*; not making equal way *1667 first
and second issues*. The alteration was probably made to avoid any imputation
of cowardice, of which Sir William Berkeley (1639–66) had been accused in
the Battle of Lowestoft: cp. *Second Advice*, 'But judg'd it safe and decent (cost
what cost) / To lose the day, since his dear brother's lost. / With his whole
squadron straight away he bore, / And like good boy, promis'd to fight no
more' (ll. 193–6; *POAS* i 45; cp. i 72). Berkeley now led the van in the
Swiftsure, which was cut off and surrounded. He fought heroically, and died
from a wound in the throat. One account says: 'Sir William Berkley had from
the June fight the year before, undergone the aspersion of a Coward . . .

68

The night comes on, we eager to pursue
270   The combat still, and they ashamed to leave:
Till the last streaks of dying day withdrew,
    And doubtful moonlight did our rage deceive.

69

In th' English fleet each ship resounds with joy,
    And loud applause of their great leader's fame;
275 In fiery dreams the Dutch they still destroy,
    And slumbering smile at the imagined flame.

70

Not so the Holland fleet, who tired and done
    Stretched on their decks like weary oxen lie:
Faint sweats all down their mighty members run,
280   (Vast bulks which little souls but ill supply).

71

In dreams they fearful precipices tread,
    Or shipwrecked labour to some distant shore;
Or in dark churches walk among the dead:
    They wake with horror, and dare sleep no more.

[which] lay like a load upon his mind, and his valour, or his rage, engaged him so far among the enemies, that neither his discretion nor his friends knew how to bring him off' (*Notes upon the June Fight* in *Letter Book* 213). But *A True Narrative* 4 confirms (and was probably the source for) D.'s original phrasing: 'the *Swiftsure* [and others] . . . staying a little behind, were cut from our Fleet'. The revision makes l. 268 less apt: Creüsa became separated from her husband Aeneas in their escape from Troy, and was killed (*Aen.* ii 735–95).

269–72. 'continuing so long as there was light enough to distinguish friends from enemies' (*An Account of the Battle* in *Letter Book* 238).

272. Cp. *per incertam lunam sub luce maligna* ('by the doubtful and malignant light of the moon'; *Aen.* vi 270).   *deceive*] frustrate (*OED* 3b).

278. Homer compares the death-throes of a warrior with those of an ox (*Iliad* xiii 571).

280. Perhaps reversing Virgil's description of the warrior bees: *ingentis animos angusto in pectore* ('great souls in narrow breasts'; *Geo.* iv 83).   *supply*] furnish with an occupant (*OED* 7b).

281–4. Perhaps suggested by Lucan's account of soldiers' dreams in an interval in the Battle of Pharsalus (vii 764–76).

72

Second day's battle.

285   The morn they look on with unwilling eyes,
      Till from their maintop joyful news they hear
    Of ships, which by their mould bring new supplies,
      And in their colours Belgian lions bear.

73

    Our watchful General had discerned from far
290   This mighty succour which made glad the foe;
    He sighed, but like a father of the war
      [1]His face spake hope, while deep his sorrows flow.

(l) His face etc: Spem vultu simulat premit alto corde dolorem. *Virg.*

74

    His wounded men he first sends off to shore,
      Never till now unwilling to obey;
295   They not their wounds but want of strength deplore,
      And think them happy who with him can stay.

75

    Then to the rest, 'Rejoice', said he, 'today
      In you the fortune of Great Britain lies:
    Among so brave a people you are they
300   Whom heaven has chose to fight for such a prize.

76

If number English courages could quell

286–8. There is no evidence that the Dutch were reinforced on the morning of the second day, though they did receive sixteen extra ships that evening (*London Gazette* lix). However, *A True Narrative* 4 says that early on the second morning 'we . . . discovered . . . 12. sayl on our Weather-bow, which we supposed a supply.'

287. mould] structural type (*OED* 11).

288. The flag of the States General of the United Provinces of the Netherlands showed a lion holding a sword and a bunch of seven arrows, one for each province (*Flags at Sea* 58–9).

291. father of the war] Davenant has the phrase 'The Father of those fights we *Lombards* fought' (*Gondibert* I v 4), but D. seems only to wish to stress Albemarle's paternal care (*Works*).

292n. Aeneas 'feigns hope in his face, and presses his grief deep down in his heart', *Aen.* i 209.

We should at first have shunned, not met our foes,
Whose numerous sails the fearful only tell:
    Courage from hearts, and not from numbers
      grows.'

77
305 He said; nor needed more to say: with haste
    To their known stations cheerfully they go;
And all at once, disdaining to be last,
    Solicit every gale to meet the foe.

78
Nor did th' encouraged Belgians long delay,
310   But bold in others, not themselves, they stood:
So thick our navy scarce could shear their way,
    But seemed to wander in a moving wood.

79
Our little fleet was now engaged so far
    That like the swordfish in the whale they fought:
315 The combat only seemed a civil war,
    Till through their bowels we our passage wrought.

80
Never had valour, no not ours before,
    Done aught like this upon the land or main,
Where not to be o'ercome was to do more
320   Than all the conquests former kings did gain.

81
The mighty ghosts of our great Harries rose,
    And armèd Edwards looked with anxious eyes

---

314. The story of the swordfish attacking the whale is traditional (see Donne, 'The Progresse of the Soule' ll. 351–60; Spenser, 'Visions of the Worlds Vanitie' ll. 62–8). No story has been found of the swordfish inside the whale, though Donne writes of fish swimming inside the whale (ll. 316–27). One report to the Royal Society spoke of 'a certain horny Fish . . . who runs its horn into the Whal's belly, . . . [and] is known, sometimes to run its horn into Ships (perhaps taking them for Whales)' (*PTRS* i (1665–6) 133) (*Works*).
321–2. Kings such as Henry V, Henry VIII, Edward I and Edward III, and Edward the Black Prince: warriors and nationalistic rulers.

To see this fleet among unequal foes,
    By which Fate promised them their Charles should
       rise.

82

325 Meantime the Belgians tack upon our rear,
    And raking chase-guns through our sterns they
       send;
  Close by their fireships like jackals appear,
    Who on their lions for the prey attend.

83

  Silent in smoke of cannons they come on
330   (Such vapours once did fiery Cacus hide);
  In these the height of pleased revenge is shown,
    Who burn contented by another's side.

84

  Sometimes from fighting squadrons of each fleet
    (Deceived themselves, or to preserve some friend)
335 Two grappling Etnas on the ocean meet,
    And English fires with Belgian flames contend.

85

  Now at each tack our little fleet grows less,
    And like maimed fowl swim lagging on the main;
  Their greater loss their numbers scarce confess,
340   While they lose cheaper than the English gain.

325–40. 'The manner of fighting at that time was, that each fleet lay in a line, and when the ships of one fleet lay with their heads to the northward, the heads of the other lay to the southward, the headmost ships of our fleet engaging first the headmost of theirs: so passing on by their fleet in a line, firing all the way, and as soon as the rear of one fleet was clear from the rear of the other, then each fleet tacked in the van, standing almost stem for stem with one another to engage again' (*An Account* in *Letter Book* 239).

326. chase-guns] guns mounted in the bows of a ship, used when pursuing an enemy.

327. jackals] They were supposed to go ahead of lions to hunt up their prey for them. The word was stressed on the second syllable (*OED*).

330. fiery Cacus] Cacus, the son of Vulcan, stole cattle from Hercules, and when pursued vomited smoke to conceal himself (*Aen.* viii 251–5).

86

Have you not seen when, whistled from the fist,
　　Some falcon stoops at what her eye designed,
And with her eagerness, the quarry missed,
　　Straight flies at check, and clips it down the wind:

87

345　The dastard crow, that to the wood made wing,
　　And sees the groves no shelter can afford,
With her loud caws her craven kind does bring,
　　Who safe in numbers cuff the noble bird.

88

Among the Dutch thus Albemarle did fare:
350　He could not conquer, and disdained to fly;
Past hope of safety, 'twas his latest care
　　Like falling Caesar decently to die.

89

Yet pity did his manly spirit move
　　To see those perish who so well had fought;
355　And generously with his despair he strove,
　　Resolved to live till he their safety wrought.

341–4. A hawk is released from the hand by whistling, cast off against the
wind in pursuit of prey, or downwind when turned loose. *stoops*] descends swiftly on its prey (*OED* 6). *flies at check*] forsakes the proper prey
and pursues baser game which crosses her flight (*OED* 6). *clips it*] flies
rapidly (*OED* 6). For D.'s precise ornithological vocabulary cp. 'Virgil's
Ninth Eclogue' ll. 16–17.

345. Cp. 'the crow / Makes wing to th' rooky wood' (*Macbeth* III ii 50–1)
(*Works*).

348. *cuff*] buffet with their wings (*OED* 2).

352. *decently*] fittingly.

353–80. 'At a Council of Flagg-Officers, his Grace the Lord Generall
resolved to draw our Fleet into a Reer-line of Battel, and make a fair Retreat
of it. Here his Grace's accustomed and excellent Conduct, as well as his
invincible Courage, was eminently seen; for, by placing his weak and
disabled Ships before in a Line, and 16. of his greatest and best in a Rank in
the Reer, as a Bulwark for them, keeping his own Ship nearest the Enemy,
such of the *Dutch* Fleet that were the best saylers of them, came first in parties
upon him, and finding it too hot service to attaque him, staid for the rest of
their Fleet' (*A True Narrative* 5).

355. *generously*] nobly.

90

Let other Muses write his prosperous fate,
   Of conquered nations tell, and kings restored;
But mine shall sing of his eclipsed estate,
360   Which like the sun's more wonders does afford.

91

He drew his mighty frigates all before,
   On which the foe his fruitless force employs;
His weak ones deep into his rear he bore,
   Remote from guns as sick men are from noise.

92

365   His fiery cannon did their passage guide,
   And following smoke obscured them from the foe:
Thus Israel safe from the Egyptian's pride
   By flaming pillars and by clouds did go.

93

Elsewhere the Belgian force we did defeat,
370   But here our courages did theirs subdue:
So Xenophon once led that famed retreat
   Which first the Asian empire overthrew.

94

The foe approached: and one for his bold sin
   Was sunk, as he that touched the ark was slain;
375   The wild waves mastered him, and sucked him in,
   And smiling eddies dimpled on the main.

357–8. Referring to the panegyrics on Monck at the Restoration (e.g. by Sir Robert Howard and Robert Wild).

360. There was an eclipse of the sun on 22 June 1666; observations of it were printed in *PTRS* i (1665–6) 295–7 (9 September 1666) and 369–72 (21 January 1667).

367–8. Exodus xiii 21: the Israelites were led through the wilderness by pillars of cloud by day and fire by night.

371–2. After the defeat of Cyrus's attempt to seize the throne of Persia, his troops were extricated by Xenophon, who led them on the long retreat described in his *Anabasis*.

374. 1 Chronicles xiii 9–10; see *AA* l. 804*n*.

95

This seen, the rest at awful distance stood,
　　As if they had been there as servants set,
To stay or to go on as he thought good,
380　　And not pursue, but wait on his retreat.

96

So Libyan huntsmen on some sandy plain,
　　From shady coverts roused, the lion chase;
The kingly beast roars out with loud disdain,
　　^mAnd slowly moves, unknowing to give place.

(m) *The simile is Virgil's*: Vestigia retro improperata refert, etc.

97

385　But if some one approach to dare his force,
　　He swings his tail, and swiftly turns him round;
With one paw seizes on his trembling horse,
　　And with the other tears him to the ground.

98

Amidst these toils succeeds the balmy night;
390　　Now hissing waters the quenched guns restore,
　　ⁿAnd weary waves, withdrawing from the fight,
　　Lie lulled and panting on the silent shore.

(n) Weary waves: *From Statius*, Sylv.: Nec trucibus fluviis idem
sonus: occidit horror aequoris, ac terris maria acclinata quiescunt.

99

The moon shone clear on the becalmèd flood,
　　Where, while her beams like glittering silver play,

377. *awful*] respectful, awe-struck.
381–4. The simile is used by Virgil of Turnus in *Aen.* ix 791–8; it is also
Homeric (*Iliad* xi 548–55; xvii 657–64).
381. *Libyan*] may recall the hunt in *Aen.* iv 151–9.
384. *unknowing to give place*] Cp. *cedere nescii* (Achilles 'not knowing how to
yield', Horace, *Carm.* I vi 6; George Loane, *N & Q* clxxxv (1943) 273).
389–93. 'At Night it proved calm' (*A True Narrative* 5).
391n. 'The boisterous waves roar no longer; the raging sea is stilled; the sea is
pillowed on the shore in slumber' (Statius, *Sylvae* V iv 5–6).

395　Upon the deck our careful General stood,
　　　　And deeply mused on the °succeeding day.

(o) *The third of June, famous for two former victories.*

100

'That happy sun', said he, 'will rise again,
　　　Who twice victorious did our navy see;
And I alone must view him rise in vain,
400　　Without one ray of all his star for me.

101

Yet like an English general will I die,
　　　And all the ocean make my spacious grave;
Women and cowards on the land may lie,
　　　The sea's a tomb that's proper for the brave.'

102

405　Restless he passed the remnants of the night,
　　　Till the fresh air proclaimed the morning nigh,
And burning ships, the martyrs of the fight,
　　　With paler fires beheld the eastern sky.

103

Third day.

But now, his stores of ammunition spent,
410　　His naked valour is his only guard:
Rare thunders are from his dumb cannon sent,
　　　And solitary guns are scarcely heard.

104

Thus far had Fortune power; here forced to stay,
　　　Nor longer durst with virtue be at strife:
415　This as a ransom Albemarle did pay
　　　For all the glories of so great a life.

395. careful] full of cares.
396n. The two former victories were those over the Dutch in 1653 and 1665.
397. happy] propitious.
402. Cp. *nunc tibi pro tumulo Carpathium omne mare est* ('now the whole Carpathian sea is your tomb', Propertius III vii 12; George Loane, *N & Q* clxxxv (1943) 272–81).
415. ransom] fine (*OED* 3).

105

For now brave Rupert from afar appears,
    Whose waving streamers the glad General knows;
With full spread sails his eager navy steers,
420   And every ship in swift proportion grows.

106

The anxious Prince had heard the cannon long,
    And from that length of time dire omens drew
Of English overmatched and Dutch too strong,
    Who never fought three days but to pursue.

107

425   Then, as an eagle (who with pious care
        Was beating widely on the wing for prey)
    To her now silent eyry does repair,
        And finds her callow infants forced away;

108

Stung with her love she stoops upon the plain,
430   The broken air loud whistling as she flies;
She stops, and listens, and shoots forth again,
    And guides her pinions by her young ones' cries:

417–20. *1667 second issue*; For now brave *Rupert*'s Navy did appear, / Whose
waving streamers from afar he knows: / As in his fate something divine there
were, / Who dead and buried the third day arose. *1667 first issue*. D. probably
made the change to remove the blasphemous comparison; but cp. ll. 453–4
and 560.
417. In the afternoon of 3 June, the third day of battle, Prince Rupert's
squadron was sighted.
423. *overmatched*] defeated by superior strength.
425–32. Cp. *The Indian Emperor* (performed 1665): 'As Callow Birds— /
Whose Mother's kill'd in seeking of the prey, / Cry in their Nest, and think
her long away; / And at each leaf that stirs, each blast of wind, / Gape for the
Food which they must never find: / So cry the people in their misery' (IV ii
39–44).
425. *pious*] Cp. l. 255*n*.
428. *callow*] unfledged.
429. *stoops*] See ll. 341–4*n*.

109

With such kind passion hastes the Prince to fight,
    And spreads his flying canvas to the sound;
435   Him whom no danger, were he there, could fright,
    Now absent every little noise can wound.

110

As in a drought the thirsty creatures cry,
    And gape upon the gathered clouds for rain,
And first the martlet meets it in the sky,
440   And with wet wings joys all the feathered train:

111

With such glad hearts did our despairing men
    Salute the appearance of the Prince's fleet;
And each ambitiously would claim the ken
    That with first eyes did distant safety meet.

112

445   The Dutch, who came like greedy hinds before
    To reap the harvest their ripe ears did yield,
Now look like those when rolling thunders roar
    And sheets of lightning blast the standing field.

113

Full in the Prince's passage hills of sand
450   And dangerous flats in secret ambush lay,
Where the false tides skim o'er the covered land,

433. kind] responding to the bonds of kinship.
435–6. From Virgil: *et me, quem dudum non ulla iniecta mouebant / tela neque
aduerso glomerati examine Grai, / nunc omnes terrent aurae, sonus excitat omnis /
suspensum* ('And I [Aeneas], whom previously no hurled weapons could
move, nor hostile ranks of Greeks, am now terrified by all noises, every
sound holds me in suspense, and I fear equally for my companion [Ascanius]
and my burden [Anchises]'; *Aen.* ii 726–9; Loane (see l. 402*n*)).
437–40. Cp. Virgil: *bucula caelum / suspiciens patulis captauit naribus auras, / aut
arguta lacus circumuolitauit hirundo* ('the cow looking up into the sky caught the
breeze in extended nostrils, or the graceful swallow swooped round the lake';
Geo. i 375–7).
443. ken] look, gaze (*OED*).
445. hinds] farm workers.
449–56. Albemarle's fleet fell 'unluckily upon a tail of the Galloper sand;

And seamen with dissembled depths betray.

114
The wily Dutch, who like fall'n angels feared
   This new Messiah's coming, there did wait,
455 And round the verge their braving vessels steered
   To tempt his courage with so fair a bait.

115
But he unmoved contemns their idle threat,
   Secure of fame whene'er he please to fight;
His cold experience tempers all his heat,
460 And inbred worth does boasting valour slight.

116
Heroic virtue did his actions guide,
   And he the substance not th' appearance chose:
To rescue one such friend he took more pride
   Than to destroy whole thousands of such foes.

117
465 But when approached, in strict embraces bound
   Rupert and Albemarle together grow:
He joys to have his friend in safety found,
   Which he to none but to that friend would owe.

118
The cheerful soldiers, with new stores supplied,
470 Now long to execute their spleenful will;

---

where most of the great ships struck, and the *Royal Prince* stuck fast, and
could not be got off. . . . So the General made sail to join with the Prince,
sending him timely notice of the dangerous sand, for his Highness had a
mind to attack the enemy then; and they had drawn out a squadron of ships,
making as if they had an intention to fight the Prince, purposely to decoy him
upon the said sand' (*An Account* in *Letter Book* 239–40).
455. *braving*] challenging, defiant (*OED* 1); vaunting (*OED* 7).
457. *contemns*] despises.
460. *slight*] disdain, disregard.
465. As D. implies, Albemarle and Rupert met on the evening of the third
day (*pace Works* i 294); *meet* in l. 475 refers to the encounter with the Dutch.
470. *spleenful*] courageous (*OED* spleen 5).

And in revenge for those three days they tried
  Wish one like Joshua's when the sun stood still.

119

Fourth day's battle.

  Thus reinforced, against the adverse fleet
    Still doubling ours, brave Rupert leads the way;
475 With the first blushes of the morn they meet,
    And bring night back upon the new-born day.

120

  His presence soon blows up the kindling fight,
    And his loud guns speak thick like angry men;
  It seemed as slaughter had been breathed all night,
480   And death new pointed his dull dart again.

121

  The Dutch too well his mighty conduct knew,
    And matchless courage since the former fight;
  Whose navy like a stiff-stretched cord did show
    Till he bore in and bent them into flight.

122

485 The wind he shares while half their fleet offends
    His open side, and high above him shows;
  Upon the rest at pleasure he descends
    And, doubly harmed, he double harms bestows.

471. *tried*] underwent (*OED* 14).

472. In Joshua x 12–14 the sun stands still while Joshua and the Israelites kill their enemies.

474. *doubling ours*] The odds were about 80:50.

476. Cp. 'And with their smoky cannons banish day' (Waller, *Of a War with Spain* l. 44).

478. *thick*] rapidly; confusedly (*OED* 3, 4).

479. *breathed*] refreshed by being given a breathing space (*OED* 13).

481–90. 'The Prince thought fit to keep the Wind, and so led the whole Line through the middle of the Enemy, the General with the rest of the Fleet following in good order . . . the Prince . . . in this Pass was environ'd with as many dangers as the Enemy could apply unto him, they raked him Fore and Aft, plyed him on both sides' (*True Narrative* 6–7).

485. *offends*] attacks (*OED* 5).

123

Behind, the General mends his weary pace,
490   And sullenly to his revenge he sails:
ᴾSo glides some trodden serpent on the grass,
And long behind his wounded volume trails.

(p) So glides etc. *From Virgil*: Cum medii nexus, extremaeque
agmina caudae solvuntur; tardosque trahit sinus ultimus orbes, etc.

124

Th' increasing sound is borne to either shore,
And for their stakes the throwing nations fear:
495   Their passion double with the cannons' roar,
And with warm wishes each man combats there.

125

Plied thick and close as when the fight begun,
Their huge unwieldy navy wastes away:
So sicken waning moons too near the sun,
500   And blunt their crescents on the edge of day.

126

And now reduced on equal terms to fight,
Their ships like wasted patrimonies show,
Where the thin scattering trees admit the light,
And shun each other's shadows as they grow.

490. sullenly] slowly.
491n. 'While the central coils and the moving tip of his tail untwine, and his last fold drags its slow coils' (Virgil, *Geo.* iii 423–4). Cp. *Aen.* v 273–9, where the damaged ship *Centaur* is compared to an injured snake.
492. volume] coil; from Latin *volumen* (coil), as in *Aen.* ii 208; it later becomes a piece of poetic diction (see *OED* 11).
495. passion double] Christie, Noyes; passion, double *1667, 1668, 1688*; passions double *Scott, Kinsley, Works*. The sense seems to be 'their passion [is *or* becomes] double'.
500. crescents] also a common battle-formation for ships. The line was ridiculed in *The Censure of the Rota* (1673) 8–9.
501. on equal terms] The Dutch were 'reduced from Eighty four, to under the number of Forty sayl' (*True Narrative* 8).

127

505 The warlike Prince had severed from the rest
      Two giant ships, the pride of all the main,
      Which with his one so vigorously he pressed
      And flew so home they could not rise again.

128

      Already battered, by his lee they lay,
510   In vain upon the passing winds they call:
      The passing winds through their torn canvas play,
      And flagging sails on heartless sailors fall.

129

      Their opened sides receive a gloomy light,
      Dreadful as day let in to shades below;
515   Without, grim death rides bare-faced in their sight,
      And urges entering billows as they flow.

130

      When one dire shot, the last they could supply,
      Close by the board the Prince's mainmast bore,
      All three now helpless by each other lie,
520   And this offends not, and those fear no more.

131

      So have I seen some fearful hare maintain
      A course, till tired before the dog she lay,

505–12. No source for this episode has been traced, unless D. is thinking of
Rupert's encounter with two fireships (*True Narrative* 7).
508. *so home*] so precisely to his target.
512. *heartless*] dispirited.
513–14. Perhaps recalling *Aen.* viii 241–6, where light is let into the cave of
Cacus.
518–19. 'His Main-stay, and Main-top-mast, being terribly shaken, came all
by the Board' (*True Narrative* 7).   *by the board*] overboard.
520. *offends*] see l. 485n.
521–8. From Ovid, *Met.* i 533–42 (the pursuit of Daphne by Apollo): *ut canis
in vacuo leporem cum Gallicus arvo / vidit, et hic praedam pedibus petit, ille salutem;
/ alter inhaesuro similis iam iamque tenere / sperat et extento stringit vestigia rostro, /
alter in ambiguo est, an sit conprensus, et ipsis / morsibus eripitur tangentiaque ora
relinquit: / sic deus et virgo est hic spe celer, illa timore, / qui tamen insequitur pennis
adiutus Amoris, / ocior est requiemque negat tergoque fugacis / imminet et crinem*

Who, stretched behind her, pants upon the plain,
  Past power to kill as she to get away:

132

525 With his lolled tongue he faintly licks his prey,
  His warm breath blows her flix up as she lies;
  She, trembling, creeps upon the ground away,
  And looks back to him with beseeching eyes.

133

  The Prince unjustly does his stars accuse,
530 Which hindered him to push his fortune on:
  For what they to his courage did refuse,
  By mortal valour never must be done.

134

  This lucky hour the wise Batavian takes,
  And warns his tattered fleet to follow home;
535 Proud to have so got off with equal stakes,
  qWhere 'twas a triumph not to be o'ercome.

(q) *From Horace*: Quos opimus fallere et effugere est triumphus.

---

sparsum cervicibus adflat. ('Just as when a Gallic hound has seen a hare in an open plain, and seeks his prey on flying feet, but the hare, safety; he, just about to fasten on her, now, even now thinks he has her, and grazes her very heels with his outstretched muzzle; but she knows not whether she be not already caught, and barely escapes from those sharp fangs and leaves behind the jaws just closing on her: so ran the god and maid, he sped by hope and she by fear. But he ran the more swiftly, borne on the wings of love, gave her no time to rest, hung over her fleeing shoulders and breathed on the hair that streamed over her neck.') For D.'s translation of these lines in *EP* (1693) see 'The First Book of Ovid's *Metamorphoses*' ll. 719–33. The simile was misquoted and ridiculed in *The Friendly Vindication of Mr. Dryden* (1673) 2–3, and defended in *Mr. Dreyden Vindicated* (1673) 3.

526. flix] dialect word for fur of hare, rabbit or cat (first example in *OED* and *English Dialect Dictionary*).

533. De Ruyter withdrew his fleet to the Dutch coast in the evening of 4 June.

535. equal stakes] The Four Days Battle cost England fourteen ships, 5,000 killed and wounded, and 3,000 prisoners. The cost to Holland was four ships and 2,000 casualties. After initial reports of an English victory, Pepys noted that 'all give over the thoughts of it as a victory, and do reckon it a great overthrow' (9 June).

536n. [The wolves] 'which it is the richest triumph for us to deceive and

135

The General's force, as kept alive by fight,
 Now, not opposed, no longer can pursue;
Lasting till heaven had done his courage right,
540 When he had conquered he his weakness knew.

136

He casts a frown on the departing foe,
 And sighs to see him quit the watery field;
His stern, fixed eyes no satisfaction show
 For all the glories which the fight did yield.

137

545 Though, as when fiends did miracles avow,
 He stands confessed ev'n by the boastful Dutch,
He only does his conquest disavow,
 And thinks too little what they found too much.

138

Returned, he with the fleet resolved to stay,
550 No tender thoughts of home his heart divide:
Domestic joys and cares he puts away,
 For realms are households which the great must
  guide.

139

As those who unripe veins in mines explore,
 On the rich bed again the warm turf lay,
555 Till time digests the yet imperfect ore,
 And know it will be gold another day:

---

escape', *Carm.* IV iv 51–2. Spoken by Hannibal, it refers to the indestructible
Romans who gain strength from every trial (see Horace's ll. 45–76). *opi-*
mus] Eds; opinius *1667, 1668, 1688.*
545. Mark iii 11, where unclean spirits call Jesus 'Son of God'.
547. *He only*] Only he.
552. Another example of D. stressing the paternal concept of rule; cp. l. 291;
'Account' l. 35; *To His Sacred Majesty* ll. 93–4*n.*
553–6. The idea that metals grew underground, gradually evolving into
gold, was a contemporary commonplace.

140

So looks our monarch on this early fight,
    Th' essay and rudiments of great success,
    Which all-maturing time must bring to light,
560   While he, like heaven, does each day's labour bless.

141

Heaven ended not the first or second day,
    Yet each was perfect to the work designed:
God and kings work when they their work survey
    And passive aptness in all subjects find.

142

His Majesty repairs the fleet.

565 In burdened vessels, first, with speedy care
    His plenteous stores do seasoned timber send;
    Thither the brawny carpenters repair,
    And as the surgeons of maimed ships attend.

143

With cord and canvas from rich Hamburg sent
570   His navy's moulted wings he imps once more;
    Tall Norway fir their masts in battle spent
    And English oak sprung leaks and planks restore.

---

558. *essay*] rehearsal (*OED* 2); first effort or draft (*OED* 7); accented on the second syllable.

560–2. See Genesis i.

565–72. The Royal Society had 'employ'd much time in examining *the Fabrick of Ships*, the forms of their *Sails*, the shapes of their *Keels*, the sorts of Timber, the planting of Firr, the bettering of Pitch, and Tarr, and Tackling. And in all *Maritime* affairs of this Nature, his *Majesty* is acknowledg'd to be the best *Judge* amongst Seamen, and Shipwrights, as well as the most powerful amongst *Princes*' (Sprat 150) (*Works*).

565. On 9 June Pepys noted 'the haste requisite to be made in getting the fleet out again', and on 13 July the fleet was 'now in all points ready to sail'.

569. Various naval supplies were imported from Hamburg (Pepys, e.g. 30 May 1665*n*, 18 March 1666*n*, 3 May 1669).

570. *imps*] Another image from falconry: to *imp* is to engraft new feathers on to the wing of a bird to improve its flight.

571. For the use of Norwegian fir see Pepys 23 June 1662 and *n*.

144

All hands employed, ʳthe royal work grows warm:
Like labouring bees on a long summer's day,
575 Some sound the trumpet for the rest to swarm,
And some on bells of tasted lilies play;

(r) Fervet opus: *the same similitude in Virgil.*

145

With gluey wax some new foundation lay
Of virgin combs which from the roof are hung;
Some armed within doors upon duty stay,
580 Or tend the sick, or educate the young.

146

So here, some pick out bullets from the sides,
Some drive old oakum through each seam and rift;
Their left hand does the caulking-iron guide,
The rattling mallet with the right they lift.

147

585 With boiling pitch another near at hand
(From friendly Sweden brought) the seams instops,

573n. Fervet opus] 'The work glows'; from *Aen.* i 430–6, where Virgil compares the Carthaginians building the walls of their city to bees.
574–6. Cp. *Aen.* vi 707–9: *ubi apes aestate serena / floribus insidunt variis, et candida circum / lilia funduntur* ('Where bees in serene summer creep into various flowers, and pour round white lilies') (*Works*).
577–80. Cp. *Geo.* iv 160–3: *lentum de cortice gluten / prima fauis ponunt fundamenta, deinde tenacis / suspendunt ceras; aliae spem gentis adultos / educunt fetus* ('lay down gluey gum from tree-bark as the first foundation of the comb, then hang aloft clinging wax; others lead out the full-grown young, the nation's hope').
578. virgin] See 'Horace: *Epode* II' l. 27n.
582–7. 'Calking is beating Okum into every seame or betwixt Planke and Planke and Okum is old Ropes torn in pieces like a Towze Match, or Hurds of Flax, which being close beat into every seame with a calking Iron and a Mallet, which is a hammer of wood and an Iron chissell, being well payed over with hot pitch' (John Smith, *The Sea-Mans Grammar* (1653) 13) (*Works*).
586. Tar was imported for the navy from Stockholm (Pepys 21 July 1662n).
instops] the only example recorded in *OED*.

Which well paid o'er the salt-sea waves withstand,
And shakes them from the rising beak in drops.

148
Some the galled ropes with dauby marling bind,
590   Or cerecloth masts with strong tarpaulin coats;
To try new shrouds one mounts into the wind,
And one below their ease or stiffness notes.

149
Our careful monarch stands in person by,
His new-cast cannons' firmness to explore:
595   The strength of big-corned powder loves to try,
And ball and cartridge sorts for every bore.

150
Each day brings fresh supplies of arms and men,
And ships which all last winter were abroad;
And such as fitted since the fight had been,
600   Or new from stocks were fall'n into the road.

151
Loyal London described.
The goodly *London* in her gallant trim
(The phoenix daughter of the vanished old)

---

587. paid] *pay* (*OED* v²) is a nautical term: to cover with pitch as a protection against water.
588. beak] prow.
589. galled] frayed.   *dauby*] like daub; sticky: apparently D.'s coinage.
marling] marline, a tarred line wound round ropes to prevent fraying.
590. cerecloth] wrap in waterproof material.
595. big-corned] large-grained; this powder was used for cannons, finer powder for small arms. The manufacture of gunpowder is described in Sprat 282–3.
600. The English fleet now had twenty-three new ships.   *fall'n into*] took their place in (*OED* 62c); cp. 'Ships from *Chatham, Harwich, &c.* come daily to encrease our strength, and some few in the River, though not yet compleatly fitted, yet are falling down, for fear they should have no share of the honour of the next Engagement' (*Current Intelligence* viii, 25–8 June 1666). *road*] anchorage.
601–16. The *London* had blown up on 7 March 1665; in her place the City built the *Loyal London*, which was to be burnt by the Dutch in the Medway in

Like a rich bride does to the ocean swim,
    And on her shadow rides in floating gold.

152

605   Her flag aloft spread ruffling to the wind,
    And sanguine streamers seem the flood to fire;
The weaver charmed with what his loom designed
    Goes on to sea, and knows not to retire.

153

With roomy decks, her guns of mighty strength
610   (Whose low-laid mouths each mounting billow
        laves),
Deep in her draught, and warlike in her length,
    She seems a sea-wasp flying on the waves.

154

This martial present, piously designed,
    The loyal city gave their best-loved King;
615   And with a bounty ample as the wind
    Built, fitted and maintained to aid him bring.

155

Digression concerning shipping and navigation.
By viewing Nature, Nature's hand-maid Art
    Makes mighty things from small beginnings grow:
Thus fishes first to shipping did impart
620   Their tail the rudder, and their head the prow.

156

Some log, perhaps, upon the waters swam
    An useless drift, which rudely cut within

June 1667. D. may have taken some hints from William Smith, *A Poem on the famous ship called the Loyal London* (1666): cp. his 'This mightier *Phoenix*' (1) and 'laves . . . waves' rhyme (5).

609. The guns in fact exploded when tested, and the ship joined the fleet without them (Pepys 26 June 1666).

621–4. Cp. *Geo.* i 136: *tunc alnos primum fluvii sensere cavatas* ('then rivers first felt the hollowed alders') (*Works*).

622. drift] floating mass (*OED* 9).

And hollowed, first a floating trough became,
And cross some riv'let passage did begin.

157

625 In shipping such as this the Irish kern
And untaught Indian on the stream did glide,
Ere sharp-keeled boats to stem the flood did learn,
Or fin-like oars did spread from either side.

158

Add but a sail, and Saturn so appeared
630 When from lost empire he to exile went,
And with the golden age to Tiber steered,
Where coin and first commerce he did invent.

159

Rude as their ships was navigation then,
No useful compass or meridian known;
635 Coasting they kept the land within their ken,
And knew no north but when the pole-star shone.

160

Of all who since have used the open sea,
Than the bold English none more fame have won:
� Beyond the year and out of heaven's highway
640 They make discoveries where they see no sun.

(s) Extra anni solisque vias. *Virg.*

624. *riv'let*] This is the spelling in *1667*; other seventeenth-century spellings (*rivlet, rivelet*: see OED) show that the word was often pronounced as disyllabic.
625. *kern*] rustic, peasant (OED 2).
626. *untaught Indian*] Cp. 'To Dr Charleton' l. 13*n*. D. repeats the adjective *untaught* from *The Indian Emperor* I i 9–10: 'No useful Arts have yet found footing here; / But all untaught and salvage does appear.'
629–32. Saturn, dethroned by his son Jove, fled to Italy, where he established the golden age of peace and justice (*Aen.* viii 319–25).
632. *commerce*] Seventeenth-century pronunciation stressed the second syllable.
639*n*. *Aen.* vi 796: 'beyond the paths of the year and the sun'; cp. *Threnodia Augustalis* l. 353.

161

But what so long in vain, and yet unknown,
　　By poor mankind's benighted wit is sought,
Shall in this age to Britain first be shown,
　　And hence be to admiring nations taught.

162

645　The ebbs of tides, and their mysterious flow,
　　We as art's elements shall understand;
And as by line upon the ocean go,
　　Whose paths shall be familiar as the land.

163

'Instructed ships shall sail to quick commerce,
650　　By which remotest regions are allied,
Which makes one city of the universe,
　　Where some may gain, and all may be supplied.

(t) *By a more exact knowledge of longitudes.*

164

Then we upon our globe's last verge shall go,
　　And view the ocean leaning on the sky;

641-4. Cp. Sprat: 'And it is a good sign, that Nature will reveal more of its secrets to the English, than to others; because it has already furnish'd them with a Genius so well proportion'd, for the receiving, and retaining its mysteries' (114-15) (*Works*).

644. *admiring*] marvelling.

645. Sir Robert Moray's account of tides in the Western Isles appeared in *PTRS* i (1665-6) 53-5 (5 June 1665). John Wallis's paper presenting a universal theory of tides was read to the Royal Society on 16 May 1666 and printed in *PTRS* i (1665-6) 263-89 (6 August), occasioning great interest.

646. *elements*] elementary knowledge; basic principles.

647. *by line*] with great accuracy (*OED* 4b).

649n. *knowledge of longitudes*] 1667, 1668; measure of Longitude 1688 (a possible revision). Despite various attempts, there was as yet no sound way of measuring longitude at sea. Major Holmes reported a successful experiment using pendulum watches to determine longitude (*PTRS* i (1665-6) 13-15 (6 March 1665)). The King was 'most ready to reward those, that shall discover the *Meridian*' (Sprat 150).

653. *last verge*] utmost limit.

655 From thence our rolling neighbours we shall know,
    And on the lunar world securely pry.

165
Apostrophe to the Royal Society.
This I foretell from your auspicious care,
    Who great in search of God and nature grow;
Who best your wise Creator's praise declare,
660   Since best to praise his works is best to know.

166
O truly royal! who behold the law
    And rule of beings in your Maker's mind,
And thence, like limbecks, rich ideas draw
    To fit the levelled use of human kind.

167
665 But first the toils of war we must endure,
    And from th' injurious Dutch redeem the seas:
War makes the valiant of his right secure,
    And gives up fraud to be chastised with ease.

168
Already were the Belgians on our coast,
670   Whose fleet more mighty every day became
By late success which they did falsely boast,
    And now by first appearing seemed to claim.

169
Designing, subtle, diligent and close,
    They knew to manage war with wise delay;

655. *rolling neighbours*] planets.
656. M. Auzout's proposals for a closer study of the moon appeared in *PTRS*
i (1665–6) 120–3 (4 December 1665).   *pry*] investigate closely (*OED* 2b);
not pejorative.
657–64. For D.'s association with the Royal Society see headnote. Sprat
noted that the Society 'principally consulted the advancement of *Navigation*'
(150). Like Sprat (345–62) D. refutes allegations of atheism and impracticality
which had been made against the Society.
664. *levelled*] aimed, directed (*OED* 6b).
669–72. De Ruyter put to sea again on 25 June, and on 1 July anchored off the
King's Channel. On 22 July the English fleet assembled at the Gunfleet.

675 Yet all those arts their vanity did cross,
    And by their pride their prudence did betray.

                    170
    Nor stayed the English long; but well supplied
    Appear as numerous as th' insulting foe:
    The combat now by courage must be tried,
680   And the success the braver nation show.

                    171
    There was the Plymouth squadron new come in,
    Which in the Straits last winter was abroad;
    Which twice on Biscay's working bay had been,
    And on the midland sea the French had awed.

                    172
685 Old expert Allin, loyal all along,
    Famed for his action on the Smyrna fleet,
    And Holmes, whose name shall live in epic song,
    While music numbers, or while verse has feet:

                    173
    Holmes, the Achates of the generals' fight,
690   Who first bewitched our eyes with Guinea gold;

---

678. 'On the 25th. the fight began with equal numbers, 90 Men of War, and
17 Fireships on each side' (*The Victory over the Fleet of the States General* (1666)
7).   *insulting*] vaunting, triumphing insolently (*OED* 1); attacking (*OED*
3).
680. *success*] result (*OED* 1).
681–4. The Plymouth squadron under the command of Sir Jeremy Smith
sailed in December 1665 for Tangier and the Straits of Gibraltar. It prevented
the French Atlantic and Mediterranean (*midland*) fleets from joining.
683. *working*] agitated, tossing (*OED* 4).
685–6. Sir Thomas Allin (1612–85) now led the van as Admiral of the White.
In December 1664 he had attacked the Dutch merchant fleet returning from
Smyrna.
687–92. Sir Robert Holmes (1622–92), Rear Admiral of the Red, led a small
expedition to the Gold Coast in 1661, and a larger one in 1664 which captured
Dutch settlements and returned with great wealth (Pepys 10 December
1664).
689. *Achates*] the faithful companion of Aeneas. Holmes accompanied the
generals, who led the Red squadron.   *generals'*] Ed.; Gen'rals 1667, which

As once old Cato in the Romans' sight
The tempting fruits of Afric did unfold.

174

With him went Spragge, as bountiful as brave,
Whom his high courage to command had
brought;
695 Harman, who did the twice-fired *Harry* save,
And in his burning ship undaunted fought.

175

Young Hollis, on a Muse by Mars begot,
Born, Caesar-like, to write and act great deeds;
Impatient to revenge his fatal shot,
700 His right hand doubly to his left succeeds.

176

Thousands were there in darker fame that dwell,
Whose deeds some nobler poem shall adorn;

---

could be singular or plural. *Works* prefers the singular, referring to Rupert, on
the grounds that Holmes was not on good terms with Albemarle. But D.
gives no hint of this, and in *AM* 'general' in the singular always refers to
Albemarle, while Rupert is always 'the Prince'.

691–2. When the Roman senators admired the figs which Cato the Censor
dropped in the Senate, he told them that 'the country where that fine fruit
grew was but three days sail from Rome' (Plutarch, *Marcus Cato* 27). He was
urging Rome into the Third Punic War.

693–4. Sir Edward Spragge (d. 1673), Vice-Admiral of the Blue, had been
knighted for gallantry in the Battle of Lowestoft.

695–6. In the Four Days Battle, the *Henry*, commanded by Sir John Harman
(d. 1673) was twice set on fire by fireships; he continued to fight, killed the
Dutch admiral with a broadside, and brought his ship into Harwich.

697–700. Sir Fretcheville Hollis (1642–72), son of the royalist officer and
antiquary Gervase Hollis, lost his left arm in the Four Days Battle. His
literary talents are unrecorded. Unflattering opinions of him are noted by
Pepys (14, 17, 25 June 1667, etc.).

697. Ridiculed in *The Friendly Vindication of Mr. Dryden* (1673) 9, and by
Buckingham in *Poetical Reflections on . . . Absalom and Achitophel* (1681) 1.

699. fatal] destructive (*OED* 6).

701. Cp. *Aen.* v 302: *multi praeterea, quos fama obscura recondit* ('many besides,
whom dark report hides').

And, though to me unknown, they, sure, fought well
    Whom Rupert led, and who were British born.

177

705 Of every size an hundred fighting sail,
    So vast the navy now at anchor rides,
That underneath it the pressed waters fail,
    And with its weight it shoulders off the tides.

178

Now anchors weighed, the seamen shout so shrill
710   That heaven and earth and the wide ocean rings;
A breeze from westward waits their sails to fill,
    And rests in those high beds his downy wings.

179

The wary Dutch this gathering storm foresaw,
    And durst not bide it on the English coast:
715 Behind their treacherous shallows they withdraw,
    And there lay snares to catch the British host.

180

So the false spider, when her nets are spread,
    Deep ambushed in her silent den does lie;
And feels far off the trembling of her thread,
720   Whose filmy cord should bind the struggling fly:

181

Then, if at last she find him fast beset,
    She issues forth and runs along her loom;
She joys to touch the captive in her net,
    And drags the little wretch in triumph home.

182

725 The Belgians hoped that with disordered haste

---

715. After the St James's Day Fight (25 July) the Dutch retreated to their
coast, taking advantage of the sandbanks which deterred the English ships,
which had a deeper draught. As Kinsley notes, D. places this retreat
before the beginning of the action, so as to emphasize Dutch cowardice and
cunning.

718. *ambushed*] lying in wait, lurking (OED 2).

Our deep-cut keels upon the sands might run;
Or if with caution leisurely were past
Their numerous gross might charge us one by one.

183

But with a fore-wind pushing them above,
730   And swelling tide that heaved them from below,
O'er the blind flats our warlike squadrons move,
And with spread sails to welcome battle go.

184

It seemed as there the British Neptune stood,
With all his host of waters at command,
735   Beneath them to submit the officious flood,
   ᵘAnd with his trident shoved them off the sand.

(u) Levat ipse tridenti, et vastas aperit syrtes, etc. *Virg.*

185

To the pale foes they suddenly draw near,
And summon them to unexpected fight:
They start like murderers when ghosts appear,
740   And draw their curtains in the dead of night.

186

Second battle.

Now van to van the foremost squadrons meet,
The midmost battles hasting up behind,

728. gross] main body (a military term).
731. blind flats] translating *vada caeca* (*Aen.* i 536; Kinsley).   *blind*] covered,
concealed from sight (*OED* 9).
735. submit] bring under control (*OED* 4).   *officious*] helpful, dutiful.
736n. Aen. i 145–6: 'With his trident [Neptune] himself lifts [the Trojan ships
off the rocks] and opens the huge quicksands'.
740. Cp. Shakespeare: 'Even such a man, so faint, so spiritless, / So dull, so
dead in look, so woe begone, / Drew Priam's curtain in the dead of night, /
And would have told him, half his Troy was burned' (*2 Henry IV* I i 70–3;
Loane (see l. 402*n*)).
741. The English fleet intended to 'engage them Van to Van'; 'half an hour
after nine, the Vans on each side came near' (*London Gazette* lxxv).   *van*]
the detachment of ships at the front of the fleet.
742. battles] A *battle* is the main body of a naval force, as distinct from the van
or rear (*OED* 9).

Who view far off the storm of falling sleet,
And hear their thunder rattling in the wind.

187

745   At length the adverse admirals appear
(The two bold champions of each country's right);
Their eyes describe the lists as they come near,
And draw the lines of death before they fight.

188

The distance judged for shot of every size,
750   The linstocks touch, the ponderous ball expires;
The vigorous seaman every porthole plies,
And adds his heart to every gun he fires.

189

Fierce was the fight on the proud Belgians' side,
For honour, which they seldom sought before;
755   But now they by their own vain boasts were tied,
And forced, at least in show, to prize it more.

190

But sharp remembrance on the English part,
And shame of being matched by such a foe,
Rouse conscious virtue up in every heart,
760   ᵂAnd seeming to be stronger makes them so.

(w) Possunt quia posse videntur. *Virg.*

743. *sleet*] i.e. shot from the guns falling like sleet.
747. *describe*] i.e. descry (*OED* 7), perceive.
748. Hollar's engraving shows each fleet drawn up in a line (reproduced in Richard Ollard, *Man of War* (1969)).
750. *linstocks*] staves for holding lighted matches.   *expires*] rushes forth (*OED* 3).
752. Cp. *dant animos plagae* (*Aen.* vii 383: 'give their souls to the blow').
759. *conscious virtue*] Cp. Virgil: *pudor incendit viris et conscia virtus* (*Aen.* v 455: 'shame and awareness of his manhood fire his strength'); and cp. *Aen.* xii 666–8.
760n. *Aen.* v 231: 'they are able because they seem to be able'. D. echoes this line again in *2 Conquest of Granada* II iii 106.

191

Nor long the Belgians could that fleet sustain
Which did two generals' fates and Caesar's bear:
Each several ship a victory did gain,
As Rupert or as Albemarle were there.

192

765 Their battered admiral too soon withdrew,
Unthanked by ours for his unfinished fight;
But he the minds of his Dutch masters knew,
Who called that providence which we called flight.

193

Never did men more joyfully obey,
770 Or sooner understood the sign to fly:
With such alacrity they bore away
As if to praise them all the States stood by.

194

O famous leader of the Belgian fleet,
Thy monument inscribed such praise shall wear
775 As Varro, timely flying, once did meet,
Because he did not of his Rome despair.

195

Behold that navy which a while before
Provoked the tardy English to the fight,
Now draw their beaten vessels close to shore,
780 As larks lie dared to shun the hobby's flight.

762. See *To His Sacred Majesty* ll. 103–4n.

763. *several*] individual.

765. De Ruyter's ship was closely engaged for several hours, and lost her topmast. 'About four *De Ruyter* made all the sail he could, and ran for it, but made frequent Tacks to fetch off his maymed ships'; his ship was 'much battered' in the retreat (*London Gazette* lxxv). This was in fact an hour after his van had turned and fled.

772. *States*] The States General was the parliament of the United Provinces.

775–6. When Varro returned to Rome after his defeat by Hannibal at the Battle of Cannae, he was thanked by the Senate for not despairing of the state (Livy xxii 41).

780. *dared*] terrified, fascinated with fear.   *hobby*] a small falcon, used to fly above larks and scare them into nets.

196

Whoe'er would English monuments survey
    In other records may our courage know;
But let them hide the story of this day,
    Whose fame was blemished by too base a foe:

197

785   Or if too busily they will enquire
          Into a victory which we disdain,
      Then let them know the Belgians did retire
          ^xBefore the patron saint of injured Spain.

(x) Patron saint: *St James, on whose day this victory was gained.*

198

Repenting England this revengeful day
790   ^yTo Philip's *manes* did an offering bring:
      England, which first by leading them astray
          Hatched up rebellion to destroy her King.

(y) Philip's *manes: Philip the Second of Spain, against whom the Hollanders rebelling were aided by Queen Elizabeth.*

199

Our fathers bent their baneful industry
    To check a monarchy that slowly grew;
795   But did not France or Holland's fate foresee,
        Whose rising power to swift dominion flew.

200

In Fortune's empire blindly thus we go,
    And wander after pathless destiny,
Whose dark resorts since prudence cannot know
800   In vain it would provide for what shall be.

201

But whate'er English to the blessed shall go,
    And the fourth Harry or first Orange meet,

790. manes] shade, ghost (Latin); disyllabic.
793–6. i.e. 'Late Tudor and early Stuart foreign policy had aimed at containing the power of Spain, but had not foreseen the commercial rise of the
Dutch Republic, or the military strength of France under Louis XIV.'
801–4. The 'Bourbon foe' is Louis XIV, disowned by Henri IV his grandfather as a foe to the English. William the Silent, the 'first Orange', detests

Find him disowning of a Bourbon foe,
    And him detesting a Batavian fleet:

202

805 Now on their coasts our conquering navy rides,
        Waylays their merchants, and their land besets:
     Each day new wealth without their care provides,
        They lie asleep with prizes in their nets.

203

     So close behind some promontory lie
810   The huge leviathans to attend their prey,
     And give no chase, but swallow in the fry
        Which through their gaping jaws mistake the way.

204

Burning of the fleet in the Vly by Sir Robert Holmes.

     Nor was this all: in ports and roads remote
        Destructive fires among whole fleets we send;
815 Triumphant flames upon the water float,
        And out-bound ships at home their voyage end.

205

     Those various squadrons, variously designed,
        Each vessel freighted with a several load;
     Each squadron waiting for a several wind,
820   All find but one, to burn them in the road.

206

     Some bound for Guinea, golden sand to find,
        Bore all the gauds the simple natives wear;

---

the fleet of Holland as employed against his benefactors. (Verrall)
804. Batavian] Dutch.
805–8. After 25 July the English fleet cruised off the Dutch coast capturing shipping.
809–12. Cp. Du Bartas tr. Sylvester: 'One (like a Pirate) onely lives of prizes / That in the Deepe he desperately surprises; / Another haunts the shoare, to feed on foame' (I v 149–51).
813–16. On 8 August Holmes attacked 170 merchantmen off Vly island; he burnt 150 and sacked the town of Terschelling.
813. roads] sheltered waters where ships may anchor in safety.
819. several] separate, different.
822. gauds] ornaments.

Some for the pride of Turkish courts designed
For folded turbans finest Holland bear.

207

825   Some English wool, vexed in a Belgian loom
    And into cloth of spungy softness made,
Did into France or colder Denmark doom
    To ruin with worse ware our staple trade.

208

Our greedy seamen rummage every hold,
830   Smile on the booty of each wealthier chest,
And, as the priests who with their gods make bold,
    Take what they like, and sacrifice the rest.

209

Transitum to the Fire of London.
But ah! how unsincere are all our joys!

824. *Holland*] i.e. Holland linen.

825–8. Kinsley notes that English wool, being finer than that of the continent, was greatly in demand, and smuggled abroad in defiance of a prohibition on its export; the French re-exported goods made from this wool to England, thus spoiling the market for home-manufactured goods. See Ogg 71–2.

825. *vexed*] worked (*OED* 6).

827. *doom*] i.e. 'Some ships condemned English wool to be carried into France or Denmark'.

829–32. Holmes's own account says that 'the common Seamen and Soldiers [returned with] their pockets well lined with Duckets and other rich spoil, which was found in great plenty, as well on board the Merchants ships, as in the Town they burnt, and was freely abandoned to them' (*London Gazette* lxxix).

829. *rummage*] a nautical term: to scrutinize and sort the contents of a ship's hold.

833. *unsincere*] impure, not unmixed. For the idea that human happiness is not unmixed, see also *AA* l. 43*n*; 'Lucretius: The Beginning of the Second Book' l. 22; 'Lucretius: Concerning the Nature of Love' l. 42; 'The Second Book of Virgil's *Georgics*' l. 584; and 'Cinyras and Myrrha' l. 259. By contrast, the medal commemorating the plague and the Fire of London bore the inscription *Mera Bonitas* ('pure goodness'), referring to God's providence (Hawkins i 525).   Transitum] Not recorded in *OED*, either separately or as a seventeenth-century spelling of *transition*. It appears to be unnaturalized Latin, but the Latin noun is *transitus*; it is not clear why D. uses the accusative, unless he mistakenly thinks it to be the nominative of a neuter noun. *1688* has *Transit*.

Which sent from heaven, like lightning make no
            stay:
835   Their palling taste the journey's length destroys,
            Or grief sent post o'ertakes them on the way.

                                210
       Swelled with our late successes on the foe,
            Which France and Holland wanted power to cross,
       We urge an unseen Fate to lay us low,
840   And feed their envious eyes with English loss.

                                211
       Each element his dread command obeys,
            Who makes or ruins with a smile or frown;
       Who as by one he did our nation raise,
            So now he with another pulls us down.

                                212
845   Yet, London, Empress of the northern clime,
            By an high fate thou greatly didst expire:
            ^zGreat as the world's, which at the death of time
            Must fall, and rise a nobler frame by fire.

(z) Cum mare cum tellus correptaque regia coeli ardeat, etc. *Ovid.*

                                213
       As when some dire usurper heaven provides
850   To scourge his country with a lawless sway;

834. lightning] Cp. ll. 849–60n for a possible echo of Marvell here.
836. post] post-haste.
841. his] The gender which D. gives to Fate is peculiar: in Latin it is neuter
(*fatum*), in Greek feminine (μοῖρα). He may intend a partial assimilation to
Christian Providence or God.
843–4. i.e. England, made mighty on the water, is laid low by fire.
846. fate] here means 'end', 'death'.
847n. In Ovid's *Met.* i 257–8, Jove, about to hurl his thunderbolts at the
world, remembers that it is in the fates that a time will come 'when sea and
land, the royal palace of heaven will catch fire and burn'.
849–60. This passage echoes Marvell's lines on the rise of Cromwell in 'An
Horatian Ode': 'like the three-fork'd Lightning, first / Breaking the Clouds
where it was nurst, / Did thorough his own Side / His fiery way divide. / . . .
Then burning through the Air he went, / And Pallaces and Temples rent: /
And *Caesars* head at last / Did through his Laurels blast. / 'Tis Madness to
resist or blame / The force of angry Heavens flame: / . . . Who, from his

His birth perhaps some petty village hides,
   And sets his cradle out of Fortune's way:

214

Till fully ripe his swelling fate breaks out,
   And hurries him to mighty mischiefs on;
855 His prince surprised at first no ill could doubt,
   And wants the power to meet it when 'tis known.

215

Such was the rise of this prodigious fire,
   Which in mean buildings first obscurely bred,
From thence did soon to open streets aspire,
860   And straight to palaces and temples spread.

216

The diligence of trades, and noiseful gain,
   And luxury, more late, asleep were laid:
All was the night's, and in her silent reign
   No sound the rest of nature did invade.

217

865 In this deep quiet, from what source unknown,
   Those seeds of fire their fatal birth disclose;

---

private Gardens, where / He liv'd reserved and austere, / . . . Could by industrious Valour climbe / To ruine the great Work of Time' (ll. 13–34) (G. de F. Lord in *John Dryden*, edited by Earl Miner (1972) 172–3). For other instances of D.'s use of this poem see *To My Lord Chancellor* ll. 39–42n.

853. Cp. 'Some unborn sorrow ripe in Fortune's womb' (Shakespeare, *Richard II* II ii 10).

855. doubt] suspect (*OED* 6b).

857–60. The Great Fire of London broke out early in the morning of 2 September 1666 in the King's baker's shop in Pudding Lane. It burnt for four days, covered 436 acres, destroyed 89 churches and about 13,200 houses and gutted St Paul's, the Guildhall and the Royal Exchange.

857. prodigious] ominous, portentous (*OED* 1).

863. All was the night's] From *omnia noctis erant, placida composta quiete* ('all was the night's, lulled to quiet rest', Varro cited in Seneca, *Controversiae* VII i 27).

866. seeds of fire] Cp. *semina flammae* (Ovid, *Met.* xv 347), and 'Horace: *Odes* I iii' l. 39.   *fatal*] bringing death (cp. l. 846).

And first, few scattering sparks about were blown,
　　Big with the flames that to our ruin rose.

218
　　Then in some close-pent room it crept along,
870　　And smouldering as it went, in silence fed;
　　Till th' infant monster, with devouring strong,
　　Walked boldly upright with exalted head.

219
　　Now like some rich or mighty murderer
　　Too great for prison, which he breaks with gold,
875　Who fresher for new mischiefs does appear,
　　And dares the world to tax him with the old:

220
　　So scapes th' insulting fire his narrow jail,
　　And makes small outlets into open air;
　　There the fierce winds his tender force assail,
880　　And beat him downward to his first repair.

221
　　ªThe winds like crafty courtesans withheld
　　His flames from burning but to blow them more,
　　And every fresh attempt he is repelled,
　　With faint denials, weaker than before.

(a) Like crafty etc.: Haec arte tractabat cupidum virum, ut illius animum inopia accenderet.

869–72. Cp. Ovid, *Met.* xv 218–24; tr. D. in 'Of the Pythagorean Philosophy' ll. 330–3.
874. Too] 1668, 1688. To 1667.
877. insulting] See l. 678n; also 'leaping' (*OED* 5; rare, from Latin *insultare*).
880. repair] dwelling place.
881n. Terence, *Heautontimorumenos* ll. 366–7 ('She handled the longing man with skill, so as to fire his heart by his failure'). Although seventeenth-century editions of Terence vary here, D. does seem to misquote: those closest to D.'s text have *virum, / Cupidum . . . incenderet.*
882. but] only.

222

885   And now no longer letted of his prey
           He leaps up at it with enraged desire,
       O'erlooks the neighbours with a wide survey
           And nods at every house his threatening fire.

223

       The ghosts of traitors from the bridge descend
890   With bold fanatic spectres to rejoice;
       About the fire into a dance they bend,
           And sing their sabbath notes with feeble voice.

224

       Our guardian angel saw them where he sate
           Above the palace of our slumbering King;
895   He sighed, abandoning his charge to Fate,
           And drooping, oft looked back upon the wing.

225

       At length the crackling noise and dreadful blaze
           Called up some waking lover to the sight,
       And long it was ere he the rest could raise,
900   Whose heavy eyelids yet were full of night.

226

       The next to danger, hot pursued by Fate,
           Half-clothed, half-naked, hastily retire,

885. *letted of*] hindered from attaining.

889–90. The heads of traitors were impaled on the Southwark gate tower of London Bridge; the fire reached the bridge on the first night, but did not spread to the south bank.   *fanatic spectres*] fifth-monarchy men and other radical insurgents executed in 1661–2.

890–92. Winn 177 suggests an echo of Psalm c in the version by Sternhold and Hopkins: 'Sing to the Lord with cheerful voice, / . . . Come ye before him and rejoice'. The description of the *fanatic spectres* thus ironically evokes one of the puritans' favourite psalms.

892. sabbath] Perhaps associating the witches' sabbath with the puritans, who strictly observed the sabbath.

893. guardian angel] D. discusses the difficulty which Christian poets have in deploying supernatural figures in epic poetry in his 'Discourse Concerning Satire' (*Works* iv 16–22).   *sate*] sat (common seventeenth-century form).

896. looked] *1688*; look *1667, 1668.*

And frighted mothers strike their breasts too late
For helpless infants left amidst the fire.

227

905 Their cries soon waken all the dwellers near:
Now murmuring noises rise in every street;
The more remote run stumbling with their fear,
And in the dark men jostle as they meet.

228

So weary bees in little cells repose,
910 But if night-robbers lift the well-stored hive
An humming through their waxen city grows,
And out upon each other's wings they drive.

229

Now streets grow thronged and busy as by day:
Some run for buckets to the hallowed choir,
915 Some cut the pipes, and some the engines play,
And some more bold mount ladders to the fire.

230

In vain: for from the east a Belgian wind
His hostile breath through the dry rafters sent;
The flames impelled soon left their foes behind
920 And forward with a wanton fury went.

231

A quay of fire ran all along the shore
ᵇAnd lightened all the river with the blaze;

903. *mothers*] *1688*; Mother *1667*, *1668*.

909–12. The simile is appropriate because those collecting honey use smoke to drive out the bees: *Geo.* iv 230.

914–15. Fire buckets were kept in churches. It was usually necessary to cut the wooden water-pipes to obtain water for fire-fighting.   *engines*] brass hand-squirts with a capacity of about a gallon (Bell, *The Great Fire* 34–6). But 'this lamentable Fire in a short time became too big to be mastered by any Engines' (*London Gazette*).

917. 'A violent Easterly wind fomented it' (*London Gazette*); it was actually north-east (Bell, *The Great Fire* 34).

922n. Aen. ii 312: 'the straits of Sigaeum light up far and wide from the fire'.

The wakened tides began again to roar,
And wondering fish in shining waters gaze.
(b) Sigaea igni freta lata relucent. *Virg.*

232

925 Old father Thames raised up his reverend head,
But feared the fate of Simois would return;
Deep in his ooze he sought his sedgy bed,
And shrunk his waters back into his urn.

233

The fire, meantime, walks in a broader gross,
930 To either hand his wings he opens wide:
He wades the streets, and straight he reaches 'cross
And plays his longing flames on th' other side.

234

At first they warm, then scorch, and then they take;
Now with long necks from side to side they feed:
935 At length grown strong their mother fire forsake,
And a new colony of flames succeed.

235

To every nobler portion of the town
The curling billows roll their restless tide;
In parties now they straggle up and down
940 As armies unopposed for prey divide.

236

One mighty squadron, with a side wind sped,

925–8. Cp. Virgil: *amnis / rauca sonans, revocatque pedem Tyberinus ab alto* (*Aen.* ix 124–5: 'Old Tyber roar'd; and raising up his Head, / Call'd back his Waters to their Oozy Bed'; tr. D. ll. 151–2).
926. The river Xanthus (near Troy) called on its tributary Simois for help and tried to drown Achilles; it was attacked by Hephaestus with fire, tormenting the fish (cp. D.'s l. 924) (*Iliad* xxi 305–82).
929. gross] body, mass.
938. Cp. *propiusque aestus incendia volvunt* (*Aen.* ii 706: 'and waves roll the fires nearer').
941–8. On 3 September the fire spread north (burning the Royal Exchange and the houses of bankers around Lombard Street) and west (towards White-

Through narrow lanes his cumbered fire does
    haste,
By powerful charms of gold and silver led
    The Lombard bankers and the Change to waste.

237

945   Another backward to the Tower would go,
    And slowly eats his way against the wind;
    But the main body of the marching foe
    Against th' imperial palace is designed.

238

    Now day appears, and with the day the King,
950   Whose early care had robbed him of his rest;
    Far off the cracks of falling houses ring,
     And shrieks of subjects pierce his tender breast.

239

    Near as he draws, thick harbingers of smoke
     With gloomy pillars cover all the place;
955   Whose little intervals of night are broke
     By sparks that drive against his sacred face.

240

    More than his guards his sorrows made him known,
     And pious tears which down his cheeks did
      shower;
    The wretched in his grief forgot their own,
960   So much the pity of a king has power.

---

hall). It also made some progress eastwards, against the prevailing wind, and drew close to the Tower on 4 September.

949–72. The King spent the whole of 4 September in the city directing the fire-fighting (Bell, *The Great Fire* 113–15). 'It is not indeede imaginable how extraordinary the vigilance & activity of the King & Duke was, even labouring in person, & being present, to command, order, reward, and encourage Workemen; by which he shewed his affection to his people, & gained theirs' (Evelyn, 6 September).

949. Perhaps recalling Cowley: 'up rose the *Sun* and *Saul*' (*Davideis* ii; *Poems* 284); and cp. 'Palamon and Arcite' iii 190.

953–4. Observers were awed by the thick pall of smoke which hung over the city; Evelyn (3 September) thought it extended for fifty miles (Bell, *The Great Fire* 67).

241

He wept the flames of what he loved so well,
　　And what so well had merited his love:
For never prince in grace did more excel,
　　Or royal city more in duty strove.

242

965　Nor with an idle care did he behold:
　　Subjects may grieve, but monarchs must redress.
He cheers the fearful and commends the bold,
　　And makes despairers hope for good success.

243

Himself directs what first is to be done,
970　　And orders all the succours which they bring:
The helpful and the good about him run
　　And form an army worthy such a King.

244

He sees the dire contagion spread so fast
　　That where it seizes all relief is vain;
975　And therefore must unwillingly lay waste
　　That country which would else the foe maintain.

245

The powder blows up all before the fire:
　　Th' amazèd flames stand gathered on a heap,
And from the precipice's brink retire,
980　　Afraid to venture on so large a leap.

246

Thus fighting fires awhile themselves consume,
　　But straight, like Turks, forced on to win or die,
They first lay tender bridges of their fume

---

965. idle] ineffectual.
977–88. The desperate measure of blowing up houses to clear a way before
the flames was eventually used on 4 September.
982. Turkish foot-soldiers in battle were half-enclosed by their cavalry, who
had orders to kill any trying to retreat (Henry Blount, *A Voyage into the
Levant,* third edition (1638) 71) (*Works*).
983. fume] smoke.

And o'er the breach in unctuous vapours fly.

247

985   Part stays for passage till a gust of wind
     Ships o'er their forces in a shining sheet;
    Part creeping under ground their journey blind,
     And climbing from below their fellows meet.

248

    Thus to some desert plain or old wood side
990   Dire night-hags come from far to dance their
      round,
    And o'er broad rivers on their fiends they ride,
     Or sweep in clouds above the blasted ground.

249

    No help avails: for hydra-like the fire
     Lifts up his hundred heads to aim his way;
995   And scarce the wealthy can one half retire
     Before he rushes in to share the prey.

250

    The rich grow suppliant, and the poor grow proud;
     Those offer mighty gain, and these ask more:
    So void of pity is th' ignoble crowd
1000   When others' ruin may increase their store.

987. blind] conceal, make difficult to trace (*OED* 3); a verb here.

989. desert] 1667's spelling *desart* indicates seventeenth-century pronunciation.

993–4. hydra] The monster with many heads (100 according to Diodorus Siculus IV xi 5), which was killed by Hercules. It is used as an image for rebellion on Rubens's ceiling in the Banqueting House, Whitehall, and in *Coriolanus* III i 93, and so continues the image of the fire as a rebel. Cp. *AA* l. 541.

995. retire] remove (*OED* 8); a transitive verb here.

997–1000. 'Any money is given for help, 5*l.* 10*l.* 20*l.* 30*l.* for a cart, to bear forth into the Fields some choice things, which were ready to be consumed; and some of the countries [i.e. countrymen] had the Conscience to accept of the highest price, which the Citizens did then offer in their extremity' (Thomas Vincent, *God's Terrible Voice in the City* (1667) 53). It was a common complaint: cp. Samuel Rolle, *The Burning of London* (1667) iii 28–33.

999. ignoble crowd] Cp. Virgil's *ignobile vulgus* (*Aen.* i 149).

251

As those who live by shores with joy behold
   Some wealthy vessel split or stranded nigh,
And from the rocks leap down for shipwrecked gold,
   And seek the tempest which the others fly:

252

1005   So these but wait the owners' last despair,
   And what's permitted to the flames invade;
   Ev'n from their jaws they hungry morsels tear,
   And on their backs the spoils of Vulcan lade.

253

The days were all in this lost labour spent,
1010   And when the weary King gave place to night
His beams he to his royal brother lent,
   And so shone still in his reflective light.

254

Night came, but without darkness or repose,
   A dismal picture of the general doom,
1015   Where souls distracted when the trumpet blows
   And half unready with their bodies come.

255

Those who have homes, when home they do repair
   To a last lodging call their wandering friends;
Their short, uneasy sleeps are broke with care,
1020   To look how near their own destruction tends.

1001–8. Rolle also condemns 'those that stole what they could in the time of the Fire' and says: 'Some living upon the Sea-coast, may, perchance, gain now and then by racks, bringing rich goods to their hands; but then, it is presumed, the owners are cast away, or cannot be known' (iii 33–5).

1006. invade] seize, usurp (*OED* 4b).

1008. lade] load.

1011–12. Cp. *To My Lord Chancellor* ll. 45–8.

1011. The Duke of York spent 4 September directing firefighting late into the night (Bell, *The Great Fire* 115).

1014–16. It was believed that at the Last Judgement (*general doom*) souls and bodies would be reunited (cp. Cowley, 'The Resurrection'; *Poems* 183).

1014. dismal] Perhaps used with overtones of its Latin origin in *dies mali* (unlucky, evil days); there were twenty-four unlucky days in the medieval calendar, including 3 September (see *OED*).

1020. tends] approaches (*OED* 1).

256

Those who have none sit round where once it was,
    And with full eyes each wonted room require,
Haunting the yet warm ashes of the place,
    As murdered men walk where they did expire.

257

1025 Some stir up coals and watch the Vestal fire,
    Others in vain from sight of ruin run,
And while through burning labyrinths they retire
    With loathing eyes repeat what they would shun.

258

The most in fields like herded beasts lie down,
1030   To dews obnoxious on the grassy floor;
And while their babes in sleep their sorrows drown,
    Sad parents watch the remnants of their store.

259

While by the motion of the flames they guess
    What streets are burning now, and what are near;
1035 An infant, waking, to the paps would press,
    And meets, instead of milk, a falling tear.

260

No thought can ease them but their sovereign's care,
    Whose praise th' afflicted as their comfort sing:
Even those whom want might drive to just despair
1040   Think life a blessing under such a King.

1022. require] seek for (*OED* 9); perhaps also 'look in vain for, miss', one of the senses of the Latin *requiro*. Like *repeat* in l. 1028, this is a somewhat unusual usage in English, and shows D.'s consciousness of Latin roots; cp. 'Account' ll. 250–63 above.

1025. Vestal fire] Vesta was the Roman goddess of the household and hearth; her cult was centred on a fire which never went out.

1028. repeat] encounter again (*OED* 4), recalling *urbem repeto* ('I seek the city again'; *Aen.* ii 749). Cp. Waller: 'the pious Trojan . . . / Repeats the danger of the burning town' ('Battle of the Summer Islands' ll. 62–4); and D.'s 'Dedication of the *Aeneis*': '*Æneas* . . . repeated all his former Dangers to have found his Wife' (*Works* v 291).

1029–32. The refugees assembled at Moorfields (Bell, *The Great Fire* 89–90).

1030. obnoxious] exposed to (*OED* 1).

261

Meantime he sadly suffers in their grief,
  Out-weeps an hermit, and out-prays a saint:
All the long night he studies their relief,
  How they may be supplied, and he may want.

262

King's Prayer.

1045 'O God', said he, 'thou patron of my days,
  Guide of my youth in exile and distress!
Who me unfriended brought'st by wondrous ways
  The kingdom of my fathers to possess;

263

Be thou my judge, with what unwearied care
1050 I since have laboured for my people's good,
To bind the bruises of a civil war
  And stop the issues of their wasting blood.

264

Thou who hast taught me to forgive the ill,
  And recompense as friends the good misled,
1055 If mercy be a precept of thy will,
  Return that mercy on thy servant's head.

265

Or if my heedless youth has stepped astray,
  Too soon forgetful of thy gracious hand;
On me alone thy just displeasure lay,
1060   But take thy judgements from this mourning land.

266

We all have sinned, and thou hast laid us low
  As humble earth from whence at first we came;

1045–60. Cp. David's prayer in the pestilence, 1 Chronicles xxi 17.
1049–52. Cp. Smith (see ll. 601–16n): 'Your watchful thoughts, and your
unwearied care, / Succeeding ages will with joy declare; / Tell, how without
th' expence of their own bloud, / Or sweat, You wisely have contriv'd their
good' (*A Poem on . . . The Loyal London* 9).
1053–6. For mercy as a characteristic of Charles cp. *Threnodia Augustalis* l.
86n.
1061. *We all have sinned*] See headnote, '*Fire*'.

Like flying shades before the clouds we show,
And shrink like parchment in consuming flame.

267

1065 O let it be enough what thou hast done,
When spotted deaths ran armed through every
street
With poisoned darts which not the good could shun,
The speedy could out-fly, or valiant meet.

268

The living few, and frequent funerals then,
1070 Proclaimed thy wrath on this forsaken place;
And now those few who are returned again
Thy searching judgements to their dwellings trace.

269

O pass not, Lord, an absolute decree,
Or bind thy sentence unconditional;
1075 But in thy sentence our remorse foresee,
And in that foresight this thy doom recall.

270

Thy threatenings, Lord, as thine, thou mayest
revoke;
But if immutable and fixed they stand,
Continue still thyself to give the stroke,
1080 And let not foreign foes oppress thy land.'

1063. 'Man . . . fleeth also as a shadow' (Job xiv 1).
1064. From Cowley: 'The wide-stretcht *Scrowl* of *Heaven* . . . / Shall crackle,
and the parts together shrink / Like *Parchment* in a fire' ('The 34. Chapter of
the Prophet *Isaiah*'; *Poems* 212) (Loane (see l. 402*n*)).
1066. D. diplomatically avoids other references to the plague of 1665, when
the King, courtiers and clergy left Londoners largely to the care of dissenting
ministers.
1069. frequent funerals] i.e. numerous corpses; D. repeats the phrase when
translating *plurima corpora* (*Aen.* ii 364–5). For the Latin poetic use of *funera*
(funerals) to mean 'corpses' cp. Horace, *Carm.* I xxviii 19.
1073–6. The vocabulary is from theological discussions of predestination; cp.
'The Cock and the Fox' ll. 507–52.
1076–82. Cp. I Chronicles xxi 13–16 (David's prayer).
1080. See quotation in l. 1084*n*.

271

Th' Eternal heard, and from the heavenly choir
　　Chose out the cherub with the flaming sword;
And bad him swiftly drive th' approaching fire
　　From where our naval magazines were stored.

272

1085　The blessèd minister his wings displayed,
　　And like a shooting star he cleft the night;
He charged the flames, and those that disobeyed
　　He lashed to duty with his sword of light.

273

The fugitive flames, chastised, went forth to prey
1090　On pious structures by our fathers reared,
By which to heaven they did affect the way
　　Ere faith in churchmen without works was heard.

274

The wanting orphans saw with watery eyes
　　Their founder's charity in dust laid low,

1081. The *London Gazette* also speaks of divine intervention: 'his miraculous
and never enough to be acknowledged Mercy in putting a stop to it when we
were in the last despair, and that all attempts for the quenching it, however
industriously pursued, seemed insufficient'.

1082. From Genesis iii 24, where Eden is guarded by cherubim and a flaming
sword.

1084. The navy's gunpowder, which had been stored in the Tower of
London, was moved to safety by Sir John Robinson, Lieutenant of the
Tower. The Tower was saved by blowing up adjoining houses (Bell, *The
Great Fire* 160). The *London Gazette* said: 'And we have further this infinite
cause particularly to give God thanks that the fire did not happen in any of
those places where his Majesties Naval stores are kept, so as tho it hath
pleased God to visit with his own hand, he hath not, by disfurnishing us with
the means of carrying on the War, subjected us to our enemies.'

1090–2. Churches and almshouses built before the Reformation, when the
doctrine of justification by faith alone, without the need for good works, was
promoted by Protestant theologians. The Restoration Church of England
was moving away from this position (see Spurr 305, 321).

1091. Cp. *Geo.* iv 562: *viamque adfectat Olympo* ('he seeks the way to Olympus'). *affect*] seek, aim at (*OED* 1); cp. *AA* l. 178.

1093–6. Parts of Christ's Hospital were burnt on 4 September; the Governors

1095   And sent to God their ever-answered cries,
        For he protects the poor who made them so.

                            275
        Nor could thy fabric, Paul's, defend thee long,
            Though thou wert sacred to thy maker's praise;
        Though made immortal by a poet's song,
1100   And poets' songs the Theban walls could raise.

                            276
        The daring flames peeped in, and saw from far
            The awful beauties of the sacred choir;
        But since it was profaned by civil war
            Heaven thought it fit to have it purged by fire.

                            277
1105   Now down the narrow streets it swiftly came,
            And widely opening did on both sides prey:
        This benefit we sadly owe the flame,
            If only ruin must enlarge our way.

                            278
        And now four days the sun had seen our woes,
1110   Four nights the moon beheld th' incessant fire;
        It seemed as if the stars more sickly rose,
            And farther from the feverish north retire.

---

had taken the precaution of moving the children to safety (Bell, *The Great Fire* 141–2).

1097–104. St Paul's Cathedral caught fire on 4 September. The fabric was in poor condition, and Wren had already made plans for its repair. He then designed the new cathedral, which was built from 1675 to 1710.

1099. poet's song] Waller's 'Upon His Majesty's Repairing of Paul's'.

1100. Amphion built the walls of Thebes by drawing stones after him by the magical music of his lyre. Cp. Waller (*ibid*, ll. 11–12): the King 'like Amphion, makes those quarries leap / Into fair figures from a confused heap'.

1102. awful] awesome.

1103. Horses were stabled in the cathedral during the Civil War.

1108. The various plans for the rebuilding of London envisaged wide, straight streets to replace the narrow winding streets of the old city.

279

In th' empyrean heaven (the blessed abode)
   The thrones and the dominions prostrate lie,
1115 Not daring to behold their angry God,
   And an hushed silence damps the tuneful sky.

280

At length th' Almighty cast a pitying eye,
   And mercy softly touched his melting breast;
He saw the town's one half in rubbish lie,
1120   And eager flames give on to storm the rest.

281

An hollow crystal pyramid he takes,
   In firmamental waters dipped above;
Of it a broad extinguisher he makes,
   And hoods the flames that to their quarry strove.

282

1125 The vanquished fires withdraw from every place,
   Or full with feeding sink into a sleep;
Each household genius shows again his face,
   And from the hearths the little Lares creep.

283

Our King this more-than-natural change beholds;
1130   With sober joy his heart and eyes abound:
To the All-good his lifted hands he folds,
   And thanks him low on his redeemèd ground.

1114. thrones . . . dominions] orders of angels (Colossians i 16).
1120. give on] assault.
1121–4. The owner of the copy of *1667* now in the library of Trinity College, Cambridge, wrote two parodies of this stanza on the endpaper; one reads: 'An Hollow far-fetcht Metaphor he takes / In non-sense dipt of his fantastick braine / Of which a broad extinguisher he makes / Which hoods his witt & stifles all his flame.' The volume was presented to Thomas Smith by Richard Duke in 1684, so the parody may be by Duke or Smith. The stanza is also criticized in *A Letter from a Gentleman to the Honourable Ed. Howard* (1668) 8–9.
1122. firmamental] of the heavens.
1127. genius] in classical religion a tutelary god or attendant spirit allotted to a person or place.
1128. Lares] Roman gods of the home and hearth (disyllabic).

284
As when sharp frosts had long constrained the earth
    A kindly thaw unlocks it with mild rain;
1135 And first the tender blade peeps up to birth,
    And straight the green fields laugh with promised
        grain:

285
By such degrees the spreading gladness grew
    In every heart which fear had froze before;
The standing streets with so much joy they view
1140   That with less grief the perished they deplore.

286
The father of the people opened wide
    His stores, and all the poor with plenty fed:
Thus God's Anointed God's own place supplied,
    And filled the empty with his daily bread.

287
1145 This royal bounty brought its own reward,
    And in their minds so deep did print the sense,
That if their ruins sadly they regard,
    'Tis but with fear the sight might drive him thence.

1133. constrained] constricted, contracted (*OED* 9); cp. 'When Winter Frosts
constrain the Field with Cold' ('The Second Book of the *Georgics*' l. 430).
1134. kindly] nurturing, fruitful (as well as 'benign').   *unlocks*] Cp.
'Lucretius: The Beginning of the First Book' l. 15*n*.
1136. laugh] The Latin *laetus* ('joyful') was used of crops and fields, meaning
'abundant' or 'fertile'.
1140. deplore] lament.
1141–8. On 5 and 6 September the King issued proclamations for the supply
and distribution of bread, and 'commanded the Victualler of his Navy to send
bread into *Moore-fields* for the relief of the poor' (*London Gazette*). On 6
September he rode out to Moorfields to address the homeless.
1141. father of the people] The title *pater patriae* ('father of the country') was
conferred on Augustus in 2 BC (Suetonius, *Divus Augustus* 58).
1145–56. The *London Gazette* told enemies abroad that 'a greater instance of
the affections of this City could never be given then hath been now given in
this sad and deplorable Accident, when if at any time disorder might have
been expected from the losses . . . yet nevertheless there hath not been
observed so much as a murmuring word to fall from any, but on the con-

288
City's request to the King not to leave them.

But so may he live long that town to sway
1150   Which by his auspice they will nobler make,
As he will hatch their ashes by his stay,
    And not their humble ruins now forsake.

289

They have not lost their loyalty by fire,
    Nor is their courage or their wealth so low
1155 That from his wars they poorly would retire,
    Or beg the pity of a vanquished foe.

290

Not with more constancy the Jews of old
    By Cyrus from rewarded exile sent,
Their royal city did in dust behold
1160   Or with more vigour to rebuild it went.

291

The utmost malice of their stars is past,
    And two dire comets which have scourged the
        town
In their own plague and fire have breathed their last,
    Or dimly in their sinking sockets frown.

292

1165 Now frequent trines the happier lights among,
    And high-raised Jove from his dark prison freed
(Those weights took off that on his planet hung)
    Will gloriously the new-laid work succeed.

---

trary, even those persons whose losses rendered their conditions most desperate, and to be fit objects of others prayers, beholding those frequent instances of his Majesties care of his people, forgot their own misery, and filled the streets with their prayers for his Majesty, whose trouble they seemed to compassionate before their own.'

1150. auspice] prosperous lead; propitious influence (*OED* 3).
1151. hatch] bring to full development (*OED* 6).
1157–60. Ezra i–iii.
1162. dire] boding ill.
1164. socket] part of a candlestick into which the candle is placed (*OED* 3).
1165–8. A *trine* is the relative position of two planets which are 120° (one-third of the zodiac) apart; this 'aspect' is benign. Jupiter is a propitious planet.

293

Methinks already from this chymic flame
1170   I see a city of more precious mould:
Rich as the town which gives the ᶜIndies name,
With silver paved, and all divine with gold.

(c) *Mexico.*

294

Already, labouring with a mighty fate,
She shakes the rubbish from her mounting brow,
1175 And seems to have renewed her charter's date
Which heaven will to the death of time allow.

295

More great than human, now, and more ᵈAugust,
New deified she from her fires does rise:
Her widening streets on new foundations trust,
1180   And opening, into larger parts she flies.

(d) *Augusta, the old name of London.*

In 1666 Jupiter had been in Pisces, its negative sign (each planet rules two signs, manifesting well in one and badly in the other). Pisces is also a sign linked with places of confinement (Simon Bentley, privately). In 1667, however, Jupiter was in Aries, where it is strongly placed, and Aries rules England. William Lilly wrote: 'The positure of *Jupiter* in *Aries,* seems to give some probability of Peace . . . it is the most promising position of Heaven for his Majesties successes against all Enemies whatsoever . . . *Mars* is . . . in a partile Trine Aspect unto the place of the last Conjunction of *Saturn* and *Jupiter,* and the benevolent *Jupiter* in Trine to the place of *Venus* in that Conjunction' (*Merlini Anglici Ephemeris* (1667) sigs B1ʳ, B5ʳ).

1168. succeed] give success to (*OED* 14).

1169–80. After the fire, Wren, Evelyn and Hooke all produced plans for a model city, but in the event rebuilding proceeded piecemeal.

1169. chymic] alchemic, transmuting. The author of *London Undone* (1666) said of London that 'She was not so much *ruin'd,* as *refin'd*'. The alchemical images in *AM* are discussed by B. A. Rosenberg in *PMLA* lxxix (1964) 254–8, J. M. Armistead, *SEL* xxvii (1987) 384–5, and Lyndy Abraham, *Marvell and Alchemy* (1990) 46, 115, 147, 301, 315.

1170. mould] earth (for its alchemical implications see Abraham 46).

1177. The name Augusta was recorded by Camden (*Britain* (1610) 80) and revived by Edmund Bolton in *London, King Charles, his Augusta* (1648).

296

Before, she like some shepherdess did show
    Who sate to bathe her by a river's side;
Not answering to her fame, but rude and low,
    Nor taught the beauteous arts of modern pride.

297

1185   Now like a maiden queen she will behold
    From her high turrets hourly suitors come:
The east with incense and the west with gold
    Will stand like suppliants to receive her doom.

298

The silver Thames, her own domestic flood,
1190   Shall bear her vessels like a sweeping train,
And often wind (as of his mistress proud)
    With longing eyes to meet her face again.

299

The wealthy Tagus and the wealthier Rhine
    The glory of their towns no more shall boast;
1195   And Seine, that would with Belgian rivers join,
    Shall find her lustre stained and traffic lost.

300

The venturous merchant who designed more far,
    And touches on our hospitable shore,
Charmed with the splendour of this northern star
1200   Shall here unlade him and depart no more.

301

Our powerful navy shall no longer meet
    The wealth of France or Holland to invade:

1185. *maiden queen*] The phrase here suggests the return of the golden age of Queen Elizabeth, the Virgin Queen.
1188. *doom*] verdict, decision.
1193. *Tagus*] 'a Famous River in *Spain*, which discharges it self into the Ocean near *Lisbone* in *Portugal*. It was held, of old, to be full of Golden Sands' (D.'s note to Juvenal's *Satire* iii (*Works* iv 142)).
1195. A reference to Louis XIV's expansionist designs on the Netherlands.
1200. *unlade*] unload.

The beauty of this town, without a fleet,
From all the world shall vindicate her trade.

302
1205 And while this famed emporium we prepare,
The British ocean shall such triumphs boast
That those who now disdain our trade to share
Shall rob like pirates on our wealthy coast.

303
Already we have conquered half the war,
1210 And the less dangerous part is left behind:
Our trouble now is but to make them dare,
And not so great to vanquish as to find.

304
Thus to the eastern wealth through storms we go,
But now, the Cape once doubled, fear no more:
1215 A constant trade-wind will securely blow,
And gently lay us on the spicy shore.

1204. vindicate] defend against encroachment (*OED* 4).
1205. emporium] Cp. Smith (see ll. 601–16*n*): 'Thou always wert the great /
Emporeum of our Kings, and royal Seat' (*A Poem on . . . the Loyal London* 10).
The word appears to have first been applied to London by Bede (*Historia
Ecclesiastica* ii 3); it is repeated by Camden (*Britannia* (1607) 304; not in the
translation). Edward Waterhouse lamented 'the spoil and loss of that once
famous place, which *Tacitus* so long ago terms, *Nobilissimum emporium &
commeatu negotiatorum maxime celebre*' (*A Short Narrative of the late Dreadful Fire
in London* (1667) 3). Waterhouse adds *emporium* to Tacitus's text in *Annales*
xiv 33.
1209. Cp. Virgil, *Ecl.* ix 59: *hinc adeo media est nobis via* ('here we have half our
way').

19 Prologue, Epilogue and Songs from *Sir Martin Mar-all*

Date and publication. The first recorded performance of the play was on 15 August 1667, by the Duke's Company at the Lincoln's Inn Fields Theatre. *Sr Martin Mar-all, or the Feign'd Innocence: A Comedy* was published by Herringman in 1668, without attribution (*SR* 24 June 1668, as 'by the Duke of Newe Castle'; *TC* November); reprinted 1668 (some copies dated 1669), 1678, 1691 (the first edition to attribute the play to D.), 1697. Song I appeared in *Westminster-Drollery* (1671, 1672), *The New Academy of Complements* (1671) and *Windsor Drollery* (1672); Song II appeared in *The New Academy of Complements*. In Nottingham UL MS Portland PwV 205 there is an anonymous song headed 'A song made by Sr Marten Marall & his man Warner to the Lady falklands tune'; it was printed as D.'s by Francis Needham in *Welbeck Miscellany* ii (1934) 46–7, but there is no evidence for this attribution.

Authorship. Pepys described the play as 'made by my Lord Duke of Newcastle, but, as everybody says, corrected by Dryden' (16 August 1667; and 1 January 1668; see also Downes 62–3). It was based on *L'Etourdi* by Molière and *L'Amant Indiscret* by Quinault. For the sources and collaboration see *Works* ix 354–69 and F. H. Moore, *SP* extra series iv (1967) 27–38. D. was associated with the King's Company at the Theatre Royal, but since the play was regarded as Newcastle's, it could be acted by the rival company. It is virtually certain that the Prologue, Epilogue and Songs are by D.

Prologue

Fools, which each man meets in his dish each day,
Are yet the great regalios of a play;
In which to poets you but just appear,
To prize that highest which costs them so dear.
5   Fops in the town more easily will pass—
One story makes a statutable ass:
But such in plays must be much thicker sown,
Like yolks of eggs, a dozen beat to one.
Observing poets all their walks invade,

¶**19**. *Prologue.*
2. *regalios*] presents of choice food or drink.
6. *statutable*] of regular or standard quality (*OED* 2).

10 As men watch woodcocks gliding through a glade;
    And when they have enough for comedy,
    They stow their several bodies in a pie:
    The poet's but the cook to fashion it,
    For, gallants, you yourselves have found the wit.
15 To bid you welcome would your bounty wrong:
    None welcome those who bring their cheer along.

Epilogue

    As country vicars, when the sermon's done,
    Run huddling to the benediction,
    Well knowing, though the better sort may stay,
    The vulgar rout will run unblessed away:
5   So we, when once our play is done, make haste
    With a short epilogue to close your taste.
    In thus withdrawing we seem mannerly,
    But when the curtain's down we peep, and see
    A jury of the wits who still stay late,
10 And in their club decree the poor play's fate;
    Their verdict back is to the boxes brought,
    Thence all the town pronounces it their thought.
    Thus, gallants, we like Lilly can foresee,
    But if you ask us what our doom will be,
15 We by tomorrow will our fortune cast,
    As he tells all things when the year is past.

10. *woodcocks*] proverbially foolish birds, easily caught (Tilley W 746; *Hamlet* I iii 115).

Epilogue.
2. *huddling*] hurrying in disorder (*OED* 7).
6. *taste*] trial, test (*OED* 2); act of tasting (*OED* 3).
9–12. Cp. 'Epilogue to *An Evening's Love*'.
11. *boxes*] See 'Prologue to *The Rival Ladies*' l. 24n.
13. *Lilly*] William Lilly (1602–81), astrologer and author of almanacs and books of prophecy.

Songs

I

Make ready fair lady tonight,
And stand at the door below,
　　For I will be there
　　To receive you with care,
5　　And to your true love you shall go.

And when the stars twinkle so bright,
Then down to the door will I creep,
　　To my love I will fly,
　　Ere the jealous can spy,
10　　And leave my old daddy asleep.

II

Blind love to this hour
Had never like me a slave under his power.
　　Then blessed be the dart
　　That he threw at my heart,
5　　For nothing can prove
A joy so great as to be wounded with love.

My days and my nights
Are filled to the purpose with sorrows and frights;
From my heart still I sigh

Song I. In Act IV Scene i Warner (played originally by Henry Harris) sings the first verse, and Millisent (Mary Davis) replies with the second.

Song II. In Act V Scene i Sir Martin (played by the comedian James Nokes), serenades Millisent. The song is sung by his servant Warner while Sir Martin mimes it; the trick is discovered when Sir Martin continues to mouth the song after Warner has finished. This episode became well known (Price, *Music in the Restoration Theatre* 25, 255). Scott noticed that the song is adapted from a song by Voiture (*Oeuvres* (1650) 37–9; printed in Day 144–5).

1–6. From Voiture's first stanza: 'L'Amour sous sa loy / N'a jamais eu d'Amant plus heureux que moy; / Benit soit son flambeau, / Son carquois, son bandeau, / Je suis amoureux, / Et le Ciel ne voit point d'Amant plus heureux.'

7–12. From Voiture's second stanza: 'Mes jours et mes nuits / Ont bien peu de repos, et beaucoup d' ennuis; / Je me meurs de langeur, / J'ay le feu dans le coeur, / Je suis . . .'.

10   And my eyes are ne'er dry,
            So that Cupid be praised,
I am to the top of love's happiness raised.

           My soul's all on fire,
So that I have the pleasure to dote and desire,
15   Such a pretty soft pain
           That it tickles each vein;
            'Tis the dream of a smart,
Which makes me breathe short when it beats at my
    heart.

           Sometimes in a pet,
20 When I am despised, I my freedom would get;
           But straight a sweet smile
           Does my anger beguile,
           And my heart does recall,
Then the more I do struggle, the lower I fall.

25   Heaven does not impart
Such a grace as to love unto everyone's heart;
           For many may wish
           To be wounded and miss:
           Then blessed be love's fire,
30 And more blessed her eyes that first taught me desire.

19–24. From Voiture's seventh stanza: 'Souvent le dépit, / Peut bien, pour quelque temps, changer mon esprit, / Je maudis sa rigeur, / Mais au fond de mon coeur, / J'en suis . . .'; and the fifth stanza: 'Les yeux qui m'ont pris, / Payeroient tous mes maux avec un soûris, / Tous leurs traits me sont doux, / Mesme dans leur courroux, / Je suis . . .'.

20 Prologue, Epilogue and Songs from *The Tempest*

Date and publication. First performed 7 November 1667 by the Duke's Company at the Lincoln's Inn Fields Theatre. It was a popular play, with seven consecutive performances in its first run, and was admired by Pepys (7 November, etc.). *The Tempest, or The Enchanted Island. A Comedy* was published by Herringman in 1670 (*SR* 8 January; *TC* 17 February). This text was not reprinted in D.'s lifetime. Song IV was printed in *Windsor-Drollery* (1672), and Songs III and IV were set by John Banister in *The Ariel's Songs in a Play Call'd The Tempest* [1675]; facsimile in Day 14–16. An operatic version of the adaptation was made (probably by Shadwell) for performance in April 1674, and was printed as *The Tempest, or the Enchanted Island* in 1674; reprinted 1676, 1690, *c.* 1692 (dated '1676') and 1695. This version included the Prologue, Epilogue and Songs from *1670* (Songs I and II in an adapted form).

Authorship. The play is an adaptation of Shakespeare's *The Tempest* made by D. and Sir William Davenant. D.'s Preface credits Davenant with devising the addition of a man who had never seen a woman, and comic dialogue for the sailors. The Prologue and Epilogue are no doubt by D.; the authorship of the Songs is uncertain.

Prologue to *The Tempest, or The Enchanted Island*

As when a tree's cut down the secret root
Lives under ground, and thence new branches shoot,
So, from old Shakespeare's honoured dust, this day
Springs up and buds a new reviving play:
5   Shakespeare, who (taught by none) did first impart
To Fletcher wit, to labouring Jonson art;
He monarch-like gave those his subjects law,

¶**20**. *Prologue.*
1–20. D. says in his Preface to *The Tempest* that it was Davenant who first taught him to admire Shakespeare (*Works* x 3). D. first offered his views on Shakespeare in *EDP* (1667), and continued his critique in *A Defence of the Epilogue* (1672; *Works* xi 203–18); the Preface to *All for Love* (1678; *Works* xiii 10–19); and the Preface to *Troilus and Cressida* (1679; *Works* xiii 225–48). In *EDP* D. stressed Shakespeare's natural intelligence: 'All the Images of Nature

And is that Nature which they paint and draw.
Fletcher reached that which on his heights did grow,
10   Whilst Jonson crept and gathered all below.
This did his love, and this his mirth digest:
One imitates him most, the other best.
If they have since out-writ all other men,
'Tis with the drops which fell from Shakespeare's pen.
15   The storm which vanished on the neighbouring shore

---

were still present to him, and he drew them not laboriously, but luckily: when he describes any thing, you more than see it, you feel it too. Those who accuse him to have wanted learning, give him the greater commendation: he was naturally learn'd; he needed not the spectacles of Books to read Nature; he look'd inwards, and found her there . . . however others are now generally preferr'd before him, yet the Age wherein he liv'd, which had contemporaries with him *Fletcher* and *Johnson*, never equall'd them to him in their esteem' (*Works* xvii 55–6). It was Jonson who inadvertently gave rise to the tradition that Shakespeare was unlearned, when in his poem in the First Folio he said that he had 'small *Latine*, and lesse *Greeke*' (Jonson viii 391); D. later called this poem 'an Insolent, Sparing, and Invidious Panegyrick' (*Works* iv 6). Milton in *L'Allegro* wrote of Shakespeare's 'native wood-notes wild' (l. 134). After 1660, Shakespeare, Jonson and Fletcher were taken to be the glory of the pre-war English stage, and there was some agreement about their respective characteristics. Richard Flecknoe wrote: '*Shakespeare* excelled in a natural Vein, *Fletcher* in Wit, and *Jonson* in Gravity and ponderousness of Style. . . . Comparing him with *Shakespeare*, you shall see the difference betwixt Nature and Art; and with *Fletcher*, the difference betwixt Wit and Judgment' (*Love's Kingdom* (1664) sig. G6ʳ). D. commended Fletcher's wit in *EDP*: 'As for Comedy, Repartee is one of its chiefest graces; the greatest pleasure of the Audience is a chase of wit kept up on both sides, and swiftly manag'd. And this our forefathers, if not we, have had in *Fletchers* Playes' (*Works* xvii 48–9); and of his gift for writing love-scenes he said: '*Shakespear* writ better betwixt man and man; *Fletcher*, betwixt man and woman: consequently, the one describ'd friendship better; the other love: yet *Shakespear* taught *Fletcher* to write love; and *Juliet*, and *Desdemona*, are Originals' (*Works* xiii 247). D. wrote of Jonson: 'I think him the most learned and judicious Writer which any Theater ever had. . . . One cannot say he wanted wit, but rather that he was frugal of it. . . . Wit and Language, and Humour also in some measure we had before him; but something of Art was wanting to the *Drama* till he came. . . . Humour was his proper Sphere, and in that he delighted most to represent Mechanick people' (*Works* xvii 57). D. expanded this criticism of Jonson in the 'Epilogue to *2 Conquest of Granada*', and it was one of the chief points of debate between him and Shadwell (see headnote to *MF*).

15–16. On 25 September 1667 the King's Company at the Theatre Royal

Was taught by Shakespeare's tempest first to roar:
That innocence and beauty which did smile
In Fletcher, grew on this enchanted isle.
But Shakespeare's magic could not copied be,
20   Within that circle none durst walk but he.
I must confess 'twas bold, nor would you now
That liberty to vulgar wits allow,
Which works by magic supernatural things:
But Shakespeare's power is sacred as a king's.
25   Those legends from old priesthood were received,
And he then writ as people then believed.
But if for Shakespeare we your grace implore,
We for our theatre shall want it more,
Who by our dearth of youths are forced t' employ
30   One of our women to present a boy.
And that's a transformation you will say
Exceeding all the magic in the play.
Let none expect in the last act to find
Her sex transformed from man to womankind.
35   Whate'er she was before the play began,
All you shall see of her is perfect man:
Or if your fancy will be farther led
To find her woman, it must be abed.

Epilogue

Gallants, by all good signs it does appear
That sixty-seven's a very damning year,
For knaves abroad, and for ill poets here.

---

staged as a rival attraction Fletcher's *The Sea Voyage* (1622) which is somewhat indebted to Shakespeare's *Tempest*. It was renamed *The Storm*.
20. In Shakespeare's play, though not in the adaptation, Alonso and his
followers are held charmed within a magic circle drawn by Prospero (V i 57).
30. Montague Summers thought that the role of Hippolito was taken by Moll
Davis, but James Winn (privately) suggests that her singing talents would
have been better used as Ariel.

Epilogue.
3. *knaves abroad*] The Dutch concluded a peace with England through the
Treaty of Breda (July 1667); but they had already been threatened in June by

Among the Muses there's a general rot,
5   The rhyming monsieur and the Spanish plot:
Defy or court, all's one, they go to pot.

The ghosts of poets walk within this place,
And haunt us actors wheresoe'er we pass,
In visions bloodier than King Richard's was.

10 For this poor wretch he has not much to say,
But quietly brings in his part o' th' play,
And begs the favour to be damned today.

He sends me only like a sheriff's man here
To let you know the malefactor's near,
15 And that he means to die *en cavalier*.

For if you should be gracious to his pen,
Th' example will prove ill to other men,
And you'll be troubled with 'em all again.

Louis XIV's invasion of the Spanish Netherlands. A defensive alliance between England and Holland was signed in January 1668.

5. *rhyming monsieur*] *Works* suggests an allusion to Orrery's *The Black Prince* (featuring King John of France) which had been performed to derision on 19 October 1667 (see Pepys). D. perhaps intends a distinction between this play and James Howard's prose comedy *The English Monsieur*, revived on 29 October.   *Spanish plot*] *Works* suggests Thomas St Serfe's *Tarugo's Wiles*, performed on 5 October, whose plot was adapted from Agustín Moreto's *No Puede Ser*. See also D.'s 'Prologue to *The Wild Gallant*' ll. 36–8n.

6. *Defy or court*] *Works* notes that St Serfe's play satirized the coffee-houses and the Royal Society, while Orrery's flattered the King.   *go to pot*] are cut up like meat for the pot.

9. Richard III's visions of the ghosts of his victims, either in Shakespeare's play (V iii) or in John Caryll's *The English Princess; or, The Death of Richard the Third* (IV ix), performed on 7 March 1667.

13. *sheriff's*] *1670* reads 'Sh'riffs'; the pronunciation is probably monosyllabic, as in the common alternative spelling 'shrieve'.

15. *en cavalier*] like a gentleman.

Songs

I

1. Where does proud Ambition dwell?
2. In the lowest rooms of hell.
1. Of the damned who leads the host?
2. He who did oppress the most.
5 1. Who such troops of damnèd brings?
2. Most are led by fighting kings:
   Kings who did crowns unjustly get,
   Here on burning thrones are set.
Chorus. Kings who did crowns *etc.*

10 1. Who are the pillars of Ambition's court?
2. Grim deaths and scarlet murthers it support.
1. What lies beneath her feet?
2.   Her footsteps tread
   On orphans' tender breasts, and brothers dead.
1. Can heaven permit such crimes should be
15   Rewarded with felicity?
2. O no! uneasily their crowns they wear,
   And their own guilt amidst their guards they fear.
   Cares when they wake their minds unquiet keep,
   And we in visions lord it o'er their sleep.
20 *Chorus.* O no! uneasily their crowns *etc.*

II

Around, around, we pace
About this cursèd place,
Whilst thus we compass in
These mortals and their sin.

III

Dry those eyes which are o'erflowing,
All your storms are overblowing;

Song I. From Act II Scene i, sung offstage by two devils: Alonzo, Antonio and Gonzalo hear it. The two devils enter and summon Pride, Fraud, Rapine and Murther. The spirits then 'fall into a round encompassing the Duke, &c' and sing Song II.
Song III. From Act III Scene ii, sung by Ariel, invisible, to Alonzo, Antonio and Gonzalo. It is an equivalent for Shakespeare's song in the masque.

While you in this isle are biding,
You shall feast without providing:
5   Every dainty you can think of,
Every wine which you would drink of
Shall be yours; all want shall shun you,
Ceres' blessing so is on you.

IV

Ferdinand.   Go thy way.
Ariel.   Go thy way.
Fer.   Why should'st thou stay?
Ar.   Why should'st thou stay?
5 *Fer.* Where the winds whistle, and where the streams creep,
      Under yond willow tree fain would I sleep.
        Then let me alone,
        For 'tis time to be gone.
Ar.   For 'tis time to be gone.
10 *Fer.* What cares or pleasures can be in this isle?
        Within this desert place
        There lives no human race;
      Fate cannot frown here, nor kind Fortune smile.
        Kind Fortune smiles, and she
15 *Ar.*   Has yet in store for thee
        Some strange felicity.
        Follow me, follow me,
        And thou shalt see.

V

We want music, we want mirth,
Up, dam, and cleave the earth;
We have now no lords that wrong us,
Send thy merry sprites among us.

Song IV. From Act III Scene iv, a dialogue between Ariel and Ferdinand. The setting by Banister extends Ariel's part. For a discussion of the relationship between the words and music see Winn, *When Beauty* 192–5. This song was parodied in Thomas Duffet's *The Mock-Tempest: or The Enchanted Castle* (1675), a burlesque of the operatic version which was staged at the rival Theatre Royal (see Winn, *When Beauty* 223).
Song V. From Act IV Scene ii, sung by Caliban.
2. *dam*] Caliban's mother, Sycorax.

21 Prologue to *Albumazar*

Date and publication. The Prologue was written for a revival of *Albumazar* on 21 February 1668. On 22 February Pepys went 'to the Duke's playhouse and there saw *Albumazar*, an old play, this the second time of acting'. It was written by Thomas Tomkis, performed at Trinity College, Cambridge, on 9 March 1615 to celebrate the visit of James I, and published later that year. It is an adaptation of *Lo Astrologo* (1606) by Giambattista della Porta, and is a satire on astrology. The Prologue was first printed anonymously in *Covent Garden Drolery* (1672, reprinted 1672); it was printed as D.'s in *MP* (1684, reprinted 1692). It also survives in two MSS: BodL MS Eng. Poet. e. 4 and Society of Antiquaries MS 330; these probably date from the early 1670s (see headnote to 'To the Lady Castlemaine'). The two MSS are virtually identical verbally, and agree in differing from *1684* in half a dozen minor substantive variants. The text in *1672* has numerous verbal variants from *1684*. Kinsley and *Works* assume that *1684* is a revised version of the original text in *1672*; they print *1672*, but emend it from *1684* wherever the texts differ in substantives. However, the agreement of MSS with *1684* (which they are not derived from, and probably predate) suggests that D.'s original text is preserved in *1684*, and that *1672* is a corrupt text, perhaps deriving from the playhouse (see the headnote to 'Prologue, Epilogue and Songs from *Marriage A-la-Mode*' for a further example of this feature of *1672*). Accordingly the present text follows *1684*, noting those readings in *1672* which may be playhouse alterations, but ignoring its minor variants and obvious errors.

The Prologue to *Albumazar*

To say this comedy pleased long ago
Is not enough to make it pass you now.
Yet, gentlemen, your ancestors had wit,
When few men censured, and when fewer writ;
5   And Jonson (of those few the best) chose this

¶**21**. 5–8. Pepys (22 February 1668) recorded that 'it is said to have been the ground of B. Johnson's *Alchymist*', but Jonson's play was staged in 1610 and printed in 1612. However, Herford and Simpson suggest that the adoption of a new motto on the title page of *The Alchemist* in the 1616 folio (*petere inde coronam, / Unde prius nulli velarint tempora Musae*: 'to seek a crown from fields whence the Muses have previously crowned no one's brows' (Lucretius i 929–30)), may have been occasioned by the appearance in the interim of *Albumazar* (*Ben Jonson* ii 96n). This motto is probably a jibe at Tomkis rather than Jonson's own defence against allegations of plagiarism. Richard Brathwait derided *Albumazar* as a poor second *Alchemist* in *A Strappado for the*

As the best model of his masterpiece:
Subtle was got by our Albumazar,
That alchemist by this astrologer;
Here he was fashioned, and we may suppose
10 He liked the fashion well who wore the clothes.
But Ben made nobly his what he did mould;
What was another's lead becomes his gold:
Like an unrighteous conqueror he reigns,
Yet rules that well which he unjustly gains.
15 But this our age such authors does afford
As make whole plays, and yet scarce write one word;
Who in this anarchy of wit rob all,
And what's their plunder their possession call;
Who, like bold padders, scorn by night to prey,
20 But rob by sunshine in the face of day:

Diuell (1615) 114–15. D. may have misunderstood the implication of Jonson's motto, or he may have heard theatrical gossip. See further the edition of *Albumazar* by H. G. Dick (1944) 48–52. As *Works* notes, the play opens with a discussion of thieving: the learned man 'steales one author from another. / This Poet is that Poets Plagiary, / And he a third's, till they end all in *Homer*. / —And *Homer* filtch't all from an Ægyptian Preestesse' (I i 19–22).

7. *Subtle*] the alchemist in Jonson's play.

9. *we may*] *1684, MSS*; I should *1672*.

10. *1684, MSS*; He likes my fashion well, that wears my Cloaths *1672*. In *EDP* D. says that Jonson was a learned plagiary of the ancients: 'you will pardon me therefore if I presume he lov'd their fashion when he wore their cloaths' (*Works* xvii 21).

13–14. Cp. *EDP*: 'But he has done his Robberies so openly, that one may see he fears not to be taxed by any Law. He invades Authours like a Monarch, and what would be theft in other Poets, is onely victory in him' (*Works* xvii 57).

15–18. Kinsley suggests an allusion to Sir Robert Howard's *The Duke of Lerma*, first performed at the Theatre Royal the previous day (Pepys 20 February). In his 'Defence of *An Essay*' (*c.* September 1668) D. says of Howard's play: 'having so much alter'd and beautifi'd it, as he has done, it can justly belong to none but him. Indeed they must be extream ignorant as well as envious, who would rob him of that Honour; for you see him putting in his claim to it, even in the first two lines. *Repulse upon repulse like waves thrown back, / That slide to hang upon obdurate rocks.* After this let detraction do its worst; for if this be not his, it deserves to be' (*Works* ix 4). A. Harbage has conjectured that Howard's play was adapted from a lost work by Ford (*MLR* xxxv (1940) 297–304). See further Winn 189–90.

19. *padders*] footpads, robbers.

Nay, scarce the common ceremony use
Of 'Stand, sir, and deliver up your Muse',
But knock the poet down, and with a grace
Mount Pegasus before the owner's face.
25   Faith, if you have such country Toms abroad,
'Tis time for all true men to leave that road.
Yet it were modest, could it but be said
They strip the living, but these rob the dead,
Dare with the mummies of the Muses play,
30   And make love to them the Egyptian way:
Or, as a rhyming author would have said,
Join the dead living to the living dead.
Such men in poetry may claim some part,
They have the licence, though they want the art;
35   And might, where theft was praised, for laureates stand,
Poets not of the head but of the hand.
They make the benefits of others' studying,
Much like the meals of politic Jack Pudding,
Whose dish to challenge no man has the courage:
40   'Tis all his own when once h' has spit i' th' porridge.
But, gentlemen, you're all concerned in this;
You are in fault for what they do amiss,
For they their thefts still undiscovered think,
And durst not steal unless you please to wink.
45   Perhaps you may award by your decree

---

25. *Toms*] 'Tom' was a standard name for a countryman.
29–30. Thorn-Drury (in his edition of *Covent Garden Drolery* (1928)) cites
Herodotus's story that after an embalmer was caught having sexual intercourse with a woman who was newly dead, it became customary for the
bodies of noble or beautiful women to be handed over for embalming only
after three or four days (ii 89; cited by Montaigne 860 and Burton III ii 1.2).
33. Such men] *1684, MSS*; Yet such *1672*.
34. want] lack.
35. 1684, MSS; Such as in *Sparta* might for Laurels stand *1672* (after press
correction). Albumazar's opening speech in praise of theft recalls that 'The
Spartans held it lawful' (I i 8; *Works*).
38. Jack Pudding] a clown assisting a mountebank.
39. 1684, MSS; Where Broth to claim, there's no one has the courage *1672*.
40. when once h'] *1684, MSS*; after he *1672*.
43. still] *1684, MSS*; will *1672*.
45–6. 1684, MSS; om. *1672*.

They should refund, but that can never be.
For should you letters of reprisal seal,
These men write that which no man else would steal.

---

47. *For should you*] 1684, *MSS*; Now should we 1672.   *letters of reprisal*] an
official warrant authorizing an aggrieved subject to exact forcible reparation
from the subjects of another state (*OED*).

22 Prologue, Epilogue and Songs from *An Evening's Love*

Date and publication. The first recorded performance of the play was on 12 June 1668, by the King's Company at the Theatre Royal, Bridges Street. *An Evening's Love, or the Mock-Astrologer* was published by Herringman in 1671 (*SR* 20 November 1668; *TC* 13 February 1671); reprinted in either 1671 or 1675 (copies of this edition have different dates on their title pages: see *Works* x 514–15) and 1691. Society of Antiquaries MS 330 has a text of the Prologue which has variants which may derive from alterations made in the playhouse (see ll. 22n, 26n). Several MS copies of the songs survive (see Beal 424). Song II was also printed in *Merry Drollery Complete* (1670, 1691), *The New Academy of Complements* (1671) and *Windsor-Drollery* (1672); set by Alphonso Marsh it appeared in *Choice Songs and Ayres for One Voyce* (1673; facsimile in Day 25) and *Choice Ayres, Songs, & Dialogues* (1675, 1676). Song III appeared in the same miscellanies (being printed twice in *Merry Drollery*), and also in *The Canting Academy* (1673) and *The Compleat Courtier* (1683); the setting by Marsh appeared in *Choice Songs* (facsimile in Day 27) and *Choice Ayres*, and also in *Wit and Mirth* (1699). Song IV was printed in *Westminster-Drollery* (1671, 1672), *The New Academy of Complements* (1671) and *Windsor-Drollery* (1672).

Reception. The play was initially quite successful, running for at least nine consecutive performances, but Herringman told Pepys that D. 'doth himself call it but a fifth-rate play' (22 June 1668). Evelyn found it 'very prophane, so as it afflicted me to see how the stage was degenerated & poluted by the licentious times' (19 June); Pepys also thought it 'very smutty' (20 June). The popularity of the songs is evident from their appearances in miscellanies, and also from several reworkings and parodies. Song III acquired two additional, more erotic, stanzas (in *The New Academy of Complements* and *The Canting Academy*), and several imitations were produced: 'Green was the garden and pleasant the walk' (*The New Academy of Complements* 289–90), 'Fair was my Mistress, and fine as a bride' (*Covent Garden Drolery* (1672) 38–9), 'Sharp was the Air, and cold was the Ground' (*Mock Songs and Joking Poems* (1675) 129–30), 'Serene was the Air, and unpearled the Fields' (*Holborn-Drollery* (1673) 50–3), and 'Bright was the morning, clear the aire' (BL MS Add 30303 f. 5ʳ). Song IV was burlesqued twice, as 'Pretty Peggy grant to me', and '*Moll*, I nere yet knew my mind' in *Mock Songs* 107–8 and 133.

Prologue

When first our poet set himself to write,
Like a young bridegroom on his wedding night
He laid about him, and did so bestir him
His Muse could never lie in quiet for him:
5   But now his honeymoon is gone and past,
Yet the ungrateful drudgery must last;
And he is bound, as civil husbands do,
To strain himself in complaisance to you,
To write in pain, and counterfeit a bliss,
10 Like the faint smackings of an after-kiss.
But you, like wives ill-pleased, supply his want;
Each writing monsieur is a fresh gallant:
And though, perhaps, 'twas done as well before,
Yet still there's something in a new amour.

¶22. *Prologue*. This suggests a rather cynical or disillusioned reaction by D. to his recent public success, and his newly-established position. Three new plays had been successfully produced in 1667, he was appointed Poet Laureate on 13 April 1668, and signed a contract with the King's Company (see l. 33*n*). See further Winn 191–4. D.'s emphasis on his being no longer a beginner as a playwright may be intended as a contrast with the recent *débuts* of Thomas Shadwell with *The Sullen Lovers* (first performed 2 May 1668) and Sir Charles Sedley with *The Mulberry Garden* (18 May); both wrote prologues which advertised that these were their first plays. These may be the subject of ll. 11–22. For the extended simile in this Prologue cp. 'Prologue to *The Wild Gallant* revived', 'Epilogue to *1 Conquest of Granada*', the anonymous Prologue to *The Mistaken Husband* (1675) (Danchin no. 172), and Shadwell's Prologue to *Psyche* (1675).

6. drudgery] The *OED* does not record a specifically sexual connotation, but there clearly was in Restoration usage: cp. 'For when his Blood no Youthful Spirits move, / He languishes and labours in his love. / . . . Dribling he drudges, and defrauds the Womb' ('The Third Book of the *Georgics*' ll. 155–8); cp. 'Epilogue to *All for Love*' l. 26; 'The Sixth Satire of Juvenal' ll. 46, 496; Rochester, 'Song: "Love a woman! you're an ass"' l. 7; and Shakespeare, *Sonnet* cli 11–12.

8. complaisance] Making oneself agreeable, obliging; accented on the first and third syllables. It was a common word in the Restoration for accommodation to the manners of society, as in the translation of Eustache du Refuge's courtesy book, *The Art of Complaisance* (1673).

14. amour] After a period when the word (naturalized from French) simply meant 'love', in the later seventeenth century it came to signify an illicit affair

15 Your several poets work with several tools,
    One gets you wits, another gets you fools:
    This pleases you with some by-stroke of wit,
    This finds some cranny that was never hit.
    But should these jaunty lovers daily come
20 To do your work, like your good man at home,
    Their fine small-timbered wits would soon decay;
    These are gallants but for a holiday.
    Others you had who oftener have appeared,
    Whom for mere impotence you have cashiered:
25 Such as at first came on with pomp and glory,
    But, overstraining, soon fell flat before ye.
    Their useless weight with patience long was born,
    But at the last you threw 'em off with scorn.
    As for the poet of this present night,   ⎫
30 Though now he claims in you an husband's right, ⎬
    He will not hinder you of fresh delight.   ⎭
    He, like a seaman, seldom will appear,
    And means to trouble home but thrice a year:

---

or intrigue; as the word was then understood as a euphemistic use of the modern French word, the accent shifted on to the second syllable, as in French (*OED*).

15. tools] The slang use of 'tool' for 'penis' dates from the sixteenth century.

16. gets] begets.

19. jaunty] well-bred, gentlemanly (*OED* 1). The spelling 'janty' in *1671* indicates a pronunciation close to that of its French original, 'gentil'.

21. small-timbered] of small bodily frame (*OED* timber 7), but no doubt with a sexual innuendo too.

22. After this line Society of Antiquaries MS adds: 'Who for once doing will expect your Praise / And court you only for a sprig of Bayes'.   *gallants*] Accented on the second syllable.

23–8. Winn 194 suggests that these lines allude to Sir Robert Howard.

26. After this line MS adds: 'Whose boystrous Nonsense ruling in the Pitt / So overaw'd you that it pass't for Witt'. These are probably playhouse variants.

33. thrice a year] It was probably early in 1668 that D. made an agreement with the King's Company to write three plays a year. After he left it in 1677 the actors complained: 'Whereas, upon Mr. Drydens binding himselfe to write 3 Playes a yeare, Hee the said Mr. Dryden was admitted & continued as a Sharer in the King's Playhouse for divers years; and received for his Share & a quarter, 3 or 4 hundred pounds, Comunibus annis; but though he received the monyes, we received not the Playes, not one in a yeare' (Osborn 204).

That only time from your gallants he'll borrow;
35 Be kind today, and cuckold him tomorrow.

Epilogue

My part being small, I have had time today
To mark your various censures of our play.
First, looking for a judgement or a wit,
Like Jews I saw 'em scattered through the pit;
5   And where a knot of smilers lent an ear
To one that talked, I knew the foe was there.
The club of jests went round; he who had none
Borrowed o' th' next, and told it for his own.
Among the rest they kept a fearful stir,
10 In whispering that he stole th' *Astrologer*;
And said, betwixt a French and English plot
He eased his half-tired Muse on pace and trot.
Up starts a monsieur new come o'er, and warm

Epilogue.

1. The speaker of the Epilogue is unknown.

3. judgement] competent critic (*OED* 8c).

4. A reference to the *diaspora* or dispersion of the Jews, initially after the Babylonian captivity.   *pit*] See 'Prologue to *The Rival Ladies*' l. 24n.

7. club] combination of contributions (*OED* 10): i.e. individuals contributed to a common stock of jests, which those who had no wit of their own could draw upon. Cp. 'Epilogue to *Sir Martin Mar-all*' ll. 9–12.

10. stole th' Astrologer] In his Preface D. says: 'I am tax'd with stealing all my Playes. . . . There is one answer which I will not make; but it has been made for me by him to whose Grace and Patronage I owe all things [i.e. Charles II] . . . that he only desir'd that they who accus'd me of theft would always steal him Playes like mine. . . . 'Tis true, that where ever I have lik'd any story in a Romance, Novel, or forreign Play, I have made no difficulty, nor ever shall, to take the foundation of it, to build it up, and to make it proper for the *English* Stage. And I will be so vain to say it has lost nothing in my hands . . . this Play . . . was first *Spanish*, and call'd *El Astrologo fingido* [by Calderon]; then made *French* by the younger *Corneille* [as *Le Feint Astrologue*]: and is now translated into *English*, and in print, under the name of the *Feign'd Astrologer*' [anon, printed 1668] (*Works* x 210–11). For the issue of plagiarism cp. 'Prologue to *Albumazar*', and headnote to *MF*.

12. For the equestrian image cp. 'Prologue to *Tyrannic Love*' l. 19n, and *EDP* (*Works* xvii 54).   *pace*] amble.

In the French stoop, and the pull-back o' th' arm;
15 'Morbleu', dit-il, and cocks, 'I am a rogue
    But he has quite spoiled the Feint Astrologue.'
    'Pox', says another, 'here's so great a stir
    With a son-of-a-whore farce that's regular,
    A rule where nothing must decorum shock!
20 Damme 'ts as dull as dining by the clock.
    An evening! why the devil should we be vexed
    Whether he gets the wench this night or next?'
    When I heard this, I to the poet went,
    Told him the house was full of discontent,
25 And asked him what excuse he could invent.
    He neither swore nor stormed as poets do,
    But, most unlike an author, vowed 'twas true.
    Yet said, he used the French like enemies,
    And did not steal their plots, but made 'em prize.
30 But should he all the pains and charges count
    Of taking 'em, the bill so high would mount,
    That, like prize-goods which through the office come,
    He could have had 'em much more cheap at home.
    He still must write, and banker-like each day

---

14. *stoop*] bow. French affectations were frequently satirized at this period, e.g. in Wycherley's *The Gentleman Dancing-Master* (1672) and James Howard's *The English Monsieur* (1666). The anonymous *Satyr against the French* (1691) 5 says: 'Their Tongues not only wag, but Hands and Feet. / Each part about them seems to move and walk; / Their Eyes, their Noses; nay, their Fingers talk' (*Works*).

15. Morbleu] a French oath ('mortdieu').   *cocks*] Either (i) struts, swaggers (*OED* 2), cp. 'Epilogue to *The Man of Mode*' l. 9; or (ii) turns up the brim of his hat (*OED* 5). This was a fashionable habit, apparently borrowed from France: 'if they like neither the Play nor the Women, they seldom stay any longer than the combing of their Perriwigs, or a whisper or two with a Friend; and then they cock their Caps, and out they strut again' (Etherege, *She wou'd if she cou'd* (first performed 6 February 1668) I ii 158–61, and cp. III iii 144–5; see also Pepys 3 June 1667).

18–22. Referring to the play's observance of the unity of time, for the action takes place in one evening. Cp. 'Prologue to *Secret Love*' ll. 1–6.

28. *like enemies*] The Triple Alliance of England, Holland and Sweden had been formed against France in January 1668.

32. *the office*] Captured ships and their goods were sold by auction at the Navy Office; Pepys thought that they were often sold far too cheaply (see 6 November 1660; 15 January 1667).

35   Accept new bills, and he must break, or pay.
      When through his hands such sums must yearly run,
      You cannot think the stock is all his own.
      His haste his other errors might excuse,
      But there's no mercy for a guilty Muse:
40   For like a mistress, she must stand or fall,
      And please you to a height, or not at all.

Songs

I

    You charmed me not with that fair face,
      Though it was all divine;
    To be another's is the grace
      That makes me wish you mine.
5   The gods and Fortune take their part,
      Who like young monarchs fight;
    And boldly dare invade that heart
      Which is another's right.
    First mad with hope we undertake
10   To pull up every bar;
    But once possessed, we faintly make
      A dull defensive war.
    Now every friend is turned a foe
      In hope to get our store;
15   And passion makes us cowards grow,
      Which made us brave before.

II

I

    After the pangs of a desperate lover,
    When day and night I have sighed all in vain,

---

35. *break*] become bankrupt.

Song I. From Act II Scene i; sung by Wildblood (Charles Hart) to Jacinta (Nell Gwyn), to 'encourage one another to a breach by the dangers of possession', as he says. Jacinta hopes 'it will go to the tune of one of our *Passa-calles*'. The *passacaglia* was a dance tune of Spanish origin in slow triple time, usually with divisions on a ground bass (*OED*; Day).
Song II. From Act II Scene i; sung by Wildblood, serenading Jacinta and

Ah what a pleasure it is to discover
In her eyes pity, who causes my pain!

2

5   When with unkindness our love at a stand is,
And both have punished ourselves with the pain,
Ah what a pleasure the touch of her hand is,
Ah what a pleasure to press it again!

3

When the denial comes fainter and fainter,
10 And her eyes give what her tongue does deny,
Ah what a trembling I feel when I venture,
Ah what a trembling does usher my joy!

4

When with a sigh she accords me the blessing,
And her eyes twinkle 'twixt pleasure and pain,
15 Ah what a joy 'tis beyond all expressing,
Ah what a joy to hear, 'shall we again?'!

III

1

Calm was the even, and clear was the sky,
    And the new budding flowers did spring,
When all alone went Amyntas and I
    To hear the sweet nightingale sing;
5   I sate, and he laid him down by me,
    But scarcely his breath he could draw;

Theodosia. He calls it 'a song al' Angloise'. This is part of a scene involving
rival serenades, a theatrical device which subsequent dramatists copied (Price,
Music in the Restoration Theatre 25–6, 255). In D.'s *Marriage A-la-Mode* (1673)
Doralice says: 'A friend of mine, who makes Songs sometimes, came lately
out of the West, and vow'd he was so put out of count'nance with a Song of
his; for at the first Countrey-Gentleman's he visited, he saw three Tailors
cross-leg'd upon the Table in the Hall, who were tearing out as loud as ever
they could sing,—*After the pangs of a desperate lover, &c.* and all that day he
heard nothing else, but the Daughters of the house and the Maids, humming
it over in every corner, and the Father whistling it' (III i 136–44).
Song III. From Act IV Scene i; sung by Beatrix (Mrs Knep) to attract
Wildblood to Jacinta.
5. *sate*] sat.

For when with a fear he began to draw near,
    He was dashed with A ha ha ha ha!

2

He blushed to himself, and lay still for a while,
10   And his modesty curbed his desire;
But straight I convinced all his fear with a smile,
    Which added new flames to his fire.
    'O Sylvia', said he, 'you are cruel,
      To keep your poor lover in awe';
15 Then once more he pressed with his hand to my breast,
    But was dashed with A ha ha ha ha.

3

I knew 'twas his passion that caused all his fear,
    And therefore I pitied his case;
I whispered him softly, 'There's nobody near',
20   And laid my cheek close to his face:
But as he grew bolder and bolder,
    A shepherd came by us and saw;
And just as our bliss we began with a kiss,
    He laughed out with 'A ha ha ha ha'.

IV

Damon.   Celimena, of my heart
      None shall e'er bereave you:
      If, with your good leave, I may
      Quarrel with you once a day,
5   I will never leave you.

2

Celimena. Passion's but an empty name
      Where respect is wanting:
      Damon you mistake your aim;
      Hang your heart, and burn your flame,
10   If you must be ranting.

Song IV. From Act V Scene i; sung by Wildblood and Jacinta: 'an old Song of
a Lover that was ever quarrelling with his Mistress'; it is sung 'for a frolick
. , . let the company be judge who sings worst.—Upon condition the best
singer shall wear the breeches.'
10. ranting] scolding (*OED* 1b; a Restoration usage).

3

Dam.   Love as dull and muddy is,
    As decaying liquor:
    Anger sets it on the lees,
    And refines it by degrees,
15   Till it works it quicker.

4

Cel.   Love by quarrels to beget
    Wisely you endeavour;
    With a grave physician's wit
    Who to cure an ague fit
20   Put me in a fever.

5

Dam.   Anger rouses love to fight,
    And his only bait is,
    'Tis the spur to dull delight,
    And is but an eager bite,
25   When desire at height is.

6

Cel.   If such drops of heat can fall
    In our wooing weather;
    If such drops of heat can fall,
    We shall have the devil and all
30   When we come together.

13–15. A metaphor from the distillation of poor wine into spirits.
29. devil] monosyllabic here.

23 Prologue, Epilogue and Songs from *Tyrannic Love*

Date and publication. The play was first performed in late June 1669 by the King's Company at the Theatre Royal, Bridges Street. Charles II probably attended a performance on 24 June (*LS* 162–3). The play occasioned a lawsuit between the company and Isaac Fuller, who had been employed to paint the scenery. The actors alleged that Fuller's work was late and shoddy, and lost them court patronage; Fuller replied that the play had actually been a great success, being acted 'about 14 days together'. The company had wanted the play for the Easter Term (18 April to 24 May). See further *Works* x 380–1. *Tyrannick Love; or the Royal Martyr* was published by Herringman in 1670 (*SR* 14 July 1669; *TC* 22 November 1670), with a dedication to the Duke of Monmouth; reprinted 1672, 1677, 1686, 1695. The words of Song III were printed in *Windsor-Drollery* (1672). An anonymous setting of Song I (dated 8 June 1681) is found in BL MS Add 19759 (facsimile in Day 19–20). Purcell's music for a revival, probably in 1694, included settings of Songs I and III, printed in *Deliciae Musicae* (1695) and *Orpheus Britannicus* (1698). Curtis Price (*Henry Purcell* 47) suggests that D. may have participated in the revision of the text for Purcell's setting.

Context. The play recounts the martyrdom of St Catharine, and was probably intended (and perhaps commissioned) as a compliment to Queen Catherine.

Sources. The Prologue shows the influence of Longinus, Περὶ Ὕψους (*On the Sublime*) in saying that (i) great geniuses are liable to stumble into faults; (ii) critics should not pay too much attention to faults; (iii) too much care can spoil a work, and make it perfect but mean: 'It will be worth our pains *first* to enquire in the Generall, whether in Poems and Orations an *irregular* and luxuriant *greatnesse* be sometimes better then a *staid proportionate* and *steddy* regulation: And withall whether *many* vertues or the *greater* ought justly to obtain the *primacy* in speech. . . . Now I observe that *excesses* of greatnesse are naturally the *least pure*, but what is *nicely exact* is in danger of *littlenesse*. Thus in *sublimities* as in *vast* estates, there must be somewhat to *contemn* and throw away. And must not this also be necessarily found, that men whose *under-standings* are of a *little making*, never adventuring themselves in *attempts* of *height*, seldome or never *fall*, but walk on sure *ground*? yet for all this it is not to be *conceal'd*, that naturally all humane things are ever rather *adjudg'd* by the *worse*, and the memory of the bad stands *fixt* and *permanent*, but that of the *good* glides away and *vanishes*. Now should I instance some no smal *faults* both of *Homer* and other *Grandees*, though for my part as I am as little pleas'd with their failings (as any man) so would I rather call them *voluntary* (errours) then offences, or (properly) failings of *carelesnesse*, heedlessly overseen by *chance* in severall places by a *noble pride* of nature' (tr. J[ohn] H[all] (1652) 60–1). Longinus may also have influenced D.'s estimate of Shakespeare (see

'Prologue to *The Tempest*'), and this Prologue shows that he was already receptive to Longinus's ideas before the publication of Boileau's translation (*Traité du Sublime*) and Rapin's *Réflexions sur la Poétique d'Aristote*, both in 1674. There is also an element of special pleading on D.'s behalf against the critics and in favour of heroic plays. For a discussion of D.'s changing views on the role of fancy and judgement in poetic creation see J. M. Aden, *PMLA* lxxiv (1959) 28–40; and R. D. Hume, *RES* xxi (1970) 295–314.

Reception. There is a parody of Song I in *The Rehearsal* (1672) V i 42–89.

Prologue

    Self-love (which never rightly understood)
    Makes poets still conclude their plays are good;
    And malice in all critics reigns so high,
    That for small errors they whole plays decry;
5   So that to see this fondness, and that spite,
    You'd think that none but madmen judge or write.
    Therefore our poet, as he thinks not fit
    T' impose upon you what he writes for wit,
    So hopes that leaving you your censures free, ⎫
10 You equal judges of the whole will be: ⎬
    They judge but half who only faults will see. ⎭
    Poets like lovers should be bold and dare,
    They spoil their business with an over-care;
    And he who servilely creeps after sense

¶**23**. *Prologue.*
1. For the right understanding of self-love, D. may have been thinking of Aristotle, *Ethics* ix 8. In the Preface to *Secret Love*, D. argues that poets may be competent judges of the design of their works, but that their judgement of their ornament may be biased by self-love (*Works* ix 115–16).
9. censures] opinions.
10. equal] impartial.
12–13. Partly an excuse for the play's hasty composition: in the Preface D. admits that it was written in seven weeks (*Works* x 111).
14–15. In a passage added to the Preface in the second edition (1672) D. says: 'For the little Critiques who pleas'd themselves with thinking they have found a flaw in that line of the Prologue . . . [ll. 14–15] as if I patroniz'd my own nonsense, I may reasonably suppose they have never read *Horace*. *Serpit humi tutus*, &c. are his words: He who creeps after plaine, dull, common sence, is safe from committing absurdities; but, can never reach any heigth, or excellence of wit' (*Works* x 112–13). D. is quoting Horace, *Ars Poetica* l.

15   Is safe, but ne'er will reach an excellence.
Hence 'tis our poet in his conjuring
Allowed his fancy the full scope and swing,
But when a tyrant for his theme he had,
He loosed the reins and bid his Muse run mad:
20   And though he stumbles in a full career,
Yet rashness is a better fault than fear.
He saw his way, but in so swift a pace
To choose the ground might be to lose the race.
They then who of each trip th' advantage take,
25   Find but those faults which they want wit to make.

Epilogue

Spoken by Mrs Ellen, when she was to be carried off dead by the bearers.

To the bearer:
    Hold, are you mad? you damned confounded dog,
    I am to rise, and speak the Epilogue.

---

28. D.'s l. 14 was echoed in *The Rehearsal*: 'he is too proud a man to creep servily after Sense' (IV ii 84–5; added in the 1675 edition).

16. conjuring] The episode in IV i where Nigrinus the conjurer summons up the spirits Nakar and Damilcar.

18–19. Later, in the Epistle Dedicatory to *The Spanish Friar* (1681) sig. A2ᵛ D. said: 'I remember some Verses of my own *Maximin* and *Almanzor* which cry, Vengeance upon me for their Extravagance, and which I wish heartily in the . . . fire.'

18. tyrant] Maximin, the 'Tyrant of Rome' who persecutes St Catharine.

19. For the image of the Muse as an impetuous horse cp. 'Epilogue to *An Evening's Love*' l. 12, and Cowley, 'The Resurrection' st. iv (*Poems* 183).

21. Cp. 'To the Memory of Mr Oldham' ll. 17–18.

22–3. Cp. 'To Mr L. Maidwell' ll. 39–40 and 'To the Memory of Mr Oldham' ll. 7–10.

24–5. 'The great Censors of Wit and Poetry, either produce nothing of their own, or what is more ridiculous than any thing they reprehend. Much of ill Nature, and a very little Judgment, go far in finding the mistakes of Writers' (D.'s Preface; *Works* x 111).

Epilogue.
Title. Ellen ('Nell') Gwyn (1642/50–87) was an orange girl in the Theatre Royal in 1663, and *c.* 1664 joined the King's Company; she was also the mistress of its leading actor, Charles Hart. After an interval as mistress of

To the audience:

  I come, kind gentlemen, strange news to tell ye,
  I am the ghost of poor departed Nelly.
5 Sweet ladies, be not frighted, I'll be civil,
  I'm what I was, a little harmless devil.
  For after death we sprites have just such natures
  We had for all the world when human creatures;
  And therefore I that was an actress here,
10 Play all my tricks in hell, a goblin there.
  Gallants, look to't, you say there are no sprites,
  But I'll come dance about your beds at nights.
  And faith, you'll be in a sweet kind of taking
  When I surprise you between sleep and waking.
15 To tell you true, I walk because I die
  Out of my calling in a tragedy.
  O poet, damned dull poet, who could prove
  So senseless to make Nelly die for love!
  Nay, what's yet worse, to kill me in the prime
20 Of Easter term, in tart and cheese-cake time!
  I'll fit the fop, for I'll not one word say

Charles Sackville (later Earl of Dorset) she became the King's mistress *c.* 1668, and bore him sons in 1670 and 1671. See J. H. Wilson, *Nell Gwyn* (1952) and Highfill vi 455–72. In *Tyrannic Love* she played Valeria, daughter of Maximin, who stabs herself in the final scene. This Epilogue became well known: cp. the anonymous Epilogue to *Piso's Conspiracy* (performed 1675): 'It is a Trick of late grown much in Vogue, / When all are Kill'd, to raise an *Epilogue*. / This, some Pert Rymer wittily contriv'd / For a Surprize, whil'st the Arch Wag believed; / 'Twould please You to see Pretty *Miss* reviv'd' (ll. 1–5; Danchin no. 201).

7. *sprites*] spirits.

13. *taking*] passion, excited state.

16. Nell Gwyn was best suited to comedy. Pepys thought her poor in the serious role of Cydaria in *The Indian Emperor* (22 August, 11 November, 26 December 1667) and praised her as Florimel in *Secret Love* (see headnote to its Prologue). In the Epilogue to Sir Robert Howard's *The Duke of Lerma* (first performed 20 February 1668) she spoke these lines: 'I know you in your hearts / Hate serious Plays, as I do serious Parts' (ll. 5–6; Danchin no. 80).

20. If the play was acted on 24 June, Easter Term had ended a month before on 24 May. In fact, Trinity Term was to end in six days on 30 June (*Works*). For the food, cp. Millisent in *Sir Martin Mar-all* (1668): 'I came up, Madam, as we Country-Gentlewomen use, at an *Easter*-Term, to the destruction of Tarts and Cheese-cakes, to see a New Play' (I i 128–30; Kinsley).

21. *fit*] punish suitably.

T' excuse his godly out-of-fashion play:
A play which if you dare but twice sit out,
You'll all be slandered, and be thought devout.
25 But farewell, gentlemen, make haste to me,
I'm sure ere long to have your company.
As for my epitaph when I am gone,
I'll trust no poet, but will write my own:
Here Nelly lies, who though she lived a slattern,
30 *Yet died a princess, acting in St Cathar'n.*

Songs

I

Nakar and Damilcar descend in clouds, and sing:
    Nak. Hark, my Damilcar, we are called below!
    Dam. Let us go, let us go!
         Go to relieve the care
         Of longing lovers in despair!
5 *Nak.* Merry, merry, merry, we sail from the east,
         Half tippled at a rainbow feast.
    Dam. In the bright moonshine while winds whistle
         loud,
         Tivy, tivy, tivy, we mount and we fly,
         All racking along in a downy white cloud:
10   And lest our leap from the sky should prove too
         far,
         We slide on the back of a new-falling star.

Songs. All three songs are from Act IV Scene i. Nakar and Damilcar are aerial spirits invoked by the conjurer Nigrinus for Placidius, who wishes to know whether the Emperor will obtain the love of St Catharine. Their names come from the appendix to Reginald Scot's *The Discovery of Witchcraft* (1665). For further details of D.'s demonology here see Maximilian E. Novak, *ELN* iv (1966) 95–8; *Works* x 421–5; Jack M. Armistead, *PLL* xxiv (1988) 367–83. For a discussion of the words and music of the songs see Price, *Henry Purcell* 44–53 and Winn, *When Beauty* 197–202.
Song I.
6. *tippled*] intoxicated (*OED*'s last example).
8. *tivy*] tantivy, at full gallop.
9. *racking*] driving before the wind.

Nak. And drop from above
   In a jelly of love!
Dam. But now the sun's down, and the element's red,
15   The spirits of fire against us make head!
Nak. They muster, they muster, like gnats in the air:
   Alas! I must leave thee, my fair,
   And to my light horsemen repair.
Dam. O stay, for you need not to fear 'em tonight;
20   The wind is for us, and blows full in their sight,
   And o'er the wide ocean we fight!
   Like leaves in the autumn our foes will fall down,
   And hiss in the water ——
Both. And hiss in the water and drown!
25 *Nak.* But their men lie securely entrenched in a cloud,
   And a trumpeter-hornet to battle sounds loud.
Dam. Now mortals that spy
   How we tilt in the sky
   With wonder will gaze,
30   And fear such events as will ne'er come to pass!
Nak. Stay you to perform what the man will have
     done.
Dam. Then call me again when the battle is won.
Both. So ready and quick is a spirit of air
   To pity the lover, and succour the fair,
35   That, silent and swift, the little soft god
   Is here with a wish, and is gone with a nod.

The clouds part, Nakar flies up, and Damilcar down.

II

Damilcar stamps, and the bed arises with St Catharine in it.
Dam. singing:
   You pleasing dreams of love and sweet delight,

13. *jelly*] The alga Nostoc, which appears as a jelly-like mass on dry soil after
rain, was sometimes supposed to be the remains of a fallen star (*OED*).
14. *element*] sky (*OED* 10).
15. *spirits of fire*] salamanders, often seen as agents of the devil.
22. A standard image: cp. Virgil, *Aen.* vi 309–10: *quam multa in siluis autumni
frigore primo / lapsa cadunt folia* ('as many as the leaves in the woods which at
the first frost of Autumn fall away and drop'); Homer, *Iliad* vi 146–9; Isaiah
xxxiv 4.
Song II. Winn compares the final song in James Shirley's *Cupid and Death*
(performed 1653 and 1659) (*When Beauty* 168).

Appear before this slumbering virgin's sight:
Soft visions set her free
From mournful piety:
5   Let her sad thoughts from heaven retire,
And let the melancholy love
Of those remoter joys above
Give place to your more sprightly fire.
Let purling streams be in her fancy seen,
10   And flowery meads, and vales of cheerful green:
And in the midst of deathless groves
Soft sighing wishes lie,
And smiling hopes fast by,
And just beyond 'em ever-laughing loves.

III

Dam. Ah how sweet it is to love,
Ah how gay is young desire!
And what pleasing pains we prove
When we first approach love's fire!
5   Pains of love be sweeter far
Than all other pleasures are.

Sighs which are from lovers blown
Do but gently heave the heart:
Ev'n the tears they shed alone
10   Cure like trickling balm their smart.
     Lovers when they lose their breath,
     Bleed away in easy death.

Love and time with reverence use,
Treat 'em like a parting friend:
15   Nor the golden gifts refuse
Which in youth sincere they send:
     For each year their price is more,
     And they less simple than before.

Love, like spring tides full and high,
20   Swells in every youthful vein:

Song III.
3. *prove*] experience.
16. *sincere*] pure, unmixed.

But each tide does less supply,
Till they quite shrink in again:
  If a flow in age appear,
  'Tis but rain, and runs not clear.

24 Prologues, Epilogues and Songs from *The Conquest of Granada*

Date and publication. Part I was first performed in December 1670, Part II early in January 1671 (*LS* 177–8), both by the King's Company at the Theatre Royal, Bridges Street. *The Conquest of Granada by the Spaniards: In Two Parts* was published by Herringman in 1672 (*SR* 25 February 1671; *TC* 7 February 1672; Thomas Blount wrote to Anthony à Wood on 6 February 1672 that it 'came out yesterday' (*Correspondence of Thomas Blount*, edited by Theo Bongaerts (1978) 125)). It has a dedication to the Duke of York, a prefatory essay 'Of Heroic Plays', commendatory verses by John, Lord Vaughan (1640–1713) and a 'Defence of the Epilogue' (see notes to 'Epilogue to the Second Part' below). It was reprinted in 1673 (with some revisions), 1678, 1687, 1695. Song I from Part I was printed in *Westminster-Drollery* (twice in the 1671 edition, once in the 1672 reprint) and *Windsor-Drollery* (1672), and set by John Banister in *Choice Songs and Ayres for One Voyce* (1673; facsimile in Day 31), *Choice Ayres, Songs, & Dialogues* (1675, 1676) and *Wit and Mirth* (1699). Song II from Part I was printed in *The New Academy of Complements* (1671), *Westminster-Drollery* (1671, 1672), *Windsor-Drollery* and *The Wits Academy* (1677). It was set by Alphonso Marsh in *Choice Songs and Ayres* (facsimile in Day 33), *Choice Ayres* and *Wit and Mirth*; for the setting by Pelham Humphrey, not printed in the period, see Day 151, who also lists two other anonymous settings. The Song from Part II was printed in *The New Academy of Complements*, *Westminster-Drollery* and *Windsor-Drollery*. The setting by Nicholas Staggins was printed in *Choice Songs and Ayres* (facsimile in Day 37), *Choice Ayres* and *Wit and Mirth*. For Purcell's music for a revival in the early 1690s see Curtis Price, *Henry Purcell* 54–5. Transcripts by Sir William Haward of the 'Epilogue to the First Part' and 'Prologue to the Second Part' in BodL MS Don.b.8 pp. 248–9 preserve readings which may derive from the playhouse (first noted by G. Thorn-Drury, *RES* i (1925) 325): for details see the notes. The present text follows the first edition of the play.

Reception. The play was extensively criticized in *The Censure of the Rota* (1673), which included objections to D.'s use of the hat and waistbelt in the 'Prologue to the First Part' and his criticism of Jonson in the 'Epilogue to the Second Part' (*Censure* 12–13). The *Censure* was followed by another attack, *The Friendly Vindication of M.ʳ Dryden* (1673), and two defences of D.: Charles Blount's *Mr. Dreyden Vindicated* (1673) and the anonymous *A Description of the Academy of the Athenian Virtuosi* (1673). See also note to 'Epilogue to the Second Part' below. The popularity of the songs is evident from the number of printed texts (there were also several MS copies: see Beal 423–4), and from various allusions and imitations. Song II from Part I was quoted in Joseph Kepple's novel *The Maiden-head Lost by Moon-Light* (1672). The Song from Part II was adapted in Edward Ravenscroft's *The Citizen Turn'd Gentleman* (1672) 40; a song with the same first line and stanza form appears in *Holborn-*

Drollery (1673) 48–5; and the Song also provides the opening and the tune for a satire on Sir Roger L'Estrange, 'How unhappy a Mastiffe am I' in *Towzer Discover'd* (1683).

Prologue to the First Part

Spoken by Mrs Ellen Gwyn in a broad-brimmed hat, and waistbelt.

This jest was first of t' other house's making,
And, five times tried, has never failed of taking:
For 'twere a shame a poet should be killed
Under the shelter of so broad a shield.
5 This is that hat whose very sight did win ye
To laugh and clap as though the devil were in ye.
As then for Nokes, so now, I hope, you'll be
So dull to laugh once more, for love of me.
'I'll write a play', says one, 'for I have got
10 A broad-brimmed hat, and waistbelt towards a plot.'
Says t' other, 'I have one more large than that':
Thus they out-write each other with a hat.
The brims still grew with every play they writ,

¶24. *Prologue to the First Part.*
Title. This device seems to have originated when James Nokes, the premier comedian of the Duke's Company, appeared before the court at Dover in May 1670 in John Caryll's *Sir Salomon*: 'The *French* Court wearing then Excessive short Lac'd Coats; some Scarlet, some Blew, with Broad wast Belts; Mr. *Nokes* having at that time one shorter than the *French* Fashion, to Act Sir *Arthur Addle* in; the Duke of *Monmouth* gave Mr. *Nokes* his Sword and Belt from his Side, and Buckled it on himself, on purpose to Ape the *French*: That Mr. *Nokes* lookt more like a Drest up Ape, than a Sir *Arthur*: Which upon his first Entrance on the Stage, put the King and Court to an Excessive Laughter' (Downes 64). Aphra Behn refers to the hat when deriding those 'Who love the Comick Hat, the Jig and Dance, / Things that are fitted to their Ignorance' (Prologue to *The Amorous Prince* ll. 25–6; Danchin no. 117; performed by the rival Duke's Company in February 1671). Nokes himself, speaking the Epilogue to Edward Howard's *The Six Days Adventure* (performed by the Duke's Company in March 1671) refers to attempts to win favour through a 'Prologue borrow'd from a Hat and Belt' (l. 10; Danchin no. 119).   *Mrs Ellen Gwyn*] See 'Epilogue to *Tyrannic Love*' n.
6. *devil*] monosyllabic.

And grew so large they covered all the wit.
15 Hat was the play: 'twas language, wit and tale,
Like them that find meat, drink and cloth in ale.
What dullness do these mongrel wits confess
When all their hope is acting of a dress!
Thus two, the best comedians of the age,
20 Must be worn out with being blocks o' th' stage.
Like a young girl who better things has known,
Beneath their poet's impotence they groan.
See now what charity it was to save!
They thought you liked, what only you forgave,
25 And brought you more dull sense—dull sense, much
  worse
Than brisk, gay nonsense, and the heavier curse.
They bring old iron and glass upon the stage,
To barter with the Indians of our age.
Still they write on, and like great authors show: ⎫
30 But 'tis as rollers in wet gardens grow   ⎬
Heavy with dirt, and gathering as they go. ⎭
May none who have so little understood
To like such trash, presume to praise what's good!
And may those drudges of the stage, whose fate
35 Is damned dull farce more dully to translate,
Fall under that excise the state thinks fit
To set on all French wares, whose worst is wit.
French farce worn out at home is sent abroad,
And, patched up here, is made our English mode.
40 Henceforth let poets, ere allowed to write,
Be searched like duellists before they fight,
For wheel-broad hats, dull humour, all that chaff,
Which makes you mourn, and makes the vulgar laugh.
For these, in plays, are as unlawful arms
45 As, in a combat, coats of mail and charms.

---

16. Proverbial: 'Good ale is meat, drink and cloth' (Tilley A103).
17. confess] disclose.
19. two] probably Nokes and Gwyn.
20. blocks] wooden moulds on which hats are made (*OED* 4).
38–9. Some French companies performed in England: the playwright in
Davenant's *The Play-house to be Let* (1663) tells the manager of a French troop:
'Your Farces are a kind of Mungril Plays. / But, Sir, I believe all *French* Farces
are / Prohibited Commodities, and will / Not pass current in *England*' (*Works*

Epilogue to the First Part

Success, which can no more than beauty last,
Makes our sad poet mourn your favours past:
For since without desert he got a name,
He fears to lose it now with greater shame.
5   Fame, like a little mistress of the town,
Is gained with ease—but then she's lost as soon.
For, as those tawdry misses soon or late
Jilt such as keep 'em at the highest rate
(And oft the lackey, or the brawny clown,
10   Gets what is hid in the loose-bodied gown):
So, Fame is false to all that keep her long,
And turns up to the fop that's brisk and young.

---

of Sr William D'avenant (1673) ii 68). But the reference is also to adaptations of French farce for the English stage (see Hume 294–5): *Tartuffe* had been adapted from Molière by Matthew Medbourne for the King's Company *c.* May 1670, and Shadwell's *The Hypocrite*, an unpublished translation from Molière, was acted for six days in June 1669 by the Duke's Company. See also *MF* l. 182*n*.

Epilogue to the First Part. BodL MS Don.b.8 records that this was spoken by Charles Hart, and that ll. 23–4, 31–2 and 35–6 were 'not spoke'. Hart (*c.* 1630–83), who played Almanzor, was one of the leading actors of his day. He acted in women's roles before the Civil War, and took part in surreptitious performances at the Cockpit in 1648; after the Restoration he joined the King's Company, and in 1662 became one of its shareholders. In 1663 he joined Michael Mohun and John Lacey as co-managers of the company. His roles for D. included Cortez in *The Indian Emperor*, Celadon in *Secret Love*, Wildblood in *An Evening's Love*, Porphyrius in *Tyrannic Love*, Palamede in *Marriage A-la-Mode*, Aurelian in *The Assignation*, Captain Towerson in *Amboyna*, Aureng-Zebe, and Antony in *All for Love* (Highfill vii 147–53). He acted Alexander in Lee's *The Rival Queens* (1677) 'with such Grandeur and Agreeable Majesty, That one of the Court was pleas'd to Honour him with this Commendation; That *Hart* might Teach any King on Earth how to Comport himself: He was no less Inferior in Comedy' (Downes 41). For the extended image in this Epilogue see 'Prologue to *An Evening's Love*' *n*.
5–12. Cp. the account of Fortune in *Heroic Stanzas* ll. 29–30*n*.
9. *clown*] rustic.
10. *Gets*] begets.
12. *turns up*] prostitutes herself (*OED* turn 80z★★★). Though the *OED* is puzzled about the meaning, it notes earlier that *turn up* can mean to lie on one's back (80i).

Some wiser poet now would leave Fame first,
But elder wits are like old lovers curst,
15 Who when the vigour of their youth is spent
Still grow more fond as they grow impotent.
This, some years hence, our poet's case may prove,
But yet, he hopes, he's young enough to love.
When forty comes, if e'er he live to see
20 That wretched, fumbling age of poetry,
'Twill be high time to bid his Muse adieu:
Well he may please himself, but never you.
Till then he'll do as well as he began,
And hopes you will not find him less a man.
25 Think him not duller for this year's delay;   ⎫
He was prepared, the women were away,   ⎬
And men, without their parts, can hardly play.   ⎭
If they, through sickness, seldom did appear,   ⎫
Pity the virgins of each theatre,   ⎬
30 For at both houses 'twas a sickly year!   ⎭
And pity us, your servants, to whose cost
In one such sickness nine whole months are lost.
Their stay, he fears, has ruined what he writ:
Long waiting both disables love and wit.
35 They thought they gave him leisure to do well:
But when they forced him to attend, he fell!
Yet though he much has failed, he begs today
You will excuse his unperforming play:
Weakness sometimes great passion does express;
40 He had pleased better, had he loved you less.

14. curst] perversely disagreeable, cantankerous (*OED* 4).
16. fond] (i) loving; (ii) foolish.
19. forty] D. was to be 40 on 9 August 1671.
20. fumbling] sexually impotent.
25. D.'s previous play *Tyrannic Love* was performed in June 1669.
26–32. Edward Howard noted that his play *The Women's Conquest* (1671), performed by the Duke's Company in 1670, was prejudiced by 'an intermission hitherto occasioned by the long absence of some principal Actresses' (sig. cᵛ). Nell Gwyn's absence was occasioned by the birth of her son by Charles II on 8 May 1670. The child was the future Duke of Somerset.
32. are] were *MS* (perhaps the original, more specific, reading).
33. stay] delay, postponement (*OED* 4).

Songs from the First Part

I

1

Beneath a myrtle shade
Which Love for none but happy lovers made,
I slept, and straight my love before me brought
Phyllis, the object of my waking thought;
5   Undressed she came my flames to meet,
     While Love strowed flowers beneath her feet;
Flowers, which so pressed by her, became more sweet.

2

From the bright vision's head
A careless veil of lawn was loosely spread;
10   From her white temples fell her shaded hair,
Like cloudy sunshine not too brown nor fair:
     Her hands, her lips did love inspire,
     Her every grace my heart did fire;
But most her eyes which languished with desire.

3

15   'Ah, charming fair', said I,
'How long can you my bliss and yours deny?
By Nature and by Love this lonely shade
Was for revenge of suffering lovers made:
     Silence and shades with love agree,
20   Both shelter you and favour me;
You cannot blush because I cannot see.'

Song I. From Act III; an entertainment for Queen Almahide. Elkanah Settle commented: 'After such a *plentiful treat* of *rank Bawdry*, of *Almahides preparing*, I need not describe *her Character*. But perhaps Mr. *Dryden* will answer that a woman of her *Quality* might keep a *Laureat*, and the *Bawdy entertainment* was her *Poets* fault; or else he may tell us, that he wrote this to *please the Age*, who are best delighted with *languishing Songs* in this *Style*: And therefore the making a *Woman of Honour*, or a *Jilt in a Comedy*, talk Bawdy, or *take pleasure in hearing it, is all alike to him*' (*Notes and Observations on the Empress of Morocco Revised* (1674) 4).

4

'No, let me die', she said,
'Rather than lose the spotless name of maid':
Faintly methought she spoke, for all the while
25   She bid me not believe her, with a smile.
        'Then die', said I; she still denied,
        And, 'Is it thus, thus, thus' she cried
    'You use a harmless maid?', and so she died!

5

    I waked, and straight I knew
30   I loved so well it made my dream prove true:
Fancy, the kinder mistress of the two,
Fancy had done what Phyllis would not do!
    Ah, cruel nymph, cease your disdain,
    While I can dream you scorn in vain;
35   Asleep or waking you must ease my pain.

II

I

Wherever I am, and whatever I do,
    My Phyllis is still in my mind:
When angry I mean not to Phyllis to go,
    My feet of themselves the way find:
5   Unknown to myself I am just at her door,
    And when I would rail, I can bring out no more,
        Than, 'Phyllis, too fair and unkind!'

2

When Phyllis I see, my heart bounds in my breast,
    And the love I would stifle is shown:
10   But asleep or awake, I am never at rest
    When from my eyes Phyllis is gone!
Sometimes a sweet dream does delude my sad mind,
But alas, when I wake and no Phyllis I find
    How I sigh to myself all alone.

22–8. *die*] a traditional *double entendre* for reaching orgasm.
Song II. From Act IV Scene ii; sung to Lyndaraxa.
12. *sweet*] *1671–2 miscellanies*; sad *1672–95 playtexts*; *sad* is probably a compositorial error, left uncorrected in later reprints.

3

15   Should a king be my rival in her I adore
        He should offer his treasure in vain;
        O let me alone to be happy and poor,
            And give me my Phyllis again:
        Let Phyllis be mine, and but ever be kind,
20   I could to a desert with her be confined,
            And envy no monarch his reign.

4

        Alas, I discover too much of my love,
            And she too well knows her own power!
        She makes me each day a new martyrdom prove,
25   And makes me grow jealous each hour:
        But let her each minute torment my poor mind,
        I had rather love Phyllis both false and unkind,
            Than ever be freed from her power.

Prologue to the Second Part

        They who write ill, and they who ne'er durst write,
        Turn critics out of mere revenge and spite:
        A playhouse gives 'em fame, and up there starts,
        From a mean fifth-rate wit, a man of parts.
5   (So common faces on the stage appear:
        We take 'em in, and they turn beauties here.)
        Our author fears those critics as his fate:

19. but] *1672 playtext;* for *1673 playtext; for* is possibly D.'s revision, but more probably the compositor's simplification.

Prologue to the Second Part. BodL MS says that this Prologue was spoken by Michael Mohun. Mohun (?1616–84) was an actor before the Civil War. He joined the King's Company in 1660, becoming a shareholder in 1661 and co-manager with Charles Hart and John Lacey in 1663. His roles for D. included the title role in *The Indian Emperor*, Philocles in *Secret Love*, Bellamy in *An Evening's Love*, Maximin in *Tyrannic Love*, Abdelmelech in *The Conquest of Granada*, Rhodophil in *Marriage A-la-Mode*, the Duke of Mantona in *The Assignation*, Mr Beaumont in *Amboyna*, the old Emperor in *Aureng-Zebe*, and Ventidius in *All for Love*; he probably retired before the union of the companies in 1682 (Highfill x 271–6).
4. parts] talents (*OED* 12).

And those he fears, by consequence, must hate.
For they the traffic of all wit invade,
10 As scriveners draw away the bankers' trade.
Howe'er, the poet's safe enough today:
They cannot censure an unfinished play.
But, as when vizard mask appears in pit,
Straight every man who thinks himself a wit

9. traffic] intercourse, business (*OED* 3).

10. scriveners] money-lenders. After this line *MS* has: 'Some of them seeme indeed ye Poetts freinds; / But 'tis, as France courts England, for her ends. / They build up this Lampoone, & th' other Songe, / And Court him, to lye still, while they grow stronge.' These lines probably derive from the play-house, and may have been written by D. but excluded from the printed texts. Kinsley suggests that the reference is to the Buckingham circle, which was preparing *The Rehearsal* for the stage in 1671 (see Macdonald 193–5). In the Dedication to Rochester of *Marriage A-la-Mode* in 1673 D. says that at court 'Few Men there have that assurance of a Friend, as not to be made ridiculous by him, when they are absent' (*Works* xi 221–2).

13–20. A sketch of the behaviour of gallants at a play is provided in *The Character of a Town-Gallant* (1680) 3: 'he advances into the middle of the *Pit*, struts about a while, to render his good parts Conspicuous, pulls out his *Comb*, *Carreens* his *Wigg*, *Hums* the *Orange-Wench*, to give her, her own rates for her *China-Fruit*, and immediately *Sacrifices* the fairest of them, to the shrine of the *next Vizor Mask*. Then gravely sits down, and falls half *asleep*, unless some *petulant Wench* hard by, keep him awake with treading on his Toe, or a wanton Complement; Yet all on a sudden to shew his *Judgment*, and prove himself at once a *Wit* and a *Critick*, he starts up, and with a Tragical Face, *Damns the Play*, though he have not *heard* (at least *understood*) two lines of it.'

13. vizard mask] masked woman. On 12 June 1663 Pepys observed Viscountess Fauconberg at the theatre, and noted: 'When the House begun to fill, she put on her vizard and so kept it on all the play—which is of late become a great fashion among the ladies, which hides their whole face.' On 18 February 1667 he heard Sir Charles Sedley talking at a play with a woman who sat 'with her mask on all the play. . . . He would fain know who she was, but she would not tell. Yet . . . did give him leave to use all means to find out who she was but pulling off her mask.' In Etherege's *She wou'd if She cou'd* (1668) Courtall says that masks were 'pretty toys, invented, first, meerly for the good of us poor Lovers to deceive the jealous, and to blind the malicious; but the proper use is so wickedly perverted, that it makes all honest men hate the fashion mortally' (II i 115–19): the phrase 'vizard mask' thus came to designate a prostitute (e.g. Wycherley, *Love in a Wood* (1672) I v 119 etc.).

15   Perks up, and managing his comb with grace,
     With his white wig sets off his nut-brown face;
     That done, bears up to the prize, and views each limb,
     To know her by her rigging and her trim:
     Then the whole noise of fops to wagers go,
20   'Pox on her, 't must be she'; and 'Dammee no'.
     Just so I prophesy these wits today
     Will blindly guess at our imperfect play:
     With what new plots our second part is filled,
     Who must be kept alive, and who be killed.
25   And as those vizard masks maintain that fashion,
     To soothe and tickle sweet imagination,
     So our dull poet keeps you on with masking,
     To make you think there's something worth your
         asking:
     But when 'tis shown, that which does now delight you
30   Will prove a dowdy, with a face to fright you.

15–16. Combing the wig in public was a foppish habit; cp. 'Prologue' in *Covent Garden Drolery* (1672) 26: 'He who comes hither with design to hiss, / And with a bum revers'd, to whisper Miss, / To comb a Perriwig, or to shew gay cloathes, / Or to vent Antique nonsence with new oathes, / Our Poet welcomes as the Muses friend; / For hee'l by irony each Play commend.' Gallants who 'like neither the Play nor the Women . . . seldom stay any longer than the combing of their Perriwigs' (*She wou'd if She cou'd* I ii 158–9). The white (powdered) wig was currently in fashion; the fop Brisk in Shadwell's *The Humorists* (1671) says: 'Here's a Perriwig, no Flax in the world can be whiter . . . if you have a fair Peruke, get by a Green or some Dark colour'd Hanging. . . . Oh it sets it off admirably' (i 221).

17. bears up] brings the vessel into the direction of the wind (*OED* 37).

19. noise] Apparently intended as a collective noun. Noise in the theatres was a frequent problem: Pepys records his vexation at the chatter of Sedley and the masked woman on 18 February 1667. Cp. 'Prologue to *Marriage A-la-Mode*' ll. 6, 27; 'Epilogue to the King and Queen'.

Epilogue to the Second Part

They who have best succeeded on the stage
Have still conformed their genius to their age.
Thus Jonson did mechanic humour show,
When men were dull, and conversation low.
5   Then comedy was faultless, but 'twas coarse:
Cob's tankard was a jest, and Otter's horse.
And as their comedy, their love was mean:
Except, by chance, in some one laboured scene

Epilogue to the Second Part. For the place of this Epilogue in D.'s criticism of
his dramatic predecessors and the debate with Shadwell, see the headnotes to
'Prologue to *The Tempest*' and *MF*. At the end of *The Conquest of Granada* D.
printed a 'Defence of the Epilogue' (*Works* xi 203–18) in which he said: 'I
have so farr ingag'd my self in a bold Epilogue to this Play, wherein I have
somewhat tax'd the former writing, that it was necessary for me either not to
print it, or to show that I could defend it' (203). He went on to argue that
both language and manners had been refined since the days of Jonson and
Fletcher. Those who subsequently attacked D. for his depreciation of Jonson
included Richard Flecknoe in *Epigrams. Of All Sorts* (1671) 51–2; Buckingham in *The Rehearsal* (1672) II i 61–4; the author of *The Censure of the Rota*
(1673) 12–13; and Rochester in 'An Allusion to Horace' (in MS, 1675–6) ll.
81–92.
1–2. These lines hit at Shadwell, who aimed to imitate Jonson, the genius of
the previous age, and argued that classical rules were universally valid.
3. mechanic] vulgar, low. Cp. *EDP*: 'Humour was his proper Sphere, and in
that he delighted most to represent Mechanick people' (*Works* xvii 57).
4. Cp. 'Defence of the Epilogue': 'The last and greatest advantage of our
writing . . . proceeds from conversation. In the Age, wherein those Poets
liv'd, there was less of gallantry than in ours; neither did they keep the best
company of theirs' (*Works* xi 215).
6. Cob] a water-bearer in *Every Man in his Humour.*   *tankard*] the large
vessel in which he carries water (see *OED* 1).   *Otter*] a land and sea captain
in *Epicoene.   horse*] See *Epicoene* III i. In the 'Defence' D. says: 'Gentlemen
will now be entertain'd with the follies of each other: and though they allow
Cob and *Tib* to speak properly, yet they are not much pleas'd with their
Tankard or with their Raggs: And, surely, their conversation can be no jest to
them on the Theatre, when they would avoid it in the street' (*Works* xi 217–
18).
7. D. says of Fletcher: 'Let us applaud his Scenes of Love; but, let us confess
that he understood not either greatness or perfect honour in the parts of any
of his women'; and of Jonson: 'Love, which is the foundation of all Comedies
in other Languages, is scarcely mention'd in any of his Playes' (*Works* xi 217).
mean] not refined.

Which must atone for an ill-written play.
10   They rose, but at their height could seldom stay.
Fame then was cheap, and the first comer sped;
And they have kept it since, by being dead.
But were they now to write when critics weigh
Each line, and every word, throughout a play,
15   None of 'em, no not Jonson in his height,
Could pass, without allowing grains for weight.
Think it not envy that these truths are told:
Our poet's not malicious, though he's bold.
'Tis not to brand 'em that their faults are shown,
20   But, by their errors, to excuse his own.
If love and honour now are higher raised,
'Tis not the poet, but the age is praised.
Wit's now arrived to a more high degree,
Our native language more refined and free.
25   Our ladies and our men now speak more wit
In conversation, than those poets writ.
Then one of these is, consequently, true:
That what this poet writes comes short of you,
And imitates you ill (which most he fears),
30   Or else his writing is not worse than theirs.
Yet, though you judge (as sure the critics will)
That some before him writ with greater skill,
In this one praise he has their fame surpassed,
To please an age more gallant than the last.

Song from the Second Part

I

He.   How unhappy a lover am I
While I sigh for my Phyllis in vain;

11. *sped*] succeeded.
14. In the 'Defence' D. makes a close analysis of passages from *Catiline*, but drops this after the first edition.
16. *grains*] A grain is the smallest English weight, 1/7000 lb.
25–6. D. comments on the wit of courtly conversation in the Dedication of *Marriage A-la-Mode* (1673) (*Works* xi 221–2).

Song. From Act IV Scene iii; in two parts. It is sung offstage, partly by

All my hopes of delight
Are another man's right,
5   Who is happy while I am in pain!

2

She. Since her honour allows no relief,
But to pity the pains which you bear,
'Tis the best of your fate
(In a hopeless estate)
10 To give o'er, and betimes to despair.

3

He. I have tried the false med'cine in vain,
For I wish what I hope not to win:
From without my desire
Has no food to its fire,
15 But it burns and consumes me within.

4

She. Yet at least 'tis a pleasure to know
That you are not unhappy alone:
For the nymph you adore
Is as wretched and more,
20 And accounts all your sufferings her own.

5

He. O ye gods, let me suffer for both;
At the feet of my Phyllis I'll lie:
I'll resign up my breath,
And take pleasure in death,
25 To be pitied by her when I die.

6

She. What her honour denied you in life,
In her death she will give to your love:
Such a flame as is true
After fate will renew,
30 For the souls to meet closer above.

Esperanza, who was played by Anne Reeves; she was possibly D.'s mistress
by this time (Winn 533).

25 Prologue, Epilogue and Songs from *Marriage A-la-Mode*

Date and publication. The play was first performed by the King's Company at the Theatre Royal, Drury Lane, probably in late November 1671 (see Robert D. Hume, *HLB* xxi (1973) 161–6). *Marriage A-la-Mode. A Comedy* was published by Herringman in 1673, with a dedication to the Earl of Rochester (*SR* 18 March; *TC* 16 June; advertised in the *London Gazette* 29 May); reprinted 1684, 1691 and 1698. The Prologue and Epilogue were previously printed in *Covent Garden Drolery* (1672, two editions) and are also found in BodL MS Top. Oxon. e 202 and Clark Library MS D779M2P96. The relationship between these texts is discussed by Paul Hammond in *PBSA* lxxxi (1987) 155–72, who argues that (i) the texts in *1672* and MSS derive from the playhouse, and preserve lines which were added in different performances, though not necessarily by D. (see 'Prologue' ll. 6*n*, 19*n*, 27*n*); (ii) *1673* has a misprint in 'Prologue' l. 4 which needs emendation from *1672* and MSS. The Epilogue similarly needs emendation in l. 13. The present text follows *1673*, with the two emendations, as that represents both the first authorized printed text and the most reliable witness to the text which D. originally authorized for performance. (The Prologue is also found in the Library of Congress copy of *The Kind Keeper* (1680): see Danchin iii 113.) Song I was printed in *New Court-Songs, and Poems* (1672), and set by Robert Smith in *Choice Songs and Ayres for One Voyce* (1673; facsimile in Day 41) and *Choice Ayres, Songs, & Dialogues* (1675; 1676). Song II was printed in *Covent Garden Drolery*, *New Court-Songs, and Poems*, *Westminster-Drollery: The Second Part* (1672), *The Canting Academy* (1673) and *The Wits Academy* (1677); it was set by Nicholas Staggins in *Choice Songs and Ayres for One Voyce* (facsimile in Day 43) and *Choice Ayres, Songs, & Dialogues*.

Reception. Imitations of Song II are found in *Covent Garden Drolery* and *New Court-Songs, and Poems*.

Prologue

Lord, how reformed and quiet we are grown,
Since all our braves and all our wits are gone:

¶**25**. *Prologue.* According to *Covent Garden Drolery* this was spoken by Charles Hart, who played Palamede. For Hart see 'Epilogue to *1 Conquest of Granada*' *n*).
1–2. The Third Dutch War was not declared until 17 March 1672, but preparations were in hand by November 1671 (Hume in *HLB*).   *braves*] bullies, bravadoes (*OED* 1b; 2).

Fop-corner now is free from civil war,
White wig and vizard mask no longer jar.
5   France and the fleet have swept the town so clear
That we can act in peace, and you can hear.
'Twas a sad sight, before they marched from home,⎤
To see our warriors in red waistcoats come   ⎬
With hair tucked up into our tiring room.   ⎦
10 But 'twas more sad to hear their last adieu;
The women sobbed, and swore they would be true;
And so they were, as long as e'er they could: ⎤
But powerful guinea cannot be withstood,   ⎬
And they were made of playhouse flesh and blood.⎦
15 Fate did their friends for double use ordain,⎤
In wars abroad they grinning honour gain,   ⎬
And mistresses, for all that stay, maintain. ⎦
Now they are gone, 'tis dead vacation here,
For neither friends nor enemies appear.
20 Poor pensive punk now peeps ere plays begin,

3. Fop-corner] Part of the pit where the fops chattered during performances
(cp. Wycherley, *The Plain-Dealer* (1677) II i 256).
4. See 'Prologue to *2 Conquest of Granada*' ll. 13n, 15–16n.   *mask*] Ed.;
Masque *MSS*; Masks *1672*; make *1673*.
6. For the noise in theatres see 'Prologue to *2 Conquest of Granada*' l. 19n.
After this line *1672* and Clark MS add: 'Those that durst fight are gone to get
renown, / And those that durst not, blush to stand in Town' (playhouse
variant).
9. hair tucked up] hair tied back in military fashion (cp. Rochester, 'Tunbridge
Wells' (in MS, 1673/4) ll. 149–50).
12–14. Echoed in the attack on D. in *The Protestant Satire* [1684], possibly by
Shadwell, ll. 172–4: 'He honest kept as long as e'er he could— / But Privy
Purse guineas cannot be withstood, / And Bayes was of Committeeman's
flesh and blood' (*POAS* iii 523).
13. Echoed in John Lacy's *Sir Hercules Buffoon* (1684) 4: 'Prithee consider,
Sister, Virtue cannot maintain thee; and when once 'tis known a handsom
Woman is in want, then as the Poet worthily says, the powerful Guinney
cannot be withstood' (Macdonald). The idea is traditional: cp. Horace, *Carm.*
III xvi 1–8; Tilley L 406 (Kinsley).
16. grinning honour] Echoes Falstaff's remark on the death of Sir Walter Blunt:
'I like not such grinning honour as Sir Walter hath. Give me life' (*1 Henry IV*
V iii 58–9) (Kinsley).
19. After this line MSS add: 'All noise is husht within our Empty walls / The
Old Cat-fac't Critick now noe longer Brawles / But vents his treadbare jests
in Hospitalls' (playhouse variant).

Sees the bare bench, and dares not venture in,
But manages her last half-crown with care,
And trudges to the Mall, on foot, for air.
Our city friends so far will hardly come,
25   They can take up with pleasures nearer home,
And see gay shows, and gaudy scenes elsewhere:
For we presume they seldom come to hear.
But they have now ta'en up a glorious trade,
And cutting Morecraft struts in masquerade.
30   There's all our hope, for we shall show today
A masking ball to recommend our play:
Nay, to endear 'em more, and let 'em see
We scorn to come behind in courtesy,
We'll follow the new mode which they begin,
35   And treat 'em with a room, and couch within:

22. half-crown] The price of admission to the pit (*LS* lxx–lxxi), and also a prostitute's charge (cp. 'Prologue to *Mithridates*' l. 24).

23. the Mall] The fashionable walk in St James's Park, London.

24–7. On 9 November 1671 the Duke's Company opened their new theatre at Dorset Garden, which was closer to the City of London than the Theatre Royal in Drury Lane, which was less accessible and in a poor quarter (Harold Love, *YES* x (1980) 36); cp. Wycherley's Prologue and Epilogue to *The Gentleman Dancing-Master* (1672). The elaborate costumes, sets and machinery of the rival company are glanced at in several of D.'s subsequent prologues and epilogues.

27. After this line Clark MS adds: 'Or if they doe, few of them will admit, / That wth old Sceanes wee can p^{r}sent new witt' (playhouse variant).

29. cutting Morecraft] The swaggering citizen, from the character of the usurer in Fletcher's *The Scornful Lady* (1616, frequently revived in the Restoration); at the end of the play 'He's turn'd Gallant . . . and is now called, *Cutting Moorecraft*' (V iv 132–4). Cp. 'Horace: *Epode* II' l. 96.   *masquerade*] During the winters of 1671–3 masquerades seem to have been particularly popular (see *Works* xi 493–5); cp. the anonymous 'Prologue to *The Widow*' (in *London Drollery* (1673); Danchin no. 153): 'But you this Winter find out other ways / To kill your selves, and to destroy our Plays, / You meet in Masquerade to pass your time / Without the help of Reason or of Rime' (ll. 3–6).

31. Act IV takes place during a masquerade at the Sicilian court.

34–5. The provision of a retiring room with a couch seems to have been a much-appreciated feature of masquerades; the 'Prologue to *The Widow*' says that many citizens believe 'that one Sceen o' th' Couch, is worth a Play' (l. 23). In *Marriage A-la-Mode* Palamede courting Doralice says: 'retire a little with me to the next room that has a couch or bed in't, and bestow your charity upon a poor dying man' (V i 209–11).

For that's one way, howe'er the play fall short,
T' oblige the town, the city and the court.

Epilogue

Thus have my spouse and I informed the nation,
And led you all the way to reformation;
Not with dull morals gravely writ, like those
Which men of easy phlegm with care compose:
5   Your poet's of stiff words, and limber sense,
Born on the confines of indifference;
But by examples drawn, I dare to say,
From most of you who hear and see the play:
There are more Rhodophils in this theatre,
10   More Palamedes, and some few wives, I fear.

37. For this tripartite division of the audience see Harold Love, *YES* x (1980) 31–3. He argues that *town* would include 'middle class' patrons such as lawyers, military officers, students, the more genteel Westminster bourgeoisie, and some whores and beaux; *city* would refer to members of the London guilds and their families, merchants, shopkeepers and apprentices; *court* would designate the royal household, office-holders, and those who identified themselves politically or culturally with the royal establishment. These divisions corresponded approximately with the physical divisions of the playhouse: the town in the pit, the city in the middle gallery, and the court in the boxes. Cp. 'Prologue to *The Rival Ladies*' l. 24*n*; 'Prologue for the Women' ll. 11–17.

Epilogue. According to *Covent Garden Drolery* the Epilogue was spoken by Michael Mohun, who played Rhodophil, Doralice's husband. Unlike the Prologue, it was evidently spoken in character. For Mohun see 'Prologue to *2 Conquest of Granada*' *n.*
2. reformation] This provides the title for Joseph Arrowsmith's play *The Reformation* (performed 1672/3; printed 1673), which is 'a systematic debunking of Dryden, and of *Marriage A-la-Mode* in particular' (Hume 292).
3–6. Kinsley notes that this refers to the opening lines of Samuel Tuke's *The Adventures of Five Hours* (1671 edition): 'How happy are the Men of easie Phlegm, / Born on the Confines of Indifference; / Holding from Nature, the securest Tenure, / The Peaceful Empire o'r themselves'.
4. phlegm] In humours physiology the cold and moist humour, producing dullness and sluggishness.
9–12. The intrigues of Rhodophil with Meleantha (Palamede's fiancée) and of Palamede with Doralice (Rhodophil's wife) are unconsummated.

But yet too far our poet would not run;
Though 'twas well offered, there was nothing done.
He would not quite the women's frailty bare,
But stripped 'em to the waist, and left 'em there:
15   And the men's faults are less severely shown,
For he considers that himself is one.
Some stabbing wits, to bloody satire bent,
Would treat both sexes with less compliment;
Would lay the scene at home, of husbands tell,
20   For wenches, taking up their wives i' th' Mall,
And a brisk bout which each of them did want,
Made by mistake of mistress and gallant.
Our modest author thought it was enough
To cut you off a sample of the stuff;
25   He spared my shame, which you, I'm sure, would not,
For you were all for driving on the plot:
You sighed when I came in to break the sport,
And set your teeth when each design fell short.
To wives and servants all good wishes lend,
30   But the poor cuckold seldom finds a friend.
Since therefore court and town will take no pity,
I humbly cast myself upon the city.

13. *women's*] Works, MSS; Women *1672*; Woman's *1673*.
19–20. 'These lines sound . . . like a description of a play called *The Mall*, in which a maid pretending to be her mistress is stripped on stage and hauled into bed by the husband, while another wife appears at what she thinks is an assignation made by her husband, and copulates with another man in the dark. Given that kind of competition, Dryden's comedy was indeed "modest"' (Winn 228). *The Mall* was printed in 1674, but might have been staged earlier.
27. Rhodophil interrupts Palamede with Doralice in III ii, IV iii and V i.
28. *set*] clench from indignation (*OED* 95).
32. The cuckolded citizen is a stock figure in seventeenth-century comedy.

Songs

I

1

Why should a foolish marriage vow
  Which long ago was made,
Oblige us to each other now
  When passion is decayed?
5 We loved, and we loved, as long as we could,
    Till our love was loved out in us both:
But our marriage is dead when the pleasure is fled:
  'Twas pleasure first made it an oath.

2

If I have pleasures for a friend,
10 And farther love in store,
What wrong has he whose joys did end,
  And who could give no more?
'Tis a madness that he should be jealous of me,
  Or that I should bar him of another:
15 For all we can gain is to give ourselves pain,
    When neither can hinder the other.

II

1

Whilst Alexis lay pressed
  In her arms he loved best,
With his hands round her neck, and his head on her breast,
He found the fierce pleasure too hasty to stay,
5 And his soul in the tempest just flying away.

Song I. Sung at the beginning of Act I by Doralice, accompanied on the lute by her maid Beliza; they retire offstage into an arbor for this song (for this theatrical device see Price, *Music in the Restoration Theatre* 46).
9. friend] lover.
13, 15. Each printed as two lines in *1673–1698*.
Song II. From Act IV Scene ii. Louis Bredvold pointed out a probable source in a French madrigal (for other analogues see Chandler B. Beall, *MLN* lxiv (1949) 461–8):

  Tirsis d'un excez de plaisir,
  Estoit sur le point de mourir

2

When Celia saw this,
With a sigh and a kiss,
She cried, 'O my dear, I am robbed of my bliss;
'Tis unkind to your love, and unfaithfully done,
10   To leave me behind you, and die all alone.'

3

The youth, though in haste,
And breathing his last,
In pity died slowly, while she died more fast;
Till at length she cried, 'Now, my dear, now let us go,
15   Now die, my Alexis, and I will die too.'

4

Thus entranced they did lie,
Till Alexis did try
To recover new breath, that again he might die:

Entre les bras de Filis qu'il adore,
Quand Filis que l'Amour range soûs méme loy,
Et que le méme feu devore,
Luy dit, ah! mon Tirsis, ah! ne meurs pas encore,
Je veux mourir avecque toy.
Tirsis alors suspend l'envie,
Qu'il avoit de perdre la vie;
Mais par cette contrainte il se met aux abois,
Et n'osant pas mourir il se meurt mille fois;
Cependant lors qu'au sein de cette jeune Amante,
Le Berger à longs traits boit l'Amoureux poison,
Elle qui sent dejâ qu'elle entre en pâmoison,
D'un régard languissant, & d'une voix tremblante,
Luy dit, mon unique soucy,
Meurs, mon Tirsis; car je me meurs aussi.
Soudain ce Berger tout en flâme,
Luy répond, comme toy je me meurs, je me pâme.
Ainsi dans les ravissements,
Moururent ces heureux Amans;
Mais d'une mort si douce & si digne d'envie,
Que pour mourir encor ils reprirent la vie.
          (*Recueil de Quelques Pieces Nouvelles et Galantes* (1663) 151) (*Works*)
10. die] common seventeenth-century image for attaining orgasm.

Then often they died, but the more they did so,
20   The nymph died more quick, and the shepherd more
       slow.

26 Song ('Farewell, fair Armida')

Date and publication. The song appeared in four miscellanies in 1672: *New Court-Songs, and Poems. By R[obert] V[eel] Gent.*; *Covent Garden Drolery* (two editions); *Westminster-Drollery* and *Windsor-Drollery*; and in *The Canting Academy* (1673). It was set by Robert Smith in *Choice Songs and Ayres* (1673; facsimile in Day 38) and *Choice Ayres, Songs, & Dialogues* (1675, 1676). The sequence of the miscellanies is uncertain (see Macdonald 78), but textually *New Court-Songs* is superior, and is followed here.

Authorship. The song was first printed as D.'s by Malone, on the basis of two references in *The Rehearsal* (1675 text). In II i 114–17 Bayes says: 'If I am to write familiar things, as Sonnets to *Armida*, and the like, I make use of Stew'd Prunes only; but, when I have a grand design in hand, I ever take Phisic, and let blood'; and in III i 90–119 Bayes sings a song which he says is 'peremptorily the very best that ever yet was written: you must know, it was made by *Tom Thimble's* first wife after she was dead . . . here's the conceit, that upon his knowing she was kill'd by an accident, he supposes, with a Sigh, that she dy'd for love of him. . . . 'Tis to the Tune of Farewel, fair *Armida*, on Seas, and in battles, in Bullets, and all that'. The song which follows ('In swords, Pikes, and Bullets') is a parody of the second stanza of 'Farewell, fair Armida'. In *A Key to the Rehearsal* in Buckingham's *Miscellaneous Works* (1704–5) ii 14, a note refers to this as 'the latter part of a Song, made by Mr. Bayes on the Death of Captain *Digby*, Son of *George* Earl of *Bristol*, who was a passionate Admirer of the Dutchess *Dowager* of *Richmond*, call'd by the Author *Armida*: he lost his Life in a Sea fight, against the *Dutch*, the 28th of May, 1672'. The song was accepted as D.'s by Scott. G. Thorn-Drury (in his edition of *Covent Garden Drolery* (1928) 126–9) rejected the attribution, but Day, in a judicious discussion (152–5) points out that the song was evidently assumed to be D.'s by the author of *The Rehearsal*, who seems to have expected the audience to concur. Day also notes that (i) Smith's setting in *Choice Songs* follows two genuine songs by D.; (ii) Smith collaborated with D. on other occasions; (iii) in *Covent Garden Drolery* 39–40 there is a parody beginning 'Farewell, dear *Revechia*, my joy and my grief', in which 'Revechia' is almost certainly intended to be D.'s mistress Anne Reeves (for whom see 'Epilogue to *Secret Love* Spoken by the Women' *n*): the parody would lack point if the original were not by D. Kinsley concurs with Day; *Works* omits the piece without discussion. Winn 533–4 reviews the evidence linking the song with D. and Reeves, but is non-committal on the authorship. The evidence assembled by Malone and Day points strongly towards D.'s authorship; at the very least it was widely believed to be his. It is not surprising that D. should not acknowledge or reprint such a slight poem which had attracted so much embarrassing comment and parody so quickly.

Reception. A reply beginning 'Blame not your Armida nor call her your grief' often follows it in the printed miscellanies (e.g. *Covent Garden Drolery* 17). In addition to the parodies already mentioned, a parody beginning 'Far-well my dear Puggy, my Pullet, my Low-bell' appears in *Mock Songs and Joking Poems* (1675) 79–80; another is found in BL MS Egerton 2623; and there was a political parody: 'Farewel, my *Tom D*[an]*by*, my Pimp and my Cheat' (*Roxburghe Ballads* edited by J. W. Ebsworth iv (1883) 82).

Song

1

Farewell, fair Armida, my joy and my grief;
In vain I have loved you, and find no relief:
Undone by your virtue, too strict and severe,
Your eyes gave me love, and you gave me despair.
5 Now called by my honour, I seek with content
The fate which in pity you would not prevent:
   To languish in love were to find by delay
   A death that's more welcome the speediest way.

2

On seas and in battles, in bullets and fire,
10 The danger is less than in hopeless desire.
My death's wound you gave me, though far off I bear
My fate from your sight, not to cost you a tear.
But if the kind flood on a wave should convey,
And under your window my body should lay,
15   The wound on my breast when you happen to see,
   You'll say with a sigh, 'It was given by me'.

¶26. *1. Armida*] The name is perhaps from Tasso, *Gerusalemme Liberata*.
6. The] *Other texts*; A *New Court-Songs*.

27 Prologue to *Wit without Money*

Date and publication. The date for the performance of this Prologue is given in BL MS Sloane 4455 as 26 February 1672. The poem was first printed in 1672 in *Covent Garden Drolery* (two editions), *Westminster-Drollery: The Second Part* and *The Last and Now Only Compleat Collection*; then in *MP* (1684, 1692). It is also found in BL MS Sloane 4455; BodL MS Eng. Poet. e.4; and Society of Antiquaries MS 330. Since the MSS were all compiled *c*. 1672, and agree with *MP* where it has substantive variants from the 1672 miscellanies, this shows that the variant readings in the 1672 miscellanies are corruptions, and that *MP* preserves the Prologue substantially as it was first performed. (One possible exception is 'While' in *MP* l. 12, where the miscellanies and MSS agree on 'Whilst'.) The present text is therefore based on *MP*.

Context. On 25 January 1672 fire destroyed the Theatre Royal in Bridges Street, with all the scenery, props and costumes belonging to the King's Company. The company moved into the old theatre in Lincoln's Inn Fields which had been vacated by the Duke's Company when it moved into the lavish new theatre in Dorset Garden. The struggles of the King's Company are evident from the subsequent 'Prologue and Epilogue to *Secret Love*, Spoken by the Women', 'Prologue for the Women' and 'Prologue to *Arviragus* revived'. Beaumont and Fletcher's *Wit without Money* (1639) was chosen as the opening production in the new quarters.

Prologue to *Wit without Money*

Spoken the first day of the King's House acting after the fire

> So shipwrecked passengers escape to land,
> So look they, when on the bare beach they stand
> Dropping and cold, and their first fear scarce o'er,
> Expecting famine on a desert shore.

¶**27**. *Title. to* Wit without Money] *1672 miscellanies; omitted in MP*. BL MS adds: 'The Curtaine being drawne up all the Actors were discover'd on the stage in Melancholick postures & Moone [i.e. Michael Mohun] advancing before the rest speaks as follows, addressing himself chiefly to ye King then present.' For Mohun see 'Prologue to *2 Conquest of Granada*' n.
1–3. Echoed in *All for Love* (1678) V 39–40; cp. also 'To the Lady Castlemaine' ll. 1–6.
3. *Dropping*] dripping.

5   From that hard climate we must wait for bread,
     Whence ev'n the natives, forced by hunger, fled.
     Our stage does human chance present to view,
     But ne'er before was seen so sadly true.
     You are changed too, and your pretence to see
10 Is but a nobler name for charity.
     Your own provisions furnish out our feasts,
     While you the founders make yourselves the guests.
     Of all mankind beside Fate had some care, ⎫
     But for poor wit no portion did prepare: ⎬
15 'Tis left a rent-charge to the brave and fair. ⎭
     You cherished it, and now its fall you mourn,
     Which blind unmannered zealots make their scorn,
     Who think that fire a judgement on the stage,
     Which spared not temples in its furious rage.
20 But as our new-built city rises higher, ⎫
     So from old theatres may new aspire, ⎬
     Since Fate contrives magnificence by fire. ⎭
     Our great metropolis does far surpass
     Whate'er is now, and equals all that was:
25 Our wit as far does foreign wit excel,
     And, like a king, should in a palace dwell.
     But we with golden hopes are vainly fed,
     Talk high, and entertain you in a shed:
     Your presence here, for which we humbly sue,
30 Will grace old theatres, and build up new.

9. pretence] professed purpose (*OED* 4).

11. Implies that the King and courtiers had, as occasionally happened, furnished the actors with their cast-off clothes (cp. Downes 52, 61).

14–15. i.e. 'Fate (like a father making a will) assigned to wit no inheritance ("portion") in ready money or ownership of land, but instead placed the burden of supporting wit upon the "brave and fair" who have an obligation to make payments out of the income from their own property (a "rent-charge")'.

17–18. Cp. 'Only the *Zealous Hypocrite*'s o'rejoyed, / To see his *Scourge* thus casually destroyed; / He cryes, *Just Judgement!*' (*On the Unhappy Conflagration of the Theatre Royal* (1672)).

20–3. Cp. *AM* ll. 845–8.

29. BodL MS marks this as spoken 'To the King'.

28 Prologue and Epilogue to *Secret Love*, Spoken by the Women

Date and publication. This revival of *Secret Love* was probably staged in the spring or early summer of 1672. The reference in 'Epilogue' l. 30 places it after Edward Ravenscroft's *The Citizen Turn'd Gentleman*; the first recorded performance of *The Citizen* was on 4 July, but Milhous and Hume 386 point out that it could have been staged as early as December 1671 or January 1672. Winn 580 suggests that *The Citizen* may have been staged in April or May, with the revived *Secret Love* following soon after. The Prologue and Epilogue were printed in *Covent Garden Drolery* (1672; two editions), and are also found in BL MS Egerton 2623.

Context. After the fire at the Theatre Royal (see 'Prologue to *Wit without Money*') the King's Company found it difficult to meet the competition from the Duke's Company in their new theatre, and these pieces suggest that the use of breeches parts was one expedient which they adopted to win popularity.

Authorship. First printed as D.'s by Scott, on the basis of the connection with D.'s play, and D.'s connection with Mrs Reeves. They are also attributed to D. in a contemporary hand in BL MS. But this evidence is not conclusive, and since D. did not include them in the collection of his prologues and epilogues in *MP* (1684) their authorship remains doubtful.

Prologue

Spoken by Mrs Boutell to *The Maiden Queen*, in man's clothes

> Women like us, passing for men, you'll cry
> Presume too much upon your secrecy.
> There's not a fop in town but will pretend
> To know the cheat himself, or by his friend.
> 5 Then make no words on't, gallants, 'tis e'en true,

¶**28**. *Prologue. Title*. Elizabeth Boutell (or 'Bowtell'), née Davenport, was a leading actress with the King's Company. She played Sabina in *Secret Love*, Donna Theodosia in *An Evening's Love*, St Catharine in *Tyrannic Love*, Benzayda in *The Conquest of Granada*, Laura in *The Assignation*, Melantha in *Marriage A-la-Mode*, and Cleopatra in *All for Love*. She made her first recorded stage appearance in August 1670 as Aurelia, a breeches part in *The*

We are condemned to look, and strut, like you.
Since we thus freely our hard fate confess,
Accept us these bad times in any dress.
You'll find the sweet on't, now old pantaloons ⎫
10   Will go as far as formerly new gowns,   ⎬
And from your own cast wigs expect no frowns. ⎭
The ladies we shall not so easily please:
They'll say, 'What impudent bold things are these,
That dare provoke, yet cannot do us right,
15   Like men with huffing looks that dare not fight!'
But this reproach our courage must not daunt, ⎫
The bravest soldier may a weapon want;   ⎬
Let her that doubts us still, send her gallant. ⎭
Ladies, in us you'll youth and beauty find,
20   All things but one, according to your mind.
And when your eyes and ears are feasted here,
Rise up and make out the short meal elsewhere.

Epilogue

Spoken by Mrs Reeves to *The Maiden Queen*, in man's clothes

What think you, sirs, was't not all well enough,
Will you not grant that we can strut, and huff?

Roman Empress, and went on to play several other breeches parts in the 1670s.
(Highfill ii 260–1; Judith Milhous, *TN* xxxix (1985) 124–34).   *in man's
clothes*] Added in *1672 second edition*.
9. *sweet*] pleasure.   *pantaloons*] breeches with immensely wide legs, pleated
into a waistband above, and reaching to the knees: 'a sort of Breeches now in
fashion, and well known' (Thomas Blount, *Glossographia* (1674); *OED*).
15. *huffing*] A huff was a disreputable, blustering gallant: 'that he may strike
terror into the fearful, he will draw upon any slight occasion not with an
intent to hurt, but to wipe off the suspition of being a Coward' (*The Canting
Academy* (1673) 98).
17. *want*] lack.
22. *make out*] supply the deficiencies of (*OED* 91d).

Epilogue.
Title. Anne Reeves was a minor actress in the King's Company *c.* 1670–5,

Men may be proud, but faith, for aught I see
They neither walk nor cock so well as we.
5 And for the fighting part we may in time
Grow up to swagger in heroic rhyme.
For though we cannot boast of equal force,
Yet at some weapons men have still the worse.
Why should not then we women act alone,⎫
10 Or whence are men so necessary grown? ⎬
Ours are so old they are as good as none.⎭
Some who have tried 'em, if you'll take their oaths,
Swear they're as arrant tinsel as their clothes.
Imagine us but what we represent,
15 And we could e'en give you as good content.
Our faces, shapes, all's better that you see,
And for the rest, they want as much as we!
O, would the higher powers be kind to us,
And grant us to set up a female house,
20 We'll make ourselves to please both sexes then:
To the men, women; to the women, men.
Here we presume our legs are no ill sight,
And they will give you no ill dreams at night.
In dreams both sexes may their passions ease,
25 You make us then as civil as you please.

---

and almost certainly D.'s mistress. She played Esperanza in *The Conquest of Granada*, Philotis in *Marriage A-la-Mode*, and Ascanio in *The Assignation* (a breeches part). See further Winn 532–9.   *Mrs*] also used in the late seventeenth century for an unmarried woman, i.e. 'Miss'.   *in man's clothes*] *Added in 1672 second edition.*

4. cock] strut, swagger.

13. tinsel] originally a rich material interwoven with gold or silver thread; later (mid-seventeenth century) a cheap imitation using copper thread (*OED* 2).

16. that] MS; than *1672.*

22. On 28 October 1661 Pepys went to the theatre, 'where a woman acted Parthenia and came afterward on the Stage in man's clothes, and had the best legs that ever I saw; and I was very well pleased with it'.

23. will] *1672 second edition, MS; would 1672 first edition.*

This would prevent the houses joining too,
At which we are as much displeased as you.
For all our women most devoutly swear ⎫
Each would be rather a poor actress here ⎬
30   Than to be made a Mamamouchi there. ⎭

26–7. No more is known of this apparent plan to merge the two companies, which actually came about in 1682. It was no doubt discussed as a way of meeting the crisis in the King's Company's fortunes.

30. *Mamamouchi*] See 'Prologue to *The Assignation*' l. 30*n*.

29 Prologue, Epilogue and Song from *The Assignation*

Date and publication. The date of the play's first performance is unknown, but it must have been between January 1672 and March 1673 (see 'Prologue' l. 30n). Milhous and Hume 385 say that it is unlikely to be later than November 1672; Winn 580 suggests early autumn. It was performed by the King's Company at Lincoln's Inn Fields. *The Assignation: Or, Love in a Nunnery* was published by Herringman in 1673 (*SR* 18 March; *TC* 16 June) and reprinted in 1678 and 1692. It was dedicated to Sir Charles Sedley. The Song was printed in *London Drollery* (1673) and *Methinks the Poor Town* (1673; two editions) and set by Robert Smith in *Choice Songs and Ayres for One Voyce* (1673; facsimile in Day 45) and *Choice Ayres, Songs, & Dialogues* (1675; 1676).

Prologue

Prologues, like bells to churches, toll you in
With chiming verse, till the dull plays begin;
With this sad difference, though, of pit and pew:
You damn the poet, but the priest damns you.
5   But priests can treat you at your own expense,
And gravely call you fools without offence.
Poets, poor devils, have ne'er your folly shown,
But, to their cost, you proved it was their own.
For, when a fop's presented on the stage,
10   Straight all the coxcombs in the town engage:
For his deliverance and revenge they join,
And grunt like hogs about their captive swine.
Your poets daily split upon this shelf:
You must have fools, yet none will have himself.
15   Or if in kindness you that leave would give,
No man could write you at that rate you live:

¶**29**. *Prologue.*
12. Works cites Edward Topsell on swine: 'when one of them is hurt or hanged fast, or bitten, then all the residue as it were in compassion condoling his misery, run to him and cry with him' (*History of Four-Footed Beasts* (1658) 522).
13. split] suffer shipwreck.   *shelf*] sandbank or submerged ledge of rock; cp. 'Horace: *Epode* II' l. 101.

For some of you grow fops with so much haste,⎤
Riot in nonsense, and commit such waste,   ⎬
'Twould ruin poets should they spend so fast. ⎦
20 He who made this observed what farces hit,
And durst not disoblige you now with wit.
But, gentlemen, you overdo the mode:
You must have fools out of the common road.
Th' unnatural, strained buffoon is only taking,
25 No fop can please you now of God's own making.
Pardon our poet if he speaks his mind,
You come to plays with your own follies lined:
Small fools fall on you, like small showers, in vain:
Your own oiled coats keep out all common rain.
30 You must have Mamamouchi, such a fop
As would appear a monster in a shop:
He'll fill your pit and boxes to the brim,
Where, rammed in crowds, you see yourselves in him.
Sure there's some spell our poet never knew,
35 In 'hullibabilah da' and 'chu, chu, chu'.
But 'marabarah sahem' most did touch ye,
That is: 'O how we love the Mamamouchi!'
Grimace and habit sent you pleased away:
You damned the poet, and cried up the play.

---

20. farces] Cp. 'Prologue to *1 Conquest of Granada*' ll. 38–9*n*.　　*hit*] succeeded.

24–5. Cp. 'Epilogue to *The Man of Mode*' ll. 1–2.

24. is only] i.e. alone is.　　*taking*] pleasing.

27. i.e. as a coat is lined (cp. l. 29).

30. Mamamouchi] The title supposedly conferred on M. Jourdain by the Sultan in Molière's *Le Bourgeois Gentilhomme*, and in Edward Ravenscroft's adaptation *The Citizen Turn'd Gentleman* which was staged by the Duke's Company at Dorset Garden in 1672 (for dates see 'Prologue and Epilogue to *Secret Love*, Spoken by the Women', headnote and l. 30). Ravenscroft's Prologue included slighting references to *Sir Martin Mar-all* and *The Conquest of Granada* ('Rhyme and Noyse with wond'rous show': Danchin no. 149, ll. 19–25). Ravenscroft replied to the present lines in his Prologue to *The Careless Lovers* in March 1673 (Danchin no. 160).

35–7. 'Hula baba la' and 'Chou, chou, chou' are supposedly Turkish phrases used in Jorden's installation as Mamamouchi. He is told that 'Marababa sahem' means 'Ah how much in love am I!' (83).

36. ye] *Works* (for the rhyme); you *1673*.

39. 'This Comedy was looked upon by the Criticks for a Foolish Play; yet it continu'd Acting 9 Days with a full House; upon the Sixth the House being

40   This thought had made our author more uneasy,
        But that he hopes I'm fool enough to please ye.
        But here's my grief: though nature joined with art
        Have cut me out to act a fooling part,
        Yet to your praise the few wits here will say,
45   'Twas imitating you taught Haines to play.

Epilogue

Some have expected from our bills today
To find a satire in our poet's play.
The zealous rout from Coleman Street did run
To see the story of the friar and nun;
5   Or tales yet more ridiculous to hear,
Vouched by their vicar of ten pounds a year,
Of nuns who did against temptation pray,
And discipline laid on the pleasant way:
Or that to please the malice of the town,   ⎫
10 Our poet should in some close cell have shown ⎬
Some sister playing at content alone.   ⎭
This they did hope; the other side did fear,
And both you see alike are cozened here.
Some thought the title of our play to blame;
15 They liked the thing, but yet abhorred the name:
Like modest punks, who all you ask afford,
But for the world they would not name that word.

---

very full: The Poet added 2 more Lines to his Epilogue, *viz. The Criticks come to Hiss, and Dam this Play, / Yet spite of themselves they can't keep away'* (Downes 70).

40–5. Joseph Haines (1648–1701) played the part of Benito, the foolish servant who thinks that he is a wit.

Epilogue.

3. zealous rout] the puritan citizens.   *Coleman Street*] In the City of London, running south from Moorgate; associated with radical puritanism throughout the seventeenth century: see Paul Seaward in *The Politics of Religion in Restoration England*, edited by Tim Harris et al., (1990) 61–3.

4. Stories about the sexual exploits of friars and nuns formed part of Restoration pornography and anti-catholic satire: see Roger Thompson, *Unfit for Modest Ears* (1979) 133–57.

Yet, if you'll credit what I heard him say,
Our poet meant no scandal in his play;
His nuns are good which on the stage are shown,
And sure, behind our scenes you'll look for none.

Song

Long betwixt love and fear Phyllis tormented,
Shunned her own wish, yet at last she consented:
But loath that day should her blushes discover,
   'Come gentle night', she said,
   'Come quickly to my aid,
   And a poor shamefaced maid
Hide from her lover.

Now cold as ice I am, now hot as fire,
I dare not tell myself my own desire;
But let day fly away, and let night haste her:
   Grant ye, kind powers above,
   Slow hours to parting love,
   But when to bliss we move,
Bid 'em fly faster.

How sweet it is to love when I discover
That fire which burns my heart, warming my lover;
'Tis pity love so true should be mistaken:
   But if this night he be
   False or unkind to me
   Let me die ere I see
That I'm forsaken.'

Song. From Act III Scene ii, sung in a masquerade.

30 Prologue for the Women

Date and publication. Spoken between 26 February 1672 and 26 March 1674, while the King's Company acted at Lincoln's Inn Fields; cp. 'Prologue to *Wit without Money*' and 'Prologue and Epilogue to *Secret Love*, Spoken by the Women'. The occasion for the present prologue is unknown. It was first printed in *MP* (1684; reprinted 1692).

Prologue for the Women

When they acted at the old theatre in Lincoln's Inn Fields

Were none of you gallants e'er driven so hard,
As when the poor kind soul was under guard,
And could not do't at home, in some by-street
To take a lodging, and in private meet?
5   Such is our case; we can't appoint our house,
The lovers' old and wonted rendezvous,
But hither to this trusty nook remove;
The worse the lodging is, the more the love.
For much good pastime, many a dear sweet hug
10   Is stol'n in garrets on the humble rug.
Here's good accommodation in the pit,
The grave demurely in the midst may sit,
And so the hot Burgundian on the side
Ply vizard mask, and o'er the benches stride:

¶**30**. *1. Were*] Eds; Where *MP*.
6. wonted] Eds; wanted *MP*.
11–17. For the division of the playhouse see 'Prologue to *The Rival Ladies*' l. 24*n*; 'Prologue to *Marriage A-la-Mode*' l. 36*n*.
13. Burgundian] proverbially violent and skilful fencers; cp. Jonson, *Every Man in his Humour* IV iv 17.
14. vizard mask] Cp. 'Prologue to *2 Conquest of Granada*' l. 13*n*.   *o'er the benches stride*] Cp. 'Prologue to *Cleomenes*' l. 8.

15 Here are convenient upper boxes too,
   For those that make the most triumphant show; ⎫
   All that keep coaches must not sit below. ⎬
                                              ⎭
   There, gallants, you betwixt the acts retire,
   And at dull plays have something to admire:
20 We who look up can your addresses mark,
   And see the creatures coupled in the ark.
   So we expect the lovers, braves, and wits:
   The gaudy house with scenes will serve for cits.

15. *upper boxes*] The Lincoln's Inn Fields playhouse probably consisted of a pit, two tiers of boxes, and a gallery. The Dorset Garden theatre was almost twice the size but was less intimate; a spectator at the back of the front boxes was some 35 feet from the stage at Lincoln's Inn Fields, but 70 feet at Dorset Garden (E. A. Langham in *The London Theatre World*, edited by Robert D. Hume (1980) 38–42; cp. Richard Leacroft, *The Development of the English Playhouse* (1973) 80–1).

22. *braves*] bullies, bravadoes (*OED* 1b, 2).

23. Cp. 'Prologue to *Arviragus* revived' ll. 1–2*n*.   *cits*] citizens.

31 Prologue to *Arviragus* revived

Date and publication. Probably spoken early in 1673 (see l. 6*n*). Lodowick Carlell's *Arviragus and Philicia* (1639) was assigned to Killigrew and the King's Company in 1669; from ll. 1–4 it appears that it was revived at Lincoln's Inn Fields after the burning of the Theatre Royal in 1672. It was printed in *MP* (1684; reprinted 1692). Another prologue for this revival appears in *London Drollery* (1673) (Danchin no. 151b).

Prologue to *Arviragus* revived

Spoken by Mr Hart

> With sickly actors and an old house too,
> We're matched with glorious theatres and new,
> And with our alehouse scenes, and clothes bare worn,
> Can neither raise old plays, nor new adorn.
> 5   If all these ills could not undo us quite,
> A brisk French troupe is grown your dear delight;
> Who with broad bloody bills call you each day
> To laugh and break your buttons at their play:
> Or see some serious piece, which we presume
> 10   Is fall'n from some incomparable plume.
> And therefore, *Messieurs*, if you'll do us grace,
> Send lackeys early to preserve your place.

¶**31**. *Title. Mr Hart*] See 'Epilogue to *1 Conquest of Granada*' *n*.
1–2. While the King's Company was making do with the old theatre at Lincoln's Inn Fields, the rival Duke's Company was playing at its new theatre in Dorset Garden, which had facilities for elaborate sets (see illustrations in Settle's *The Empress of Morocco* (1673)).
6. A company of French comedians came over in December 1672 and left in May 1673; another troupe from the Palais Royal, led by the Italian Tiberio Fiorelli (known as 'Scaramouche') acted at Whitehall from April or May to September 1673 (*LS* 197–8; E. Boswell, *The Restoration Court Stage* (1932) 118–19).
7. bloody bills] i.e. playbills printed in red.
9–10. piece . . . plume] Both words are slightly unusual at this date in English in their French senses of 'play' and 'pen'.
11. grace] favour.

We dare not on your privilege intrench,
Or ask you why you like 'em—they are French.
15 Therefore some go with courtesy exceeding,
Neither to hear nor see, but show their breeding:
Each lady striving to out-laugh the rest,
To make it seem they understood the jest.
Their countrymen come in, and nothing pay,
20 To teach us English where to clap the play:
Civil egad!—our hospitable land
Bears all the charge for them to understand.
Meantime we languish, and neglected lie,
Like wives, while you keep better company;
25 And wish for our own sakes, without a satire,
You'd less good breeding, or had more good nature.

---

13. *intrench*] encroach.
20. *clap*] The pun is ubiquitous in Restoration prologues and epilogues.
25. *satire*] The original spelling 'satyr' suggests a good rhyme with 'nature'.

32 Prologue, Epilogue and Songs from *Amboyna*

Date and publication. The play, which depicts the massacre of English sailors by the Dutch at Amboyna in 1623, was staged by the King's Company at Lincoln's Inn Fields as a contribution to anti-Dutch feeling during the Third Dutch War. Scholarly opinion has been divided between spring 1672 and spring 1673 as the most probable date for the first performance of the play. Charles E. Ward in *PMLA* li (1936) 786–92 argued for May 1672, assuming that D. set to work soon after the declaration of war on 17 March 1672; Ward added that in November 1672 Anthony di Voto announced a performance of *The Dutch Cruelties at Amboyna*, and was promptly forbidden by the Lord Chamberlain to produce plays or parts of plays acted at the main theatres. But it is not certain that di Voto was pirating D.'s play. The allusion to Amboyna in *Covent Garden Drolery* (1672) 33 noted by Noyes is probably to the original event rather than D.'s play. Milhous and Hume 385 agree with Ward, citing the long interval between production and publication which was usual for D.'s plays at this period. However, topical propaganda is likely to have been rushed into print, and the arguments for spring 1673 seem stronger. Malone, Kinsley, *LS* and Winn all argue for a date around May or June 1673. Colin Visser argues for 1673 because of sets available in the theatre at Lincoln's Inn Fields after the fire at the Theatre Royal in 1672 (*RECTR* xv (1976) 1–11). Winn 580–1 notes that the pamphlet which D. used as a source was not reprinted until late spring of 1672 (*TC* June), and that in the advertisement to *King Arthur*, where D. lists his plays in the order of composition, *Amboyna* is placed after *The Assignation* (probably autumn 1672). Winn also suggests that the play was staged soon after Parliament returned from its long prorogation on 4 February 1673, 'when propaganda was even more urgent . . . than at the outset of the war'. As Anne Barbeau Gardiner points out, in a convincing argument for spring 1673 on the basis of several allusions to political events from 1672 and early 1673, opposition to the war had been stirred up in March 1673 by the publication of the pamphlet *Englands Appeale from the Private Caballe at Whitehall*, which aroused old fears of France and Catholicism and turned opinion against Charles's alliance with France to make war on the Protestant Dutch (*RECTR* second series v (1990) 18–27). Additional evidence is that the transcript of the Prologue and Epilogue in BodL MS Don.b.8 was made *c.* July 1673. *Amboyna: A Tragedy* was published by Herringman in 1673 (*SR* 26 June; *TC* 24 November); reprinted 1691. It was dedicated to Lord Clifford. The text of the Prologue and Epilogue in BodL MS probably preserves playhouse variants (see 'Prologue' l. 16*n*, and for a full collation see Kinsley); for other MSS see Beal 400, 410–11. In *POAS* (1704) lines from the Prologue and Epilogue were combined to form a 'Satyr upon the Dutch' (Macdonald 320). Song I appeared in *Methinks the Poor Town* (1673) and *London Drollery* (1673), and was set by Robert Smith in *Choice Songs and Ayres for One Voyce* (1673; facsimile in Day 47) and

Choice Ayres, Songs, & Dialogues (1675; 1676). Song II appeared in *Methinks the Poor Town* (1673).

Prologue

As needy gallants in the scrivener's hands
Court the rich knave that gripes their mortgaged lands,
The first fat buck of all the season's sent,
And keeper takes no fee in compliment:
5   The dotage of some Englishmen is such
To fawn on those who ruin them—the Dutch.
They shall have all, rather than make a war
With those who of the same religion are.
The Straits, the Guinea trade, the herrings too;
10 Nay, to keep friendship, they shall pickle you.
Some are resolved not to find out the cheat,
But cuckold-like love him who does the feat.
What injuries soe'er upon us fall,
Yet still the same religion answers all:
15 Religion wheedled you to civil war,
Drew English blood, and Dutchmen's now would
     spare.
Be gulled no longer, for you'll find it true,
They have no more religion, faith, than you;

¶**32**. *Prologue.*
1. *scrivener*] money-lender.
5–8. *Englands Appeale* stirred up the feeling that England should not be making war on another Protestant country.
9. England's inferior position in her maritime rivalry with the Netherlands was exemplified by the passage of Dutch merchant ships through the Straits of Dover, the success of the Dutch in excluding England from trade with West Africa, and the collapse of English attempts to establish a herring fishery to compete with the Dutch. Cp. *AM* ll. 1–20. In Act II Fiscal says to the Englishman Beaumont: 'for your Fishery at home, you'r like Dogs in the Manger, you will neither manage it your selves, nor permit your neighbours; so that for your Soveraignty of the *Narrow Seas*, if the Inhabitants of 'em, the Herrings, were capable of being Judges, they wou'd certainly award it to the *English*, because they were then sure to live undisturb'd' (21).
12. *love*] BodL MS, Kinsley; *loves* 1673, 1691.
16. After this line BodL MS adds: 'One would haue thought, you should haue growne more wise, / Then to be caught with yᵉ same bargaine twice.'

Interest's the god they worship in their state,
20 And you, I take it, have not much of that.
Well monarchies may own religion's name,
But states are atheists in their very frame.
They share a sin, and such proportions fall
That like a stink 'tis nothing to 'em all.
25 How they love England you shall see this day:
No map shows Holland truer than our play.
Their pictures and inscriptions well we know;
We may be bold one medal sure to show.

19. In Act II Beaumont says: 'your Religion . . . is only made up of Interest: at home, ye tolerate all Worships, in them who can pay for it; and abroad, you were lately so civil to the Emperor of *Pegu*, as to do open sacrifice to his Idols' (22). As Gardiner notes, the Test Act of March 1673 had removed the *de facto* toleration of prominent Catholics by excluding them from public office. The Dutch were accused of irreligion and apostasy in several contemporary pamphlets: see Anne Barbeau Gardiner, *HLQ* liv (1991) 235–52.

22–4. The United Provinces of the Netherlands was a republic of independent provinces with a federal parliament, the States General. Its system of government was oligarchic rather than democratic, but Charles I called it 'popular and without discretion' (David Ogg, *Europe in the Seventeenth Century* (1943) 409). The Dutch distrust of centralization prevented the creation of an established state church.   *states*] republics (*OED* 28b). In *The State of Innocence* (1677, written 1674) Lucifer calls his followers the 'States-General of Hell' (4).

26. Dutch national identity was promoted through the publication of maps and emblems (Simon Schama, *The Embarrassment of Riches* (1987) 50–6, 69–71). Gardiner (*RECTR* second series v (1990) 23) notes that maps by Nickolaes Visscher which labelled the North Sea *Mare Germanicum* and the Channel *La Manche* were available in England, and would have irritated English people.

27–8. Pepys heard that the Dutch circulated cartoons of Charles II: 'One way is with his pockets turned the wrong side outward, hanging out empty—another, with two courtiers picking of his pocket—and a third, leading of two ladies, while others abuse him' (28 November 1663). Charles was particularly incensed by the medal which the Dutch struck to commemorate the Treaty of Breda which ended the Second Dutch War in 1667 (see Anne Barbeau Gardiner, *The Medal* vii (1990) 11–15). The declaration of war in 1672 said that the Dutch were 'so bold with Our Royal Person, and the Honour of this Nation' that there was 'scarce a Town within their Territories that is not filled with abusive Pictures, and false Historical Medals and Pillars' (*His Majesties Declaration against the States Generall of the United Provinces* (1672) 5–6). Details of the abusive emblems which the Dutch had circulated were given by Henry Stubbe in *A Justification of the Present War against the*

View then their falsehoods, rapine, cruelty,
30   And think what once they were they still would be.
But hope not either language, plot or art:
'Twas writ in haste, but with an English heart.
And least hope wit: in Dutchmen that would be
As much improper as would honesty.

Epilogue

A poet once the Spartans led to fight,
And made 'em conquer in the Muses' right:
So would our poet lead you on this day,
Showing your tortured fathers in his play.
5   To one well-born th' affront is worse and more
When he's abused and baffled by a bore.
With an ill grace the Dutch their mischiefs do,
They've both ill nature and ill manners too.
Well may they boast themselves an ancient nation,
10   For they were bred ere manners were in fashion;
And their new commonwealth has set 'em free
Only from honour and civility.

United Netherlands (1672) 40 and *A Further Justification* (1673) 3 (pictures reproduced in Schama, *Embarrassment of Riches* 272). Burnet thought that these objections were mere excuses for a war already resolved upon for other reasons (i 546–7; Kinsley), as did Marvell (*An Account of the Growth of Popery and Arbitrary Government in England* (1677) 32).

32. In the Dedication D. says that the play was written in a month.

Epilogue.

1–2. The Greek elegiac poet Tyrtaeus led the Spartans to victory in the war against Messene. Gardiner (*RECTR* second series v (1990) 21) notes that he rallied them when they were on the point of abandoning a long siege, suggesting that the allusion is particularly appropriate after a year of war.

6. bore] Punning on 'boor' and 'Boer'; cp. l. 16*n*, and Marvell's *The Character of Holland* (written 1653; printed 1665; reprinted 1672) l. 80.

9–12. Dutch political philosophers (e.g. Grotius) used the Batavians, who rebelled against the Romans in AD 69, as a legitimising precedent for the seventeenth-century Dutch nation (see Schama, *Embarrassment of Riches* 75–81); cp. Marvell ll. 81–4.

11. new commonwealth] The Dutch republic was formed at the end of the sixteenth century after a war of independence against Philip II of Spain.

Venetians do not more uncouthly ride
Than did their lubber state mankind bestride.
15   Their sway became 'em with as ill a mien
As their own paunches swell above their chin:
Yet is their empire no true growth, but humour,
And only two kings' touch can cure the tumour.
As Cato did his Afric fruits display,
20   So we before your eyes their Indies lay;
All loyal English will like him conclude:
Let Caesar live, and Carthage be subdued.

Songs

I

Epithalamium

The day is come, I see it rise
Betwixt the bride's and bridegroom's eyes,
That golden day they wished so long,
Love picked it out amidst the throng;
5   He destined to himself this sun,
And took the reins and drove him on;
In his own beams he dressed him bright,
Yet bid him bring a better night.

14. lubber] a big, clumsy, stupid person.
16. The supposed greed of the Dutch was a commonplace: cp. *The Dutch Boare Dissected, or a Description of Hogg-Land* (1665).
17. humour] fluid in the body.
18. two kings] Charles II and Louis XIV, allies in the war against Holland. *touch*] English kings, including Charles II, touched sufferers from 'the King's Evil' (scrofula) in a ceremony which was thought to cure the disease.
19–22. The comparison of Holland with Carthage had been made during the First and Second Dutch Wars: see *AM* ll. 17–20*n*.   *Cato*] See *AM* ll. 691–2*n*. The climax of Cato's speech, *Delenda est Carthago* ('Carthage must be destroyed') was quoted by Shaftesbury in a speech against Holland on 5 February 1673.   *Caesar*] i.e. Charles II. D. is mixing his classical references, since Cato (234–149 BC) lived under the Republic, long before either Julius (100–44 BC) or Augustus Caesar (63 BC to AD 14).

Song I. From Act III.

The day you wished arrived at last,
10   You wish as much that it were past,
One minute more and night will hide
The bridegroom and the blushing bride.
The virgin now to bed does go:
Take care, O youth, she rise not so;
15   She pants and trembles at her doom,
And fears and wishes thou wouldst come.

The bridegroom comes, he comes apace
With love and fury in his face;
She shrinks away, he close pursues,
20   And prayers and threats at once does use;
She softly sighing begs delay,
And with her hand puts his away;
Now out aloud for help she cries,
And now despairing shuts her eyes.

II

The Sea Fight

Who ever saw a noble sight,
That never viewed a brave sea fight:
Hang up your bloody colours in the air,
Up with your fights and your nettings prepare,
5   Your merry mates cheer with a lusty bold spright,
Now each man his brindice, and then to the fight:
'St George, St George' we cry,
The shouting Turks reply.
O now it begins, and the gunroom grows hot,
10   Ply it with culverin and with small shot;

22. *puts*] *1691*; put *1673*.
Song II. From Act III.
4. *fights*] screens used to protect the crew.   *nettings*] for protection against missiles and debris, and to prevent boarding.
5. *spright*] spirit.
6. *brindice*] cup in which a health is drunk (*OED*'s only example is from *Amboyna* Act I).
10. *culverin*] large cannon.

Hark, does it not thunder? no 'tis the guns' roar,
The neighbouring billows are turned into gore.
Now each man must resolve to die,
For here the coward cannot fly.
15   Drums and trumpets toll the knell,
And culverins the passing bell.
Now, now they grapple, and now board amain,
Blow up the hatches, they're off all again.
Give 'em a broadside, the dice run at all,
20   Down comes the mast and yard, and tacklings fall.
She grows giddy now like blind Fortune's wheel,
She sinks there, she sinks, she turns up her keel.
Who ever beheld so noble a sight
As this so brave, so bloody sea fight!

19. dice] cube-shaped bullets.
20. tacklings] rigging.

33 Prologue and Epilogue at Oxford, 1673 ('What Greece . . .')

Date and publication. Spoken in July 1673; the year is established by allusions in the Epilogue, and the date 1673 in Folger MS D347. The poems were first printed in *MP* (1684; reprinted 1692); for several MS copies see Beal 402, 415.

Context. London companies visited Oxford at the time of the annual Act in mid-July, and this is the first of the prologues and epilogues which D. wrote for visits by the King's Company (see Macdonald 137–9). The flattering tone of this and subsequent Oxford pieces has been seen as part of a campaign by D. for preferment there, but prologues and epilogues by other writers also express appreciation for the attentive reception which the actors received there in comparison with London (cp. Danchin nos. 123–4). In the early summer of 1673 D. wrote to Rochester: 'I have sent Your Lordship a prologue and epilogue which I made for our players when they went down to Oxford. I heare, since they have succeeded; And by the event your Lordship will judge how easy 'tis to passe any thing upon an University; and how grosse flattery the learned will endure' (*Letters* 10). For the players' visits to Oxford see W. J. Lawrence, *TLS* 16 January 1930 43, and Sybil Rosenfeld, *RES* xix (1943) 366–75.

Prologue to the University of Oxon

Spoken by Mr Hart at the acting of *The Silent Woman*

¶33. *Prologue.* This Prologue contributes to the controversy between D. and Shadwell over Jonson and the function of drama: Shadwell argued that comedy should instruct, while D. stressed its power to delight (see Richard L. Oden, *Dryden and Shadwell* (1977)). D. had previously praised Shakespeare's natural genius and criticized Jonson in 'Prologue to *The Tempest*', 'Epilogue to *2 Conquest of Granada*' and especially *Defence of the Epilogue* (1672; *Works* xi 203–18). In changing his emphasis here and insisting that learning and artistry are essential for the dramatist who wishes to anatomize human nature, D. is not contradicting but complementing his earlier arguments, and by implication still criticizing those (like Shadwell) who too readily take up Jonson's mantle without his skill (cp. *MF* ll. 165–78). D. may be replying to the distortion of his views presented in the anonymous 'Prologue to *Julius Caesar*' in *Covent Garden Drolery* (1672) (see Paul Hammond, *ES* lxv (1984) 409–19).

Title. For Hart see 'Epilogue to *1 Conquest of Granada*' n.   The Silent Woman] *Epicoene, or The Silent Woman,* by Ben Jonson.

What Greece, when learning flourished, only knew,
Athenian judges, you this day renew.
Here too are annual rites to Pallas done,
And here poetic prizes lost or won.
5   Methinks I see you crowned with olives sit,
And strike a sacred horror from the pit.
A day of doom is this of your decree,
Where ev'n the best are but by mercy free:
A day which none but Jonson durst have wished to see.
10 Here they who long have known the useful stage
Come to be taught themselves to teach the age:
As your commissioners, our poets go
To cultivate the virtue which you sow;
In your Lyceum first themselves refined,
15 And delegated thence to human kind.
But as ambassadors when long from home
For new instructions to their princes come,
So poets who your precepts have forgot
Return, and beg they may be better taught:
20 Follies and faults elsewhere by them are shown,
But by your manners they correct their own.
Th' illiterate writer, emp'ric-like, applies
To minds diseased, unsafe, chance remedies:
The learned in schools, where knowledge first began,
25 Studies with care th' anatomy of man;
Sees virtue, vice and passions in their cause,
And fame from science, not from fortune draws.
So poetry, which is in Oxford made

1–4. In Athens the annual spring festival of the Great Dionysia included a competition between three poets who each offered three tragedies and a satyr play. Plato writes that originally the judgement of performances 'was not left, as it is today, to the catcalls and discordant outcries of the crowd, nor yet to the clapping of applauders; the educated made it their rule to hear the performances through in silence'; this is seen as part of a trend to lawlessness and mob-rule (*Laws* 700c–701c).
3. *Pallas*] Pallas Athena, goddess of wisdom.
6. *horror*] awe, reverend fear (*OED* 4).
7. *doom*] judgement.
14. *Lyceum*] the garden at Athens where Aristotle taught philosophy.
22. *emp'ric-like*] like an untrained doctor acting by trial and error; cp. 'To Dr Charleton' l. 7.
27. *science*] knowledge.

An art, in London only is a trade.
30 There haughty dunces whose unlearnèd pen
Could ne'er spell grammar, would be reading men.
Such build their poems the Lucretian way:
So many huddled atoms make a play,
And if they hit in order by some chance,
35 They call that nature, which is ignorance.
To such a fame let mere town-wits aspire,
And their gay nonsense their own cits admire.
Our poet, could he find forgiveness here,
Would wish it rather than a plaudit there.
40 He owns no crown from those Praetorian bands,
But knows *that* right is in this Senate's hands.
Not impudent enough to hope your praise, ⎫
Low at the Muses' feet his wreath he lays, ⎬
And where he took it up resigns his bays. ⎭
45 Kings make their poets whom themselves think fit,
But 'tis your suffrage makes authentic wit.

Epilogue

Spoken by the same

No poor Dutch peasant, winged with all his fear,
Flies with more haste when the French arms draw near,

30–5. Winn 255 suggests that these lines are an attack on Elkanah Settle; in the *Notes and Observations on the Empress of Morocco* (1674) D. called Settle's play 'a confus'd heap of false Grammar, improper *English*, strain'd Hyperboles, and downright Bulls' (*Works* xvii 84).
32–3. Lucretius taught that matter arose from the chance encounter of atoms; cp. 'To Sir Robert Howard' ll. 29–32.
37. cits] citizens.
40–1. Roman emperors were technically appointed by the Senate, but the power of nomination lay increasingly with the Praetorian Guard, instituted by Augustus as the imperial bodyguard. Its loyalty had to be secured by donatives of up to five times the annual pay on the accession of each emperor.
43. Muses'] 'Muses' in *MP* could be either a singular or plural possessive.
46. suffrage] approval (*OED* 5).

Epilogue.
1–2. France invaded Holland in June 1672; after considerable initial success

Than we with our poetic train come down
For refuge hither from th' infected town;
5   Heaven for our sins this summer has thought fit
To visit us with all the plagues of wit.
    A French troupe first swept all things in its way,
But those hot monsieurs were too quick to stay;
Yet to our cost in that short time we find
10   They left their itch of novelty behind.
    Th' Italian Merry-Andrews took their place,
And quite debauched the stage with lewd grimace;
Instead of wit and humours, your delight
Was there to see two hobby-horses fight;
15   Stout Scaramoucha with rush lance rode in,
And ran a tilt at centaur Arlequin.
For love you heard how amorous asses brayed,
And cats in gutters gave their serenade.
Nature was out of countenance, and each day
20   Some new-born monster shown you for a play.
    But when all failed, to strike the stage quite dumb
Those wicked engines called machines are come.
Thunder and lightning now for wit are played,
And shortly scenes in Lapland will be laid:
25   Art magic is for poetry professed,
And cats and dogs, and each obscener beast

---

the French troops were hampered by the deliberate flooding and resistance
led by William of Orange. France was acting in alliance with England.
7–20. For the foreign actors see 'Prologue to *Arviragus* revived' l. *6n.*
8, 10. hot . . . itch] with sexual innuendo.
11. Merry-Andrews] clowns (*OED*'s first example).
13. humours] i.e. Jonsonian humours comedy.
16. Arlequin] This spelling in *MP* recalls the original Italian *arlecchino*, a
character in Italian *commedia dell'arte.*
22–30. Davenant's *Macbeth*, staged by the Duke's Company at Dorset Garden in February 1673, used elaborate stage machinery: cp. Anon, 'Epilogue
to *The Ordinary*' (*c.* April 1673): 'Now empty shows must want of sense
supply, / Angels shall dance, and *Macbeths* Witches fly: / You shall have
storms, thunder & lightning too / And Conjurers raise spirits to your view:'
(Danchin no. 161).
24. Lapland] supposedly the abode of witches; cp. *PL* ii 665.
25. Art magic] the magic art (*OED* 11a).
26–7. The Egyptians' worship of animals, including cats and dogs; derided
by Juvenal in *Satire* xv 1–8.

To which Egyptian dotards once did bow
Upon our English stage are worshipped now.
Witchcraft reigns there, and raises to renown
30   Macbeth, the Simon Magus of the town.
Fletcher's despised, your Jonson out of fashion,
And wit the only drug in all the nation.
In this low ebb our wares to you are shown, ⎫
By you those staple authors' worth is known, ⎬
35   For wit's a manufacture of your own. ⎭
When you, who only can, their scenes have praised,
We'll boldly back, and say their price is raised.

30. Simon Magus] the sorcerer in Acts viii 9.
31. There are no recorded performances of Jonson or Fletcher in the (admittedly very incomplete) evidence in *LS* for the first half of 1673.
32. drug] commodity in no demand (*OED* 2).

34 Prologue and Epilogue at the Opening of the New House

Date and publication. Spoken 26 March 1674. First printed in *MP* (1684; reprinted 1692). MS copies in Huntington Library MS EL 8923 and 8925 (fully collated in *Works*) and MS Nicholas Fisher (privately owned, not in Beal) preserve variants which probably derive from the playhouse.

Context. The new Theatre Royal Drury Lane, designed by Wren, was opened with a revival of *The Beggar's Bush* by John Fletcher. Whereas the Duke's Theatre in Dorset Garden had cost £9,000, this theatre cost £4,000 and was far from elaborate, lacking the scenic facilities of its rival (see Richard Leacroft, *The Development of the English Playhouse* (1973) 89–97). A reply to this prologue, defending the expense of the Duke's Company productions, was composed (perhaps by Shadwell) for the operatic *Tempest* in April 1674 (BL MS Egerton 2623; Danchin no. 175c).

A Prologue spoken at the Opening of the New House, Mar. 26. 1674

A plain-built house after so long a stay
Will send you half unsatisfied away,
When, fall'n from your expected pomp, you find
A bare convenience only is designed.
5 You who each day can theatres behold
Like Nero's palace, shining all with gold,
Our mean ungilded stage will scorn, we fear,
And for the homely room disdain the cheer.
Yet now cheap druggets to a mode are grown, ⎫
10 And a plain suit (since we can make but one) ⎬
Is better than to be by tarnished gaudery known. ⎭

¶**34**. *Prologue*.
6. Nero built a huge palace called the *Domus Aurea* ('Golden House'), parts of which were inlaid with gold. It was designed with angled vistas and buildings giving the effect of cities, comparable to elaborate stage sets (Suetonius, *Nero* 31). Nero was also notorious for his patronage of, and participation in, extravagant dramatic performances.   *gold*] The Duke's Theatre had a carved and gilded proscenium arch.
9. *druggets*] coarse woollen cloths; cp. Wycherley: 'the vain fopps will take up Druggets, and embroider 'em' (*The Country Wife* V iv 74–5; composed *c*. 1672–4).

They who are by your favours wealthy made,
With mighty sums may carry on the trade:
We, broken bankers, half destroyed by fire, ⎫
15   With our small stock to humble roofs retire; ⎬
Pity our loss, while you their pomp admire. ⎭
For fame and honour we no longer strive,
We yield in both, and only beg to live;
Unable to support their vast expense
20   Who build and treat with such magnificence,
That like th' ambitious monarchs of the age,
They give the law to our provincial stage.
Great neighbours enviously promote excess,
While they impose their splendour on the less:
25   But only fools, and they of vast estate, ⎫
Th' extremity of modes will imitate, ⎬
The dangling knee-fringe, and the bib-cravat. ⎭
Yet if some pride with want may be allowed,
We in our plainness may be justly proud:
30   Our royal master willed it should be so,
Whate'er he's pleased to own can need no show:
That sacred name gives ornament and grace,
And like his stamp makes basest metals pass.
'Twere folly now a stately pile to raise,
35   To build a playhouse while you throw down plays;
Whilst scenes, machines, and empty operas reign,
And for the pencil you the pen disdain;
While troops of famished Frenchmen hither drive,
And laugh at those upon whose alms they live:
40   Old English authors vanish, and give place
To these new conquerors of the Norman race;

12–16. Answered in the Prologue to the operatic *Tempest*: 'Wee, as the ffathers of the stage have said, / To treat you here, a Vast expence have made: / What they have gott from you in Chests is laid, / Or is for purchac'd Lands, or houses paid' (ll. 1–4; Danchin no. 175). For other attacks by Duffett and Fane on the lavish productions at the Duke's Theatre, see Danchin nos. 166, 181 and 196.

27. knee-fringe] the trimming on pantaloons; see C. W. Cunnington and P. Cunnington, *Handbook of English Costume in the Seventeenth Century* (1966) 150; the *bib-cravat* is illustrated on 141.

37. pencil] paint brush.

38–9. For visiting French troupes see 'Prologue to *Arviragus* revived' and

More tamely than your fathers you submit,
You're now grown vassals to 'em in your wit.
Mark, when they play, how our fine fops advance ⎤
45 The mighty merits of these men of France,   ⎬
Keep time, cry '*Ben*', and humour the cadence: ⎦
Well, please yourselves, but sure 'tis understood
That French machines have ne'er done England good.
I would not prophesy our house's fate,
50 But while vain shows and scenes you over-rate,
'Tis to be feared——
That as a fire the former house o'erthrew,
Machines and tempests will destroy the new.

Epilogue

Though what our prologue said was sadly true, ⎤
Yet, gentlemen, our homely house is new,   ⎬
A charm that seldom fails with wicked you.   ⎦
A country lip may have the velvet touch,   ⎤
5   Though she's no lady you may think her such: ⎬
A strong imagination may do much.   ⎦
But you, loud sirs, who through your curls look big,
Critics in plume and white vallancy wig,
Who lolling on our foremost benches sit,

'Epilogue at Oxford, 1673'. The opera *Ariane* was performed in French by
the Royal Academy of Music at the Theatre Royal on 30 March 1674 (see
Danchin no. 174).
46. Ben] i.e. Bien, 'well'; *MSS* have 'bon' ('good').   *humour*] adapt to, fit.
cadence] accent (*OED* 2c), here stressed on the second syllable, as in the
French; cp. *Marriage A-la-Mode* V i 16.
48. French machines] with a pun on political 'machinations' (cp. *OED* v. 1);
Works suggests that the phrase also meant 'dildoes', but without evidence.
53. Machines and tempests] Tempests and Operas *MSS*, probably a playhouse
variant. The operatic *Tempest* was being prepared at the Duke's Theatre for
production in April (though Winn 583–4 suggests that it was already on stage
by the date of this prologue).

Epilogue.
7. through] thro' *MSS*; tho' *MP* (probably a misprint).
8. white] shock *MSS*; i.e. with rough, thick hair (*OED*'s first example 1681);

10   And still charge first, the true forlorn of wit,
     Whose favours, like the sun, warm where you roll,
     Yet you, like him, have neither heat nor soul;
     So may your hats your foretops never press,
     Untouched your ribbons, sacred be your dress;
15   So may you slowly to old age advance,
     And have th' excuse of youth for ignorance;
     So may fop-corner full of noise remain,
     And drive far off the dull attentive train;
     So may your midnight scourings happy prove,
20   And morning batteries force your way to love;
     So may not France your warlike hands recall,
     But leave you by each other's swords to fall:
     As you come here to ruffle vizard punk
     When sober, rail and roar when you are drunk.
25   But to the wits we can some merit plead,
     And urge what by themselves has oft been said:
     Our house relieves the ladies from the frights

---

probably a playhouse variant.   *vallancy*] *OED*, citing only this instance,
explains it as 'a form of wig' from the surname Vallancey; Kinsley glosses it
as 'fringing the face' from 'valance'.

10. forlorn] forlorn hope, vanguard.

12. Walter Charleton argued that bodies, such as the sun, which had '*Atoms of Heat*, or *Calorifick Atoms*' were not hot in themselves but only had a power to create heat: 'when they do Actually emit them . . . then may they be said to be *Actually Hot* . . . but while they contain them within themselves . . . they are Hot only *Potentially*' (*Physiologia Epicuro-Gassendo-Charletoniana* (1654) 294).

13. 'There are some well-bred Gentlemen have so much Reverence for their Perruque, that they wou'd refuse to be Grandees of your *Spain*, for fear of putting on their Hats' (Wycherley, *Gentleman Dancing-Master* (performed 1672) IV i 140–2); cp. D.'s 'Epilogue to *The Man of Mode*' ll. 25–6.

14. ribbons] either the decorations on pantaloon breeches, or the bows which sometimes tied the front locks on wigs (Cunnington and Cunnington, *Handbook of English Costume* 150–2, 164).

17. fop-corner] See 'Prologue to *Marriage A-la-Mode*' l. 3n.

19–20. scourings] Oldham writes of 'the drunken Scowrers of the Street, / Flush'd with success of warlike Deeds perform'd, / Of Constables subdu'd, and Brothels storm'd' ('A Satyr, In Imitation of the Third of Juvenal' ll. 406–8; written 1682).

23. vizard punk] See 'Prologue to *2 Conquest of Granada*' l. 13n.

27–30. This was answered in the Prologue to the operatic *Tempest*: 'They

Of ill-paved streets, and long dark winter nights;
The Flanders horses from a cold bleak road,
30   Where bears in furs dare scarcely look abroad;
The audience from worn plays and fustian stuff
Of rhyme, more nauseous than three boys in buff.
Though in their house the poets' heads appear,
We hope we may presume their wits are here.
35   The best which they reserved they now will play, ⎫
For, like kind cuckolds, though w' have not the way ⎬
To please, we'll find you abler men who may.   ⎭
If they should fail, for last recruits we breed   ⎫
A troop of frisking monsieurs to succeed: ⎬
40   You know the French sure cards at time of need. ⎭

scoff at us, & Libell the high wayes. / Tis fitt we, for our faults, rebukes
should meet, / The Citty ought to mend those of ye street' (ll. 32–4).

30. Echoes Orrery's *Mustapha* (II i 230), where Solyman recalls campaigns in
winter 'When in thick Furs, Bears durst not look abroad'. The play was first
performed in 1665, but remained in the repertory of the Duke's Company
(*Works*).

31. Also answered: 'Had we not for your pleasure found new wayes, / You
still had rusty Arras had, & thredbare playes' (ll. 25–6).

32. Noyes suggests a reference to the droll, *The Three Merry Boys*, adapted
from Fletcher's *Rollo Duke of Normandy* and printed in *The Wits* (1662, 1672).

33. The Dorset Garden theatre was decorated with portraits of poets.

33–4. Also answered: 'With the best poets heads our house we gracd, /
Which we in honour to the Poets placd. / "Too much of the old witt they
have; 'Tis true; / But they must look for little of the new.' (ll. 35–8). The
King's Company did indeed have rights to a larger share of pre-Restoration
drama than the Duke's Company (*LS* 140, 151–2). The only new play which
they are known to have produced before the end of the season was Lee's *The
Tragedy of Nero*; their other recorded productions were revivals of Shirley and
D. (*LS* 214–17).

40. i.e. 'You know that anything French is a sure winning card to play'.

35 Song from *The State of Innocence*

Date and publication. The play was composed in spring 1674, probably to provide an opera to compete with the operatic *Tempest* and other spectacular productions at the Duke's Theatre. It was not performed, probably because of the expense of the staging (Winn 262). Though it was not published in 1674 by being performed, and was not printed until 1677, it appears at this point in the chronological sequence because MS copies circulated, 'many hundred' according to D. in his Preface to *1677*. For the eight surviving MS copies see Beal 426–7, and for a discussion of their textual significance see Marion H. Hamilton, *SB* vi (1954) 237–46. *The State of Innocence, and Fall of Man: An Opera* was published by Herringman in 1677 (*SR* 17 April 1674; *TC* 12 February 1677; advertised in the *London Gazette* 8–12 February); reprinted 1678, 1684 (three times), 1690, 1692, 1695 (twice). No music survives, but for the musicality of the Song see Winn, *When Beauty* 219–21.

Sources. The opera is based on *PL*, and this passage from Act III representing Eve's dream before her fall is drawn from *PL* v 28–93. For D.'s general interest in Milton see J. R. Mason.

Song

A vision, where a tree rises loaden with fruit; four spirits rise with it, and draw a canopy out of the tree; other spirits dance about the tree in deformed shapes; after the dance an angel enters with a woman habited like Eve.

Angel, singing. Look up, look up and see
       What heaven prepares for thee;
       Look up, and this fair fruit behold,
       Ruddy it smiles, and rich with streaks of
        gold.

5   The loaded branches downward bend,
       Willing they stoop, and thy fair hand attend;
       Fair mother of mankind, make haste
       And bless, and bless thy senses with the taste.
Woman.   No; 'tis forbidden, I
10   In tasting it shall die.
Angel.   Say who enjoined this harsh command.
Woman.   'Twas heaven, and who can heaven
       withstand?

Angel.   Why was it made so fair, why placed in
                sight?
              Heaven is too good to envy man's delight.
15   See, we before thy face will try
              What thou so fear'st, and will not die.

The angel takes the fruit and gives to the spirits who danced; they immediately put off their deformed shapes and appear angels.

Angel, singing. Behold what a change on a sudden is here!
              How glorious in beauty, how bright they
                appear!
              From spirits deformed they are deities made,
20   Their pinions at pleasure the clouds can
                invade;

The angel gives to the woman, who eats.

              Till equal in honour they rise
              With him who commands in the skies:
              Then taste without fear, and be happy and
                wise.

Woman.   Ah, now I believe; such a pleasure I find
25   As enlightens my eyes, and enlivens my
                mind.

The spirits who are turned angels fly up when they have tasted.

              I only repent
              I deferred my consent.

Angel.   Now wiser experience has taught you to
                prove
              What a folly it is
30   Out of fear to shun bliss.
              To the joy that's forbidden we eagerly move,
              It enhances the price, and increases the love.

Chorus of both. To the joy, etc.

Two angels descend; they take the woman each by the hand and fly up with her out of sight. The angel who sung and the spirits who held the canopy at the same instant sink down with the tree.

¶**35**. *17. Angel*] Ed.; Angels *1677*.
20. pinions] wings.

36 Prologue and Epilogue at Oxford, 1674 ('Poets, your subjects . . .')

Date and publication. The Prologue was spoken 6 July and Epilogue 18 July 1674 according to MS copy in Northants Record Office I.L. 4101 (Beal 401, 414); the year is confirmed by the title in *MP*. *MP* (1684) prints the Prologue and two texts of the Epilogue (269–71 (hereafter '*MPa*') and 275–7 ('*MPb*')); in the second edition of *MP* (1692) only *MPa* is reprinted. The reason for the duplication is unclear. *MPa* is followed here, with substantive variants from *MPb* noted. For the MSS copies see Beal 400–1, 414. In BodL MS Rawl. Poet. 81 the Prologue and Epilogue are conflated to form a single 'Epilogue to yᵉ University' (Danchin no. 177c); as it replaces the compliment to Bathurst with one to Edmund Boldero, Vice-Chancellor of Cambridge in 1674, Danchin concludes that this text was put together for a performance at Cambridge in that year. There is no evidence that D. was responsible for the revision.

Context. The 1674 visit of the King's Company to the annual Act at Oxford was the subject of a letter from the King to the Vice-Chancellor requesting that their stay be extended from twelve to twenty days (Sybil Rosenfeld, *RES* xix (1943) 368).

Prologue to the University of Oxford, 1674

Spoken by Mr Hart

Poets, your subjects, have their parts assigned
T' unbend and to divert their sovereign's mind;
When tired with following nature, you think fit
To seek repose in the cool shades of wit,
5   And from the sweet retreat with joy survey
What rests, and what is conquered, of the way.
Here free yourselves from envy, care and strife,
You view the various turns of human life:
Safe in our scene, through dangerous courts you go,
10   And undebauched the vice of cities know.
Your theories are here to practice brought,

¶**36**. *Prologue. Title.* For Hart see 'Epilogue to *1 Conquest of Granada*' *n.*

As in mechanic operations wrought;
And man the little world before you set,
As once the sphere of crystal showed the great.
15 Blessed sure are you above all mortal kind,
If to your fortunes you can suit your mind;
Content to see, and shun, those ills we show,
And crimes on theatres alone to know.
With joy we bring what our dead authors writ,
20 And beg from you the value of their wit,
That Shakespeare's, Fletcher's and great Jonson's claim
May be renewed from those who gave them fame.
None of our living poets dare appear,
For Muses so severe are worshipped here
25 That conscious of their faults they shun the eye,⎫
And as profane from sacred places fly,   ⎬
Rather than see th' offended god, and die.   ⎭
We bring no imperfections but our own,
Such faults as made, are by the makers shown;
30 And you have been so kind that we may boast
The greatest judges still can pardon most.
Poets must stoop when they would please our pit,
Debased ev'n to the level of their wit,
Disdaining that which yet they know will take,
35 Hating themselves what their applause must make:
But when to praise from you they would aspire,

---

12. mechanic] practical.
14. sphere of crystal] either Merlin's globe (*FQ* III ii 19) or Archimedes' sphere (cp. 'Upon the Death of the Lord Hastings' l. *30n*).
19, 23. Cp. 'Epilogue at the Opening of the New House' ll. 33–4*n*.
24. Cp. *nobis non licet esse tam disertis, / qui Musas colimus severiores* ('we who cultivate the severer Muses are not permitted to be so witty': Martial IX xi 16–17).
26. profane] not initiated into esoteric knowledge (*OED* 1b), with echoes of Horace, *odi profanum vulgus* ('I hate the profane crowd': *Carm.* III i 1) and Virgil, *procul este, profani* ('far hence be souls profane' (D.'s translation): *Aen.* vi 258).
27. Cp. Exodus xxxiii 20.
34. take] please.
35. Hating themselves] i.e. themselves hating.

Though they like eagles mount, your Jove is higher;
So far your knowledge all their power transcends,
As what *should be* beyond what *is* extends.

Epilogue

Spoken by Mrs Marshall

Oft has our poet wished this happy seat
Might prove his fading Muse's last retreat:
I wondered at his wish, but now I find
He sought for quiet and content of mind,
5 Which noiseful towns and courts can never know,
And only in the shades like laurels grow.
Youth, ere it sees the world, here studies rest,
And age, returning thence, concludes it best.
What wonder if we court that happiness
10 Yearly to share, which hourly you possess,

---

37. The eagle was Jove's bird.

Epilogue. Title. Mrs Marshall] *MPb, MP (1692)*; Mrs Boutell *MPa, Northants MS. Mrs Marshall*] Rebecca Marshall (*fl.* 1660–83), actress with the King's Company from the early 1660s. Her roles for D. included Lyndaraxa in *The Conquest of Granada*, Doralice in *Marriage A-la-Mode*, Lucretia in *The Assignation*, Isabinda in *Amboyna* and Nourmahal in *Aureng-Zebe* (Highfill x 106–8). *Mrs Boutell*] See 'Prologue to *Secret Love*, Spoken by the Woman' *n*. *1–2*. These lines have often been read as autobiographical on D.'s part (e.g. by Roswell G. Ham, *MLN* xlix (1934) 324–32; Winn 270), and there is no doubt that D. was increasingly attracted by the possibility of retirement from the pressures of having to please courtiers and audiences: see the Dedications to *Marriage A-la-Mode* (1673) and *Aureng-Zebe* (1675), 'Prologue and Epilogue at Oxford, 1673' and 'Prologue at Oxford, 1675'. However, in prologues and epilogues 'our poet' normally refers to the playwright, not the author of the prologue or epilogue, and the identity of the playwright in this instance is unknown; from 'Prologue' ll. 19–23 he was evidently not a contemporary. If the play was by Jonson, as it had been in 1673 and might be again (see 'Prologue' l. 21), the reference might recall Jonson's famous dedication of *Volpone* to the University of Oxford, and Oxford's exceptional award of an honorary degree to Jonson in 1619. See also 'Prologue at Oxford, 1676' ll. 36–7*n*.
4. sought for] *MPa*; here sought *MPb*.

Teaching e'en you, while the vexed world we show,
Your peace to value more, and better know.
'Tis all we can return for favours past,
Whose holy memory shall ever last,
15 For patronage from him whose care presides
O'er every noble art, and every science guides:
Bathurst, a name the learned with reverence know,
And scarcely more to his own Virgil owe;
Whose age enjoys but what his youth deserved,
20 To rule those Muses whom before he served.
His learning, and untainted manners too,
We find, Athenians, are derived to you;
Such ancient hospitality there rests   ⎫
In yours, as dwelt in the first Grecian breasts, ⎬
25 Whose kindness was religion to their guests. ⎭
Such modesty did to our sex appear,   ⎫
As had there been no laws we need not fear, ⎬
Since each of you was our protector here: ⎭
Converse so chaste, and so strict virtue shown,
30 As might Apollo with the Muses own.
Till our return we must despair to find
Judges so just, so knowing, and so kind.

16. science] area of knowledge.
17. Bathurst] Ralph Bathurst (1620–1704), FRS, President of Trinity College, Oxford, Vice-Chancellor 1673–6. He wrote some English and Latin poems, had been a student of medicine, and was a member of the group led by John Wilkins which encouraged the new science in the late 1650s.
22. Athenians] Cp. 'Prologue at Oxford, 1673' ll. 1–4*n*.   *derived*] conveyed, transmitted (*OED* 4).
24–5. The Greeks held hospitality to be a sacred duty.
25. Whose] *MPa*; Where *MPb*.

37 Epilogue to *Calisto*

Date and publication. The masque was composed in the autumn of 1674, and after some delays was performed at court on 15 and 16 February 1675. The Epilogue was first printed in *MP* (1684, reprinted 1692) without attribution; it was not included in the 1675 edition of *Calisto*, which had Crowne's own Epilogue. Though D.'s Epilogue may not have been spoken in 1675, it seems appropriate to include it at this point in the chronological sequence rather than under 1684.

Context. Calisto was written by John Crowne at the command of the Duke of York to provide a text for seven court ladies to act, and depicts Jupiter's unsuccessful attempt to seduce the chaste nymph Calisto. For its staging see E. Boswell, *The Restoration Court Stage* (1932) 177–227.

Authorship. The poem was first attributed to D. in *MP* (1702). W. B. Gardner (*Prologues and Epilogues of John Dryden* (1951) 341–5) questioned D.'s authorship on four counts: (i) since D., the Poet Laureate, had been passed over for this commission in favour of Crowne, he is unlikely to have contributed an Epilogue; (ii) parallels between this poem and Crowne's own Epilogue printed with the play suggest common authorship; (iii) the Epilogue in *MP* may have been the original one which was dropped because of undiplomatic references to the Dutch War in ll. 21–8; (iv) the 1702 attribution could have been an attempt by Tonson to enhance the value of his publication after D.'s death and 'about the time of Crowne's death'. Kinsley convincingly countered these claims: (i) Crowne admits in his preface that the commission was exceptionally troublesome, and says that the play would have been much better if D. had written it; so Crowne had reason to seek D.'s help with an Epilogue, and D. little reason to resent not having the commission himself; (ii) Crowne's Epilogue and the Epilogue in *MP* bear only a general resemblance; (iii) ll. 21–8 are not undiplomatic, but complimentary; (iv) Crowne did not die until 1712. Winn 271 points out that Crowne and D. were friendly, for they had just collaborated on the *Notes and Observations on The Empress of Morocco* (1674), and that when the Epilogue was printed in 1684 Henrietta Wentworth had become Monmouth's mistress, an association from which D. might well wish to distance himself by keeping the poem anonymous. We may also note that although the poem is a late addition to *MP*, and is not printed with D.'s other prologues and epilogues, it is listed with them (out of its proper sequence) on the contents page. *Works* omits the poem silently, but the weight of the evidence is thus firmly in favour of D.'s authorship.

Epilogue intended to have been spoken by the Lady Henr. Mar. Wentworth when *Calisto* was acted at court

As Jupiter I made my court in vain,
I'll now assume my native shape again.
I'm weary to be so unkindly used,
And would not be a god to be refused.
5   State grows uneasy when it hinders love,
A glorious burden which the wise remove.
Now as a nymph I need not sue nor try
The force of any lightning but the eye.
Beauty and youth more than a god command;
10 No Jove could e'er the force of these withstand.
'Tis here that sovereign power admits dispute,
Beauty sometimes is justly absolute.
Our sullen Catos, whatsoe'er they say,
Even while they frown and dictate laws, obey.
15 You, mighty Sir, our bonds more easy make,
And gracefully what all must suffer take,
Above those forms the grave affect to wear,
For 'tis not to be wise to be severe.
True wisdom may some gallantry admit,
20 And soften business with the charms of wit.
These peaceful triumphs with your cares you bought,
And from the midst of fighting nations brought;
You only hear it thunder from afar,
And sit in peace the arbiter of war.

¶**37**. *Title*. Lady Henrietta Maria Wentworth (1660–86), who played Jupiter in the masque, was Maid of Honour to the Duchess of York; she later became the mistress of the Duke of Monmouth and possibly also of the Earl of Mulgrave (see *Court Satires of the Restoration*, edited by J. H. Wilson (1976) 82, 103).

8. lightning] taken as a sign of Jupiter's power.

13. Catos] Cato the Censor (234–149 BC) promoted stern traditional morality and conservative legislation in Rome.

15. You] the King.

17. Above] i.e. You are above.

21–4. The Third Dutch War, begun in 1672, had been ended by the Treaty of

25 Peace, the loathed manna which hot brains despise,
You knew its worth, and made it early prize;
And in its happy leisure sit and see
The promises of more felicity:
Two glorious nymphs of your one godlike line,
30 Whose morning rays like noontide strike and shine;
Whom you to suppliant monarchs shall dispose,
To bind your friends and to disarm your foes.

Westminster (9 February 1674), and peace was confirmed by a maritime treaty in December 1674, securing free commerce. This left the Dutch still at war with France.

25. *manna*] the food from heaven which the Israelites ate in the wilderness (Exodus xvi).

29–32. Referring to the Duke of York's two daughters: Mary (aged 12) played Calisto, and Anne (aged 10) played Psyche. As Mary was second in line to the throne, her marriage was an important political question, and alliances with William of Orange and the Dauphin of France had already been mooted. She married William in 1677; Anne married Prince George of Denmark in 1683.

29. one] probably the seventeenth-century spelling of 'own' (see *OED*), as well as forming an antithesis to *two*.

38 Epitaph on the Marquis of Winchester

Date and publication. The inscription on the monument in the church at Englefield, Berkshire (see Plate 4), probably dates from soon after the Marquis's death on 5 March 1675. The lines were first printed in *Miscellaneous Poems and Translations by Several Hands*, published by Bernard Lintott in 1712. The present text is taken from the monument.

Context. John Paulet, Marquis of Winchester (1598–1675), a Roman Catholic and strong supporter of Charles I, defended Basing House, Hampshire, against the Parliamentarian forces in a famous siege from August 1643 to October 1645. After the Restoration he retired to his house at Englefield. Milton, Jonson and others had written lines on the death of his first wife in 1631.

Epitaph on the Marquis of Winchester

He who in impious times untainted stood,
And 'midst rebellion durst be just and good;
Whose arms asserted, and whose sufferings more
Confirmed the cause for which he fought before,
5 Rests here, rewarded by an heavenly Prince
For what his earthly could not recompense.
Pray, reader, that such times no more appear,
Or, if they happen, learn true honour here.
Ark of thy age's faith and loyalty,
10 Which, to preserve them, heaven confined in thee,
Few subjects could a King like thine deserve,
And fewer such a King so well could serve.
Blessed King, blessed subject, whose exalted state
By sufferings rose, and gave the law to fate.
15 Such souls are rare: but mighty patterns given
To earth were meant for ornaments to heaven.

¶**38**. *Title.* Ed.; Epitaph on the Monument of the Marquis of Winchester *1712; no title on monument.*
1. untainted] *monument*; undaunted *1712.*

39 Prologue and Epilogue to *Aureng-Zebe*

Date and publication. The play was first performed 17 November 1675 by the King's Company at the Theatre Royal. *Aureng-Zebe: A Tragedy* was published by Herringman in 1676 (*SR* 29 November 1675; *TC* 5 May 1676; advertised in the *London Gazette* 17–21 February 1676); reprinted 1685, 1690, 1692, 1694, 1699. It was dedicated to the Earl of Mulgrave. For Purcell's later song for this play see Curtis Price, *Henry Purcell* 55–7.

Prologue

Our author by experience finds it true,
'Tis much more hard to please himself than you;
And out of no feigned modesty this day
Damns his laborious trifle of a play:
5 Not that it's worse than what before he writ,
But he has now another taste of wit;
And to confess a truth (though out of time)
Grows weary of his long-loved mistress, rhyme.
Passion's too fierce to be in fetters bound,
10 And nature flies him like enchanted ground.
What verse can do, he has performed in this,
Which he presumes the most correct of his;
But spite of all his pride, a secret shame
Invades his breast at Shakespeare's sacred name:
15 Awed when he hears his godlike Romans rage,
He in a just despair would quit the stage,

¶**39**. *Prologue.*
5–22. *Aureng-Zebe* was the last of D.'s rhymed heroic plays. In the Epistle Dedicatory he says: 'I desire to be no longer the *Sisyphus* of the Stage; to rowl up a Stone with endless labour (which to follow the proverb, *gathers no Mosse*) and which is perpetually falling down again. I never thought my self very fit for an Employment, where many of my Predecessors have excell'd me in all kinds; and some of my Contemporaries, even in my own partial Judgment, have out-done me in *Comedy*' (sig. A4ʳ).
10. Cp. Morat in *Aureng-Zebe*: 'like inchanted ground, / Flies from my sight, before 'tis fully found' (69).
11. verse] rhyming couplets.

And to an age less polished, more unskilled,
Does with disdain the foremost honours yield.
As with the greater dead he dares not strive,
20   He would not match his verse with those who live:
Let him retire, betwixt two ages cast,
The first of this, and hindmost of the last.
A losing gamester, let him sneak away,
He bears no ready money from the play.
25   The fate which governs poets thought it fit
He should not raise his fortunes by his wit.
The clergy thrive, and the litigious bar;
Dull heroes fatten with the spoils of war:
All southern vices, heaven be praised, are here,
30   But wit's a luxury you think too dear.
When you to cultivate the plant are loath,
'Tis a shrewd sign 'twas never of your growth:
And wit in northern climates will not blow,
Except, like orange trees, 'tis housed from snow.
35   There needs no care to put a playhouse down,
'Tis the most desert place of all the town.
We and our neighbours, to speak proudly, are
Like monarchs, ruined with expensive war,
While, like wise English, unconcerned you sit,
40   And see us play the tragedy of wit.

---

17. For these criticisms of Elizabethan and Jacobean drama cp. 'Epilogue to *2 Conquest of Granada*'.

18. disdain] indignation, vexation (*OED* 2).

24. 'His contract with the King's Company had now become a liability: as an independent playwright, he would have received the third day's profits, but as a sharer, he had to suffer from the general indebtedness of the company' (Winn 276).

27–30. Quoted in *Poeta De Tristibus* (1682) among examples of contemporary poets' 'unmerciful damnings both of the Times and one another' (sig. A2ᵛ); cp. 'Epilogue to *The Unhappy Favourite*' ll. 3–11, 16–19.

29. southern vices] Italian music and French opera (Winn).

33. blow] flourish.

36. desert] The spelling *desart* in *1676* reflects contemporary pronunciation.

37. our neighbours] The Duke's Company; but the King's Company was in much greater financial difficulties (Winn, *When Beauty* 244–5).

38. See 'Epilogue to *Calisto*' ll. 21–4*n*.

Epilogue

A pretty task! and so I told the fool,
Who needs would undertake to please by rule:
He thought that, if his characters were good,
The scenes entire, and freed from noise and blood,
5   The action great, yet circumscribed by time,
The words not forced, but sliding into rhyme,
The passions raised and calmed by just degrees,
As tides are swelled, and then retire to seas;
He thought, in hitting these, his business done,
10   Though he, perhaps, has failed in every one:
But, after all, a poet must confess
His art's like physic, but a happy guess.
Your pleasure on your fancy must depend:
The lady's pleased, just as she likes her friend.
15   'No song! no dance! no show!' he fears you'll say:
You love all naked beauties but a play.
He much mistakes your methods to delight, ⎫
And like the French abhors our target fight: ⎬
But those damned dogs can never be i' th' right. ⎭
20   True English hate your monsieur's paltry arts,
For you are all silk-weavers in your hearts.
Bold Britons at a brave bear-garden fray
Are roused, and clattering sticks cry, 'Play, play, play.'

Epilogue.

4. entire] continuous; the play follows the French practice of *la liaison des scènes*.

12. For the image cp. 'Prologue at Oxford, 1673' ll. 22–7.   *but*] only, merely.

18. Sounds of fighting offstage are heard between Acts I and II, following the French habit of not staging battles. This was a change of mind by D., for in 'Of Heroic Plays' (prefixed to *The Conquest of Granada* (1672)) he defended his representation of fighting by citing the example of Shakespeare (*Works* xi 13–14).

21. silk-weavers] Hostile to France because English silk manufacturers at this date could not compete with French producers. In August 1675 a group of London weavers attacked the immigrant Huguenot weavers, 'broke all their materials, and defaced several of their houses' (*CSPD 1675–6* 253).

22–3. For prize-fighting at the Bear Garden in Southwark see Pepys, 27 May, 9 September 1667; 12 April 1669.

Meantime, your filthy foreigner will stare,
25 And mutter to himself, 'Ha, gens barbare!'
And, Gad, 'tis well he mutters; well for him—
Our butchers else would tear him limb from limb.
'Tis true, the time may come your sons may be
Infected with this French civility,
30 But this in after-ages will be done:
Our poet writes a hundred years too soon.
This age comes on too slow, or he too fast,
And early springs are subject to a blast!
Who would excel, when few can make a test
35 Betwixt indifferent writing and the best?
For favours cheap and common who would strive,
Which, like abandoned prostitutes, you give?
Yet scattered here and there I some behold
Who can discern the tinsel from the gold:
40 To these he writes; and if by them allowed,
'Tis their prerogative to rule the crowd.
For he more fears, like a presuming man,
Their votes who cannot judge, than theirs who can.

25. *gens barbare*] 'barbarous people'.
39. *tinsel*] See 'Epilogue to *Secret Love*' l. 13*n*.
40. *allowed*] approved.

40 Epilogue to *The Man of Mode*

Date and publication. The first recorded performance of Etherege's play was on 11 March 1676, by the Duke's Company at Dorset Garden. *The Man of Mode, or, Sʳ Fopling Flutter* was published by Herringman in 1676 (licensed 3 June; *SR* 15 June); reprinted 1684, 1693. There are four MS copies of the Epilogue: BL MSS Sloane 203 and 1458; BodL MS Don.b.8; Nottingham UL MS Portland PwV 203. In Sloane 1458 the lines are in this order: 1–12, additional couplet (see l. 14*n*), 13–14, 17–20, 15–16, 21–2, 27–30, 23–4, 31–4 (25–6 omitted). Kinsley's use of some MS readings to emend *they* to *it* in l. 6, and *vow* to *now* in l. 10, was mistaken, since both readings in *1676* have independent MS support.

Context. Sir George Etherege (?1636–?92) had already written *The Comical Revenge* (1664) and *She wou'd if She cou'd* (1668). Etherege and D. were evidently friends, though the evidence is scarce: D. mentions him in 1673 in a letter to Rochester (*Letters* 10); in 1676 he refers to him as 'gentle George' in *MF* l. 151; and in 1686 D. writes the verse letter 'To Sir George Etherege'. This Epilogue for the Duke's Company may signal D.'s interest in a move from the troubled King's Company; see Winn 285 and 'Prologue to *Aureng-Zebe*' l. 24*n*. According to BL MS Sloane 1458 it was spoken by William Smith, who played Sir Fopling.

The Epilogue

Most modern wits such monstrous fools have shown,
They seemed not of heaven's making, but their own.
Those nauseous harlequins in farce may pass,
But there goes more to a substantial ass!
5 Something of man must be exposed to view,
That, gallants, they may more resemble you.
Sir Fopling is a fool so nicely writ
The ladies would mistake him for a wit,

¶**40**. *1–2*. Cp. 'Prologue to *The Assignation*' ll. 24–5.
3. harlequins] The troupe led by Scaramouche had played at court from June to October 1675; cp. Duffett's 'Prologue to *Every Man Out of his Humour*' (July 1675; Danchin no. 199), and D.'s 'Epilogue at Oxford, 1673' l. 16.
4. there goes more to] more is needed for the making of.
6. they] The antecedent is *fools*.
7. nicely] exactly, discerningly.

And when he sings, talks loud, and cocks, would cry,
10   'I vow, methinks he's pretty company,
    So brisk, so gay, so travelled, so refined!'
    As he took pains to graff upon his kind:
    True fops help nature's work, and go to school
    To file and finish God A'mighty's fool.
15   Yet none Sir Fopling him or him can call:
    He's knight o' the shire, and represents ye all.
    From each he meets he culls whate'er he can,
    Legion's his name, a people in a man.
    His bulky folly gathers as it goes,
20   And, rolling o'er you, like a snowball grows.
    His various modes from various fathers follow,
    One taught the toss, and one the new French wallow.
    His sword-knot this, his cravat this designed,
    And this, the yard-long snake he twirls behind.
25   From one the sacred perriwig he gained,
    Which wind ne'er blew, nor touch of hat profaned.
    Another's diving bow he did adore,

9. talks loud] Cp. 'alwayes talking; especially too if it be loud and fast, is the sign of a Fool' (Wycherley, *The Plain Dealer* (performed December 1676) V ii 185–6).   *cocks*] (i) struts (ii) cocks his hat (cp. 'Prologue to *An Evening's Love*' l. 15*n*).

12. i.e. 'as if he took pains to graft new accomplishments on to what Nature gave him'.

14. After this line BodL MS adds: 'Labour to put in more, as Master Bayes / Thrumms in Additions to his ten-yeares playes' (so too BL MS Sloane 1458 (subst.) after l. 12). This refers to Buckingham's *The Rehearsal* (1672, third edition revised 1675), which included a caricature of D. as Mr Bayes. The authorship of the couplet is unknown.

15–16. Contemporaries admitted that the play depicted manners accurately, and there were attempts to identify the originals of some characters (see edition by John Barnard (1979) xiii–xiv).

16, 18. Marvell applies these lines to Francis Turner in *Mr. Smirke. Or, The Divine in Mode* (June 1676) 8.

16. knight o' the shire] Member of Parliament for a county.

18. Legion] From Mark v 9; at V ii 350 Mrs Loveit calls Sir Fopling 'Legion of fools, as many devils take thee!'

22. toss] i.e. of the head (*OED*'s first example).   *wallow*] rolling walk (*OED*'s only example).

23. sword-knot] ribbon or tassel tied to the hilt of a sword.

24. snake] a long curl or tail attached to a wig (*OED*'s first example).

26. Cp. 'Epilogue at the Opening of the New House' l. 13*n*.

Which with a shog casts all the hair before,
Till he with full decorum brings it back,
30   And rises with a water spaniel shake.
As for his songs (the ladies' dear delight),
Those sure he took from most of you who write.
Yet every man is safe from what he feared,
For no one fool is hunted from the herd.

28. shog] shake, jerk.

41 Prologue at Oxford, 1676 ('Though actors cannot . . .')

Date and publication. Spoken in July 1676 at the annual Act in Oxford. The year is given in the copy in BodL MS Eng. Poet e.4. It was printed in *MP* (1684; reprinted 1692).

Prologue to the University of Oxford

Though actors cannot much of learning boast,
Of all who want it, we admire it most.
We love the praises of a learnèd pit,
As we remotely are allied to wit.
5 We speak our poet's wit, and trade in ore
Like those who touch upon the golden shore;
Betwixt our judges can distinction make,
Discern how much, and why, our poems take;
Mark if the fools, or men of sense, rejoice,
10 Whether th' applause be only sound, or voice.
When our fop gallants, or our city folly
Clap over-loud, it makes us melancholy:
We doubt that scene which does their wonder raise,
And for their ignorance contemn their praise.
15 Judge then if we who act and they who write
Should not be proud of giving you delight.
London likes grossly, but this nicer pit
Examines, fathoms all the depths of wit:
The ready finger lays on every blot,
20 Knows what should justly please, and what should not.
Nature herself lies open to your view,
You judge by her what draft of her is true;
Where outlines false, and colours seem too faint,

¶**41**. *2. want*] lack.
8. take] please (*OED* 10); succeed (*OED* 11).
10. voice] expressed judgement (*OED* 3), as distinct from mere *sound*.
11. For the divisions in the audience see 'Epilogue to *Marriage A-la-Mode*' l. 37*n*.
14. contemn] scorn, disdain.
17. nicer] more discriminating.

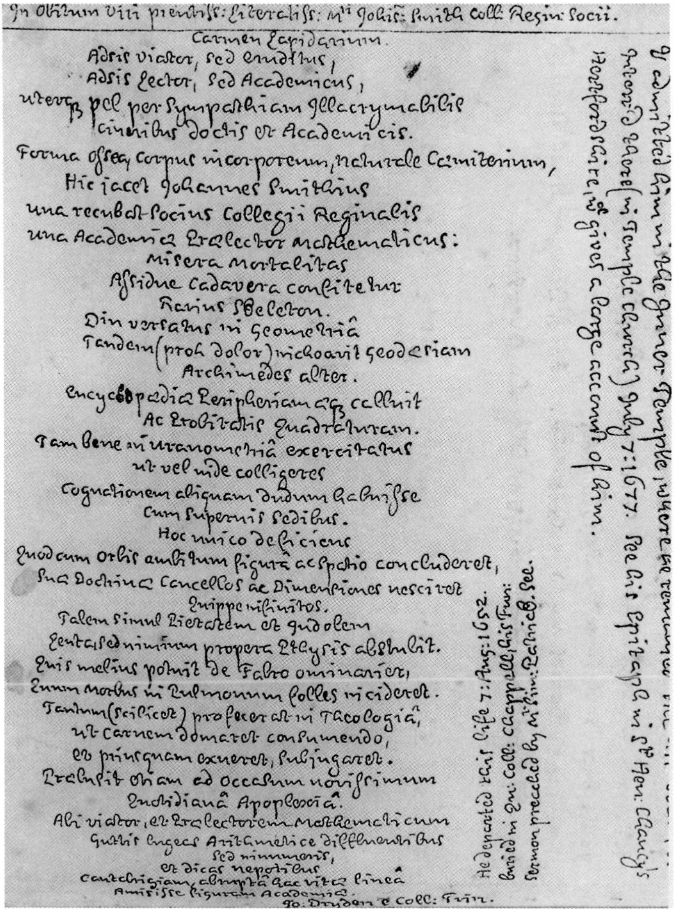

Plate 1. Thomas Baker's transcript of Dryden's 'Carmen Lapidarium', in Cambridge University Library MS Mm1.36 page 406. Reproduced by permission of the Syndics of Cambridge University Library.

Heroïque Stanza's,
Consecrated to the glorious ~~memorie~~ memorie
Of his most Serene & Renowned Highness
OLIVER
Late Lord Protector of this Common-wealth. &c.
Written after the Celebration of his funeralls.

1

And now 'tis time; for theire officious hast
Who would before haue borne him to the sky
Like Eager Romans, ere all rites were past
Did let too soone the sacred Eagle fly.

2

Though our best notes are treason to his fame
Joynd with the loud applause of publique voice;
Since Heav'n what praise wee offer to his name
Hath render'd too authentiq by its choise;

3

Though in his praise no Arts can liberall bee,
And they whose Muses haue the highest floune
Add not to his immortall memorie;
But do an Act of friendship to theire own:

4

Yet 'tis our duty and our intrest too
Such monuments as wee can build to raise;
Lest all the world prevent what wee should do
And claime a title in him by theire praise.

5

How shall I then begin or where conclude
To draw a fame so truly Circular?
For in a round what order can bee shewd
Where all the parts so equall perfect are?

6

His grandeur hee deriv'd from Heav'n alone;
For hee was great ere Fortune made him so:
And Warrs, like mists that rise against the Sunne,
Made him but greater seeme, not greater grow.

Plate 2. The first page of the autograph manuscript of Dryden's
Heroic Stanzas, from British Library MS Lansdowne 1045 f.101ʳ.
Reproduced by permission of the British Library Board.

ANNVS MIRABILIS:

The Year of

WONDERS,
1 6 6 6.

AN HISTORICAL

POEM:

CONTAINING

The Progrefs and various Succeffes of our Naval
War with *Holland*, under the Conduct of His
Highnefs Prince RUPERT, and His Grace the
Duke of ALBEMARL.

And defcribing

THE FIRE
OF
LONDON.

By JOHN DRYDEN, Efq;

Multùm intereft res pofcat, an homines latius imperare velint.
Trajan. Imperator. ad Plin.

Urbs antiqua ruit, multos dominata per annos. Virg

London, Printed for *Henry Herringman,* at the Anchor in the Lower Walk of the *New Exchange.* 1667.

Plate 3. Title page of the first edition of *Annus Mirabilis* (1667), from a
copy in the Brotherton Collection, Leeds University Library.
Reproduced by permission of the Librarian.

He, who in impious times vntainted stood,
And mid'st Rebellion durst be just and good;
Whose Armes asserted, and whose sufferings more
Confirm'd the cause for which he fought before,
Rests here, rewarded by an Heav'nly Prince
For what his Earthly could not recompence.
Pray (Reader) that such times no more appeare,
Or, if they happen, learn true Honour here

Ark of thy Age's faith and Loyalty
(Which to preserve them) Heav'n confin'd in thee,
Few Subjects could a King like thine deserve,
And fewer such a King so well could serve
Blest King, blest Subject, whose exalted state
By suffrings rose, and gave the law to fate
Such Soules are rare but mighty patterns given
To Earth, were meant for ornaments in Heaven.

By John Dryden, Poet Laureat

Plate 4. The monument to the Marquis of Winchester in Englefield church, showing the epitaph composed by Dryden. Photograph by Mr Ian Maclean.

ABSALOM

AND

ACHITOPHEL.

A

POEM.

XLII . 7. 15.

-------*Si Propiùs ſtes*
Te Capiet Magis---------

L O N D O N,
Printed for *J. T.* and are to be Sold by *W. Davis* in
Amen-Corner, 1 68 1.

Plate 5. Title page from the first issue of the first edition of *Absalom and Achitophel* (1681), from a copy in the Brotherton Collection, Leeds University Library. Reproduced by permission of the Librarian.

Some by their Monarch's fatal mercy grown,
From Pardon'd Rebels, Kinsmen to the Throne;
Were rais'd in Power and publick Office high:
Strong Bands, if Bands ungratefull men cuold tye.
of Shaftsbury. Of these the false *Achitophel* was first:
A Name to all succeeding Ages Curst.
For close Designs, and crooked Counsell fit;
Sagacious, Bold, and Turbulent of wit:
Restless, unfixt in Principle and Place;
In Power unpleas'd, impatient of Disgrace.
A fiery Soul, which working out its way,⎫
Fretted the Pigmy Body to decay:⎬
And o'r inform'd the Tenement of Clay.⎭
A daring Pilot in extremity;
Pleas'd with the Danger, when the Waves went high
He sought the Storms; but for a Calm unfit,
Would Steer too nigh the Sands, to boast his Wit.
Great Wits are sure to Madness near ally'd;
And thin Partitions do their Bounds divide:
Else, why should he, with Wealth and Honour blest,
Refuse his Age the needful hours of Rest?
Punish a Body which he coud not please;
Bankrupt of Life, yet Prodigal of Ease?
And all to leave, what with his Toyl he won,
To that unfeather'd, two Leg'd thing, a Son:
Got, while his Soul did hudled Notions try;
And born a shapeless Lump, like Anarchy.
In Friendship False, Implacable in Hate:
Resolv'd to Ruine or to Rule the State.
To Compass this the Triple Bond he broke;⎫
The Pillars of the publick Safety shook:⎬
And fitted *Israel* for a Foreign Yoke.⎭
Then, seiz'd with Fear, yet still affecting Fame,
Assum'd a Patriott's All-attoning Name.

Not

Plates 6 and 7. Pages 6–7 from the first issue of the first edition of
Absalom and Achitophel (1681). Page 6 shows the original readings
'Kold', 'Kody' and 'Patron's' corrected by hand to 'Bold', 'Body'
and 'Patriott's'. Pages 6 and 7 together show the passage on

7

Oh, had he been content to serve the Crown,
With vertues only proper to the Gown;
Or, had the rankness of the Soyl been freed
From Cockle, that oppreſt the Noble ſeed:
David, for him his tunefull Harp had ſtrung,
And Heaven had wanted one Immortal ſong.
But wilde Ambition loves to ſlide, not ſtand;
And Fortunes Ice prefers to Vertues Land:
Achitophel, grown weary to poſſeſs
A lawfull Fame, and lazy Happineſs,
Diſdain'd the Golden fruit to gather free,
And lent the Croud his Arm to ſhake the Tree.
Now, manifeſt of Crimes, contriv'd long ſince,
He ſtood at bold Defiance with his Prince:
Held up the Buckler of the Peoples Cauſe,
Againſt the Crown; and ſculk'd behind the Laws.
The wiſh'd occaſion of the Plot he takes,
Some Circumſtances finds, but more he makes.
By buzzing Emiſſaries, fills the ears
Of liſtning Crowds, with Jealoſies and Fears
Of Arbitrary Counſels brought to light,
And proves the King himſelf a *Jebuſite*:
Weak Arguments! which yet he knew fulwell,
Were ſtrong with People eaſie to Rebell.
For, govern'd by the *Moon*, the giddy *Jews*
Tread the ſame track when ſhe the Prime renews:
And once in twenty Years, their Scribes Record,
By natural Inſtinct they change their Lord.
Achitophel ſtill wants a Chief, and none
Was found ſo fit as Warlike *Abſolon*:
Not, that he wiſh'd his Greatneſs to create,
(For Politicians neither love nor hate:)
But, for he knew, his Title not allow'd,
Would keep him ſtill depending on the Crowd:

                                            That

Shaftesbury as it was before the addition of the present lines 180–91.
From a copy in the Brotherton Collection, Leeds University Library,
reproduced by permission of the Librarian.

Mac Flecкno.

All human things are Subject to decay;
And, when Fate Summons, Monarchs must obey:
This Fleckno found; who, like Augustus, young
Was call'd to Empire, and had Govern'd long;
In Prose and Verse was own'd, without dispute,
Through all the Realm of Nonsence, absolute.
The aged Prince now flourishing in peace,
And blest with Issue of a large increase,
Worn out with Bus'ness, did at length debate
To settle the Succession of the State;
And, pond'ring which of all his Sons were fit
To Reign, and wage immortal War with Wit:
Cry'd, 'tis resolv'd; for Nature pleads that he
Should only Rule that most resembles Me:
Shadwell alone my perfect Image bears;
Mature in Dulness from his tender years:
Shadwell alone, of all my Sons, is he
Who stands confirm'd in full stupidity;
The rest, to some faint meaning make pretence,
But Shadwell never deviates into Sence.

Some

Plate 8. First page of *Mac Flecknoe* from Leeds University Library,
Brotherton Collection MS Lt 54 page 1. Reproduced by permission
of the Librarian. The manuscript is a scribal miscellany compiled
c. 1680, and illustrates the circulation of the poem before its first
appearance in print in 1682.

Where bunglers daub, and where true poets paint.
25   But by the sacred Genius of this place,
      By every Muse, by each domestic Grace,
      Be kind to wit, which but endeavours well,
      And where you judge, presumes not to excel.
      Our poets hither for adoption come,
30   As nations sued to be made free of Rome:
      Not in the suffragating tribes to stand,
      But in your utmost, last, provincial band.
      If his ambition may those hopes pursue
      Who with religion loves your arts and you,
35   Oxford to him a dearer name shall be
      Than his own mother university.
      Thebes did his green, unknowing youth engage,
      He chooses Athens in his riper age.

25. *Genius*] guardian spirit.
30–2. Citizenship was gradually extended to Rome's provinces and allies; an intermediate stage was *civitas sine suffragio* ('citizenship without voting rights'). *suffragating*] voting (*OED*'s first example).
35–8. D. was educated at Cambridge, though this was not necessarily an autobiographical remark: cp. 'Epilogue at Oxford, 1674' ll. 1–2*n*. It was interpreted autobiographically, however, by the anonymous author of 'On the University of Cambridge. A Dialogue Between Tutor and Pupil. By an Unknown Hand, *Anno* 84', who wrote: 'In *Dryden*'s Mighty self she claims a part, / Tho he to *Oxford* has resign'd his heart; / *Thebes* did his green unknowing youth ingage, / But he chose *Athens* in his riper Age;' (*Miscellany*, edited by Aphra Behn (1685) 249).   *Thebes . . . Athens*] Cp. 'Prologue at Oxford, 1673' ll. 1–2, 'Epilogue at Oxford, 1674' l. 22.

42 Mac Flecknoe

Date and publication. Written July–August 1676. The date of *MF* has been much debated, but was definitively established by David M. Vieth in *Evidence in Literary Scholarship*, edited by René Wellek and Alvaro Ribiero (1979) 63–87. Vieth shows that *MF* alludes to a number of Shadwell's works up to and including the printed text of *The Virtuoso* (advertised in the *London Gazette* 3–6 July 1676), but none thereafter; the reference to Ogilby (l. 174), who died on 4 September 1676, implies that he is still alive; and there are probable borrowings from *MF* by Settle in the Preface to *Ibrahim* (licensed 4 May 1676; *SR* 7 July; *TC* November). George McFadden (*PQ* xliii (1964) 55–72) suggested that D. borrowed from Settle's Preface, and that *MF* was conceived over a period of several years, after the controversy over Settle's *Empress of Morocco* (1673); this is unlikely, for *MF* is richly specific to Shadwell and to 1676, as Vieth shows.

Soon after its composition *MF* was given a restricted form of publication by being circulated in MS copies. Seventeen MSS are known to survive: Beal 407–8 lists fifteen, to which should be added National Library of Ireland MS 2093, and Badminton MS FmE 3/12 (described by Michael Brennan and Paul Hammond in *EMS* v (1993), forthcoming). Of particular interest is BodL MS Rawl. Poet 123, transcribed in 1678 by John Oldham. Two have been published in facsimile: Leeds UL Brotherton Collection MS Lt 54, reproduced by Paul Hammond in *PLPLS* xviii (1982) 287–96, and the first page also reproduced here as Plate 8; and Royal Library Stockholm MS Vu. 69 reproduced as *The Gyldenstolpe Manuscript Miscellany of Poems by John Wilmot, Earl of Rochester, and other Restoration Authors*, edited by Bror Danielsson and David M. Vieth, *Stockholm Studies in English* 17 (1967). The poem reached print in a pirated text of no authority in 1682 entitled *Mac Flecknoe, or a Satyr upon the True-Blew-Protestant Poet*, *T.S.*; the subtitle is the bookseller's attempt to make the poem politically topical in the light of the controversy between D. and Shadwell in 1682 over *The Medal*, and is not attributable to D. himself. *MF* was printed in an authorized text in *MP* 1684 (reprinted 1692), and reprinted in 1692 as part of Tonson's uniform series of D.'s major poems. The relationship between the MSS and printed texts is established by David M. Vieth in *HLB* xxiv (1976) 204–45, supplemented by Paul Hammond in *PLPLS*, and by Paul Hammond and Michael Brennan in *EMS*. Vieth's discussion corrects and supersedes the provisional piece by G. B. Evans in *HLB* vii (1953) 32–54 and the mistaken argument for extensive authorial revision propounded by Vinton A. Dearing in *SB* vii (1955) 85–102 and again in *Works* ii 428–30. The collation and stemma given in *Works* ii 430–9 are also superseded by those of Vieth and Hammond. Comparison of *1684* with the MSS and *1682* shows that the only indisputable revision which D. made for *1684* was to change *rustic* to *Norwich* in l. 33. It is possible that the original 1676 text may also have read *poppy* (l. 126), *heaven* (l. 139) and *after ages* (l. 159). Otherwise D. did not revise *MF* between 1676 and 1684. In the 1676 text all the proper names were spelt out in full, whereas *1684* prints many simply as initials and dashes. In order to present *MF* as it was first read in 1676, the present text is based on *1684* but restores *rustic* and spells out the names.

Context. Thomas Shadwell (1642–92), a leading dramatist with the Duke's Company, was the author of *The Sullen Lovers* (1668), *The Royal Shepherdess* (1669), *The Hypocrite* (produced 1670? not printed), *The Humorists* (1671), *The Miser* (1672), perhaps the operatic adaptation of *The Tempest* (1674), the opera *Psyche* (1675), *The Libertine* (1676) and *The Virtuoso* (1676). He continued to write plays after the appearance of *MF*, but had none produced from the union of the companies in 1682 until 1688. We know of no personal animosity between D. and Shadwell before 1676, nor is there yet any political difference: that does not become apparent until 1682, with Shadwell's *The Medal of John Bayes* and D.'s lines on Shadwell in 2*AA* ll. 457–509. The dispute is a literary one, and *MF* is the culmination of a critical debate between D. and Shadwell which had begun in 1668. The debate is well summarized by R. Jack Smith in *RES* xx (1944) 29–44, and the relevant documents are reproduced with an introduction by Richard L. Oden in *Dryden and Shadwell* (1977). As Smith says, the matters at issue were: (i) the relative merits of the comedy of repartee, practised by D., and the comedy of humours, advocated by Shadwell; (ii) the right of an author to borrow from ancient and modern writers; (iii) the proper estimate of Ben Jonson; (iv) the rationale of heroic tragedy; (v) the relative importance of pleasing the public and instructing it. The debate begins with the Preface to *The Sullen Lovers*. Here Shadwell derides heroic tragedy, where 'they strein Love and Honour to that Ridiculous height, that it becomes Burlesque', and the comedy of wit, where 'the two chief persons are most commonly a Swearing, Drinking, Whoring, Ruffian for a Lover, and an impudent ill-bred *tomrig* for a Mistress'; by contrast, the Jonsonian comedy of humours offers 'perfect Representations of Humane Life' (Shadwell, *Works* i 11). He attacks those who had been 'so Insolent to say, that *Ben Johnson* wrote his best *Playes* without Wit', replying to D.'s *EDP*, published earlier that year, where D. said of Jonson that 'one cannot say he wanted wit, but rather that he was frugal of it' (*Works* xvii 57; and cp. 'Prologue to *The Tempest*'). To Shadwell, however, Jonson 'is the man, of all the World, *I* most passionately admire for his Excellency in Drammatick-*Poetry*' (i 11). In his Preface to *The Royal Shepherdess* Shadwell returned to his attack on the comedy of repartee, which encourages vice 'by bringing the Characters of debauch'd People upon the Stage, and making them pass for fine Gentlemen, who openly profess Swearing, Drinking, Whoring, breaking Windows, beating Constables, &c.' (i 100); the creators of such characters plead that they are pleasing the people, but 'he that debases himself to think of nothing but pleasing the Rabble, loses the dignity of a Poet, and becomes as little as a Jugler, or a Rope-Dancer' (i 100). D. replied in the Preface to *An Evening's Love* (1671), saying that in comedy 'the faults and vices are but the sallies of youth, and the frailties of humane nature, and not premeditated crimes'; consequently such characters need not be punished. As for pleasing the people, 'the first end of Comedie is delight, and instruction only the second'. D. says that he is not an enemy of Jonson, but 'I do not admire him blindly, and without looking into his imperfections: . . . I admire and applaud him where I ought: those who do more do but value themselves in their admiration of him: and, by telling you they extoll *Ben Johnson*'s way, would insinuate to you that they can practice it' (*Works* x 209, 205). Nor is D. a plagiarist: he may take the outline of his story from romance, novel or play, but he transforms it, as others, including Shakespeare and Jonson, have done. The exchange continued along these lines in Shadwell's Preface to *The Humorists* (1671), D.'s 'Epilogue to *2 Conquest of Granada*' and its 'Defence' (1672), Shadwell's Epilogue to *The Miser* (1672), D.'s 'Prologue at Oxford, 1673', Shadwell's Prologue to *Psyche* (1675) and Prologue and Epilogue to *The Virtuoso* (1676). All of these critical issues are taken up in *MF*: (i) wit, repartee and humours: ll. 12, 21, 89, 150, 161, 181–2, 188–90, 196; (ii) plagiarism: ll. 157–64, 183–6; (iii) Jonson: ll. 80, 172–96, and several verbal echoes; (iv) heroic tragedy: ll. 75–8 and the imagery of kingship made burlesque throughout; (v) comedy pleasing or instructing: ll. 150–6, 182, and the imagery of dullness throughout. Shadwell had claimed to be the heir of Ben Jonson, and through his frequent quotations from Horace had appropriated the classical heritage; D. in *MF* derides that claim by casting him as the true heir not of Jonson but of Flecknoe.

As Vieth saw, the immediate occasion of *MF* was the publication of *The Virtuoso*. Its Dedication (dated 26 June 1676) attacks comedies which rely upon 'downright silly folly' or 'the affectation of some *French* words', and defends his work against 'some Women, and some Men of Feminine understandings, who like slight Plays onely, that represent a little tattle sort of Conversation, like their own; but true Humour is not liked or understood by them, and therefore even my attempt towards it is condemned by them. But the same people, to my great comfort, damn all Mr. *Johnson*'s Plays, who was incomparably the best Drammatick Poet that ever was, or, I believe, ever will be; and I had rather be Authour of one Scene in his best Comedies, than of any Play this Age has produced' (iii 101–2). Vieth (1979) 85–6 notes that *MF* is not only a review of Shadwell's career, but also a selective review of the theatrical season of 1675–6, in which the most successful plays were Etherege's *The Man of Mode* (performed in March with an Epilogue by D.) and *The Virtuoso*; there had also been three performances of *Psyche*, and a revival of D.'s *Tyrannic Love* (cp. l. 78). Shadwell may have irritated D. in other ways. Aline M. Taylor suggests that Shadwell's possible role in the lucrative adaptation of the D.–Davenant *Tempest* into an opera in 1674 may have rankled (*SP* extra series iv (1967) 39–53). Michael W. Alssid argues that the character Drybob in *The Humorists* was a humours portrayal of D. which prompted D. to turn Shadwell into a humour (of dullness) in *MF* (*SEL* vii (1967) 387–402). Richard Perkin (unpublished PhD thesis, Leeds 1980) notes that the MS of *The Humorists* included the part of Button, Drybob's mistress, which is missing from the printed text. If performed, it would clearly have irritated D., whether or not he was already involved with Anne Reeves. Perkin also suggests that the poet Crambo in Newcastle's *The Triumphant Widow* (partly written by Shadwell: performed 1674; printed 1677) may be a caricature of D. Crambo constantly laments how dull he is; when he falls sick, Codshead jokes that he is 'big with Muse, and cannot be delivered' (55: cp. *MF* ll. 41, 148), and the doctor, having suggested applying various poets as remedies, finally suggests applying Jonson's works 'to the head'. Crambo recoils: 'Oh, I hate *Johnson*, oh oh, dull dull, oh oh no Wit.' The doctor says that Jonson will purify his language. Characters also accuse Crambo of plagiarism (60–1).

Richard Flecknoe (*c.* 1605–*c.* 77) is the other chief figure in *MF*. Despite *DNB* he was not Irish, but born in Northamptonshire; he is often said to have died in 1678, but this claim is based on two errors, (i) that *MF* was written in 1678, (ii) that *MF* is concerned with his death. He was a Roman Catholic priest, traveller and writer. His epigrams and prose characters appeared in many editions from 1653 to 1677; he wrote the plays *Love's Dominion* (1654; cp. ll. 122–5n) and *Erminia* (1661), satirical attacks upon Thomas Killigrew (*The Life of Tomaso the Wanderer* (1667)) and Sir William Davenant (*Sr William D'avenant's Voyage to the Other World* (1668)), and *A True and Faithful Account of . . . Ten Years Travels* (1665). He has sometimes been credited with the attack on D. by one 'R.F.', *A Letter from a Gentleman to the Honourable Ed. Howard Esq.* (1668); the attribution may be wrong, but we do not know D.'s view. Flecknoe included laudatory verses on D. in his *Epigrams of all Sorts* (1670) 70: '*DReyden* the Muses darling and delight, / Than whom none ever flew so high a flight. / Some have their vains so drosie, as from *earth*, / Their Muses onely seem to have tane their birth. / Others but *Water-Poets* are, have gon / No farther than to th' *Fount of Helicon*: / And they're but *aiery ones*, whose *Muse* soars up / No higher than to mount *Pernassus* top; / Whilst thou, with thine, dost seem to have mounted higher, / Then he who fetcht from *Heaven* Celestial fire: / And dost as far surpass all others, as / *Fire* does all other Elements surpass.' But there were several reasons why D. might have regarded Flecknoe as an archetypally bad writer: (i) his prolific output included the recycling of old material and the reissuing of sheets of unsold books under new titles; (ii) he had attacked D.'s colleagues Killigrew and Davenant, and suggested that Shakespeare would have resented the alteration of his plays by Davenant (and, implicitly, by D., his collaborator on *The Tempest*); (iii) he contributed to the debate between D. and Shadwell by attacking Jonson's critics and defending him against modern 'wit' (*Epigrams. Of All Sorts* (1671) 51–2); (iv) his output of epigrams and criticism lays claim to the classical heritage in the Jonsonian mould. It was Flecknoe's claim to be an heir of Jonson which allowed D. to cast Shadwell in the role of son of Flecknoe instead of son of Jonson. Flecknoe provided an apt image for the writer about to retire, since he had announced his retirement in 'L'Envoy' (*Epigrams Made at Several Times* (1673) 98; Novak) and three times subsequently. Flecknoe was already a by-word for a bad writer. Marvell had written of him in '*Flecknoe, an English Priest at Rome*'; this encounter would have been *c.* 1646, but the date of the poem's composition is unknown, and it was first printed in Marvell's *Miscellaneous Poems* (1681); however, D. could have seen a copy in MS (as he did with Marvell's 'An Horatian Ode'). Flecknoe was 'very well jeer'd' in *The Session of the Poets* (in MS, 1668; *POAS* i 329), and a poem on Edward Howard begins: 'Thou damn'd antipodes to common sense! / Thou foil to Flecknoe! Prithee tell from whence / Does all this mighty stock of dullness spring' (in MS, 1671; *POAS* i 340). Shadwell in his verse letter to Wycherley in 1671 derides Flecknoe (v 228). Shadwell owned a copy of Flecknoe's *Enigmaticall Characters* (1658), now in Cambridge UL (E. E. Duncan-Jones, privately). For the links between D., Shadwell and Flecknoe see further Maximillian E. Novak, *BNYPL* lxxii (1968) 499–506; Paul Hammond, *EIC* xxxv (1985) 315–29; Ian Donaldson, *SRev* xviii (1985) 314–27; for Flecknoe's life, see his *Prose Characters*, edited by Fred Mayer (1987) ix–cxix.

Authorship. Only two MSS (Illinois MS and Yale MS Osborn b. 105) attribute *MF* to D., so the poem probably circulated anonymously at first. *1682* describes it as being 'By the Author of *Absalom & Achitophel*'. Mulgrave attributes *MF* to 'The Laureat' in *An Essay upon Poetry* (1682) 10. It was printed anonymously in *1684*, but following on from *AA* and *The Medal*, forming a clearly defined group; in the 1692 reprint of *MP* the three satires were attributed to D. on the contents page but not in the text, and in the following year (after Shadwell's death) D. acknowledged his authorship of *MF* in the 'Discourse Concerning Satire' (*Works* iv 48). For the significance of the anonymous publication see Paul Hammond, *SC* viii (1993) 124–7.

Sources. The chief sources for *MF* are the works of Shadwell and Flecknoe themselves, as the notes show. Shadwell's claim to be heir to the classical heritage in general, and to Jonson's achievement in particular, gave D. the reason for using the classical references and the image of succession. Jonson himself had called his followers 'sons'. Flecknoe had announced his retirement more than once (ll. 7–10n), and had also provided an image of himself as king at a Twelfth Night feast in a letter to Mademoiselle de Beauvais: 'Think me not now one of those who change their natural Condition, with the condition of Fortune, and wax proud with their honours. . . . I promise you on my *Royal* word, my Subjects here shall have cause to rejoice whilst I reign over them, my raign shall be nothing but one continued Feast, which they shall celebrate with joyful acclamation, nothing shall be consum'd but in the Kitchen; and nothing be exhausted but the Cellar'; the lady replied with an address 'To his Flecknotique Majesty' (*A Relation Of ten Years Travells* [1656] 137–9).

The idea of a poet being crowned goes back to the coronation of Petrarch as laureate in 1341, but D. may have known about two burlesque poetic coronations which took place later under the aegis of Pope Leo X (1475–1521). Camillo Querno came from Apulia to Rome to make his fortune, and was invited to a symposium at which he was made to drink and sing alternately. He was then crowned with a wreath of vine leaves, cabbage and laurel, and given the title of arch-poet. Baraballo of Gaeta considered himself a second Petrarch, and rode through the streets of Rome mounted on an elephant; after reciting his verses to the Pope he was led away to the sound of drums and trumpets, but on the return journey the elephant shied on the bridge of St Angelo and deposited the poet on the pavement. The stories are told by Paulo Giovio in *Elogia Doctorum Virorum* (1557).

The question of *MF*'s genre and antecedents is complex. D. himself included *MF* in a discussion of Varronian satire in his 'Discourse Concerning Satire' in 1693 (*Works* iv 48); other examples which he mentions include Petronius's *Satyricon*, some of Lucian's dialogues, Apuleius's *Golden Ass*, Seneca's *Apocolocyntosis* (the mock deification of the Emperor Claudius), Barclay's *Euphormio*, Erasmus's *Moriae Encomium* and Spenser's *Mother Hubbard's Tale*. Michael West (*SEL* xiii (1973) 437–49) points to the continental background to *MF*. The poem has affinities with the paradoxical encomium (on which see Henry Knight Miller, *MPh* liii (1956) 145–78), exemplified not only by Erasmus's *Moriae Encomium* but by other humanists' panegyrics to the louse, ant, ass, elephant, egg, shade and gout. In his 'Discourse' (1693; *Works* iv 84–5) D. praises *Le Lutrin* (1674) by Nicolas Boileau-Despréaux, a satire on a battle for precedence in a chapel, and the *Secchia Rapita* (1622) by Alessandro Tassoni; according to an anecdote by Lockier D. once said that he valued *MF* 'because 'tis the first piece of ridicule written in heroics' and was then forced by Lockier to admit the precedence of Tassoni and Boileau (Spence i 274–5).

There had already been several verse satires on Restoration writers before *MF*, including the *Sessions of the Poets* (in MS, 1668; *POAS* i 327–37), some satires on Edward Howard (*POAS* i 338–41), ?Etherege's *Ephelia to Bajazet* and Rochester's reply *A Very Heroical Epistle in Answer to Ephelia* (in MS, 1675; *POAS* i 342–7), Rochester's *An Allusion to Horace* (in MS, 1675) and his *An Epistolary Essay from M.G. to O.B.* (in MS, 1676). George McFadden has shown that *MF* has some ideas in common with D.'s contributions to *Notes and Observations on the Empress of Morocco* (1674) (*PQ* xliii (1964) 55–72). Michael West (*SEL* xviii (1978) 457–64) suggests that D. may have been influenced by the example of Thomas Duffett's burlesque dramas; the operatic *Tempest* was travestied in Duffett's *The Mock Tempest* (performed 1674), and Shadwell's opera *Psyche* was burlesqued by Duffett in *Psyche Debauch'd* (performed 1675). Both burlesques are set amid London low-life.

As these examples indicate, *MF* can be thought of as combining a number of modes or genres: the paradoxical encomium, the personal lampoon and the satirical discussion of literary values and writers. Ian Jack in *Augustan Satire* (1952) 43–52 defines *MF* as 'mock heroic'; in this mode heroic language and incident are applied to an unworthy subject. This is distinct from burlesque, exemplified by Butler's *Hudibras* (1663–78), which employs a low style. *MF* may be the first poem in English to attempt quite this manner, though Boileau's *Le Lutrin* showed what might be done, and its first appearance in his *Oeuvres Diverses* (1674) just two years before D. wrote *MF* may have been

an important stimulus to D.'s imagination. In his 'Discourse Concerning
Satire' (1693) D. commented that the double rhyme used in *Hudibras* 'is not
so proper for Manly Satire, for it turns Earnest too much to Jest, and gives us
a Boyish kind of Pleasure . . . when we know he cou'd have given us a better,
and more solid.' He compares this form of satire with that of Boileau, who
'had read the Burlesque Poetry of *Scarron*, with some kind of Indignation, as
witty as it was. . . . He writes it in the *French* Heroique Verse, and calls it an
Heroique Poem: His Subject is Trivial, but his Verse is Noble. I doubt not
but he had *Virgil* in his Eye, for we find many admirable Imitations of him,
and some *Parodies*. . . . This, I think . . . to be the most Beautiful, and most
Noble kind of Satire. Here is the Majesty of the Heroique, finely mix'd with
the Venom of the other; and raising the Delight which otherwise wou'd be
flat and vulgar, by the Sublimity of the Expression' (*Works* iv 81–4). This
seems to describe the effect which D. aimed at in both *MF* and *AA*.

The heroic manner of *MF* is indebted to Virgil (see R. A. Brower, *PQ* xviii
(1939) 211–17, *PMLA* lv (1940) 119–38, *ELH* xix (1952) 38–48); to Milton
(see Michael Wilding, *EIC* xix (1969) 355–70; and J. R. Mason); and to
Cowley (see A. L. Korn, *HLQ* xiv (1950–1) 99–127), whose *Davideis*, along
with the Bible, provides the images of Flecknoe and Shadwell as prophets,
priests and kings.

Reception. There are probable borrowings from *MF* in the Preface to Settle's
Ibrahim (1676): see above. If 'A Session of the Poets' is correctly dated to
November or December 1676, then the description of Shadwell in ll. 26–36
may owe something to *MF* (*POAS* i 353). The date on Oldham's transcript,
1678, is probably the year in which he copied the poem; there are echoes of
MF in his *Satyrs upon the Jesuits* iii 657–63, 665 (written summer 1679), and 'A
Satyr, in Imitation of the Third of Juvenal' ll. 176–7 (written 1682), while 'A
Satyr' ["Spenser's Ghost"] (written 1682–3) has some comparable material.
Vieth (1979) 67–9 collects echoes of *MF* in D'Urfey's *Sir Barnaby Whigg*
(performed 1681?), *The Tory-Poets* (1682) and *Rochester's Farewell* (in MS,
written 1680), and an apparent allusion in *Advice to Apollo* (written 1677;
POAS i 392–4). *The Loyal Protestant*, 9 February 1682, remarks: 'he would
send him [Shadwell] his Recantation next morning, with a *Mac-Flecknoe*, and
a brace of Lobsters for his Breakfast; All which he knew he had a singular
aversion for.' This relatively meagre evidence, and the comparatively small
number of extant MSS (few of which can be dated with certainty to before
1682), suggests that the circulation of *MF* before 1682 was confined to
London literary circles, and perhaps Oxford and Cambridge. It seems not to
have made a great impact in these early years. Mulgrave in *An Essay upon
Poetry* (1682) 10 commends *MF* as an example of how to write sharp satire in
an elegant way. *MF* l. 178 is echoed by Tonson in his poem on Oldham in
Sylvae (1685) 473.

Mac Flecknoe

All human things are subject to decay,
And, when Fate summons, monarchs must obey:
This Flecknoe found, who like Augustus young
Was called to empire, and had governed long;
5   In prose and verse was owned without dispute
Through all the realms of nonsense absolute.

¶42. *Title. Mac*] Son [of] (Gaelic). Shadwell protested at D. 'giving me the *Irish* name of *Mack*, when he knows I never saw *Ireland* till I was three and twenty years old, and was there but four Months' (Dedication of *The Tenth Satyr of Juvenal* (1687); v 292). The Irish have been proverbially represented by the English as comic failures lacking intelligence and culture; Rochester included 'Hibernian learning' in his poem *Upon Nothing* l. 47. See also l. 213*n*.

1. Cp. Waller: 'Well sung the Roman bard, "All human things / Of dearest value hang on slender strings" ' ('Of the danger His Majesty . . . escaped' ll. 163–4; the reference is to Ovid, *omnia sunt hominum tenui pendentia filo* (*Ex Ponto* IV iii 35).

3. This *Flecknoe found*] Echoes 'This Caesar found' (Waller, 'A Panegyric to my Lord Protector' l. 149).   *Augustus*] Gaius Octavius (63 BC to AD 14), first of the Roman emperors, whose leading role in Rome began with his appointment as consul in 43 BC.

3–4. young / Was called to empire] Flecknoe's first book was his poem *Hierothalamium. Or, the heavenly nuptialls of our Saviour* (1626), published when he was about 21.

4, 6. empire . . . realms] For the image cp. Shadwell's Preface to *Psyche* where he says that some writers 'are very much offended with me, for leaving my own Province of *Comedy*, to invade their Dominion of *Rhime*' (ii 279; Michael W. Alssid, *SEL* vii (1967) 387–402). D. plays later with the titles of Flecknoe's plays *Love's Dominion* and *Love's Kingdom* (ll. 122, 141, 143). See also headnote, '*Sources*', for a tradition of poetic coronations. Thomas Carew had said that Donne ruled 'The universall Monarchy of wit' (*Poems* 74). Cowley also uses the image of the poet's empire in 'To Sir *William Davenant*' and 'On *Orinda's* Poems' (*Poems* 42–3, 406).

6. nonsense] This word is first used by Jonson: in *Bartholomew Fair* the game of vapours 'is *non sense*. Euery man to oppose the last man that spoke: whether it concern'd him, or no' (IV iv 27*n*), and in *Discoveries* he says: 'Many Writers perplexe their Readers, and Hearers with meere *Non-sense*. Their writings need sunshine' (ll. 1868–70). Shadwell in his Preface to *The Humorists* laments the fact that the rabble are 'more pleased with the extravagant and unnatural actions the trifles, and fripperies of a Play, or the trappings and ornaments of Nonsense, than with all the wit in the world' (i 185), and in the Epilogue he says: 'Yet if you hiss, he knows not where the harm is, / He'll not defend his Nonsense *Vi & Armis*' (ll. 40–1). For Jonson the spectacles produced by Inigo

> This agèd prince, now flourishing in peace,
> And blessed with issue of a large increase,
> Worn out with business, did at length debate
> 10   To settle the succession of the state;
> And pondering which of all his sons was fit
> To reign, and wage immortal war with wit,

Jones were instances of nonsense because they lacked the profound art of the poet: 'O Showes! Showes! Mighty Showes! / The Eloquence of Masques! What need of prose / Or Verse, or Sense t' express Immortall you?' ('An Expostulation with Inigo Jones' ll. 39–41); whereas 'In all speech, words and sense, are as the body, and the soule. The sense is as the life and soule of Language, without which all words are dead. Sense is wrought out of experience, the knowledge of humane life, and actions, or of the liberall Arts' (*Discoveries* ll. 1884–9). Shadwell is an enemy of sense (ll. 20, 89, 117, 156, 194) and, like Inigo Jones, has devoted his energies to spectacle in his opera *Psyche* (Ian Donaldson, *SRev* xviii (1985) 314–27). The contrasting idea of *sense* is complex. In part it has echoes of the French principle of *le bon sens* (see Boileau, *L' Art Poétique* (1674) i 28). As J. R. Crider notes (*Brno Studies in English* ix (1970) 11–16), in neo-classical criticism wit (or imagination) and sense (or judgement) were the two elements in the creative process. Shadwell does not possess the steady, restraining quality of sense or judgement. But neither does he possess *wit* (ll. 12, 89), which denotes both 'imagination' (*OED* 7), 'verbal brilliance' (*OED* 8) and, more generally, 'intelligence' (*OED* 5). So Shadwell is presented as an enemy not only of the comedy of wit (see headnote) but also of poetic inventiveness and intelligence. For D.'s deployment of these terms in his criticism see John M. Aden, *PMLA* lxxiv (1959) 28–40 and Robert D. Hume, *RES* xxi (1970) 295–314.   *absolute*] (i) perfect, free from deficiency (*OED* 4); (ii) having absolute power (*OED* 8).

7–10. Flecknoe announced his own retirement in 'The *Remembrance*': 'Now aged grown, does in some *hermitage,* / Desire to end the *remnant* of his age' (*A Treatise of the Sports of Wit* (1675) 15 *bis*; cp. 'The Adue', ibid. 7).

8. Flecknoe published over thirty books. The phrasing may come from Deuteronomy xvi 15: 'the Lord thy God shall bless thee in all thine increase' (A. L. Korn, *HLQ* xiv (1950–1) 99–127).   *increase*] The noun was stressed on the second syllable.

9. business] with a play on the meaning 'sexual intercourse' (*OED* 19b); perhaps also recalling Charles II's tireless devotion to such 'business'.   *debate*] deliberate, consider with himself (*OED* 5b).

10. In 1676 the question of the succession to Charles II was not yet as contentious as it was to be from 1679, though anxiety about the religion of James and his children was voiced in Parliament in 1674 (Haley 358–60).

12. Satan in *PL* resolves 'to wage by force or guile eternal war' against God (i 121; *Works*) and vows 'immortal hate' (i 107; Michael Wilding, *EIC* xix (1969) 355–70).   *wit*] See l. 6n.

Cried, ' 'Tis resolved; for Nature pleads that he
Should only rule who most resembles me:
15   Shadwell alone my perfect image bears,
Mature in dullness from his tender years;
Shadwell alone, of all my sons, is he
Who stands confirmed in full stupidity.
The rest to some faint meaning make pretence,
20   But Shadwell never deviates into sense.
Some beams of wit on other souls may fall,
Strike through and make a lucid interval,

15–17. Korn (185–6) notes that these lines echo Cowley's repetition of the
name Abdon in *Davideis* iv: '*Abdon* alone his gen'erous purpose knew; / . . .
Abdon alone did on him now attend' (*Poems* 385).
15. Shadwell] all MSS independent of *1684*; Shad— *1682*; Sh— *1684*. Although
the form 'Sh—' is particularly effective here (and at ll. 47–8, 103) in associating Shadwell with shit (as Wilding observes), the MS evidence shows that D.
originally spelt out the name in full (Vieth (1976) 227).   *perfect image*] Sin is
the 'perfect image' of Satan (*PL* ii 764), and Christ is the 'image' of God the
Father (*PL* iii 63; *PR* iv 596).
16. dullness] Rochester had described D.'s poetry as dull in *An Allusion to
Horace* (in MS, early 1676) l. 2, and said that D. called Jonson dull (l. 81).
Crambo laments his own dullness, and calls Jonson dull (*The Triumphant
Widow* 22, 37, 46, 61; see headnote). D. repeats the charge of Shadwell's
dullness in *2AA* l. 477.
20. sense] See l. 6n.
21–4. Echoes the description of hell in Cowley's *Davideis*: 'There is a place
deep, wondrous deep below, / Which genuine *Night* and *Horrour* does o're-
flow; / . . . Here no dear glimpse of the *Suns* lovely face, / Strikes through the
Solid darkness of the place; / No dawning *Morn* does her kind reds display; /
One slight weak beam would here be thought the *Day*' (*Poems* 244; Van
Doren). Cp. also Boileau: 'Il est certains Esprits, dont les sombres pensées /
Sont d'un nuage épais toûjours embarrassées. / Le jour de la raison ne le
sçauroit percer' (*L' Art Poétique* (1674) i 147–9). Ken Robinson and Clare
Wenley cite Burton's account of windy, hypochondriacal melancholy: 'from
these crudities, windy vapours ascend up to the brain, which trouble the
imagination, and cause fear, sorrow, dullness, heaviness, many terrible con-
ceits and chimeras, as Lemnius well observes, *lib.* 1, *cap.* 16: "As a black and
thick cloud covers the sun, and intercepts his beams and light, so doth this
melancholy vapour obnubilate the mind, enforce it to many absurd thoughts
and imaginations"' (*Anatomy of Melancholy* 1.3.2.2; *DUJ* lxxv (1983) 25–30).
22. lucid interval] period of temporary sanity between attacks of lunacy (*OED*
lucid 3). The idea that the urge to write is a form of madness may be traced
back to Horace (*Epist.* II i 117–18; Gillian Manning, *N & Q* ccxxxv (1990)
295–6).

> But Shadwell's genuine night admits no ray,
> His rising fogs prevail upon the day.
> 25 Besides, his goodly fabric fills the eye,
> And seems designed for thoughtless majesty:
> Thoughtless as monarch oaks that shade the plain,
> And, spread in solemn state, supinely reign.
> Heywood and Shirley were but types of thee,
> 30 Thou last great prophet of tautology:
> Ev'n I, a dunce of more renown than they,

23. genuine] natural, not acquired (*OED* 1); cp. D. and Lee's *Oedipus* (1679): 'a sudden darkness covers all, / True genuine Night' (III i 293–4).

24–5. Pandaemonium, 'a fabric huge / Rose like an exhalation' (*PL* i 710–11).

25. goodly] of good appearance (*OED* 1); of considerable size (*OED* 2). It was often applied to 'fabric' or 'frame' in admiration of the earth and heavens (*OED* fabric 3a; *PL* vii 15; *Hamlet* II ii 298).   *fabric*] frame (*OED* 3b; the first example of 'fabric' used for the body is from 1695). D. ridicules Shadwell's size again in *2AA* ll. 456–65.

26. thoughtless] unmindful, careless (*OED* 1); devoid of ideas (*OED* 2, first example).

27. For the oak see *Geo.* ii 290–7, translated in 'The Second Book of the *Georgics*' ll. 397–409. Adding to Virgil, D. says that '*Joves* own Tree . . . holds the Woods in awful Sov'raignty' and 'His Shade protects the Plains'. Flecknoe had compared his patron to 'some goodly Oak . . . / Long time the pride and glory of the Wood' ('The Portrait of William Marquis of Newcastle', *Heroick Portraits* (1660) sig. E6ʳ). There is probably also a reference to the Royal Oak in which Charles hid during his escape from the Battle of Worcester; it was featured in one of the arches in his coronation entry: see John Ogilby, *The Entertainment of his Most Excellent Majestie Charles II* (1662) 37.

28. supinely] indolently (*OED* 2).

29. Heywood] Thomas Heywood (*c.* 1574–1641), prolific writer of plays and of pageants for the Lord Mayor's Show.   *Shirley*] James Shirley (1596–1666), also a prolific dramatist, particularly noted for comedy. Tom H. Towers argues that D.'s references to Heywood, Shirley and Dekker (l. 87) link Shadwell to the theatrical tradition exemplified by Christopher Beeston's company at the Red Bull, which specialized in spectacular and vulgar productions; in the Restoration the Duke's Company (for which Shadwell wrote) used more spectacle than the less well-equipped King's Company for which D. wrote (*SEL* iii (1963) 323–34).   *types*] A 'type' is a person, object or event in the OT which is taken to prefigure some person or thing fully revealed in the NT.

30. tautology] D. implies that the repetition of the same idea is a characteristic of Shadwell's plays and prefaces. Shadwell admitted that 'Another Objection, that has been made by some, is, that there is the same thing over and

Was sent before but to prepare thy way,
And coarsely clad in rustic drugget came
To teach the nations in thy greater name.
35 My warbling lute, the lute I whilom strung
When to King John of Portugal I sung,
Was but the prelude to that glorious day

---

over' (*The Sullen Lovers*; i 10). Repetition is certainly a characteristic of
Flecknoe. Settle was also accused of tautology in *Notes and Observations*
(*Works* xvii 90, 92).
32. So John the Baptist preceded Christ as 'the voice of one crying in the
wilderness, Prepare ye the way of the Lord' (Matthew iii 3).
33. coarsely clad] 'And the same John had his raiment of camel's hair, and a
leathern girdle about his loins' (Matthew iii 4). The homely dress is appropriate for Flecknoe, who had commented on the simple dress worn by the King
of Portugal: 'the *King* is an honest plain man . . . faring as homely as any
Farmer, and going as meanly clad as any *Citizen*, neither did he ever make use
of any of the Crown Wardrope, since he came unto the Crown' (*A Relation of
Ten Years Travells* [1656] 56; Paul Hammond, *EIC* xxxv (1985) 315–29).
Flecknoe assigned different clothing to different styles of satire: 'I would
cloath *Satyr* in hair-cloath, *jeering* in homespun-stuff, *jesting* in motley, and
Raillerie in silk' ('Of Railerie', *Prose Characters* 102). *rustic*] all MSS independent of *1684* (with some corruptions), *1682*; Norwich *1684*. This change from
rustic in the original text to *Norwich* in *1684* is D.'s only undoubted revision in
MF. Shadwell was a Norfolk man (though Flecknoe, who is wearing the
drugget, was from Northamptonshire). *drugget*] Cloth of wool, wool and
silk, or wool and linen; not necessarily coarse at this date (see *OED*). There
seems to be no evidence for the statement (Scott, Kinsley, *Works*) that 'Norwich drugget' was a coarse cloth. A writer in *The Gentleman's Magazine* xv
(1745) 99 drew on this line when recalling that D. in his early years in London
wore 'one uniform clothing of *Norwich* drugget' (Scott).
35–6. In *A Relation* Flecknoe recalls how in Portugal the Secretary of State
noticed his lute and informed the king: 'he sent for me to Court . . . where
after some two or three hours tryal of my skill, (especially in the compositive
part of Musick, in which his Majesty chiefly exceeded) I past *Court* Doctor'
(50–1); and in 'The *Remembrance*' he says: '*His Majesty* never danc'd, nor
Dutchess sung; / But he with's *Lute* or *Viol* still was one' (*A Treatise of the
Sports of Wit* (1675) 15 bis). Marvell described Flecknoe playing his lute in
'*Flecknoe*, an English Priest at *Rome*' (printed 1681) ll. 36–44. Wilding
observes that the lute of Flecknoe and Shadwell is a parody of the biblical
King David's lyre.
37–42. The episode referred to here is unknown, but Mrs E. E. Duncan-
Jones points out (privately) that the royal barge which Shadwell was accom-
panying might well have carried Queen Catharine, who was Portuguese,
thus providing a pointed comparison with Flecknoe's serenading of the King

> When thou on silver Thames didst cut thy way
> With well-timed oars before the royal barge,
> 40 Swelled with the pride of thy celestial charge,
> And big with hymn, commander of an host,
> The like was ne'er in Epsom blankets tossed.
> Methinks I see the new Arion sail,

of Portugal. The passage also alludes to Aeneas's voyage up the Tiber (Virgil, *Aen.* viii 86–101). Shadwell refers to his own musical ability in the Preface to *Psyche*: 'In all the words which are sung, I did not so much take care of the Wit or Fancy of 'em, as the making of 'em proper for Musick; in which I cannot but have some little knowledge, having been bred, for many years of my Youth, to some performance in it' (ii 280). See also the Prefaces to *The Sullen Lovers* and *The Humorists*.

38. Cp. Waller: 'On the smooth back of silver Thames to ride' ('Of the danger' l. 62; Noyes, citing N. H. Oswald; also for the following references to Waller).

39–40. Cp. Waller: 'These mighty Peers plac'd in the guilded Barge, / Proud with the burden of so brave a charge; / With painted oars . . .' ('Of the danger' ll. 39–41).

40. celestial charge] If the speculation in ll. 37–42*n* is correct, this would refer to the Queen (who would be degraded by being named in a satire). *charge*] responsibility (*OED* 12); person for whom one has responsibility (*OED* 14).

41. big with hymn] Echoing the description of the poet Crambo as 'big with Muse' (see headnote).   *hymn*] Primarily Shadwell's song of praise to the personage in the royal barge; possibly also associating him with the inspiration (suspect in D.'s opinion) claimed by Protestant zealots, since hymn singing was associated with radical nonconformist sects (see Christopher Hill, *A Turbulent, Seditious, and Factious People* (1988) 261–3).

42. On 17 June 1676 in Epsom a group of rakes including Rochester, Etherege and Capt. Downs tossed in a blanket some fiddlers who refused to play for them; the subsequent skirmish with the watch led to Downs's death (David M. Vieth, *Attribution in Restoration Poetry* (1963) 143). There is a subsidiary reference to Act II of Shadwell's *The Virtuoso*, where Sir Samuel Hearty, who 'by the help of humourous, nonsensical By-Words, takes himself to be a Wit', is tossed in a blanket. Editors have seen a further reference to Shadwell's *Epsom-Wells*, but this seems to lack any point.

43. Cp. Waller: 'While to his harp divine, *Arion* sings' ('Of the danger' l. 11). *Arion*] In Greek legend a musician, expert on the lyre; when he returned by ship from a music festival his prizes excited the greed of the sailors, who decided to force him overboard. Arion mounted on the prow of the ship, and sung a song which attracted a school of dolphins, one of which carried him safely ashore. Arion appears in the preface to Flecknoe's *Ariadne Deserted by Theseus* (1654; Towers).

The lute still trembling underneath thy nail:
45   At thy well-sharpened thumb from shore to shore
The treble squeaks for fear, the basses roar;
Echoes from Pissing Alley "Shadwell" call,
And "Shadwell" they resound from Aston Hall.
About thy boat the little fishes throng,
50   As at the morning toast that floats along.
Sometimes as prince of thy harmonious band
Thou wield'st thy papers in thy threshing hand:
St André's feet ne'er kept more equal time,

45–6. Cp. Waller: 'Healths to both Kings attended with the rore / Of Cannons eccho'd from th' affrighted shore' ('Of the danger' ll. 7–8).
47–8. Echoes Virgil, *Geo.* iv 526–7: *a miseram Eurydicen! anima fugiente uocabat: / Eurydicen toto referebant flumine ripae* (' "ah wretched Eurydice" [Orpheus] cried with his last voice; "Eurydice" the banks replied along the whole river') (Legouis).
47. Pissing Alley] John Ogilby and William Morgan list three Pissing Alleys in *London Survey'd* (1677) 22, 34, 35; the nearest one ran between the Strand and the Thames.
48. Aston Hall] *most MSS, 1682*; Ashton Hall *some MSS*; A— Hall *1684*. It is clear that D. wrote *Aston* or *Ashton*, so no emendation is required (*pace* Pat Rogers, who suggests 'Arm'rers Hall' (*Scriblerian* xvi (1984) 184–5)). No such place has been found in London. The reference is probably to Col. Edmund Ashton, the minor satirist and rake, who in May 1671 entertained Shadwell at his home in Lancashire; from this '*Hall* yclepped *Chaderton*' Shadwell sent Wycherley a verse letter (G. de F. Lord in *POAS* i 388; David M. Vieth, *Attribution* 257, 264; q.v. 249–70 for a life of Ashton).
49. Cp. Waller: 'With the sweet sound of this harmonious lay / About the keele delighted Dolphins play:' ('Of the danger' ll. 33–4). Flecknoe says that on his voyage from Lisbon to Brazil 'our ship being all incompast with *Dorado's* or shining Fishes (somwhat like *Dolphins*) hunting the Flying Fishes, which you might see on Top of the water, fluttering to escape . . . nor wanted we Musick to our Feast . . . the Mariners having some *Fiddles* amongst them' (*A Relation* 61–3; Hammond in *EIC* (1985)).
52. threshing] beating violently as with a flail (simply a variant spelling of 'thrashing' which some MSS have).
53–4. Shadwell's opera *Psyche* was staged by the Duke's Company at Dorset Garden in February 1675, with music by Draghi, elaborate scenery, machines, and dances arranged by the French dancing master St André. In the Preface, Shadwell apologized for his venture into rhyme, and said that 'the great Design was to entertain the Town with variety of Musick, curious Dancing, splendid Scenes and Machines: And that I do not, nor ever did, intend to value my self upon the writing of this Play' (ii 279). As Donaldson notes, Jonson would have heartily despised this production (cp. l. 6*n*).

Not ev'n the feet of thy own *Psyche*'s rhyme,
55   Though they in number as in sense excel:
So just, so like tautology they fell
That pale with envy Singleton forswore   ⎤
The lute and sword which he in triumph bore,   ⎬
And vowed he ne'er would act Villerius more.'   ⎦
60   Here stopped the good old sire, and wept for joy
In silent raptures of the hopeful boy.
All arguments, but most his plays, persuade
That for anointed dullness he was made.
Close to the walls which fair Augusta bind
65   (The fair Augusta, much to fears inclined),
An ancient fabric raised t' inform the sight
There stood of yore, and Barbican it hight:
A watchtower once, but now, so Fate ordains,
Of all the pile an empty name remains.
70   From its old ruins brothel-houses rise,
Scenes of lewd loves, and of polluted joys;
Where their vast courts the mother-strumpets keep,
And undisturbed by watch, in silence sleep.

55. *they*] the feet.   *number*] rhythm.
56. *they*] the papers.
57–9. John Singleton (d. 1686) was one of the King's musicians, who were
often employed in the theatre (see Pepys 20 November 1660). Villerius is a
character in Davenant's *The Siege of Rhodes* (1656; restaged at Whitehall some
time before 1673). The combination of lute and sword had been ridiculed in
The Rehearsal (1672), where Bayes makes two soldiers 'come out in Armor
Cap-a-pea, with their Swords drawn' but with each holding a lute, to 'play
the battel in *Recitativo*' (V 186–98).
61. *hopeful*] promising (*OED* 2).   *boy*] Shadwell was 34 (b. 1642). He is
described as 'so bonny a lad' in *A Session of the Poets* l. 30 (in MS, *c*. November 1676; *POAS* i 353).
64–73. Michael West, *SEL* xiii (1973) 442–3 suggests that this setting is
reminiscent of hell in Quevedo's *The Visions*.
64–5. Cp. Crowne: '*Augusta* is inclin'd to fears' ('Prologue to *Calisto*' (1675)
l. 45).   *Augusta*] the ancient name for London: see *AM* l. 1177*n*.   *fears*]
of plots by Catholics or radical Protestants, as well as foreign invasion.
66–9. The Barbican was in the parish of St Giles, Cripplegate, which also
included Grub Street; the area was associated with nonconformity, plague,
licentiousness and madness: see Pat Rogers, *Grub Street* (1972) 18–37.
66. *inform*] inspire, impress (*OED* 3).
67. *hight*] was called.
72–3. Echoes Cowley's description of hell in the *Davideis*: 'Where their vast
Court the *Mother-waters* keep, / And undisturb'd by *Moons* in silence sleep'

Near these a nursery erects its head,
75 Where queens are formed, and future heroes bred;
Where unfledged actors learn to laugh and cry, ⎤
Where infant punks their tender voices try,   ⎬
And little Maximins the gods defy.   ⎦
Great Fletcher never treads in buskins here,
80 Nor greater Jonson dares in socks appear;
But gentle Simkin just reception finds
Amidst this monument of vanished minds.

(*Poems* 244; Christie). That the reference was familiar is shown by the reversion to the reading 'mother waters' in MS Harvard fMS Eng 636. D. had previously echoed these lines in *To His Sacred Majesty* ll. 113–14. In 'The Authors Apology for Heroique Poetry, and Poetique Licence' prefixed to *The State of Innocence* (1677), D. quotes these lines by Cowley and says: 'How easie 'tis to turn into ridicule, the best descriptions, when once a man is in the humour of laughing, till he wheezes at his own dull jest! but an Image which is strongly and beautifully set before the eyes of the Reader, will still be Poetry, when the merry fit is over: and last when the other is forgotten' (sig. c1ᵛ).

74. nursery] A theatre for the training of young actors was built in the Barbican by Lady Davenant in 1671, despite opposition from the residents (Hotson 176–94). On 23 November 1671 Joseph Williamson noted that the two nurseries in Barbican and Bunhill were a source of opposition to the government (*CSPD 1671* 581; W. J. Cameron).

75. queens] punning on 'quean' (also spelt 'queen'), prostitute.

76–7. Echoes Cowley: 'Beneath the dens where *unfletcht Tempests* lye, / And infant *Winds* their tender *Voyces* try' (*Poems* 244). For a subsequent echo see 'The Tenth Book of the *Aeneis*' ll. 149–50.

77. punks] prostitutes.

78. Maximin is the ranting, atheist emperor in D.'s *Tyrannic Love* (1670). In his dedication to *The Spanish Friar* (1681) D. expresses regret for Maximin's extravagances (sig. A2ᵛ; Kinsley).

79–80. John Fletcher (1579–1625) and Ben Jonson (?1572–1637), the major Jacobean dramatists to whom Restoration criticism looks back (e.g. in D.'s *EDP* (1668)).   *buskins*] boots supposedly worn by actors in Greek tragedy.   *socks*] low shoes supposedly worn by actors in Greek comedy. Buskins and socks stand for tragedy and comedy in Jonson's 'To the memory of my beloved, The Author Mr. William Shakespeare' ll. 36–7; and cp. Milton, 'L' Allegro' l. 132.

81. gentle] well-born (ironic here).   *Simkin*] the clown in *The Humours of Simpkin* (printed in Francis Kirkman's *The Wits, or Sport upon Sport* (1672)); generally, a simpleton (*OED*). In Shadwell's *The Miser* Timothy enjoys '*Simkin* in the Chest' and other 'Pretty harmless Drolls' (ii 53; Kinsley).

82. In Davenant's *Gondibert* (1651) there is a repository of books, 'a structure

Pure clinches the suburbian Muse affords,
And Panton waging harmless war with words.
85 Here Flecknoe, as a place to Fame well known,
Ambitiously designed his Shadwell's throne;
For ancient Dekker prophesied long since ⎤
That in this pile should reign a mighty prince, ⎬
Born for a scourge of wit, and flail of sense, ⎦

. . . long knowne to Fame, / And cald, *The Monument of vanish'd Mindes*' (II v
36; Noyes, citing J. C. Collins).

83. clinches] puns, word-play (*OED*).   *suburbian*] At this period the suburbs
were often associated with squalor and licentiousness; cp. Flecknoe: 'He is so far
from a courtly Wit, as his breeding seems only to have been i' th' Suburbs; or at
best, he seems onely graduated good companion in a Tavern' (*Prose Characters*
42); see also examples in *OED*, and Pat Rogers, *Grub Street passim*.

84. Panton] Probably Capt. Edward Panton (suggested by E. E. Duncan-
Jones, privately). He wrote *Speculum Juventutis* (1671), a treatise on the education of the nobility which stresses the need for the rulers of empires not to
be ignorant, and says that their natural abilities should be improved by art.
However, he also argues for the precedence of arms over arts, and devotes
much attention to the proper conduct of duels. In 1676 (the year of *MF*) he
published *A Publick and Pious Design for the Preserving the Generous Youth, and
Consequently the Nation from Ruine*, in which he sets out plans to found a
'Royal Academy' at Chelsea or another place near London to educate the sons
of the nobility; his scheme includes a promise to teach them 'to Speak &
Write Proper and Short, Without Tautology or Repetition' (3; cp. *MF* ll. 30,
56).

85. a place to Fame well known] Cp. l. 82n.

86. Ambitiously] Ambition is a characteristic of Satan (*PL* i 262 etc).   *designed*] design also has Satanic connotations (*PL* i 646 etc).

87. Dekker] Thomas Dekker (*c.* 1572–1632), dramatist and City poet (cp. l.
29n). Dekker, once a rival and antagonist of Jonson, is seen as a forerunner
and prophet of Shadwell. In Dekker's *Satiromastix* (1602), an attack on Jonson, Horace (who represents Jonson) prophesies 'That we to learned eares
should sweetly sing, / But to the vulger and adulterate braine, / Should loath
to prostitute our Virgin straine' (II ii 57–9). G. B. Evans notes that *Satiromastix* (which means 'a whipping of the satire', cp. *flail* in l. 89) was performed
by the Children of Paul's, and may therefore have been associated by D. with
an earlier kind of nursery (*MLN* lxxvi (1961) 598–600). When attacking
Settle in *Notes and Observations on the Empress of Morocco* (1673; *Works* xvii 84)
D. had said: 'I knew indeed that to Write against him, was to do him too
great an Honour: But I consider'd *Ben. Johnson* had done it before to *Decker*,
our Authors Predecessor, whom he chastis'd in his *Poetaster* . . . and brought
him in Vomiting up his Fustian and Non-sense' (Donaldson).

89. flail] Pace S. H. Monk (*N & Q* ccv (1960) 67–8) *MF* is too early for this to

90   To whom true dullness should some *Psyches* owe,
      But worlds of *Misers* from his pen should flow;
      Humourists and *Hypocrites* it should produce,
      Whole Raymond families, and tribes of Bruce.
      Now Empress Fame had published the renown
95   Of Shadwell's coronation through the town.
      Roused by report of Fame, the nations meet
      From near Bunhill and distant Watling Street.
      No Persian carpets spread th' imperial way,
      But scattered limbs of mangled poets lay:
100 From dusty shops neglected authors come,
      Martyrs of pies, and relics of the bum.
      Much Heywood, Shirley, Ogilby there lay,
      But loads of Shadwell almost choked the way.
      Bilked stationers for yeomen stood prepared,
105 And Herringman was captain of the guard.

---

allude to the 'Protestant flail' which was used during the Popish Plot (1678–
9).   *sense*] See l. 6n.

90–3. Alludes to Shadwell's plays *Psyche* (see ll. 53–4*n*), *The Miser*, based on
Molière's *L'Avare*, *The Hypocrite* (never printed), presumably based on
Molière's *Tartuffe*, and *The Humorists*. Raymond and Bruce are gentlemen of
wit in *The Humorists* and *The Virtuoso* respectively.

94. Fame] Rumour, as in Virgil, *Aen.* iv 173–7.

97. Bunhill] Bunhill Fields, on the edge of Cripplegate, a burial ground for
nonconformists (not, *pace Works*, for plague victims: see Rogers, *Grub Street*
29). It was already associated with bad poetry by Dekker in his preface to
Satiromastix, where he writes of the world of poetry from 'all mount *Helicon*
to *Bun-hill*' (Evans).   *Watling Street*] in the heart of the City.

101. Martyrs of pies] In *EDP* (1668) D. said of Robert Wild: 'they have bought
more Editions of his Works then would serve to lay under all their Pies at the
Lord Mayor's *Christmass*' (*Works* xvii 12; Kinsley).   *relics of the bum*] In his
Advertisement to *Poems, and Translations* (1683) Oldham says: 'If it be their
Fate to perish, and go the way of all mortal Rhimes, 'tis no great matter . . .
whether *Ode*, *Elegy*, or *Satyr* have the honor of Wiping first' (*Poems* 161).

102. Ogilby] John Ogilby (1600–76), friend of Shirley, dancing master,
Master of the Revels in Ireland, founder of the theatre in Dublin; translator of
Virgil (1649), Aesop (1651), the *Iliad* (1660) and *Odyssey* (1665); publisher of
atlases (1670–75; cp. l. 47*n*); author of 'the poetical part' of *The Entertainment
of . . . Charles II* (1662) describing the King's coronation entry and ceremony.

104. Bilked] cheated, unpaid.   *stationers*] publishers.

105. Herringman] Henry Herringman was the publisher of D.'s works to

The hoary prince in majesty appeared,
High on a throne of his own labours reared.
At his right hand our young Ascanius sate,
Rome's other hope, and pillar of the state:
110　His brows thick fogs, instead of glories, grace,
And lambent dullness played around his face.
As Hannibal did to the altars come,
Sworn by his sire a mortal foe to Rome,
So Shadwell swore, nor should his vow be vain,
115　That he till death true dullness would maintain,
And in his father's right, and realm's defence,
Ne'er to have peace with wit, nor truce with sense.

1678, of Shadwell's plays from *Epsom-Wells* (1673) to *Timon of Athens* (1678), and of Flecknoe's *The Diarium* (1656).

107. Echoes *PL* ii 1, where Satan sits 'High on a throne of royal state'.

108–9. Echoes Virgil, *Aen.* xii 168: *iuxta Ascanius, magnae spes altera Romae* ('And by his [Aeneas's] side *Ascanius* took his place, / The second Hope of *Rome*'s Immortal Race': 'The Twelfth Book of the *Aeneis*' ll. 253–4). The phrase *Magnae Spes Altera Romae* is said to have been used of Virgil by Cicero (see Knightly Chetwood's 'Preface to the Pastorals' in *Works* v 41), and is inscribed on a medal of Virgil reproduced in D.'s copy of *P. Virgilii Maronis Opera* (1636) acquired in 1685 (now in Cambridge UL). 'Spes Altera' was the motto assigned to the Duke of York in the coronation entry (Ogilby, *The Entertainment* 93).

108. Ascanius] the son of Aeneas.　　　*sate*] common seventeenth-century spelling of 'sat'.

109. pillar of the state] Beelzebub is called 'a pillar of state' (*PL* ii 302; Wilding).

110–11. Echoes Virgil, *Aen.* ii 682–4: *ecce leui summo de uertice uisus Iuli / fundere lumen apex, tactuque innoxia mollis / lambere flamma comas et circum tempora pasci* ('from young *Iulus* [i.e. Ascanius's] Head / A lambent Flame arose, which gently spread / Around his Brows, and on his Temples fed.': 'The Second Book of the *Aeneis*' ll. 930–2). The flame around the head of Ascanius is a sign of divine approval and protection. For the phrasing of l. 111 cp. Cowley: 'Like harmless *Lambent Fires* about my Temples play' ('The Extasie', *Poems* 204).

110. glories] circles of light, haloes (*OED*).

111. lambent] playing lightly over the surface (*OED*; first example is from Cowley, 1647).

112–13. When Hannibal was about nine years old, his father Hamilcar took him to the altar and made him swear that he would become an enemy to Rome (Livy xxi 1).

The king himself the sacred unction made,
As king by office, and as priest by trade:
120 In his sinister hand, instead of ball
He placed a mighty mug of potent ale;
Love's Kingdom to his right he did convey,
At once his sceptre and his rule of sway,
Whose righteous lore the prince had practised young,
125 And from whose loins recorded *Psyche* sprung.

118. unction] the oil used to anoint the king as part of the coronation ceremony.

119. Kings were traditionally held to have priestly attributes (see E. H. Kantorowicz, *The King's Two Bodies* (1957)). Flecknoe was himself a Roman Catholic priest, here seen as merely a 'trade'; cp. the pejorative 'priestcraft' in *AA* l. 1.

120–3. In the coronation ceremony the orb ('ball') is placed in the monarch's left hand, and the sceptre in the right.

120. sinister] left; accented on the second syllable in the seventeenth century.

121. potent ale] Flecknoe's reign as king at Twelfth Night was characterized by abundant drink (see headnote), and he wrote an epigram 'In Execration of small [i.e. weak] Beer' (*Epigrams of All Sorts* (1669) 13–14). Shadwell's verse letter to Wycherley begins with an invocation of ale: 'Inspir'd with high and mighty Ale, / That does with stubborn Muse prevail: / Ale, that makes Tinker mighty Witty, / And makes him Droll out merry Ditty' (v 227; Wilding). Shadwell and Flecknoe are Jonson's heirs in their drinking, if not in their wit (Hammond in *EIC* (1985)). D. has a portrait of Shadwell drunk in *2AA* ll. 457–66.

122–5. Love's Kingdom] Flecknoe's 'Pastoral Trage-Comedy', originally published as *Love's Dominion* (1654), was revised, retitled and printed in 1664; reissued 1674. When staged by the Duke's Company in 1664 'it had the misfortune to be damn'd by the Audience' (Langbaine). *Psyche*, as a pastoral opera, is its offspring.

123. Cp. Cowley: 'At once his *Murder* and his *Monument*' (*Davideis* i; *Poems* 247).

124. righteous lore] The title page of *Love's Dominion* claims: 'Full of Excellent Moralitie; Written as a Pattern for the Reformed Stage'. In his Preface Flecknoe says: 'I have endeavoured here the clearing of it [the stage], and restoring it to its former splendor, and first institution; (of teaching *Virtue*, reproving *Vice*, and amendment of *Manners*,)' (sig. A4ᵛ). *Love's Kingdom* is prefaced by 'A Short Discourse of the English Stage'. Flecknoe's emphasis on the moral responsibility of the drama is consistent with the line taken by Shadwell in his debate with D.

125. recorded] rendered in song, warbled (*OED* 2); probably facetious, since the word was applied mainly to birds, and was becoming obsolete. James Winn (privately) notes that Matthew Locke's music for *Psyche* has prominent parts for recorders. In his Preface to *Psyche*, Shadwell says that 'in all the

His temples last with poppies were o'erspread,
That nodding seemed to consecrate his head.
Just at that point of time, if Fame not lie,
On his left hand twelve reverend owls did fly:
130   So Romulus, 'tis sung, by Tiber's brook
Presage of sway from twice six vultures took.
Th' admiring throng loud acclamations make,
And omens of his future empire take.
The sire then shook the honours of his head,
135   And from his brows damps of oblivion shed
Full on the filial dullness; long he stood   ⎫
Repelling from his breast the raging god;   ⎬
At length burst out in this prophetic mood: ⎭

words which are sung, I did not so much take care of the Wit or Fancy of
'em, as the making of 'em proper for Musick' (ii 280).
126. poppies] The poppy is (i) soporific (e.g. *Aen.* iv 486, and the cave of sleep
in *Met.* xi 605); (ii) parching and sterilizing (e.g. *Geo.* i 78); (iii) aphrodisiac
but not fertilizing (e.g. Thomas Browne, *Pseudodoxia Epidemica* (1646) vii 7;
Kinsley). Shadwell was addicted to opium (*2AA* l. 482; Scott).
129. owls] signifying apparent wisdom but actual stupidity (*OED* 2).
130. Romulus and Remus agreed to settle a dispute about the site of Rome by
observing the flight of birds of omen. Remus saw six vultures and Romulus
twelve (Plutarch, *Romulus* ix 4–5).
132. admiring throng] Wilding notes echoes of the devils entering Pandaemonium in *PL*: 'the hasty multitude / Admiring entered', and 'all access was
thronged' (i 730–1, 761).   *admiring*] wondering, marvelling.
134–6. Echoes Cowley's *Davideis*: 'He saw the reverend *Prophet* boldly shed /
The *Royal Drops* round his *Enlarged Head*', and 'He tells the mighty *Fate* to
him assign'd, / And with great rules fills his *capacious mind*. / Then takes the
sacred *Viol*, and does shed / A *Crown* of mystique drops around his head'
(*Poems* 245, 375, describing the anointing of David by Samuel; Korn). Wilding observes that 'the "damps" and "dullness" have extinguished and darkened the dignity of the light and enlightenment of *Paradise Lost*, where the
Father "on his Son with Rays direct / Shon full" prior to Christ's enthrone-
ment' (*PL* vi 719–20).
134. shook the honours] 'Honours, that is, *Beauties*, which make things
Honoured' (Cowley, *Davideis* ii n. 1; *Poems* 306). The usage is Virgilian, as in
laetos oculis adflarat honores (*Aen.* i 591; 'she had breathed beauty into his
eyes'). In 'The Tenth Book of the *Aeneis*' l. 172 D. says that Jupiter 'shook the
sacred Honours of his Head' (translating *adnuit*, 'he nodded': *Aen.* x 115).
135. damps] fogs (*OED* 2).
136. the filial dullness] For the Miltonic echoes cp. 'the filial Godhead' (*PL* vi
722, vii 175) and 'the filial power arrived, and sate him down' (*PL* vii 587).
137–8. Echoes Virgil, *Aen.* vi 77–82, on the Sibyl, the frenzied prophetess: *at*

'Heavens bless my son: from Ireland let him reign
140 To far Barbados on the western main;
Of his dominion may no end be known,
And greater than his father's be his throne.
Beyond *Love's Kingdom* let him stretch his pen;'
He paused, and all the people cried, 'Amen'.
145 Then thus continued he, 'My son, advance
Still in new impudence, new ignorance.
Success let others teach; learn thou from me

Phoebi nondum patiens immanis in antro / bacchatur uates, magnum si pectore possit / excussisse deum; tanto magis ille fatigat / os rabidum, fera corda domans, fingitque premendo. ('Strugling in vain, impatient her Load, / And lab'ring underneath the pond'rous God, / The more she strove to shake him from her Breast, / With more, and far superior Force he press'd: / Commands his Entrance, and without Controul, / Usurps her Organs, and inspires her Soul.': 'The Sixth Book of the *Aeneis*' ll. 120–5; Brower).

139. Ireland] See Title, *n.*

140. Echoes Cowley, *Davideis*: 'From sacred *Jordan* to the *Western main*' (*Poems* 366; Korn).   *Barbados*] Probably thought of as the setting for the D.–Davenant version of *The Tempest* (1674) which Shadwell had turned into an opera (Aline M. Taylor, *SP* extra series iv (1967) 39–53); also proverbially remote and uncivilized (cp. Wycherley, *The Gentleman Dancing-Master* (1672) II i 460–6; Alan Roper in *Works*). Flecknoe's journeys took him to Brazil, but not to Barbados.

141. Echoes Isaiah ix 7: 'Of the increase of his government and peace there shall be no end' (interpreted as a prophecy of the Messiah).   *dominion*] See l. 6*n.*

143. pen] For the pun on 'penis' cp. 'I'll mar the young clerk's pen' (*The Merchant of Venice* V i 237).

144. Cp. Nehemiah viii 6: 'And all the people answered, Amen' (Korn).

145. Ed.; Then thus, continued he, my Son advance *1684*. The commas in *1684* (which does not use inverted commas to mark speech) imply that *Then thus* are the opening words of Flecknoe's speech, but *1682* and all the MSS have no comma after *thus*, which is therefore probably a compositorial error.   *advance*] Cp. Shadwell's 'Prologue to the King and Queen' from *Epsom-Wells*: 'Poets and Souldiers used to various chance, / Cannot expect they should each day advance' (ll. 1–2; ii 105).

147–8. Echoes Aeneas's advice to Ascanius in *Aen.* xii 435–6: *disce, puer, uirtutem ex me uerumque laborem, / fortunam ex aliis* ('boy, learn virtue and true labour from me, good fortune from others'; G. C. Loane, *N & Q* clxxxv (1943) 275).

Pangs without birth, and fruitless industry.
Let *Virtuosos* in five years be writ,
150 Yet not one thought accuse thy toil of wit.
Let gentle George in triumph tread the stage,
Make Dorimant betray, and Loveit rage;
Let Cully, Cockwood, Fopling charm the pit,
And in their folly show the writer's wit;
155 Yet still thy fools shall stand in thy defence,
And justify their author's want of sense.
Let 'em be all by thy own model made
Of dullness, and desire no foreign aid,
That they to future ages may be known
160 Not copies drawn, but issue of thy own.
Nay, let thy men of wit too be the same,
All full of thee, and differing but in name.

148. Echoes Shadwell's Epilogue to *The Virtuoso*: 'You know the pangs and many labouring throws, / By which your Brains their perfect births disclose' (ll. 36–7; iii 182; Noyes, citing Oswald). Cp. Crambo's supposed pregnancy in *The Triumphant Widow* (see headnote).

149. In his Prologue to *The Virtuoso*, Shadwell says that wit 'requires expence of time and pains, / Too great, alas, for Poets slender gains. / For Wit, like *China*, should long buri'd lie, / Before it ripens to good Comedy: / . . . Now Drudges of the Stage must oft appear, / They must be bound to scribble twice a year' (ll. 7–14; iii 103). Rochester in *An Allusion to Horace* (in MS, winter 1675–6; l. 46) calls Shadwell 'hasty'. Shadwell claimed that *The Libertine* took him three weeks (iii 21). The suggestion that *The Virtuoso* took five years may be a deliberate misreading of Shadwell's reference in his Dedication to 'the *Humorists*, written five Years since' (iii 102) (Kinsley).

151–4. These lines refer to Sir George Etherege (?1636–?92) and several characters from his plays: Dorimant, Mrs Loveit and Sir Fopling Flutter from *The Man of Mode* (staged 11 March 1676), Sir Nicholas Cully from *The Comical Revenge, or, Love in a Tub* (1664), and Sir Oliver Cockwood from *She wou'd if She cou'd* (1668).

151. gentle] This epithet is again applied to Etherege in *A Session of the Poets* l. 16 (in MS *c.* November 1676; *POAS* i 353).

155–6. This is a retort to Shadwell's comment on himself in the Prologue to *The Virtuoso*: 'He's sure in Wit he cann't excel the rest, / He'd but be thought to write a Fool the best' (ll. 23–4; iii 103; *Works*).

160. Vieth compares the Epilogue to *The Humorists*: 'All that have since [Jonson] been writ, if they be scan'd, / Are but faint Copies from that Master's Hand' (ll. 24–5; i 254). Donaldson observes that Jonson had said of Shakespeare: 'Looke how the fathers face / Liues in his issue' ('To the memory of . . . Mr. William Shakespeare' ll. 65–6).

But let no alien Sedley interpose
To lard with wit thy hungry Epsom prose,
165 And when false flowers of rhetoric thou wouldst cull,
Trust nature, do not labour to be dull;
But write thy best, and top, and in each line
Sir Formal's oratory will be thine:
Sir Formal, though unsought, attends thy quill,
170 And does thy northern dedications fill.

163–4. Rumour had it that *Epsom-Wells* was not Shadwell's unaided work, and in his 'Prologue to the King and Queen' he said: 'If this for him had been by others done, / After this honour sure they'd claim their own' (ll. 16–17), and printed it with this note: 'These two Lines were writ in answer to the calumny of some impotent and envious Scriblers, and some industrious Enemies of mine, who would have made the Town and Court believe, though I am sure they themselves did not, that I did not write the Play; but at last it was found to be so frivolous a piece of malice, it left an impression upon few or none' (ii 105). Sir Charles Sedley wrote a Prologue for *Epsom-Wells*; later he corrected Shadwell's *A True Widow* (1679) for him (Noyes; Kinsley). Vieth notes that Rochester's *Timon* (in MS, 1674) refers to 'Shadwell's unassisted former scenes' (l. 16).

164. Burton says of writers who pilfer from others: 'They lard their lean books with the fat of others' works' (*The Anatomy of Melancholy* 23). *hungry*] not satisfying one's hunger (*OED* 3a); not rich or fertile (*OED* 6).

165. flowers of rhetoric] See l. 168n.

166. Shadwell in the Preface to *The Virtuoso* writes of 'those, who are not Coxcombs by Nature, but with great Art and Industry make themselves so' (iii 102). Cp. Rochester: 'Shadwell's unfinished works do yet impart / Great proofs of force of nature, none of art' (*An Allusion to Horace* ll. 44–5). Flecknoe in 'Of a Dull-fellow' says: 'if he say any thing like a *pump*, he labours for it', and in 'Of Wit': 'it is . . . not acquired by *Art* and *Study*, but *Nature* and *Conversation*' (*Prose Characters* 269, 521). Flecknoe admitted that writing epigrams and characters suited him because they are 'a short and easy kind of writing; and therefore most fit for me, who Love not long discourses, and cannot take pains in anything' (*Epigrams of All Sorts* (1669) sig. A3ʳ⁻ᵛ). See also ll. 175–6n and Shadwell's Preface to *Timon of Athens*. The basic antithesis between art and nature in poetic creativity goes back to Horace, *Ars Poetica* ll. 408–18. Tonson echoed D.'s line in 'On the Death of Mr. Oldham': 'sweated not to be correctly dull' (*Sylvae* (1685) 472); cp. l. 178n.

168. Sir Formal Trifle in *The Virtuoso* is 'the greatest Master of Tropes and Figures: The most *Ciceronian* Coxcomb: the noblest Orator breathing; he never speaks without Flowers of Rhetorick: In short, he is very much abounding in words, and very much defective in sense' (iii 107).

170. northern dedications] Shadwell dedicated *The Sullen Lovers*, *Epsom-Wells*, *The Virtuoso* and *The Libertine* to the Duke of Newcastle. Flecknoe had

Nor let false friends seduce thy mind to fame
By arrogating Jonson's hostile name:
Let father Flecknoe fire thy mind with praise,
And uncle Ogilby thy envy raise.
175 Thou art my blood, where Jonson has no part;
What share have we in nature or in art?
Where did his wit on learning fix a brand,

---

dedicated *Love's Kingdom* to the Duke, *A Farrago of Several Pieces* (1666) to the
Duchess, and *The Damoiselles A La Mode* (1667) to both Duke and Duchess;
he also addressed several poems to them. The Duke returned the compliment
with commendatory poems for *Rich. Flecknoe's Ænigmaticall Characters*
(1665). Newcastle had been patron of Jonson and Shirley; he had collaborated
with D. on *Sir Martin Mar-all* (1668), and D. dedicated *An Evening's Love*
(1671) to him. See further Harold Love, *PLL* xxi (1985) 19–27, though
Love's suggestion that *MF* was originally a satire on Newcastle is implausible.

173–4. Echoes *Aen.* iii 342–3: *ecquid in antiquam uirtutem animosque uirilis / et
pater Aeneas et auunculus excitat Hector?* ('do his father Aeneas and his uncle
Hector rouse him [Ascanius] to ancient virtue and manly spirit?'; Kinsley).

174. envy] desire to equal another in achievement (without malevolent feelings) (*OED* 4).

175–6. Echoes Jonson on Shakespeare: 'Yet must I not giue Nature all: Thy
Art, / My gentle *Shakespeare*, must enioy a part' ('To the memory of . . . Mr.
William Shakespeare' ll. 55–6; Donaldson). The antithesis between nature
and art had informed the debate over the relative merits of Shakespeare and
Jonson; Flecknoe wrote: '*Shakespear* excelled in a natural Vein, . . . *Johnson* in
Gravity and ponderousness of Style; whose onely fault was, he was too
elaborate; and had he mixt less erudition with his Playes, they had been more
pleasant and delightful then they are. Comparing him with *Shakespear*, you
shall see the difference betwixt Nature and Art' (*Love's Kingdom* sig. G5ʳ).
Cp. also D.'s 'Prologue to *The Tempest*' ll. 5–8, and Rochester, quoted in l.
166*n*.

177–8. (i) As in Flecknoe's criticism of Jonson's learning (see ll. 175–6*n*); (ii)
as in *The Virtuoso*, in so far as it might be construed as caricaturing the new
science (for an argument that the play does not attack true virtuosi see Joseph
M. Gilde, *SEL* x (1970) 469–90); (iii) as in Shadwell's disparagement of the
art of heroic drama, e.g. in the Epilogue to *The Virtuoso*: 'sniveling Heroes
sigh, and pine, and cry. / Though singly they beat Armies, and huff Kings, /
Rant at the Gods, and do impossible things' (ll. 14–16; iii 181; Vieth); (iv) as
in Shadwell's criticism of the comedy of wit in his debate with D. (see
headnote).

177. brand] Jonson had written of Inigo Jones: 'Thy Forehead is too narrow
for my Brand' ('To a ffriend an Epigram Of Him' l. 14), and cp. Martial XII
lxi 11 (Donaldson).

And rail at arts he did not understand?
Where made he love in Prince Nicander's vein,
180   Or swept the dust in *Psyche*'s humble strain?
Where sold he bargains, "whip-stitch, kiss my arse",
Promised a play and dwindled to a farce?

178. understand] Jonson frequently stressed the need for readers to understand his work, e.g. 'Pray thee, take care, that tak'st my booke in hand, / To reade it well: that is, to vnderstand' (*Epigrammes* i), and the preface to *The Alchemist*: 'To the Reader. If thou beest more, thou art an Vnderstander, and then I trust thee.' (v 291). Donaldson notes that in the Dedication to *The Assignation* (1673) D. said: 'I know I honour *Ben Johnson* more than my little Critiques, because without vanity I may own, I understand him better' (*Works* xi 322). Snarl in *The Virtuoso* says of young men that 'they are all forward and positive in things they understand not; they laugh at any Gentleman that has Art or Science' (iii 131). D.'s line was echoed by Tonson on Oldham: 'And censur'd what they did not understand' (*Sylvae* 473).
179. Nicander pursues Psyche with 'Industrious Love' and high rhetoric (Kinsley). D.'s phrase echoes Falstaff, who promises to play Henry IV 'in King Cambyses' vein' (*1 Henry IV* II iv 383); and cp. Buckingham's Prologue to *The Rehearsal* (1672): 'There strutting Heroes, with a grim fac'd train, / Shall brave the Gods, in King *Cambyses* vein' (ll. 9–10).
180. humble] Shadwell says in the Prologue to *Psyche*: 'You must not here expect exalted Thought, / Nor lofty Verse, nor Scenes with labor wrought: / His Subject's humble, and his Verse is so' (ll. 12–14; ii 281; Noyes, citing Oswald).
181. i.e. 'Where did Jonson use coarse repartee such as "whip-stitch, kiss my arse"?' D. is continuing the debate with Shadwell over wit and humours (see headnote). D. had used repartee in his comedies, and defended it; here he convicts the would-be Jonsonian Shadwell of using repartee coarser than D.'s, and without precedent in Jonson.   *sold . . . bargains*] To sell someone bargains was to make a fool of them (*OED* 7), specifically to give a coarse reply to a question: in the Prologue to *The Debauchee* (1677), boorish men are told: 'to be brisk, and free, / You sell 'em Bargains for a Repartee' (ll. 42–3; Danchin no. 229), and Sir Carr Scrope's Prologue to Lee's *The Rival Queens* (1677) says that the sparks in the theatre 'with loud Non-sense drown the Stages Wit: / . . . And witty Bargains to each other sell' (ll. 24–6; Danchin no. 231).   *"whip-stitch, kiss my arse"*] Quoting Sir Samuel Hearty in *The Virtuoso*: 'Prethee, *Longvil*, hold thy peace, with a whip-stitch, your nose in my breech' (iii 119). From being a stitch in needlework, *whip-stitch* came to mean 'suddenly' (*OED*). Kinsley notes that Settle says that 'Whip stitch, your Nose in my Breech' are 'Link-boy phrases' (Preface to *Ibrahim* (1677) sig. a3ʳ).
182. In the Dedication to *The Virtuoso* Shadwell says: 'I have endeavoured, in this Play, at Humour, Wit, and Satyr, which are . . . the life of a Comedy. . . .

When did his Muse from Fletcher scenes purloin,
As thou whole Eth'rege dost transfuse to thine?
185   But so transfused as oil on water's flow,

Nor do I count those Humours which . . . consist in using one or two By
words . . . I say nothing of impossible, unnatural Farce Fools, which some
intend for Comical, who think it the easiest thing in the World to write a
Comedy' (iii 101; Noyes). D. had expressed his contempt for the contemporary fashion for farce in the Preface to *An Evening's Love* (1671; *Works* x 202–4)
and 'Prologue to *1 Conquest of Granada*' ll. 35–9, and his *Marriage A-la-Mode*
(1673) is an attempt to elevate the tone of comedy (see Hume 277). For verbal
parallels to l. 182 cp. 'this Huff, like all those in his Play, dwindles, when
examin'd, into non-sense or nothing' and 'has debased Tragedy into farce'
(*Notes and Observations*; *Works* xvii 88, 90).

184. Noyes shows that there are similarities between some characters and
plot-devices in Etherege's *She wou'd if She cou'd* (1668) and *Epsom-Wells*
(1673); Vieth (1979) 75 shows that similar roles and incidents are used again in
The Virtuoso (1676), and points out that *She wou'd* was revived *c.* February
1676 and would therefore have been fresh in the minds of the audience of *The
Virtuoso*. Ironically, Flecknoe had attacked Etherege's play as offering 'sparks
of wit, as much as you'd desire, / But sparks alone, as far from solid fire' ('On
the Play, of she wou'd, if she cou'd', *Epigrams of All Sorts* (1669) 10–
11).   *transfuse*] Vieth (1979) 75 suggests that D. alludes to Sir Nicholas
Gimcrack's transfusions of blood between a mangy spaniel and a sound
bulldog in *The Virtuoso* (iii 128).

185–6. Perhaps recalling Cowley: 'That *Oyl* mixt with any other liquor, still
gets uppermost, is perhaps one of the chiefest *Significancies* in the *Ceremony of
Anointing Kings* and *Priests*' (*Davideis* iv n. 28; *Poems* 399; Korn).

185. oil on water's flow] Noyes; Oyl on Waters flow *1684*. The line has always
been problematic, as Vieth's collation of the MSS shows. *1684* is either (i)
textually correct and grammatically correct; or (ii) textually correct but
grammatically incorrect; or (iii) textually corrupt and grammatically incorrect. If (i), then Noyes's proposal that *flow* is a noun is the only possible
interpretation of the line. In this case *1684* requires no emendation but only
modernization (*Waters* could be modernized to either *water's* or *waters'*). Elsewhere D. does use *flow* as a noun, meaning the opposite of ebb (e.g. *AM* l.
645), but he more frequently uses it as a verb (e.g. 'Prologue to *All for Love*'
ll. 25–6, q.v. for a parallel), while in *RL* l. 341 it could be taken either way. If
(ii), then D. wrote *Oyl . . . flow*, wrongly allowing the verb *flow* to take a
plural form under the influence of *Waters* and of the rhyme. In seventeenth-
century English, plural subjects often take singular verbs, but the reverse is
very rare (Manfred Görlach, *Introduction to Early Modern English* (1991) 88 has
only one example, from 1591; information from Jonathan Hope); though
unlikely, this interpretation is possible. Both (i) and (ii) assume that *Oyl* is the
textually correct reading. In favour of this is the fact that *Oyl* is supported by

His always floats above, thine sinks below.
This is thy province, this thy wondrous way,
New humours to invent for each new play.
This is that boasted bias of thy mind,
190 By which one way, to dullness, 'tis inclined,
Which makes thy writings lean on one side still,
And in all changes that way bends thy will.
Nor let thy mountain belly make pretence

---

three MSS independent of *1684*, and (as Vieth (1976) 228 argues) the agreement of *1684* with one or more independent MSS is good testimony that their reading was present in the original 1676 text. If (iii), then *flow* is a verb, and *Oyl* is a textual corruption of *Oyls*, as Evans argues. In favour of this is that *1682* and nine MSS read *Oyls*. But in textual criticism the number of witnesses to a reading is no indication of its authority, and *Oyls* is a suspiciously easy resolution of the crux (which other MSS attempt to solve by emending *on* to *and*, *of* or *in*). If the original reading was indeed *Oyls* it is difficult to explain how *1684* and three MSS arrived at the harder reading *Oyl*. The textual evidence therefore points to D. having written *Oyl* in 1676; this produced a difficult line which most MSS tried to regularize in various ways; and the line stood unrevised in *1684*. On textual grounds, then, (iii) seems the least likely explanation. The grounds for deciding between (i) and (ii) can only be one's assumptions about D.'s grammar. In favour of (i) is that a grammatical error is unlikely to have eluded D. both in 1676 and when rereading *MF* for *1684*; in favour of (ii) is that the syntax leads one to expect a verb, and D. was not infallible. The argument is inconclusive, and Noyes's solution is adopted here since it produces a grammatical line without altering *1684*. Kinsley and *Works* are silent on this crux.

186. sinks below] When Sir Formal disappears down the trap in Act III of *The Virtuoso* the stage direction reads 'He sinks below' (iii 145).

187. province] See ll. 4, 6n.

188. Cp. the Preface to *The Virtuoso*: 'Four of the Humors are entirely new; and (without vanity) I may say, I ne'er produc'd a Comedy that had not some natural Humour in it not represented before, nor I hope I ever shall' (iii 101; Noyes).

189–92. Parodies Shadwell's Epilogue to *The Humorists*: 'A Humor is the Byas of the Mind, / By which with violence 'tis one way inclin'd: / It makes our Actions lean on one side still, / And in all Changes that way bends the Will' (ll. 15–18; i 254; Noyes).

193. mountain belly] Jonson refers to his 'mountaine belly' in 'My Picture left in *Scotland*' l. 17 (*The Vnder-wood* ix). For Shadwell's bulk see l. 25n. Flecknoe describes a man with a mountain belly in *The Diarium* (1656) 44–6.

Of likeness; thine's a tympany of sense:
195 A tun of man in thy large bulk is writ,
But sure thou'rt but a kilderkin of wit.
Like mine thy gentle numbers feebly creep,
Thy tragic Muse gives smiles, thy comic sleep.

194. likeness] i.e. to Jonson.   *tympany*] swelling, tumour (*OED* 1); figuratively something big or pretentious but empty or vain; often used of style (*OED* 2).

195. A tun of man] echoes the description of Falstaff: 'a tun of man is thy companion' (*1 Henry IV* II iv 442).   *tun*] a large cask for wine, ale or beer, usually holding 210 gallons (*OED*).

196. kilderkin] cask holding 16 or 18 gallons (*OED*).

197–208. This passage seems to represent Shadwell as a fusion of the two bad poets (generally thought to be Robert Wild and Flecknoe) discussed in *EDP*: 'I ask you if one of them does not perpetually pay us with clenches upon words and a certain clownish kind of raillery . . . wresting and torturing a word into another meaning . . . one who is so much a well-willer to the Satire, that he intends, at least, to spare no man . . . though he cannot strike a blow to hurt any . . . my other extremity of Poetry . . . is one of those who having had some advantage of education and converse, knows better then the other what a Poet should be, but puts it into practice more unluckily then any man; his stile and matter are every where alike; he is the most calm, peaceable Writer you ever read: he never disquiets your passions with the least concernment, but still leaves you in as even a temper as he found you; he is a very Leveller in Poetry, he creeps along with ten little words in every line . . . when he writes the serious way, the highest flight of his fancy is some miserable *Antithesis*, or seeming contradiction; and in the Comick he is still reaching at some thin conceit, the ghost of a Jest, and that too flies before him, never to be caught' (*Works* xvii 10–11).

197. Cp. Shadwell's Prologue to *Psyche*: 'He would not soar too high, nor creep too low' (l. 31; ii 281; Noyes, citing Oswald). In commendatory verses prefixed to *A Relation Of ten Years Travells* the Marquis of Newcastle had commended the lofty flight of Flecknoe's Muse: '*Flecknoe* thy verses are too high for me, / Though they but justly fit thy Muse and thee, / . . . Though *Homers* blush, and *Virgils* lofty stile: / For thy Poetique Flame is so much higher, / Where it should warm, 't consumes us with thy fire. / Thy vaster fancy does imbrace all things' (sig. A4ʳ). Flecknoe's epigram on D. commends his high-flying Muse (see headnote), and the 1675 revision of it adds these lines: 'Nor ever any's *Muse* so high did soar / Above the Poets *Empyreum* before. / Some are so *low* and *creeping*, they appear / But as the *reptils* of *Parnassus* were;' (*Euterpe Revived* (1675) 77).

198. Cp. Buckingham's Prologue to *The Rehearsal* (1672): 'Our Poets make us laugh at Tragoedy, / And with their Comedies they make us cry' (ll. 13–14; Michael Wilding in *John Dryden*, edited by Earl Miner (1972) 194–5).

With whate'er gall thou sett'st thyself to write,
200   Thy inoffensive satires never bite:
In thy felonious heart though venom lies,
It does but touch thy Irish pen, and dies.
Thy genius calls thee not to purchase fame
In keen iambics, but mild anagram.
205   Leave writing plays, and choose for thy command
Some peaceful province in acrostic land:
There thou mayest wings display and altars raise,
And torture one poor word ten thousand ways.
Or if thou wouldst thy different talents suit,
210   Set thy own songs, and sing them to thy lute.'

200, 204. bite . . . keen iambics] Cp. Cleveland: 'Come keen *Iambicks*, with your Badgers feet, / And Badger-like, bite till your teeth do meet' ('The Rebell *Scot*' ll. 27–8; W. J. Cameron, *N & Q* cciii (1957) 39); *keen iambics* may be a translation of *celeres iambos* (Horace, *Carm.* I xvi 24; R. Martin, *N & Q* ccii (1956) 505).

201. venom] 'Iambus' was falsely derived from the Greek 'ιός 'poison' (R. C. Elliott, *The Power of Satire* (1960) 23).

202. Irish] Probably because St Patrick was said to have banished snakes from Ireland, so there was no venom there; cp. Cleveland: 'No more let *Ireland* brag, her harmless Nation / Fosters no Venome' ('The Rebell *Scot*' ll. 37–8). See also Title *n* for alleged Irish characteristics.

204–8. One of Robert Burton's remedies for melancholy was: 'he may apply his mind, I say, to heraldry, antiquity, invent impresses, emblems; make epithalamiums, epitaphs, elegies, epigrams, *palindroma epigrammata*, anagrams, chronograms, acrostics upon his friends' names . . . and rather than do nothing, vary a verse a thousand ways with Putean, so torturing his wits' (*The Anatomy of Melancholy* (1621) II ii 4; *Works*). Figure poems originated in Greek poetry, and were given currency in the Renaissance in the *Planudean Anthology* (1494). Poems in the shape of wings and altars abound in English Renaissance Latin poetry; in English the best-known examples are George Herbert's poems 'Easter-wings' and 'The Altar' in *The Temple* (1633). Flecknoe in *A Treatise of the Sports of Wit* (1675) describes the word-games which he devised for the amusement of his royal patrons: 'The next Nights sport . . . was the Acting of Proverbs . . . some which cause laughter without any *Wit*, others more studious then delightful as *Ridles, Rebus's*, and *Anagrams*' (25; Hammond in *EIC* (1985)).

206. province] See ll. 4, 6n.

He said; but his last words were scarcely heard, ⎤
For Bruce and Longvil had a trap prepared,   ⎬
And down they sent the yet declaiming bard.   ⎦
Sinking he left his drugget robe behind,
215   Born upwards by a subterranean wind.
The mantle fell to the young prophet's part
With double portion of his father's art.

211–13. In *The Virtuoso* Act III Clarinda and Miranda dispose of Sir Formal through a trapdoor while he is in the middle of a flight of oratory; E. E. Duncan-Jones points out (privately) that Bruce and Longvil are merely spectators, not authors, of the trick.

213. bard] Michael Wilding (*John Dryden*, edited by Earl Miner (1972) 193–4) notes that *bard* at this date specifically applied to Irish poets (*OED* 1), who according to Spenser praised licentious and lawless men: 'Theare is amongst the Irishe a certen kinde of people Called Bardes which are to them in steade of Poets whose profession is to sett fourthe the praises and dispraises of menne in their Poems or Rymes. . . . But these Irishe Bardes are for the moste parte . . . so farre from instructinge yonge men in morrall discipline that they themselues doe more deserue to be sharpelye discipled for . . . whom soeuer they finde to be moste . . . daungerous and desperate in all partes of disobedience and rebellious disposicion him they set vp and glorifye in their Rymes' (*A View of the Present State of Ireland* (1633) in *Spenser's Prose Works*, edited by Rudolf Gottfried (1949) 124–5).

214–17. Echoes the disappearance of Elijah: 'Elijah said unto Elisha, Ask what I shall do for thee, before I be taken away from thee. And Elisha said, I pray thee, let a double portion of thy spirit be upon me . . . and Elijah went up by a whirlwind into heaven. . . . And Elisha saw it, and he cried, My father, my father. . . . He took up also the mantle of Elijah that fell from him' (2 Kings ii 9–13). Unlike Elijah, Flecknoe disappears downwards. The rapid disappearance of a butt of satire is also a feature of Seneca's *Apocolocyntosis*, Erasmus's *Julius Exclusus* and Marvell's 'Tom May's Death'.

214. See l. 186*n*.

215. subterranean wind] A. S. Borgman (*Thomas Shadwell* (1928) 51) notes an echo of a song sung by a devil in Shadwell's operatic *Tempest*: 'Arise, arise! ye subterranean winds, / More to disturb their guilty minds. / And all ye filthy damps and vapours rise, / Which use t' infect the Earth, and trouble all the Skies; / Rise you, from whom devouring plagues have birth: / You that i' th' vast and hollow womb of Earth, / Engender Earthquakes, make whole Countreys shake, / And stately Cities into Desarts turn; / . . . Cause Fogs and Storms' (ii 224). Wilding observes an echo of *PL*, where Satan lands on ground which appears as if wrecked by 'the force / Of subterranean wind' (i 231).

43 Prologue to *Circe*

Date and publication. The date of the first recorded performance of *Circe* by the Duke's Company at Dorset Garden is 12 May 1677. Charles Davenant (1656–1714) was the eldest son of Sir William, with whom D. had collaborated on *The Tempest*. The play had an epilogue by the Earl of Rochester. *Circe, A Tragedy* by Charles Davenant was published by Richard Tonson in 1677 (*SR* 19 June; *TC* 5 July); reprinted 1685. For ll. 1–10 reused in an Epilogue see the next poem.

The Prologue

Were you but half so wise as you're severe,
Our youthful poet should not need to fear;
To his green years your censures you would suit,
Not blast the blossom, but expect the fruit.
5 The sex that best does pleasure understand
Will always choose to err on t' other hand:
They check not him that's awkward in delight,
But clap the young rogue's cheek, and set him right;
Thus heartened well, and fleshed upon his prey,
10 The youth may prove a man another day.
For your own sakes instruct him when he's out,
You'll find him mend his work at every bout.
When some young lusty thief is passing by, ⎫
How many of your tender kind will cry: ⎬
15 'A proper fellow, pity he should die.   ⎭
He might be saved, and thank us for our pains,
There's such a stock of love within his veins.'
These arguments the women may persuade,
But move not you, the brothers of the trade,
20 Who scattering your infection through the pit ⎫
With aching hearts and empty purses sit   ⎬
To take your dear five shillings worth of wit. ⎭
The praise you give him in your kindest mood
Comes dribbling from you, just like drops of blood;

¶**43**. *9. fleshed*] rewarded and made eager for prey by the taste of blood (*OED* 1); initiated (*OED* 2).
22. five shillings] The standard price of admission to the boxes was four shillings, but this was occasionally raised to five (*LS* lxx–lxxi).

25   And then you clap so civilly, for fear
     The loudness might offend your neighbour's ear,
     That we suspect your gloves are lined within
     For silence sake, and cottoned next the skin.
     From these usurpers we appeal to you,
30   The only knowing, only judging few:
     You who in private have this play allowed
     Ought to maintain your suffrage to the crowd.
     The captive once submitted to your bands
     You should protect from death by vulgar hands.

31. allowed] approved.
32. suffrage] approval (*OED* 5).
33. bands] fetters (*OED* 1); custody (*OED* 1b).

44 Epilogue ('Were you but half so wise as you're severe')

Date and publication. This epilogue uses ll. 1–10 of the 'Prologue to *Circe*' (1677), but its occasion is unknown. It was first printed in *MP* (1684; reprinted 1692).

An Epilogue

Were you but half so wise as you're severe,
Our youthful poet should not need to fear;
To his green years your censures you would suit,
Not blast the blossom, but expect the fruit.
5 The sex that best does pleasure understand
Will always choose to err on t' other hand:
They check not him that's awkward in delight,
But clap the young rogue's cheek, and set him right;
Thus heartened well, and fleshed upon his prey,
10 The youth may prove a man another day.
Your Ben and Fletcher in their first young flight
Did no *Volpone*, no *Arbaces* write,
But hopped about, and short excursions made ⎫
From bough to bough, as if they were afraid, ⎬
15 And each were guilty of some *Slighted Maid*. ⎭
Shakespeare's own Muse her *Pericles* first bore:
The Prince of Tyre was elder than the Moor.
'Tis miracle to see a first good play,
All hawthorns do not bloom on Christmas Day.
20 A slender poet must have time to grow,

¶**44**. *11–12.* Jonson (b. 1572) wrote *Volpone* in 1606; Fletcher (b. 1579) wrote *A King and No King* (in which the principal character is Arbaces) *c.* 1618.
15. Sir Robert Stapylton's comedy *The Slighted Maid* (1663) of which D. said, 'there is no Scene in the first Act, which might not by as good reason be in the fifth' ('The Grounds of Criticism in Tragedy' (1679); *Works* xiii 230).
16–17. D.'s assumption seems to be based on the plays' relative merits; modern scholars date *Othello* to 1604 and *Pericles* 1606–8.
19. The thorn at Glastonbury was supposed to flower at Christmas, and other examples were reported (Sir Thomas Browne, *Pseudodoxia Epidemica* II vi 4; edited by R. Robbins (1981) 150, 776).

And spread and burnish as his brothers do;
Who still looks lean, sure with some pox is cursed,
But no man can be Falstaff-fat at first.
Then damn not, but indulge his stewed essays,
25   Encourage him, and bloat him up with praise,
That he may get more bulk before he dies—
He's not yet fed enough for sacrifice.
Perhaps if now your grace you will not grudge,
He may grow up to write, and you to judge.

21. *burnish*] grow plump, spread out (*OED* v²).
24. *stewed*] sweated, laboured.

45 To Mr Lee, on his *Alexander*

Date and publication. The *Rival Queens, or The Death of Alexander the Great*, by Nathaniel Lee, was published by James Magnes and Richard Bentley in 1677 (*TC* 26 November) and reprinted in 1684, 1694, and 1699. It included an Epistle Dedicatory by Lee to the Earl of Mulgrave, D.'s poem, and a Prologue by Sir Carr Scrope.

Context. The *Rival Queens* was first performed on 17 March 1677 by the King's Company at the Theatre Royal; it was the first play by Lee (?1649–92) who, like D., had been educated at Trinity College, Cambridge, and possibly also at Westminster School. He contributed commendatory verses to D.'s *The State of Innocence* (February 1677), as D. notes here in ll. 3–4. D. subsequently collaborated with Lee on *Oedipus* (1679) and *The Duke of Guise* (1683), and contributed prologues or epilogues to Lee's *Mithridates King of Pontus* (1678), *Caesar Borgia* (1680), *Sophonisba* (1681) and *Constantine the Great* (1684). Lee contributed a commendatory poem to *AA*.

To Mr Lee, on his *Alexander*

> The blast of common censure could I fear,
> Before your play my name should not appear;
> For 'twill be thought, and with some colour too,
> I pay the bribe I first received from you:
> 5 That mutual vouchers for our fame we stand,
> To play the game into each other's hand;
> And as cheap penn'worths to ourselves afford
> As Bessus and the brothers of the sword.
> Such libels private men may well endure,
> 10 When states, and kings themselves, are not secure:
> For ill men, conscious of their inward guilt,
> Think the best actions on by-ends are built.

¶**45**. *8*. In Beaumont and Fletcher's play *A King and No King* (1619) Bessus and two 'gentlemen o' th' sword' vouch for one another's courage and honour. The play was popular on the Restoration stage, and was reprinted in 1676.

10. Perhaps a reference to the marriage of William of Orange to Princess Mary (announced on 22 October 1677); Charles II may have agreed to the match because this alliance with a Protestant country would allay suspicions of his covert Catholicism (Ogg 546–7).

12. by-ends] covert, selfish purposes.

And yet my silence had not scaped their spite:
Then envy had not suffered me to write;
15 For since I could not ignorance pretend,
Such worth I must or envy or commend.
So many candidates there stand for wit,
A place in court is scarce so hard to get;
In vain they crowd each other at the door,
20 For ev'n reversions are all begged before.
Desert, how known so e'er, is long delayed,
And then, too, fools and knaves are better paid.
Yet, as some actions bear so great a name
That courts themselves are just, for fear of shame,
25 So has the mighty merit of your play
Extorted praise, and forced itself a way.
'Tis here, as 'tis at sea: who farthest goes,
Or dares the most, makes all the rest his foes;
Yet when some virtue much outgrows the rest,
30 It shoots too fast and high to be oppressed;
As his heroic worth struck envy dumb
Who took the Dutchman, and who cut the boom.
Such praise is yours while you the passions move,
That 'tis no longer feigned, 'tis real love,
35 Where nature triumphs over wretched art;
We only warm the head, but you the heart.
Always you warm! and if the rising year,
As in hot regions, bring the sun too near,
'Tis but to make your fragrant spices blow
40 Which in our colder climates will not grow.
They only think you animate your theme
With too much fire who are themselves all phlegm:
Prizes would be for lags of slowest pace
Were cripples made the judges of the race.

16. *or . . . or*] either . . . or.
20. *reversions*] rights of succession to an office.
32. Admiral Sir Edward Spragge served in the Second Dutch War (cp. *AM* ll.
693–4*n*) and on 8 May 1671 attacked the Algerine pirate fleet in Bugia Bay,
first cutting through the boom which protected it. He was drowned during a
battle with the Dutch on 11 August 1673.
39. *blow*] flourish, bloom (*OED* v² 2).
42. *phlegm*] in humours physiology, the cold and moist humour, producing
dullness and sluggishness.

45   Despise those drones who praise while they accuse
     The too much vigour of your youthful Muse:
     That humble style which they their virtue make
     Is in your power: you need but stoop and take.
     Your beauteous images must be allowed
50   By all but some vile poets of the crowd;
     But how should any signpost-dauber know
     The worth of Titian, or of Angelo?
     Hard features every bungler can command;
     To draw true beauty shows a master's hand.

46. Cp. 'To the Memory of Mr Oldham' ll. 17–18.
49. *allowed*] approved.
52. The Italian painters Titian (?1480–1576) and Michelangelo (1475–1564).

46 Prologue and Epilogue to *All for Love*

Date and publication. The play (dramatizing the story of Antony and Cleopatra) was completed by July 1677 (*Letters* 12) but not performed until late in the year. Milhous and Hume 386 doubt the authenticity of the evidence for a performance on 12 December. It was D.'s last play for the King's Company at the Theatre Royal. *All for Love: or, The World well Lost. A Tragedy* was published by Herringman in 1678 (*SR* 31 January; advertised in the *London Gazette* 21–5 March); reprinted 1692, 1696. It was dedicated to the Earl of Danby, and included a preface attacking the wits, particularly Rochester.

Prologue to *Antony and Cleopatra*

What flocks of critics hover here today, ⎫
As vultures wait on armies for their prey, ⎬
All gaping for the carcass of a play! ⎭
With croaking notes they bode some dire event,
5   And follow dying poets by the scent.
Ours gives himself for gone; y' have watched your
        time!
He fights this day unarmed, without his rhyme,
And brings a tale which often has been told,
As sad as Dido's, and almost as old.
10 His hero, whom you wits his bully call,
Bates of his mettle, and scarce rants at all:
He's somewhat lewd, but a well-meaning mind,
Weeps much, fights little, but is wondrous kind.
In short, a pattern and companion fit

¶**46**. *Prologue.*
7. *without his rhyme*] This was D.'s first unrhymed tragedy; in the Preface he says: 'In my Stile I have profess'd to imitate the Divine *Shakespeare*; which that I might perform more freely, I dis-incumber'd my self from Rhyme. Not that I condemn my former way, but that this is more proper to my present purpose' (*Works* xiii 18). Cp. 'Prologue to *Aureng-Zebe*' ll. 8–9.
10. bully] good friend (*OED* 1); perhaps also 'blustering gallant' (*OED* 2, first example 1688).
11. Bates of] decreases in.
13. kind] contemporary meanings included 'sexually compliant'.

15 For all the keeping Tonies of the pit.
    I could name more: a wife, and mistress too, ⎤
    Both (to be plain) too good for most of you— ⎬
    The wife well-natured, and the mistress true. ⎦
       Now, poets, if your fame has been his care,
20 Allow him all the candour you can spare.
    A brave man scorns to quarrel once a day,
    Like hectors in at every petty fray.
    Let those find fault whose wit's so very small
    They've need to show that they can think at all:
25 Errors like straws upon the surface flow;
    He who would search for pearls must dive below.
    Fops may have leave to level all they can,
    As pygmies would be glad to lop a man.
    Half-wits are fleas, so little and so light
30 We scarce could know they live, but that they bite.
    But as the rich, when tired with daily feasts
    For change become their next poor tenant's guests,
    Drink hearty draughts of ale from plain brown bowls,
    And snatch the homely rasher from the coals:
35 So you, retiring from much better cheer,
    For once may venture to do penance here:
    And since that plenteous autumn now is past,
    Whose grapes and peaches have indulged your taste,
    Take in good part from our poor poet's board
40 Such rivelled fruits as winter can afford.

Epilogue

    Poets, like disputants when reasons fail,
    Have one sure refuge left, and that's to rail:
    'Fop', 'coxcomb', 'fool' are thundered through the pit,
    And this is all their equipage of wit.
5   We wonder how the devil this diff'rence grows
    Betwixt our fools in verse and yours in prose:

---

15. keeping Tonies] foolish fellows (colloquial application of 'Anthony') who keep mistresses.
22. hectors] swaggering braggarts; cp. 'Prologue to *Secret Love*' l. *22n.*
31–4. Cp. 'Horace: *Odes* III xxix' ll. *22–5.*
40. rivelled] dried up, wrinkled.

For, 'faith, the quarrel rightly understood
'Tis civil war with their own flesh and blood.
The thread-bare author hates the gaudy coat,
10   And swears at the gilt coach, but swears afoot:
For 'tis observed of every scribbling man
He grows a fop as fast as e'er he can,
Prunes up, and asks his oracle the glass
If pink or purple best become his face.
15   For our poor wretch, he neither rails nor prays, ⎫
Nor likes your wit just as you like his plays: ⎬
He has not yet so much of Mr Bayes.   ⎭
He does his best, and if he cannot please
Would quietly sue out his writ of ease.
20   Yet if he might his own grand jury call,
By the fair sex he begs to stand or fall.
Let Caesar's power the men's ambition move,
But grace you him who lost the world for love.
Yet if some antiquated lady say
25   The last age is not copied in his play,
Heaven help the man who for that face must drudge
Which only has the wrinkles of a judge.
Let not the young and beauteous join with those,
For should you raise such numerous hosts of foes,
30   Young wits and sparks he to his aid must call:
'Tis more than one man's work to please you all.

Epilogue.
7. *'faith*] in faith.
13. *Prunes up*] dresses up, decks out himself (*OED* 2b).
17. *Mr Bayes*] The dramatist, partly based on D., satirized in Buckingham's
play *The Rehearsal* (revised 1675), who railed at his unappreciative audience.
19. i.e. apply to a court for his certificate of discharge from employment.
23. *grace*] show favour to (*OED* 1).   *him*] Antony.
25. *The last age*] the Jacobean and Caroline period; cp. the title of Thomas
Rymer's *The Tragedies of the Last Age Consider'd* (1677).
26. *drudge*] with sexual connotations: cp. 'Prologue to *An Evening's Love*' l.
6n.

47 Epilogue to *Mithridates*

Date and publication. Probably first performed in February 1678; the play was staged by the King's Company at the Theatre Royal. For D.'s association with Lee see 'To Mr Lee, on his *Alexander*'. Lee's *Mithridates King of Pontus, A Tragedy* was published by James Magnes and Richard Bentley in 1678 (licensed 28 March; *TC* June); reprinted 1685, 1693. It was dedicated to the Earl of Dorset.

Epilogue

You've seen a pair of faithful lovers die, }
And much you care, for most of you will cry, }
' 'Twas a just judgement on their constancy.' }
For, heaven be thanked, we live in such an age
5   When no man dies for love but on the stage,
And ev'n those martyrs are but rare in plays,
A cursèd sign how much true faith decays.
Love is no more a violent desire,
'Tis a mere metaphor, a painted fire.
10 In all our sex, the name examined well
Is pride to gain, and vanity to tell.
In woman, 'tis of subtle interest made:
Curse on the punk that made it first a trade!
She first did wit's prerogative remove,
15 And made a fool presume to prate of love.
Let honour and preferment go for gold,
But glorious beauty is not to be sold:
Or, if it be, 'tis at a rate so high
That nothing but adoring it should buy.
20 Yet the rich cullies may their boasting spare:
They purchase but sophisticated ware.

¶**47**. *1. lovers*] Ziphares (Mithridates' son) and Semandra.
10. i.e. 'In men, what is called "love" is, when closely examined, just pride in gaining a woman and vanity in boasting of it.'   *our sex*] The Epilogue is spoken by a man, probably either Hart (who played Ziphares) or Mohun (Mithridates).
13. punk] prostitute.
20. cullies] dupes.
21. sophisticated] adulterated, impure.

'Tis prodigality that buys deceit,
Where both the giver and the taker cheat.
Men but refine on the old half-crown way,
25   And women fight, like Switzers, for their pay.

---

24. *half-crown*] the price of a prostitute's services (cp. 'Prologue to *Marriage A-la-Mode*' l. 22).
25. *Switzers*] Swiss mercenaries.

48 Prologue, Epilogue and Songs from *The Kind Keeper*

Date and publication. The play was drafted in summer 1677 (*Letters* 11) and first performed on 11 March 1678 at Dorset Garden, the first of D.'s plays to be staged by the Duke's Company. It was stopped after three performances, for reasons which remain obscure, but probably because its satire of contemporary sexual *mores* was thought to reflect on some prominent public figure (see Susan Staves, *RECTR* xiii (1974) 1–11; Winn 589–91; and cp. 'Prologue to *Caesar Borgia*' ll. 7–10). *The Kind Keeper; or, Mr. Limberham: A Comedy* was published by Bentley and Magnes in 1680 (*TC* November 1679); reprinted 1690. It was dedicated to John, Lord Vaughan.

Prologue

    True wit has seen its best days long ago,
    It ne'er looked up since we were dipped in show,
    When sense in doggerel rhymes and clouds was lost,
    And dullness flourished at the actors' cost.
5   Nor stopped it here: when tragedy was done, ⎤
    Satire and humour the same fate have run, ⎬
    And comedy is sunk to trick and pun. ⎦
    Now our machining lumber will not sell, ⎤
    And you no longer care for heaven or hell; ⎬
10 What stuff will please you next, the Lord can tell. ⎦
    Let them who the rebellion first began, ⎤
    To wit restore the monarch if they can; ⎬
    Our author dares not be the first bold man. ⎦

¶**48**. *Prologue.*
1–10. For this complaint cp. 'Prologue to *Troilus and Cressida*'.
3. clouds] The fashion for such scenic effects is mocked by Buckingham in *The Rehearsal* (revised 1675) Act V, where 'The two right Kings of *Brentford* descend in the Clouds', and by Rochester in his Epilogue to Sir Francis Fane's *Love in the Dark* (1675): 'Players turn puppets now at your desire: / In their mouths nonsense, in their tails a wire, / They fly through clouds of clouts and showers of fire' (ll. 10–12). Shadwell's *Psyche* (1675) is Rochester's target, though Buckingham's scene satirizes D.'s *Tyrannic Love*.
9. Perhaps a reference to Shadwell's *Psyche* (1675), Act V of which included settings for heaven and hell (Kinsley). D.'s own unstaged *The State of Innocence* would have required similarly elaborate staging.

He, like the prudent citizen, takes care
15 To keep for better marts his staple ware—
His toys are good enough for Stourbridge Fair.
Tricks were the fashion; if it now be spent,
'Tis time enough at Easter to invent:
No man will make up a new suit for Lent.
20 If now and then he takes a small pretence
To forage for a little wit and sense,
Pray pardon him, he meant you no offence.
Next summer Nostradamus tells, they say,
That all the critics shall be shipped away,
25 And not enow be left to damn a play.
To every sail beside, good heaven be kind,
But drive away that swarm with such a wind
That not one locust may be left behind.

Epilogue

Spoken by Limberham

I beg a boon, that ere you all disband,
Someone would take my bargain off my hand;
To keep a punk is but a common evil,

---

16. *Stourbridge Fair*] the fair held annually at Cambridge from 18 September to 10 October.
18–19. The play was staged during Lent: in 1678 Ash Wednesday fell on 13 February and Easter on 31 March.
23. *Nostradamus*] Michel de Nostradame (1503–66), the author of the prophetic *Centuries* (1555; English translation 1672).
25. *enow*] enough.
27–8. Exodus x 19.

Epilogue.
Title. Mr Limberham is betrayed by his kept mistress Mrs Tricksy, but eventually marries her 'to give good Example to all Christian keepers' (65).

To find her false, and marry, that's the devil.
5 Well, I ne'er acted part in all my life,
But still I was fobbed off with some such wife.
I find the trick: these poets take no pity
Of one that is a member of the city.
We cheat you lawfully, and in our trades:
10 You cheat us basely with your common jades.
Now I am married I must sit down by it,
But let me keep my dear-bought spouse in quiet:
Let none of you damned Woodalls of the pit
Put in for shares to mend our breed in wit;
15 We know your bastards from our flesh and blood—
Not one in ten of yours e'er comes to good.
In all the boys their father's virtues shine,
But all the female fry turn pugs like mine.
When these grow up, Lord! with what rampant gadders
20 Our counters will be thronged, and roads with padders.
This town two bargains has not worth one farthing:
A Smithfield horse, and wife of Covent Garden.

Songs

I

I

'Gainst keepers we petition,
Who would enclose the common:

---

11. sit down by] put up with, be content with (*OED* 21b).
13. Woodall] a rake in D.'s play.
18. pugs] Limberham uses this as a term of endearment for Mrs Tricksy; it is also (as here) a term for a mistress or courtesan (*OED* 1 and 2).
20. counters] compters, debtors' prisons (*OED* 7).   *padders*] footpads.
22. Smithfield horse] Pepys commented on the 'knaveries and tricks' of the horse-dealers at Smithfield market (11 December 1668).   *Covent Garden*] The area around Covent Garden was frequented by prostitutes; Pepys noted them particularly in Long Acre and Drury Lane (17, 22 February 1664; 14 March 1666). The remark was also proverbial (Tilley W 276).

Song I. From Act I, sung by Mrs Tricksy and Judith.

'Tis enough to raise sedition
In the free-born subject woman.
5   Because for his gold
I my body have sold,
He thinks I'm a slave for my life;
He rants, domineers,
He swaggers and swears,
10   And would keep me as bare as his wife.

2

'Gainst keepers we petition, etc.
'Tis honest and fair,
That a feast I prepare;
But when his dull appetite's o'er,
15   I'll treat with the rest
Some welcomer guest,
For the reck'ning was paid me before.

II

I my own gaoler was, my only foe,
Who did my liberty forgo;
I was a pris'ner, 'cause I would be so.

III

A Song from the Italian

By a dismal cypress lying,
Damon cried, all pale and dying,
'Kind is death that ends my pain,
But cruel she I loved in vain.
5   The mossy fountains
Murmur my trouble,
And hollow mountains
My groans redouble:
Every nymph mourns me,

Song II. From Act II, sung by Mr Limberham.
Song III. From Act III, sung by Judith. The Italian source is unknown.

10   Thus while I languish,
        She only scorns me
        Who caused my anguish,
        No love returning me, but all hope denying.'
        By a dismal cypress lying,
15   Like a swan, so sung he dying:
        'Kind is death that ends my pain,
        But cruel she I loved in vain.'

49 Prologue to *A True Widow*

Date and publication. The play was probably first performed in March 1678. The date 21 March mentioned in Act I may be that of the première. The political and literary allusions help to confirm this date (see ll. 11–14*n*, 16–18*n*); see also Winn 310–11. *Works* argues for a date in late 1678 or early 1679, based on the publication date, but by then the allusions would be stale. Milhous and Hume 387 are noncommittal, but note that a long interval between performance and publication is not unusual for plays which failed, as this did. Thomas Shadwell's *A True Widow. A Comedy* was published by Benjamin Tooke in 1679 (Dedication to Sir Charles Sedley dated 16 February 1679; *TC* May); reissued with new title page 1689. D.'s Prologue was reprinted in Aphra Behn's *The Widdow Ranter* (1690).

Context. The play was staged at Dorset Garden by the Duke's Company, for which D. was now writing. 'In contributing the prologue . . . Dryden merely fulfilled a normal playhouse duty carrying no implications concerning his personal relationship with Shadwell. His prologue does not refer specifically to Shadwell's play' (David M. Vieth in *Evidence in Literary Scholarship* edited by René Wellek and Alvero Ribiero (1979) 78). For D.'s previous relations with Shadwell see headnote to *MF*.

Prologue

> Heaven save ye, gallants, and this hopeful age,
> Y' are welcome to the downfall of the stage:
> The fools have laboured long in their vocation,
> And vice (the manufacture of the nation)
> 5 O'er-stocks the town so much, and thrives so well,
> That fops and knaves grow drugs and will not sell.
> In vain our wares on theatres are shown
> When each has a plantation of his own.
> His cruse ne'er fails, for whatsoe'er he spends
> 10 There's still God's plenty for himself and friends.

¶**49**. *1. hopeful*] promising.
6. drugs] commodities in no demand (*OED* 2).
8. plantation] Perhaps a glance at Shaftesbury, who had a profitable plantation in South Carolina (Winn).
9. cruse] See 1 Kings xvii 12–16.

Should men be rated by poetic rules,
Lord, what a poll would there be raised from fools!
Meantime poor wit prohibited must lie
As if 'twere made some French commodity.
15 Fools you will have, and raised at vast expense,
And yet, as soon as seen they give offence.
Time was when none would cry, 'That oaf was me!'
But now you strive about your pedigree:
Bauble and cap no sooner are thrown down,
20 But there's a muss of more than half the town;
Each one will challenge a child's part at least,
A sign the family is well increased.
Of foreign cattle there's no longer need,
When w'are supplied so fast with English breed.
25 Well! flourish, countrymen: drink, swear and roar,
Let every free-born subject keep his whore,
And wandering in the wilderness about
At end of forty years not wear her out.
But when you see these pictures, let none dare
30 To own beyond a limb, or single share:
For where the punk is common, he's a sot
Who needs will father what the parish got.

11–14. The Poll Act which passed the Commons on 18 February 1678 (not 1676, as *Works* says) and came into effect on 20 March provided for a poll tax to be used for the war with France, and for 'prohibiting several French commodities' including wine, brandy, vinegar, linen and silk, for a three-year period (Ogg 437, 550–1).

11. rated] assessed for taxation.

12. poll] poll tax.

16–18. Probably alluding to objections made to *The Kind Keeper* (q.v.), staged on 11 March; cp. also 'Epilogue to *The Man of Mode*'.

20. muss] a game in which small objects were thrown down to be scrambled for; a scramble (*OED*).

25. drink, swear and roar] Cp. the advice to Og (Shadwell) in *2AA* l. 478.

27–8. See Exodus xvi 35.

31. punk] prostitute.

50 Prologue, Epilogue and Songs from *Oedipus*

Date and publication. Staged in Autumn 1678; the exact date of the first performance is unknown. It was staged by the Duke's Company at Dorset Garden. *Oedipus: A Tragedy* was published by Bentley and Magnes in 1679 (licensed 3 January 1679; advertised in the *London Gazette* 10–13 March; *TC* May), and reprinted in 1682, 1687, 1692 and [1696]. Song I was printed in *The Compleat Courtier* (1683) and Song III was set by Purcell for a revival *c.* 1692 (see Price, *Henry Purcell* 105–11).

Authorship. The play was a collaboration between D. and Lee (for whom see 'To Mr Lee, on his *Alexander*'); D. said that he wrote Acts I and III, and Lee Acts II, IV and V (*Works* xiii 443). There is no actual evidence for D.'s authorship of the Prologue and Epilogue, but they have generally been accepted as his. Songs II and III may reasonably be assigned to D., as they occur in Act III; Kinsley thought that Song I 'has at least something of his manner'.

Prologue

When Athens all the Grecian state did guide,
And Greece gave laws to all the world beside,
Then Sophocles with Socrates did sit,
Supreme in wisdom one, and one in wit;
5   And wit from wisdom differed not in those
But as 'twas sung in verse, or said in prose.
Then *Oedipus* on crowded theatres
Drew all admiring eyes and listening ears;
The pleased spectator shouted every line,
10   The noblest, manliest, and the best design!

¶**50**. *Prologue.*
1–3. In the fifth and fourth centuries BC, Athens was the cultural centre of Greece, renowned for tragedians such as Sophocles (*c.* 496–406 BC) and philosophers such as Socrates (469–399 BC).
4. wit] quickness of intellect, liveliness of imagination (*OED* 7); apt association of thought and expression in writing (*OED* 8).
6. Greek tragedy was chanted; Socrates taught philosophy largely through spoken dialogues.
9. Athenian audiences were vocal in their approval or disapproval of particular lines, as well as whole performances (Arthur Pickard-Cambridge, *The Dramatic Festivals of Athens*, second edition (1968) 272–5).

And every critic of each learnèd age
By this just model has reformed the stage.
Now, should it fail (as heaven avert our fear!)
Damn it in silence, lest the world should hear:
15   For were it known this poem did not please,
You might set up for perfect savages;
Your neighbours would not look on you as men,
But think the nation all turned Picts again.
Faith, as you manage matters, 'tis not fit
20   You should suspect yourselves of too much wit:
Drive not the jest too far, but spare this piece,
And, for this once, be not more wise than Greece.
See twice! Do not pell-mell to damning fall,
Like true-born Britons, who ne'er think at all:
25   Pray be advised; and though at Mons you won,
On pointed cannon do not always run.
With some respect to ancient wit proceed;
You take the four first councils for your creed:
But when you lay tradition wholly by, ⎤
30   And on the private spirit alone rely, ⎬
You turn fanatics in your poetry. ⎦

11–12. In his Preface D. says that *Oedipus* was 'the most celebrated piece of all
Antiquity'; *Works* notes that he is following Corneille and others in this
opinion (*Works* xiii 115, 470, 473). Rymer in *Tragedies of the Last Age* (1678;
issued November 1677) said that Sophocles gave 'the utmost *perfection* to
Tragedy', and in *A Short View of Tragedy* (1693) called Sophocles' *Oedipus* the
only perfect tragedy (*Critical Works* 22, 83).
16. savages] The original spelling here is 'salvages'.
25–6. The army of William of Orange engaged the French in a bloody and
indecisive battle at Mons in August 1678. The *London Gazette* carried reports
of the action which emphasized the bravery of the English contingent led by
the Earl of Ossory (mcccxxviii, 8–12 August 1678).
28. The first four Oecumenical Councils (Nicaea (325), Constantinople (381),
Ephesus (431) and Chalcedon (451)) were accepted with special reverence by
the Church of England according to the *Reformatio Legum Ecclesiasticarum*
(1553), confirmed by statute of Elizabeth I.
29–31. Rymer says that some claim that poetry 'is *blind* inspiration, is pure
enthusiasm, is *rapture* and *rage* all over. . . . Those who object against reason,
are the *Fanaticks* in Poetry, and are never to be sav'd by their good works'
(*Tragedies of the Last Age*; *Critical Works* 20); cp. Oldham, 'Horace His Art of
Poetry' ll. 465–8 and 'Upon the Works of Ben. Johnson' ll. 52–8.
30. spirit] monosyllabic (perhaps 'sprite').
31. fanatics] extreme nonconformist Protestants.

If, notwithstanding all that we can say,   ⎫
You needs will have your pen'worths of the play, ⎬
And come resolved to damn, because you pay;   ⎭
35 Record it, in memorial of the fact,
The first play buried since the Woollen Act.

Epilogue

What Sophocles could undertake alone,
Our poets found a work for more than one;
And therefore two lay tugging at the piece,
With all their force, to draw the ponderous mass
from Greece:
5   A weight that bent ev'n Seneca's strong Muse,
And which Corneille's shoulders did refuse.
So hard it is th' Athenian harp to string!
So much two consuls yield to one just king.
Terror and pity this whole poem sway,
10 The mightiest machines that can mount a play.
How heavy will those vulgar souls be found,
Whom two such engines cannot move from ground!
When Greece and Rome have smiled upon this birth,
You can but damn for one poor spot of earth;

---

36. A new Act required everyone to be buried in woollen shrouds from 1 August 1678.

Epilogue.
1–6. The chief sources for *Oedipus* were Sophocles' *Oedipus Tyrannos*, Seneca's *Oedipus* and Corneille's *Oedipe*.
5–6. Echoes Horace: *sumite materiam vestris, qui scribitis, aequam / viribus, et versate diu, quid ferre recusent, / quid valeant umeri* ('you who write should choose material equal to your strength, and ponder long what your shoulders refuse and what they can bear': *Ars Poetica* ll. 38–40; J. C. Maxwell, *N & Q* ccvii (1962) 384–5).
6. Corneille's] trisyllabic.
9. Terror and pity] the emotions raised by tragedy according to Aristotle (*Poetics* 1449b).
10. machines] contrivances (*OED* 7, first example); stressed on the first syllable, as often in the seventeenth century.

15 And when your children find your judgement such,
    They'll scorn their sires, and wish themselves born
        Dutch;
    Each haughty poet will infer with ease
    How much his wit must under-write to please.
    As some strong churl would brandishing advance
20 The monumental sword that conquered France,
    So you by judging this, your judgements teach
    Thus far you like, that is, thus far you reach.
    Since then the vote of full two thousand years
    Has crowned this plot, and all the dead are theirs,
25 Think it a debt you pay, not alms you give,
    And in your own defence let this play live.
    Think 'em not vain, when Sophocles is shown,
    To praise his worth; they humbly doubt their own:
    Yet as weak states each other's power assure,
30 Weak poets by conjunction are secure.
    Their treat is what your palates relish most:
    Charm, song, and show! a murder and a ghost!
    We know not what you can desire or hope
    To please you more, but burning of a pope.

Songs

I

Song to Apollo
Phoebus, god beloved by men,
At thy dawn every beast is roused in his den,

---

16. *Dutch*] proverbially dull; cp. 'Prologue to *Amboyna*' ll. 33–4.
18. *under-write*] write below his usual level (*OED* v²2, only example is from 1766).
19–20. Probably referring to the sword of Edward the Black Prince, which is represented on his monument in Canterbury Cathedral.
21–2. i.e. 'Your judgement of this play reveals not only what you like, but what you are capable of appreciating.'
34. Pope-burning processions took place in the 1670s on 17 November, the anniversary of Queen Elizabeth's accession (see Sheila Williams, *JWCI* xxi (1958) 104–18).

Song I. From Act II. Apollo is invoked by the blind prophet Tiresias.

At thy setting all the birds of thy absence complain,
And we die, all die till the morning comes again;
5   Phoebus, god beloved by men!
Idol of the eastern kings,
Awful as the god who flings
His thunder round, and the lightning wings;
God of songs, and Orphean strings,
10 Who to this mortal bosom brings
All harmonious heavenly things!
Thy drowsy prophet to revive,
Ten thousand thousand forms before him drive;
With chariots and horses all o' fire awake him,
15 Convulsions and furies and prophecies shake him:
Let him tell it in groans, though he bend with the load,
Though he burst with the weight of the terrible god.

II

Tiresias.	Choose the darkest part o' th' grove,
	Such as ghosts at noonday love;
	Dig a trench, and dig it nigh
	Where the bones of Laius lie.
5	Altars raised of turf or stone
	Will th' infernal powers have none.
	Answer me, if this be done?
All Priests.	'Tis done.
Tiresias.	Is the sacrifice made fit?
10	Draw her backward to the pit:
	Draw the barren heifer back,
	Barren let her be and black.
	Cut the curlèd hair that grows
	Full betwixt her horns and brows;
15	And turn your faces from the sun:
	Answer me, if this be done?
All Priests.	'Tis done.
Tiresias.	Pour in blood, and blood-like wine
	To mother earth and Proserpine:
20	Mingle milk into the stream,
	Feast the ghosts that love the steam;
	Snatch a brand from funeral pile,

Songs II and III. From Act III. Tiresias and the priests prepare to raise the ghost of Laius.

            Toss it in to make 'em boil;
            And turn your faces from the sun:
25   Answer me, if all be done?
All Priests. All is done.
Peal of thunder, and flashes of lightning; then groaning below the stage.

III

    1. Hear, ye sullen powers below;
         Hear, ye taskers of the dead:
    2. You that boiling cauldrons blow,
         You that scum the molten lead;
5 *3.* You that pinch with red-hot tongs;
    1.   You that drive the trembling hosts
         Of poor, poor ghosts
         With your sharpened prongs;
    2. You that thrust 'em off the brim,
10 *3.* You that plunge 'em when they swim,
    1. Till they drown;
         Till they go
         On a row
         Down, down, down
15   Ten thousand thousand, thousand fadoms low.
Chorus. Till they drown, etc.
    1. Music for a while
         Shall your cares beguile,
         Wond'ring how your pains were eased;
20 *2.* And disdaining to be pleased,
    3. Till Alecto free the dead
         From their eternal bands;
         Till the snakes drop from her head,
         And whip from out her hands.
25 *1.* Come away
         Do not stay,
         But obey
         While we play,
         For hell's broke up, and ghosts have holiday.
Chorus.   Come away, etc.
A flash of lightning: the stage is made bright, and the ghosts are seen passing betwixt the trees.
    1. Laius! *2.* Laius! *3.* Laius!
    1. Hear! *2.* Hear! *3.* Hear!

Tiresias.	Hear and appear:
	By the fates that spun thy thread!
Chorus.	Which are three,
Tiresias.	By the furies fierce and dread!
Chorus.	Which are three,
Tiresias.	By the judges of the dead!
Chorus.	Which are three,
40	Three times three!
Tiresias.	By hell's blue flame,
	By the Stygian lake,
	And by Demogorgon's name,
	At which ghosts quake,
45	Hear and appear.

The ghost of Laius rises armed in his chariot, as he was slain. And behind his chariot sit the three who were murdered with him.

43–4. Demogorgon] In Statius, Tiresias threatens the ghost with an unnamed god, identified by the scholiast as Demogorgon (*Thebaid* iv 514–16; cp. *FQ* I i 37 and *PL* ii 965).

51 Prologue, Epilogue and Song from *Troilus and Cressida*

Date and publication. Performed *c*. 1679; the exact date of the première is unknown. It was staged by the Duke's Company at Dorset Garden. *Troilus and Cressida, or, Truth Found too Late. A Tragedy* was published by Jacob Tonson in 1679 (*SR* 14 April; *TC* November); reprinted 1695 (with some copies misdated '1679': see Fredson Bowers, *HLB* iii (1949) 278–88). This was the beginning of D.'s long association with Tonson. The play had a dedication to the Earl of Sunderland, a Preface which included 'The Grounds of Criticism in Tragedy', and a commendatory poem by Richard Duke. The Song occurs in *The Compleat Courtier* (1683) and *Choice Ayres and Songs* (1681; set by Thomas Farmer).

The Prologue

Spoken by Mr Betterton, representing the ghost of Shakespeare

> See, my loved Britons, see your Shakespeare rise,
> An awful ghost confessed to human eyes!
> Unnamed, methinks distinguished I had been
> From other shades by this eternal green,
> 5 About whose wreaths the vulgar poets strive,
> And with a touch their withered bays revive.
> Untaught, unpractised, in a barbarous age
> I found not, but created first the stage;
> And if I drained no Greek or Latin store
> 10 'Twas that my own abundance gave me more:

¶**51**. *Prologue.*
Title. Thomas Betterton (?1635–1710) played Troilus; he was the leading actor in the Duke's Company, which he joined in 1660 as a shareholder; he was its manager from 1668. His roles for D. included Torrismond in *The Spanish Friar.* He became co-manager with William Smith of the United Company in 1682 (Highfill ii 73–99). *ghost*] The ghost of Jonson had spoken the prologue to Edward Howard's *The Womens Conquest* (1671; Danchin no. A104).
2. *awful*] awesome. *confessed*] disclosed.
4. *green*] Cp. 'Prologue to *The Tempest*' ll. 1–4.
7–10. Cp. 'Prologue to *The Tempest*' l. 5 and headnote.
7. *unpractised*] inexpert.

On foreign trade I needed not rely,
Like fruitful Britain, rich without supply.
In this my rough-drawn play you shall behold
Some master-strokes, so manly and so bold
15 That he who meant to alter found 'em such
He shook, and thought it sacrilege to touch.
Now, where are the successors to my name?
What bring they to fill out a poet's fame?
Weak, short-lived issues of a feeble age,
20 Scarce living to be christened on the stage!
For humour, farce; for love, they rhyme dispense,
That tolls the knell for their departed sense.
Dullness might thrive in any trade but this:
'Twould recommend to some fat benefice.
25 Dullness, that in a playhouse meets disgrace,
Might meet with reverence in its proper place.
The fulsome clench that nauseates the town ⎤
Would from a judge or alderman go down, ⎬
Such virtue is there in a robe and gown! ⎦
30 And that insipid stuff which here you hate ⎤
Might somewhere else be called a grave debate: ⎬
Dullness is decent in the church and state. ⎦
But I forget that still 'tis understood
Bad plays are best decried by showing good.
35 Sit silent then, that my pleased soul may see
A judging audience once, and worthy me.
My faithful scene from true records shall tell
How Trojan valour did the Greek excel;
Your great forefathers shall their fame regain,
40 And Homer's angry ghost repine in vain.

13–15. In his Preface D. says that he 'undertook to remove that heap of Rubbish, under which many excellent thoughts lay wholly bury'd' (*Works* xiii 226).

23–32. Cp. Horace's argument in *Ars Poetica* ll. 366–73 that while other professions tolerate mediocre achievement, poetry does not.

27. fulsome] excessive (OED 7).   *clench*] play on words.

37. records] stressed on the second syllable.

39. forefathers] alluding to the legend that Britain was founded by the Trojan Brutus.

The Epilogue

Spoken by Thersites

These cruel critics put me into passion,
For in their louring looks I read damnation:
Y' expect a satire, and I seldom fail—
When I'm first beaten, 'tis my part to rail.
5 You British fools of the old Trojan stock,
That stand so thick one cannot miss the flock;
Poets have cause to dread a keeping pit,
When women's cullies come to judge of wit.
As we strew ratsbane when we vermin fear,
10 'Twere worth our cost to scatter fool-bane here.
And after all our judging fops were served,
Dull poets too should have a dose reserved—
Such reprobates as past all sense of shaming
Write on, and ne'er are satisfied with damning.
15 Next, those to whom the stage does not belong,
Such whose vocation only is to song,
At most to prologue, when for want of time
Poets take in for journey-work in rhyme.
But I want curses for those mighty shoals

Epilogue.
Title. Thersites was played by Cave Underhill, who specialized in low comedy. His other roles included the curate in *The Duke of Guise* and Pedro in *The Spanish Friar.*
7. a keeping pit] i.e. one which keeps mistresses.
8. cullies] dupes.
12–14. These lines make no specific references, but *Works* (xiii 565) suggests allusions to Settle and Shadwell, whom D. had damned in *Notes and Observations on the Empress of Morocco* (1674) and *MF* [1676]. Settle had subsequently staged *The Conquest of China* in 1675 and *Ibrahim* in 1676. Shadwell had recently staged *Timon of Athens* (1678) and *The True Widow* (1678).
15–22. These lines are also generalized, but point towards courtiers such as Rochester and Sedley. Both wrote songs to Chloris and Phyllis, and prologues and epilogues; both dabbled in drama: Sedley's *Antony and Cleopatra* was performed in 1677, and *c.* 1676 Rochester had contributed a scene to Sir Robert Howard's unfinished play *The Conquest of China*. He also adapted Fletcher's *Valentinian* (posthumously published in 1685).
18. journey-work] work done for daily wages; hack work.
19. want] lack.

20   Of scribbling Chloris's and Phyllis' fools;
     Those oafs should be restrained, during their lives,
     From pen and ink, as madmen are from knives.
     I could rail on, but 'twere a task as vain
     As preaching truth at Rome, or wit in Spain;
25   Yet to huff out our play was worth my trying—
     John Lilburne scaped his judges by defying.
     If guilty, yet I'm sure o' th' church's blessing,
     By suffering for the plot without confessing.

Song

1

     Can life be a blessing,
      Or worth the possessing,
   Can life be a blessing if love were away?
   Ah no! though our love all night keep us waking
5   And though he torment us with cares all the day,
   Yet he sweetens, he sweetens our pains in the taking,
   There's an hour at the last, there's an hour to repay.

2

     In every possessing
      The ravishing blessing,
10   In every possessing the fruit of our pain,

---

25. huff] inflate, puff.

26. At his trial for treason in 1649, the Leveller John Lilburne defied his judges and appealed to the jury: 'you that call yourselves judges of the law are no more but Norman intruders; and indeed and in truth, if the jury please, are no more but ciphers to pronounce their verdict'. The jury acquitted him (H. N. Brailsford, *The Levellers and the English Revolution* (1961) 598–602).

27–8. Alluding to the trial and execution of Catholics for alleged complicity in the Popish Plot. The trials had begun with that of Edward Coleman in November 1678 and continued through 1679. For Thersites' joke cp. his speech in V ii 74–5: 'I shall be mistaken for some valiant Asse, and dye a Martyr, in a wrong Religion!'.

Song. In Act III Scene ii; sung by musicians hired by Pandarus to serenade Troilus and Cressida. *The Compleat Courtier* prints a third verse.

Poor lovers forget long ages of anguish,
Whate'er they have suffered and done to obtain;
'Tis a pleasure, a pleasure to sigh and to languish,
When we hope, when we hope to be happy again.

52 Prologue to *Caesar Borgia*

Date and publication. Staged *c.* May 1679 (*LS* 276–7). The play was performed by the Duke's Company at Dorset Garden. Nathaniel Lee's *Caesar Borgia; Son of Pope Alexander the Sixth: A Tragedy* was published by Bentley and Magnes in 1680 (*TC* November 1679), dedicated to the Earl of Pembroke; there were two issues, in the first of which D.'s Prologue was anonymous. It was reprinted in 1696.

Prologue

Th' unhappy man who once has trailed a pen
Lives not to please himself but other men;
Is always drudging, wastes his life and blood,
Yet only eats and drinks what you think good:
5 What praise soe'er the poetry deserve,
Yet every fool can bid the poet starve.
That fumbling lecher to revenge is bent
Because he thinks himself or whore is meant:
Name but a cuckold, all the city swarms,
10 From Leadenhall to Ludgate is in arms.
Were there no fear of Antichrist or France,
In the best times poor poets live by chance.
Either you come not here, or as you grace ⎫
Some old acquaintance, drop into the place, ⎬
15 Careless and qualmish with a yawning face. ⎭
You sleep o'er wit, and by my troth you may—
Most of your talents lie another way.
You love to hear of some prodigious tale,

¶**52.** *1.* Cp. the expression 'trailed a pike' for 'served as a soldier'.
5–6. deserve . . . starve] a perfect rhyme: cp. 'Prologue at Oxford, 1679' ll. 34–5.
7–8. A reference to the unfavourable reception of D.'s *The Kind Keeper* (1678).
9–10. The area from Leadenhall Street at the east end of Cornhill to Ludgate Hill at the west end of St Paul's comprises the City of London. For cuckolded citizens cp. 'Epilogue to *Marriage A-la-Mode*' ll. 30–2.
11. Antichrist] The Pope was represented as Antichrist in Protestant propaganda.
15. qualmish] faint, lacking appetite.

The bell that tolled alone, or Irish whale.
20 News is your food, and you enough provide
Both for yourselves and all the world beside.
One theatre there is of vast resort,
Which whilom of Requests was called the Court.
But now the great Exchange of News 'tis hight,
25 And full of hum and buzz from noon till night.
Upstairs and down you run as for a race,
And each man wears three nations in his face.
So big you look, though claret you retrench,
That armed with bottled ale you huff the French.
30 But all your entertainment still is fed
By villains in our own dull island bred.
Would you return to us, we dare engage
To show you better rogues upon the stage:
You know no poison but plain ratsbane here;
35 Death's more refined and better bred elsewhere.
They have a civil way in Italy   ⎫
By smelling a perfume to make you die,   ⎬
A trick would make you lay your snuffbox by.⎭
Murder's a trade so known and practised there

19. Stories of this kind abounded in contemporary newspapers (see James Sutherland, *The Restoration Newspaper* (1986) 99–104), and in ballads. In [Aphra Behn], *The Revenge* (1680) 23–4, a story about whales coming ashore at Gravesend is used to mock the credulity of London citizens about popish plots.

20–31. Several prologues and epilogues in the politically tense autumn of 1679 viewed newsmongering with suspicion: 'Not only opposition, but any presumptuous interest in politics is condemned, for government is the business of the King and his ministers' (Owen 86). Cp. Shadwell, Prologue to *The Woman Captain* (*c.* September 1679; Danchin no. 273); anon. Prologue to *Fools have Fortune* (*c.* January 1680; Danchin no. A278).

23. The Court of Requests sat in the White Hall of Westminster Palace until its demise in 1642.   *whilom*] once upon a time.

28. *retrench*] do without (*OED* 5b). Imports of French wines had been prohibited.

30–1. Referring to the Popish Plot, but non-committal as to whether the villains are Oates and his associates or the Catholics. Lee's play and Epilogue are more explicitly anti-Catholic (Owen 57–62).

36–8. In Act IV Machiavel kills Adorna by having her smell a pair of poisoned gloves.

40   That 'tis infallible as is the chair.
      But mark their feasts, you shall behold such pranks—
      The Pope says grace, but 'tis the devil gives thanks.

40. Referring (i) to the infallibility claimed by the Pope, who occupies the
chair of St Peter; (ii) to Act V, where the Duke of Gandia is tied to a chair,
tortured and killed.
41–2. The Pope and the devil often appeared together in Pope-burning
processions in 1679–81: cp. 'Prologue to *The Loyal Brother*' ll. 18–40*n*.
41. *But*] only.
42. *devil*] monosyllabic here.

53 Prologue at Oxford, 1679 ('Discord and plots . . .')

Date and publication. Spoken in July 1679 (Winn 592; not 1680 (*Works*; Danchin) or 1681 (Kinsley)) at the annual Act at Oxford. The year is established by the references in l. 4 (see *n*). The players were the King's Company. It was first printed in *MP* (1684; reprinted 1692).

Prologue to the University of Oxford

Discord and plots which have undone our age
With the same ruin have o'erwhelmed the stage.
Our house has suffered in the common woe,
We have been troubled with Scotch rebels too:
5   Our brethren are from Thames to Tweed departed,
And of our sisters, all the kinder hearted
To Edinborough gone, or coached or carted.
With bonny bluecap there they act all night
For Scotch half-crown, in English three-pence hight.
10 One nymph, to whom fat Sir John Falstaff's lean,
There with her single person fills the scene;
Another, with long use and age decayed,
Dived here old woman, and rose there a maid.

¶**53**. *1–2.* The Popish Plot controversy began in October 1678 and continued through 1679. There is evidence that the theatres did badly during the crisis as a result of public anxieties; cp. Prologue to Aphra Behn's *The Feign'd Curtizans* (March 1679): 'The devil take this cursed plotting Age, / 'T has ruin'd all our Plots upon the Stage' (ll. 1–2; Danchin no. 267).

4. Scotch rebels] After dissension in the King's Company a group of the younger players went to Edinburgh in 1679 and acted there, returning in February 1680 (Hotson 262–3). Cp. Edward Ravenscroft's 'Prologue, Spoken before the Long Vacation' ll. 48–50 (1679; printed in his *Titus Andronicus* (1687); Danchin no. 356c). On 22 June 1679 the Duke of Monmouth defeated an army of Scottish rebels at Bothwell Bridge.

7. or . . . or] either . . . or.   *carted*] Carts were used for parading bawds and prostitutes (*Works*).

8. bluecap] Scotsman (from the traditional headgear).

9. half-crown] the price of a prostitute (cp. 'Prologue to *Marriage A-la-Mode*' l. 22).   *hight*] called.

10–11. Perhaps Katherine Corey (*Works*).

12–13. Perhaps Mrs Knepp (J. H. Wilson, *Mr Goodman the Player* (1964) 70).

Our trusty door-keepers of former time
15   There strut and swagger in heroic rhyme.
Tack but a copper-lace to drugget suit,
And there's a hero made without dispute;
And that which was a capon's tail before
Becomes a plume for Indian emperor:
20   But all his subjects, to express the care
Of imitation, go like Indians bare.
Laced linen there would be a dangerous thing, ⎤
It might perhaps a new rebellion bring: ⎬
The Scot who wore it would be chosen king. ⎦
25   But why should I these renegades describe,
When you yourselves have seen a lewder tribe:
Teg has been here, and to this learnèd pit
With Irish action slandered English wit;
You have beheld such barb'rous Macs appear
30   As merited a second massacre;
Such as like Cain were branded with disgrace,
And had their country stamped upon their face.
When strollers durst presume to pick your purse,

15. heroic rhyme] now unfashionable: D.'s last rhymed heroic play was *Aureng-Zebe* (1676); cp. l. 19*n*.
16. copper-lace] a cheap imitation of gold (*OED* 9c).   *drugget*] coarse woollen cloth (cp. 'Prologue at the Opening of the New House' l. 9*n*).
19. Kinsley notes that D.'s *The Indian Emperor* (1667) was performed in Edinburgh during the Duke of York's residence at Holyrood (November 1680 to March 1682).
22–4. Cleveland also jested at the Scots' lack of linen: 'Lord! what a goodly thing is want of shirts!' (*The Rebell Scot* l. 101; *Works*).
27–8. An Irish company whose patron was the Duke of Ormonde (Lord Lieutenant of Ireland and Chancellor of Oxford University) played at the Act in 1677: see the Epilogue spoken then by John Haines (Danchin no. 242). Ormonde unsuccessfully requested that his players perform at the Act in 1680 (see Sybil Rosenfeld, *RES* xix (1943) 369–70).   *Teg*] (also Teague) a nickname for an Irishman.
29. Macs] Irishmen; cp. Rochester, *Tunbridge Wells* l. 71.
30. second massacre] The Irish rebellion in November 1641 included atrocities against Protestant settlers which were widely reported in England.
31. Cain] See Genesis iv 15.
33. strollers] strolling players.

We humbly thought our broken troupe not worse;
35 How ill soe'er our action may deserve,
Oxford's a place where wit can never starve.

36. *starve*] The spelling in *MP* is 'sterve'; 'deserve' / 'starve' was a perfect
rhyme, as in 'Prologue to *Caesar Borgia*' ll. 5–6.

54 Prologue to *The Loyal General*

Date and publication. Probably staged in December 1679. The play was performed by the Duke's Company at Dorset Garden. For D.'s association with Tate see headnote to *2AA*. Nahum Tate's *The Loyal General, a Tragedy* was published by Henry Bonwicke in 1680 (*TC* February), with a dedication to Edward Tayler which includes complimentary references to D.'s criticism of Shakespeare. For the problematic royalism of Tate's play see Owen 113–20.

Prologue

    If yet there be a few that take delight   ⎫
    In that which reasonable men should write, ⎬
    To them alone we dedicate this night.   ⎭
    The rest may satisfy their curious itch
5   With city gazettes or some factious speech,
    Or whate'er libel for the public good
    Stirs up the Shrovetide crew to fire and blood!
    Remove your benches, you apostate pit,
    And take above twelve pennyworth of wit;
10 Go back to your dear dancing on the rope,
    Or see what's worse, the devil and the Pope!

¶**54**. *4. The rest*] D. associates the Whig members of the audience with vulgar literary taste. This was a common topic of prologues at this date (Owen 85–6).

5. gazettes] accented on the first syllable in the late seventeenth century.
factious speech] On 13 September 1679 Sir Thomas Player, accompanied by several hundred citizens, made a speech at the Guildhall in London, saying 'that it was apparent, what Advantage and Encouragement the Duke of YORK's being a PAPIST, gave to the Rise and Progress of this Horrid and Damnable PLOT', and asking for the guards to be doubled (*An Account of the Proceedings at the Guild-hall* [1679]). The speech provoked a pamphlet controversy for a few months.

7. Shrove Tuesday was traditionally an apprentices' holiday marked by rowdy behaviour such as attacks on brothels. The apprentices were staunch Protestants. See Tim Harris, *London Crowds in the Reign of Charles II* (1987).

8. Remove] move from.

9. The pit was supposedly the preserve of the wits; the price of the cheapest seats (in the gallery, used by servants) was one shilling.

10. Rope dancing was a popular entertainment at Bartholomew Fair.

11. For the Pope-burning ceremonies see 'Prologue to *The Loyal Brother*' ll. 18–40.

The plays that take on our corrupted stage
Methinks resemble the distracted age:
Noise, madness, all unreasonable things
15 That strike at sense as rebels do at kings!
The style of forty-one our poets write,
And you are grown to judge like forty-eight.
Such censures our mistaking audience make
That 'tis almost grown scandalous to take!
20 They talk of fevers that infect the brains,
But nonsense is the new disease that reigns.
Weak stomachs with a long disease oppressed
Cannot the cordials of strong wit digest:
Therefore thin nourishment of farce ye choose,
25 Decoctions of a barley-water Muse;
A meal of tragedy would make ye sick,
Unless it were a very tender chick.
Some scenes in sippets would be worth our time,
Those would go down—some love that's poached in
    rhyme.
30 If these should fail——
We must lie down, and after all our cost
Keep holiday, like watermen in frost,
Whilst you turn players on the world's great stage,
And act yourselves the farce of your own age.

12, 19. take] please, be popular (*OED* 10).

16. The year 1641, which saw the Irish Rebellion and rumours of a Popish Plot, was thought of after the Restoration as the beginning of the Civil War, and the parallel of 1641 with 1681 became a commonplace.

17. The trial and execution of Charles I took place in 1648, old style.

24. farce] This appealed not only to city audiences: the King and court were being entertained at Newmarket with farces such as *The Merry Milkmaid of Islington* (Owen 90).

25. Decoctions] liquors in which something (e.g. a vegetable) had been boiled (*OED* 4).   *barley-water*] a soothing drink for invalids.

26. a meal of tragedy] Winn 325 suggests a reference to the poor reception of *Troilus and Cressida* in the Spring.

28. sippets] pieces of toast or fried bread served in soup.

55 Preface to *Ovid's Epistles*

Date and publication. *Ovid's Epistles, Translated by Several Hands* was published by Jacob Tonson in 1680 (advertised in *Protestant Intelligence* 6 February); reprinted 1681, 1683, 1688, 1693.

Context. This translation from the *Heroides* was the first of the many translations from the classics on which D. and Tonson collaborated; for the early stages of this association see Stuart Gillespie, *Restoration* xii (1988) 10–19. D. contributed the Preface and three translations, one of them in collaboration with the Earl of Mulgrave. For the other contributors see Appendix B. For D.'s previous comments on Ovid see the 'Account' prefixed to *AM*. Since then his thinking had been affected by Rapin (see ll. 154ff). The statements on translation form D.'s first discussion of a subject to which he returned frequently, and his division of translation into three kinds proved influential, even though his own practice as a translator tended to mix the three modes. For his later views see 'Preface to *Sylvae*'.

Sources. Bottkol was the first scholar to establish D.'s working methods as a translator from Latin sources. D. worked from the edition of Ovid by Borchard Cnipping (1670), and probably also that by Heinsius (1629), whose notes are often quoted by Cnipping. For his translations of the *Heroides* he used the English translations by George Turberville, *The Heroycall Epistles* (1567); Wye Saltonstall, *Ovids Heroicall Epistles* (1636); John Sherburne, *Ovids Heroical Epistles* (1639); and Thomas Heywood, *Troia Britanica* (1609), for which see David Hopkins, *N & Q* ccxxii (1977) 218–19. D. also used the French translation by Marolles, *P. Ovidii Nasonis . . . Heroidum Liber. Cum interpretatione et notis M. de Marolles* (1661). The present notes record only D.'s more significant departures from the Latin and uses of editorial glosses and previous translations. Besides the borrowings noted here, D. often takes rhyme words from his predecessors. For antecedents to D.'s theory of translation in his Preface see Thomas R. Steiner, *Comparative Literature Studies* vii (1970) 50–81.

Reception. Two parodies confirm the collection's popularity: *Ovid Travestie* by Alexander Radcliffe (1680; revised 1681; both published by Tonson), and Matthew Stevenson, *The Wits Paraphras'd* (1680; reprinted 1680). John Oldham acknowledged that his translation of 'The Passion of Byblis' from Ovid's *Met.* was prompted by this collection (Advertisement to his *Satyrs upon the Jesuits* (1681)); so too was Thomas Hoy's translation of Ovid's *Ars Amatoria* in his *Two Essays* (1682), where D.'s Preface is particularly praised. Matthew Prior in 'A Satyr on the Modern Translators' (1685) ridicules the volume, esp. D.'s collaboration with Mulgrave, and Behn's ignorance of Latin. For D.'s own later affectionate view of these translations see Dedication to *EP* (*Works* iv 369).

The Preface to *Ovid's Epistles*

The life of Ovid being already written in our language before the translation of his *Metamorphoses*, I will not presume so far upon myself to think I can add anything to Mr Sandys his undertaking. The English reader may
5 there be satisfied that he flourished in the reign of Augustus Caesar; that he was extracted from an ancient family of Roman knights; that he was born to the inheritance of a splendid fortune; that he was designed to the study of the law, and had made considerable progress in
10 it before he quitted that profession for this of poetry, to which he was more naturally formed. The cause of his banishment is unknown, because he was himself unwilling further to provoke the Emperor by ascribing it to any other reason than what was pretended by
15 Augustus, which was the lasciviousness of his *Elegies* and his *Art of Love*. 'Tis true they are not to be excused in the severity of manners, as being able to corrupt a larger empire, if there were any, than that of Rome; yet this may be said in behalf of Ovid, that no man has ever
20 treated the passion of love with so much delicacy of thought and of expression, or searched into the nature of it more philosophically than he. And the Emperor who condemned him had as little reason as another man to punish that fault with so much severity, if at least he
25 were the author of a certain epigram, which is ascribed to him, relating to the cause of the first civil war betwixt himself and Mark Anthony the Triumvir, which is more fulsome than any passage I have met

¶55. *1–2. Ovid's Metamorphosis Englished* by George Sandys (1626, revised 1632) includes a life of the poet.
11–12. The cause of Ovid's banishment in AD 8 to Tomis on the Black Sea is unknown, but has been the subject of much speculation.
15. Elegies] The *Amores*, which, like the *Ars Amatoria*, offended against Augustus's moral legislation.
20. D. returns to the poetic analysis of the psychology of love in his discussion of Lucretius in 'Preface to *Sylvae*' ll. 372–425.
25. epigram] Martial XI xx contains six lines of verse attributed to Augustus.
28. fulsome] obscene.

with in our poet. To pass by the naked familiarity of his
30   expressions to Horace, which are cited in that author's
life, I need only mention one notorious act of his in
taking Livia to his bed, when she was not only married,
but with child by her husband then living. But deeds, it
seems, may be justified by arbitrary power, when
35   words are questioned in a poet. There is another guess
of the grammarians, as far from truth as the first from
reason: they will have him banished for some favours
which they say he received from Julia, the daughter of
Augustus, whom they think he celebrates under the
40   name of Corinna in his *Elegies*; but he who will observe
the verses which are made to that mistress, may gather
from the whole contexture of them that Corinna was
not a woman of the highest quality. If Julia were then
married to Agrippa, why should our poet make his
45   petition to Isis for her safe delivery, and afterwards
condole her miscarriage, which for aught he knew
might be by her own husband? Or indeed, how durst he
be so bold to make the least discovery of such a crime,
which was no less than capital, especially committed
50   against a person of Agrippa's rank? Or if it were before
her marriage, he would surely have been more discreet
than to have published an accident which must have
been fatal to them both. But what most confirms me
against this opinion, is that Ovid himself complains that
55   the true person of Corinna was found out by the fame
of his verses to her: which if it had been Julia he durst
not have owned, and besides, an immediate punishment

29–31. Suetonius (*Vita Horati*) reports that Augustus called Horace *purissi-mum penem* ('most immaculate libertine' (lit. 'penis')).

32. Livia] The wife of Tiberius Claudius Nero, who divorced her in 39 BC so that she could marry Octavian (Augustus); Drusus, her son by her first husband, was born around the time of her remarriage.

35–9. As reported in Cnipping: *Tandem cum venisset in suspicionem Augusti, creditus sub nomine Corinnae amasse Juliam, in exilium missus est* (sig. *6ᵛ) ('when he at length came to be suspected by Augustus, who believed him to have loved Julia under the name of Corinna, he was sent into exile').

44. Agrippa] Marcus Vispanius Agrippa married Augustus's daughter Julia in 21 BC; she bore him five children.

45–6. petition . . . condole] *Amores* II xiii–xiv.

54. himself complains] *Amores* III xii 7–14.

must have followed. He seems himself more truly to
have touched at the cause of his exile in those obscure
60   verses,

> *Cur aliquid vidi, cur noxia lumina feci? etc.*

Namely, that he had either seen, or was conscious to
somewhat which had procured him his disgrace. But
neither am I satisfied that this was the incest of the
65   Emperor with his own daughter; for Augustus was of a
nature too vindicative to have contented himself with so
small a revenge, or so unsafe to himself, as that of
simple banishment, and would certainly have secured
his crimes from public notice by the death of him who
70   was witness to them. Neither have histories given us
any sight into such an action of this Emperor; nor
would he (the greatest politician of his time) in all probability have managed his crimes with so little secrecy as
not to shun the observation of any man. It seems more
75   probable that Ovid was either the confidant of some
other passion, or that he had stumbled by some inad-
vertency upon the privacies of Livia, and seen her in a
bath: for the words

> *Nudam sine veste Dianam*

80   agree better with Livia, who had the fame of chastity,
than with either of the Julias who were both noted of
incontinency. The first verses which were made by him
in his youth, and recited publicly according to the
custom, were, as he himself assures us, to Corinna; his

---

61. 'Why did I see something? Why did I make my eyes guilty?' (*Tristia* II
103).

64. incest] Thus Heinsius: *Tradunt quidam, quod cum filia Augustum parum
honeste jacentem vidisset* (sig. ★★2ʳ⁻ᵛ) ('some say that he had seen Augustus
lying shamefully with his own daughter'). The story originates in Suetonius,
Caligula 23.

72. politician] schemer; cp. *AA* l. 223n.

79. 'Diana naked and unclothed' (*Tristia* II 105). *1681* drops *Nudam*, which is
not in Ovid's text: D. may have been quoting from memory, and subsequently corrected his slip.

81. the Julias] (i) Augustus's daughter Julia; (ii) her daughter by Agrippa.
Both were notoriously promiscuous, and both were banished for adultery.

82. first verses] *Amores* III xii 15–18.

85 banishment happened not till the age of fifty, from
which it may be deduced with probability enough that
the love of Corinna did not occasion it: nay he tells us
plainly that his offence was that of error only, not of
wickedness: and in the same paper of verses also that the
90 cause was notoriously known at Rome, though it be left
so obscure to after ages.

But to leave conjectures on a subject so incertain, and
to write somewhat more authentic of this poet: that he
frequented the court of Augustus, and was well
95 received in it, is most undoubted; all his poems bear the
character of a court, and appear to be written as the
French call it *cavalièrement*; add to this, that the titles of
many of his *Elegies*, and more of his letters in his banishment, are addressed to persons well known to us, even
100 at this distance, to have been considerable in that court.

Nor was his acquaintance less with the famous poets
of his age than with the noblemen and ladies; he tells
you himself, in a particular account of his own life, that
Macer, Horace, Tibullus, Propertius and many others
105 of them were his familiar friends, and that some of them
communicated their writings to him; but that he had
only seen Virgil.

If the imitation of nature be the business of a poet, I
know no author who can justly be compared with ours,
110 especially in the description of the passions. And to
prove this, I shall need no other judges than the gener-
ality of his readers; for all passions being inborn with
us, we are almost equally judges when we are concerned in the representation of them: now I will appeal
115 to any man who has read this poet, whether he find not
the natural emotion of the same passion in himself,
which the poet describes in his feigned persons? His
thoughts which are the pictures and results of those
passions are generally such as naturally arise from those
120 disorderly motions of our spirits. Yet, not to speak too

87–8. tells us plainly] In *Tristia* IV iv 37, 39 he insists that the cause of his exile
was not *scelus* ('crime') but *aut timor aut error* ('either timidity or a mistake').
103. account of his own life] *Tristia* IV x 43–54.

partially in his behalf, I will confess that the copiousness
of his wit was such that he often writ too pointedly for
his subject, and made his persons speak more elo-
quently than the violence of their passion would admit:
125 so that he is frequently witty out of season; leaving the
imitation of nature, and the cooler dictates of his judgement, for the false applause of fancy. Yet he seems to
have found out this imperfection in his riper age: for
why else should he complain that his *Metamorphosis* was
130 left unfinished? Nothing sure can be added to the wit of
that poem, or of the rest; but many things ought to have
been retrenched, which I suppose would have been the
business of his age, if his misfortunes had not come too
fast upon him. But take him uncorrected as he is trans-
135 mitted to us, and it must be acknowledged in spite of
his Dutch friends the commentators, even of Julius
Scaliger himself, that Seneca's censure will stand good
against him—

> *Nescivit quod bene cessit relinquere:*

140 he never knew how to give over, when he had done
well; but continually varying the same sense an hundred
ways, and taking up in another place what he had more
than enough inculcated before, he sometimes cloys his
readers instead of satisfying them; and gives occasion to
145 his translators, who dare not cover him, to blush at the
nakedness of their father. This then is the allay of
Ovid's writing, which is sufficiently recompensed by
his other excellencies; nay this very fault is not without
its beauties: for the most severe censor cannot but be
150 pleased with the prodigality of his wit, though at the
same time he could have wished that the master of it

121–27. For the ancestry of this criticism of Ovid's over-ready wit see 'Preface to *Sylvae*' l. 90n.

130. unfinished] *Tristia* I vii 11–16.

137. Scaliger] Heinsius says: *Julius in Rhetoricis . . . tanquam absolutum &
perfectum omni ex parte exemplum, scripta ejus proponebat* ('Julius Scaliger in his
Rhetoric put forward his writings as an absolute and perfect model'; quoted by
Cnipping, sig. ★6ʳ⁻ᵛ).

139. Seneca, *Controversiae* IX v 17.

146. allay] inferior metal mixed with one of greater value.

149. censor] judge, critic.

had been a better manager. Everything which he does
becomes him, and if sometimes he appear too gay, yet
there is a secret gracefulness of youth which accompa-
155   nies his writings, though the staidness and sobriety of
age be wanting. In the most material part, which is the
conduct, 'tis certain that he seldom has miscarried: for if
his *Elegies* be compared with those of Tibullus and Propertius, his contemporaries, it will be found that those
160   poets seldom designed before they writ; and though the
language of Tibullus be more polished, and the learning
of Propertius, especially in his fourth book, more set
out to ostentation; yet their common practice was to
look no further before them than the next line: whence
165   it will inevitably follow, that they can drive to no
certain point, but ramble from one subject to another,
and conclude with somewhat which is not of a piece
with their beginning:

> *Purpureus late qui splendeat, unus et alter*
170   *Assuitur pannus:*

as Horace says, though the verses are golden they are
but patched into the garment. But our poet has always
the goal in his eye, which directs him in his race; some
beautiful design, which he first establishes, and then
175   contrives the means which will naturally conduct it to
his end. This will be evident to judicious readers in this
work of his *Epistles*, of which somewhat, at least in
general, will be expected.

The title of them in our late editions is *Epistolae Heroi-*
180   *dum, The Letters of the Heroines.* But Heinsius has judged

---

154–6, 172–6. Cp. René Rapin, comparing the elegies of Ovid with those by
Tibullus and Propertius: 'il a des jeunesses, qu'on auroit de la peine à luy
pardonner, sans la vivacité de son esprit . . . on y trouve toujours un tour
secret qui en fait le dessein, et c'est d'ordinaire ce tour qui fait la principale
beauté' (*Réflexions sur la Poétique* (1674; edited by Dubois (1970) 91, 35;
Works).

157. *conduct*] management of the parts of a work (*OED* 6d; first example
1758).

169–70. 'One or two purple patches are sewn on, to shine far and wide'
(Horace, *Ars Poetica* ll. 15–16).

179–85, 199–203. The title in Cnipping's edition is *Epistolarum Heroidum
Liber*; he quotes Heinsius: *Caeterum quod Ovidius versibus paulo ante prolatis se*

more truly, that the inscription of our author was barely, *Epistles*; which he concludes from his cited verses,
where Ovid asserts this work as his own invention, and
not borrowed from the Greeks, whom (as the masters
185 of their learning) the Romans usually did imitate. But it
appears not from their writers that any of the Grecians
ever touched upon this way, which our poet therefore
justly has vindicated to himself. I quarrel not at the
word *Heroidum*, because 'tis used by Ovid in his *Art of*
190 *Love*:

> *Jupiter ad veteres supplex heroidas ibat.*

But sure he could not be guilty of such an oversight, to
call his work by the name of heroines, when there are
divers men or heroes, as namely Paris, Leander, and
195 Acontius, joined in it. Except Sabinus, who writ some
answers to Ovid's letters,

> *(Quam celer e toto rediit meus orbe Sabinus)*

I remember not any of the Romans who have treated
this subject, save only Propertius, and that but once, in
200 his Epistle of Arethusa to Lycotas, which is written so
near the style of Ovid that it seems to be but an imitation, and therefore ought not to defraud our poet of the
glory of his invention.

Concerning this work of the *Epistles*, I shall content
205 myself to observe these few particulars. First, that they
are generally granted to be the most perfect piece of

---

auctorem primum atque inventorem facit hujus generis epistolarum, liquet hinc, eam
Arethusae ad Lycotam, quae apud Propertium lib. 4 extat, ad imitationem nostri
fuisse conscriptam, Nasonique solidam Heroidum pangendarum ac principem gloriam
omnino deberi. (1) ('Ovid, in the lines cited a little earlier, makes himself the
first author and inventor of this form of epistle; it is clear that the one from
Arethusa to Lycotas which is found in Propertius' Book IV was written in
imitation of Ovid, and that the principal and substantial credit for composing
letters from heroines belongs entirely to Ovid.').

188. vindicated to] claimed for (*OED* 7, first example).

191. 'Jupiter used to approach the heroines of ancient times as a suppliant'
(*Ars Amatoria* i 713).

197. 'How quickly my friend Sabinus returned from the ends of the earth'
(*Amores* II xviii 27).   *celer e*] Thus Heinsius and Cnipping; *cito de* is the
reading of Schrevelius and modern editors of Ovid.

Ovid, and that the style of them is tenderly passionate and courtly, two properties well agreeing with the persons which were heroines and lovers. Yet where the
210   characters were lower, as in Oenone and Hero, he has kept close to nature in drawing his images after a country life, though perhaps he has Romanized his Grecian dames too much, and made them speak sometimes as if they had been born in the city of Rome, and under
215   the empire of Augustus. There seems to be no great variety in the particular subjects which he has chosen, most of the epistles being written from ladies who were forsaken by their lovers; which is the reason that many of the same thoughts come back upon us in divers
220   letters: but of the general character of women, which is modesty, he has taken a most becoming care, for his amorous expressions go no further than virtue may allow, and therefore may be read, as he intended them, by matrons without a blush.
225   Thus much concerning the poet, whom you find translated by divers hands, that you may at least have that variety in the English which the subject denied to the author of the Latin. It remains that I should say somewhat of poetical translations in general, and give
230   my opinion (with submission to better judgements) which way of version seems to me most proper.
      All translation I suppose may be reduced to these three heads.
      First, that of metaphrase, or turning an author word
235   by word, and line by line, from one language into another. Thus, or near this manner, was Horace his *Art of Poetry* translated by Ben Jonson. The second way is that of paraphrase, or translation with latitude, where the author is kept in view by the translator, so as never
240   to be lost, but his words are not so strictly followed as his sense, and that too is admitted to be amplified, but

---

231. version] process of translating (*OED* 1).
236–7. Jonson's translation of the *Ars Poetica* was published in 1640 and included in Alexander Brome's collaborative *Poems of Horace* (1666, reprinted 1671) but dropped from the 1680 reprint. It was criticized for being too literal by Roscommon in the preface to his version, *Horace's Art of Poetry* (1680).

not altered. Such is Mr Waller's translation of Virgil's
fourth *Aeneid*. The third way is that of imitation, where
the translator (if now he has not lost that name) assumes
245 the liberty not only to vary from the words and sense,
but to forsake them both as he sees occasion; and taking
only some general hints from the original, to run division on the ground-work as he pleases. Such is Mr
Cowley's practice in turning two odes of Pindar, and
250 one of Horace, into English.

Concerning the first of these methods, our master
Horace has given us this caution,

> *Nec verbum verbo curabis reddere, fidus*
> *Interpres—*

255 *Nor word for word too faithfully translate*, as the Earl of
Roscommon has excellently rendered it. Too faithfully
is indeed pedantically; 'tis a faith like that which proceeds from superstition, blind and zealous: take it in the
expression of Sir John Denham to Sir Rich. Fanshawe,
260 on his version of the *Pastor Fido*:

> *That servile path thou nobly do'st decline*
> *Of tracing word by word and line by line;*
> *A new and nobler way thou do'st pursue,*
> *To make translations, and translators too:*
265 *They but preserve the ashes, thou the flame,*
> *True to his sense, but truer to his fame.*

242–3. The Passion of Dido (1658) by Edmund Waller and Sidney Godolphin.
247–8. run division on the ground-work] execute a variation or descant on a theme.
249–50. Cowley's 'Pindarique Odes' in *Poems* (1656) include versions of Pindar's second Olympian and first Nemean odes, and Horace's *Carm*. IV ii. In his preface he says: 'If a man should undertake to translate *Pindar* word for word, it would be thought that *one Mad-man* had translated *another*; . . . It does not at all trouble me that the *Grammarians* perhaps will not suffer this libertine way of rendring foreign Authors, to be called *Translation*; . . . I have in these two *Odes* of *Pindar* taken, left out, and added what I please; nor make it so much my aim to let the Reader know precisely what he spoke, as what was his *way* and *manner* of speaking' (*Poems* 155–6).
253–4. Ars Poetica ll. 133–4.
261–6. D. quotes ll. 15–16, 21–4 of Sir John Denham's prefatory verses to Sir Richard Fanshawe's *Il Pastor Fido* (1647).

'Tis almost impossible to translate verbally and well
at the same time; for the Latin (a most severe and compendious language) often expresses that in one word
270 which either the barbarity or the narrowness of modern
tongues cannot supply in more. 'Tis frequent also that
the conceit is couched in some expression which will be
lost in English.

Atque iidem venti vela fidemque ferent.

275 What poet of our nation is so happy as to express this
thought literally in English, and to strike wit or almost
sense out of it?

In short the verbal copier is encumbered with so
many difficulties at once, that he can never disentangle
280 himself from all. He is to consider at the same time the
thought of his author, and his words, and to find out
the counterpart to each in another language: and besides
this he is to confine himself to the compass of numbers,
and the slavery of rhyme. 'Tis much like dancing on
285 ropes with fettered legs: a man may shun a fall by using
caution, but the gracefulness of motion is not to be
expected; and when we have said the best of it, 'tis but a
foolish task, for no sober man would put himself into a
danger for the applause of scaping without breaking his
290 neck. We see Ben Jonson could not avoid obscurity in
his literal translation of Horace, attempted in the same
compass of lines; nay Horace himself could scarce have
done it to a Greek poet.

Brevis esse laboro, obscurus fio.

295 Either perspicuity or gracefulness will frequently be
wanting. Horace has indeed avoided both these rocks in
his translation of the three first lines of Homer's
Odysses, which he has contracted into two:

       Dic mihi Musa virum captae post tempora Troiae
300   *Qui mores hominum multorum vidit et urbes.*

---

271. in] *1681*; it *1680*.
274. *Heroides* vii 8; tr. D. in *Dido to Aeneas* l. 9.
294. 'I strive to become brief, I become obscure', *Ars Poetica* ll. 25–6.
299–300. *Ars Poetica* ll. 141–2.

Muse, speak the man, who since the siege of Troy,
So many towns, such change of manners saw.

                                    Earl of Rosc.

But then the sufferings of Ulysses, which are a con-
305 siderable part of that sentence, are omitted.

Ὃς μάλα πολλὰ πλάγχθη.

The consideration of these difficulties in a servile,
literal translation, not long since made two of our
famous wits, Sir John Denham and Mr Cowley, to
310 contrive another way of turning authors into our
tongue, called by the latter of them 'imitation'. As they
were friends, I suppose they communicated their
thoughts on this subject to each other, and therefore
their reasons for it are little different, though the prac-
315 tice of one is much more moderate. I take imitation of
an author in their sense to be an endeavour of a later
poet to write like one who has written before him on
the same subject: that is, not to translate his words, or
to be confined to his sense, but only to set him as a
320 pattern, and to write as he supposes that author would
have done, had he lived in our age and in our country.
Yet I dare not say that either of them have carried this
libertine way of rendering authors (as Mr Cowley calls
it) so far as my definition reaches. For in the *Pindaric*
325 *Odes* the customs and ceremonies of ancient Greece are
still preserved: but I know not what mischief may arise
hereafter from the example of such an innovation, when
writers of unequal parts to him shall imitate so bold an
undertaking; to add and to diminish what we please,
330 which is the way avowed by him, ought only to be
granted to Mr Cowley, and that too only in his translation of Pindar, because he alone was able to make him
amends by giving him better of his own whenever he refused his author's thoughts. Pindar is generally known
335 to be a dark writer, to want connexion (I mean as to
our understanding), to soar out of sight and leave his
reader at a gaze: so wild and ungovernable a poet cannot
be translated literally, his genius is too strong to bear a

306. Odyssey i 1–2: 'who wandered very many ways'.

chain, and Samson-like he shakes it off; a genius
340 so elevated and unconfined as Mr Cowley's was but
necessary to make Pindar speak English, and that was to
be performed by no other way than imitation. But if
Virgil or Ovid, or any regular intelligible authors be
thus used, 'tis no longer to be called their work, when
345 neither the thoughts nor words are drawn from the
original, but instead of them there is something new
produced, which is almost the creation of another hand.
By this way, 'tis true, somewhat that is excellent may
be invented perhaps more excellent than the first
350 design, though Virgil must be still excepted, when that
perhaps takes place: yet he who is inquisitive to know
an author's thoughts will be disappointed in his expectation. And 'tis not always that a man will be contented
to have a present made him, when he expects the pay-
355 ment of a debt. To state it fairly, imitation of an author
is the most advantageous way for a translator to show
himself, but the greatest wrong which can be done to
the memory and reputation of the dead. Sir John Denham (who advised more liberty than he took himself)
360 gives this reason for his innovation, in his admirable
preface before the translation of the second *Aeneid*:
'Poetry is of so subtle a spirit, that in pouring out of one
language into another it will all evaporate; and if a new
spirit be not added in the transfusion, there will remain
365 nothing but a *caput mortuum*'. I confess this argument
holds good against a literal translation, but who defends
it? Imitation and verbal version are in my opinion the
two extremes, which ought to be avoided; and therefore when I have proposed the mean betwixt them, it
370 will be seen how far his argument will reach.
   No man is capable of translating poetry, who besides
a genius to that art is not a master both of his author's
language and of his own: nor must we understand the

362–5. D. quotes from Denham's Preface to *The Destruction of Troy* (1656), a
major statement of the theory of translation.
365. caput mortuum] the worthless residue remaining after the distillation of
a substance.

language only of the poet, but his particular turn of
375 thoughts, and of expression, which are the characters
that distinguish, and as it were individuate him from all
other writers. When we are come thus far, 'tis time to
look into ourselves, to conform our genius to his, to
give his thought either the same turn if our tongue will
380 bear it, or if not, to vary but the dress, not to alter or
destroy the substance. The like care must be taken of
the more outward ornaments, the words: when they
appear (which is but seldom) literally graceful, it were
an injury to the author that they should be changed; but
385 since every language is so full of its own proprieties that
what is beautiful in one is often barbarous, nay sometimes nonsense in another, it would be unreasonable to
limit a translator to the narrow compass of his author's
words: 'tis enough if he choose out some expression
390 which does not vitiate the sense. I suppose he may
stretch his chain to such a latitude, but by innovation of
thoughts methinks he breaks it. By this means the spirit
of an author may be transfused, and yet not lost; and
thus 'tis plain that the reason alleged by Sir John Den-
395 ham has no farther force than to expression: for
thought, if it be translated truly, cannot be lost in
another language, but the words that convey it to our
apprehension (which are the image and ornament of
that thought) may be so ill chosen as to make it appear
400 in an unhandsome dress, and rob it of its native lustre.
There is therefore a liberty to be allowed for the expression, neither is it necessary that words and lines
should be confined to the measure of their original. The
sense of an author, generally speaking, is to be sacred
405 and inviolable. If the fancy of Ovid be luxuriant, 'tis his
character to be so, and if I retrench it, he is no longer
Ovid. It will be replied that he receives advantage by
this lopping of his superfluous branches, but I rejoin
that a translator has no such right: when a painter copies
410 from the life, I suppose he has no privilege to alter
features and lineaments under pretence that his picture
will look better; perhaps the face which he has drawn
would be more exact if the eyes or nose were altered,
but 'tis his business to make it resemble the original. In
415 two cases only there may a seeming difficulty arise, that

is if the thought be notoriously trivial or dishonest; but
the same answer will serve for both, that then they
ought not to be translated.

              ——*Et quae*
420   *Desperes tractata nitescere posse, relinquas.*

    Thus I have ventured to give my opinion on this
subject against the authority of two great men, but I
hope without offence to either of their memories, for I
both loved them living, and reverence them now they
425 are dead. But if after what I have urged, it be thought
by better judges that the praise of a translation consists
in adding new beauties to the piece, thereby to recompense the loss which it sustains by change of language, I
shall be willing to be taught better, and to recant. In the
430 mean time it seems to me that the true reason why we
have so few versions which are tolerable, is not from
the too close pursuing of the author's sense, but because
there are so few who have all the talents which are
requisite for translation; and that there is so little praise
435 and so small encouragement for so considerable a part
of learning.

    To apply in short what has been said to this present
work, the reader will here find most of the translations
with some little latitude or variation from the author's
440 sense: that of Oenone to Paris is in Mr Cowley's way of
imitation only. I was desired to say that the author, who
is of the fair sex, understood not Latin. But if she does
not, I am afraid she has given us occasion to be ashamed
who do.

445   For my own part I am ready to acknowledge that I
have transgressed the rules which I have given, and
taken more liberty than a just translation will allow. But

<hr>

419–20. 'And those things which you despair of making brilliant if you treat
of them, you should abandon' (Horace, *Ars Poetica* ll. 149–50; the usual text
of Horace is *desperat . . . relinquit*).

441. the author] Aphra Behn. She had addressed the question of women's
learning, and complimented D. on his own learning, in her 'Epistle to the
Reader' before *The Dutch Lover* (1673); see Winn, *When Beauty* 423–5.

447. just] corresponding exactly (*OED* 10).

so many gentlemen whose wit and learning are well known being joined in it, I doubt not but that their 450 excellencies will make you ample satisfaction for my errors.

J. Dryden

56 Canace to Macareus

For headnote see 'Preface to *Ovid's Epistles*'.

Canace to Macareus

The Argument

Macareus and Canace, son and daughter to Aeolus, god of the
winds, loved each other incestuously. Canace was delivered
of a son, and committed him to her nurse, to be secretly
conveyed away. The infant crying out, by that means was
discovered to Aeolus, who, enraged at the wickedness of his
children, commanded the babe to be exposed to wild beasts
on the mountains; and withal sent a sword to Canace with
this message, that her crimes would instruct her how to use it.
With this sword she slew herself; but before she died, she writ
the following letter to her brother Macareus, who had taken
sanctuary in the temple of Apollo.

> If streaming blood my fatal letter stain,
> Imagine, ere you read, the writer slain:
> One hand the sword, and one the pen employs,
> And in my lap the ready paper lies.
> 5 Think in this posture thou behold'st me write:
> In this my cruel father would delight.
> O were he present, that his eyes and hands
> Might see and urge the death which he commands;
> Than all his raging winds more dreadful, he
> 10 Unmoved, without a tear, my wounds would see.
> Jove justly placed him on a stormy throne—
> His people's temper is so like his own.
> The north and south, and each contending blast

¶**56**. *Argument*] This and the following arguments are translated from the
Latin prose summaries found in Cnipping and other seventeenth-century
editions.
1. In all three epistles D. follows Heinsius and Cnipping in rejecting the
opening couplet found in some MSS of Ovid.
4. 'And in my lap the limber paper lies' (Sherburne; *Works*).
5. 'This is my posture whilst to thee I write' (Sherburne; *Works*).

Are underneath his wide dominion cast:
15 Those he can rule; but his tempestuous mind
Is, like his airy kingdom, unconfined.
Ah, what avail my kindred gods above,
That in their number I can reckon Jove!
What help will all my heavenly friends afford,
20 When to my breast I lift the pointed sword?
That hour which joined us came before its time:
In death we had been one without a crime.
Why did thy flames beyond a brother's move?
Why loved I thee with more than sister's love?
25 For I loved too, and knowing not my wound
A secret pleasure in thy kisses found;
My cheeks no longer did their colour boast,
My food grew loathsome, and my strength I lost;
Still ere I spoke a sigh would stop my tongue,
30 Short were my slumbers, and my nights were long.
I knew not from my love these griefs did grow,
Yet was, alas, the thing I did not know.
My wily nurse by long experience found,
And first discovered to my soul its wound.
35 ' 'Tis love', said she; and then my downcast eyes
And guilty dumbness witnessed my surprise.
Forced at the last, my shameful pain I tell,
And, O, what followed we both know too well!
When half denying, more than half content,
40 Embraces warmed me to a full consent:
Then with tumultuous joys my heart did beat,
And guilt that made them anxious, made them great.
    But now my swelling womb heaved up my breast,
And rising weight my sinking limbs oppressed.
45 What herbs, what plants, did not my nurse produce
To make abortion by their powerful juice?
What medicines tried we not, to thee unknown?
Our first crime common, this was mine alone.

---

14. underneath his wide dominion] sub imperio suo (Cnipping).
37–42. D.'s addition.
39–42. Inverted commas at the beginning of each line in *1680* mark this as a
sententia, or notable piece of expression.
43. Editorial paragraph.
44. limbs oppressed] Turberville (*Works*).

But the strong child, secure in his dark cell,
50   With nature's vigour did our arts repell.
And now the pale-faced empress of the night
Nine times had filled her orb with borrowed light:
Not knowing 'twas my labour, I complain
Of sudden shootings, and of grinding pain;
55   My throes came thicker, and my cries increased,
Which with her hand the conscious nurse suppressed.
To that unhappy fortune was I come,
Pain urged my clamours, but fear kept me dumb.
With inward struggling I restrained my cries,
60   And drunk the tears that trickled from my eyes.
Death was in sight, Lucina gave no aid,
And ev'n my dying had my guilt betrayed.
Thou cam'st, and in thy count'nance sate despair;
Rent were thy garments all, and torn thy hair.
65   Yet feigning comfort which thou couldst not give,
Pressed in thy arms, and whispering me to live,
'For both our sakes', said'st thou, 'preserve thy life;
Live, my dear sister, and my dearer wife.'
Raised by that name, with my last pangs I strove:
70   Such power have words, when spoke by those we
        love.
The babe, as if he heard what thou hadst sworn,
With hasty joy sprung forward to be born.
What helps it to have weathered out one storm?
Fear of our father does another form.
75   High in his hall, rocked in a chair of state,
The King with his tempestuous council sate:

49. *secure in his dark cell*] D.'s addition, partly from 'en seureté' (Marolles).
50. *vigour*] 'l'enfant vigoureux' (Marolles).
55. *thicker*] more quickly.
56. *with her hand*] D.'s addition, from 'sa main' (Marolles).   *conscious*]
party to the secret.
59–60. 'cries / And dranke the teares that flow'd downe from my eies'
(Saltonstall; *Works*).
61. *Lucina*] goddess of childbirth.
63. D.'s addition.   *sate*] sat.
65. D.'s addition.
67–8. D. abbreviates Ovid's word-play in ll. 59–62.
69–78. D. elaborates Ovid's bare account in ll. 63–6.
75–6. Cp. *MF* ll. 107–9.

Through this large room our only passage lay,
By which we could the new-born babe convey.
Swathed in her lap the bold nurse bore him out,
80   With olive branches covered round about;
And muttering prayers, as holy rites she meant,
Through the divided crowd unquestioned went.
Just at the door th' unhappy infant cried:
The grandsire heard him, and the theft he spied.
85   Swift as a whirlwind to the nurse he flies,
And deafs his stormy subjects with his cries.
With one fierce puff he blows the leaves away:
Exposed the self-discovered infant lay.
The noise reached me, and my presaging mind
90   Too soon its own approaching woes divined.
Not ships at sea with winds are shaken more,
Nor seas themselves when angry tempests roar,
Than I, when my loud father's voice I hear:
The bed beneath me trembled with my fear.
95   He rushed upon me, and divulged my stain;
Scarce from my murther could his hands refrain.
I only answered him with silent tears;
They flowed; my tongue was frozen up with fears.
His little grandchild he commands away
100 To mountain wolves and every bird of prey.
The babe cried out as if he understood,
And begged his pardon with what voice he could.
By what expressions can my grief be shown
(Yet you may guess my anguish by your own)
105 To see my bowels, and what yet was worse,
Your bowels too, condemned to such a curse!
Out went the King; my voice its freedom found,
My breasts I beat, my blubbered cheeks I wound.
    And now appeared the messenger of death,
110 Sad were his looks, and scarce he drew his breath
To say, 'Your father sends you—' (with that word
His trembling hands presented me a sword)
'Your father sends you this: and lets you know
That your own crimes the use of it will show.'

85–90. D.'s expansion of Ovid's ll. 73–4.
86. deafs] drowns a sound with a louder one (*OED* 3).
109. Editorial paragraph.

115   Too well I know the sense those words impart:
        His present shall be treasured in my heart.
        Are these the nuptial gifts a bride receives?
        And this the fatal dower a father gives?
        Thou god of marriage, shun thy own disgrace,
120   And take thy torch from this detested place:
        Instead of that, let furies light their brands,
        And fire my pile with their infernal hands.
        With happier fortune may my sisters wed,
        Warned by the dire example of the dead.
125   For thee, poor babe, what crime could they pretend?
        How could thy infant innocence offend?
        A guilt there was; but O that guilt was mine!
        Thou suffer'st for a sin that was not thine:
        Thy mother's grief and crime! But just enjoyed,
130   Shown to my sight, and born to be destroyed!
        Unhappy offspring of my teeming womb,
        Dragged headlong from thy cradle to thy tomb!
        Thy unoffending life I could not save,
        Nor weeping could I follow to thy grave;
135   Nor on thy tomb could offer my shorn hair,
        Nor show the grief which tender mothers bear.
        Yet long thou shalt not from my arms be lost,
        For soon I will o'ertake thy infant ghost.
        But thou, my love, and now my love's despair,
140   Perform his funerals with paternal care.
        His scattered limbs with my dead body burn,
        And once more join us in the pious urn.
        If on my wounded breast thou dropp'st a tear,
        Think for whose sake my breast that wound did bear,
145   And faithfully my last desires fulfil,
        As I perform my cruel father's will.

---

136. D. omits Ovid's l. 118: 'greedy wild beasts are tearing to pieces the child
of my womb.'
146. 'My cruell fathers will' (Turberville; *Works*).

57 Helen to Paris

For headnote see 'Preface to *Ovid's Epistles*'.

Authorship. John Sheffield, Earl of Mulgrave (1648–1721) wrote *An Essay upon Satire* which circulated in MS in 1679, and was attributed by some to D.; this probably occasioned the Rose Alley attack on D. on 18 December 1679. Mulgrave also wrote *An Essay upon Poetry* (1682). D. dedicated *Aureng-Zebe* to him in 1676. See also *AA* ll. 877–81n. Mulgrave may have had the major share in 'Helen to Paris': D.'s 'To the Earl of Roscommon' ll. 59–62n attributes it to him, and it was omitted from Tonson's 1701 folio edition of D.

Helen to Paris

By the Right Honourable the Earl of Mulgrave and Mr Dryden

The Argument

Helen, having received the foregoing epistle from Paris, returns the following answer: wherein she seems at first to chide him for his presumption in writing as he had done, which could only proceed from his low opinion of her virtue; then owns herself to be sensible of the passion which he had expressed for her, though she much suspect his constancy; and at last discovers her inclinations to be favourable to him. The whole letter showing the extreme artifice of womankind.

> When loose epistles violate chaste eyes,
> She half consents who silently denies.
> How dares a stranger with designs so vain,
> Marriage and hospitable rights profane?
> 5 Was it for this your fate did shelter find
> From swelling seas and every faithless wind?
> (For though a distant country brought you forth,
> Your usage here was equal to your worth.)

¶**57**. *Argument. foregoing epistle*] This epistle is preceded in Ovid by one to Helen from Paris, son of Priam the King of Troy, written while he is her guest, and her husband Menelaus is away.
5. 'was it for this' (Sherburne).

       Does this deserve to be rewarded so?
10   Did you come here a stranger, or a foe?
       Your partial judgement may perhaps complain,
       And think me barbarous for my just disdain;
       Ill-bred then let me be, but not unchaste,
       Nor my clear fame with any spot defaced:
15   Though in my face there's no affected frown,
       Nor in my carriage a feigned niceness shown,
       I keep my honour still without a stain,
       Nor has my love made any coxcomb vain.
       Your boldness I with admiration see;
20   What hope had you to gain a queen like me?
       Because a hero forced me once away,
       Am I thought fit to be a second prey?
       Had I been won, I had deserved your blame,
       But sure my part was nothing but the shame:
25   Yet the base theft to him no fruit did bear,
       I scaped unhurt by anything but fear;
       Rude force might some unwilling kisses gain,
       But that was all he ever could obtain.
       You on such terms would ne'er have let me go,
30   Were he like you we had not parted so.
       Untouched the youth restored me to my friends,
       And modest usage made me some amends.
       'Tis virtue to repent a vicious deed;
       Did he repent that Paris might succeed?
35   Sure 'tis some fate that sets me above wrongs,
       Yet still exposes me to busy tongues.
       I'll not complain, for who's displeased with love
       If it sincere, discreet and constant prove?
       But that I fear; not that I think you base,
40   Or doubt the blooming beauties of my face;
       But all your sex is subject to deceive,
       And ours, alas, too willing to believe.

16. *niceness*] coyness (*OED* 4).
17. 'without a staine: / ' (Sherburne; *Works*).
18. *coxcomb*] fool.
19. *admiration*] astonishment (*OED* 1).
21. *a hero*] Theseus.
23. 'Had I been wonne' (Sherburne; *Works*).
38. Renders Ovid's 'if it is not feigned love' (l. 36).

Yet others yield; and love o'ercomes the best,
But why should I not shine above the rest?
45 Fair Leda's story seems at first to be
A fit example ready found for me;
But she was cozened by a borrowed shape,
And under harmless feathers felt a rape.
If I should yield, what reason could I use?
50 By what mistake the loving crime excuse?
Her fault was in her powerful lover lost,
But of what Jupiter have I to boast?
Though you to heroes and to kings succeed,
Our famous race does no addition need;
55 And great alliances but useless prove
To one that's come herself from mighty Jove.
Go then, and boast in some less haughty place
Your Phrygian blood and Priam's ancient race,
Which I would show I valued, if I durst;
60 You are the fifth from Jove, but I the first.
The crown of Troy is powerful, I confess,
But I have reason to think ours no less.
Your letter filled with promises of all
That men can good, or women pleasant call,
65 Gives expectation such an ample field
As would move goddesses themselves to yield.
But if I e'er offend great Juno's laws,
Yourself shall be the dear, the only cause;
Either my honour I'll to death maintain,
70 Or follow you, without mean thoughts of gain.
Not that so fair a present I despise:
We like the gift, when we the giver prize.
But 'tis your love moves me, which made you take
Such pains, and run such hazards for my sake;
75 I have perceived (though I dissembled too)

43. 'Let others sinne:' (Sherburne).
45–8. Helen's mother, Leda, was possessed by Jupiter in the shape of a swan.
50. *loving crime*] rendering Ovid's *crimen* ('crime').
55–6. D.'s abbreviation of Ovid's ll. 53–6.
62. 'I thinke ours are no lesse' (Sherburne). After this line D. omits Ovid's ll.
63–4 (*Works*).
64–5. D.'s addition.
67. *Juno*] goddess of marriage.

A thousand things that love has made you do;
Your eager eyes would almost dazzle mine,
In which (wild man) your wanton thoughts would
    shine.
Sometimes you'd sigh, sometimes disordered stand,
80 And with unusual ardour press my hand;
Contrive just after me to take the glass:
Nor would you let the least occasion pass,
Which oft I feared I did not mind alone,
And blushing sate for things which you have done;
85 Then murmured to myself, 'He'll for my sake
Do anything, I hope 'twas no mistake.'
Oft have I read within this pleasing grove
Under my name those charming words, 'I love';
I frowning seemed not to believe your flame,
90 But now, alas, am come to write the same.
If I were capable to do amiss,
I could not but be sensible of this.
For O! your face has such peculiar charms,
That who can hold from flying to your arms?
95 But what I ne'er can have without offence,
May some blessed maid possess with innocence.
Pleasure may tempt, but virtue more should move,
O learn of me to want the thing you love.
What you desire is sought by all mankind;
100 As you have eyes, so others are not blind;
Like you they see, like you my charms adore,
They wish not less, but you dare venture more.
O! had you then upon our coasts been brought,
My virgin love when thousand rivals sought,
105 You had I seen, you should have had my voice,
Nor could my husband justly blame my choice.
For both our hopes, alas, you come too late!
Another now is master of my fate.

80. D.'s addition; he omits Ovid's ll. 81–2.
83. *I did not mind alone*] i.e. I was not the only one who noticed.
84. *sate*] sat.
87. 'Oft have I read' (Sherburne).   *within . . . grove*] for Ovid's 'on the
round table' (*Works*).
92. *sensible*] aware.
98. *want*] ambiguous: (i) go without (ii) wish for.

More to my wish I could have lived with you,
110 And yet my present lot can undergo.
Cease to solicit a weak woman's will,
And urge not her you love to so much ill;
But let me live contented as I may,
And make not my unspotted fame your prey.
115 Some right you claim, since naked to your eyes
Three goddesses disputed beauty's prize;
One offered valour, t' other crowns, but she
Obtained her cause who smiling promised me.
But first I am not of belief so light
120 To think such nymphs would show you such a sight.
Yet granting this, the other part is feigned:
A bribe so mean your sentence had not gained.
With partial eyes I should myself regard
To think that Venus made me her reward:
125 I humbly am content with human praise;
A goddess's applause would envy raise.
But be it as you say, for 'tis confessed
The men who flatter highest please us best.
That I suspect it ought not to displease,
130 For miracles are not believed with ease.
One joy I have, that I had Venus' voice,
A greater yet, that you confirmed her choice,
That proffered laurels, promised sovereignty,
Juno and Pallas you contemned for me.
135 Am I your empire, then, and your renown?
What heart of rock but must by this be won?
And yet bear witness, O you powers above,
How rude I am in all the arts of love!
My hand is yet untaught to write to men;
140 This is th' essay of my unpractised pen:
Happy those nymphs whom use has perfect made;
I think all crime, and tremble at a shade.
Even while I write, my fearful conscious eyes

121. 'the latter part is fain'd' (Saltonstall; *Works*).
122. sentence] verdict.
134. contemned] despised.
136. After this line D. omits Ovid's ll. 137–40.
138. rude] naïve, untaught.
143. conscious] sharing in the secret, guilty.

Look often back, misdoubting a surprise.
145 For now the rumour spreads among the crowd,
     At court in whispers, but in town aloud:
     Dissemble you, whate'er you hear 'em say; ⎫
     To leave off loving were your better way, ⎬
     Yet if you will dissemble it, you may.   ⎭
150 Love secretly: the absence of my lord
     More freedom gives, but does not all afford.
     Long is his journey, long will be his stay,
     Called by affairs of consequence away.
     To go or not when unresolved he stood,
155 I bid him make what swift return he could;
     Then kissing me, he said, 'I recommend
     All to thy care, but most my Trojan friend'.
     I smiled at what he innocently said,
     And only answered, 'You shall be obeyed'.
160 Propitious winds have borne him far from hence,
     But let not this secure your confidence.
     Absent he is, yet absent he commands;
     You know the proverb, princes have long hands.
     My fame's my burden, for the more I'm praised
165 A juster ground of jealousy is raised.
     Were I less fair, I might have been more blessed:
     Great beauty through great danger is possessed.
     To leave me here his venture was not hard,
     Because he thought my virtue was my guard.
170 He feared my face, but trusted to my life,
     The beauty doubted, but believed the wife.
     You bid me use th' occasion while I can,
     Put in our hands by the good easy man:
     I would, and yet I doubt, 'twixt love and fear;
175 One draws me from you, and one brings me near.
     Our flames are mutual; and my husband's gone:
     The nights are long; I fear to lie alone.
     One house contains us, and weak walls divide,
     And you're too pressing to be long denied.
180 Let me not live, but everything conspires
     To join our loves, and yet my fear retires.

168. *venture*] something which is ventured or put at risk (*OED* 4b).
177. D. alters Ovid: contrast 'you without a wife doe lye alone' (Saltonstall).
181. *retires*] dissuades, restrains (*OED* 9b).

You court with words, when you should force
    employ,
A rape is requisite to shamefaced joy.
Indulgent to the wrongs which we receive,
185 Our sex can suffer what we dare not give.
What have I said! for both of us 'twere best
Our kindling fires if each of us suppressed.
The faith of strangers is too prone to change,
And like themselves their wandering passions range.
190 Hypsipyle and the fond Minoan maid
Were both by trusting of their guests betrayed.
How can I doubt that other men deceive,
When you yourself did fair Oenone leave?
But lest I should upbraid your treachery,
195 You make a merit of that crime to me.
Yet grant you were to faithful love inclined,
Your weary Trojans wait but for a wind.
Should you prevail, while I assign the night
Your sails are hoisted, and you take your flight:
200 Some bawling mariner our love destroys,
And breaks asunder our unfinished joys.
But I with you may leave the Spartan port
To view the Trojan wealth and Priam's court:
Shown while I see, I shall expose my fame,
205 And fill a foreign country with my shame.
In Asia what reception shall I find,
And what dishonour leave in Greece behind?
What will your brothers, Priam, Hecuba,
And what will all your modest matrons say?
210 Ev'n you, when on this action you reflect,
My future conduct justly may suspect,
And whate'er stranger lands upon your coast
Conclude me, by your own example, lost.
I from your rage a strumpet's name shall hear,
215 While you forget what part in it you bear;
You my crime's author will my crime upbraid:
Deep under ground, O let me first be laid!
You boast the pomp and plenty of your land,

190. Hypsipyle was abandoned by Jason, and Ariadne by Theseus.
200. D.'s addition.

And promise all shall be at my command;
220   Your Trojan wealth, believe me, I despise;
My own poor native land has dearer ties. ·
Should I be injured on your Phrygian shore,
What help of kindred could I there implore?
Medea was by Jason's flattery won:
225   I may like her believe and be undone.
Plain honest hearts, like mine, suspect no cheat,
And love contributes to its own deceit.
The ships about whose sides loud tempests roar,
With gentle winds were wafted from the shore.
230   Your teeming mother dreamed a flaming brand
Sprung from her womb consumed the Trojan land;
To second this, old prophecies conspire
That Ilium shall be burnt with Grecian fire.
Both give me fear, nor is it much allayed
235   That Venus is obliged our loves to aid:
For they who lost their cause revenge will take,
And for one friend two enemies you make.
Nor can I doubt but should I follow you
The sword would soon our fatal crime pursue:
240   A wrong so great my husband's rage would rouse,
And my relations would his cause espouse.
You boast your strength and courage, but alas!
Your words receive small credit from your face.
Let heroes in the dusty field delight,
245   Those limbs were fashioned for another fight:
Bid Hector sally from the walls of Troy,
A sweeter quarrel should your arms employ.
Yet fears like these should not my mind perplex,
Were I as wise as many of my sex.
250   But time and you may bolder thoughts inspire,
And I perhaps may yield to your desire.
You last demand a private conference;

---

219. After this line D. omits Ovid's ll. 223–4.
225. After this line D. omits Ovid's ll. 231–2.
230. teeming] Hecuba was the mother of nineteen sons.
232. conspire] agree (*OED* 4).
239. After this line D. omits Ovid's ll. 246–8.
252. 'private conference' (Sherburne; *Works*).

These are your words, but I can guess your sense.
Your unripe hopes their harvest must attend:
255 Be ruled by me, and time may be your friend.
This is enough to let you understand,
For now my pen has tired my tender hand:
My woman knows the secret of my heart,
And may hereafter better news impart.

58 Dido to Aeneas

For headnote see 'Preface to *Ovid's Epistles*'.

Dido to Aeneas

The Argument

Aeneas, the son of Venus and Anchises, having at the destruction of Troy saved his gods, his father, and son Ascanius from the fire, put to sea with twenty sail of ships, and having been long tossed with tempests, was at last cast upon the shore of Libya, where Queen Dido, flying from the cruelty of Pygmalion her brother, who had killed her husband Sychaeus, had lately built Carthage. She entertained Aeneas and his fleet with great civility, fell passionately in love with him, and in the end denied him not the last favours. But Mercury admonishing Aeneas to go in search of Italy (a kingdom promised to him by the gods), he readily prepared to obey him. Dido soon perceived it, and having in vain tried all other means to engage him to stay, at last in despair writes to him as follows.

> So, on Mæander's banks, when death is nigh,
> The mournful swan sings her own elegy:
> Not that I hope (for O, that hope were vain!)
> By words your lost affection to regain;
> 5   But having lost whate'er was worth my care,
> Why should I fear to lose a dying prayer?
> 'Tis then resolved poor Dido must be left
> Of life, of honour, and of love bereft!
> While you, with loosened sails and vows, prepare
> 10   To seek a land that flies the searcher's care.
> Nor can my rising towers your flight restrain,
> Nor my new empire, offered you in vain.
> Built walls you shun, unbuilt you seek; that land
> Is yet to conquer, but you this command.
> 15   Suppose you landed where your wish designed,
> Think what reception foreigners would find.

¶**58**. *1. Mæander*] a winding river in Phrygia.

What people is so void of common sense
To vote succession from a native prince?
Yet there new sceptres and new loves you seek,
20 New vows to plight, and plighted vows to break.
When will your towers the height of Carthage know?
Or when your eyes discern such crowds below?
If such a town and subjects you could see,
Still would you want a wife who loved like me.
25 For, O, I burn, like fires with incense bright;
Not holy tapers flame with purer light.
Aeneas is my thoughts' perpetual theme,
Their daily longing, and their nightly dream.
Yet he ungrateful and obdurate still:
30 Fool that I am to place my heart so ill!
Myself I cannot to myself restore;
Still I complain, and still I love him more.
Have pity, Cupid, on my bleeding heart,
And pierce thy brother's with an equal dart.
35 I rave: nor canst thou Venus' offspring be—
Love's mother could not bear a son like thee.
From hardened oak, or from a rock's cold womb,
At least thou art from some fierce tigress come,
Or on rough seas, from their foundation torn,
40 Got by the winds, and in a tempest born;
Like that which now thy trembling sailors fear,
Like that whose rage should still detain thee here.
Behold how high the foamy billows ride!
The winds and waves are on the juster side.
45 To winter weather and a stormy sea
I'll owe what rather I would owe to thee.
Death thou deserv'st from heaven's avenging laws,
But I'm unwilling to become the cause.
To shun my love, if thou wilt seek thy fate
50 'Tis a dear purchase, and a costly hate.
Stay but a little, till the tempest cease,
And the loud winds are lulled into a peace.

17–18. D.'s addition, alluding to the Exclusion Crisis (see *AA* headnote).
24. *want*] lack.
29. *obdurate*] stressed on the second syllable.
34. After this line D. omits Ovid's ll. 33–4.
46. 'Though for thy stay I had rather owe to thee' (Saltonstall).

May all thy rage, like theirs, unconstant prove!
And so it will, if there be power in love.
55 Know'st thou not yet what dangers ships sustain:
So often wrecked, how dar'st thou tempt the main?
Which, were it smooth, were every wave asleep,
Ten thousand forms of death are in the deep.
In that abyss the gods their vengeance store
60 For broken vows of those who falsely swore.
There wingèd storms on sea-born Venus wait
To vindicate the justice of her state.
Thus I to thee the means of safety show,
And, lost myself, would still preserve my foe.
65 False as thou art, I not thy death design:
O rather live to be the cause of mine!
Should some avenging storm thy vessel tear
(But heaven forbid my words should omen bear),
Then in thy face thy perjured vows would fly,
70 And my wronged ghost be present to thy eye:
With threatening looks think thou behold'st me stare,
Gasping my mouth, and clotted all my hair.
Then should forked lightning and red thunder fall,
What couldst thou say, but 'I deserved 'em all'?
75 Lest this should happen, make not haste away:
To shun the danger will be worth thy stay.
Have pity on thy son, if not on me;
My death alone is guilt enough for thee:
What has his youth, what have thy gods deserved,
80 To sink in seas, who were from fires preserved?
But neither gods nor parent didst thou bear
(Smooth stories all, to please a woman's ear):
False was the tale of thy romantic life;
Nor yet am I thy first deluded wife.
85 Left to pursuing foes Creüsa stayed,
By thee, base man, forsaken and betrayed.
This, when thou told'st me, struck my tender heart,
That such requital followed such desert.
Nor doubt I but the gods for crimes like these

79–80. 'What hath *Ascanius*, or thy gods deserv'd? / Shal waves devoure
them, late from flames preserv'd?' (Sherburne; Saltonstall has similar phrasing; *Works*).
83. *romantic*] like a romance, heroic.

90 Seven winters kept thee wandering on the seas.
Thy starved companions, cast ashore, I fed,
Thyself admitted to my crown and bed.
To harbour strangers, succour the distressed,
Was kind enough; but O too kind the rest!
95 Cursed be the cave which first my ruin brought,
Where from the storm we common shelter sought!
A dreadful howling echoed round the place,
The mountain nymphs, thought I, my nuptials grace.
I thought so then, but now too late I know
100 The furies yelled my funerals from below.
O chastity and violated fame,
Exact your dues to my dead husband's name!
By death redeem my reputation lost,
And to his arms restore my guilty ghost.
105 Close by my palace, in a gloomy grove,
Is raised a chapel to my murdered love:
There, wreathed with boughs and wool his statue
    stands,
The pious monument of artful hands.
Last night methought he called me from the dome,
110 And thrice with hollow voice cried, 'Dido, come'.
She comes: thy wife thy lawful summons hears,
But comes more slowly, clogged with conscious fears.
Forgive the wrong I offered to thy bed:
Strong were his charms who my weak faith misled.
115 His goddess mother, and his agèd sire
Borne on his back, did to my fall conspire.
O such he was, and is, that were he true
Without a blush I might his love pursue.
But cruel stars my birthday did attend,
120 And as my fortune opened it must end.
My plighted lord was at the altar slain,
Whose wealth was made my bloody brother's gain:

92. and bed] D.'s addition.
94. kind] the second occurrence invokes the sense 'sexually compliant'.
103–4, 108. D.'s additions.
108. artful] artistic.
109. dome] chapel.
110. thrice] Ovid has quater ('four times').
112. conscious] guilty.

Friendless, and followed by the murderer's hate,
To foreign countries I removed my fate,
125 And here, a suppliant, from the natives' hands
I bought the ground on which my city stands,
With all the coast that stretches to the sea—
Ev'n to the friendly port that sheltered thee;
Then raised these walls which mount into the air,
130 At once my neighbours' wonder and their fear.
For now they arm, and round me leagues are made
My scarce-established empire to invade.
To man my new-built walls I must prepare,
An helpless woman and unskilled in war.
135 Yet thousand rivals to my love pretend,
And for my person would my crown defend;
Whose jarring votes in one complaint agree
That each unjustly is disdained for thee.
To proud Hiarbas give me up a prey
140 (For that must follow if thou goest away);
Or to my husband's murderer leave my life,
That to the husband he may add the wife.
Go then, since no complaints can move thy mind:
Go perjured man, but leave thy gods behind.
145 Touch not those gods by whom thou art forsworn,
Who will in impious hands no more be borne.
Thy sacrilegious worship they disdain,
And rather would the Grecian fires sustain.
Perhaps my greatest shame is still to come,
150 And part of thee lies hid within my womb:
The babe unborn must perish by thy hate,
And perish guiltless in his mother's fate.
Some god, thou sayest, thy voyage does command:
Would the same god had barred thee from my land.
155 The same, I doubt not, thy departure steers
Who kept thee out at sea so many years,
Where thy long labours were a price so great
As thou to purchase Troy wouldst not repeat.
But Tiber now thou seek'st, to be at best
160 When there arrived, a poor precarious guest.

137. votes] aspirations, desires (OED 3).
139. Hiarbas] a local ruler wishing to marry Dido.

Yet it deludes thy search: perhaps it will
To thy old age lie undiscovered still.
A ready crown and wealth in dower I bring,
And without conquering here thou art a king:
165   Here thou to Carthage may'st transfer thy Troy,
Here young Ascanius may his arms employ,
And while we live secure in soft repose
Bring many laurels home from conquered foes.
By Cupid's arrows, I adjure thee, stay;
170   By all the gods, companions of thy way:
So may thy Trojans, who are yet alive
Live still, and with no future fortune strive;
So may thy youthful son old age attain,
And thy dead father's bones in peace remain,
175   As thou hast pity on unhappy me,
Who know no crime but too much love of thee.
I am not born from fierce Achilles' line,
Nor did my parents against Troy combine.
To be thy wife if I unworthy prove,
180   By some inferior name admit my love:
To be secured of still possessing thee,
What would I do, and what would I not be!
Our Libyan coasts their certain seasons know,
When free from tempests passengers may go:
185   But now with northern blasts the billows roar,
And drive the floating sea-weed to the shore.
Leave to my care the time to sail away;
When safe, I will not suffer thee to stay.
Thy weary men would be with ease content;
190   Their sails are tattered, and their masts are spent.
If by no merit I thy mind can move,
What thou deniest my merit give my love.
Stay, till I learn my loss to undergo,
And give me time to struggle with my woe.
195   If not, know this: I will not suffer long;
My life's too loathsome, and my love too strong.
Death holds my pen, and dictates what I say,
While 'cross my lap thy Trojan sword I lay:
My tears flow down, the sharp edge cuts their flood,

161. *deludes*] eludes (OED 4).
196–7. D.'s addition.

200   And drinks my sorrows that must drink my blood.
      How well thy gift does with my fate agree!
      My funeral pomp is cheaply made by thee.
      To no new wounds my bosom I display:
      The sword but enters where love made the way.
205   But thou, dear sister, and yet dearer friend,
      Shalt my cold ashes to their urn attend.
      'Sychaeus' wife' let not the marble boast,
      I lost that title when my fame I lost.
      This short inscription only let it bear:
210   'Unhappy Dido lies in quiet here.
      The cause of death, and sword by which she died,
      Aeneas gave: the rest her arm supplied.'

201. 'How well thy gifts doe with my fate agree!' (Sherburne; *Works*).
210. D.'s addition.

59 Prologue at Oxford, 1680
('Thespis, the first professor . . .')

Date and publication. Spoken in July 1680 (not 1679, as in *Works*) at the visit of the King's Company to the annual Act in Oxford. The year is given in the title in *MP*, and confirmed by the reference in l. 18. The play was Settle's *The Female Prelate*, which had been given its London première on 31 May 1680. The Prologue was printed in *MP* (1684; reprinted 1692); a variant version of it had previously been printed in the second edition of Lee's *Sophonisba: or, Hannibal's Overthrow, A Tragedy*, published by Bentley and Magnes in 1681 (*TC* May), reprinted 1685, 1691, 1693, 1697. It had not appeared in the first edition, 1676. The origin of the *1681* version is unknown, but two possibilities are: (i) The Prologue which was originally written for *The Female Prelate* at Oxford in July 1680 could have been adapted for a performance of *Sophonisba* at Oxford in March 1681 during the exceptional visit of the King's Company there for the Oxford Parliament. *Tamerlane* and *The Plain Dealer* are known to have been staged then, but we do not know how many plays were normally performed during such visits; in 1674 the players offered 'several tragedies and comedies' (Sybil Rosenfeld, *RES* xix (1943) 368). (ii) *Sophonisba* could have been produced at Oxford in July 1680 along with *The Female Prelate*, the same prologue serving (with adaptations) for both plays. Winn 595 suggests that Settle's crude play displeased the Oxford audience, and that when the actors decided to perform Lee's play instead, D. wrote a prologue which referred to the failure of *The Female Prelate*. But since the *MP* text is clearly spoken by one of Settle's cardinals (see l. 22), the Prologue was evidently written originally for Settle's play, then adapted (not necessarily by D.) for Lee's. The second hypothesis also fails to explain the removal of the topical references in ll. 17–18. Whatever the date of the adapted prologue, it appears that *MP* preserves the text as originally spoken for Settle's play in 1680; the version in *1681* removes the topical reference to the Oxford bells (ll. 17–18), along with the self-reference in ll. 21–4 by an actor in Settle's play, and adds further lines possibly alluding to a hostile reception given to that play (see l. 30*n*). The present edition therefore follows *MP*, giving the variant readings from *1681* in the notes.

The Prologue at Oxford, 1680

Thespis, the first professor of our art,
At country wakes sung ballads from a cart.
To prove this true, if Latin be no trespass,
Dicitur et plaustris vexisse poemata Thespis.
5   But Aeschylus, says Horace in some page,
Was the first mountebank that trod the stage;
Yet Athens never knew your learnèd sport
Of tossing poets in a tennis court;
But 'tis the talent of our English nation,
10 Still to be plotting some new reformation;
And few years hence, if anarchy goes on,
Jack Presbyter shall here erect his throne,
Knock out a tub with preaching once a day,
And every prayer be longer than a play.
15 Then all you heathen wits shall go to pot
For disbelieving of a popish plot;
Your poets shall be used like infidels,

¶**59**. *Title. Prologue to the University of Oxford 1681* (no date given).
1–4. Ignòtum tragicae genus invenisse Camenae / dicitur et plaustris vexisse poemata
Thespis ('Thespis is said to have discovered the tragic muse, a type unknown
before, and to have carried his pieces in wagons': Horace, *Ars Poetica* ll. 275–
6).
2. from] in *1681*.
5–6. Post hunc personae pallaeque repertor honestae / Aeschylus et modicis instravit
pulpita tignis ('After him Aeschylus, inventor of the mask and comely robe,
laid a stage of small planks': *Ars Poetica* ll. 278–9).
6. that] e're *1681*.
8. In 1680 the company performed in Robert Wood's tennis court (*Life and*
Times of Anthony Wood, 5 vols (1891–1900) ii 490). Previously they had used
Thomas Burnham's New Tennis Court (Sybil Rosenfeld, *RES* xix (1943)
368).
11. few] some *1681.   goes*] go *1681.*
12. Jack Presbyter] A generic name for a nonconformist; on 5 November 1681
Jack Presbyter was burnt in effigy by Westminster schoolboys instead of the
Pope (Wood ii 558).   *shall*] will *1681.*
13. Nonconformists were debarred from preaching from church pulpits.
16. Belief in the Popish Plot, at its height in the winter of 1678–9, was now
waning.
17–18. omitted in 1681.

And worst the author of the *Oxford Bells*:
Nor should we scape the sentence, to depart
20   Ev'n in our first original, a cart.
No zealous brother there would want a stone
To maul us cardinals, and pelt Pope Joan.
Religion, learning, wit would be suppressed,
Rags of the Whore, and trappings of the Beast.
25   Scot, Suarez, Tom of Aquin must go down
As chief supporters of the triple crown;
And Aristotle's for destruction ripe:

18. Oxford Bells] On 8 April 1680 Great Tom, the bell of Christ Church, was recast after three unsuccessful attempts; the bells of Merton were also recast in 1680 (Wood ii 484, 508). The poem 'Oh the Merry *Christ-Church* Bells' occurs in *Wit and Drollery* (1682) 301–2, followed by a parody. Though the words were anonymous, the music was by Henry Aldrich (1648–1710), subsequently Dean of Christ Church (W. G. Hiscock, *Henry Aldrich of Christ Church* (1960)). Latin verses on the recasting of Great Tom, attributed to 'Mr Sparks', are found in BodL MS Add B 106.

19–20. Carts were used to transport criminals to prison or execution.

19. scape] want *1681*.

21–4. omitted in 1681.

22. Pope Joan] The legendary ninth- or tenth-century female Pope, who featured in Settle's play *The Female Prelate*. A staple of anti-Catholic propaganda, the story had recently been retold in *A Present for a Papist: or the Life and Death of Pope Joan* (1675).

24. The Whore of Babylon and the Beast of the Apocalypse (both from Revelation xvii) were epithets applied to the papacy in Protestant propaganda.

25. Occam, Dun, Scotus must, though learn'd, go down *1681*. William of Occam (*c*. 1285–1347) and Johannes Duns Scotus (*c*. 1265–1308), scholastic theologians who taught at Oxford; Francisco de Suarez (1548–1617), the Spanish Jesuit whose works included the *Defensio Fidei* (1613) against the Church of England; the philosopher Thomas Aquinas (*c*. 1225–74). All these Catholic theologians featured in the seventeenth-century Oxford and Cambridge curriculum (W. T. Costello, *The Scholastic Curriculum at Early Seventeenth-Century Cambridge* (1958)).

26. triple crown] the papal tiara.

27. Aristotle's] Aristotle *1681*.

Some say he called the soul an organ-pipe,
Which by some little help of derivation
30   Shall then be proved a pipe of inspiration.

28–30. Since some Puritans opposed organs (and all prized divine inspiration) they might interpret Aristotle's remark as envisaging the soul as the instrument through which God inspires man.   *organ-pipe*] Perhaps referring to *On the Soul* ii 8, where Aristotle says that the voice is the sound produced by a creature which possesses a soul. Charles Blount says that the ancients thought of the Spirit of the World as being like wind in organ pipes (*Anima Mundi* [1679] 25).

30. then be proved] thence be call'd *1681*. After l. 30 *1681* adds: 'Your wiser Judgments farther penetrate, / Who late found out one Tare amongst the Wheat. / This is our comfort, none e're cry'd us down, / But who dislik'd both *Bishop* and a *Crown*.' Winn suggests that this may refer to an unfavourable reception given to *The Female Prelate*.

60 Prologue and Songs from *The Spanish Friar*

Date and publication. The play was first performed *c.* 1 November 1680 by the Duke's Company at Dorset Garden (*LS* 292). *The Spanish Fryar or, The Double Discovery* was published by Tonson in 1681 (advertised in *The Protestant Mercury* 9–12 March 1681; *TC* June); reprinted 1686 (omitting some politically sensitive lines), 1690 (restoring the omissions and adding further lines) and 1695. The play was dedicated to John, Lord Haughton, and had an Epilogue 'By a Friend of the Author's' (Robert Wolseley, according to Macdonald 123). One copy of *1695* apparently has a MS note attributing the last couplet of the Epilogue to D. himself (Macdonald). The Epilogue (except for ll. 1–4) appeared in *POAS* (1704) as 'Satyr upon Romish Confessors. By Mr. Dryden'. Song II was printed in *Wit and Drollery* (1682), *Female Poems on Several Occasions. Written by Ephelia*, second edition (1682) and *The Compleat Courtier* (1683). A setting by Captain Pack is found in BL MS Add 19759. For an expanded version see *The Roxburghe Ballads* edited by J. W. Ebsworth (1889) vi 21–2. An altered version ('Farewell thou false Philander') was printed as a single sheet (BL G. 307 (186)). Purcell composed a song to words by Godfrey Finger for a revival in 1695 (Price, *Henry Purcell* 86–9).

Prologue

    Now luck for us, and a kind hearty pit;
    For he who pleases never fails of wit.
    Honour is yours——
    And you, like kings at city treats, bestow it;
5   The writer kneels, and is bid rise a poet:
    But you are fickle sovereigns, to our sorrow,
    You dub today, and hang a man tomorrow;
    You cry the same sense up, and down again,
    Just like brass money once a year in Spain;
10 Take you i' th' mood, whate'er base metal come,

¶**60**. *Prologue.*
9. Throughout the seventeenth century the Spanish copper vellon fluctuated markedly in value, and was frequently 'cried up' and 'cried down'; on 10 February 1680, after a year of rapid inflation, the tariff of the vellon was halved in a deflationary move which stabilized its value for a few years (E. J. Hamilton, *War and Prices in Spain 1651–1800* (1947) 9–35).

You coin as fast as groats at Bromingam:
Though 'tis no more like sense in ancient plays
Than Rome's religion like St Peter's days.
In short, so swift your judgements turn and wind,
15   You cast our fleetest wits a mile behind.
'Twere well your judgements but in plays did range,
But ev'n your follies and debauches change
With such a whirl, the poets of your age
Are tired, and cannot score 'em on the stage,
20   Unless each vice in shorthand they indite,
Ev'n as notched prentices whole sermons write.
The heavy Hollanders no vices know
But what they used a hundred years ago;
Like honest plants, where they were stuck, they grow:
25   They cheat, but still from cheating sires they come;
They drink, but they were christened first in Mum.
Their patrimonial sloth the Spaniards keep,
And Philip first taught Philip how to sleep.
The French and we still change, but here's the curse,
30   They change for better, and we change for worse;
They take up our old trade of conquering,
And we are taking theirs, to dance and sing;

11. Tories 'styled the adversary *Birmingham* Protestants, alluding to false Groats counterfeited at that Place' (Roger North, *Examen* (1740) 321; Kinsley).

12–13. omitted in *1686.*

21. Cp. Mrs Marwood in Congreve's *The Way of the World* (1700): 'What, and have your Name prostituted in a publicke Court; . . . And then to have my young Revellers of the *Temple* take Notes, like Prentices at a *Conventicle*' (Act V; Kinsley). The London apprentices were traditionally keen Protestants.   *notched*] with unevenly or closely cropped hair.

22–6. For other attacks on the Dutch cp. 'Prologue and Epilogue to *Amboyna*'.

26. Mum] a kind of beer originally brewed in Brunswick.

27. Rochester refers ironically to 'Spaniards' dispatch' in 'Upon Nothing' l. 48.

31. The war which followed France's invasion of Holland in 1672 was concluded by the Peace of Nymegen (1678), under which France received Franche Comté but little else. But in 1680 Louis XIV used the Treaty as a pretext for further annexations.

Our fathers did for change to France repair,
And they for change will try our English air.
35 As children, when they throw one toy away,
Straight a more foolish gewgaw comes in play:
So we, grown penitent on serious thinking,
Leave whoring, and devoutly fall to drinking.
Scouring the watch grows out-of-fashion wit
40 Now we set up for tilting in the pit,
Where 'tis agreed by bullies, chicken-hearted,
To fright the ladies first, and then be parted.
A fair attempt has twice or thrice been made
To hire night-murth'rers, and make death a trade.
45 When murther's out, what vice can we advance?

33. Cp. Oldham: 'In vain for health to forein Countries we repair, / And change our *English* for *Mompellier* Air' ('Paraphrase upon Horace. Book II. Ode XIV' (1681; *Poems* 121, 423)).

36. gewgaw] trifle, plaything.

39. Scouring] To 'scour' was to roam around drunkenly at night, breaking windows and attacking the watch; cp. Oldham: 'you meet / Some of the drunken Scowrers of the Street, / Flush'd with success of warlike Deeds perform'd, / Of Constables subdu'd, and Brothels storm'd:' ('A Satyr, in Imitation of the Third of Juvenal' (1683) ll. 405–8); and D.'s 'Prologue to *The Wild Gallant* revived' ll. 10–12*n*.

40. Quarrels in the pit had become notorious, such as the one between Churchill and Otway in June 1679 (Montague Summers, *The Restoration Theatre* (1934) 77–81; Aphra Behn, 'Prologue to *The Young King*' (1679), Danchin no. 274). More recently, in February 1680 'happened a great dispute in the Duke's Play-house, some Gentlemen in their Cupps entring into the Pitt, flinging Links at the Actors, and using several reproachfull speeches against the Dutchess of P[ortsmouth] and other persons of Honour' (*Mercurius Anglicus* 4–7 February). On 26 February 'Mrs Ellen Gwyn being at the dukes playhouse, was affronted by a person who came into the pitt and called her whore; whom Mr Herbert, the earl of Pembrokes brother, vindicating, there were many swords drawn, and a great hubbub in the house' (Luttrell i 34–5) (*LS* 284–5). D.'s lines are echoed by Nahum Tate in 'The Battle of the B[aw]d's in the Theatre Royal. December the 3d 1680': 'Give ore ye Tilters of the Pit, give ore, / Frighten the Boxes and your selves no more; / Two Amazons of Scandalous renown, / Have with dire Combat made this Field their own' (*Poems Written on Several Occasions* (1684) 153). The problem continued: see D.'s 'Epilogue Spoken to the King and Queen' ll. 29–34*n*.

41. bullies] blustering gallants.

44. Recalling the attack on D. in Rose Alley on 18 December 1679.

Unless the new-found pois'ning trick of France:
And when their art of ratsbane we have got,
By way of thanks, we'll send 'em o'er our plot.

Songs

I

A procession of priests and choristers in white, with tapers, followed by the Queen and ladies, goes over the stage, the choristers singing.

Look down, ye blessed above, look down,
   Behold our weeping matrons' tears,
   Behold our tender virgins' fears,
And with success our armies crown.

5 Look down, ye blessed above, look down:
   O! save us, save us, and our state restore;
   For pity, pity, pity we implore;
For pity, pity, pity we implore.

II

A Song

I

Farewell ungrateful traitor,
   Farewell my perjured swain;
Let never injured creature
   Believe a man again;
5 The pleasure of possessing
Surpasses all expressing,

---

46. The Marquise de Brinvilliers had been found guilty of poisoning four of her family in 1676, and Catherine Deshayes had been executed in February 1680 (Kinsley). See *A Narrative of the Process against Madam Brinvilliers* (1676). Cp. Oldham: 'And we shall have their Pois'ning too e're long' ('A Satyr, in Imitation of the Third of Juvenal' l. 93).

Song I. From Act I.
Song II. From Act V. Sung to the Queen as 'the Song which poor *Olympia* made / When false *Bireno* left her' (see Ariosto, *Orlando Furioso* X).

But 'tis too short a blessing,
And love too long a pain.

2

'Tis easy to deceive us
10   In pity of your pain,
But when we love you leave us
To rail at you in vain.
Before we have descried it
There is no bliss beside it,
15   But she that once has tried it
Will never love again.

3

The passion you pretended
Was only to obtain,
But when the charm is ended
20   The charmer you disdain.
Your love by ours we measure
Till we have lost our treasure,
But dying is a pleasure
When living is a pain.

10. your] *1686, 1690, 1695*; our *1681.*

61 Epitaph on Sir Palmes Fairborne

Date and publication. The inscription on the monument in Westminster Abbey probably dates from late 1680. An incomplete text of the epitaph (omitting ll. 23–4) was printed in *Poetical Recreations . . . Part II* (1688), and the full text in *EP*. It is silently omitted from *Works*, but the attribution to D. in *EP* seems unimpeachable. The present text is taken from the monument, but with two emendations from *EP*.

Context. Sir Palmes Fairborne (1644–80) was the governor of Tangier. On 24 October 1680 he rode outside the town to observe the besieging Moorish army; 'as he was riding without the Walls with a Party of Horse to observe what the Moors were doing, was shot by one of them, and being mortally wounded, fell from his Horse' (*London Gazette* mdlxvii 22–5 November 1680). He died on 27 October after witnessing the defeat of the Moors (*DNB*).

Sacred to the Immortal Memory of Sir Palmes Fairborne, K^t, Governor of Tangier

In execution of which command he was mortally wounded by a shot from the Moors then besieging the town, in the 46 year of his age, Octob. 24th 1680

> Ye sacred relics which your marble keep,
> Here undisturbed by wars in quiet sleep;
> Discharge the trust which when it was below ⎫
> Fairborne's undaunted soul did undergo,   ⎬
> 5 And be the town's palladium from the foe. ⎭

¶**61**. *Title. 46*] a slip for 36.

2. Echoes Cowley: 'And undisturb'd by *Moons* in silence sleep' (*Davideis* i; *Poems* 244).

4. *undaunted*] *monument before correction*, EP; disdaunted *monument after correction*; 'disdaunted' is not in the *OED*, and may be an erroneous alteration on the monument, perhaps influenced by the 'dis' in *undisturbed* and *discharge*.

5. *palladium*] the image of Pallas Athene kept at Troy, regarded as the city's security against destruction.

Alive and dead these walls he will defend,
Great actions great examples must attend.
The Candian siege his early valour knew,
Where Turkish blood did his young hands imbrue.
10 From thence returning with deserved applause, ⎱
Against the Moors his well-fleshed sword he draws: ⎰
The same the courage, and the same the cause.
His youth and age, his life and death combine, ⎱
As in some great and regular design, ⎰
15 All of a piece throughout, and all divine.
Still nearer heaven his virtues shone more bright, ⎱
Like rising flames expanding in their height, ⎰
The martyr's glory crowned the soldier's fight.
More bravely British general never fell,
20 Nor general's death was e'er revenged so well,
Which his pleased eyes beheld before their close,
Followed by thousand victims of his foes.
To his lamented loss for times to come,
His pious widow consecrates this tomb.

---

8. Candian siege] As a young man Fairborne had taken part in the defence of
Candia (Crete) against the Turks.
15. All of a piece throughout] D. repeats this phrase in 'The Secular Masque'
l. 92.
16. virtues] *EP*; Vertue *monument* (the plural seems required by *flames* in l. 17).
23. times] *monument*; time *EP*. For the plural cp. Shakespeare, *Sonnet* lx: 'And
yet to times in hope my verse shall stand' (l. 13).

62 Epilogue to *Tamerlane the Great*

Date and publication. The play was staged *c.* February 1681. In March 1681 it was performed at Oxford (see 'Epilogue Spoken to the King') and a prior production at Drury Lane seems likely. Charles Saunders's *Tamerlane the Great. A Tragedy* was published by Bentley and Magnes in 1681 (*TC* May). It has a prefatory poem by J. Bankes and D.'s Epilogue.

Context. Charles Saunders, like D., went up to Trinity College, Cambridge, from Westminster School (elected 1680, aged 17); he did not graduate. In his Preface he says that the play 'receiv'd some Rules for Correction from Mr. *Dryden* himself, who also was pleas'd to Grace it with an Epilogue, to which it ows no small part of its success' (sig. a^r).

Epilogue

Ladies, the beardless author of this day
Commends to you the fortune of his play.
A woman wit has often graced the stage,
But he's the first boy-poet of our age.
5 Early as is the year his fancies blow,
Like young Narcissus peeping through the snow;
Thus Cowley blossomed soon, yet flourished long;
This is as forward, and may prove as strong.
Youth with the fair should always favour find,
10 Or we are damned dissemblers of our kind.
What's all this love they put into our parts?
'Tis but the pit-a-pat of two young hearts.
Should hag and grey-beard make such tender moan, ⎫
Faith, you'd e'en trust 'em to themselves alone, ⎬
15 And cry, 'Let's go, here's nothing to be done.' ⎭

¶**62**. *3. A woman wit*] Aphra Behn, thirteen of whose plays had now been performed.
5. blow] flower.
7. Abraham Cowley published his *Poetical Blossoms* in 1633 at the age of 15. Sprat in his life of Cowley says: 'with . . . extraordinary hopes he was remov'd to *Trinity* Colledge in *Cambridge*, where by the progress and continuance of his Wit, it appear'd that . . . it was both early-ripe and lasting' (Cowley, *Works* (1668) sig. A2^r); Bankes in his prefatory poem also compares Saunders with Cowley (sig. a2^r).
10. we] Evidently the Epilogue was spoken by a woman.

Since love's our business, as 'tis your delight,
The young, who best can practise, best can write.
What though he be not come to his full power,
He's mending and improving every hour.
20   You sly she-jockeys of the box and pit
Are pleased to find a hot unbroken wit;
By management he may in time be made,
But there's no hopes of an old battered jade;
Faint and unnerved he runs into a sweat,
25   And always fails you at the second heat.

20–5. This image plays on 'ride' meaning 'copulate' (*OED* 3).
24. unnerved] made weak (*OED* 1); also playing on 'nerve' meaning 'penis'
(*OED* 1b) from the Latin *nervus*.

63 Epilogue Spoken to the King

Date and publication. Spoken 19 March 1681. Charles II arrived in Oxford on 14 March for the crucial Parliament which opened on 21 March to consider the Exclusion Bill. The King's Company also moved to Oxford and opened their season on 19 March with a performance of Saunders's *Tamerlane the Great*, at which the King, the Duchess of Portsmouth and Nell Gwyn were present (*True Protestant Mercury* xxv (19–23 March)).

There were two contemporary printings of the Epilogue, each on a folio half-sheet: (1) *The Epilogue Spoken to the King at the opening the Play-House at Oxford on Saturday last. Being March the Nineteenth 1681* (no imprint). This was probably printed in Oxford by Leonard Lichfield jr, printer to the university. The only known copy is in Christ Church, Oxford. (2) *The Epilogue.* [in margin:] 'Writ by Mr. *Dreyden*, Spoke before His Majesty at *Oxford, March* 19. 1680' [i.e. 1680/1]. This was printed by Richard Royston in London. The Oxford printing is followed here, as it seems superior at the two points where the texts differ, ll. 17 and 23.

The Epilogue

Spoken to the King at the opening the playhouse at Oxford on Saturday last, being March the nineteenth 1681

As from a darkened room some optic glass
Transmits the distant species as they pass,
The world's large landscape is from far descried,
And men contracted on the paper glide;
5   Thus crowded Oxford represents mankind,
And in these walls Great Britain seems confined.
Oxford is now the public theatre,
And you both audience are, and actors here.
The gazing world on the new scene attend,
10 Admire the turns, and wish a prosperous end.
This place, the seat of peace, the quiet cell

¶**63**. *1–4.* Robert Hooke described the operation of a camera obscura, which made the picture of an object or landscape from outside appear on the wall of a room (*PTRS* iii (1668) 741–3).
2. species] images of things.
10. Admire] wonder at.   *turns*] changes of events.

Where arts removed from noisy business dwell,
Should calm your wills, unite the jarring parts,
And with a kind contagion seize your hearts.
15 O may its genius like soft music move,
And tune you all to concord and to love!
Our ark that has in tempests long been tossed
Could never land on so secure a coast.
From hence you may look back on civil rage,
20 And view the ruins of the former age.
Here a new world its glories may unfold,
And here be saved the remnants of the old.
But while your days on public thoughts are bent,
Past ills to heal, and future to prevent,
25 Some vacant hours allow to your delight; ⎫
Mirth is the pleasing business of the night, ⎬
The King's prerogative, the people's right. ⎭
Were all your hours to sullen cares confined,
The body would be jaded by the mind.
30 'Tis wisdom's part betwixt extremes to steer:
Be gods in senates, but be mortals here.

15. genius] special character.
17–18. Cp. *To His Sacred Majesty* ll. *1–8n.*
17. has in tempests] *Oxford*; hath in Tempest *London.*
18–20. Oxford had been Charles I's headquarters during the Civil War.
23. days on] *Oxford*; Day-sun *London.*
30. As Aristotle counselled (*Ethics* 1108b–1109b).

64 Prologue and Epilogue to *The Unhappy Favourite*

Date and publication. The play was performed *c.* May 1681 (see the allusions in the Epilogue). The occasion on which the King and Queen saw this play at the Theatre Royal is unknown. John Banks's *The Unhappy Favourite: Or The Earl of Essex. A Tragedy* was published by Bentley and Magnes in 1682 (*TC* November 1681), and reprinted 1685, 1693 and [1699]. It was dedicated to Princess Anne and had a 'Prologue Spoken by Major Mohun, The First Four Dayes', the Prologue and Epilogue by D., and a 'Prologue, Intended to be spoken, Written by the Author'. D.'s Epilogue was reprinted with revisions in *MP* (1684; reprinted 1692). The present text follows *1682* (the text as first spoken), but records the revisions made for *MP*.

Context. Beyond the fact that both men wrote for the King's Company, nothing is known of the relations between Banks and D., and the pieces were probably written as part of D.'s duties to the Company. Banks's previous plays were *The Rival Kings* (1677) and *The Destruction of Troy* (1679). In *Vertue Betray'd* (1682) he describes D. as 'the best of *Laureats*' (Macdonald 159).

Prologue

Spoken to the King and Queen at their coming to the house, and written on purpose by Mr Dryden

When first the ark was landed on the shore,
And heaven had vowed to curse the ground no more,
When tops of hills the longing patriarch saw,
And the new scene of earth began to draw;
5   The dove was sent to view the waves' decrease,
And first brought back to man the pledge of peace:
'Tis needless to apply, when those appear
Who bring the olive, and who plant it here.

¶64. *Prologue.*
1–6. Cp. *To His Sacred Majesty* ll. 1–8n. Winn 596 suggests a recollection of Edward Ecclestone's opera *Noah's Flood* (1679).
5. waves' decrease] The apostrophe is editorial; without it, 'decrease' could be a verb.

      We have before our eyes the royal dove,
10   Still innocence is harbinger to love;
      The ark is opened to dismiss the train,
      And people with a better race the plain.
      Tell me you powers, why should vain man pursue ⎫
      With endless toil each object that is new,   ⎬
15   And for the seeming substance leave the true; ⎭
      Why should he quit for hopes his certain good,
      And loathe the manna of his daily food?
      Must England still the scene of changes be,   ⎫
      Tossed and tempestuous like our ambient sea? ⎬
20   Must still our weather and our wills agree?   ⎭
      Without our blood our liberties we have;
      Who that is free would fight to be a slave?
      Or what can wars to after times assure,
      Of which our present age is not secure?
25   All that our monarch would for us ordain
      Is but t' enjoy the blessings of his reign.
      Our land's an Eden, and the main's our fence
      While we preserve our state of innocence;
      That lost, then beasts their brutal force employ,
30   And first their lord, and then themselves destroy:
      What civil broils have cost we know too well;
      O let it be enough that once we fell,
      And every heart conspire with every tongue
      Still to have such a King, and this King long.

Epilogue

We act by fits and starts, like drowning men,

13–22. Cp. *The Medal* ll. 123–34.
31. know] *1685*; knew *1682.*
34. Verbally identical to Jonson's *A Panegyre on the Happie Entrance of James*
l. 162, itself a rendering of Martial's *dux tibi sit semper talis, et iste diu* (*Ep.* XII
vi 5, l. 6; Steven N. Zwicker, *N & Q* ccxiii (1968) 105–6).

Epilogue.
Title. 1682. An Epilogue for the Kings House *MP.*
1. Between February and June 1681 the King's Company's audiences were

But just peep up, and then dop down again.
Let those who call us wicked change their sense,
For never men lived more on providence:
5   Not lottery cavaliers are half so poor,
Nor broken cits, nor a vacation whore;
Not courts, nor courtiers living on the rents
Of the three last ungiving parliaments:
So wretched, that if Pharaoh could divine,
10   He might have spared his dream of seven lean kine,
And changed the vision for the Muses nine.
The comet, which they say portends a dearth,
Was but a vapour drawn from playhouse earth,
Pent here since our last fire, and Lilly says
15   Foreshows our change of state, and thin third days.
'Tis not our want of wit that keeps us poor,

---

often so small that receipts did not cover costs, and the company would cease acting (Hotson 266–7). In spring 1682 the King's Company merged with the Duke's.

2. dop] dip suddenly.

3–11, 16–19. Quoted in *Poeta De Tristibus* (1682) sig. A3ᵛ as examples of contemporary poets' 'unmerciful damnings both of the Times and one another'; cp. 'Prologue to *Aureng-Zebe*' ll. 27–30.

5. At the Restoration the monopoly of lotteries was granted for six years to 'Truly Loyal Indigent Commissioned Officers' who had served Charles I, but in 1674 they complained to the Privy Council that the commissioners appointed to administer the lotteries on their behalf had defrauded them of the profit, and that the crown had ignored their monopoly by granting lotteries to others (Ogg 164).

6. cits] citizens, traders.

8. None of the last three Parliaments (March–May 1679; October 1680 to January 1681; March 1681) had voted money for the King's use.

9–10. Genesis xli.

11. the¹] *1682; his MP.*

12. A comet was seen by Evelyn on 12 December 1680: 'very much in shape like the blade of a sword. . . . What this may Portend (for it was very extraordinarie) God onely knows.' Cp. *Remarkable Observations on the Comet, in the Year 1680* (1682).   *which*] *1682; that MP.*

13. Cp. *AM* ll. 65–72n.

14. here] *1682; there MP.   our last fire*] The previous Theatre Royal had been burnt down on 25 January 1672.   *Lilly*] William Lilly, the astrologer (d. 9 June 1681).

15. third days] The playwright took the third day's net receipts (*LS* lxxxi).

For then the printers' press would suffer more.
Their pamphleteers their venom daily spit,
They thrive by treason, and we starve by wit.
20 Confess the truth: which of you has not laid
                                To the Upper Gallery.
Four farthings out to buy the Hatfield Maid?
Or, what is duller yet, and more to spite us,
Democritus his wars with Heraclitus?
These are the authors that have run us down,
25 And exercise you critics of the town.
Yet these are pearls to your lampooning rhymes,
Y' abuse yourselves more dully than the times.
Scandal, the glory of the English nation,

17–19. The expiry of the 1662 Printing Act on 10 June 1679 brought about a marked increase in political pamphleteering, followed by government attempts to curtail opposition publishers through court actions (see Timothy Crist, *Publishing History* v (1979) 49–77). In April 1681 Luttrell noted: 'the presse abounds with all sorts of pamphlets and libells; one side running down the papists and upholding the dissenters; the other side cryeing down both . . .; publick intelligencers or pamphlets of news abounding, every day spawning two, sometimes three, filling the town and country with notorious falsehoods' (i 76). *Poeta De Tristibus* complains that 'since the Press has lately had / Its Liberty', good poets have suffered while hacks and booksellers flourish: 'when for *Dryden*'s Works I came, / They vow'd they never heard his Name' (2–3).
18. their venom daily] *1682*; each day their Venom *MP*.
20. To the Upper Gallery] *1682*; Looking above *MP*. The upper gallery was used by servants.
21. Refers to a pamphlet called *A True and Perfect Relation of Elizabeth Freeman of Bishops-Hatfield in the County of Hertford, Of a Strange and Wonderful Apparition Which Appeared to her several times and Commanded Her to declare a Message to his Most Sacred Majesty. January 27. 1680* [i.e. 1680/1]. The message was that 'the Royal Blood' would be poisoned on 15 May, and that the King should not move Parliament to Oxford. The King 'was pleased to bid her, *Go home and to serve God, and she should see no more such Visions*' (James Sutherland, *The Restoration Newspaper* (1986) 168).
22. what . . . to] *1682*; which . . . would *MP*.
23. Heraclitus Ridens, the Tory paper, ran from 1 February 1681 to 22 August 1682; it was answered by the Whig paper *Democritus Ridens*, 14 March to 13 June 1681.
24. These . . . that] *1682*; Such . . . who *MP*.
25. exercise] *1682*; Exercis'd *MP*.
26–37. Satires against court ladies seem to have been particularly in vogue in 1680–1: see *Court Satires of the Restoration*, edited by J. H. Wilson (1976) 32–

Is worn to rags, and scribbled out of fashion:
30   Such harmless thrusts, as if, like fencers wise,
You had agreed your play before the prize:
Faith, you may hang your harps upon the willows,
'Tis just like children when they box with pillows.
Then put an end to civil wars, for shame,
35   Let each knight errant who has wronged a dame
Throw down his pen, and give her if he can
The satisfaction of a gentleman.

---

67. In 'An Answer to the Satire on the Court Ladies' (1680) D. is praised for
not lampooning women: 'There's Dryden, though a devil at his pen, / In all
his satires pecks at only men' (ll. 13–14; Wilson 42). Cp. 'Another Epilogue
to *The Duke of Guise*' ll. 30–6n.
31. *You . . . your . . . the*] *1682*; They . . . their . . . their *MP.*   *prize*]
contest.
32. Psalm cxxxvii 2.   *you . . . your*] *1682*; they . . . their *MP.*
36. *if*] *1682*; as *MP.*

65 Prologue at Oxford, 1681 ('The famed Italian Muse . . .')

Date and publication. Spoken in July 1681, at the visit of the King's Company to Oxford for the annual Act. Printed in *EP* (1693).

Prologue to the University of Oxford, 1681

The famed Italian Muse, whose rhymes advance
Orlando, and the paladins of France,
Records that when our wit and sense is flown,
'Tis lodged within the circle of the moon
5   In earthen jars, which one who thither soared
Set to his nose, snuffed up, and was restored.
Whate'er the story be, the moral's true:
The wit we lost in town we find in you.
Our poets their fled parts may draw from hence,
10   And fill their windy heads with sober sense.
When London votes with Southwark's disagree,

¶65. *1–6.* Ariosto, *Orlando Furioso* xxxiv. D. echoes Harington's translation (1591): Men's wits are 'layd up . . . in the circle of the Moone' (st. 72); Astolfo soared there, and finding the vessel containing his own wit, he 'set the vessels mouth but to his nose, / And to his place he snuft up all his wit' (st. 85). He then took the jar containing Orlando's wit and put it to Orlando's nostrils: 'He drawing breath, this miracle was wrought: / . . . And he restored unto his perfect wit' (xxxix 55).
1–2. Echoes Drayton: 'The *Thuskan* Poet doth advance, / The franticke *Paladine* of *France*' (*Nymphidia* ll. 193–4; W. B. Gardner).
11. In the February 1681 election London returned the same predominantly Whig members that it had sent to the two previous Parliaments, but Southwark elected two Tory MPs, rejecting the Whig candidates Slingsby Bethel and Edward Smith. In May 1681 the Borough of Southwark presented a petition to the King thanking him for dissolving Parliament (R. R. Sharpe, *London and the Kingdom*, 3 vols (1894–5) ii 463–6). The political contrast between London and Southwark is depicted by Robert Hearne in *Obsequium et Veritas: or A Dialogue Between London and Southwark* (1681), where 'Veritas' (Truth) scorns 'popular Applause' and claims to be 'a good honest *Southwark* Borough, and I thank God, we love our King, and our Country; and our

Here they may find their long-lost loyalty.
Here busy senates, to th' old cause inclined,
May snuff the votes their fellows left behind:
15   Your country neighbours, when their grain grows dear,
May come and find their last provision here:
Whereas we cannot much lament our loss,
Who neither carried back, nor brought one cross;
We looked what representatives would bring,
20   But they helped us just as they did the King.
Yet we despair not, for we now lay forth
The Sibyl's books to those who know their worth;
And though the first was sacrificed before,
These volumes doubly will the price restore.
25   Our poet bade us hope this grace to find,
To whom by long prescription you are kind.

Publick Peace, Utility, and Order' (2). See also the Tory manifesto, *The Southwark Address Presented . . . on Friday March 18* (1681).

12. In February 1681 Oxford University had returned two Tory Members of Parliament, Dr Charles Perrot and Sir Leoline Jenkins; the latter led the court's opposition to Shaftesbury. The town, however, returned two Whig members, Brome Whorwood and William Wright, due partly to the support of the Duke of Buckingham (*Life and Times of Anthony Wood* (1892) ii 516, 523).

13. *th' old cause*] also called 'The Good Old Cause': extreme Protestantism.

14. *snuff*] inhale.   *their fellows*] the Members of the Parliament which Charles I summoned at Oxford in January 1644, in defiance of the Long Parliament sitting at Westminster.

15. In May–June 1681 a drought had sent up the price of grain around Oxford (Wood ii 538).

17–18. The actors' visit to Oxford in March 1681 had evidently been unprofitable, because of the sudden dissolution of Parliament on 28 March.   *cross*] a coin stamped with a cross.

20. The Oxford Parliament had not voted any taxes for the King.

21–4. The Cumaean Sibyl offered to sell nine books of prophecy to Tarquinius Priscus, who refused because the price was too high. She then burned three of the books and offered him the remaining six at the same price. Again he refused. She burned three more books and offered him the remaining three at the original price, to which he agreed (Dionysus of Halicarnassus iv 62).

He whose undaunted Muse, with loyal rage,
Has never spared the vices of the age,
Here finding nothing that his spleen can raise,
30 Is forced to turn his satire into praise.

27–30. D.'s plays, prologues and epilogues had continually satirized the political disloyalty and the private vices of the Londoners, but had been complimentary to the Oxford audiences.

66 Prologue and Epilogue Spoken at *Mithridates*

Date and publication. Spoken in mid–October 1681 at a revival of Lee's play by the King's Company at the Theatre Royal. D. had contributed an Epilogue for the play's first run in 1678. The poems were first printed anonymously on a folio half-sheet headed *A Prologue spoken at Mithridates King of Pontus, the First Play Acted at the Theatre Royal this year, 1681*, printed for J. Sturton (siglum: '*S*'). Narcissus Luttrell wrote the date of acquisition (13 February 1681/2) and a number of marginal corrections ('*L*') on his copy, now in the Huntington Library. Richard Janeway's Whig paper *The Impartial Protestant Mercury* liv (28 October 1681) reported that 'a Revised Play was some days since Acted on an Eminent Publick Theatre, and the Prologue is extreamly talked of, some Verses whereof are' and then follow 'Prologue' ll. 24–41 ('*J*'). On 29 October Nathaniel Thompson's Tory paper *The Loyal Protestant, and True Domestick Intelligence* lxx replied: 'Whereas Mr. *Janeway* in his *Partial Protestant* of yesterday, is pleased to make use of a *Prologue* to a reviv'd Play lately acted at the *Theatre Royal*, with this grave Authors Animadversions upon the same. By his good leave, I'll incert a part of the Epilogue to the same Play, and leave it to the chewing of the Brotherhood'; then follow 'Epilogue' ll. 1–7 ('*T*'). J. H. Smith (*PMLA* lxviii (1953) 251–67) argued that *S* derives from a shorthand transcription made in the theatre; that *J* and *T* derive from a rival broadside printing (now lost) which was itself produced from a shorthand transcription in the theatre, made independently of the one which formed the basis for *S*; and that *L*'s alterations are corrections derived from some authoritative source, perhaps D.'s MS as revised for publication, which could have been shown to Luttrell by his friend Tonson. However, the hypothesis of a second, lost broadside seems unnecessarily complicated; there is no reason to suppose that *J* and *T* were working from the same source; and a MS provided by the actors is a possible alternative to one produced through shorthand transcription. Nevertheless, Smith's argument seems correct in outline: *S* and *J* do indeed appear to derive from performances, as is suggested by the occasional colloquial roughness of their text compared with the refinements in *L*, and by readings which may be due to mishearings (e.g. 'Epilogue' ll. 22, 40). Smith's suggestion that *L*'s revisions derive from some authoritative text is strengthened by the support given to *L* by *T*, and also by a MS (not hitherto collated by editors) which also seems to derive from a performance: Chetham's Library Manchester MS A.4.14. The present edition follows *S*, but emends wherever the other witnesses agree against it. (Exceptions are 'Prologue' l. 33, where the plural noun seems unnecessary and the verb is properly a subjunctive; and 'Epilogue' l. 28, where *MS* alone supplies a spelling which is necessary for the rhyme.) All the variants are recorded, since some (particularly in *S*, *J* and *MS*) may provide evidence of playhouse usage (e.g. 'Prologue' ll. 6, 19, 39; 'Epilogue' ll. 7, 10, 17, 30, 32);

others, however, may simply be errors in transmission (e.g. 'Prologue' ll. 21, 28, 41; 'Epilogue' ll. 23, 40).

Authorship. The poems are attributed to D. by Luttrell on his copy; in a MS note on the BL copy (Ashley 4805); and in the Chetham MS.

A Prologue Spoken at *Mithridates King of Pontus*

The first play acted at the Theatre Royal this year, 1681

> After a four months' fast we hope at length
> Your queasy stomachs have recovered strength,
> That you can taste a play (your old coarse mess)
> As honest and as plain as an address:
> 5   And therefore welcome from your several parts,

¶66. *Prologue.*
Title. Epilogue *MS.*   *year*] i.e. theatrical season.
1–4. Cp. 'Prologue to *The Loyal General*' ll. 22–4.
1. *a four months' fast*] the Long Vacation from mid-June to mid-October. *four*] *S*; two *MS.*   *we*] *S*; I *MS.*
3. *That you can*] *S*; To *MS.*   *mess*] dish.
4. *address*] A Tory declaration of support for the King's actions, e.g. thanking him for dissolving Parliament; the Whig equivalents were called 'petitions'. A royal proclamation of 12 December 1679 forbade petitions against the prorogation or dissolution of Parliament, but on 27 October 1680 the Commons resolved that petitioning was the inalienable right of the subject (Ogg 602). Shaftesbury orchestrated a Whig campaign of petitioning for Parliament to be allowed to meet in January 1680; a petition 300 feet long with some 50,000 names from Westminster and Southwark was presented to the King on 13 January, and another with 30,000 names from Wiltshire was presented by Thomas Thynne nine days later. Others followed (Haley 559–64). In July 1681 Luttrell commented on the different reception which the King gave to 'addressers and petitioners: those meet with a kind reception at any time, these are alwaies distasteful; these petition him in these times of danger to call the representative body of the nation, and those give him thanks for dissolving them' (Luttrell i 108). Cp. D'Urfey's Prologue to *The Royalist* (1682): the Tory '*Addresses* loves, to all Mankind is civil; / But hates *Petitions* as he hates the Devil' (ll. 28–9; Danchin no. 315). Cp. *AA* l. 986 and 'Prologue to *The Loyal Brother*' ll. 7, 9.

You that have stol'n kind country wenches' hearts,
Have watched returning milkmaids in the dark,
And sinned against the pales of every park.
Welcome fair ladies of unblemished faith,
10   That left town bagnios for the fruitful bath;
For when the season's hot, and lover's there,
The waters never fail to make an heir.
Welcome kind men that did your wives attend,
And welcome he that was the husband's friend,
15   Who holding chat did silently encroach
With treacherous hand to grabble in the coach.
Hail you Newmarket brothers of the switch,
That use cast strumpets, full of pox and itch,
A leap more dangerous than the Devil's Ditch.
20   Last welcome you who never did appear,
Gave out i' the country, but lay fluxing here;

6. *stol'n*] L, stole *MS*; gain'd *S*.

10. *That*] *S*; Which *MS*.   *bagnios*] Turkish baths: the royal bagnio opened in London in 1680 (see *A True Account of the Royal Bagnio* (1680)).   *bath*] After Queen Catherine took the waters at Bath and Tunbridge in the hope of curing her infertility, the spas became fashionable resorts.

11–12. A common joke; cp. Rochester: 'here walk Cuff and Kick, / With brawny back and legs, and potent prick, / Who more substantially will cure thy wife, / And on her half-dead womb bestow new life. / From these the waters got the reputation / Of good assistants unto generation.' (*Tunbridge Wells* (in *MS*, 1673–4) ll. 143–8).

12. *make*] L, *MS*; get *S*.

13. *kind*] complacent (cp. *AA* l. 572n).   *men*] *S*; S^{rs} *MS*.

15. *Who*] *S*; That *MS*.

16. *grabble*] grope.

17. The professional jockeys who had followed the King when he returned from Newmarket on 12 October (cp. 'Epilogue', Title *n*.).

18. *use cast*] L, *MS*; leap left *S*.   *cast*] Cp. 'cast Punk' in Oldham's 'A Satyr' [Spenser's Ghost] l. 258 (written 1682–3).

19. *the Devil's Ditch*] The post-Roman Devil's Ditch (or Dyke) runs across Newmarket Heath. J. H. Smith suggests that the name may also have been applied to a jump on the racecourse (citing Edward Howard's play *The Man of Newmarket* (1678) Act IV). After l. 19 *MS* adds: 'Whose Day delight was in a Smoaky Roome / To tope wth Jockeys & corrupt a Groome'.

20. *who*] *S*; y^{t} *MS*.

21. i.e. 'gave out the report that you were in the country, but stayed in London being treated for venereal disease'.   *Gave out i' the country*] *S*; omitted in *MS*.   *the*] L; th' *S*.

Now crawl abroad with stick, lean-chapt and thin,
And fair as lady that hath new lain in.
This winter let us reckon you our own,
25 For all wise men will let the state alone:
The Plot's removed, a witness of renown
Has lodged it safe at t' other end o' th' town,
And that it ne'er may fail, some pious whore ⎫
Has cast her mite, and fairly at his door   ⎬
30 Laid two small squalling evidences more, ⎭
Which well instructed, if we take their words,
In time may grow to hang two Popish lords;
Heaven grant the babes may live, for faith, there's need, ⎫
Swearers fall off so fast, if none succeed   ⎬
35 The land's in danger quite to lose the breed: ⎭

---

23. *hath . . . lain*] S; has . . . layd *MS*.

26–30. Titus Oates moved from Whitehall to the City in August 1681, and was said to have taken lodgings with a Quaker in Lombard Street. 'Since the *Salamanca* Dr's removal into the City, the *Whigs* are so generous in their supplies, that Pigs, Geese, and Capons fly in at his Windows in as great Plenty as ever they did to Dr. *Faustus*; nay, his Magick is so great, that it hath attracted two Infants in their Swaddling-Cloaths to lie at his Door. . . . The one will be Christen'd *Titus*, and the other *Oates*' (*The Loyal Protestant*, 10 and 20 September 1681); see also *A New Ballad upon D*ʳ *Oates his Retreat from White-Hall, Into the City* (1681), and *A Dialogue between Two Porters. Upon D*ʳ. *O-s's removing from White-hall into the City* (1681).

28. *ne'er may*] S; nere might *MS*; may ne'er *J*.

30. *evidences*] witnesses.

32. In October 1678 five Catholic lords were imprisoned, accused by Oates of complicity in the Popish Plot. Viscount Stafford was tried and executed in December 1680; Lord Petre died in the Tower on 4 January 1684, and the rest were released in February 1685.   *grow*] S, J, MS; come L.

33. *Heaven*] S; Heavens *J, MS*.

34. *Swearers*] S, MS; Swearing *J*.

Unless we break an Act, which were a sin,
And for recruit let Irish cattle in.
Well; after all 'twere better to compound
Than let the foolish frolic still go round;
40   Both sides have lost, and by my computation
None but Jack Ketch has gained in all the nation.

Epilogue

Pox on this playhouse, 'tis an old tired jade,
'Twill do no longer, we must force a trade;
What if we all turn witnesses o' th' Plot?
That's overstocked, there's nothing to be got.

36–7. The 1666 Act against importing Irish cattle had been renewed in 1681.
Irish witnesses figured prominently in the Popish Plot trials. Luttrell reports
that the Catholic David Fitzgerald 'has been often heard to say that he could
have as many witnesses as he pleased from Ireland to forswear themselves for
2s. 6d. each' (i 89–90). Shaftesbury also employed witnesses: see *AA* ll. 679,
922*n*, 1012*n*. Aphra Behn in the 'Prologue to *The Roundheads*' (performed
c. December 1681) has the regicide Huson say: 'Pay well your Witnesses, they
may not run / To the right side and tell who set 'em on / Pay 'em so well, that
they may ne'er Recant / And so turn Honest meerly out of Want' (ll. 19–22;
Danchin no. 311).
36. we] *J, MS*; you *S*.
38. compound] settle differences.
39. foolish] *S, J*; silly *MS*.
40. by my] *S, MS*; so by *J*.
41. Jack Ketch] the hangman.   *all*] *L, MS, J* ('hath gain'd of all'); *omitted in S*.

Epilogue.
Title. 'Prologue to yᵉ King upon his return from Newmarket in yᵉ year 1681
. . .' *MS*. The Epilogue is begun by Cardell Goodman (1653–after 1713), a
leading actor in the King's Company which he joined in 1673; his roles for D.
included Alexas in *All for Love*. On his return from a season in Edinburgh
(1679–80) he signed a new agreement with Charles and Henry Killigrew,
giving him a share in the company and a chance to play leading roles (see
Highfill vi 258–66; J. H. Wilson, *Mr. Goodman the Player* (1964)).
1. The King's Company was by now in severe difficulties: cp. 'Epilogue to
The Unhappy Favourite' l. 1*n*.   *on this*] *S*; o' this *MS*; o' th' *T*.
3. witnesses o' th'] *L, T*; wittnesses of 'the *MS*; Witness of the *S*.

5   Shall we take orders? That will parts require, ⎤
    Our colleges give no degrees for hire—   ⎬
    Would Salamanca were a little nigher.   ⎦
    Will nothing do? O now 'tis found, I hope:
    Have you not seen the dancing of the rope?
10 When Andrew's wit was clean run off the
        score,·
    And Jacob's capering tricks could do no more,
    A damsel does to the ladder's top advance,
    And with two heavy buckets drags a dance.
    The yawning crowd perked up to see the sight,
15 And slavered at the mouth with vast delight:
    O friends, there's nothing to enchant the mind,
    Nothing like that cleft sex to draw mankind:
    The foundered horse that switching will not
        stir,
    Trots to the mare afore without a spur.
20 Faith, I'll go scour the scene room and engage

5. *will*] would *MS.*   *parts*] abilities.

6. *Our*] *L, T, MS*; And *S.*

7. *Salamanca*] where Oates claimed to have received a DD (cp. *AA* ll. 657–
9).   *were*] *T, MS*; was *S.*

9–15. Entertainments at Bartholomew Fair (see Pepys 29 August, 21 September 1668). *MS* offers an alternative syntax for these lines, taking the
whole passage to be governed by 'Have you not seen', with a question mark
after l. 13; it also has some readings which seem more vivid than those in *S.*
But in the absence of support from *L* these readings are reluctantly rejected,
since they may simply be unauthorized scribal or playhouse alterations.

10. Andrew] a merry-andrew, clown.   *clean*] *S*; quite *MS.*   *run off the
score*] exceeded his credit.

11. Jacob] Jacob Hall, the popular rope-dancer.   *do*] *S*; draw *MS.*

12. does] *S*; *omitted in MS.*

13. drags] *S*; dragg *MS.*

14. perked] *L*, pearch't *S* (variant form of 'perked'); perks *MS.*   *see*] *S*;
omitted in *MS.*

15. slavered] *S*; slavers *MS.*   *with*] *L, MS*; for *S.*

17. cleft] *L*; deaf *MS* (probably mishearing or misreading of *cleft*); sweet *S.*
For the sexual connotations of *cleft* see *OED* 2a, and Shakespeare, *Troilus and
Cressida* V ii 11.   *draw*] *S*; charm *MS.*

18–19. omitted in MS.

18. foundered] fallen to the ground (*OED* 4).

Some toy within to prop the falling stage.   *Exit.*
          Re-enters with Mrs Cox.
Who have we here again, what numps i' th' stocks?
Your most obedient slave, sweet Madam Cox.
You'd best be coy, and blush for a pretence;
25   For shame, say something in your own defence.
Mrs Cox   What shall I say? I have been hence so long
I've e'en almost forgot my mother tongue;
If I can act, I wish I were ten fadom
Beneath—
Mr Goodman —O Lord, pray, no swearing, Madam.
Mrs Cox   If I had sworn, yet sure to serve the nation
I could find out some mental reservation.
Well, in plain terms, gallants, without a sham,
Will you be pleased to take me as I am;
Quite out of countenance, with a downcast look,
35   Just like a truant that returns to book?
Yet I'm not old, but if I were this place
Ne'er wanted art to piece a ruined face.

---

21. prop] L, MS; save S.

21. s.d. omitted in MS.   Mrs Cox] Elizabeth Cox (?1639–?1688), actress with the King's Company from 1671. Her roles for D. included Palmyra in *Marriage A-la-Mode*, Violetta in *The Assignation*, and Indamora in *Aureng-Zebe*. She was off the stage 1676–81, returning for this season. She was apparently Goodman's mistress at this date (Highfill iv 17–18).

22. again, what numps] what Numps again *MS.*   *numps*] L, MS; Nymphs S. A foolish person (i.e. for joining a failing company). In Jonson's *Bartholomew Fair* (1614) Cokes derides Humphrey Waspe for having been punished in the stocks: 'O *Numps*, i' the Stocks, *Numps*?' (V iv 106).

23. slave] L, MS; Servant S.

24–5. omitted in MS.

26. shall] S; should MS.

28. fadom] MS ('faddam'); Fathom S.

30. L, MS; Why Sir, If I had sworn, to save the Nation S.

31. Both Dissenters and Catholics were thought to swear oaths with mental reservations.   *could*] S; would MS.

32. in plain terms, gallants] S; Gallants in plain Terms MS.

36. but] S; or MS.

37. piece] repair (OED 1).

When greybeards governed I forsook the stage,
You know 'tis piteous work to act with age;
40   Though there's no sense amongst these
        beardless boys,
There's what we women love, that's mirth and
        noise;
These young beginners may grow up in time,
And the devil's in't if I am past my prime.

38–40. In the 1670s the King's Company was led by Charles Hart and Michael Mohun, who were excluded when Goodman and his associates took over in 1680.
40. there's] *S*; here's *MS*.   *sense*] *L, MS*; sex *S*.
43. I am past] *Ed.*; I'me past *S*; I have lost *MS*.

67 Absalom and Achitophel

Date and publication. The statement in *The Second Part of Miscellany Poems* (1716) that *AA* was begun 'in the year 1680' has been accepted by some scholars (e.g. Howard H. Schless, *POAS* iii 278–9), but is unlikely. Malone took it to mean before 25 March 1681 (i.e. 1680 in the old calendar), which would be before the dissolution of the Oxford Parliament. It is more probable that the dissolution prompted D. to begin the poem, and that he worked at it over the summer of 1681. *Absalom and Achitophel. A Poem* was published by Tonson in 1681 (advertised in *The Loyal Protestant* 19 November; Luttrell's copy (in the Huntington) is dated 17 November, and was given him by Tonson). This first edition, in folio (siglum: *F*) had one misprint on p. 5 and four (plus an incorrect catchword) on p. 6. The errors on p. 6 were corrected as the book was going through the press, resulting in four different issues (Macdonald nos. 12a (i)–(iv)). The folio edition was reprinted (partly reset) in 1681 (*F2*), and some copies of this printing have an extra leaf with commendatory verses by Nathaniel Lee and Richard Duke (Macdonald 12d). 'The Second Edition; Augmented and Revised', in quarto (*Q*), was published in 1681, adding twelve lines on Shaftesbury (ll. 180–91) and four on Monmouth (ll. 957–60), and making several verbal alterations which appear to be D.'s revisions (Macdonald 12e (i)–(ii)). Noyes 959 conjectured that ll. 180–91 might have been in D.'s original MS but omitted in order to sharpen the satire on Shaftesbury; Vinton A. Dearing (*Works* ii 411–12) developed this into an elaborate hypothesis about royal censorship and last-minute revision; a rival hypothesis about revision was proposed by E. L. Saslow (*SB* xxviii (1975) 276–83). Another hypothesis is that ll. 180–91 and 957–60 were added when D. saw that it was both safe and advantageous for the King's supporters to appear reasonable and magnanimous. The present editor thinks that Noyes was right in supposing that ll. 180–91 were in the original MS, but that they were omitted accidentally: ll. 180–91 do not form a coherent unit, since ll. 180–5 are a strongly worded development of the point in l. 179 about private ambition masquerading as public service, while ll. 186–91 make a generous concession about Shaftesbury's probity as a judge, and lead smoothly into ll. 192–3. It is therefore unlikely that this passage would have been seen as a unit and omitted in *F* to sharpen the satire, or composed as a block to be added in *Q* to show magnanimity. It is more likely that ll. 180–91 were in D.'s original MS but accidentally omitted in *F* (they would have come between the foot of p. 6 and the top of p. 7, and other errors and signs of haste affected p. 6); they would then have been restored when the poem was reset in a new format for *Q*. Lines 957–60 need not have had the same textual history as ll. 180–91: they could well have been added in *Q* to soften the presentation of Monmouth. *Q* was reprinted in 1682 with the addition of verses by Nahum Tate (Macdonald 12f), and twice again in the same year (Macdonald 12g and h). *AA* was then reprinted in *MP* (reprinted 1692) and again in 1692 along with *The Medal* and *MF* as part of Tonson's series of D.'s poems in a uniform format. Two undated editions appeared, probably in Dublin (Macdonald 12b and c), and there is a pirated edition called *Absalom and Achitpohel* [*sic*] (1681). The poem was also reprinted (n.p., n.d.) with a key (Macdonald 12l). The present text is based on *F*, incorporating the press corrections, but emended from *Q* to include the additional lines and revisions. The passage on Shaftesbury as it stood in the first edition is reproduced as Plates 6–7. For a justification of this policy see Introduction, pp. xiv–xv above. There is no evidence that D. revised the poem after *Q*. Paragraphing has been added at ll. 150, 543 and 630. For the commendatory poems see Appendix C.

Context. In the late 1670s there was growing anxiety about the succession to Charles II, who had no legitimate children. His heir, his brother James, Duke of York, was a Roman Catholic, and the prospect of a Catholic king made many Englishmen fear for their political and religious liberties. Fears were accentuated by the allegations made by Titus Oates in October 1678 that there was a Popish Plot to assassinate Charles and establish Catholicism. Proposals were discussed for excluding James from the succession: either by enabling Charles to divorce Catherine of Braganza and remarry; or by making Charles's son James, Duke of Monmouth, legitimate; or by establishing a regency over James, Duke of York; or by having the crown pass to either James's daughter Mary or her husband William of Orange. Exclusion Bills were debated by Parliament in April–May 1679 and November 1680; in March 1681 the King summoned Parliament to meet at Oxford, but dissolved it before another Exclusion Bill could be passed. Opposition to the court had begun to take the form of a loose party which became known as the Whigs. One of the chief Whigs, though not a formal leader, was the Earl of Shaftesbury, and after the political tide turned in favour of Charles in the summer of 1681 Shaftesbury was arrested on 2 July and imprisoned in the Tower of London on a charge of treason. A preliminary hearing of his case began on 24 November, and a jury picked by Whig sheriffs returned a verdict of *ignoramus* ('we do not know'), by which the crown's evidence was rejected as insufficient for the case to proceed to a full trial by the House of Lords, which would almost certainly have convicted him. The publication of *AA* on 17 November seems timed to influence public opinion at a critical moment (the first edition shows signs of hasty production), but Phillip Harth (*SECC* iv (1975) 13–29) refutes the common notion that *AA* was written or published to affect the outcome of Shaftesbury's trial: a verdict favourable to Shaftesbury was regarded as inevitable a few weeks before *AA* was published, so the poem was designed to influence public opinion generally. For studies of the political machinations of this period see Ogg 559–631; J. R. Jones, *The First Whigs* (1970); K. H. D. Haley, *The First Earl of Shaftesbury* (1968); Tim Harris, *London Crowds in the Reign of Charles II* (1987); and Hutton, *Charles the Second*. For the debate over political theory see Richard Ashcraft, *Revolutionary Politics and Locke's 'Two Treatises of Government'* (1986); and Jonathan Scott, *Algernon Sidney and the Restoration Crisis, 1677–*

1683 (1991). Some contemporary political materials are reprinted in *Contexts 3: Absalom and Achitophel*, edited by Robert W. McHenry Jr (1986). Tonson in *The Second Part of Miscellany Poems* (1716) reported that *AA* was written 'upon the Desire of King *Charles* the Second'; a letter from Richard Mulys in November 1681 claims that Edward Seymour commissioned it (*HMC Ormonde* vi 233; Wallace Maurer, *PQ* xl (1961) 130–8); another report says that D. was paid £100 for it (*HMC* X iv 175; Winn).

Authorship. *AA* was published anonymously, and never appeared over D.'s name in his lifetime (it was attributed to him on the contents page of *MP* (1692) but not in the text); for the significance of this see Paul Hammond, *SC* viii (1993) 138–9. D.'s authorship was quickly guessed (by Mulys, cited above; and in *Correspondence of the Family of Hatton* (1878) ii 10, dated 22 November 1681), but D. acknowledged it (with *MF*) only in 'A Discourse Concerning Satire' (1693).

Sources. The story of Absalom's rebellion against King David comes from 2 Samuel xiii–xviii, though D. adds some names from other parts of the OT and there are many allusions to both OT and NT (see Barbara K. Lewalski, *ELN* iii (1965) 29–35). The names which D. adopts vary in the precision with which they suit the contemporary characters, and some of the allusions are not clearly determinable. Robert Aylett's poem *David's Troubles Remembred* (1638) is a possible source for *AA* (see Barbara K. Lewalski, *N&Q* ccix (1964) 340–43), as is Cowley's *Davideis* (1656). The application of the story to English politics is not new, as R. F. Jones showed (*MLN* xlvi (1931) 211–18). Nathaniel Carpenter in *Achitophel, or the Picture of a Wicked Politician* (1627) wrote of '*David* an anointed King: *Absolon* an ambitious prince: *Achitophel* a wicked politician, and *Hushai* a loyal subject'. During the parliamentary debates on the eve of the Civil War 'Achitophel' was applied to some of Charles I's ministers; and Henry King's 'An Elegy upon the most Incomparable King *Charls* the First' employs many OT parallels, including Absalom, David and Zimri (*Poems, Elegies, Paradoxes, and Sonnets* (1664) 18–38). At the Restoration the parallel between Charles II and David was used widely in sermons and poems (see *Astraea Redux* l. 79; Carolyn A. Edie, *BJRL* lxii (1979–80) 81). Simon Ford remarked: 'It is a matter of greatest wonder to me to observe how exactly the *two Histories* run *parallel*. Insomuch that it were no hard matter for an *ingenious phancy*, by altering the Names of *David, Absalom, Joab, Abishai, Zadock, Abiathar, Ziba, Mephibosheth, Jordan*, &c. into others proper to our late affairs, to insert *verbatim* the *greatest part of the Chapter* into a *Chronicle of these Times*' (Παράλληλα; . . . *A Sermon Preached at All-Saints Church in Northampton, Jun. 28. 1660* (1660) 1–2). The form of service for 29 May (Charles's birthday and return) in the *Book of Common Prayer* (1662) includes verses from the Psalms which give thanks for David's preservation, and the first lesson is from 2 Samuel xix. In 1667 Robert Creighton, who had been at Westminster and Trinity with D., preached a sermon before the King 'against the sins of the Court, and particularly against adultery, over and over instancing how for that single sin in David, the whole nation was undone' (Winn 185). In 1677 Nathaniel Lee, in a poem prefixed to D.'s *The State of Innocence*, had suggested that D. should 'The troubles of majestic Charles sat [i.e. set] down: / Not David vanquish'd more to reach a crown. / Praise him as Cowley did that Hebrew King; / Thy theme's as great, do thou as greatly sing.' (E. S. de Beer, *RES* xvii (1941) 300). In his 5 November commemorative sermon in 1678 Aaron Baker implied a connection between Absalom and Monmouth, without naming the Duke (*Achitophel befool'd* (1678) 3–4) and said that Achitophel was 'of *David*'s Privy-Councill, a great Statesman, and a cunning Politician, and therefore a very dangerous and remarkable Conspirator' (11); see also l. 163*n*. In Thomas Jordan's 1678 Lord Mayor's Show, *London in Luster*, the story of David and Bathsheba is linked with that of Cain and Abel as a topical comment on Exclusion (Owen 111–12).

During the Exclusion Crisis the story was used several times in pamphlets. *A Letter to His Grace the D. of Monmouth, this 15th. of July, 1680* warns Monmouth against advisers who would have him seek the crown, comparing them with the advisers of Absalom: 'these Principled Men were they that set on *Absalom* to steal away the Hearts of the People from the King; . . . And These were the Men that led him into Actual Rebellion against his Father, and to be destroy'd by some of the very Hands that had assisted him in those pernicious Councels' (3). The writer of *Absalom's Conspiracy; or, The Tragedy of Treason* (1680; dated June in Cambridge UL copy) cites the story as 'a particular Caveat to all young men, to beware of such Counsellors, as the old *Achitophel*, lest while they are tempted with the hopes of a Crown, they hasten on their own Destiny, and come to an untimely End' (1). Shaftesbury is linked with Achitophel in *An Answer to a Paper* (1681; probably July) and in the Whig pamphlet *Some Memoirs* (1681; October or November, according to Wood's MS note in BodL copy): 'What was said of *Achitophel* (that bad man, yet of a deep reach) may better be said of this better Gentleman (*That his Counsel was as if a Man had enquired at the Oracle of God*)' (4). This pamphlet also has an extensive comparison of Shaftesbury with Job, and remarks: 'This *Comparison* must not therefore be accounted ridiculous, because it cannot *in omnibus quadrare* [be an exact parallel at all points], or have a happy Hit in ev'ry punctilio. . . . There is never a *congruity*, either in Civil or sacred History, which will not well enough admit of some unlikeness thereunto in some circumstantial Adjuncts' (7). See also the citations from *A Seasonable Invitation* in ll. 229*n* and 267–9*n* below. Several poems used these references. Thomas D'Urfey's *The Progress of Honesty* (1680; Luttrell's copy dated 11 October) calls Shaftesbury Achitophel and gives OT names to some of his followers. *Satyr Unmuzzled* (in MS, 1680; *POAS* ii 209–16) characterizes Shaftesbury and Monmouth as Absalom and Achitophel in ll. 86–101; so too does *The Waking Vision* (1681; probably April–June; *POAS* ii 419–24) in ll. 7–19. In *A Vision in the Tower* (1681; dated 22 July on Luttrell's copy; *POAS* ii 435–9), l. 8 refers to Shaftesbury as Achitophel. [John Dean's] *The Badger in the Fox-Trap* (?July 1681; see R. H. Levy, *ELN* (1964) 253–6) reports that some call Shaftesbury Achitophel. *A Dialogue between Nathan and Absolome* (in MS, 1680; *POAS* ii 269–72; see Howard H. Schless, *PQ* xl (1961) 139–43) casts Monmouth as Absalom. These and other contemporary poems supplied D. with hints, particularly for the characters of the opposition leaders, as the notes below indicate. The idea of a series of character sketches may go back to the *Advice to a Painter* genre, while previous political allegories using OT stories were John Caryll's *Naboth's Vinyard* (1679), 'E. P. Philopatris', *News from Hell* (1680), and Anon, *A Poem on the History of Queen Hesther* [1680]. For discussions of D.'s use of biblical imagery see Hoffman 72–91; Miner 106–43; Zwicker 83–101; G. R. Levine, *ECS* i (1968) 291–312; L. M. Guilhamet, *SEL* ix (1969) 395–413; Dustin Griffin, *PQ* lvii (1978) 359–82. For the relation of *AA* to contemporary political pamphlets see W. K. Thomas, *The Crafting of 'Absalom and Achitophel'* (1978) and Phillip Harth, *Pen for a Party* (1993), the latter published too late to be used in this edition. Altogether the ideas, images and rhetoric of *AA* are much more indebted to contemporary polemics than has previously been realized, and the notes below illustrate this. However, it is not always possible, particularly with the many works dated 1681, to know whether a particular parallel constitutes a source for *AA*, an analogue to it, or a borrowing from it.

AA also draws upon classical poetry and history: the use of classical allusion is discussed by Reuben A. Brower in *ELH* xix (1952) 38–48; of Virgil by Brower, *PMLA* lv (1940) 132–3; of Virgil and Sallust by R. G. Peterson, *PMLA* lxxxii (1967) 236–44; and of Ovid by A. Poyet, *N&Q* ccxxvi (1981) 52–3. The roll call of champions on each side is a classical device, e.g. in *Aen.* vii. D.'s use of Milton, esp. *PL*, was pointed out by A. W. Verrall; Morris Freedman sketched the relationship between *AA* and Milton's epics in *JEGP* lvii (1958) 211–19; A. B. Chambers briefly noted the associations of Achitophel with the Miltonic Satan in *MLN* lxxiv (1959) 592–6. L. L. Brodwin (*JEGP* lxviii (1969) 24–44) discusses in detail the extensive parallels with *PL*, *PR* and *Samson Agonistes*, suggesting that the first part of *AA* (ll. 1–753) is structured on *PL* i, and that D.'s allusions ironically enlist Milton in the campaign against his own political heirs. A. D. Ferry in *Milton and the Miltonic Dryden* (1968) discusses the different kinds of Miltonic allusion and imitation which D. uses in *AA*, and suggests that the seductive rhetoric of Achitophel has a Satanic precedent. For a wider discussion of D.'s use of Milton see J. R. Mason.

The form and genre of *AA* have been much debated; affinities have been noted with epic, classical oration, and painting: for a survey and bibliography see A. E. Wallace Maurer, *PLL* xxvii (1991) 320–37.

Reception. Many readers annotated their copies with identifications of the characters and brief comments (particularly interesting marginalia from a Whig reader are on Folger Shakespeare Library, Washington, copy D2212). On 3 December 1681 the Duke of Beaufort wrote to his wife: 'I most humbly thanke you for the bookes I like Mr Dreyden very well, I hope hee will goe on wth it, tis somewhat obrupt as it is an I am sure hee hath left out some of the Kings best friends; I wish his patron may make out the caracter hee gives of him' (Badminton Muniments Room MS FmE 4/1/14; reference supplied by Michael Brennan). *AA* attracted a number of rejoinders: [Henry Care ?], *Towser The Second A Bull-Dog* (1681; Luttrell's copy dated 10 December); *Poetical Reflections on a Late Poem Entituled Absalom and Achitophel* (1681; Luttrell's copy dated 14 December); *A Panegyrick On the Author of Absolom and Achitophel, occasioned by his former writing of an Elegy in praise of Oliver Cromwell, lately reprinted* (1681; Luttrell's copies dated 19 and 20 December; reprinted 1682); Christopher Nesse, *A Whip for the Fools Back* (1681; Luttrell's copy dated 24 December), and *A Key (With the Whip) To open the Mystery & Iniquity of the Poem called, Absalom & Achitophel* (1682; Luttrell's copy dated 13 January); [Samuel Pordage], *Azaria and Hushai* (1682; Luttrell's copy dated 17 January; reprinted 1682); *Absolon's IX Worthies* ([1682]; Luttrell's copy dated 10 March); [Elkanah Settle], *Absalom Senior: or, Achitophel Transpros'd* (1682; Luttrell's copy dated 6 April; reprinted 1682). In *A Loyal Congratulation to the Right Honourable Anthony, Earl of Shaftsbury* (1681), published soon after the *ignoramus* verdict, the writer says: 'Let them with their Poetick Malice swell, / Falsly apply the Story, known so well, / Of *Absalom*, and of *Achitophel*'. There are also adverse comments on D. and *AA* in *Directions to Fame, about an Elegy On the Late Deceased Thomas Thynn, Esq.* (1682). 'A short Reply to *Absalon* and *Achitophel*' appeared in *Rome Rhym'd to Death* (1683). As *A Panegyrick* states, D.'s enemies attempted to embarrass him by reprinting his *Heroic Stanzas* as *An Elegy on the Usurper O.C. By the Author of Absalom and Achitophel, published to shew the Loyalty and Integrity of the Poet* (1681; two other reprints in 1682), with a self-incriminating postscript attributed to D. Two Latin translations of *AA* were published in 1682, one by William Coward, the other by Francis Atterbury and Francis Hickman. A few examples must suffice to illustrate the wide influence of the rhetoric of *AA*. The name 'Achitophel' is used in many pamphlets and poems. *A Congratulatory Poem Upon the Happy Arrival of . . . James Duke of York* (1682) 2 echoes *AA* ll. 82–4 and uses the names Absalom and Corah. The sermon *Ahitophel's Policy Defeated* (1683) applies the biblical story to the Rye House Plot. The prose attack on Shaftesbury in the form of a novel, *The Fugitive Statesman* (1683), makes substantial use of *AA* (see Paul Salzman, *Restoration* iv (1980) 11–13). The verse satire *Massinello* (1683) echoes *AA* verbally and structurally. Thomas D'Urfey's *The Malecontent* (1684) 22 echoes *AA* l. 547, and its roll call of heroes and villains also recalls *AA*, while other echoes of *AA* may be found in *The Polititian's Downfall; or Potapski's Arrival at the Netherlands* (1684).

Absalom and Achitophel
A Poem

——Si propius stes
Te capiet magis——

To the Reader

'Tis not my intention to make an apology for my poem:
some will think it needs no excuse, and others will receive
none. The design, I am sure, is honest, but he who draws
his pen for one party must expect to make enemies of the
5 other: for wit and fool are consequents of Whig and Tory,
and every man is a knave or an ass to the contrary side.
There's a treasury of merits in the fanatic church as well as
in the papist; and a pennyworth to be had of saintship,
honesty and poetry for the lewd, the factious and the
10 blockheads: but the longest chapter in Deuteronomy has

¶**67**. *Epigraph*. Si . . . magis] 'If you stand nearer, it will please you more'
(Horace, *Ars Poetica* ll. 361–2).
5. consequents] consequences.   *Whig and Tory*] This is D.'s first use of these
words. Both terms seem to have been applied to the emerging parties in the
first months of 1681, and popularized by L'Estrange in *The Observator* from 2
July 1681 onwards (R. Willman, *HJ* xvii (1974) 247–64, correcting *OED*).
Whig was originally applied to the Scottish rebels of 1648; *Tory* originally
applied to the dispossessed Irish who became outlaws, thence to any Irish
Catholic or Royalist in arms. Luttrell wrote in September 1681: 'Ever since
the dissolution of the last parliament, the presse has abounded with pamphlets of all sorts, so that there has been a violent paper scuffle; some, on the one
side, branding the two late parliaments, and standing very highly for the
church; the other side defending the parliament, and cryeing up (as they call
it) the true protestant religion, and opposing a popish successor: whence the
latter party have been called by the former, whigs, fanaticks, covenanters,
bromigham protestants, &c.; and the former are called by the latter, tories,
tantivies, Yorkists, high flown church men, &c.' (i 124).
7. treasury of merits] The Roman Catholic doctrine that the merits of Christ
and the saints are laid up as a treasury which can be drawn upon in aid of
ordinary sinners.   *fanatic*] extreme Protestant; dissenting.
10. the longest chapter in Deuteronomy] ch. xxviii, containing curses for disobedience to the law.

not curses enough for an Anti-Bromingham. My comfort
is, their manifest prejudice to my cause will render their
judgement of less authority against me. Yet if a poem
have a genius it will force its own reception in the world:
15 for there's a sweetness in good verse which tickles even
while it hurts; and no man can be heartily angry with him
who pleases him against his will. The commendation of
adversaries is the greatest triumph of a writer, because it
never comes unless extorted. But I can be satisfied on
20 more easy terms: if I happen to please the more moderate
sort I shall be sure of an honest party, and, in all probability, of the best judges, for the least concerned are
commonly the least corrupt; and, I confess, I have laid in
for those by rebating the satire (where justice would allow
25 it) from carrying too sharp an edge. They who can criti-
cize so weakly as to imagine I have done my worst may be
convinced, at their own cost, that I can write severely
with more ease than I can gently. I have but laughed at
some men's follies when I could have declaimed against
30 their vices; and other men's virtues I have commended as
freely as I have taxed their crimes. And now, if you are a
malicious reader, I expect you should return upon me that
I affect to be thought more impartial than I am. But if men
are not to be judged by their professions, God forgive you
35 Commonwealthsmen for professing so plausibly for the
government. You cannot be so unconscionable as to
charge me for not subscribing of my name, for that would
reflect too grossly upon your own party, who never dare,
though they have the advantage of a jury to secure them.
40 If you like not my poem, the fault may, possibly, be in my

11. enough] *Q*; *enow F*.   *Anti-Bromingham*] Tory; see 'Prologue to *The
Spanish Friar*' l. 11*n*.
14. genius] power appropriate for its task (*OED* 4).
15. sweetness] pleasing artistic effect (*OED* 5).
23. laid in] provided.
24. rebating] blunting (*OED* 4b).
34. professions] professed aims and beliefs.
35. Commonwealthsmen] Cp. l. 82*n*.
38–9. There had been several recent convictions of Whig writers and publishers, notably of the booksellers Francis Smith and Benjamin Harris; in
January 1681 'an indictment was brought against Francis Smith the elder, for
publishing a seditious paper entituled A Speech of a noble Peer, (pretended to

writing (though 'tis hard for an author to judge against
himself): but, more probably, 'tis in your morals, which
cannot bear the truth of it. The violent on both sides will
condemn the character of Absalom, as either too favoura-
45 bly or too hardly drawn. But they are not the violent
whom I desire to please. The fault, on the right hand, is to
extenuate, palliate and indulge; and, to confess freely, I
have endeavoured to commit it. Besides the respect which
I owe his birth, I have a greater for his heroic virtues, and
50 David himself could not be more tender of the young
man's life than I would be of his reputation. But since the
most excellent natures are always the most easy, and, as
being such, are the soonest perverted by ill counsels, especially when baited with fame and glory, 'tis no more a
55 wonder that he withstood not the temptations of Achitophel than it was for Adam not to have resisted the two
devils, the serpent and the woman. The conclusion of the
story I purposely forbore to prosecute, because I could not
obtain from myself to show Absalom unfortunate. The
60 frame of it was cut out but for a picture to the waist, and if
the draft be so far true, 'tis as much as I designed.

Were I the inventor, who am only the historian, I
should certainly conclude the piece with the reconcilement
of Absalom to David. And who knows but this may come
65 to pass? Things were not brought to an extremity where I
left the story. There seems yet to be room left for a composure; hereafter there may only be for pity. I have not so
much as an uncharitable wish against Achitophel, but am
content to be accused of a good natured error, and to hope
70 with Origen that the devil himself may, at last, be saved.

---

be a speech of the earl of Shaftesburies in the lords house;) but the jury
brought in an ignoramus thereon' (Luttrell i 64). London juries were selected
by the Whig sheriffs.
52. *easy*] easily persuaded, compliant (*OED* 12).
57. *conclusion*] In 2 Samuel xviii Absalom, riding on a mule, is caught in the
branches of an oak tree, and killed by Joab.
66. *composure*] agreement, settlement (*OED* 4).
70. *Origen*] The Alexandrian theologian and biblical critic (*c.* 185–*c.* 254); he
believed that the devil was a fallen angel, and that the evil powers had
retained freedom and reason; no being is totally depraved, and even Satan can
repent at the end. Cp. *RL* Preface ll. 48–50*n*.

For which reason, in this poem he is neither brought to set his house in order, nor to dispose of his person afterwards, as he in wisdom shall think fit. God is infinitely merciful, and his vicegerent is only not so because he is not infinite. 75 The true end of satire is the amendment of vices by correction. And he who writes honestly is no more an enemy to the offender than the physician to the patient when he prescribes harsh remedies to an inveterate disease: for those are only in order to prevent the chirur- 80 geon's work of an *ense rescindendum*, which I wish not to my very enemies. To conclude all, if the body politic have any analogy to the natural, in my weak judgement an Act of Oblivion were as necessary in a hot, distempered state as an opiate would be in a raging fever.

72. In 2 Samuel xvii 23 'when Ahitophel saw that his counsel was not followed, he . . . put his household in order, and hanged himself'.

74. *his vicegerent*] the King.

79. *chirurgeon*] surgeon.

80. ense rescindendum] *cuncta prius temptanda, sed inmedicabile curae / ense rescindendum, ne pars sincera trahatur* ('all means should first be tried, but what does not respond to treatment must be cut away with the knife, lest the untainted part also draw infection': Ovid, *Met.* i 190–1; the context is Jove's speech after the rebellion of the giants and the rejection of piety and justice by men).

Absalom and Achitophel
A Poem

In pious times, ere priestcraft did begin,
Before polygamy was made a sin,
When man on many multiplied his kind,

1–10. G. B. Evans suggests a parallel with Plutarch's life of Antony, translated by North: 'Nobility was multiplyed [cp. l. 3] amongst men by the Posterity of Kings, when they left of their seed in divers places: and that by this means his first Ancestor was begotten of *Hercules*, who had not left the hope and continuance of his Line and Posterity in the womb of one onely woman, fearing *Solons* Laws, or regarding the Ordinances of men touching the procreation of children: but that he gave it unto nature, and established the foundation of many noble Races and Families in divers places' (*Lives of the Noble Grecians and Romans* (1676) 767; *N & Q* ccxxxii (1987) 331).

1–6. Kinsley compares Donne: 'How happy were our Syres in ancient time, / Who held plurality of loves no crime! / With them it was accounted charity / To stirre up race of all indifferently;' ('Variety' ll. 37–40). Cp. also Don John in Otway's *Don Carlos* (1676): 'How vainly would dull Moralists Impose / Limits on Love, whose Nature brooks no Laws: / Love is a God, and like a God should be / Inconstant: with unbounded liberty / Rove as he list.– . . . How wretched then's the man who . . . Confin'd to one, / Is but at best a pris'ner on a Throne.' (III i 1–5, 18–20); for another parallel see ll. 19–20*n*.

1. This is an example of D.'s ambiguous chronology and selective use of biblical material, since the priestly caste originated with Aaron, long before David (Barbara K. Lewalski, *ELN* iii (1965) 30).   *priestcraft*] (i) the profession of priesthood; (ii) the deceitful cunning of priests. This is the *OED*'s first example, but Mark Goldie cites an instance in James Harrington's *Pian Piano* (1657), and argues that it is part of the vocabulary of Whig anticlericalism; he suggests that in *AA* D. uses it to allude to 'the scoffing Whig's habit of treating the laws of marriage as amongst priestly inventions' (*Political Discourse in Early Modern Britain*, edited by Nicholas Phillipson and Quentin Skinner (1993) 216–18). It may therefore be an instance not of D.'s anticlericalism, but of his habit of turning his opponents' vocabulary against them.

2. Polygamy was practised in early Judaism, but monogamy had become the norm by the time of Christ. Milton and others had advocated polygamy during the Commonwealth (Christopher Hill, *Milton and the English Revolution* (1977) 136–9, 287–8). D. often discussed the relation between nature and law in the field of sexual behaviour, e.g. in *Aureng-Zebe* IV i 71–167; *Oedipus, passim*; 'The Cock and the Fox' ll. 56–64 (q.v. for its political allusions); and 'Cinyras and Myrrha' (on which see David Hopkins, *MLR* lxxx (1985) 786–801).

Ere one to one was cursedly confined;
5   When nature prompted, and no law denied
Promiscuous use of concubine and bride;
Then Israel's monarch, after heaven's own heart,
His vigorous warmth did variously impart
To wives and slaves: and wide as his command
10   Scattered his maker's image through the land.
Michal, of royal blood, the crown did wear,
A soil ungrateful to the tiller's care:
Not so the rest, for several mothers bore
To godlike David several sons before;
15   But since like slaves his bed they did ascend
No true succession could their seed attend.
Of all this numerous progeny was none
So beautiful, so brave as Absolon:

4. Cp. 'Since Liberty, Nature for all has design'd, / A pox on the Fool who to one is confin'd' (Shadwell, *The Libertine* (1676); iii 43). Winn (*When Beauty* 17) notes that D.'s line is echoed by Creech in his translation of Lucretius (1682) 171: 'When One to One confin'd in chast embrace'; cp. ll. 53–6n.
6. *Promiscuous*] without distinction (*OED* 2); English law, however, distinguished between the children of a wife and those of a mistress.
7. *Israel's monarch*] Here Charles II. King David had several wives, including Bathsheba, whose previous husband Uriah had been killed at David's instigation (2 Samuel xi). Samuel told Saul that 'the Lord hath sought him a man after his own heart' (1 Samuel xiii 14).
11. *Michal*] Catherine of Braganza (1638–1705), the Portuguese princess who married Charles in 1662. She had no children. The biblical Michal was Saul's daughter, and 'had no child unto the day of her death' (2 Samuel vi 23).
12. The image was a commonplace: cp. Shakespeare, *Sonnets* iii 5–6. *ungrateful*] not responding to cultivation (*OED* 1c, first example; a sense of the Latin *ingratus*). Cp. ground 'ungrateful to the Plough' ('The Second Book of the *Georgics*' l. 262).
13–14. Charles had fourteen acknowledged illegitimate children (GEC, *Complete Peerage*, 13 vols (1910–40) vi 706–8). His affection for them was well known.
17–18. Cp. 'In all the kingdoms of the east not one / Was found, for beauty, like to Absalon' (Aylett 2; Schilling).
18–30. *Absolon*] A variant seventeenth-century spelling which D. uses for the rhyme; it is kept here in the form given in *F*. James Scott (1649–85), son of Charles II and Lucy Walter; created Duke of Monmouth in 1663. 2 Samuel iv 25 says that 'in all Israel there was none to be so much praised as Absalom for his beauty: from the sole of his feet even to the crown of his head there was no blemish in him'. Evelyn wrote of Monmouth that he was 'the darling of

Whether, inspired by some diviner lust,
20   His father got him with a greater gust,

---

his Father, and the Ladys, being extraordinarily handsome, and adroit: an
excellent souldier, & dauncer, a favorite of the people, of an Easy nature,
debauched by lust, seduc'd by crafty knaves' (*Diary* 15 July 1685). Monmouth served at sea in 1664–6; he commanded the English troops fighting
with the French against the Dutch in 1672–3, and those fighting with the
Dutch against the French in 1678. In 1679 he defeated the Scottish rebels at
the battle of Bothwell Bridge. His military career was characterized by his
personal bravery. In 1678–9 Monmouth became a focus for opposition to the
court, and was sent to Holland by Charles in September 1679, but returned in
November, probably at the instance of Shaftesbury. He received an enthusiastic welcome from the people of London, but incurred the wrath of the
King, who stripped him of all his posts and pensions. After rumours that the
King had been married to Lucy Walter, and that Monmouth was therefore
legitimate, Charles issued a declaration on 2 June 1680 that he had never been
married to anyone but the Queen. In July 1680 Monmouth embarked on a
popular tour of the West Country (see ll. 729–44*nn*); in November he voted
for the Exclusion Bill, making a speech about the dangers to Charles's life,
which caused the King to remark, 'The kiss of Judas!' (Haley 602). See
further Elizabeth D'Oyley, *James Duke of Monmouth* (1938). D. had dedicated
The Indian Emperor (1667) to the Duchess of Monmouth, who acted with the
Duke in a performance of the play at court in 1668 (Winn 188); D. dedicated
Tyrannic Love (1670) to the Duke, saying: 'Heaven has already taken care to
form you for an Heroe. You have all the advantages of Mind and Body, and
an Illustrious Birth, conspiring to render you an extraordinary Person . . .
Youth, Beauty, and Courage (all which you possess in the height of their
perfection) are the most desirable gifts of Heaven: and Heaven is never
prodigal of such Treasures, but to some uncommon purpose. So goodly a
Fabrick was never framed by an Almighty Architect for a vulgar Guest. He
shewed the value which he set upon your Mind, when he took care to have it
so nobly and so beautifully lodg'd. To a graceful fashion and deportment of
Body, you have joyned a winning Conversation, and an easie Greatness,
derived to you from the best, and best-belov'd of Princes' (*Works* x 107–8). In
The Vindication . . . of . . . The Duke of Guise (1683) D. acknowledges his
obligations to Monmouth for 'his Countenance, his Favour, his good Word,
and his Esteem; all which I have likewise had in a greater measure from his
excellent Dutchess, the Patroness of my poor unworthy Poetry' (20).
19–20. Cp. the King's illegitimate son Don John in Otway's *Don Carlos*: 'My
Glorious Father got me in his heat, / When all he did was eminently great' (II
i 10–11); cp. ll. 1–6*n*.
19. by] Q; *with* F.
20. gust] keen relish (*OED* 4).

Or that his conscious destiny made way
By manly beauty to imperial sway.
Early in foreign fields he won renown,
With kings and states allied to Israel's crown:
25 In peace the thoughts of war he could remove,
And seemed as he were only born for love.
Whate'er he did was done with so much ease,
In him alone 'twas natural to please:
His motions all accompanied with grace,
30 And paradise was opened in his face.
With secret joy indulgent David viewed
His youthful image in his son renewed;
To all his wishes nothing he denied,
And made the charming Annabel his bride.
35 What faults he had (for who from faults is free?)
His father could not, or he would not see.
Some warm excesses which the law forbore
Were construed youth that purged by boiling o'er;
And Amnon's murther by a specious name
40 Was called a just revenge for injured fame.
Thus praised and loved the noble youth remained,

21. *conscious*] aware of itself (*OED* 10).

30. Cp. 'Paradis stood formed in hire yën' (Chaucer, *Troilus and Criseyde* v
817); Dante, *Paradiso* xviii 21; Samuel Pordage, *Mundorum Explicatio* (1661)
77: 'Paradise doth open in the heart'. D.'s line was parodied as 'For Baud is
always open'd in thy Face' in 'M^rs. Nelly's Complaint, 1682' (BodL MS Firth
c 15 p. 131].

34. *Annabel*] Anne, Countess of Buccleuch (1651–1732), who married Monmouth in 1663. Shadwell in *The Medal of John Bayes* (1682) 9–10 says that the
Duchess's patronage brought D. the favour of the court, and that his only
gratitude to her was to traduce her husband. See further Winn (*When Beauty*
408–11).

38. *construed*] accented on the first syllable until the nineteenth century
(*OED*).   *purged*] purified itself (*OED* 7, first example).

39–40. *Amnon's murther . . . injured fame*] Amnon's murder was arranged by
Absalom to avenge the rape of his sister Tamar by Amnon (2 Samuel xiii).
There are two possible contemporary applications: (i) In the early hours of 26
February 1671 a beadle named Peter Vernell was murdered in a brothel in
Whetstones Park by the Dukes of Monmouth, Albemarle and Somerset, and
Viscount Dunbar; they received pardons, but the affair became a scandal: see
'On the Three Dukes Killing the Beadle' and 'Upon the Beadle' in *POAS* i
172–6. 'Upon the Beadle' ll. 43–54 presents Monmouth as being enraged by
the beadle's effrontery in opposing him. (ii) A savage, but not fatal, attack on

While David undisturbed in Sion reigned.
But life can never be sincerely blessed:
Heaven punishes the bad, and proves the best.
45   The Jews, a headstrong, moody, murmuring race
As ever tried th' extent and stretch of grace,
God's pampered people, whom, debauched with
    ease,
No king could govern, nor no god could please
(Gods they had tried of every shape and size

Sir John Coventry was carried out on 21 December 1670 by the King's Horseguards, of which Monmouth was captain; he is blamed for the assault in 'A Song' in BodL MS Don.b.8 pp. 210–11. In this case the 'injured fame' would be that of Charles II: when a proposal in the Commons for a tax on the playhouses was objected to because 'the Players were the King's servants, and a part of his pleasure', Coventry asked 'If the King's pleasure lay among the men or women Players?' (Grey i 332). Kinsley (*RES* vi (1955) 292) notes that Coventry was attacked on his way home from a tavern, while Amnon was murdered when he was 'merry with wine'; neither Absalom nor Monmouth actually took part in the assault, but exhorted their followers to action; and both David and Charles condemned the offence. It seems impossible to choose between these two explanations, both of which would have occurred to contemporaries.

42. Sion] a biblical name for Jerusalem; here applied to London.

43. sincerely] completely, purely (*OED* 4b).

44. proves] tests.

45. The Jews] The English. Supporters of the Commonwealth had often represented England as an elect nation, a second Israel (Zwicker 84; and Zwicker in *Millenarianism and Messianism . . . 1650–1800*, edited by Richard H. Popkin (1988) 42–7). Sir Edward Turner had used this parallel to describe the ingratitude of the English people: 'The *Children of Israel*, when they were in the Wilderness, though they were fed with Gods own hand . . . yet they surfeited, and murmured, and rebelled against *Moses*. The same unthankfull spirit dwelt in this Nation for divers years last past; the men of that Age were weary of the Government' (*The Several Speeches of Sr. Edward Turner Kt. Speaker of the honourable House of Commons* (1661) 7). Some writers at the Restoration had compared those who were responsible for Charles I's execution with the Jews who called for Jesus's crucifixion (see Jonathan Sawday, *SC* vii (1992) 192–3).

47. Cp. 'no Disease / Is like a Surfeit of Luxurious Ease' (*A Dialogue Between the Ghosts of the Two last Parliaments* (1681)).   *pampered*] Cp. the quotation from *The Character of a Leading Petitioner* (1681) in ll. 51–6n.   *debauched*] (i) corrupted morally (*OED* 2); (ii) seduced from proper allegiance (*OED* 1), as in 'the People are debauched with false Representations, and Rebellious Principles' (*The Character of a Rebellion* (1681) 4).

50   That god-smiths could produce, or priests devise);
      These Adam-wits, too fortunately free
      Began to dream they wanted liberty,

50. god-smiths] apparently D.'s coinage.

51–6. In the Epistle Dedicatory to *All for Love* (1678) D. expresses 'a loathing to that specious Name of a *Republick*: that mock-appearance of a Liberty, where all who have not part in the Government, are Slaves: and Slaves they are of a viler note than such as are Subjects to an absolute Dominion. For no Christian Monarchy is so absolute, but 'tis circumscrib'd with Laws. . . . And yet there are not wanting Malecontents amongst us, who surfeiting themselves on too much happiness, wou'd perswade the People that they might be happier by a change. 'Twas indeed the policy of their old Forefather, when himself was fallen from the station of Glory, to seduce Mankind into the same Rebellion with him, by telling him he might yet be freer than he was: that is, more free than his Nature wou'd allow, or (if I may so say) than God cou'd make him. We have already all the Liberty which Free-born Subjects can enjoy; and all beyond it is but License' (*Works* xiii 6–7); cp. *Astraea Redux* ll. 43–8 (Kinsley). Sir Edward Turner said of the English under the Commonwealth: 'Liberty they called it, but it was *Libertas quidlibet audendi* [a liberty of daring to do what they liked] (*Several Speeches* 8). Sir Robert Filmer objected to those 'who magnify liberty as if the height of human felicity were only to be found in it, never remembering that the desire of liberty was the cause of the fall of Adam' (*Patriarcha* (1680), edited by Peter Laslett (1949) 53). The charge that the Whigs are pursuing a specious liberty is common in contemporary Tory pamphlets, e.g.: 'I chang'd True Freedom for the Name of Free, / And grew Seditious for Variety' (*A Dialogue Between the Ghosts of the Two last Parliaments* (1681)); 'How greadily this Petitional *Animal* catcheth at the seeming gilded bait of that imaginary *Liberty* that betrays him; He repines when he's hungry, and murmurs when he's full, no sooner has a *Moses* redeliver'd him from slavery, and pamper'd him with the *Manna* of peace and plenty, but the High-fled Blockhead grows senseless of his happiness, and industriously contrives for misery and want' (*The Character of a Leading Petitioner* (1681) 1–2); 'where he can find no real Faults, he Feigns imaginary ones . . . He Amuses the freest Nation in the *Universe*, with wild Rumours and extravagant Apprehensions of *Slavery*' (*The Character of a Disbanded Courtier* (1681) 1). For discussions of the Whig rhetoric of 'liberty' see Ashcraft, *passim*, but esp. 208–14, and Tim Harris in *The Politics of Religion in Restoration England*, edited by Tim Harris, Paul Seaward and Mark Goldie (1990) 217–41.

51. Adam-wits] Those who, like Adam, were not satisfied with their God-given freedom, and rebelled against their imagined constraint. For the image of the Fall cp. ll. 202–3*n*.

52. wanted] lacked.

And when no rule, no precedent was found
Of men, by laws less circumscribed and bound
55 They led their wild desires to woods and caves,
And thought that all but savages were slaves.
They who when Saul was dead, without a blow,
Made foolish Ishbosheth the crown forgo,
Who banished David did from Hebron bring
60 And with a general shout proclaimed him King:
Those very Jews, who, at their very best
Their humour more than loyalty expressed,
Now wondered why so long they had obeyed
An idol monarch which their hands had made;
65 Thought they might ruin him they could create,

53–6. Echoes Lucretius's account of primitive man: *nemora atque cavos montis silvasque colebant . . . nec commune bonum poterant spectare, neque ullis / moribus inter se scibant nec legibus uti* (*De Rerum Natura* v 955, 958–9: 'they dwelt in the woods and forests and mountain caves, . . . they could not look to the common good, they did not know how to govern their intercourse by custom and law'). Cp. also *Aen.* v 677–8, describing the flight of the women who had madly burnt Aeneas's ships: *silvasque et sicubi concava furtim / saxa petunt* ('Dispers'd, to Woods and Caverns take their flight': 'The Fifth Book of the *Aeneis*' l. 885).

56. See *Astraea Redux* ll. 46–8n. D. can also imagine savages as innocent and noble (perhaps following Montaigne in *Des Cannibales*), as in *1 Conquest of Granada* I i 203–9, which is probably the first occurrence in English of the phrase 'the noble savage', anticipating Rousseau.

57–60. After his death, Saul was succeeded as King of Israel by his son Ishbosheth, who ruled for two years, while David became King of Judah and ruled in Hebron for seven and a half years; after the murder of Ishbosheth the tribes of Israel came to David in Hebron and anointed him King of Israel (2 Samuel ii–v). Oliver Cromwell was succeeded as Lord Protector in September 1658 by his son Richard, who ruled for eight months; Charles II was recalled from exile in Holland in May 1660.

58. Ishbosheth] Q; Isbosheth F.

59. Hebron] Either Scotland (as in *2AA* l. 320), since Charles was crowned King of Scots on 1 January 1651, nine and a half years before his recall to England; or (stressing '*from* Hebron') Brussels, whence Charles was summoned in 1660, though his place of exile is called 'Gath' at l. 264.

62. humour] temporary mood (*OED* 5); whim, caprice (*OED* 6).

64. idol] The Jews were forbidden to worship idols (Exodus xx 4). *which their hands had made]* Whereas early Stuart political theory had insisted that kings were appointed by God and were not accountable to the people (see James I, *The Trew Law of Free Monarchies* (1598)), the theories which were

Or melt him to that golden calf, a state.
But these were random bolts: no formed design
Nor interest made the factious crowd to join;
The sober part of Israel, free from stain,
70 Well knew the value of a peaceful reign,
And looking backward with a wise affright
Saw seams of wounds dishonest to the sight;
In contemplation of whose ugly scars
They cursed the memory of civil wars.
75 The moderate sort of men, thus qualified,
Inclined the balance to the better side,
And David's mildness managed it so well
The bad found no occasion to rebel.
But when to sin our biased nature leans,
80 The careful devil is still at hand with means,
And providently pimps for ill desires:
The Good Old Cause revived a plot requires;

prevalent during the Commonwealth tended to argue that rulers were created by the people, who transferred their rights to them (thus Hobbes, *Leviathan* (1651)) or entrusted them with authority which could be taken back by the people if the rulers abused their trust (thus Milton, *The Tenure of Kings and Magistrates* (1649)); cp. ll. 409–12.

66. golden calf] While Moses was receiving instructions from God on Mt Sinai, the Israelites built a golden calf, which they worshipped (Exodus xxxii).   *state*] republic (*OED* 28b).

67. bolts] shots; ventures (*OED* 1b).

68. crowd] For the importance of the London crowd in contemporary politics, see Harris, *London Crowds*.

71–4. The parallel between 1641 and 1681 was frequently made on all sides. *The Weekly Discovery of the Mystery of Iniquity* recounted events in England in 1641 in thirty issues from February to August 1681, while 'Theophilus Rationalis' compared the 1640s and 1680s parliaments in *Multum in Parvo* (1681).

71. affright] fear, terror (*OED* 2).

72. seams] the joining of the edges of a wound by sewing (*OED* 1b).   *dishonest*] hideous (*OED* 3); from *inhonesto vulnere* (*Aen.* vi 497; cp. 'The Sixth Book of the *Aeneis*' l. 668; Kinsley).

75. qualified] moderated (*OED* 8); calmed (*OED* 9); brought into a proper condition (*OED* 10).

79. biased] the image is from the bias in a bowl which makes it run in a curve away from the straight path; cp. *MF* l. 189.

82. The Good Old Cause] The Commonwealth. The Whigs were often accused of working for the restoration of a republic. Shaftesbury himself wanted a monarchy rather than a republic, but said in the Privy Council on 7

Plots, true or false, are necessary things
To raise up commonwealths and ruin kings.
85   Th' inhabitants of old Jerusalem
Were Jebusites, the town so called from them,
And theirs the native right——
But when the chosen people grew more strong,
The rightful cause at length became the wrong,
90   And every loss the men of Jebus bore
They still were thought God's enemies the more.
Thus worn and weakened, well or ill content,
Submit they must to David's government:
Impoverished, and deprived of all command,
95   Their taxes doubled as they lost their land,
And, what was harder yet to flesh and blood,

June 1679 that 'if the King so governed as that his estate might with safety be transmitted to his son, as it was by his father to him, and he might enjoy the known rights and liberties of the subjects, he would rather be under kingly government, but if he could not be satisfied of that he declared he was for a Commonwealth' (Haley 536; cp. 312, 517). In *The Waking Vision* (1681) Shaftesbury (as 'Achitophel') boasts that he 'fought and prosper'd in the Good Old Cause', and says that to stir up fears of Popery 'of a Bad Old Cause a Good one makes' (ll. 24, 63; *POAS* ii 420–1). Cp. the title of *The Good Old Cause Revived* (MS date 2 February 1680 on BL copy).

83. Plots] (i) The Popish Plot of 1678–9 (see l. 108*n*); (ii) the alleged Popish Plot of 1640, in which the Jesuits were supposedly plotting to kill Charles I and bring England under the Church of Rome; this allegation strengthened suspicion of Charles I in the Commons (see *A True Narrative of the Popish-Plot against King Charles I. and the Protestant Religion* (1680); Caroline Hibbard, *Charles I and the Popish Plot* (1983)).

86. Jebusites] Roman Catholics (perhaps with a pun on 'Jesuits'). 'As for the Jebusites the inhabitants of Jerusalem, the children of Judah could not drive them out: but the Jebusites dwell with the children of Judah at Jerusalem unto this day' (Joshua xv 63). Jerusalem is called Jebus in Judges xix 10–11 and 1 Chronicles xi 4. D. also recalls England's Catholic past in *His Majesties Declaration Defended* (1681; *Works* xvii 210).

87. An imitation of the Virgilian hemistich (Brower); but in his 'Dedication of the *Aeneis*' (1697) D. argues that Virgil's half-lines were simply unfinished, not deliberate effects (*Works* v 332).

88. the chosen people] Protestants, recalling Calvin's doctrine of election.

94–5. Under an Act of James I the crown had power to seize two-thirds of recusants' estates; the Test Act of 1673 barred all who were not Anglican communicants from holding office under the crown; and Catholics paid double taxes.

Their gods disgraced, and burned like common
   wood.
This set the heathen priesthood in a flame,
For priests of all religions are the same:
100   Of whatsoe'er descent their godhead be,
Stock, stone or other homely pedigree,
In his defence his servants are as bold
As if he had been born of beaten gold.
The Jewish rabbins, though their enemies,
105   In this conclude them honest men and wise;
For 'twas their duty, all the learnèd think,
T' espouse his cause by whom they eat and drink.
From hence began that plot, the nation's curse,
Bad in itself, but represented worse;
110   Raised in extremes, and in extremes decried,
With oaths affirmed, with dying vows denied;
Not weighed or winnowed by the multitude,

97. There was widespread destruction of religious images, particularly
wooden statues, at the Reformation.

101. Stock] block of wood (*OED* 1b).

104. Jewish rabbins] Anglican theologians.

108. plot] The Popish Plot. On 13 August 1678 Charles was informed by
Israel Tonge of a plot to assassinate him; Tonge was working in an uneasy
alliance with Titus Oates (see ll. 632–81*nn*). The allegations widened to
implicate many Catholics in a conspiracy against the King and the Protestant
religion, masterminded by the Jesuits. Most of the allegations were lies, but
there were enough correct details and lucky guesses for the whole story to
alarm a nation always susceptible to rumour and afraid of a Catholic coup.
Oates was examined by the Privy Council on 28–9 September, and when
Parliament assembled on 21 October it established committees to investigate.
The papers of Edward Coleman, secretary to the Duchess of York (and
previously to the Duke) were seized and proved highly suspicious: he was
tried for treason and executed on 3 December 1678. Altogether some 35
people had been executed by July 1681. Charles told Burnet in December
1678 that 'the greatest part of the evidence was a contrivance. But he suspected some had set on Oates, and instructed him, and named the earl of
Shaftesbury' (ii 179). Shaftesbury is unlikely to have manipulated Oates
directly, but the affair suited his political purposes. See further J. P. Kenyon,
The Popish Plot (1972).

111. Oates gave his evidence on oath to the Privy Council, to Sir Edmund
Berry Godfrey, and at the trials; many of those convicted protested their
innocence at their execution.

But swallowed in the mass, unchewed and crude.
Some truth there was, but dashed and brewed with
    lies,
115 To please the fools and puzzle all the wise.
Succeeding times did equal folly call
Believing nothing, or believing all.
Th' Egyptian rites the Jebusites embraced,
Where gods were recommended by their taste:
120 Such savoury deities must needs be good
As served at once for worship and for food.
By force they could not introduce these gods,
For ten to one in former days was odds,
So fraud was used (the sacrificer's trade):
125 Fools are more hard to conquer than persuade.
Their busy teachers mingled with the Jews,
And raked for converts ev'n the court and stews;
Which Hebrew priests the more unkindly took
Because the fleece accompanies the flock.
130 Some thought they God's anointed meant to slay
By guns, invented since full many a day:
Our author swears it not, but who can know
How far the devil and Jebusites may go?
This plot, which failed for want of common sense,

113. *crude*] raw, uncooked (*OED* 2).

114. *dashed*] mingled (*OED* 5).   *brewed*] diluted (*OED* 2).

118–21. Egyptian] Catholic French. D. also alludes to the Egyptians' animal gods derided by Juvenal (*Satire* xv 1–13). The Catholic doctrine of transubstantiation was often mocked during the Popish Plot trials, e.g. by Chief Justice Scroggs: 'They eat their God, they kill their King, and saint the murderer!' (Kenyon 146); cp. John Oldham, *Satyrs upon the Jesuits* (1681) iv 259–72; *Poems* 52.

120–1. Such . . . As] i.e. 'deities of such a kind which'.

121. As] Q; And F.

123. ten to one] In the mid-seventeenth century there were roughly 60,000 Catholics in England and Wales out of a population of about 5 million, i.e. 1 per cent; only in Lancashire and Monmouth did the proportion approach 10 per cent (John Bossy, *The English Catholic Community 1570–1850* (1975) 188–9, 404–5).   *odds*] balance of advantage, superior position (*OED* 4).

127. stews] brothels.

130–1. According to Oates's and Tonge's first allegations, the Benedictine Thomas Pickering and a Jesuit lay brother, John Grove, had vowed to shoot Charles.

135　Had yet a deep and dangerous consequence:
　　For, as when raging fevers boil the blood
　　The standing lake soon floats into a flood,
　　And every hostile humour which before
　　Slept quiet in its channels, bubbles o'er;
140　So several factions from this first ferment
　　Work up to foam, and threat the government.
　　Some by their friends, more by themselves thought
　　　wise,
　　Opposed the power to which they could not rise.
　　Some had in courts been great, and thrown from
　　　thence
145　Like fiends, were hardened in impenitence.
　　Some by their monarch's fatal mercy grown

136–9. For the disease imagery cp. 'I can by no ways approve of those of our Physitians who use such violent means to wake us out of our Security, as if there were no Cure for a Lethargy but casting us into a Raving Frenzy. And indeed such has been the Physick of our State Mountebanks . . . since they have possest the people with so desperate a madness' (*An Answer to a late Pamphlet; Entituled, A Character of a Popish Successor* (1681) 2); and in *The Badger in the Fox-Trap* [July 1681], Shaftesbury is made to say that some call him 'the Scab, from whence the Infection Breeds' (1). Cp. Theophilus Rationalis, *Multum in Parvo* (1681): 'To see how boldly you infect the blood / Of Prince and People, which much like a floud / Of lofty Billows, purposely to drown / Our Ship, our Pilate, and our Captains Crown'. For the political connotations of the image of a river overflowing its banks cp. Denham, *Cooper's Hill* ll. 173–6.

137. lake] channel of water (*OED sb.*³).　　*floats*] undulates.

138. humour] one of the fluids thought to determine physical and mental qualities.

140. several factions] See ll. 491–4*n.*　　*ferment*] The noun was accented on the second syllable (cp. Jonson, *The Alchemist* II ii 3).

141. work up to] are agitated into (*OED* 39l, first example, but cp. *OED* 34 where a stormy sea 'works').

144–5. Homer's story of how Hephaistos was thrown from heaven by Zeus (*Iliad* i 591–5) is echoed in Milton's account of the fallen angels throwing themselves over the walls of heaven (*PL* vi 864–6; cp. i 740–2).

146. fatal mercy] For Charles II's possibly unwise tendency to show mercy to his opponents cp. *Threnodia Augustalis* l. 86*n.*

From pardoned rebels, kinsmen to the throne,
Were raised in power and public office high—
Strong bands, if bands ungrateful men could tie.
150   Of these the false Achitophel was first:
A name to all succeeding ages cursed.

150–99. Achitophel] Anthony Ashley Cooper (1621–83) fought initially on
the royalist side in the Civil War, but went over to Parliament in 1644, and
held various military and civil posts in Dorset. In January 1652 he was
appointed to Parliament's commission on legal reform, and in July 1653 was
elected to the Council of State, which he left in January 1655. He rejected
overtures from Charles II, then in exile. The recalled Rump Parliament
elected him to the new Council of State in May 1659, and he was instrumental in persuading Monck to force it to readmit the secluded members. Early in
1660 he began to incline towards the restoration of the monarchy, and re-
sponded positively to an emissary from Charles in April. He sat in the
Convention Parliament as Member of Parliament for Wiltshire, and was one
of twelve commissioners sent to The Hague to invite Charles to return. He
was appointed a Privy Councillor, and in April 1661 created Lord Ashley and
appointed Chancellor of the Exchequer; in May 1667 he became one of the
commissioners of the Treasury. He was created Earl of Shaftesbury in March
1672, and in September made President of the new Council of Trade and
Plantations, an area in which he already had private interests (cp. 'Prologue to
the King and Queen' ll. 2–5*n*); in November he became Lord Chancellor, but
was dismissed on 9 November 1673. Thereafter he was a member of the
opposition, or 'country party'. In February 1677 Shaftesbury was one of four
lords (including Buckingham) who argued that Parliament stood dissolved,
as it had been prorogued for more than twelve months, but the House of
Lords disagreed and committed all four to the Tower; Shaftesbury was not
released until February 1678. He was one of the organizers of the Exclusion
Bills, and was not converted when the King attempted to defuse the opposition by bringing Shaftesbury and some others back into the Privy Council.
The parliamentary attempts to exclude James from the succession were accompanied by vigorous propaganda which Shaftesbury encouraged, assisted
by John Locke. After the sudden dissolution of the Oxford Parliament in
March 1681 the Whigs' position weakened, and Shaftesbury was arrested on
a charge of high treason on 2 July. The jury at the preliminary hearing on 24
November refused to find a true bill, and he was released on bail (Monmouth
offering surety, which was refused). The year 1682 saw the struggle for
control of the City of London (cp. 'Prologue and Epilogues to *The Duke of
Guise*'), and the Rye House Plot to assassinate Charles laid by Shaftesbury's
associates. In danger of arrest, he went into hiding and left secretly for
Holland in late November 1682. He died in Amsterdam on 21 January 1683.
See Haley *passim*.

For close designs and crooked counsels fit,
Sagacious, bold, and turbulent of wit;
Restless, unfixed in principles and place,
155 In power unpleased, impatient of disgrace.

152–5. This is a partisan view, shared by the author of *The Character of a Disbanded Courtier* (1681; second edition 1682): He 'thought all the Favors, and Honours, he enjoy'd, were less then the reward of his Merit; that Thought puff'd him up with Pride, such a sort of Pride, as is usually attended with an irrecoverable fall . . . like that of *Lucifer*, his Predecessor. . . . He would fain be reputed as constant as the *Sun*; and yet this Age has produced nothing beneath the *Moon*, more fickle and variable, for he never was, and 'tis like never will be true to anything; save onely the Eternal Resolution of doing Mischeif' (1–3; *Works*). L'Estrange agreed: 'his very *Inclination* prompted him to *Mischief*, Even for *Mischiefs sake*. It was his *Way*, and his *Humour*, to *Tear All to pieces*, where he could not be the *First Man in Bus'ness Himself*. And yet All this while, his *Faculty*, was rather a *Quirking* way of *Wit*, then a *Solidity* of *Judgment*; and he was *much Happier* at *Pulling-down*, then at *Building-up*. In One Word; He was a man of *Subtlety*, not of *Depth*; and his *Talent* was *Fancy*, rather than *Wisdom*' (*A Brief History of the Times* (1687) i 131–2). But Shaftesbury's own view of himself was of 'one that, in all these variety of changes of this last Age, was never known to be either bought or frighted out of his publick Principles' (*A Letter from a Person of Quality, to his Friend in the Country* (1675) 9; probably written by Locke at Shaftesbury's direction). A supporter concurred: his 'Policy was always founded upon the solid Basis of Piety and Judgment; upon which firm Foundation he endeavour'd to raise the admirable superstructure of Royal Government in the Prince, free from all manner of arbitrary severity, and a willing subjection in the People, without any kind of force or compunction; so uniting the Interest of the Governour with that of the governed' (*Rawleigh Redivivus* (1683) 4; *Works*). The latter view is probably closer to the truth.
152–3. Echoes John Caryll, *Naboth's Vinyard* (1679): 'nature furnish'd him with parts and wit, / For bold attempts and deep intriguing fit' (ll. 145–6, on Scroggs; *POAS* ii 88).
152. counsels] Q; Counsell F.
153. Peterson suggests an echo of Sallust's character of Catiline: *animus audax, subdolus, varius, cuius rei lubet simulator ac dissimulator* ('a bold spirit, crafty, changeable, able to simulate and dissimulate'; *Bellum Catilinae* 5); cp. l. 545n.
154. principles] Q; Principle F.

A fiery soul, which working out its way ⎫
Fretted the pigmy body to decay,   ⎬
And o'erinformed the tenement of clay. ⎭

156–8. Cp. Carew: 'The purest Soule that e're was sent / Into a clayie
tenement / Inform'd this dust, but the weake mold / Could the great guest no
longer hold' (Second 'Epitaph on the Lady Mary Villiers' ll. 1–4). J. D. Jump
also cites uses of 'tenement of clay' in Thomas Philipott, *Poems* (1646) 6, 11
(*N & Q* cxcvi (1951) 535–6). Winn (311–12) suggests that D. had previously
caricatured Shaftesbury in the character of Creon in *Oedipus* (1679): '*Creon.*
Am I to blame if Nature threw my body / In so perverse a mould? . . . to
revenge / Her bungled work she stampt my mind more fair: / And as from
Chaos, huddled and deform'd, / The God strook fire, and lighted up the
Lamps / That beautify the sky, so he inform'd / This ill-shap'd body with a
daring soul: / . . . *Euryd.* No; thou art all one errour; soul and body; / . . . Thy
crooked mind within hunch'd out thy back' (I i 145–59). Mulgrave in *An
Essay upon Satire* (circulating in MS, 1679) writes of Shaftesbury: 'His limbs
are crippl'd and his body shakes, / Yet his hard mind, which all this bustle
makes, / No pity of his poor companion takes. / What gravity can hold from
laughing out / To see that drag his feeble legs about / . . . Yet this false
comfort never gives him o'er, / That whilst he creeps his vig'rous thoughts
can soar' (ll. 104–14; *POAS* i 406–7). Cp. also *The Cabal* (in MS, 1680):
'Double with head to tail he crawls apart, / His body's th' emblem of his
double heart' (ll. 87–8; *POAS* ii 331); *The Badger in the Fox-Trap*: 'A perfect
Monster both in Soul and Body' (1); and D'Urfey, *The Progress of Honesty*
16–17. Shaftesbury was short in stature, and suffered from poor health
throughout his life; in June 1668 he was operated on at the direction of his
friend John Locke for a hydatid cyst of the liver. D. drew attention to
Shaftesbury's body again in *Albion and Albanius* (1685) III ii *s.d.* (*Works* xv 53).
The emphasis on Shaftesbury's deformity (and that of Oates in ll. 646–9)
suggests that these opposition leaders will deform the body politic and rival
the sacred body of the King (see Paul Hammond in *Culture, Politics and Society
in Britain 1660–1800*, edited by Jeremy Black and Jeremy Gregory (1991) 38–
40).
157. Fretted] devoured, consumed (*OED* 3b).   *pigmy*] He is called a
'Pigmy Lord' in *Sejanus: or the Popular Favourite* [summer 1681] 3.
158. o'erinformed] over-animated (*OED*'s first example; from 'inform' 3c, 'to
impart life or spirit to').   *tenement*] often applied to the body as the dwelling place of the soul (*OED* 3b).

A daring pilot in extremity:
160 Pleased with the danger, when the waves went high
He sought the storms; but for a calm unfit
Would steer too nigh the sands to boast his wit.
Great wits are sure to madness near allied,

159–62. The image of the ship of state which needs to be carefully steered recurs in the pamphlet literature; several writers picture Shaftesbury as an unreliable pilot: 'Like a vile sculler he abjures the realm, / And sinks the bark 'cause he's not chief at helm; / . . . if he got through / Secure himself, he drowns the ship and crew. / If to the ocean back again he's bent, / The rabble, he's in his own element' (*The Cabal* ll. 65–74; *POAS* ii 331–2); 'being injoyn'd by duty, and qualyfi'd by education, to shew himself an industrious *Terpawlin* [i.e. common sailor], when the billows of the troubl'd State furiously heave, yet He'l saucily presume to give directions to his *Pilate*, and regardless of his own respective Office, will boldly aym at the management of the Helm' (*The Character of a Leading Petitioner* 1); 'Whilst on the Purpl'd Ocean thou didst ride, / And Tack about still with the Wind and Tide: / This floating Bark, he now again would Steer, / Ah! treacherous Pilot, and false Mariner; / The Kingdom's yet scarce mended Hulk to save, / Would launch again into the Purple wave:' (*Sejanus* 2). For other applications of the image cp. *A Dialogue Between the Ghosts of the Two last Parliaments*; *A Congratulatory Poem on the meeting together of the Parliament* (1680); *The Good Old Cause Revived.* The image also belongs in a moralist tradition: Joseph Hall's presumptuous man 'hois[t]eth saile in a tempest, & sayth never any of his Ancestors were drowned' (*Characters of Vertues and Vices* (1608) 141). See also *The Medal* ll. 79–80n.

159. daring] Shaftesbury had applied this epithet to himself: 'the E. of *Schaftsbury*, a man as daring but more able' (*A Letter from a Person of Quality* 3). Cp. also the quotation from *Oedipus* in ll. 156–8n.

161. He sought the storms] Cp. Virgil: *in patriam, loca feta furentibus Austris, / Aeoliam uenit* (*Aen.* i 51–2: 'Thus rag'd the Goddess, and with Fury fraught, / The restless Regions of the Storms she sought', 'The First Book of the *Aeneis*' ll. 76–7).

163. Echoes Seneca: *nullum magnum ingenium sine mixtura dementiae fuit* ('there was no great wit without an element of madness'; *De Tranquillitate Animi* xvii 10, following Aristotle, *Problemata* xxx 1). In *Sir Martin Mar-all* (1668) Rose says: 'your greatest wits have ever a touch of madness and extravagance in them' (V i 61–2). Joseph Hall had commented on the 'mixture . . . of wisdom and madness' in the biblical Achitophel (*Contemplations upon . . . the Old Testament* in his *Works* (1837) i 437–8; A. B. Chambers, *MLN* lxxiv (1959) 593). Aaron Baker said of Achitophel: 'The greatest Wits prove most Pernicious, when they are misimploy'd' (*Achitophel befool'd* (1678) 11). Ruth Wallerstein relates D.'s character of Shaftesbury to Renaissance attitudes towards melancholy and the imagination (*HLQ* vi (1942–3) 445–71).

And thin partitions do their bounds divide:
165   Else why should he, with wealth and honour blessed,
       Refuse his age the needful hours of rest?
       Punish a body which he could not please,
       Bankrupt of life, yet prodigal of ease?
       And all to leave what with his toil he won
170   To that unfeathered, two-legged thing, a son:
       Got while his soul did huddled notions try,
       And born a shapeless lump, like anarchy.
       In friendship false, implacable in hate,
       Resolved to ruin or to rule the state;

165–6. In 1676 Charles had told Shaftesbury to cease his involvement in public affairs and retire to his home in the country; Shaftesbury declined (Haley 404).

168. ease] Often used by D. with positive connotations of rest and refreshment (cp. 'Horace: *Epode* II' l. 54), unlike the 'ignoble ease' advocated by Belial in *PL* ii 227. Classical and Renaissance writers were divided as to whether *ease* (*otium* in Latin; the opposite of *negotium*, 'business') was to be approved or censured: see Brian Vickers, *RS* iv (1990) 1–37, 107–54.

170. Applying the definition of man as 'a two-legged unfeathered animal', which is attributed to Plato by Diogenes Laertius (vi 40). Cp. 'The Cock and the Fox' ll. 459–62. Shaftesbury's son Anthony (1652–99) had poor health and was politically insignificant (Haley 221–2).

171–2. For a comparable jibe cp. *The Character of a Modern Whig* (1681): 'his Father begetting him in the hot Zeal of this Persuasion, and his Dam all that while fixing her teeming Fancy with Adulterous lust on their able Holderforth, he was moulded a strong *Presbyterian* in the very Womb' (1). In Crowne's *The Ambitious Statesman* (1679) 52 the villainous Constable envisages producing chaotic children: 'I ought not to get Children of a Woman, / I ought to mix with nothing but a Chaos, / And get Confusion to the Universe, / And then the Children wou'd be like the Father.'

171. huddled] concealed (*OED v.* 1); heaped in confusion (*OED v.* 2).

172. lump] Used of the unformed mass of the body without shape or soul: cp. Cowley: '*Nature* herself, whilst in the *womb* he was, / Sow'd *Strength* and *Beauty* through the *forming Mass*, / They mov'ed the *vital Lump* in every part' ('Nemeaean Ode', *Poems* 172). Cp. D.'s 'Lucretius: Against the Fear of Death' l. 10 and 'The First Book of Ovid's *Metamorphoses*' ll. 10–11.

174. Cp. the quotations from L'Estrange in ll. 152–5*n*, and *The Cabal* in ll. 159–62*n*.

175   To compass this the triple bond he broke, ⎫
The pillars of the public safety shook,   ⎬
And fitted Israel for a foreign yoke.   ⎭
Then, seized with fear, yet still affecting fame,
Usurped a patriot's all-atoning name.

175. The Triple Alliance between England, Holland and Sweden had been formed in 1668, but in May 1670 Charles (with the knowledge of Arlington and Clifford) signed the secret Treaty of Dover with Louis XIV, under which Charles was to receive 1 million livres (£150,000) from Louis, to declare himself a Catholic when circumstances permitted (receiving 6,000 French troops to suppress any revolt), and to join the French in a war against the Dutch. In December a treaty with France was signed by Shaftesbury along with Clifford, Arlington, Buckingham and Lauderdale; this *traité simulé* committed England to an alliance with France without revealing the secret clauses in the earlier treaty. Shaftesbury seems to have been the last of Charles's ministers to accept this switch of alliances, though he became particularly associated with it in the popular mind, largely through his vehement speech against the Dutch in February 1673 (cp. 'Epilogue to *Amboyna*' ll. 19–22*n*); the responsibility for initiating the change was, however, the King's, and the secret treaty tied him to France in ways that Shaftesbury could not suspect and would have repudiated (Haley 282–3). For the charge that Shaftesbury and his colleagues 'gave rise to the present greatness of the *French*' see D.'s *His Majesties Declaration Defended* (1681; *Works* xvii 202).

176. For the image cp. *The Character of a Disbanded Courtier*: Shaftesbury knew 'that the *Mighty Fabrick* can never be shaken, till its Main Pillars and Supporters be by Cunning and Sly Stratagem, either destroy'd or undermined' (2).

178. affecting] aiming at (*OED* 1).

179. Cp. 'Having lost his Honour with his Prince, and Reputation with the best of Men, he Cringes, and Creeps, and Sneaks, to the lowest and Basest of the People; to procure himself among them an empty, vainglorious, and undeserved name, the *Patriot* of his Country' (*The Character of a Disbanded Courtier* 2; Kinsley). The rhetoric of patriotism was part of the Whig claim to be defending the country against subversion. D. had already attacked this rhetoric in *Troilus and Cressida* (1679): 'While secret envy, and while open pride, / Among thy factious Nobles discord threw; / While publique good was urg'd for private ends, / And those thought Patriots, who disturb'd it most;' (V ii 317–20). For another echo of this speech see ll. 1028–31*n*. D.'s suspicion of politicians' claims to patriotic motives continued: cp. 'such only merit to be call'd Patriots, under whom we see their Country Flourish' ('Dedication of the *Georgics*'; *Works* v 141) and 'Some Patriot Fools to pop'lar Praise aspire, / By Publick Speeches, which worse Fools admire' ('The Second Book of the *Georgics*' ll. 730–1). Cp. ll. 497, 965–8. *Usurped*] Q; Assumed *F*. H. Buchan notes that both words occur in Adam's denunciation

180   [So easy still it proves in factious times
       With public zeal to cancel private crimes:
       How safe is treason, and how sacred ill,
       Where none can sin against the people's will;
       Where crowds can wink, and no offence be known,
185   Since in another's guilt they find their own.
       Yet fame deserved no enemy can grudge:
       The statesman we abhor, but praise the judge.
       In Israel's courts ne'er sat an Abbethdin
       With more discerning eyes, or hands more clean:
190   Unbribed, unsought, the wretched to redress,
       Swift of despatch, and easy of access.]
       O, had he been content to serve the crown
       With virtues only proper to the gown,
       Or had the rankness of the soil been freed
195   From cockle that oppressed the noble seed,
       David for him his tuneful harp had strung,
       And heaven had wanted one immortal song.

---

of the tyrant Nimrod: 'to himself assuming / Authority usurped, from God
not given' (*PL* xii 65–6; *YES* vii (1977) 87).   *patriot's*] Q, F *corrected state*;
Patron's F *uncorrected state*. Buchan argues that 'patron' in the sense of protector or advocate is likely to have been D.'s first idea, but it seems more likely
to have been a compositorial error.

180–91. Added in Q; not in F. See headnote, '*Date and publication*'.

181. zeal] a quality associated with extreme Protestants.

184. wink] close one's eyes (*OED* 1), i.e. to something improper.

187–91. Shaftesbury's record as Lord Chancellor does seem to have been
creditable (Haley 309–10); his integrity as a judge is emphasized in the Whig
broadside *The Character of a Loyal Statesman* (1680).

188. Abbethdin] 'father of the court of justice', one of two presiding judges of
the Jewish civil court. D. could have found the term in Thomas Godwin,
Moses and Aaron (1625) (E. S. de Beer, *RES* xvii (1941) 303).

190. unsought] To seek (*OED* 5) is to approach someone for help; i.e. he did
not need to be bribed or begged before helping someone.

191. access] accented on the second syllable in the seventeenth century.

194. rankness] fertility (*OED* rank 11).

195. cockle] A weed which grows in cornfields (see *OED*). D. echoes the
parable of the wheat and the tares, where 'the good seed are the children of
the kingdom; but the tares are the children of the wicked one' (Matthew xiii
24–30, 38–40). Kinsley notes a reference to 'the cockle of rebellion, insol-
ence, sedition' in *Coriolanus* III i 69.

196–7. i.e. 'David would have sung his praises instead of writing a psalm,
and so Heaven would have had one immortal song the less' (Nichol Smith).

But wild ambition loves to slide, not stand,
And fortune's ice prefers to virtue's land.
200 Achitophel, grown weary to possess
A lawful fame and lazy happiness,
Disdained the golden fruit to gather free,
And lent the crowd his arm to shake the tree.
Now, manifest of crimes contrived long since
205 He stood at bold defiance with his prince;
Held up the buckler of the people's cause
Against the crown, and skulked behind the laws.
The wished occasion of the plot he takes,
Some circumstances finds, but more he makes.

The song may be either Psalm cix, which some seventeenth-century commentators saw as a prediction of God's judgements on Absalom and Achitophel (H. Hammond, *RES* v (1954) 60–2), or 2 Samuel xxii, David's song of thanksgiving towards the end of his reign (W. Maurer, *N&Q* cciii (1958) 341–3). *wanted*] lacked.

198–9. Cp. 'Greatnesse, on Goodnesse loues to slide, not stand, / And leaues for Fortunes ice, Vertues firm land' (Richard Knolles, *The Generall Historie of the Turkes* (1621) 1370, lines under a portrait of Mustapha I; Macaulay, 'Sir William Temple' in *Lord Macaulay's Essays* (1899) 454). Hall's presumptuous man 'walks on weake ice, and never thinks, what if I fall? but, What if I runne over, and fall not?' (*Characters* 141).

198. wild ambition] D. had used this phrase in Ulysses' speech on 'the observance due to rule' in *Troilus and Cressida* I i 45. Ambition is also the force which drives Creon in D. and Lee's *Oedipus* (1679): see V i 393, and cp. ll. 156–8*n* above. Ambition is frequently denounced in Tory writing, e.g. Otway, *The History and Fall of Caius Marius* (1680) 9, 66. See also 'Horace: *Odes* I iii' headnote, '*Context*'.

199. fortune] See ll. 252–61*n*.

202–3. Cp. 'In his whole Paradice one only Tree / He had excepted by a strict Decree; / A *Sacred Tree* which *Royal Fruit* did bear, / Yet It in pieces I Conspir'd to tear;' (*A Dialogue between the Ghosts of the Two last Parliaments*). Like Milton (*PL* iv 250) D. associates the fruit of the forbidden tree in Eden with the golden apples of the Hesperides gathered by Heracles.

204. manifest of] evidently guilty of (*OED* 2, first example; a Latinate construction).

207. skulked behind the laws] The Whigs used carefully picked juries to frustrate Charles's attempts to use the courts against the opposition (see ll. 584–629*n*, 606–9*n*).

208–9. Shaftesbury did not instigate Oates's revelations, but took full advantage of them, particularly to discredit James; he was active in the House of Lords committees which investigated the Plot, and may have encouraged Oates behind the scenes, though some of Oates's testimony was tangential or

210 By buzzing emissaries fills the ears
     Of listening crowds with jealousies and fears
     Of arbitrary counsels brought to light,
     And proves the King himself a Jebusite.
     Weak arguments! which yet he knew full well
215 Were strong with people easy to rebel:
     For, governed by the moon, the giddy Jews
     Tread the same track when she the prime renews;
     And once in twenty years, their scribes record,
     By natural instinct they change their lord.
220 Achitophel still wants a chief, and none
     Was found so fit as warlike Absolon:
     Not that he wished his greatness to create

---

unhelpful to Shaftesbury's interests. Oates's *The Popes Ware-house, or the Merchandise of the Whore of Rome* (1679) was dedicated to Shaftesbury as his 'affectionate good Friend, and singular good Lord' (sig. A^r) as were his *An Exact Discovery of the Mystery of Iniquity* (1679) and *The Witch of Endor* (1679). The Tory pamphlet *A Brief Account of the Commitment of the Earl of Sh.* (1681) comments: 'But now People begin to find out the Mystery, and are pretty well satisfyed, that his Lordship did not promote the Discovery of the *Popish* Plot out of any extraordinary Zeal he had for the good either of the King or Kingdom, but was resolv'd to make a good hand of this Hellish Conspiracy, to advance another of his own' (1).

210. buzzing] To *buzz* is to move about busily (*OED* 2); murmur busily (*OED* 3); spread a rumour (*OED* 5); incite by suggestions (*OED* 7). Cp. *Titus Andronicus*: 'these disturbers of our peace / Buzz in the people's ears' (IV iv 6–7).

211. jealousies] indignation (*OED* 1); suspicions, apprehensions of evil, mistrust (*OED* 5).

212–13. One of the charges against Shaftesbury when he was arrested was that 'he used great endeavours to possess the People that His Majesty is a *Papist*, and designs to introduce *Popery* and *Arbitrary Power*' (*A Brief Account* 1).

215. easy] not unwilling, ready (*OED* 12b).

217. prime] the lunar cycle of nineteen years (*OED* 4b).

218. once in twenty years] i.e. at the outbreak of the Civil War in 1641–2, at the restoration of the monarchy in 1660, and now in 1680–1.

219. instinct] stressed on the second syllable in the seventeenth century.

220–1. Monmouth was not a consistent supporter of exclusion, nor did Shaftesbury ever commit himself to Monmouth's succession, though he did propose it privately to the King during the Oxford Parliament. But the two men were close politically and met frequently (Haley 633–4; Ashcraft 177).

220. wants] lacks.

222, 224. he] Shaftesbury.   *his*] Monmouth's.

(For politicians neither love nor hate),
But for he knew his title not allowed
225 Would keep him still depending on the crowd,
That kingly power, thus ebbing out, might be
Drawn to the dregs of a democracy.
Him he attempts with studied arts to please,
And sheds his venom in such words as these:
230 'Auspicious Prince! at whose nativity
Some royal planet ruled the southern sky;

223. politicians] predominantly a pejorative word in the seventeenth century: 'schemers, plotters' (*OED* 1).

224–5. An Appeal from the Country to the City (1679) advocated the claims of Monmouth, since 'his Life and Fortune depends upon the same bottom with yours: he will stand by you, therefore ought you to stand by him. And remember, the old Rule is, *He who hath the worst Title, ever makes the best King*; as being constrain'd by a gracious Government, to supply what he wants in Title; that instead of *God and my Right*, his Motto may be, *God and my People*' (25; Kinsley).

224. allowed] acknowledged to be valid (*OED* 4).

227. Echoes Marchamont Needham: 'It is decreed, we must be drain'd (I see) / Down to the dregs of a *Democracie*' (*Lachrymae Musarum* (1649) 81); see 'Upon the Death of the Lord Hastings', headnote; and cp. *HP* i 211. *Drawn*] contracted, shrunk (*OED* 6); made to flow (like beer from a cask) (*OED* 40).   *democracy*] often pejorative in the seventeenth century, implying mob rule, as when Shaftesbury said that without the secure privileges of the House of Lords 'the *Monarchy* cannot long support, or keep it self from tumbling into a *Democratical Republique*' (*Two Speeches. I. The Earl of Shaftesbury's Speech in the House of Lords the 20th of October, 1675 . . .* (1675) 7).

229. venom] Cp. 'Caballing Devils; who, like cursed *Achitophel*, are ever pouring Poison in the Ears of Young *Absolom*' (*A Seasonable Invitation for Monmouth to Return to Court* (1681) 1). Satan sheds his 'venom' into the ear of Eve in *PL* iv 804.

230–61. Bruce King (*EA* xvi (1963) 251–4) suggests that this speech echoes *The Prince*, chs xxv–xxvi, in which Machiavelli writes of Fortune, and urges Cesare Borgia to liberate Italy. Garrison relates it to the tradition of panegyric (228–36).

230–1. The royal planet would be the sun, moon or Jupiter; the southern sky is the zenith or midheaven of the horoscope. Monmouth, born on 9 April 1649, had the sun in Aries, its exaltation sign. William Lilly writes: '[The Sun] and [the Moon] in the very degree of their Exaltation . . . are arguments unto the Native of obtaining a Kingdom, if he be capable thereof' and they portend 'Kingly Preferment, if the Native be of Kingly Progeny' (*Christian Astrology* (1659) 617; *Works*; Simon Bentley, privately).

230. Auspicious] well-omened. Garrison 230 identifies the term as a common

Thy longing country's darling and desire,
Their cloudy pillar and their guardian fire;
Their second Moses, whose extended wand
235   Divides the seas, and shows the promised land;
Whose dawning day in every distant age
Has exercised the sacred prophets' rage;
The people's prayer, the glad diviner's theme,
The young men's vision, and the old men's dream!
240   Thee, saviour, thee, the nation's vows confess,
And never satisfied with seeing, bless.
Swift, unbespoken pomps thy steps proclaim,
And stammering babes are taught to lisp thy name.
How long wilt thou the general joy detain,
245   Starve and defraud the people of thy reign;
Content ingloriously to pass thy days
Like one of virtue's fools that feeds on praise,
Till thy fresh glories which now shine so bright
Grow stale and tarnish with our daily sight?
250   Believe me, royal youth, thy fruit must be
Or gathered ripe, or rot upon the tree.
Heaven has to all allotted, soon or late,

---

feature of panegyric, e.g.: *Auspiciis iterum sese regalibus annus / induit et nota fruitur iactantior aula* ('Once more the year opens under royal auspices and enjoys in fuller pride its famous prince'; Claudian, *Panegyricus De Quarto Consulatu Honorii Augusti* ll. 1–2); 'Auspicious *Star* again arise', Cowley, *Ode Upon His Majesties Restoration and Return* l. 23. For D.'s usage of the word see Paul Hammond, *MLR* lxxx (1985) 772–3.

233–5. The Israelites were led through the wilderness by a pillar of cloud by day and fire by night; when they came to the Red Sea, God told Moses: 'lift thou up thy rod, and stretch out thine hand over the sea, and divide it' (Exodus xiii 21, xiv 16).

235. Divides] Q; Shuts up F (echoing Job xxxviii 8).

237. rage] prophetic enthusiasm or inspiration (*OED* 8).

239. From Joel iii 28: 'your old men shall dream dreams, your young men shall see visions'.

240. Thee, saviour, thee] Cp. 'Lucretius: The Beginning of the First Book' l. 7n. *confess*] acknowledge.

242. unbespoken] not arranged, spontaneous (*OED*'s first example). *pomps*] triumphal processions; splendid displays along a route (*OED* 2).

244. detain] hinder, delay (*OED* 5).

251. Or . . . or] Either . . . or.

252–63. Achitophel's stress on Fortune (or 'Occasion'), rather than divine Providence, associates him with Machiavelli's advice to the Prince to seize his

Some lucky revolution of their fate;
Whose motions, if we watch and guide with skill
255　(For human good depends on human will),
Our Fortune rolls, as from a smooth descent,
And from the first impression takes the bent:
But if unseized, she glides away like wind,
And leaves repenting folly far behind.
260　Now, now she meets you with a glorious prize,
And spreads her locks before her as she flies.
Had thus old David, from whose loins you spring,
Not dared, when Fortune called him, to be King,
At Gath an exile he might still remain,
265　And heaven's anointing oil had been in vain.
Let his successful youth your hopes engage,

---

opportunities (see *The Prince* ch. xxv, and *Heroic Stanzas* ll. 29–30*n*). His assumption in l. 263 that Charles II was given his crown by Fortune is a denial of the hand of God in his restoration. This passage uses details from the emblem-book tradition. G. E. Wilson cites the emblem 'Of Occasion' in Geoffrey Whitney's *A Choice of Emblemes* (1586) 181: 'What creature thou? *Occasion I doe showe.* / On whirling wheel declare why doste thou stande? / *Bicause, I still am tossed too, and froe.* / . . . What meanes long lockes before? *that suche as meete,* / *Maye houlde at firste, when they occasion finde.* / Thy head behinde all balde, what telles it more? / *That none shoulde houlde, that let me slippe before*'; cp. *1 Conquest of Granada* III i 265–7 (*PLL* xi (1975) 199–203). For this and other examples of D.'s thinking about Fortune see Paul Hammond, *MLR* lxxx (1985) 769–85. The motif of Fortune's dealings with Monmouth is used in 'On the Election of yᵉ Duke of Monmouth to be Chancellor of yᵉ University of Cambridge' (1674; BodL MS Don.b.8 pp. 506–7). Milton's Satan, tempting Christ 'to sit upon thy father David's throne', says: 'zeal and duty are not slow; / But on occasion's forelock watchful wait' (*PR* iii 153, 172–3).
253. *revolution*] alteration (*OED* 6).
257. *bent*] direction of motion (*OED* 6d).
262–5. To escape Saul, David went into exile in Gath (1 Samuel xxvii 1–7). Charles II's exile was spent chiefly in Germany and the Netherlands, particularly Brussels.
265. *heaven's anointing oil*] After God rejected Saul, Samuel anointed the boy David (1 Samuel xvi 13).
266. *engage*] invite (*OED* 8).

But shun th' example of declining age:
Behold him setting in his western skies,
The shadows length'ning as the vapours rise.
270 He is not now, as when on Jordan's sand ⎫
The joyful people thronged to see him land, ⎬
Cov'ring the beach, and black'ning all the strand: ⎭
But like the Prince of Angels from his height
Comes tumbling downward with diminished light;
275 Betrayed by one poor plot to public scorn
(Our only blessing since his cursed return):
Those heaps of people which one sheaf did bind
Blown off and scattered by a puff of wind.
What strength can he to your designs oppose,
280 Naked of friends, and round beset with foes?

267–9. Cp. *A Seasonable Invitation*: Achitophel tells Absalom: 'The *King* (his Father) grows Old and Weak, and that He is easily subdued; that the *Mobile* grow weary of His Government, and fall off from Him; that he himself hath so much the Hearts of the People, as that he can immediately Raise *Twelve* Thousand Men and that the *King* being left Desolate, he will strike Him: And all this, that *Absolom* may be King, and the People may live in Peace' (1).

267. *declining age*] Charles (b. 29 May 1630) was 51, old in seventeenth-century terms.

268–9. Kinsley compares *Aureng-Zebe* (1676) 3: '*Solyman*. [He] Wishes each Minute he could unbeget / Those Rebel-Sons, who dare t' usurp his Seat: / To sway his Empire, with unequal Skill, / And mount a Throne, which none but he can fill. / *Arimant*. Oh! had he still that Character maintain'd, / Of valour, which in blooming Youth he gain'd, / He promis'd in his East a Glorious Race; / Now sunk from his Meridian, sets apace.'

269. *vapours*] mists (*OED* 2b).

270–2. Cp. Virgil: *migrantis cernas totaque ex urbe ruentis: / ac velut ingentem formicae farris acervum / cum populant hiemis memores tectoque reponunt, / it nigrum campis agmen* (*Aen.* iv 401–4; 'The Beach is cover'd o're / With *Trojan* Bands that blacken all the Shore: / On ev'ry side are seen, descending down, / Thick swarms of Souldiers loaden from the Town. / Thus, in Battalia, march embody'd Ants / Fearful of Winter, and of future Wants', 'The Fourth Book of the *Aeneis*' ll. 578–83; R. M. Ogilvie, *N&Q* ccxv (1970) 415–16); cp. *Astraea Redux* ll. 276–9.

270. *Jordan's sand*] Dover beach; see 2 Samuel xix 15.

273–4. 'How art thou fallen from heaven, O Lucifer, son of the morning! how art thou cut down to the ground, which didst weaken the nations! For thou hast said in thine heart, I will ascend into heaven, I will exalt my throne above the stars of God' (Isaiah xiv 12–13; cp. Luke x 18).

If Pharaoh's doubtful succour he should use,
A foreign aid would more incense the Jews:
Proud Egypt would dissembled friendship bring,
Foment the war, but not support the King;
285 Nor would the royal party e'er unite
With Pharaoh's arms t' assist the Jebusite;
Or if they should, their interest soon would break,
And with such odious aid make David weak.
All sorts of men by my successful arts
290 Abhorring kings, estrange their altered hearts
From David's rule; and 'tis the general cry
"Religion, Commonwealth and Liberty".
If you as champion of the public good
Add to their arms a chief of royal blood,
295 What may not Israel hope, and what applause
Might such a general gain by such a cause?
Not barren praise alone, that gaudy flower
Fair only to the sight, but solid power:
And nobler is a limited command
300 Given by the love of all your native land,
Than a successive title, long and dark,
Drawn from the mouldy rolls of Noah's ark.'
    What cannot praise effect in mighty minds,
When flattery soothes, and when ambition blinds!
305 Desire of power, on earth a vicious weed,
Yet, sprung from high, is of celestial seed:
In God 'tis glory; and when men aspire
'Tis but a spark too much of heavenly fire.
Th' ambitious youth, too covetous of fame,
310 Too full of angel's metal in his frame,
Unwarily was led from virtue's ways,

281. *Pharaoh*] Louis XIV.

287. *interest*] participation (*OED* 1d).   *break*] dissolve (*OED* 8b, quoting this line).

295. *What may not Israel hope*] Cp. Marvell: 'What may not then our *Isle* presume' ('An Horatian Ode' l. 97); see ll. 353–4*n*.   *applause*] Distrusted by D.; cp. 'Lucretius: Against the Fear of Death' l. 203.

302. *rolls*] The descent of English kings was shown in genealogical parchment rolls (e.g. BodL MS Rolls 3).

310. *angel*] (i) ominously, in view of the Luciferian precedent; (ii) with a pun on the gold coin, last minted by Charles I, which was presented to patients touched by the monarch for the King's Evil (*OED*; W. K. Thomas, *The*

Made drunk with honour, and debauched with
    praise.
Half loath, and half consenting to the ill
(For loyal blood within him struggled still),
315 He thus replied: 'And what pretence have I
To take up arms for public liberty?
My father governs with unquestioned right,
The faith's defender, and mankind's delight:
Good, gracious, just, observant of the laws,
320 And heaven by wonders has espoused his cause.
Whom has he wronged in all his peaceful reign?
Who sues for justice to his throne in vain?
What millions has he pardoned of his foes,
Whom just revenge did to his wrath expose?
325 Mild, easy, humble, studious of our good,
Inclined to mercy, and averse from blood.
If mildness ill with stubborn Israel suit,
His crime is God's belovèd attribute.

Crafting of 'Absalom and Achitophel').   metal] 'metal' and 'mettle' are originally the same word, and both could be spelt 'metal' in the seventeenth
century, as here.

312. debauched] See l. 47n.

318. The faith's defender] echoing the King's title *Fidei Defensor*, originally
granted to Henry VIII by Pope Leo X for his treatise against Luther.   *mankind's delight*] Suetonius calls Titus *amor ac deliciae generis humani* ('the love and
delight of mankind', viii 1; Christie). Thomas D'Urfey has the same comparison: '*Titus* the Second reigns, he whose celestial mind / Stiles him the joy
of human kind' (*The Progress of Honesty* (1681) 7). Cp. also George Berkeley,
Historical Applications, third edition (1680) 90–1. For the phrasing cp. 'Lucretius: The Beginning of the First Book' l. 1 (used of Venus).

320. See *Threnodia Augustalis* l. 90n.

323–4. The general pardon offered by Charles in the Declaration of Breda (4
April 1660) was implemented in the Act of Indemnity (29 August 1660)
which offered a general pardon for all treasons, felonies and numerous other
offences committed since 1 January 1637; 51 individuals, chiefly regicides,
were excepted from the pardon (Ogg 154–5).

326. Although Charles allowed the law to take its usual course during the
Popish Plot, he regretted some of the executions, and occasionally remitted
the more savage punishments for treason. 'The King like a Just and Excellent
Prince, who like Heavens Monarch delights in Mercy, suspends the Rigors
and Severities of the Penal Laws against them; this they construe to be Fear
and not Favour' (*The Character of a Rebellion* (1681) 2).

What could he gain, his people to betray,
330 Or change his right for arbitrary sway?
Let haughty Pharaoh curse with such a reign
His fruitful Nile, and yoke a servile train.
If David's rule Jerusalem displease,
The dog-star heats their brains to this disease.
335 Why then should I, encouraging the bad,
Turn rebel, and run popularly mad?
Were he a tyrant who by lawless might
Oppressed the Jews and raised the Jebusite,
Well might I mourn; but nature's holy bands
340 Would curb my spirits and restrain my hands:
The people might assert their liberty,
But what was right in them were crime in me.
His favour leaves me nothing to require,
Prevents my wishes, and outruns desire.
345 What more can I expect while David lives?
All but his kingly diadem he gives,
And that—' But there he paused, then sighing said,
'Is justly destined for a worthier head.
For when my father from his toils shall rest,
350 And late augment the number of the blessed,
His lawful issue shall the throne ascend,
Or the collateral line where that shall end.

329–30. In his speech to the Oxford Parliament on 20 March 1681 Charles said: 'I, who will never use arbitrary government myself, am resolved not to suffer it in others. . . . It is much my interest, and it shall be as much my care as yours, to preserve the liberty of the subject; because the Crown can never be safe when that is in danger. And I would have you likewise be convinced, that neither your liberties nor properties can subsist long, when the just rights and prerogatives of the Crown are invaded, or the honour of the government brought low and into disreputation' (*Letters, Speeches and Declarations of King Charles II*, edited by Arthur Bryant (1935) 317–18; Kinsley).

334. Sirius, the dog-star, rises around 11 August, and the previous forty days (dog-days) were said to bring unpleasantly hot weather and malignant influences.

336. run popularly mad] run mad and pander to the people.

344. Prevents] anticipates.

349. toils] Charles II notoriously preferred pleasure to business. For the sexual connotations of *toil* cp. Lady Fidget in Wycherley's *The Country-Wife*: 'I have been toyling and moyling, for the pretti'st piece of China' (IV iii 177–8).

His brother, though oppressed with vulgar spite,
Yet dauntless and secure of native right,
355 Of every royal virtue stands possessed,
Still dear to all the bravest, and the best.
His courage foes, his friends his truth proclaim,
His loyalty the King, the world his fame.
His mercy ev'n th' offending crowd will find,
360 For sure he comes of a forgiving kind.
Why should I then repine at heaven's decree,
Which gives me no pretence to royalty?

353–60. James, Duke of York, 'cunningly unnamed' by D. (Winn 357).
Suspicion of him intensified during the Popish Plot; though he was not
alleged to be implicated personally, the discovery of Coleman's correspondence was embarrassing, and it was fortunate that no one discovered that
there had in fact been a meeting of the Jesuits in James's own apartments. On
3 November 1678 it was decided that James should cease to attend the Privy
Council and its committees, and on 27 April 1679 the House of Commons
resolved 'That the Duke of *Yorke*'s being a Papist, and the Hopes of his
coming such to the Crown, has given the greatest Countenance and Encouragement to the present Conspiracies and Designs of the Papists against the
King, and the Protestant Religion' (*Commons' Journals* ix 605). James spent
some time away from London: March to September 1679 in Brussels, and
November 1679 to February 1680 and October 1680 to March 1681 in Scotland. D. had praised James in the Dedication of *The State of Innocence* (1677)
to the Duchess of York, as a prince 'whose Conduct, Courage, and Success in
War, whose Fidelity to His Royal Brother, whose Love for His Countrey,
whose Constancy to His Friends, whose Bounty to His Servants, whose
Justice to Merit, whose Inviolable Truth, and whose Magnanimity in all His
Actions, seem to have been rewarded by Heaven by the gift of You' (sig.
A2ʳ). Lines in *The Duke of Guise* (1683) also reflect on James: '*King.* I know
my Brother's nature, 'tis sincere, / Above deceit, no crookedness of thought,
/ Says, what he means, and what he says performs: / Brave, but not rash;
successful, but not proud. / So much acknowledging that he's uneasie, / Till
every petty service be o're paid. / *Archb.* Some say revengeful. / *King.* Some
then libel him: / But that's what both of us have learnt to bear. / He can
forgive, but you disdain Forgiveness' (62). Cp. also 'Epilogue to *Albion and
Albanius*' (Kinsley).
353–4. Echoing Marvell: 'Nor call'd the *Gods* with vulgar spight / To vindicate his helpless Right' ('An Horatian Ode' ll. 61–2, of Charles I). This is one
of a cluster of echoes of the Ode in *AA*; see also ll. 295*n*, 387–8*n*, 805–8*n*,
887*n*; Paul Hammond, *N & Q* ccxxxvi (1988) 172–3.
360. kind] race (*OED* 10).
362. pretence] claim (*OED* 1).

Yet O that Fate, propitiously inclined,
Had raised my birth, or had debased my mind;
365 To my large soul not all her treasure lent,
And then betrayed it to a mean descent.
I find, I find my mounting spirits bold,
And David's part disdains my mother's mould.
Why am I scanted by a niggard birth?
370 My soul disclaims the kindred of her earth,
And made for empire whispers me within,
"Desire of greatness is a godlike sin." '
       Him staggering so when hell's dire agent found,
While fainting virtue scarce maintained her ground,
375 He pours fresh forces in, and thus replies:
       'Th' eternal God, supremely good and wise,
Imparts not these prodigious gifts in vain;
What wonders are reserved to bless your reign!
Against your will your arguments have shown
380 Such virtue's only given to guide a throne.
Not that your father's mildness I condemn,
But manly force becomes the diadem.
'Tis true, he grants the people all they crave,

363–72. Cp. Torrismond in *The Spanish Friar* (1681) 20: 'Good Heav'ns, why gave you me a Monarch's Soul, / And crusted it with base Plebeian Clay! / Why gave you me Desires of such extent, / And such a Span to grasp 'em? Sure my lot / By some o'er-hasty Angel was misplac'd, / In Fate's Eternal Volume!' (Kinsley).

363–4. Cp. 'Ah mighty prince! By too great Birth betray'd, / Borne to those Fortunes, which you might have made; / Had Fate been kind, she would have plac'd you lowe, / That to your selfe you might your Greatnesse owe' ('On the Election of y⁰ Duke of Monmouth . . .', BodL MS Don.b.8. p. 506).

366. mean] lowly.

368. mould] (i) earth, regarded as the material of the body (*OED sb¹* 4; cp. *earth* in l. 370); (ii) the body as a matrix for creating a child (*OED sb²* 4).

369. scanted] inadequately supplied (*OED* 3); confined, restricted (*OED* 6).

373. A quasi-Miltonic line.   *staggering*] beginning to doubt or waver (*OED* 2).   *hell's dire agent*] D. associates Shaftesbury with the Satan of *PL*, for which cp. the Epistle Dedicatory to *All for Love*, quoted in ll. 51–6*n*; but he had already been presented as a devil in the pamphlet literature, most viciously in *A Seasonable Invitation* 2. Cp. 'Some call me Devil, some his Foster-Brother' (*The Badger in the Fox-Trap* 1). Monmouth is seduced by 'Hells curst Agents' in *The Progress of Honesty* 11.

376–80. Cp. D.'s Dedication to *Tyrannic Love*, quoted in ll. 18–30*n* (Bruce King, *ES* xlvi (1965) 332–3).

And more perhaps than subjects ought to have:
385 For lavish grants suppose a monarch tame,
And more his goodness than his wit proclaim.
But when should people strive their bonds to break,
If not when kings are negligent or weak?
Let him give on till he can give no more,
390 The thrifty Sanhedrin shall keep him poor:
And every shekel which he can receive
Shall cost a limb of his prerogative.
To ply him with new plots shall be my care,
Or plunge him deep in some expensive war;
395 Which when his treasure can no more supply
He must with the remains of kingship buy.
His faithful friends our jealousies and fears
Call Jebusites, and Pharaoh's pensioners;
Whom when our fury from his aid has torn
400 He shall be naked left to public scorn.
The next successor, whom I fear and hate,
My arts have made obnoxious to the state,
Turned all his virtues to his overthrow,
And gained our elders to pronounce a foe.
405 His right for sums of necessary gold
Shall first be pawned, and afterwards be sold;
Till time shall ever-wanting David draw
To pass your doubtful title into law:
If not, the people have a right supreme

---

385. *suppose*] imply, presuppose (*OED* 10).

386. *wit*] intelligence.

387–8. Echoing Marvell: 'But those [antient Rights] do hold or break / As Men are strong or weak' ('An Horatian Ode' ll. 39–40).

390. *Sanhedrin*] The highest court of justice in Jerusalem; applied here to Parliament; see 'Epilogue to *The Unhappy Favourite*' l. 8*n*.

394–6. Recalling the Third Anglo-Dutch War (1672–4) which Shaftesbury had helped to promote. The Commons voted money for it, but at the same time challenged the King's prerogative right to suspend penal laws against dissenters; Charles cancelled his Declaration of Indulgence, and the Money Bill was passed. Another outcome of this session was the Test Act, which disqualified from public office anyone refusing to take the oath of allegiance and supremacy and the Anglican sacrament (Ogg 365–8).

398. *Pharaoh's pensioners*] Louis XIV's ambassadors in London spent considerable sums of money to influence both court and Parliament.

409–12. See ll. 759–810*nn*.

410   To make their kings, for kings are made for them.
     All empire is no more than power in trust,
     Which when resumed can be no longer just.
     Succession, for the general good designed,
     In its own wrong a nation cannot bind:
415   If altering that the people can relieve,
     Better one suffer than a nation grieve.
     The Jews well know their power: ere Saul they chose
     God was their King, and God they durst depose.
     Urge now your piety, your filial name,
420   A father's right, and fear of future fame;
     The public good, that universal call
     To which ev'n heaven submitted, answers all.
     Nor let his love enchant your generous mind:
     'Tis nature's trick to propagate her kind.
425   Our fond begetters, who would never die,
     Love but themselves in their posterity.
     Or let his kindness by th' effects be tried,
     Or let him lay his vain pretence aside.
     God said he loved your father: could he bring
430   A better proof than to anoint him King?

---

412. i.e. when the people take back the power which they had entrusted to a ruler, he no longer has any just claim to it.

414. i.e. a nation cannot be bound by arrangements for the succession which will cause it harm.

416. Echoes John xviii 14: 'it was expedient that one man [i.e. Christ] should die for the people'. Sir Thomas Player, a Whig, used a similar argument in the Commons on 4 January 1681: 'I have read *That one man died for the People*, but never that three Kingdoms must die for one man' (Grey viii 236). *nation*] Q; Million F.

417–18. Saul was the first king of Israel, and the people's demand for a king was seen as a rejection of the rule of God (1 Samuel viii 4–8, 18–19). D. refers to the replacement of the Commonwealth by the quasi-monarchical Protectorate under Cromwell ('Saul') on 16 December 1653. Vavasor Powell denounced the change, saying: 'Lord wilt Thou have Oliver Cromwell or Jesus Christ to reign over us?' (*CSPD 1653–4* 306).

419. piety] reverence and obedience to God (*OED* 2) and parents (*OED* 3); cp. *AM* l. 255n.

421–2. Applying the dictum *salus populi suprema lex* ('the safety of the people is the supreme law').

423. generous] noble.

427–8. Or . . . Or] Either . . . Or.

It surely showed he loved the shepherd well
Who gave so fair a flock as Israel.
Would David have you thought his darling son?
What means he then to alienate the crown?
435   The name of godly he may blush to bear:
'Tis after God's own heart to cheat his heir.
He to his brother gives supreme command:
To you, a legacy of barren land;
Perhaps th' old harp on which he thrums his lays,
440   Or some dull Hebrew ballad in your praise.
Then the next heir, a prince severe and wise,
Already looks on you with jealous eyes;
Sees through the thin disguises of your arts,
And marks your progress in the people's hearts.
445   Though now his mighty soul its grief contains,
He meditates revenge who least complains;

431. shepherd] David had been a shepherd boy (1 Samuel xvi 11); the reference
also carries connotations of Christ as the good shepherd (John x 11–15).
434. alienate] transfer to the ownership of another (*OED* 2).
435–6. i.e. 'Charles may blush to call himself "godly" when he declines to
cheat the Duke of York of his succession, to do which would be "after God's
own heart"' (Christie). The 'cheat' would be acceptable to God because it
would preserve Protestantism. D. may be recalling that David had his son
Solomon anointed king to thwart his elder son Adonijah, who had begun to
behave as king (1 Kings i).
438. Probably a reference to the Border estates of Monmouth's wife (Kinsley).
439. Charles was a lover of music, particularly of the guitar: see Richard
Luckett, 'Music' in Pepys, *Diary* x 264–7, 274.
441. severe] not inclined to indulgence: often seen as a proper attribute of
princes: cp. 'He who the sword of heaven will bear / Should be as holy as
severe' (*Measure for Measure* III ii 254–5).
442. jealous] See l. 211n.
445. grief] feeling of having been wronged; displeasure; anger (*OED* 4).

And like a lion slumbering in the way,
Or sleep dissembling while he waits his prey,
His fearless foes within his distance draws,
450 Constrains his roaring and contracts his paws;
Till at the last, his time for fury found,
He shoots with sudden vengeance from the ground,
The prostrate vulgar passes o'er and spares,
But with a lordly rage his hunters tears.
455 Your case no tame expedients will afford:
Resolve on death, or conquest by the sword,
Which for no less a stake than life you draw;
And self-defence is nature's eldest law.

447–54. Cp. Lucan: *sicut squalentibus arvis / Aestiferae Libyes viso leo comminus hoste / Subsedit dubius, totam dum colligit iram; / Mox, ubi se saevae stimulavit verbere caudae / Erexitque iubam et vasto grave murmur hiatu / Infremuit* ('So on the untilled fields of sultry Libya, when the lion sees his foe at hand, he crouches down at first uncertain till he gathers all his rage; but soon, when he has maddened himself with the cruel lash of his tail, and made his mane stand up, and sent forth a roar from his cavernous jaws . . .'; *Pharsalia* i 205–10; R. M. Ogilvie, *N&Q* ccxv (1970) 415–16). D.'s rhymes also point to a recollection of Cowley's *Davideis*: 'A *Lyon* prickt with rage and want of food, / Espies out from afar some well-fed beast, / And brustles up preparing for his feast; / If that by swiftness scape his gaping jaws; / His bloody eyes he hurls round, his sharp paws / Tear up the ground; then runs he wild about, / Lashing his angry tail, and roaring out. / . . . *Silence* and *horror* fill the place around. / *Eccho* it self dares scarce repeat the sound' (*Poems* 258).

447. like a lion] Cp. Col. Titus's speech in the Commons, 7 January 1681: 'If a Lion was in the Lobby, and we were to consider which way to secure ourselves from him, and conclude it is best to shut the Door, and keep him out, "No," says another, "let us chain him, and let him come in;" but I should be loth to put the chain on' (Grey viii 279). James is referred to as 'the Popish Lyon' in the Tory beast-fable *Grimalkin, or, the Rebel-Cat* (1681); and *The White Rose: or A Word for the House of York* (1680) remarks: 'From the secret instincts of *Nature*, Birds and Beasts are taught to obey the *Eagle* and the *Lyon*' (2). For examples of political beast-fables at this period see Paul Hammond, *N&Q* ccxxvii (1982) 55–7; Ashcraft 401; and ll. *527–8n.*

448. sleep dissembling] F2; Sleep-dissembling F, Q.

453. From Pliny: *Leoni tantum ex feris clementia in supplices; prostratis parcit* ('The lion alone of wild animals shows mercy to suppliants; it spares persons prostrated in front of it'; *Naturalis Historia* viii 19 (Kinsley)); so too Edward Topsell, *The History of Four-footed Beasts* (1658) 365.

458. So Hobbes: 'The Right of Nature . . . is the Liberty each man hath, to use his own power, as he will himselfe, for the preservation of his own Nature; that is to say, of his own Life' (*Leviathan* (1651) 64; Kinsley).

     Leave the warm people no considering time,
460   For then rebellion may be thought a crime:
     Prevail yourself of what occasion gives,
     But try your title while your father lives;
     And that your arms may have a fair pretence,
     Proclaim you take them in the King's defence,
465   Whose sacred life each minute would expose
     To plots from seeming friends and secret foes.
     And who can sound the depth of David's soul?
     Perhaps his fear his kindness may control.
     He fears his brother though he loves his son
470   For plighted vows too late to be undone.
     If so, by force he wishes to be gained,
     Like women's lechery, to seem constrained.
     Doubt not, but when he most affects the frown
     Commit a pleasing rape upon the crown;
475   Secure his person to secure your cause:
     They who possess the prince possess the laws.'
       He said; and this advice above the rest
     With Absalom's mild nature suited best:
     Unblamed of life (ambition set aside),
480   Not stained with cruelty, nor puffed with pride;

461. Prevail] avail (*OED* 4c).   *occasion*] See ll. 252–61*n*.

464. This claim had been made by Parliament in the early stages of the Civil War.

468. i.e. 'Perhaps his fear of James may restrain the natural affection arising from his kinship to you.'

470. plighted vows] See ll. 18–30*n*.

472. Proverbial: Tilley W 660; Ovid, *Ars Amatoria* i 664, 672, 698 (Poyet).

473. Doubt] hesitate, scruple, delay (*OED* 3).

474. rape] (i) violent theft (*OED* 1); (ii) sexual violation (*OED* 3c). The latter sense was commonly used politically, e.g. in *King John*: 'Thou hast under-wrought [i.e. undermined] his lawful king, / Cut off the sequence of posterity, / . . . and done a rape / Upon the maiden virtue of the crown' (II i 95–8). Rape was used as a political trope in the Exclusion Crisis by several dramatists, as Susan Owen shows: to the Whigs it could figure tyranny, to the Tories, rebellion. Examples are Creon in *Oedipus*, a rebel leader who contemplates rape in a temple; the tyrant Tarquin who rapes Lucrece in Lee's *Lucius Junius Brutus*; and the attempted rape of Belvidera by Renault in Otway's *Venice Preserv'd* (Owen 29–30, 267–70 and *SEL* xxxi (1991) 474–6).

479. Unblamed of life] a Latin construction, translating *integer vitae* (Horace, *Carm.* I xxii 1).

How happy had he been if destiny
Had higher placed his birth, or not so high!
His kingly virtues might have claimed a throne,
And blessed all other countries but his own;
485   But charming greatness since so few refuse
'Tis juster to lament him than accuse.
Strong were his hopes a rival to remove,
With blandishments to gain the public love;
To head the faction while their zeal was hot,
490   And popularly prosecute the plot.
To farther this, Achitophel unites
The malcontents of all the Israelites,
Whose differing parties he could wisely join
For several ends, to serve the same design.
495   The best, and of the princes some were such,
Who thought the power of monarchy too much,
Mistaken men, and patriots in their hearts,
Not wicked, but seduced by impious arts:
By these the springs of property were bent,
500   And wound so high they cracked the government.
The next for interest sought t' embroil the state,

481–2. Cp. ll. 363–4*n*.

491–4. The Whigs were a coalition of different interests. J. R. Jones (10–16) divides them into five groups: (i) 'The old Presbyterians', distinguished by zeal for religious reform and Protestant unity, sympathetic to dissenters, and advocates of toleration; (ii) 'The country opposition', who valued the law, honest government, consultation with parliament, financial retrenchment and the defence of Protestantism: cp. D.'s ll. 495–500; (iii) 'The adventurers', who criticized ministers in the hope of supplanting them: cp. D.'s ll. 501–4; (iv) 'Monmouth and his circle', bound together by personal interests; (v) 'The radicals', the survivors and successors of the republicans of the 1650s: cp. D.'s ll. 511–14. Ashcraft says of L'Estrange's propaganda that 'like Dryden, L'Estrange perceived the "contradictory" interests united in the Whig political movement, and he hoped to break apart the unity of the movement by showing that some classes (tradesmen and merchants) would benefit greatly at the expense of others (nobility and gentry) if the Whigs achieved their political objectives' (242). See also Gary S. De Krey in Harris, Seaward and Goldie (cited in ll. 51–6*n*) 133–62, for the London Whigs.

497. patriots] a designation claimed by the Whigs: cp. l. 179*n*, ll. 965–8.

499. property] See l. 536*n*.

501–4. The Whigs drew strong support from merchants and traders, and much Whig propaganda was aimed at their interests (Ashcraft 230–3).

501. interest] advantage, profit (*OED* 2b); faction, political party (*OED* 4);

To sell their duty at a dearer rate;
And make their Jewish markets of the throne,
Pretending public good, to serve their own.
505 Others thought kings an useless, heavy load,
Who cost too much, and did too little good:
These were for laying honest David by
On principles of pure good husbandry.
With them joined all th' haranguers of the throng
510 That thought to get preferment by the tongue.
Who follow next a double danger bring,
Not only hating David, but the King—
The Solymæan rout, well versed of old
In godly faction, and in treason bold;
515 Cowering and quaking at a conqueror's sword,
But lofty to a lawful prince restored,
Saw with disdain an ethnic plot begun,
And scorned by Jebusites to be outdone.
Hot Levites headed these, who pulled before
520 From th' ark, which in the Judges' days they bore,
Resumed their cant, and with a zealous cry
Pursued their old beloved theocracy,
Where Sanhedrin and priest enslaved the nation
And justified their spoils by inspiration;

selfish pursuit of one's own welfare (*OED* 5).   *embroil the state*] Echoes
[Roger L'Estrange]: 'Nor is't at all th' *Intent of Their Debate* / To fix Religion,
but t' embroyl the *State*' (*The Committee; or Popery in Masquerade* (1680)).
513. *Solymæan rout*] London rabble. Tory pamphleteers often accused the
Whigs of appealing to the rabble (Ashcraft 301–3). See Harris, *London
Crowds, passim.*   *Solymæan*] of Jerusalem (from the Latin *Solyma* for *Hiero-
solyma*, Jerusalem), *OED*'s only example.
517. *ethnic*] Gentile (*OED* 1); here, Roman Catholic.
519. *Levites*] Jewish priests; here, the dissenting clergy who were deprived of
their benefices by the Act of Uniformity (1662).
520. *Judges*] the leaders of Israel between the death of Joshua and the election
of Saul as king.
521. *cant*] peculiar phraseology of a religious sect (*OED* 4c; first example).
522. *theocracy*] form of government in which God is recognized as king, and
the country is administered by a priestly order; applied particularly to Israel
from the Exodus to the election of Saul (*OED*); here, the Commonwealth of
England.

525   For who so fit for reign as Aaron's race
       If once dominion they could found in grace?
       These led the pack, though not of surest scent
       Yet deepest-mouthed against the government.
       A numerous host of dreaming saints succeed,
530   Of the true old enthusiastic breed;
       'Gainst form and order they their power employ,
       Nothing to build, and all things to destroy.
       But far more numerous was the herd of such
       Who think too little, and who talk too much.
535   These, out of mere instinct, they knew not why,
       Adored their fathers' god, and property;

525. Aaron's race] The clergy; the Jewish priesthood was hereditary in the line of Aaron.

526. Cp. *The Character of a Fanatick* (1675): 'he makes his Doctrine suitable to his Text, and owns above-board, that Dominion is founded in Grace, not Nature: That the Goods of this World are properly the Elects' (Kinsley).

527–8. Cp. *The Progress of Honesty*: 'Their deep mouth'd Oaths to th' lofty Skies were sent / That there would be a Change in Government' (12); the image is also applied to the Tories in *The Character of a Tory* (1681) 2: 'Whilst we were Hunting down their *Plot* with a full Cry, they slipt in their *Deep-mouth'd* Hound, who spending on a *false Scent* diverted the Chase, and so the *Popish Puss squats safe in her Form*'.   *deepest-mouthed*] with the deepest or most sonorous voices (of dogs).

530. enthusiastic] 'Enthusiasm' first meant possession by a god, supernatural inspiration (*OED* 1); thence fancied inspiration, extravagant religious fervour (*OED* 2). See Susie I. Tucker, *Enthusiasm: A Study in Semantic Change* (1972).

535. instinct] accented on the second syllable.

536. The Whigs 'included a considerable proportion of both the landed nobility and the landed gentry, as well as many city merchants and rich Dissenters. From these constituent elements can be deduced two of their fundamental principles—sanctity of private property and religious toleration' (Ogg 611; Kinsley). The Whigs feared that James as king would appropriate the former church lands which had been in private ownership since the Reformation, and generally would not respect property rights (Ashcraft 202–3). Buckingham voiced this fear in the Lords in 1675: 'There is a thing called *Property*, (whatever some men may think) *that* the People of *England* are fondest *of*. It is *that* they will never part with, and it is *that* His *Majesty* in his *Speech* has promised to take particular care of. *This*, my Lords, in my opinion, can never be done, without an *Indulgence to all Protestant dissenters*' (*Two Speeches . . .* 13); cp. 'Think how your Magistrates are murder'd before your eyes, for supporting that Liberty and Property whereby alone you subsist! That Property which entitles you to something you may call your own, which having enjoy'd your self, you may bequeath to your Posterity

And by the same blind benefit of fate
The devil and the Jebusite did hate:
Born to be saved, ev'n in their own despite,
540 Because they could not help believing right.
Such were the tools, but a whole hydra more
Remains, of sprouting heads too long to score.
 Some of their chiefs were princes of the land:
In the first rank of these did Zimri stand;

after you: That Property which satisfies your hunger and thirst with whole-som and substantial food, as good Beef, Mutton, &c. meats unknown to any in an absolute Monarchy, under the degree of the Nobility' (*A Character of Popery and Arbitrary Government* [early 1681] 2); cp. also *The Case of Protestants in England under a Popish Prince* (1681) 10; Henry Neville, *Plato Redivivus* (1681) 134, 141. See further Harris, cited in ll. 51–6*n*; Ashcraft 255–7; and Judith Richards et al., *JHI* xlii (1981) 29–51.

539–40. The Calvinist doctrine that the righteous are justified by faith, not works, and are elected for salvation from before their birth.

541. hydra] The mythical many-headed snake whose heads grew as fast as they were cut off; it was eventually killed by Heracles. In *The Badger in the Fox-Trap* Shaftesbury says: 'Some call me *Hydra* with a hundred Heads' (1). Cp. *Threnodia Augustalis* l. 464. It was traditionally an image of the unruly mob, e.g. in *Coriolanus* III i 92; see further C. A. Patrides, *Shakespeare Quarterly* xvi (1965) 241–6.

542. score] count.

544–68. Zimri] George Villiers (1628–87), second Duke of Buckingham. There are two biblical Zimris: (i) In Numbers xxv 6–15 Zimri is 'a prince of a chief house among the Simeonites' who openly takes a Midianite mistress, Cozbi; they are both killed by the outraged priest Phinehas. This parallel suggests a reference to Buckingham's notoriously open affair with the Countess of Shrewsbury which led to her husband's death after a duel with Buckingham in 1668. Kinsley notes that this reference is developed in *Absolon's IX Worthies* (1682): 'T' enjoy his *Cosbi*, He her Husband kill'd; / The rest 'oth story waits to be fulfill'd'. (ii) In 1 Kings xvi 8–20 Zimri is the servant of Elah, king of Israel, and captain of half his chariots; he conspired against Elah, killed him, and reigned as king for seven days; when the people rose up against him, Zimri 'went into the palace of the king's house, and burnt the king's house over him with fire, and died'. In 2 Kings ix 31 Jezebel asks, 'Had Zimri peace, who slew his master?'. Buckingham had been a close friend of Charles II in boyhood and exile, and became his chief minister after the fall of Clarendon in 1667 (see Pepys 27 November), though as a member of the 'Cabal' ministry he was less important than he imagined. In January 1674 the Commons voted to ask the King to remove Buckingham 'from all his employments that are held during his Majesty's pleasure, and from his Presence and Councils for ever'; the main charges were that he had broken the Triple Alliance (see l. 175*n*), arranged the alliance with France, and endeavoured 'to take away the affections of the King's good subjects, by saying, "that the King was an arrant knave, and unfit to govern"'; he was also accused of attempting 'a horrid sin not to be named; not to be named at *Rome*, where their other practices are horrid' (Grey ii 270, 245–6). Buckingham aligned himself with the opposition, cultivated radical associates (Harris (cited in ll. 51–6*n*) 11), and was one of the lords committed to the Tower in 1677 (see ll. 150–99*n*). He was prominent in the investigations into the Popish Plot, but his political power waned; he was not among the opposition leaders brought into the Privy Council in 1679, and did not attend the Oxford Parliament of 1681. His character was described thus by Burnet: 'He had a great liveliness of wit, and a peculiar faculty of turning all things into ridicule, with bold figures and natural descriptions. He had no sort of literature: only he was drawn into chemistry, and for some years he thought he was very near the finding the philosopher's stone. . . . He had no principles either of religion, virtue, or friendship. Pleasure, frolic, and extravagant diversions, was all that he laid to heart. He was true to nothing: for he was not true to himself. He had no steadiness nor conduct. . . . He could never fix his thoughts, nor govern his estate, though then the greatest in England. . . . He also ruined body and mind, fortune and reputation equally . . . since at last he became contemptible and poor, sickly, and sunk in his parts, as well as in all other respects, so that his conversation was as much avoided as ever it had been courted' (i 182). Samuel Butler wrote: 'Continual Wine, Women, and Music put false Values upon Things, which by Custom become habitual, and debauch his Understanding so, that he retains no right Notion nor Sense of Things. . . . He is as inconstant as the Moon, which he lives under. . . . His Mind entertains all Things very freely, that come and go; but like Guests and Strangers they are not welcome, if they stay long— This lays him open to all Cheats, Quacks, and Imposters, who apply to every particular Humour while it lasts, and afterwards vanish. . . . His Ears are perpetually drilled with a Fiddlestick. He endures Pleasures with less Patience, than other Men do their Pains' ('A Duke of Bucks' in *Genuine Remains* (1759) ii 73–5). Members of Parliament commented in the Commons in January 1673 on the beliefs and wit of Buckingham and his associates: Mr Russel feared 'the danger the King and the nation are in, from a knot of persons that meet at the Duke's, who have neither Morality nor Christianity, who turn our Saviour and Parliaments into ridicule'; while Mr Sawyer said: 'This new light, a thing called wit, is little less than fanaticism, one degree below madness— Of *Democritus*'s family, he laughs always at all Religion and true Wisdom— We come here to take away examples of such things; such as this Duke, as great as any. This kind of Wit's best ornament is most horrid blasphemy, oaths, and imprecations' (Grey ii 256–7). Buckingham satirized D. in *The Rehearsal* (performed 1671). In 1673 D. wrote to Rochester about Buckingham: 'I hope your Lordship will not omitt the occasion of laughing at the Great Duke of B— who is so oneasy to [him]self by pursueing the honour of Lieutenant Generall which flyes him, that he can enjoy nothing he possesses. Though at the same time, he is so unfit to command an Army, that he is the onely Man in the three Nations who does not know it. Yet he still picques him self, like his father, to find another Isle of Rhe in Zealand: thinkes this dissappointment an injury to him which is indeed a favour, and will not be satisfyed but with his own ruine and with ours. Tis a strange quality in a man to love idlenesse so well as to destroy his Estate by it; and yet at the same time to pursue so violently the most toilesome, and most unpleasant part of businesse. These observations would easily run into lampoon, if I had not forsworn that dangerous part of wit' (*Letters* 9–10). In 1693 D. commented: 'The Character of *Zimri* in my *Absalom*, is, in my Opinion, worth the whole Poem: 'Tis not bloody, but 'tis ridiculous enough. And he for whom it was intended, was too witty to resent it as an injury. If I had rail'd, I might have suffer'd for it justly: But I manag'd my own Work more happily, perhaps more dextrously. I avoided the mention of great Crimes, and apply'd my self to the representing of Blind-sides, and little Extravagancies: To which, the wittier a Man is, he is generally the more obnoxious [i.e. impervious]. It succeeded as I wish'd; the Jest went round, and he was laught at in his turn who began the Frolick' ('Discourse Concerning Satire', *Works* iv 71). But Buckingham himself wrote lines 'To Dryden' in his commonplace book: 'As witches images of wax invent / To torture those theyr bid to Represent. / And as the true live substance do's decay / Whilst that slight Idoll melts in flames away / Such, & no lesser witchcraft wounds my name / So thy ill made Resemblance wasts my fame. / So as the charmed brand consumd ith' fire / So did Meleagers vitall heat expire. / Poor name! w^t medicine for thee can I finde / But thus with stronger charms, thy charme t' unbinde?' (*Buckingham: Public and Private Man*, edited by Christine Phipps (1985) 168). See further J. H. Wilson, *A Rake and His Times* (1954); Winn esp. 178–89.

545–52. This passage is modelled on Juvenal's character of the timeserving Greek in Rome: *quemuis hominem secum attulit ad nos: / grammaticus, rhetor, geometres, pictor, aliptes, / augur, schoenobates, medicus, magus, omnia nouit / Graeculus esuriens* (*Satire* iii 75–8: 'Who bears a Nation in a single Man? / A Cook, a Conjurer, a Rhetorician, / A Painter, Pedant, a Geometrician, / A Dancer on the Ropes, and a Physician. / All things the hungry *Greek* exactly knows', 'The Third Satire of Juvenal' ll. 136–40). Buckingham's volatility is similarly described in several earlier satires: 'At variance with himself, whose youth and age / Confronted in a mortal feud engage, / A court-spy and an evil counsellor, / A soph-divine, a mock-philosopher, / Many in one, one from himself another, / Two States, two Churches in the same false brother' (Christopher Wase, *Divination* (in MS, 1666) ll. 105–10; *POAS* i 59–60); 'Would fain be something if he knew but what? / A commonwealth's man he owns himself to be, / And, by and by, for absolute monarchy, / Then neither likes, but, some new knicknacks found, / Nor fish nor flesh, nor square is nor yet round. / Venetian model pleaseth him at night; / Tomorrow, France is only in the right. / Thus, like light butterflies, much flutter makes, / Sleeps of one judgment, and of another wakes. / Zealous in morn, he doth a bishop

Who made new porridge for the paschal lamb.
Let friendship's holy band some names assure;
Some their own worth, and some let scorn secure.
Nor shall the rascal rabble here have place,
580 Whom kings no titles gave, and God no grace:
Not bull-faced Jonas, who could statutes draw
To mean rebellion, and make treason law.
But he, though bad, is followed by a worse,
The wretch who heaven's anointed dared to curse:

576. porridge] soup made from stewed vegetables or meat (*OED* 1); hotch-potch, unsubstantial stuff, contemptuously applied to the Prayer Book since 1642 (*OED* 3a); in 1662 Pepys heard that 'there hath been a disturbance in a church in Friday-street; a great many young [people] knotting together and crying out "porridge" often and seditiously in the church; and took the Common Prayer-Book, they say, away; and some say did tear it' (24 August).

579. rascal] belonging to the rabble (*OED* B1).

581. Jonas] Jonah, who was angry when God spared Ninevah after he had prophesied its destruction. Here, Sir William Jones (1631–82); as Attorney-General 1675–9 he directed the Plot prosecutions, and as Member of Parliament 1680–1 promoted, and perhaps drafted, the Exclusion Bills. He was reputedly the author of *A Just and Modest Vindication of the Proceedings of the Two Last Parliaments* (1682) which answered *His Majesties Declaration* defending the dissolution of the Oxford Parliament (Burnet ii 257, 282, 284, 289). Burnet wrote: 'He was raised to that high post merely by merit, and by his being thought the greatest man of the law: for as he was no flatterer, but a man of a morose temper, so he was against all the measures that they took at court' (ii 106). Referring to Jones's promotion of the Exclusion Bill, a Tory pamphleteer wrote: 'Since *He* the *Jonas* is that rais'd the *Storm*, / Fling Him o'er-Board' (*A Vote for Moderate Counsels* (1681; Luttrell's copy dated 11 May) 12; W. K. Thomas 121–2). See also 'On the Bishops throwing out the Bill of Exclusion' (1679) in BodL MS Firth c 15 p. 45. The Jonah/Jones parallel hardly extends beyond the verbal echo, but a possible link is their ingratitude: 'Ungrateful *Jonas* next to *Nineveh* / Pleads Treason *gratis*, that's without his Fee; / Which he n'eer did before for King or Clown; / That got most by't, yet most disgrac'd the Crown' (*Absolon's IX Worthies*).

584–629. Shimei] When David was fleeing after Absalom's rebellion, he was cursed by Shimei, one of the house of Saul, who said, 'come out, thou bloody man, and thou man of Belial . . . the Lord hath delivered the kingdom into the hand of Absalom thy son.' David prevented one of his followers from killing him, saying, 'It may be that the Lord will requite me good for his cursing this day' (2 Samuel xvi 5–13). In *The True Presbyterian Without Disguise* (1680) the Presbyterian is described thus: '*Shimei* like, to all the Men he meets, / He spews his Frantick Venom in the streets: / And tho' he sayes

585   Shimei, whose youth did early promise bring
      Of zeal to God, and hatred to his King,
      Did wisely from expensive sins refrain,
      And never broke the sabbath but for gain:

the spirit moves him to it, / The Devil is that spirit made him do it.' D.'s
Shimei is Slingsby Bethel (1617–97), a successful merchant who lived in
Hamburg from 1637 to December 1649; elected Member of Parliament for
Knaresborough in 1659 he opposed the Protectorate of Richard Cromwell on
republican grounds. A member of the Council of State in January 1660, he
lived a retired life after the Restoration; on 24 June 1680 he and Henry
Cornish were elected sheriffs for London and Middlesex, but they were
unable to serve because they had not sworn the oaths of allegiance required
by the Corporation Act. A second election took place on 14 July, by which
time they had qualified, and both were elected again. The sheriffs were
responsible for the selection of juries, and notoriously Whig juries returned
ignoramus verdicts, refusing to indict Stephen College in July 1681 and Shaftesbury in November (cp. 'Prologue to *The Duke of Guise*' ll. 42*n*, 43*n*). In
February 1681, with Buckingham's support, Bethel stood for election to
Parliament for Southwark, but came bottom of the poll. The polling was
rowdy, as one Tory pamphlet relates: 'He must thank himself, if by threatening to pull the King's Watermans Coat over his Ears, he provok'd him to
reply, *Ay, Sir, so perhaps you would my Masters too, if it were in your Power*'
(*How and Rich* (1681) 2). Tried in October for his assault on the waterman,
Bethel was convicted, but fined only five marks by the jury. Burnet wrote:
'Bethel was a man of knowledge, and had writ a very judicious book of the
interests of princes: but as he was a known republican in principle, so he was
a sullen and wilful man, and run the way of a sheriff's living into the extreme
of sordidness, which was very unacceptable to the body of the citizens, and
proved a great prejudice to the party. . . . The court was very jealous of this,
and understood it to be done on design to pack juries, so that the party should
be always safe, whatever they might engage in, and it was said that the king
would not have common justice done him hereafter against any of them,
how guilty soever. The setting up Bethel gave a great colour to this jealousy;
for it was said he had expressed his approving the late king's death in very
indecent terms. These two persons had never before received the sacrament
in the church, being independents, but they did it now to qualify themselves
for this office, which gave great advantages against the whole party: it was
said that the serving an end was a good resolver of all cases of conscience, and
purged all scruples' (ii 254). On D.'s presentation of Bethel, see Robert
McHenry, *HLQ* xlvii (1984) 253–72.
585. *youth did early*] Q; early Youth did *F*.
586. *hatred to his King*] In *The Vindication of Slingsby Bethel Esq.* (1681) Bethel
denied the allegation that 'being at *Hambrough* at such time as the late Kings
Death was resolved of in *England*, I did there say, That rather than he should
want an Executioner, I would come thence to perform the Office' (3).

Nor ever was he known an oath to vent,
590   Or curse, unless against the government.
      Thus heaping wealth by the most ready way
      Among the Jews, which was to cheat and pray;
      The city to reward his pious hate
      Against his master, chose him magistrate:
595   His hand a vare of justice did uphold,
      His neck was loaded with a chain of gold.
      During his office treason was no crime,
      The sons of Belial had a glorious time:
      For Shimei, though not prodigal of pelf,
600   Yet loved his wicked neighbour as himself.

589. *oath*] playing on Bethel's not having taken the oath of allegiance.
595. *vare*] staff carried as a symbol of office.
598. *sons of Belial*] (i) rebels (e.g. in Deuteronomy xiii 13; 1 Samuel x 27; 2 Samuel xx 1; 2 Chronicles xiii 7); (ii) false witnesses (1 Kings xxi 10: the story of Naboth's vineyard, which John Caryll used in his poem about the perjured witnesses to the Plot; Robert McHenry, *ELN* xxii.2 (1984) 27–30); (iii) the other connotation, of debauchery, seems irrelevant (Judges xix 22; Milton, *PL* i 500–5). Cp. the collect at Evening Prayer on 30 January, the commemoration of King Charles the Martyr: 'We thy sinful people fall down before thee, confessing that thy judgments were right in permitting cruel men, sons of Belial, this day to imbrue their hands in the bloud of thine Anointed; we having drawn down the same upon our selves, by the great and long provocations of our sins against thee' (*Book of Common Prayer* (1662); *Works*). Several Tory pamphlets use the phrase: *A Letter to the Earl of Shaftesbury . . . From Tom Tell-Troth* (1680) attributes the execution of Charles I and the Civil War to 'such pernicious Counsels and Designs, as are now hatching by these Sons of Belial, to the present disturbance, if not ruine of our flourishing Church and Kingdoms' (1); Oates is called 'the *First Son* of Belial' (*The Character of an Ignoramus Doctor* (1681) 1); the Parliamentarian armies are referred to as 'those Sons of *Belial* [who] fought / Against their King' (*The Glory of the English Nation* (1681); MS date 30 May 1681 on BL copy); and in *The Progress of Honesty* 'Two wretched Sons of *Belial* rose / Unhappy Resolution to oppose' (12). But the Whigs also used the phrase, as in *The Freeholders Choice* [1681]: ''Tis these Sons of *Belial* who in all ages have endeavoured to corrupt and stain the generous minds of Princes with Arbitrary and unmanly Maxims of Government and State, and have framed for them the weak Policies of Cruelty, Craft, Treachery, and formal Devotion, instead of Protection, Wisdom, Justice, and Righteousness, which alone can establish a Nation' (3).
599. *pelf*] riches.
600. Playing on Matthew xix 19.

When two or three were gathered to declaim ⎫
Against the monarch of Jerusalem,   ⎬
Shimei was always in the midst of them; ⎭
And if they cursed the King when he was by,
605   Would rather curse than break good company.
If any durst his factious friends accuse,
He packed a jury of dissenting Jews,
Whose fellow-feeling in the godly cause
Would free the suffering saint from human laws;
610   For laws are only made to punish those
Who serve the King, and to protect his foes.
If any leisure time he had from power
(Because 'tis sin to misemploy an hour)
His business was, by writing, to persuade
615   That kings were useless, and a clog to trade:
And that his noble style he might refine,

601–3. Playing on Christ's promise, 'For where two or three are gathered together in my name, there am I in the midst of them' (Matthew xviii 20).

606–9. When the jury returned a verdict of *ignoramus* in the case of Stephen College, tried in London in July 1681 for seditious words and actions, 'The Lord Chief Justice asked the foreman if he did not believe the evidence. He answered he was not bound to give any reasons. The foreman was one John Wilmer, a professed fanatic, and hackney-bail for all almost that of late have been committed for treason and have had bail. . . . The Lord Chief Justice told the Sheriffs that it was not fit that such a person should be a juryman. Bethel answered he was a stranger in the City, and therefore must take others advice' (*HMC Ormonde*, n.s. vi 96; McHenry, *HLQ* 260).

614–15. Bethel wrote a series of tracts exploring the political and social conditions which advance trade. He does not make the argument attributed to him here, though he does say that the Netherlands flourished more as a federation of autonomous provinces than when they were under the rule of a standing General or Governor (*The Interest of Princes and States* (1680) 110–11; *Works*). An approximation to D.'s charge may be found in *The Present Interest of England Stated* (1671), where Bethel says that 'the Domestick Interest of England . . . lyeth in the advancement of Trade, by removing all obstructions both in City and Country . . . especially in giving Liberty of Conscience to all Protestant Non-conformists, and denying it to Papists' (34).

No Rechabite more shunned the fumes of wine.
Chaste were his cellars, and his shrieval board
The grossness of a city feast abhorred:
620 His cooks with long disuse their trade forgot;
Cool was his kitchen, though his brains were hot.
Such frugal virtue malice may accuse,
But sure 'twas necessary to the Jews,
For towns once burnt such magistrates require
625 As dare not tempt God's providence by fire.
With spiritual food he fed his servants well,
But free from flesh that made the Jews rebel;
And Moses' laws he held in more account
For forty days of fasting in the mount.
630 To speak the rest, who better are forgot,
Would tire a well-breathed witness of the plot.
Yet Corah, thou shalt from oblivion pass:

617–21. Bethel had attacked the custom of public feasting long before
becoming sheriff: 'I am not of their opinion, who think popular feastings and
good fellowship, called Hospitality, to be the Interest of the Nation. . . . For,
besides the provoking of the Judgments of God by such inordinate living,
Excess weakens mens bodies, spends vainly their time, dulls their wits, and
makes them unfit for action and business' (*The Present Interest* 12). Answering
the charge that '*I live in a Garret, and keep no House*', Bethel said: 'The Truth
is, being a single Person (as I have been for many years) and having neither
the Concerns of a Family nor of Trade lying upon me, that I might have a
settled and known Being for such time of the Year as I commonly spend in
Town, without the trouble and inconveniency which commonly attends the
shifting of Lodgings: I took the House I now live in, (not the Garrets but) all
save the Garrets, Cellars, and one small Room upon the first Floor, with
accommodations suffiecient for a Gentleman of better Quality than my self'
(*The Vindication* 4–5). At the Southwark election 'some Waggs, by the Emb-
lematical Black-Pudding and the famish'd Mouse, intended an abusive Representation of the Gentleman-Strangers Nine-penny Ordinary abroad, and
his empty Cupboard at home' (*How and Rich* 2).
617. The Rechabites, following the command of their ancestor, drank no
wine (Jeremiah xxxv).
618. *shrieval*] of the sheriff.
629. See Exodus xxxiv 28.
630–2. Echoes *Dr. Otes his Vindication* (1680): 'Let not the name of *Otes* live,
let it dye, / And in the Grave of dark Oblivion lye: / Let *Bedloe, Otes* and
Dugdale be forgot, / For they were not discoverers of this Plot'.
631. *well-breathed*] well exercised; in training.
632–77. *Corah*] Korah, Dathan and Abiram rebelled against the priestly auth-

ority of Moses and Aaron, and were punished: 'the earth opened her mouth, and swallowed them up, and their houses, and all the men that appertained unto Korah, and all their goods' (Numbers xvi). Moses prayed God not to destroy the people who had followed Korah, and urged them to stand apart. Abraham Wright commented thus on the passage: 'The same Tongue that prayed against the Conspirators prayes for the people: as lewd men think to carry it with number; *Corah* had so far prevail'd, that he had drawn the multitude to his side. God the avenger of Treasons would have consumed them at once; *Moses* and *Aaron* pray for the Rebels; although they were worthy of Death, and nothing but Death could stop their mouths, yet their merciful Leaders will not buy their own peace with the loss of such Enemies. O rare and inimitable mercy! the people rise up against their Governors, their Governors fall *on their faces to God for the people*' (*A Practical Commentary or Exposition upon the Pentateuch* (1662) 158; *Works*). D.'s Corah is Titus Oates (1649–1705), the chief witness in the Popish Plot. His father, Samuel, was a weaver, a chaplain in the New Model Army, and an Anabaptist, who in 1660 was presented to the living of All Saints, Hastings. Titus attended Westminster School and Merchant Taylors' School, from which he was expelled; then Gonville and Caius College, Cambridge, from which he was expelled after two terms, and St John's College, which he left without a degree in 1669 after a dispute with his tutor over a tailor's bill. He then took orders, and after a curacy at Sandhurst, Surrey, was presented to the living of Bobbing, Kent, in March 1673. His parishioners complained of his drunkenness and his 'very indecent expressions concerning the mysteries of the Christian religion', and before the end of the year he was ejected. Joining his father in Hastings, he took up Samuel's quarrel with the local Parker family, accusing the elder Parker of treasonable words, and his son of sodomy. The former charge was dismissed by the Privy Council, and the latter by local magistrates; Oates then faced an action for £1,000 damages from the son, and a charge of perjury. He promptly signed up as chaplain on a frigate bound for Tangier, but on its return was dismissed for sodomy. Early in 1677 he was appointed chaplain to the Catholic Earl of Norwich's household in London, was dismissed, and on 3 March 1677 was received into the Roman Catholic church. He was sent to Valladolid to study, but was soon sent back to England when his ignorance of Latin was discovered; after a month in London he entered the college at St Omers in northern France in December, but was expelled in June 1678. Returning to London, he took up with his old acquaintance Israel Tonge, and the two concocted the allegations of a Popish Plot which were put before the King in August 1678 (see l. 108n). Though Oates received a pension and lodgings in Whitehall during the height of the panic, his standing declined in the summer of 1681; his evidence for the defence at College's trial in August was sarcastically handled by Judge Jeffreys; he was moved out of his lodgings in Whitehall, and in September his allowance from the King was stopped (cp. 'Prologue Spoken at *Mithridates*' ll. 26–30n). In May 1684 Oates was convicted of *scandalum magnatum* for calling James a traitor, and fined £100,000, and in May 1685 he was convicted of perjury, fined, whipped,

Erect thyself, thou monumental brass,
High as the serpent of thy metal made,
635 While nations stand secure beneath thy shade.
What though his birth were base, yet comets rise
From earthy vapours ere they shine in skies:
Prodigious actions may as well be done

---

pilloried and imprisoned for life. Released in December 1688 he was granted
a pension by William III. See Kenyon, *The Popish Plot, passim,* and Jane Lane,
Titus Oates (1949).

633–5. When the people of Israel complained against God and Moses for
bringing them out of Egypt into the wilderness, God punished them by
sending fiery serpents; the people repented, and Moses 'made a serpent of
brass, and put it upon a pole, and it came to pass, that if a serpent had bitten
any man, when he beheld the serpent of brass, he lived' (Numbers xxi 5–9).
Robert Rowles notes (privately) that the example of the brazen serpent was
used in the *Homily against Idolatry* (in *Certain Sermons or Homilies* (1676) 139)
in an official Anglican argument against Catholic claims for miracles
wrought by relics and images; its use here may therefore imply that Oates has
become an idol, about whose salvific powers specious claims are being made.

633. Erect thyself] This *double entendre* is the closest D. comes to joining in the
vilification of Oates's homosexuality which was frequent in Tory pamphlets,
particularly after the tide had turned against him, e.g. *A Hue and Cry after Dr.
T.O.* (1681): 'He seldom frequents the Company of Women, but keeps
private Communication with four *Bums*, to make good the old Proverb,
*Lying together makes Swine to love . . . with a Masculine Chamber-maid, which he
keeps to scour his Yard*'. McFadden 261–2 notes that Corah is associated with
the men of Sodom in the Epistle of Jude (4–11), where they are denounced as
'ungodly men, turning the grace of our God into lasciviousness.'   *brass*]
This has several connotations: (i) effrontery, impudence (*OED* 4); cp. 'In his
Brazen Forehead is writ *ABOMINATION*' (*The Character of an Ignoramus
Doctor* (1681) 1); (ii) in the OT it denotes people impudent in sin, e.g. in
Jeremiah vi 28: 'They are all grievous revolters, walking with slanders: they
are brass and iron; they are all corrupters' (Kinsley); (iii) in the Civil War,
royalist propaganda called a parliamentary spokesman a 'brazen Head as
often as they bid Him speak in defamation of the Kings side' and 'the states
trumpet; for then he does not preach, but is blown; proclaims news, very
loud, the trumpet and his forehead being both of one metal' (P. W. Thomas,
Sir John Berkenhead (1969) 119); (iv) echoes Horace, *Carm.* III xxx 1: *exegi
monumentum aere perennius* ('I have completed a monument more durable than
brass'; Reuben A. Brower, *ELH* xix (1952) 42).

636–7. Comets were thought ominous, often portending national disaster;
the one which appeared in December 1680 was interpreted thus by one Whig
writer: 'This present Comet (it's true) is of a menacing Aspect, but if the *New
Parliament* (for whose Convention so many good men pray) continue long to

By weaver's issue as by prince's son.
640   This arch-attestor for the public good
By that one deed ennobles all his blood.
Who ever asked the witnesses' high race
Whose oath with martyrdom did Stephen grace?
Ours was a Levite, and as times went then
645   His tribe were God Almighty's gentlemen.
Sunk were his eyes, his voice was harsh and loud,

---

sit, I fear not but the *Star* will lose its virulence and malignancy' (*The Petitioning-Comet* (1681) sig. A^r). For contemporary views of the origins of comets see *The Wonderful Blazing Star* (1681) and *AM* ll. 65–72n.

639. weaver's issue] 'He is one that preached *B—y* before the Weavers, in respect to his Father being one of the same Trade and Tribe' (*A Hue and Cry*); 'The *Monster* was begot (as some will have it) by the Gyant *Typhon*, in the shape of a *Broken Tub-preaching Weaver*' (*The Character of an Ignoramus Doctor* 1).

641. Embarrassed by his origins, Oates 'would needs be descended from some Ancient and worshipful stock. . . . Heralds were sent for, to make out his Pedigree, and give him a Blazon. . . . And it was engraved on his Table and other Plate' (Roger North, *Examen* (1740) 223 (Kinsley); cp. Lane, *Titus Oates* 167–8; William Smith, *Intrigues of the Popish Plot Laid Open* (1685) 15 bis).

642–3. Acts vi 9–15.

644–5. Korah was a Levite, one of the tribe which provided the priests.

646–9. The Jesuit John Warner recalled: 'Oates had an extremely stupid mind, a babbling tongue, the speech of the gutter, and a strident and sing-song voice, so that he seemed to wail rather than to speak. His memory was bad, never repeating accurately what had been said; his brow was low, his eyes small and sunk deep in his head; his face was flat, compressed in the middle so as to look like a dish or a discus; on each side were prominent ruddy cheeks; his nose was snub, his mouth in the very centre of his face, for his chin was almost equal in size to the rest of his face. His head scarcely protruded from his body and was bowed towards his chest. The rest of his figure was equally grotesque; more like a beast's than human, it filled people with contempt' (*The History of English Persecution of Catholics and the Presbyterian Plot*, edited by T. A. Birrell, tr. J. Bligh, Catholic Record Society xlvii–xlviii (1953–5) ii 415–16; Kinsley). Caricature seems superfluous, but cp. *Hue and Cry*: 'His marks are as followeth; The off Leg behind something shorter than the other, and cloven Foot on the nether side; His Face Rain-bow-colour, and the rest of his Body black: Two slouching Ears, ready to be cropp'd the next Spring, if they do not drop off before; His Mouth is in the middle of his Face, exactly between the upper part of his Forehead and the lower part of his Chin; He hath a short Neck, which makes him defie the Pillory; A thin Chin, and somewhat sharp, bending up almost to his Nose;

Sure signs he neither choleric was, nor proud:
His long chin proved his wit, his saintlike grace
A church vermilion and a Moses' face.
650 His memory, miraculously great,
Could plots exceeding man's belief repeat;
Which therefore cannot be accounted lies,
For human wit could never such devise.
Some future truths are mingled in his book,
655 But where the witness failed, the prophet spoke.
Some things like visionary flights appear:
The Spirit caught him up, the Lord knows where,
And gave him his rabbinical degree
Unknown to foreign university.
660 His judgement yet his memory did excel,

He hath few or no Teeth on the upper Jaw, but bites with his *Tongue*; His voice something resembles that of the *Guinney*-Pigs. . . . His eyes are very small, and sunk, and is suppos'd to be either thick-ey'd, or Moon-blind'; and *The Character of an Ignoramus Doctor*: 'His Eyes are *Murdering* as the *Basilisk*'s; tho' *Blindish* too as the *Batt*'s. With his *Screech-Owl*'s *Voice*, he bodes Death and Destruction' (1). But these portraits also correspond to a literary type, e.g. *The Phanatick Anatomized* (1672): 'His forehead high, and hard beyond all Story: / His Chin is an extended Promontory. / His Eyes are small, yet one bigger then t' other, / . . . His Nose is sharp, and very quick of scent, / . . . His Ears are long, one always hanging down'.

647. choleric] Choler was one of the four humours, causing irascibility. Burton characterized choleric men as 'bold and impudent, and of a more haire-braine disposition . . . furious, impatient in discourse, stiffe, irrefragable and prodigious in their tenents, and if they be moved, most violent, outrageous, and ready to disgrace, provoke any, to kill themselves and others, Arnoldus [adds,] starke mad by fits' (*The Anatomy of Melancholy* (1621) I iii 1. 3; Kinsley).

649. church vermilion] Clerical countenances have traditionally been depicted as rosy.   *Moses' face*] When Moses came down from Mount Sinai 'the skin of his face shone' (Exodus xxxiv 29).

654. his book] *A True Narrative of the Horrid Plot* (1679).

655. L'Estrange commented: 'He has certainly a strange *Fore-sight*' (*The Observator* xxxv (20 July 1681)).

656–9. Cp. 'he should (like Dr. *Faustus*) fly over the World, *Unseen*; and converse *Invisibly* with *Grandees* at *Rome, Paris, Madrid, Salamanca*' (*The Character of an Ignoramus Doctor* 2). Oates claimed to hold the degree of Doctor of Divinity from Salamanca, but the university denied it. L'Estrange printed the university's denial (dated 30 April 1682) in *The Observator* ccxxv (17 October 1682).

> Which pieced his wondrous evidence so well,
> And suited to the temper of the times
> Then groaning under Jebusitic crimes.
> Let Israel's foes suspect his heavenly call,
665 And rashly judge his writ apocryphal;
> Our laws for such affronts have forfeits made:
> He takes his life who takes away his trade.
> Were I myself in witness Corah's place
> The wretch who did me such a dire disgrace
670 Should whet my memory, though once forgot,
> To make him an appendix of my plot.
> His zeal to heaven made him his prince despise,
> And load his person with indignities:
> But zeal peculiar privilege affords,
675 Indulging latitude to deeds and words;
> And Corah might for Agag's murther call
> In terms as coarse as Samuel used to Saul.
> What others in his evidence did join

661. *pieced*] put together from pieces (*OED* 2).

665. *writ*] Q; wit F.

666–71. It was dangerous to cross Oates. In 1679 his former servant John Lane charged him with sodomy; when the jury returned a verdict of *ignoramus*, Oates had Lane indicted and convicted on a charge of trying to stifle the discovery of the Plot, and sued him for heavy damages. See *The Reputation of Dr. Oates . . . Clear'd* (1679) and *An Exact and Faithful Narrative of the Horrid Conspiracy of Thomas Knox, William Osborne, and John Lane, to Invalidate the Testimonies of Dr. Titus Oates, and Mr. William Bedloe* (1680). Adam Elliot also became embroiled with Oates: see his *A Modest Vindication of Titus Oates the Salamanca-Doctor from Perjury: or an Essay to Demonstrate him only forsworn in several Instances* (1682).

667. Cp. 'you take my life / When you do take the means whereby I live' (*The Merchant of Venice* IV i 372–3), and Ecclesiasticus xxxiv 22. Kenyon reckons that Oates gained comparatively little financial reward from the Plot: the lodgings and a maintenance allowance, £116 17s in expenses, royal bounty of £297 10s, and some money from his publications; but none of this lasted (277–8).

671. *appendix*] Oates appended a list of the alleged conspirators to his *A True Narrative of the Horrid Plot* (1679).

672–3. Oates made no direct charges against the King, but he did accuse the Queen of high treason, and her physician Sir George Wakeman with complicity in a plot to poison Charles with her approval (Kinsley).

676–7. *Agag's murther*] Samuel told Saul that God commanded him to destroy

Israel's enemies, the Amalekites; Saul did so, but spared their king, Agag. Samuel then rejected Saul for disobeying God, and Samuel himself 'hewed Agag in pieces before the Lord in Gilgal' (1 Samuel xv). D.'s application of this story has been much disputed. There are several general problems: (i) how close a parallel with the OT story should we expect? (ii) how much emphasis is to be put on 'might' (but did not?), 'call' for (but not achieve?), 'coarse' (do we have to find examples of coarse words from Oates? indeed, were Samuel's words coarse?), and 'murther' (literally, or metaphorically?)? (iii) is 'Agag' Oates's opprobrious term, which we see to be inappropriate, or is it D.'s identification, like the other names? (iv) does the poem's mode demand a single clear reference, or does it admit of generalities, or mischievously contrived ambiguities? Four candidates for 'Agag' have been proposed: (i) Sir Edmund Berry Godfrey, suggested in contemporary MS annotations and in the 1716 Key. But Godfrey was not the leader of an enemy people or group, and Oates did not call for his murder—rather, he called for it to be avenged. Nevertheless, many seventeenth-century readers evidently thought that D. was implying that Oates arranged Godfrey's murder in order to blame it on the Catholics. (ii) Lord Chief Justice Scroggs, proposed by E. S. de Beer (*RES* xvii (1941) 298–309). After Scroggs had cast doubts on Oates's evidence at Wakeman's trial, Oates brought a charge of misdemeanour before the Privy Council, which was rejected. Yet this scarcely amounts to a call for his murder, nor is there any apparent parallel between Scroggs and Agag. (iii) Lord Stafford, proposed by Kinsley (*RES* vi (1955) 295–6, and debate in vii (1956) 411–15). Oates gave the testimony to the Commons on which Stafford was arrested, and was a witness at his trial; he was therefore instrumental in Stafford's death. As a Catholic Stafford would be seen by Oates as one of a hostile faction, though he was by no means their leader. It is not clear that D. would have regarded Stafford's death as murder. (iv) James, Duke of York, identified as Agag by Christopher Nesse: 'Where did he [Oates] with affronts the *King* Annoy, / Or threaten him *his Brother* to Destroy? / As *Samuel* did *Saul* for *Agags* Death' (*A Key* 34). W. K. Thomas (135–6) supports this identification by saying that 'Oates repeatedly called for his murder or execution for treason'. Thomas cites no evidence, but Roger L'Estrange quotes Oates as having called James a traitor and said 'He shall be hang'd' (*A Brief History of the Times* (1687) i 151–2), and *The Account of the Manner of Executing a Writ of Inquiry* (1684) 12–13, which reports Oates's trial for *scandalum magnatum*, cites evidence that Oates had called for James to be hanged. Thomas suggests that by making Oates refer to James as Agag, D. exposes Oates's exaggerated view of Roman Catholics as enemies. J. R. Crider notes that Charles I had been called 'Agag' by his opponents, so that Oates's attack on James is associated with the execution, or murder, of Charles I (*ELN* xxi (1983) 34–42). It is impossible now to be certain about this reference, but James seems the best suggestion, particularly since the immediately preceding lines refer to Oates's offensive handling of the King and Queen: this charge is the culmination of the passage on Oates, and an allusion to anyone but James would be anticlimactic.

(The best that could be had for love or coin)
680   In Corah's own predicament will fall,
For witness is a common name to all.
   Surrounded thus with friends of every sort,
Deluded Absalom forsakes the court;
Impatient of high hopes, urged with renown,
685   And fired with near possession of a crown;
Th' admiring crowd are dazzled with surprise,
And on his goodly person feed their eyes.
His joy concealed, he sets himself to show,
On each side bowing popularly low;
690   His looks, his gestures and his words he frames,
And with familiar ease repeats their names.
Thus, formed by nature, furnished out with arts,
He glides unfelt into their secret hearts;
Then with a kind compassionating look,
695   And sighs bespeaking pity ere he spoke,
Few words he said, but easy those and fit,
More slow than Hybla drops, and far more sweet:
   'I mourn, my countrymen, your lost estate,
Though far unable to prevent your fate;
700   Behold a banished man, for your dear cause
Exposed a prey to arbitrary laws!

---

679. coin] See l. 922*n.*

681. Echoes '*Homo*, is a commune name to all men', William Lily and John Colet, *A Shorte Introduction of Grammar* (1549) 7; a familiar seventeenth-century tag, as in *1 Henry IV* II i 94.

686. admiring] wondering.

688. His joy concealed] Q; Dissembling Joy F.

690. frames] adapts to the occasion.

693–7. Cp. Spenser: Despair's 'subtill tongue, like dropping honny, mealt'th / Into the hart, and searcheth euery vaine' (*FQ* I ix 31 ll. 5–6; David Hopkins, privately).

697. Hybla] a town in Sicily celebrated for its honey (cp. Virgil, *Ecl.* vii 37).

698. estate] legal right to property (*OED* 11); political constitution (*OED* 8).

699. far unable] far from able (*OED* far 4b, a seventeenth-century idiom).

700. a banished man] Monmouth had been banished from England by Charles in 1679, but his absence from London in 1680 was part of his campaign to attract popular support (see ll. 18–30*n*, 729–38*n*).

701. arbitrary laws] The Whigs alleged that Charles was intent upon arbitrary government, i.e. rule without consultation with Parliament, and using the royal prerogative to suspend laws.

Yet O that I alone could be undone,
Cut off from empire, and no more a son!
Now all your liberties a spoil are made,⎫
705   Egypt and Tyrus intercept your trade,   ⎬
And Jebusites your sacred rites invade. ⎭
My father, whom with reverence yet I name,
Charmed into ease, is careless of his fame;
And bribed with petty sums of foreign gold
710   Is grown in Bathsheba's embraces old;
Exalts his enemies, his friends destroys,
And all his power against himself employs.
He gives, and let him give my right away,
.   But why should he his own, and yours, betray?
715   He only, he can make the nation bleed,

705. Egypt and Tyrus] France and Holland. Dutch merchant ships had established a strong position in transporting the products of other countries; this commercial rivalry led to three Dutch wars (see *AM* ll. 1–6 and headnote; Ogg 221–2). From France many luxury goods were imported into England, resulting in an annual trade deficit of about £1 million (Ogg 221). Ezekiel xxvii describes the glories of Tyre as a trading city, and its destruction.

709. Charles received extensive subsidies from Louis XIV, and although these were secret, the fact that he had asked for them was revealed in the House of Commons on 19 December 1678, when Ralph Montagu, formerly ambassador in Paris, produced letters which he had received earlier that year from the Earl of Danby, saying that the King expected to have 6 million livres (£300,000) annually for three years on making peace with France (Grey vi 348).

710. Bathsheba] The biblical Bathsheba was one of David's wives; the parallel does not extend to the way David acquired her, which was by arranging the death of her husband Uriah (2 Samuel xi). Here, Louise de Kéroualle (1649–1734). A Breton, she was maid of honour to Charles's sister Henrietta (1668–70) and then to Queen Catherine. She became Charles's mistress in October 1671. In 1673 she was created Duchess of Portsmouth, with apartments in Whitehall and an income of some £10,000 a year. She was suspected of influencing Charles in the French interest. During the Popish Plot she was subjected to much abuse: some Members of Parliament drafted articles of impeachment against her, and there was an attempt to prosecute her as a common prostitute. She contemplated leaving for France, but stayed and weathered the storm. Although she had advised Charles to exile Monmouth in 1679, she effected a rapprochement with Monmouth and Shaftesbury in 1680, and favoured Exclusion (Haley 502–3, 588, 599). She was the subject of many satires directed particularly against her influence over the King. *Britannia and Raleigh* (in MS, 1674–5), perhaps by John Ayloffe, says that Charles's 'fair soul, transform'd by that French dame, / Had lost all sense of honor,

And he alone from my revenge is freed.
Take then my tears' (with that he wiped his eyes),
'Tis all the aid my present power supplies.
No court informer can these arms accuse,
720 These arms may sons against their fathers use;
And 'tis my wish the next successor's reign
May make no other Israelite complain.'
    Youth, beauty, graceful action seldom fail,
But common interest always will prevail:
725 And pity never ceases to be shown
To him who makes the people's wrongs his own.
The crowd (that still believe their kings oppress)
With lifted hands their young Messiah bless,   .
Who now begins his progress to ordain
730 With chariots, horsemen and a numerous train.
From east to west his glories he displays,
And like the sun the promised land surveys.

---

justice, fame. / Like a tame spinster in's seragl' he sits, / Besieg'd by whores,
buffoons, and bastard chits; / Lull'd in security, rolling in lust, / Resigns his
crown to angel Carwell's trust' (ll. 117–22; *POAS* i 233). *Colin*, by the Earl
of Dorset (in MS, 1679; *POAS* ii 167–75), depicts her selling her place as
royal mistress. The *Satire on Old Rowley* (in MS, 1680) refers to 'slimy
Portsmouth's creatures / . . . Who would reform this brutal nation, / And
bring French slavery in fashion' (ll. 20–4), and the same poem presents
Charles in terms which state more viciously Absalom's charge in *AA* ll. 708–
10: 'Silly and sauntering he goes / From French whore to Italian; / Unlucky
in what'er he does, / An old ill-favor'd stallion. / Fain the good man would
live at ease, / And ev'ry punk and party please' (ll. 7–12; *POAS* ii 184–5).
Rochester's Farewell (in MS, 1680) comments on her political moves: 'O
Portsmouth, foolish Portsmouth! not to take / The offer the great faction
once did make, / When cringing at thy feet e'en Monmouth bow'd, / The
golden calf that's worship'd by the crowd: / But then for York (who now
despises thee) / To leave both him and pow'rful Shaftesbury!' (ll. 206–11;
POAS ii 227). See also *The King's Answer* and *A Satire* (*POAS* ii 255, 291).
717. Cp. the gesture of the duplicitous Ulysses in Ovid, *Met.* xiii 132–3 (D.
W. Hopkins, *N & Q* ccxxiv (1979) 523).
723. *action*] gesture, oratorical management of the body and features (*OED*
6a); histrionic personation (*OED* 12).
727. *believe*] Q; believes F.
728. *With lifted hands*] the OT posture for blessing (e.g. in Leviticus ix 22).
729–38. In July and August 1680 Monmouth made a triumphal progress
from London through the West Country, defying Charles's prohibition
(D'Oyley 168–74; Ogg 645; *A True Narrative of the Duke of Monmouth's Late*

Fame runs before him as the morning star,
And shouts of joy salute him from afar;
735 Each house receives him as a guardian god,
And consecrates the place of his abode:
But hospitable treats did most commend
Wise Issachar, his wealthy western friend.
This moving court that caught the people's eyes,
740 And seemed but pomp, did other ends disguise:
Achitophel had formed it with intent
To sound the depths, and fathom, where it went,
The people's hearts, distinguish friends from foes,
And try their strength before they came to blows.
745 Yet all was coloured with a smooth pretence
Of specious love, and duty to their prince;
Religion, and redress of grievances,
Two names that always cheat and always please,
Are often urged; and good King David's life
750 Endangered by a brother and a wife.
Thus in a pageant show a plot is made,

Journey into the West (1680)). Cp. 2 Samuel xv 1–6: 'Absalom prepared him chariots and horses, and fifty men to run before him . . . Absalom said moreover, Oh that I were made judge in the land, that every man which hath any suit for cause might come unto me, and I would do him justice! . . . so Absalom stole the hearts of the men of Israel'.

733. morning star] The planet Venus, which precedes the rising of the sun; Christ is described as the morning star in Revelation xxii 16, and Satan is a misleading morning star in *PL* v 708–10.

738. Issachar] Thomas Thynne (1648–82), of Longleat, Wiltshire, a wealthy supporter of Monmouth who entertained him on his western progress. In Genesis xlix 14–15 Jacob describes his son Issachar as 'a strong ass couching down between two burdens: And he saw that rest was good, and the land that it was pleasant; and bowed his shoulder to bear, and became a servant unto tribute.' Kinsley suggests that Thynne's 'two burdens' were his financial support of Monmouth and his unhappy marriage to Lady Ogle (*RES* vi (1955) 296–7).

741–4. It seems likely that Shaftesbury planned Monmouth's expedition in order to demonstrate his popular support (Haley 586–7).

742. depths] Q; depth F.

747. These had been Parliament's concerns before the outbreak of the Civil War.

749–50. Oates did not include James among the Popish Plot conspirators, but Stephen Dugdale did implicate him in March 1679, and the resulting alarm led to the Commons' resolution of 27 April (see ll. 353–60n; Kenyon, *The*

And peace itself is war in masquerade.
O foolish Israel! never warned by ill,
Still the same bait, and circumvented still!
755 Did ever men forsake their present ease,
In midst of health imagine a disease,
Take pains contingent mischiefs to foresee,
Make heirs for monarchs, and for God decree?
What shall we think? Can people give away

Popish Plot 176–7). The Queen was implicated by Oates in Sir George Wakeman's alleged plot to poison the King (Kenyon 125–31).

752. masquerade] Whigs accused Tories of being 'masqueraders' in concealing their political and religious aims: see D'Urfey's Prologue to *Sir Barnaby Whigg* (staged autumn 1681) l. 23 (Danchin no. 308).

754. circumvented] outwitted (*OED* 3).

759–810. In this passage D. examines the political theories underlying the Exclusion Crisis. The discussion falls into four parts: see ll. 759–64*n*; ll. 765–76*n*; ll. 777–94*n*; ll. 795–810*n*. The passage is well analysed by M. J. Conlon, *JEGP* lxxviii (1979) 17–32.

759–64. D. begins with one of the main Whig arguments, that the fundamental rights of the people need to be safeguarded against the threat of arbitrary power represented by James. One Whig wrote: 'Our Ancestors might refrain and limit us in the usage of those things which we derive from them; yet they could not refrain and limit us in those things which we have a right unto by the Law of Nature' (*A Letter from a Gentleman in the City* (1680) 14; Conlon 21). D. concedes that there is a danger in the absolutist monarchical theory as expounded by Hobbes in *Leviathan* (1651), who had argued that the people emerge from a state of nature (in which every man had a right to everything) by transferring their natural rights to a single sovereign; this theory makes the people completely vulnerable to their sovereign, since his power is unbounded and he is accountable only to God. Such a view was still held by some Tories: 'After the People have conveyed their Power unto a person to be King; there remains no superintendent power in them over him; for they have divested themselves of all power by the conveyance; if it were conveyed with conditions, then under those conditions it may be held against them; if absolutely, then it may be held absolutely over them' (*Antidotum Britannicum* (1681) 19). D. dissociates himself from such extreme positions, and 'by affirming the native rights and privileges of English subjects, Dryden gains a moral frame of reference for his subsequent argument against Exclusion. Rights and privileges conferred by the law of nature cannot be limited or resumed arbitrarily from one generation to the next. This much the reader must grant, and Dryden can now apply this shared assumption to the subject of Exclusion, an act that implied the power of subjects to revoke or resume the king's title from one generation to the next' (Conlon 21).

759–60. D. returns to this point in 'The Tenth Satire of Juvenal' ll. 128–9.

760   Both for themselves and sons, their native sway?
       Then they are left defenceless to the sword
       Of each unbounded arbitrary lord:
       And laws are vain by which we right enjoy,
       If kings unquestioned can those laws destroy.
765   Yet if the crowd be judge of fit and just,

765–76. D. now considers the Whig argument that kings are only entrusted with power by the people, who may resume it at will (cp. ll. 409–12); this argument assumes that the people had included terms allowing for their resumption of power in the original contract by which kingship was set up (which D. implies is unlikely). Rather, D.'s view is that all succeeding generations are bound by the original establishment of government as firmly as they are implicated in the original sin of Adam (and many seventeenth-century writers thought that it was the Fall which rendered government necessary in the first place: Conlon 23–5). The idea that kings are only entrusted with power had a republican ancestry. Conlon notes that John Bradshaw told Charles I at his trial that the King was 'but an officer in trust and he ought to discharge that trust for the people, and if he do not they are to take order for the . . . punishment of such an offending governor' (22–3). Milton, in *The Tenure of Kings and Magistrates* (1649), insisted that 'the power of Kings and Magistrates is nothing else, but what is only derivative, trans-ferr'd and committed to them in trust from the People, to the Common good of them all, in whom the power yet remaines fundamentally, and cannot be tak'n from them, without a violation of thir natural birthright' (*Complete Prose Works* iii 202). For the influence of Milton on Whig thought see George F. Sensabaugh, *That Grand Whig Milton* (1952). Henry Neville in *Plato Redivi-vus* (1681) says: 'our Prince has no Authority of his own, but what was first intrusted in him by the Government, of which he is Head' (119; and cp. the reply to Neville, *Antidotum Britannicum* 14). The idea was also advanced by Locke in his *Two Treatises of Government* (composed 1679–80; published 1689; edited by Peter Laslett (1970) 444–5; for Locke on 'trust' see 112–14). Whig thinkers argued that because the King had abrogated the people's right to redress of grievances through Parliament, he had forfeited his trust and could therefore be resisted as a private individual who had no authority (Ashcraft 322; 336; 403–4). This argument is countered by W. P., who says that 'The King hath His Title to the Crown, and to His Kingly Office and Power, not by way of Trust from the People, but by inherent Birthright, immediately from God, Nature, and the Law' (*The Divine Right of Kings Asserted* [c. 1680] 2). Conlon notes that D. uses the conventional explanation for the origins of government in Adam's fall to undermine the idea of an original contract or covenant, invoking a providential view of history which is at odds with the voluntarist principles of trust, covenant and consent (24–5).

765, 778. crowd] a sly shift from 'people'.

And kings are only officers in trust,
Then this resuming cov'nant was declared
When kings were made, or is for ever barred:
If those who gave the sceptre could not tie
770 By their own deed their own posterity,
How then could Adam bind his future race?
How could his forfeit on mankind take place?
Or how could heavenly justice damn us all,
Who ne'er consented to our father's fall?
775 Then kings are slaves to those whom they command,
And tenants to their people's pleasure stand.
Add that the power for property allowed
Is mischievously seated in the crowd:
For who can be secure of private right
780 If sovereign sway may be dissolved by might?
Nor is the people's judgement always true:
The most may err as grossly as the few,
And faultless kings run down by common cry

---

772. *take place*] take effect (*OED* 27a).

777–94. Milton in *The Tenure* had argued that 'to say, as is usual, the King hath as good right to his Crown and dignitie, as any man to his inheritance, is to make the Subject no better than the Kings slave, his chattel, or his possession that may be bought and sould' (iii 203). According to the Whig view, no man can be secure and free in a system where sovereign power is the birthright of one man. But D. now turns this question on its head, suggesting that 'if the king can be deprived of his right by a *de facto* power, then no man's right is secure. This was another royalist tactic, designed to show that the king's prerogatives were the best guarantee of the subject's privileges. . . . These lines effect a deliberate inversion of the commonwealth argument, suggesting that the threat of arbitrary rule comes from Whig attempts to transform the king's office into a fiduciary power, not from the Stuart succession' (Conlon 25–6). D. also counters the Whig stress on 'property' (see l. 536*n*). One Tory writer had represented a Whig as arguing: 'the natural part of the Government of *England,* which is Power, is by means of Property in the hands of the People; and they having the greatest interest in the Property, they will and must have it in the Empire' (*Antidotum Britannicum* 30). D.'s argument shows that Whig theory would actually lead to the destruction of 'property'—in the sense both of 'material possessions' and 'political rights'— by mob rule.

777. *Add that the power*] Q; That Pow'r, which is F.

<blockquote>

For vice, oppression and for tyranny.
785   What standard is there in a fickle rout,
Which flowing to the mark runs faster out?
Nor only crowds, but Sanhedrins may be
Infected with this public lunacy,
And share the madness of rebellious times
790   To murther monarchs for imagined crimes.
If they may give and take whene'er they please,
Not kings alone (the Godhead's images)
But government itself at length must fall
To nature's state, where all have right to all.
795   Yet grant our lords the people kings can make,
What prudent men a settled throne would shake?

</blockquote>

784. These charges had been levelled at Charles in many poems from the late 1660s onward; see *POAS* i and ii *passim*, and Paul Hammond (cited in ll. 156–8*n*).

785. standard] principle, means of judgement (*OED* 10b).

786. i.e. which fluctuates like the tides: 'the higher the tide and consequently the greater the distance between high and low water-mark (the interval of time between tides remaining the same), the more rapid is the fall of the water at the ebb' (Verrall 87).

788. lunacy] The moon was thought to produce madness as well as influencing the tides (Verrall).

794. Cp. Hobbes's description of the state of nature: 'during the time men live without a common Power to keep them all in awe, they are in that condition which is called Warre; and such a warre, as is of every man, against every man. . . . It is consequent also to the same condition, that there be no Propriety [i.e. property], no Dominion, no *Mine* and *Thine* distinct; but onely that to be every mans that he can get; and for as long, as he can keep it' (*Leviathan* (1651) 62–3). Whig thinkers made the concept of the state of nature an important part of their political philosophy, since it implied a contractual theory of government (e.g. Henry Neville, *Plato Redivivus* 29). Locke considered that England in 1681 had been reduced to a state of nature, since the King was governing by force without Parliament; similarly one of the arguments for Exclusion was that a Catholic king would be at war with his people, returning the country to a state of nature (Ashcraft 330–1, 190–6 and *passim*). The Whigs saw absolutism returning England to a state of nature: D. typically reverses his opponents' point, seeing the state of nature resulting from their policies.

795–810. Finally D. appeals for peace and quiet (cp. *RL* ll. 446–50); minor reforms may be permissible, but to change a settled government runs the risk of destroying it completely. D. 'proceeds to locate monarchy within the tradition of England's ancient constitution in a manner that mutes the absolutist implications of divine right but retains the divine source of the king's

For whatsoe'er their sufferings were before,
That change they covet makes them suffer more.
All other errors but disturb a state,
800   But innovation is the blow of fate.
If ancient fabrics nod, and threat to fall,
To patch the flaws and buttress up the wall
Thus far 'tis duty; but here fix the mark,
For all beyond it is to touch our ark.
805   To change foundations, cast the frame anew,
Is work for rebels who base ends pursue,
At once divine and human laws control,
And mend the parts by ruin of the whole.

---

authority. . . . The idea of an ancient constitution had evolved out of the history of English common law. Both the king and parliament were thought to be subject to the fundamental or common laws of the realm, which, in turn, formed and informed its constitution. Throughout the seventeenth century, moderate royalists accepted the idea of the ancient constitution, but insisted that the king's prerogatives were as essential to the constitution as were the powers of parliament' (Conlon 28; see also J. G. A. Pocock, *The Ancient Constitution and the Feudal Law* (1957, 1987)). Kinsley cites the Epistle Dedicatory to *All for Love* (1678) where D. says: 'Neither is it enough for them to answer that they only intend a Reformation of the Government, but not the Subversion of it: On such pretences all Insurrections have been founded: 'Tis striking at the Root of Power, which is Obedience. Every Remonstrance of private Men, has the seed of Treason in it' (*Works* xiii 7).

799. but] only.

800. innovation] (i) the alteration of what is established (*OED* 1 and 2; all its sixteenth- and seventeenth-century examples are pejorative); (ii) revolution, insurrection (*OED* 1b and 2b).

801. nod] sway away from the perpendicular (*OED* 3).

803. mark] boundary, limit (*OED* 1).

804. touch our ark] The Ark of the Covenant was a wooden coffer containing the stone tablets of the law which Moses had brought down from Mount Horeb. When it was being moved by David to Jerusalem, Uzzah put out his hand to steady it, as the oxen were making it tilt, and was struck dead by God for presuming to touch it (1 Chronicles xiii 9–10); cp. Preface to *RL*, l. 14). In this case the *ark* stands for the ancient constitution.

805–8. Echoing Marvell: 'To ruine the great Work of Time, / And cast the Kingdome old / Into another Mold' ('An Horatian Ode' ll. 34–6); D. echoes Marvell's lines again in 'Of the Pythagorean Philosophy' ll. 264–5.

807. control] challenge, find fault with (*OED* 3b).

The tampering world is subject to this curse,
810 To physic their disease into a worse.
Now what relief can righteous David bring?
How fatal 'tis to be too good a King!
Friends he has few, so high the madness grows;
Who dare be such must be the people's foes.
815 Yet some there were, ev'n in the worst of days,
Some let me name, and naming is to praise.
In this short file Barzillai first appears:
Barzillai crowned with honour and with years.
Long since the rising rebels he withstood
820 In regions waste beyond the Jordan's flood,
Unfortunately brave to buoy the state,
But sinking underneath his master's fate.
In exile with his godlike prince he mourned,
For him he suffered, and with him returned.
825 The court he practised, not the courtier's art;
Large was his wealth, but larger was his heart,
Which well the noblest objects knew to choose,

809. *tampering*] scheming, plotting (*OED* 2); meddling (esp. medically, *OED* 4b; cp. l. 810).
810. *physic*] medicate.
817–59. *Barzillai*] In the OT an old man of Gilead loyal to David during Absalom's rebellion (2 Samuel xvii 27–9; xix 31–9). Here, James Butler, Duke of Ormonde (1610–88). He commanded Charles I's army against the Irish rebels in 1641, and was Lord Lieutenant of Ireland from 1644 until he was forced into exile in 1650. During the Commonwealth he was a close adviser to Prince Charles, and suffered severe financial hardship; in 1660 he was rewarded with a dukedom and recouped some of his losses. He served again as Lord Lieutenant 1661–9 (removed at Buckingham's instigation) and 1677–85, surviving strong Whig criticism. Thomas Carte recorded that 'Once in a quarter of a year, he used to have the Marquis of *Hallifax*, the Earls of *Mulgrave*, *Dorset* and *Danby*, Mr. *Dryden*, and others of that set of men at supper, and then they were merry and drank hard' (*An History of the Life of James, Duke of Ormonde*, 3 vols (1735–6) ii 554). In 1683 D. dedicated to Ormonde the collaborative translation of Plutarch which he had supervised.
825. *practised*] performed the duties of (*OED* 2; cp. 'to practise religion'), rather than 'frequent, haunt' (*OED* 7b, citing this line; Kinsley). Ormonde was punctilious in maintaining the dress and hospitality appropriate to his position. Burnet commented: 'a man every way fitted for a court, of a graceful appearance, a lively wit, and a cheerful temper: a man of great expense, decent even in his vices, for he always kept up the forms of religion' (i 170; Kinsley).

The fighting warrior and recording Muse.
His bed could once a fruitful issue boast,
830   Now more than half a father's name is lost.
His eldest hope, with every grace adorned,
By me (so heaven will have it) always mourned,
And always honoured, snatched in manhood's prime
By' unequal Fates, and providence's crime.
835   Yet not before the goal of honour won,
All parts fulfilled of subject and of son;
Swift was the race, but short the time to run.

829–30. Seven of Ormonde's eight sons had now died; his two daughters survived him (Carte, *An History* ii 551).

831–53. Thomas, Earl of Ossory (1634–80), Ormonde's eldest son. He distinguished himself in the Second and Third Dutch Wars, and fighting for the Dutch against France in 1677–8. Ossory defended his father vigorously against attacks by Shaftesbury in the Lords. On his death Evelyn wrote: 'Surely his Majestie never lost a worthier Subject; nor Father, a better, & more dutifull sonn, a loving, goodnatured, generous and perfectly obliging friend, & one who had don innumerable kindnesses to severall persons, before they so much as knew it; nor advanc'd he any but such as were worthy; None more brave, more modest, none more humble, sober, & every way virtuous: O unhapy *England*! in this illustrious persons losse' (*Diary*, 26 July 1680). In 1683 D. wrote to Ormonde: 'Never was one Soul more fully infus'd into anothers breast: Never was so strong an impression made of vertue, as that of your Graces into him: But though the stamp was deep, the subject which receiv'd it was of too fine a composition to be durable. Were not priority of time and nature in the case, it might have been doubted which of you had been most excellent: But Heaven snatch'd away the Copy to make the Original more precious. I dare trust my self no farther on this subject; for after years of mourning, my sorrow is yet so green upon me, that I am ready to tax Providence for the loss of that Heroick Son: Three Nations had a general concernment in his Death, but I had one so very particular, that all my hopes are almost dead with him; and I have lost so much that I am past the danger of a second Shipwreck. But he sleeps with an unenvy'd commendation: And has left your Grace the sad Legacy of all those Glories which he deriv'd from you' (*Works* xvii 229–30). D. dedicated the *Fables* (1700) to Ossory's son, the second Duke of Ormonde.

832–4. From Virgil: *iamque dies, nisi fallor, adest, quem semper acerbum, / semper honoratum (sic di voluistis) habebo* (*Aen.* v 49–50; 'already, if I am not mistaken, the day is at hand which I shall keep always as a day of grief, always as one of honour (such, O gods, was your will)'; Christie).

834. unequal Fates] From Virgil's *fatis iniquis* (*Aen.* ii 257, x 380).   *unequal*] unjust, unfair (*OED* 4).

835–7. Cp. 'To the Memory of Mr Oldham' ll. 7–10*n*.

836. Cp. 'Hee entered well, by vertuous parts, / . . . A perfect Patriot, and a

O narrow circle, but of power divine,
Scanted in space, but perfect in thy line!
840 By sea, by land, thy matchless worth was known,
Arms thy delight, and war was all thy own:
Thy force infused the fainting Tyrians propped,
And haughty Pharaoh found his fortune stopped.
O ancient honour, O unconquered hand,
845 Whom foes unpunished never could withstand!
But Israel was unworthy of thy name:
Short is the date of all immoderate fame.
It looks as heaven our ruin had designed,
And durst not trust thy fortune and thy mind.
850 Now free from earth, thy disencumbered soul
Mounts up and leaves behind the clouds and starry
    pole.
From thence thy kindred legions mayest thou bring
To aid the guardian angel of thy King.
Here stop my Muse, here cease thy painful flight,
855 No pinions can pursue immortal height:

---

noble friend, / But most, a vertuous Sonne' (Ben Jonson, 'To the immortall memorie, and friendship of that noble paire, Sir Lucius Cary, and Sir H. Morrison' ll. 33, 46–7).

838–9. The circle was an image of perfection; cp. 'Upon the Death of the Lord Hastings' l. 27n.

839. Scanted in space] Cp. 'For, what is life, if measur'd by the space, / Not by the act?' (Jonson ll. 21–2).   *Scanted*] limited (*OED* 3c).

844–5. Cp. Virgil's tribute to Marcellus: *heu pietas, heu prisca fides invictaque bello / dextera! non illi se quisquam impune tulisset / obvius armato* (*Aen.* vi 878–80; 'alas for piety, alas for ancient honour and the right hand invincible in war! no one would have advanced unscathed against him in arms'; Reuben A. Brower, *PMLA* lv (1940) 133).

846–7. name . . . fame] Q; Birth . . . Worth F.

847. Translates Martial VI xxix 7: *immodicis brevis est aetas, et rara senectus* ('short is the life of those who are uncommonly endowed, and they rarely reach old age'); cp. 'To Anne Killigrew' l. 147.

850–1. Echoes Virgil: *Candidus insuetum miratur limen Olympi / sub pedibusque videt nubes et sidera Daphnis* (*Ecl.* v 56–7: 'Daphnis in radiant beauty marvels at Heaven's unfamiliar threshold, and beneath his feet beholds the clouds and the stars'; Brower 133).

855. pinions] wings.

Tell good Barzillai thou canst sing no more,
And tell thy soul she should have fled before:
Or fled she with his life, and left this verse
To hang on her departed patron's hearse?
860 Now take thy steepy flight from heaven, and see
If thou canst find on earth another he;
Another he would be too hard to find,
See then whom thou canst see not far behind.
Zadok the priest, whom, shunning power and place,
865 His lowly mind advanced to David's grace;
With him the Sagan of Jerusalem,
Of hospitable soul and noble stem;

858–9. Friends often attached epitaphs to a hearse, the structure which was erected over a bier to carry arms and devices (Kinsley).

860. steepy] precipitous (*OED*'s first example of the word applied to movement rather than place).

864–5. Zadok] When David fled during Absalom's rebellion, Zadok the priest and the Levites took the ark and followed him, but David sent them back to Jerusalem (2 Samuel xv 24–9). D.'s Zadok is William Sancroft (1617–93), appointed Dean of St Paul's in 1664, where he was energetic in promoting the rebuilding of the cathedral after the Great Fire, and Archbishop of Canterbury in 1678. Burnet wrote sourly of him: 'He was a man of a solemn deportment, had a sullen gravity in his looks, and was considerably learned. He had put on a monastic strictness, and lived abstracted from much company. These things, together with his living unmarried, and his being fixed in the old maxims of high loyalty, and a superstitious valuing little things, made the court conclude that he was a man who might be entirely gained to serve all their ends, or, at least, that he would be an unactive speculative man, and give them little opposition in any thing that they might attempt' (ii 100). But D. is correct in saying that Sancroft lacked personal ambition; he was a devoted guardian of the Church of England who attempted to convert James from Catholicism, and, after 1688, was a courageous non-juror.

866–7. the Sagan of Jerusalem] Henry Compton (1632–1713), son of the Earl of Northampton; Bishop of London since 1675. Burnet commented: 'He was a humble and modest man: he applied himself more to his function than bishops had commonly done. . . . He was a great patron of the converts from popery. . . . He was as a property to lord Danby, and was turned by him as he pleased. The duke [of York] hated him; but lord Danby persuaded both the king and him, that, as his heat did no great hurt to any person, so the giving way to it helped to lay the jealousies of the church party' (ii 98–100). He supervised the Protestant education of James's children, but was an opponent of Exclusion. Compton was well known for his hospitality and charity (*DNB*).   *Sagan*] the Jewish high priest's deputy.

Him of the western dome, whose weighty sense
Flows in fit words and heavenly eloquence:
870 The prophets' sons by such example led,
To learning and to loyalty were bred,
For colleges on bounteous kings depend,
And never rebel was to arts a friend.
To these succeed the pillars of the laws,
875 Who best could plead, and best can judge a cause.
Next them a train of loyal peers ascend:
Sharp-judging Adriel the Muses' friend,
Himself a Muse; in Sanhedrin's debate

868–9. *Him of the western dome*] John Dolben (1625–86), Dean of Westminster since 1662 (later Archbishop of York 1683–86). He fought for the King in the Civil War, and was wounded at Marston Moor and at the siege of York. Burnet, who bore him a grudge, said that he was 'a man of more spirit than discretion; an excellent preacher, but of a free conversation, which laid him open to much censure in a vicious court' (ii 430–1). His preaching was much admired; Evelyn called it 'most passionat & pathetic' (*Diary*, 28 March 1673). *dome*] church; see *To His Sacred Majesty* l. 61n.
870. *The prophets' sons*] the boys at Westminster School.
872–3. P. W. Thomas notes that this link between culture and political allegiance has its roots in Civil War propaganda (*Sir John Berkenhead* (1969) 102–3).
877. *Adriel*] Saul's son-in-law (1 Samuel xviii 19). There is no apparent point in D.'s choice of this name for John Sheffield, Earl of Mulgrave (1648–1721). D. had dedicated *Aureng-Zebe* (1676) to him, thanking him for 'the care you have taken of my Fortune; which you have rescu'd, not onely from the power of others, but from my worst of Enemies, my own modesty and Laziness' (sig. A3ʳ). Mulgrave showed the draft of *Aureng-Zebe* to the King, and also gave D. an opportunity of discussing his plans for an epic poem on English history with the King and the Duke of York (A4ᵛ). Mulgrave was the author of *An Essay upon Satire* (in MS, 1679) and *An Essay upon Poetry* (1682); D. was suspected of having a hand in the former, and this was the probable cause of the attack on him in Rose Alley on 18 December 1679 (see *POAS* i 396–401). The two men collaborated on 'Helen to Paris' in *Ovid's Epistles* (1680) and D. dedicated his *Aeneis* to Mulgrave in 1697. In 1701 John Dennis praised Mulgrave for his patronage of D.: 'you generously began to espouse him, when he was more than half oppress'd, by a very formidable Party in the Court of King *Charles* II. a Faction that wanted neither Power nor Authority to crush him [e.g. Buckingham and Rochester] . . . Your Lordship, in Consideration of that rising Merit, cherish'd his Person, not-withstanding his pretended Frailties; and while others, to express their Malice to the Man, would have hindred the Advancement, even of that Art, which

True to his prince, but not a slave of state;
880 Whom David's love with honours did adorn
That from his disobedient son were torn.
Jotham, of piercing wit and pregnant thought,
Endued by nature, and by learning taught
To move assemblies, who but only tried
885 The worse awhile, then chose the better side;
Nor chose alone, but turned the balance too—
So much the weight of one brave man can do.

they pretended to esteem so much; your Lordship . . . cherish'd the Man on purpose, to make him instrumental in advancing the Art' (*Critical Works*, edited by E. N. Hooker (1939) i 198).

879. not a slave of state] D. told Mulgrave: 'Your mind has always been above the wretched affectation of Popularity. A popular man is, in truth, no better than a Prostitute to common Fame, and to the people' (*Aureng-Zebe* sig. A2ᵛ).

880–1. When Charles deprived Monmouth of his offices in 1679, Mulgrave was made Lord Lieutenant of the East Riding, and Governor of Hull.

882–7. Jotham] In Judges ix Jotham protests against the attempt by the men of Shechem to make the usurper Abimelech king. Here, George Savile (1633–95), created Viscount (1668) and Marquis of Halifax (1682). 'He was a man of a great and ready wit, full of life, and very pleasant, much turned to satire. . . . A severe jest was preferred by him to all arguments whatsoever; and he was endless in consultations. For when after much discourse a point was settled, if he could find a new jest to make even that which was suggested by himself seem ridiculous, he could not hold, but would study to raise the credit of his wit, though it made others call his judgment in question' (Burnet i 484–5). Halifax had been associated with Shaftesbury, his uncle by marriage, and supported the impeachment of Danby, but they parted company in 1679 (Haley 530–1). Although he had remarked that no man would use the hereditary principle to select his coachman, Halifax opposed the Exclusion Bill, and spoke energetically against it in the Lords in November 1680, when 'he gained great honour in the debate, and had a visible superiority to lord Shaftesbury in the opinion of the whole house' (Burnet ii 259). D. dedicated *King Arthur* (1691) to Halifax, remarking that Halifax had been a trusted friend of Charles II in the King's last years, and recalling that 'formerly I have shadow'd some part of your Virtues under another Name; but the Character, though short and imperfect, was so true, that it broke through the Fable, and was discover'd by its Native Light' (sig. A4ʳ).

882. piercing] Q; ready F.

887. Echoing Marvell: 'So much one Man can do, / That does both act and know' ('An Horatian Ode' ll. 75–6).

Hushai, the friend of David in distress,
In public storms of manly steadfastness;
890 By foreign treaties he informed his youth,
And joined experience to his native truth.
His frugal care supplied the wanting throne,
Frugal for that, but bounteous of his own;
'Tis easy conduct when exchequers flow,
895 But hard the task to manage well the low,
For sovereign power is too depressed or high
When kings are forced to sell, or crowds to buy.
Indulge one labour more, my weary Muse,
For Amiel, who can Amiel's praise refuse?

888–97. The OT Hushai offered to join David in exile during Absalom's rebellion, but David persuaded him to stay in Jerusalem and provide intelligence of Absalom's plans; he did so, and also gave Absalom misleading advice to destroy him (2 Samuel xv 32–7, xvi 16–19, xvii 5–16). Here, Laurence Hyde (1642–1711), Clarendon's son, first Earl of Rochester of the second creation (1682). In 1676 he was sent as ambassador to the King of Poland and assisted in negotiating a settlement with the Turks; in 1677 he was one of the ambassadors at the negotiations at the Congress of Nimeguen. Hyde was First Lord of the Treasury 1679–84, and opposed Exclusion at the cost of being accused of popery by the Commons. Burnet wrote: 'He was thought the smoothest man in the court: and during all the dispute concerning his father, he made his court so dexterously, that no resentments appeared on that head. When he came into business, and rose to high posts, he grew both violent and insolent: but was thought by many an incorrupt man. He has high notions of government, and thinks it must be maintained with great severity' (i 463). D. wrote to him *c.* 1683 in an attempt to have part of his salary paid (*Letters* 20–2); in 1685 he referred to his 'particular obligations' to Hyde ('Preface to *Sylvae*' ll. 545–6) and dedicated 'Horace: *Odes* III xxix' to him. D. also dedicated *The Duke of Guise* (1683) and *Cleomenes* (1692) to Hyde; in the latter D. wrote: 'I shall be proud to hold my Dependance on you in Chief, as I do part of my small Fortune in *Wiltshire*. Your Goodness had not been wanting to me, during the Reign of my two Masters. And even from a bare Treasury, my Success has been contrary to that of Mr. *Cowley*; and *Gideon's* Fleece has then been moisten'd, when all the Ground has been dry about it' (sig. A3^v).
898. Cp. Virgil: *extremum hunc, Arethusa, mihi concede laborem* (*Ecl.* x 1; 'concede to me this final labour, Arethusa'; Brower, *PMLA* lv (1940) 132).
899–913. Amiel] The father of Machir, who with Barzillai brought David supplies (2 Samuel xvii 27–9; alternatively, the gatekeeper mentioned in 1 Chronicles xxvi 5). Here, Edward Seymour (1633–1708), a descendant of the first Duke of Somerset, Protector to Edward VI. He was Navy Treasurer 1673–81. As Speaker of the House of Commons 1673–8 he was adept at

900   Of ancient race by birth, but nobler yet
       In his own worth, and without title great:
       The Sanhedrin long time as chief he ruled,
       Their reason guided and their passion cooled;
       So dexterous was he in the crown's defence,
905   So formed to speak a loyal nation's sense,
       That as their band was Israel's tribes in small
       So fit was he to represent them all.
       Now rasher charioteers the seat ascend,
       Whose loose careers his steady skill commend:
910   They like th' unequal ruler of the day

managing business to the advantage of the court: 'He knew the house and every man in it so well, that by looking about he could tell the fate of any question. So if any thing was put when the court party were not well gathered together, he would have held the house from doing any thing, by a wilful mistaking or mistating the question, so that he gave time to those who were appointed for that mercenary work, to go about and gather in all their party. And he would discern when they had got the majority, and then he would very fairly state the question, when he saw he was sure to carry it' (Burnet ii 80). When Parliament met in March 1679 Seymour was again elected Speaker, but Danby, with whom Seymour had quarrelled, persuaded Charles to veto the nomination, provoking a furious reaction from the MPs. Seymour was active in opposing Exclusion, and in the course of 1681 attempted unsuccessfully to make himself Charles's chief minister (Haley 504; J. R. Jones, *Charles II: Royal Politician* (1987) 141, 174–5).

908–11. Seymour was succeeded as Speaker by William Gregory in March 1679; that Parliament was prorogued in May and dissolved in July. When the new Parliament that was elected in October 1679 eventually met in October 1680, William Williams was elected Speaker, and was re-elected for the Oxford Parliament of March 1681. He was no friend of the court, and attracted particular notice for the blunt terms in which he expelled Sir Robert Peyton from the House after his alleged complicity in the Meal Tub Plot (Grey viii 148–9; *POAS* ii 305–8).

910–11. Phaëton, son of Apollo, persuaded his father to allow him to drive the chariot of the sun across the sky for one day; he was unable to control it, and was on the verge of destroying the earth when Jupiter killed him with a thunderbolt (Ovid, *Met.* ii 1–328). The story had been given a political application by Henry King in 'An Elegy upon the most Incomparable King *Charls* the First': 'Whilst blind Ambition by successes fed / Hath You beyond the bound of Subjects led, / . . . Needs must you with unskilfull *Phaeton* / Aspire to guid the Chariot of the Sun, / Though your ill-govern'd height with lightning be / Thrown headlong from his burning Axle-tree' (ll. 309–10, 16–18; Kinsley).

910. unequal] inadequate for the task (*OED* 2).

Misguide the seasons and mistake the way,
While he withdrawn at their mad labour smiles,
And safe enjoys the sabbath of his toils.
  These were the chief, a small but faithful band⎤
915 Of worthies, in the breach who dared to stand,   ⎬
And tempt th' united fury of the land.   ⎦
With grief they viewed such powerful engines bent
To batter down the lawful government,
A numerous faction with pretended frights
920 In Sanhedrins to plume the regal rights,
The true successor from the court removed,
The plot by hireling witnesses improved.
These ills they saw, and as their duty bound
They showed the King the danger of the wound:
925 That no concessions from the throne would please,
But lenitives fomented the disease;
That Absalom, ambitious of the crown,
Was made the lure to draw the people down;
That false Achitophel's pernicious hate
930 Had turned the plot to ruin church and state;
The council violent, the rabble worse,
That Shimei taught Jerusalem to curse.
  With all these loads of injuries oppressed,
And long revolving in his careful breast
935 Th' event of things, at last his patience tired,
Thus from his royal throne by heaven inspired
The godlike David spoke: with awful fear
His train their maker in their master hear:
  'Thus long have I, by native mercy swayed,
940 My wrongs dissembled, my revenge delayed;
So willing to forgive th' offending age,

920. plume] pluck the feathers from (*OED* 2).
922. hireling witnesses] See 'Prologue Spoken at *Mithridates*' ll. 36–7*n*; but the
King had money too: see l. 1012*n*.
926. lenitives] soothing medicines.
928. An image from hawking: the lure is an artificial bird from which the
hawk is fed, used to draw down the hawk.
931. The Privy Council, which had been enlarged in 1679 to include opposition leaders, was often the forum for heated discussions (Haley 536–7).
939–1025. David's speech has resemblances to *His Majesties Declaration to all
His Loving Subjects* (8 April 1681; reprinted in *Works* xvii 513–16), rather than
to the King's speech opening the Oxford Parliament, as Spence reported

So much the father did the King assuage.
But now so far my clemency they slight,
Th' offenders question my forgiving right.
945 That one was made for many they contend,
But 'tis to rule, for that's a monarch's end.
They call my tenderness of blood my fear,
Though manly tempers can the longest bear.
Yet since they will divert my native course,
950 'Tis time to show I am not good by force.
Those heaped affronts that haughty subjects bring
Are burthens for a camel, not a King:
Kings are the public pillars of the state,
Born to sustain and prop the nation's weight;
955 If my young Samson will pretend a call
To shake the column, let him share the fall.
[But O that yet he would repent and live,
How easy 'tis for parents to forgive!
With how few tears a pardon might be won

(*Observations, Anecdotes and Characters*, edited by J. M. Osborn (1966) 28–9, 614; see G. Davies, *HLQ* x (1946) 69–82). D. was probably responsible for the anonymous tract *His Majesties Declaration Defended* (June 1681; *Works* xvii 195–225).

942. Cp. Ovid: *in rege tamen pater est* ('however the father is in the king'; *Met.* xiii 187; Poyet).

944. In an attempt to prevent the trial of the Earl of Danby, Charles gave him a pardon on 1 March 1679. When the King informed the Commons of this on 22 March he told them: 'I never denied it to any of my servants or Ministers, when they quitted their places, as Lord *Shaftsbury* and the Duke of *Buckingham* well know'. But the Commons attacked the pardon, and disputed the King's right to grant it (Grey vii 19–30). When Viscount Stafford was condemned in December 1680 the King commuted the penalty of hanging, drawing and quartering to one of beheading; the sheriffs Cornish and Bethel disputed the validity of the King's action and sought the advice of the Commons, which directed them to follow the King's writ (Grey viii 204–5, 209–10).

945. Cp. 'all his actings without himself are only as a King, and in his Politick capacity he ought not to Marry, Love, Hate, make War Friendship or Peace, but as a King and agreeable to the People, and their Interest he governs' (*A Letter from a Person of Quality to his Friend concerning His Majesties late Declaration* [1681] 6; *Works*).

955–6. Samson destroyed both himself and the Philistines by pulling down the two pillars which supported their house (Judges xvi 21–31).

957–60. Q; *not in* F. Cp. 'Prologue to His Royal Highness' ll. 27–9.

960 From nature, pleading for a darling son!]
Poor pitied youth, by my paternal care
Raised up to all the height his frame could bear:
Had God ordained his fate for empire born,
He would have given his soul another turn;
965 Gulled with a patriot's name, whose modern sense
Is one that would by law supplant his prince;
The people's brave, the politician's tool,
Never was patriot yet, but was a fool.
Whence comes it that religion and the laws
970 Should more be Absalom's than David's cause?
His old instructor, ere he lost his place,
Was never thought endued with so much grace.
Good heavens, how faction can a patriot paint!
My rebel ever proves my people's saint.
975 Would they impose an heir upon the throne?
Let Sanhedrins be taught to give their own.
A King's at least a part of government,
And mine as requisite as their consent;
Without my leave a future King to choose
980 Infers a right the present to depose:
True, they petition me t' approve their choice,
But Esau's hands suit ill with Jacob's voice.

965–6. See l. *179n.*
966. supplant] Q; destroy F.
967. brave] warrior (*OED* 1); bravo, bully, hired assassin (*OED* 1b).
976. their own] what is theirs to give (Kinsley).
979–80. Cp. 'We have reason to believe, by what pass'd in the last Parliament at *Westminster*, that if We could have been brought to give Our consent to a Bill of Exclusion, the Intent was not to rest there, but to pass further, and to attempt some other Great and Important Changes even in Present' (*His Majesties Declaration*; Kinsley). L'Estrange made the same point: 'His Majesty will not agree to the Disinheriting his Brother, contrary to Honour, Justice and Conscience; nor to the Erecting of such a Doctrine or Precedent, in the Excluding of his Royall Highness, as may be apply'd, in Consequence, to the Deposing of Himself' (*Observator* xxvi (22 June 1681); *Works*).
982. Jacob tricked his blind father Isaac into giving him the blessing which was due to his elder brother Esau, by covering his hands and neck with goatskin to make them feel like Esau's; Isaac 'felt him, and said, The voice is Jacob's voice, but the hands are the hands of Esau' (Genesis xxvii). The image had been used in the Whig poem *The Protestants Congratulation to the City for*

My pious subjects for my safety pray,
Which to secure they take my power away.
985 From plots and treasons heaven preserve my years,
But save me most from my petitioners.
Unsatiate as the barren womb or grave,
God cannot grant so much as they can crave.
What then is left, but with a jealous eye
990 To guard the small remains of royalty?
The law shall still direct my peaceful sway,
And the same law teach rebels to obey.
Votes shall no more established power control,
Such votes as make a part exceed the whole:
995 No groundless clamours shall my friends remove,
Nor crowds have power to punish ere they prove.
For gods and godlike kings their care express,
Still to defend their servants in distress.
O that my power to saving were confined;
1000 Why am I forced, like heaven, against my mind
To make examples of another kind?
Must I at length the sword of justice draw?
O cursed effects of necessary law!

their Excellent Choice of Members to Serve in Parliament (1679): 'But Thanks, brave *City*, which well Understands, / To Judge 'twixt *Jacob*'s Voice and *Esau*'s Hands'.

983–4. Cp. 'while they pretended a care of his Person on the one hand, were plucking at his Scepter with the other' (*His Majesties Declaration Defended, Works* xvii 209).

986. petitioners] See 'Prologue Spoken at *Mithridates*' l. 4*n*.

987. From Proverbs xxx 15–16: 'four things say not, It is enough: The grave; and the barren womb; the earth that is not filled with water; and the fire that saith not, It is enough' (Christie).

993–4. Cp. 'By which Vote, without any regard to the Laws establish'd, they [the Commons] assumed to themselves a Power of Suspending Acts of Parliament' (*His Majesties Declaration*).

995–6. His Majesties Declaration refers to 'Strange illegal Votes, declaring divers eminent Persons to be enemies to the King and Kingdom, without any Order or Process of Law, any hearing of their Defence, or any Proof so much as offer'd against them'. Whig objections to this passage were countered by D. in *His Majesties Declaration Defended*: 'They who will have a thing done, and give no reason for it, assume to themselves a manifest Arbitrary Power. Now this Power cannot be in the Representatives, if it be not in the People: or if it be in them, the People is absolute' (*Works* xvii 215).

       How ill my fear they by my mercy scan;
1005   Beware the fury of a patient man.
       Law they require; let law then show her face:
       They could not be content to look on grace
       Her hinder parts, but with a daring eye
       To tempt the terror of her front, and die.
1010   By their own arts 'tis righteously decreed
       Those dire artificers of death shall bleed.
       Against themselves their witnesses will swear,
       Till viper-like their mother plot they tear,
       And suck for nutriment that bloody gore
1015   Which was their principle of life before.

1004. scan] form an opinion of.
1007–9. i.e. 'They could not be content with experiencing just grace and
mercy, which are the hind parts of the law, but insisted on challenging the
law face to face.' The image is based on Exodus xxxiii 20–3, where God says
to Moses: 'Thou canst not see my face: for there shall no man see me, and
live. And the Lord said, Behold, there is a place by me, and thou shalt stand
upon a rock: And it shall come to pass, while my glory passeth by, that I will
put thee in a clift of the rock, and will cover thee with my hand while I pass
by: And I will take away mine hand, and thou shalt see my back parts: but
my face shall not be seen.' Cp. *Astraea Redux* ll. 262–5.
1010–11. From Ovid: *neque enim lex aequior ulla, / quam necis artifices arte perire
sua* (*Ars Amatoria* i 655–6: 'for there is no juster law than that contrivers of
death should perish by their own contrivances').
1012. Several of those who had been used by the Whigs as witnesses against
Catholics in earlier trials (including Dugdale and Turberville who had sworn
against Stafford) found it expedient and profitable to testify in the King's
interest at the trial of Stephen College in August 1681, and were now being
prepared to testify at Shaftesbury's trial (Haley 652–4). Cp. *The Medal*,
'Epistle' l. 186.
1013–15. Cp. 'Oh! of *themselves,* they're e'en a *Vip'rous Brood; / Begot* in
Discord, and *brought up* with *Blood. / . . .* the *Ungrateful Brats* devour'd their
Dam.' ([Sir Roger L'Estrange], *The Committee; or Popery in Masquerade*
(1680)). The idea that the viper's young are born by eating their way out of
their mother's belly is traditional (see Edward Topsell, *The History of Four-
footed Beasts and Serpents* (1658) 802). James I cites the viper as an image of
rebellion in *The Trew Law of Free Monarchies* (1598) (*The Political Works of
James I,* edited by C. H. McIlwain (1918) 65). Du Bartas cites the viper as an
example of God's providence in setting man's enemies mutually at strife
(*Divine Weeks and Works,* tr. Sylvester (1605) I vi 233–40). For other allegori-
cal applications see Spenser, *FQ* I i 25–6 (Error) and Milton, *PL* ii 653–9
(Sin).

Their Belial with their Belzebub will fight,
Thus on my foes my foes shall do me right.
Nor doubt th' event, for factious crowds engage
In their first onset all their brutal rage;
1020   Then let 'em take an unresisted course,
Retire and traverse, and delude their force:
But when they stand all breathless, urge the fight,
And rise upon 'em with redoubled might;
For lawful power is still superior found,
1025   When long driven back, at length it stands the
                                                       ground.'
He said. Th' Almighty, nodding, gave consent,
And peals of thunder shook the firmament.
Henceforth a series of new time began,
The mighty years in long procession ran;
1030   Once more the godlike David was restored,
And willing nations knew their lawful lord.

1018. event] outcome.

1021. retire] i.e. let us retire.   *traverse*] tack (*OED* 14); move from side to side, dodge (*OED* 15).   *delude*] elude, evade, frustrate the purposes of (*OED* 4).

1026. nodding] as in Homer, Virgil (*Aen.* ix 106) and Ovid (*Met.* i 179–80; Poyet).

1028–31. Cp. the end of D.'s *Troilus and Cressida* (1679): 'Now peacefull order has resum'd the reynes, / Old time looks young, and Nature seems renew'd: / Then, since from homebred factions ruine springs, / Let Subjects learn obedience to their kings' (V ii 323–6).

1028–9. Cp. Virgil: *magnus ab integro saeclorum nascitur ordo* ('the great order of the centuries starts again from the beginning': *Ecl.* iv 5; Brower, *PMLA* lv (1940) 132); and cp. *Astraea Redux* ll. 292–3*n*.

Appendix A

The Authorial Manuscript Text of *Heroic Stanzas*

This is the text of *Heroic Stanzas* as it appears in Dryden's autograph fair copy (BL MS Lansdowne 1045 ff. 101ʳ–103ᵛ). Foliation and line numbers have been added in square brackets.

[f. 101ʳ]
Heroique Stanza's,
Consecrated to the glorious [& happy *deleted*]
    memorie
Of his most Serene & Renowned Highness
    OLIVER
Late Lord Protector of this Common=wealth. &c.
    Written after the Celebration of his Funeralls

And now t'is time; for theire officious hast
Who would before haue borne him to the Sky
Like Eager Romans, e're all rites were past
Did let too soone the sacred Eagle fly.

2
[5] Though our best notes are treason to his fame
Joyn'd with the loud applause of publique voice,
Since Heav'n what praise wee offer to his name
Hath render'd too authentique by its choise;

3
Though in his praise no Arts can liberall bee,
[10] And they whose Muses haue the highest flowne
Add not to his immortall memorie;
But do an Act of friendship to theire own:

4
Yet tis our duty and our in'trest too
Such Monuments as wee can build to raise;
[15] Least all the World prevent what wee should do
And claime a title in him by theire praise.

5

How shall I then begin or where conclude
To draw a fame so truly Circular?
For in a round what order can bee shewd,
[20]   Where all the parts so equall perfect are?

6

His grandeur hee deriv'd from Heav'n alone;
For hee was great e're Fortune made him so:
And Warrs, like Mists that rise against the Sunne,
Made him but greater seeme, not greater grow.

[f. 101ᵛ]
[25]   No Borrow'd Bayes his Temples did adorne
But to our Crowne hee did fresh Jewells bring:
Nor was his vertue poison'd soone as borne
With the too early thoughts of beeing King.

8

Fortune, (that easy Mistresse of the younge,
[30]   But to her ancient Servants coy and hard;)
Him at that age her favo'urites ranck'd among
When shee her best lov'd Pompey did discard.

9

Hee, private, mark'd the faults of others sway
And set as Sea=markes for him selfe to shun;
[35]   Not like rash Monarques who theire youth betray
By acts theire age too late would wish undone.

10

And yet Dominion was not his designe,
Wee owe that blessing not to him but Heaven,
Which to faire acts unsought rewards did joine;
[40]   Rewards, that lesse to him then us were given.

11

Our former Chiefs like Sticklers of the Warre
First sought t' inflame the parties, then to poize;
The quarrell lov'd, but did the cause abhorre,
And did not strike to hurt, but make a noise.

12

[45] Warre, our Consumption, was theire gainfull trade;
Wee inward bled whilst they prolong'd our paine:
Hee fought to end our fighting and assay'd
To stanch the blood by breathing of the veine.

13

Swift and Resistlesse through the Land hee past
[50] Like that bold Greeke who did the East subdue;
And made to Battailes such heroique hast
As if on Wings of Victorie hee flew.

[f. 102ʳ]

Hee fought secure of Fortune as of Fame
Till by new Maps the Island might bee showne
[55] Of Conquests, which hee strew'd where e're hee
came,
Thicke as the Galaxie with Starr's is sowne.

15

His Palmes, though under weight they did not stand
Still thriv'd; no winter could his Lawrells fade;
Heav'n in his portraict shew'd a Workmans hand
[60] And drew it perfect, yet without a shade.

16

Peace was the prize of all his toiles and care
Which Warre had banish'd, and did now restore;
Bolognia's walls thus mounted in the Ayre
To seat them selves more surely then before.

17

[65] Her safety, rescu'd Ireland to him owes;
And treach'rous Scotland to no Int'rest true,
May blesse that Fate which did his Armes dispose
Her Land to civilize as to subdue.

18

Nor was hee like those Starrs which onely shine
[70] When to pale Mariners they stormes portend;
Hee had his calmer influence, and his Mine
Did Love and Majesty together blend.

19

T'is true, his Count'nance did imprint an awe,
And nat'urally all Soules to his did bowe;
[75]   As Wands of Divination downward draw
And point to beds where soveraigne Gold doth
        grow.

20

When past all off'erings to Feretrian Jove
Hee Mars depos'd, & Armes to Gownes made yield,
Successfull Councells did him soone approove
[80]   As fit for close Intrigues as open field.

21

[f. 102ᵛ]

To suppliant Holland hee vouchsaf'd a peace,
Our once bold Rivall in the British Maine,
Now tamely glad her unjust Claime to cease,
And buy our friendship with her Idoll gaine.

22

[85]   Fame of th' asserted Sea through Europe blowne
Made France and Spaine ambitious of his loue:
Each knew that side must conquer hee would own
And for him fiercely as for Empire strove.

23

Nor sooner was the Frenchmans cause embrac'd
[90]   Then th' ayery Monsieur the grave Don outweighd;
His fortune turn'd the Scale where it was cast
Though Indian Mines were in the other layd.

24

When absent, yet wee conquer'd in his right;
For though some meaner Artists skill were showne
[95]   In Mingling colours or in placeing light,
Yet still the faire designment was his own.

25

For from all tempers hee could service draw
The worth of each with its allay hee knew;
And as the Confident of Nature saw

[100]   How shee Complexions did divide and brew.

26

Or hee theire single vertues did survay
by Intuition in his own large brest,
Where all the rich Idea's of them lay
That were the rule and measure to the rest.

27

[105]   When such Heroique vertue Heav'n sets out
The Starr's like Commons sullenly obay;
Because it draines them when it comes about
And therefore is a Taxe they seldome pay.

[f. 103^r]

From this high Spring our forraigne Conquests flow
[110]   Which yet more glorious triumphs do portend,
Since theire Commencement to his Armes they owe,
If Springs as high as Fountaines may ascend.

29

Hee made us Freemen of the Continent
Whom Nature did like Captives treat before;
[115]   To nobler prey's the English Lion sent,
And taught him first in Belgian walkes to roare.

30

That old, unquestion'd Pirate of the Land
Proud Rome, with dread the fate of Dunkirke h'ard,
And trembling wish'd behinde more Alpes to stand
[120]   Although an Alexander were her guard.

31

By his command wee boldly cross'd the Line
And bravely fought where Southerne Starrs arise;
Wee trac'd the farre fetch'd gold unto the mine,
And that which brib'd our Fathers, made our Prize.

32

[125]   Such was our Prince, yet own'd a Soule, aboue
The highest Acts it could produce to showe;
Thus poore Mechanique Arts in publique moove

Whilst the deepe Secrets beyond practice goe.

33

Nor dy'd hee when his ebbing fame went lesse
[130]   But when fresh Laurells courted him to live:
Hee seem'd but to prevent some new successe;
As if above what triumphs Earth could giue.

34

His latest Victories still thickest came,
As neere the Center Motion does increase:
[135]   Till hee prest downe by his own weighty name
Did like the Vestall under spoiles decease.

[f. 103ᵛ]

But first the Ocean as a tribute sent
That Gyant Prince of all the watry heard;
And th' Isle, when her Protecting Genius went
[140]   Upon his Obsequyes loud sighes conferr'd.

36

No Civill broyles haue since his death arose
But faction now by habit does obey;
And Warrs haue that respect for his repose
As winds for Halcyon's when they breed at Sea.

37

[145]   In peacefull Urne his sacred Ashes rest,
His name a great Example stands, to show
How strangely, high Endeavours may bee blest
Where Piety and vallour jointly goe.

Appendix B

The Contents of *Ovid's Epistles*

While this edition presents Dryden's translations in the context of his other poems, they were initially read as part of a different canon in the miscellanies and composite translations published by Tonson. For the contents of *Miscellany Poems* (1684) and *Sylvae* (1685) see Volume II Appendix A.

Attributions are supplied inside square brackets where the original publication was anonymous.

Ovid's Epistles (1680)

Sappho to Phaon	Sir Carr Scrope
Canace to Macareus	John Dryden
Phyllis to Demophoon	Ed. Pooley
Hypermnestra to Linus	[James] Wright (Macdonald 17)
Ariadne to Theseus	[John Somers] (*Works* i 341)
Hermione to Orestes	[John] Pulteney (Macdonald 17)
Leander to Hero	Nahum Tate
Hero to Leander	Nahum Tate
Laodamia to Protesilaus	Thomas Flatman
Phyllis to Demophoon	Ed. Floyd
Oenone to Paris	Aphra Behn (a second translation, by John Cooper, is added in the 1681 edition; Behn's is retained)
Paris to Helen	Richard Duke
Helen to Paris	John Sheffield, Earl of Mulgrave, and John Dryden
Penelope to Ulysses	Thomas Rymer
Hypsipyle to Jason	Elkanah Settle
Medea to Jason	Nahum Tate
Phaedra to Hippolytus	Thomas Otway
Dido to Aeneas	John Dryden
Dido to Aeneas	[John Somers] (*Works* i 341)
Briseis to Achilles	John Caryll
Deianeira to Hercules	Anon
Acontius to Cydippe	Richard Duke
Cydippe to Acontius	Samuel Butler

Appendix C
Commendatory Poems on *Absalom and Achitophel*

Absalom and Achitophel

The first edition of *Absalom and Achitophel* carried no commendatory poems; the second London edition in folio (1681; Macdonald no. 12d) included unsigned poems which were later attributed to Nathaniel Lee and Richard Duke (Macdonald 23). For Dryden's association with Lee see 'To Mr Lee, on his *Alexander*'. Richard Duke (1658–1711) was (like Dryden) educated at Westminster School and Trinity College, Cambridge; he contributed to *Ovid's Epistles* and *Miscellany Poems* (see Appendix B and Volume II Appendix A), and to the Dryden–Tonson Juvenal of 1693; he had also written commendatory verses to Dryden's *Troilus and Cressida* (1679). In the 'third edition' of *Absalom and Achitophel* (1682; Macdonald no. 12f) Duke's poem is signed with his initials, and a third poem, signed 'N.T.' (Nahum Tate) is added. For Dryden's association with Tate see 'To Mr L. Maidwell', headnote.

To the Unknown Author of this Excellent Poem

    Take it as earnest of a faith renewed,
    Your theme is vast, your verse divinely good:
    Where, though the Nine their beauteous strokes repeat,
    And the turned lines on golden anvils beat,
5   It looks as if they struck 'em at a heat.
    So all serenely great, so just, refined,
    Like angels' love to human seed inclined,
    It starts a giant, and exalts the kind.
    'Tis spirit seen, whose fiery atoms roll,
10 So brightly fierce each syllable's a soul.
    'Tis miniature of man, but he's all heart;
    'Tis what the world would be, but wants the art:
    To whom ev'n the fanatics altars raise,
    Bow in their own despite, and grin your praise:
15 As if a Milton from the dead arose,
    Filed off his rust, and the right party chose.

Nor, sir, be shocked at what the gloomy say,
Turn not your feet too inward, nor too splay.
'Tis gracious all, and great: push on your theme,
20 Lean your grieved head on David's diadem:
David that rebel Israel's envy moved,
David by God and all good men beloved.
    The beauties of your Absalom excel,
But more the charms of charming Annabel;
25 Of Annabel, than May's first morn more bright,
Cheerful as summer's noon, and chaste as winter's
    night;
Of Annabel the Muses' dearest theme,
Of Annabel the angel of my dream.
Thus let a broken eloquence attend,
30 And to your masterpiece these shadows send.
                    [Nathaniel Lee]

To the Unknown Author of this Admirable Poem

I thought, forgive my sin, the boasted fire
Of poets' souls did long ago expire;
Of folly or of madness did accuse
The wretch that thought himself possessed with Muse;
5 Laughed at the god within, that did inspire
With more than human thoughts the tuneful choir;
But sure 'tis more than fancy, or the dream
Of rhymers slumbering by the Muses' stream.
Some livelier spark of heaven, and more refined
10 From earthly dross, fills the great poet's mind.
Witness these mighty and immortal lines,
Through each of which th' informing genius shines.
Scarce a diviner flame inspired the King
Of whom thy Muse does so sublimely sing.
15 Not David's self could in a nobler verse
His gloriously offending son rehearse,
Though in his breast the prophet's fury met
The father's fondness, and the poet's wit.
    Here all consent in wonder and in praise,
20 And to the unknown poet altars raise,

Which thou must needs accept with equal joy
As when Aeneas heard the wars of Troy,
Wrapped up himself in darkness and unseen,
Extolled with wonder by the Tyrian Queen.
25   Sure thou already art secure of fame,
Nor want'st new glories to exalt thy name:
What father else would have refused to own
So great a son as godlike Absalon?

                                R[ichard] D[uke]

To the Concealed Author of this Incomparable Poem

Hail heaven-born Muse! hail every sacred page!
The glory of our isle and of our age.
Th' inspiring sun to Albion draws more nigh,
The north at length teems with a work to vie
5   With Homer's flame and Virgil's majesty.
While Pindus' lofty heights our poet sought
(His ravished mind with vast ideas fraught)
Our language failed beneath his rising thought:
This checks not his attempt, for Maro's mines
10   He drains of all their gold t' adorn his lines,
Through each of which the Mantuan genius shines.
The rock obeyed the powerful Hebrew guide,
Her flinty breast dissolved into a tide:
Thus on our stubborn language he prevails,
15   And makes the Helicon in which he sails;
The dialect, as well as sense, invents,
And with his poem a new speech presents.
Hail then, thou matchless bard, thou great unknown,
That give your country fame, yet shun your own!
20   In vain—for everywhere your praise you find,
And not to meet it you must shun mankind.
Your loyal theme each loyal reader draws,
And ev'n the factious give your verse applause,
Whose lightning strikes to ground their idol cause:
25   The cause for whose dear sake they drank a flood
Of civil gore, nor spared the royal blood:
The cause whose growth to crush our prelates wrote

In vain, almost in vain our heroes fought:
Yet by one stab of your keen satire dies,
30 Before your sacred lines their shattered Dagon lies.
O! if unworthy we appear to know
The sire to whom this lovely birth we owe,
Denied our ready homage to express,
And can at best but thankful be by guess,
35 This hope remains: may David's godlike mind
(For him 'twas wrote) the unknown author find;
And having found, shower equal favours down
On wit so vast as could oblige a crown.

N[ahum] T[ate]

Index of Titles

Index of First Lines